The Ultimate

MINOR ★ LEAGUE ★ BASEBALL ★ ROAD ★ TRIP

Josh Pahigian

The Ultimate

MINOR ★ LEAGUE ★ BASEBALL
ROAD ★ TRIP

A Fan's Guide to AAA, AA, A, and Independent League Stadiums

THE LYONS PRESS

Guilford, Connecticut

An imprint of The Globe Pequot Press

To buy books in quantity for corporate use
or incentives, call **(800) 962–0973,**
or e-mail **premiums@GlobePequot.com.**

The Lyons Press is an imprint
of The Globe Pequot Press.

10   9   8   7   6   5   4   3   2   1

Printed in the United States of America

Book design by Diane Gleba Hall

ISBN: 978-1-59921-024-7

Library of Congress Cataloging-in-Publication Data
is available.

CONTENTS

SECTION 2
THE SOUTH

Kentucky, North Carolina, Tennessee, South Carolina, Georgia, Florida, Alabama, Mississippi, Louisiana, Arkansas

CONTENTS

SECTION 3
THE MIDWEST

Texas, Oklahoma, Kansas, Missouri, Illinois, Indiana, Ohio, Michigan, Wisconsin, Nebraska, Iowa

SECTION 4
THE WEST
Colorado, New Mexico, Arizona, Utah, Nevada,
California, Oregon, Washington

SECTION 5
SHORT-SEASON, ROOKIE, AND INDEPENDENT LEAGUES

INTRODUCTION

IF YOU'RE LIKE ME and you love baseball in all of its many forms, then surely the minor league version of the game holds a special place in your heart. Each summer, scores of "bush league" ballparks open across the United States, welcoming millions of fans, who turn out to enjoy cozy, fan-friendly environments. The promotions are goofy, the players are friendly, and best of all you don't have to pawn your Roger Clemens rookie card in order to afford a seat down near the field. Minor league baseball's ballparks offer a happy medium between the bright lights and packed stadiums of the major leagues and the wooden bleachers and chain-link fences of the amateur game.

Minor league ballparks are as diverse and varied as the towns and cities they represent. Many date back to the middle part of the last century, existing as monuments to a simpler, more innocent time for the game and for the nation—a time that fans gladly hearken back to on warm summer nights when the home plate ump yells "Play ball," and the smell of boiling hot dogs fills the air. On the other end of the spectrum, many modern parks have been built in recent years, as minor league baseball's surging popularity has spurred a wave of stadium construction projects across the country. These parks provide all the consumer comforts found at the state-of-the-art major league stadiums, though on a smaller scale and at a fraction of the price.

Every minor league ballpark is endowed with its own treasure chest of stories and memories related to the players who have graced its dugouts, the fans who have filled its seats, and the games that have been played on its lawn. And each offers its own unique experience for fans to enjoy. At ancient Holman Stadium in Vero Beach, Florida, the fans sit in the shade of live oak trees that grow intermittently between the seats, while the players sit on uncovered aluminum benches in the sun.

Meanwhile, in Rome, Georgia, State Mutual Stadium offers more than one hundred televisions mounted above its concourses, ensuring fans don't miss a single pitch while making hot dog and beer runs.

At Sam Lynn Ballpark in Bakersfield, California, fans find a center field wall that measures just 354 feet from home plate. Fans in Bakersfield also find games frequently delayed by the sun, because the ballpark was built facing west instead of east, forcing batters to peer directly into the center of the solar system at twilight. At Legends Field in Tampa, Florida, the left field fence follows the same path as the fence in Yankee Stadium's famous Death Valley, and the ballpark has a miniature Monument Park to boot.

At the Eastern League ballpark in Portland, Maine, a 37-foot-high "Green Monster" rises high above left field, mimicking the famous wall at Fenway Park. At the South Atlantic League ballpark in Greenville, South Carolina, there stands another dead-ringer for the Green Monster. Meanwhile, the California League ballpark in Lake Elsinore, California, throws its own hat into the faux Fenway fray too, but places its Monster in right field.

In Salem, Virginia, fans enjoy breathtaking views of the Blue Ridge Mountains spanning majestically beyond the local park's right field fence. In Davenport, Iowa, fans enjoy views of the Mighty Mississippi meandering along beyond the left field fence. At Appalachian Power Park in Charleston, West Virginia, a committed fan sits behind home plate making toast with an electric toaster to celebrate every strikeout for the home team's pitchers. At Bright House Networks Field in Clearwater, Florida, fans enjoy authentic Philly cheesesteaks while they root for the Phillies minor leaguers.

And so on.

While every minor league ballpark is special in its own distinct way, the parks all hold certain things in common. They all offer the chance to watch baseball at its idyllic best. At the minor league level, winning and losing is not as important as in the major leagues. The experience is what matters most, both for the fans and for the players. This is baseball without the superstar egos, without the $100 box seats, without the $6.00 sodas, without the pregame traffic jams, and without the long lines at the urinals. The stakes are lower, sure, and the game is not played as flawlessly as at the big league level, but you can actually relax and enjoy yourself at any minor league ballpark, which is not always easy to do at the major league stadiums. Undeniably, sometimes things fall into place and the major league parks live up to our expectations, but it's not a guarantee. Some days you shell out $300 for four tickets, fight through rush hour traffic to get to the ballpark, spend another $50 for hot dogs and drinks, and then realize you're sitting 500 feet from home plate, the home team is already losing 7–0 in the second inning, and you think that if you had it all to do over again you'd just as soon be home watching *Walker, Texas Ranger* reruns on the Hallmark Channel.

Thankfully, minor league baseball never leaves us pining for an evening on the couch watching Chuck Norris and Noble Willingham redefine bad acting. Minor league baseball always delivers, and that's why more than just attending your local ballpark a few times each summer you should consider getting out and experiencing the wonders of the many ballparks across the country. Whether you take the parks by storm, loading up the family truckster and hitting the road for a whirlwind tour, or visit a few parks each summer, or tackle them one by one as your business trips bring you to new cities, I guarantee you'll find your bush league adventures rewarding and enlightening.

As for me, I've chipped away at the minor league ballparks over the past several seasons, and now I've written this book in the hope that my insights will help readers plan their own minor league adventures and maximize their enjoyment of their own experiences. This book devotes a separate chapter to each of the ballparks currently serving the Class-A, Double-A, and Triple-A classifications, as well as a few chapters at the very end that provide information about and driving directions to the ballparks of the short-season, rookie, and independent leagues.

The chapters are sorted first by region, then by state within each region. You will notice that the book begins with my "home" ballpark, Hadlock Field in Portland, Maine. This is not reflective of any East Coast bias on my part. It's just where my road trip began, and I had to start the book somewhere. Wherever you choose to begin your own trip, I hope this book will help make your adventures as fulfilling and memorable as possible.

Each chapter details the history of the local minor league team and of its ballpark. In gathering this information, I relied heavily on local fans and ballpark employees, who generously delved into their personal memory banks to tell me about the special players—some destined to achieve major league stardom, others to become furniture salesmen— who helped create their team's unique history, and about the special community members who made sure those players always had a decent place to play. Each chapter also provides a physical description of the local ballpark and discusses its quirks and nuances. Each chapter also offers a quick synopsis of the gameday experience at each park, and a few words about the special things the home team does to entertain its fans.

In addition to providing driving directions to each of the parks, each chapter devotes a page or so to describing the seating layout and to offering menu suggestions related to the concession stands. If your sensitive buttocks require the luxury of a stadium chair, as opposed to the unfor-giving expanse of a cold metal bleacher bench, this book will give you a heads-up, so that you can order tickets in advance when necessary. If you've never tried a hot dog topped with pickled okra before, this book will tell you when and where to belly up to the bar and order one.

Finally, at the end of each chapter, I've written a few paragraphs about the peripheral destinations near each ballpark that might enhance your road trip. Here you'll find information about sports bars and restau-rants where fans tend to congregate before and after games, as well as information related to still-standing historic ballparks that you might find worth visiting, cemeteries where former big league stars are buried, and baseball museums. I have also included information about nearby inde-pendent league and short-season league stadiums. Finally, this section mentions amusement parks, beaches, national parks, and other tourist sites that you may choose to visit along the way.

I leave the rest up to you. Spend a few weeks reading about all of the different minor league ballparks and figuring out which ones you'd most like to see, then surf the Internet going to www.minorleaguebaseball. com, where you'll find the updated schedules for all of the minor league teams, and plot your itinerary. After that, check your oil, rotate your tires, fill up your tank, and hit the road. Chant "You Are Toast" alongside the Toast Man in Charleston, as a visiting player dejectedly walks back to the dugout; take a ride on the outfield carousel in Bowie; cheer along with the fans in Reading as the miniature train makes its way atop the right field fence; shake your keys with the fans in Frederick during the seventh-inning stretch; high-five Louie the LumberKing in Clinton; chow down on a Swimming Pig in Grand Rapids. Experience the magic of baseball's bush leagues as you create memories that will last a lifetime. Drive safely, have a few hot dogs for me along the way, and enjoy!

Your friend and tour guide,
Josh Pahigian

SECTION 1

THE EAST

Maine, New Hampshire, Rhode Island, Connecticut,
New York, Ontario, New Jersey, Pennsylvania,
Delaware, Maryland, West Virginia, Virginia

HADLOCK FIELD
Portland Sea Dogs

Class AA, Eastern League
(BOSTON RED SOX)

Hadlock Field
271 Park Avenue
Portland, Maine
207–879–9500

The Eastern League team in Portland celebrated the signing of a new player development contract with the Boston Red Sox in 2002 by outfitting team mascot "Slugger the Sea Dog" with a new uniform that favored blue and red instead of the teal and white he had worn during the Sea Dogs' first eight years of existence—when they were a Florida Marlins affiliate. Then the Sea Dogs and the city of Portland ambitiously spent the winter outfitting Hadlock Field with a replica of Fenway Park's famous left field wall. Just like the "Green Monster" in Boston, the "Maine Monster" rises 37 feet above the playing field and is topped by a Citgo sign and gigantic Coke bottle. And just like at Fenway, a scoreboard appears in the middle of the wall, providing a line score of the game.

The Maine Monster is distinct from the Green Monster in a few ways though. First, the scoreboard on the wall in Maine is of the electric sort, while the one in Boston is manually operated. Second, the Maine Monster is a darker shade of green than the original. And third, there are no seats atop the wall at Hadlock, just a screen like the one that used to run atop the wall at Fenway. Still, the Maine Monster is the closest thing you'll find to the actual Green Monster north of the replica Monsters that stands at Bucky Dent's baseball school in Delray Beach, Florida, and at West End Field in Greenville, South Carolina. And that's saying something, because New Englanders have been building faux Fenways in their backyards for generations now.

Hadlock Field was built in time for the 1994 debut of the Sea Dogs. The park was designed and constructed by Portland municipal employees. Inside, the seating bowl relies more heavily on aluminum than most newer parks do, as the second level is set in an aluminum base rather than in concrete. There is no roof over the grandstand, but fans find plenty of dry and shaded space on the concourse that runs at ground level beneath the grandstand. On the street outside, Hadlock Field projects a redbrick façade that blends in with the circa-1915 Exposition Building next door. The "Expo" looms over the field along the first baseline and is bombarded by foul balls on a nightly basis. Aside from serving as a schoolboy and schoolgirl basketball mecca, the old building houses the Sea Dog clubhouses and indoor batting cages in its basement.

As fans approach Hadlock Field, they are welcomed at the main entrance by a larger than life statue of Slugger. Inside, the Maine Monster dominates the view, while fans can spy a stretch of I–295 beyond the fence in left-center. In right-center, an inflatable LL Bean boot—a replica of the one that sits outside the original LL Bean store in Freeport, Maine—sits atop three levels of advertising signs. And beyond the fences in right field lies Fitzpatrick Stadium, the home of the Portland High School football and soccer teams.

When Hadlock Field opened in 1994—bearing the name of longtime Portland High School baseball coach Edson B. Hadlock Jr.—it returned minor league baseball to Maine for the first time since 1988. That was the year the International League's Maine Guides played their final game at Old Orchard Park in Old Orchard Beach before moving to Scranton-Wilkes/Barre, Pennsylvania, to become the team currently known as the Red Barons. The Guides, who lasted just five years in Maine, never established a fan base among the tourists populating Maine's premiere summer vacation destination.

During their affiliation with the Marlins, the Sea Dogs treated their fans to glimpses of future major leaguers like Josh Beckett, A. J. Burnett, Luis Castillo, Alex González, Livián Hernández, Kevin Millar, Charles Johnson, and Edgar Rentería. On August 8, 1999, Brad Penny and Luis Arroyo combined to no-hit the Trenton Thunder after the two teams sat through a rain delay of three and one-half hours. Another highlight came on June 29, 2000, when the Marlins came to Portland to play an exhibition game against the Sea Dogs, and Ross Gload hit for the cycle against his big league cousins. Meanwhile, the Sea Dogs out-slugged the Marlins in the pregame home run hitting contest as Portland manager Rick Rentería stepped to the plate and cracked five long balls. Since becoming a Red Sox affiliate, the Sea Dogs have sent alums like Kevin Youkilis, Jonathan Papelbon, Manny Delcarmen, Jon Lester, Craig Hansen, and Hanley Ramírez to the major leagues. The Sea Dogs honor all team alumni currently on the Red Sox by hanging their jerseys on the face of the press box behind home plate.

In addition to your humble author, who lives just 15 miles from Hadlock Field, other celebrity guests who frequently turn out at the ballpark in Portland include horror author Stephen King and former president George H. W. Bush. The Bush family owns a vacation home in nearby Kennebunkport, and the former president threw out the ceremonial first pitch when the Sea Dogs hosted the Eastern League All-Star Game in 2005.

Game Day

Getting to the Park

From I–295 North, take exit 5A and merge onto Congress Street. At the first set of lights, take a left onto St. John Street, then at the next set of lights merge right onto Park Avenue. The ballpark will appear immediately on your left. From I–295 South, take exit 6A, merge onto Forest Avenue, and follow Forest to the Park Avenue intersection. Turn right onto Park and the ballpark will appear on your right after about a mile. Parking is available at the Maine Medical Center, Fitzpatrick Stadium, King Middle School, and at several other privately operated lots near the stadium that all charge between $3.00 and $5.00 per car. Early arrivals can park for free at curbside on Route 25 on either side of the bridge that spans I–295.

Inside the Park

In 2006 the Sea Dogs added some seats in home run territory in right field that increased Hadlock's capacity to 7,368. Tickets are usually available for games in April and May, but nearly all games sell out once school ends and the weather warms up in June.

While golfers might describe Hadlock Field's seating bowl as a dogleg right, perhaps it is best described for baseball fans as a fishhook, given the Sea Dogs affinity for the nearby Atlantic Ocean. Due to the presence of the Expo in right field foul territory, the seating bowl extends barely to first base on the right side, while across the diamond the bowl extends into medium-depth left. Section 101 is behind the Sea Dogs dugout on the first base side, Sections 105 and 106 are behind home plate, and Section 114 is the last section out in left field.

The Box Seats are between the field and an interior walkway. The Reserved Seats are the

Hadlock Field

first several rows behind the walkway. The General Admission seats are the bleachers with backs that appear above the Reserved Seats. And the final few rows atop the seating bowl are comfortable stadium chairs that belong to the indoor/outdoor luxury boxes that ring the top of the stadium. There are seventeen luxury boxes and each is named after a famous Red Sox player, like Ted Williams, Carl Yastrzemski, Carlton Fisk, Jim Rice, Fred Lynn, Harry Hooper, Johnny Pesky, and others.

Beyond the seating bowl in deep left, a bank of bleachers that was added in 1995 provides room for 500 General Admission ticket holders. Meanwhile, above the Sea Dogs bull pen in right field home run territory, the U.S. Cellular Pavilion, which was added in 2006, seats 400 fans in nine steeply rising rows. A covered group picnic area is tucked between the right field foul line and Expo building.

The concession stands are located on the concourse beneath the grandstand. Here fans find a taste of Maine in the form of a deep fried fish sandwich, as well as popcorn chicken and steamed Kayem deli dogs. An outdoor grill on the first base side serves Italian sausages, steak sandwiches, and chicken sandwiches, all with generous helpings of peppers and onions. This area on the first base side also offers several different microbrews and imports, including Red Hook, Guinness, Shipyard, Geary's Pale Ale, and Harp. The dessert of choice at Hadlock Field is a Sea Dog Biscuit, which is an ice-cream sandwich made of two chocolate chip cookies and vanilla ice cream, courtesy of Shain's of Maine.

While on the concourse, check out the many team photos that hang on the third base side. It's fun to examine these and pick out the future big leaguers in each year's Sea Dog edition. Meanwhile, the first base side of the concourse displays large color photographs of every stadium in the Eastern League.

Kids find Slugger's Workshop on the concourse behind home plate, an interactive area where they can make their own stuffed animals for a small price.

The Hadlock Field Experience

Aside from the faux Green Monster, Hadlock Field's other trademark feature is the lighthouse that sits out of sight behind the fence in right-center until a member of the Sea Dogs hits a home run. Then the lighthouse slowly rises amidst a cloud of fog and flashes a rotating white light while a foghorn sounds. After the conquering Portland player completes his trot around the bases, the lighthouse rescinds behind the wall.

Another local tradition is the nightly lobster toss. Competing between innings down on the field, a tandem of fans maneuvers a wooden lobster trap while ballpark employees use lacrosse sticks to lob lobsters their way. If the fans catch enough crustaceans, they win a gift certificate to Newick's Seafood Restaurant. Before any PETA sympathizers send angry letters to the Sea Dogs, I should tell you that no lobsters are harmed in the orchestration of this promotion. The lobsters they toss around Hadlock Field are made of plastic.

Slugger, the zany mascot, enters the ballpark on a four-wheeler midway through the first inning each night. He loves to steal Sea Dog Biscuits from unsuspecting fans and to dance on top of the dugout roofs. He also enjoys racing young fans around the bases, although he always manages to fall down or pull up lame or find some other way to lose at the absolute last minute.

The team's other mascots are Trash Monsters, fishlike creatures that roam the stands allowing fans to cram garbage into their oversized mouths. This is a unique way to trick fans into cleaning up the ballpark. A highlight of the 2005 season occurred when a young lady wearing one of the Trash Monster suits proposed to her boyfriend during a game and he said yes . . . as long as she cleaned up her act.

In true Red Sox tradition, the Sea Dogs fans sing Neil Diamond's "Sweet Caroline" between the eighth and ninth innings, just like the fans do at Fenway Park.

On the Town

The "Old Port" entertainment district offers lively nightlife and a multitude of fine restaurants. For a post-game brew, try **Bull Feeney's** (375 Fore Street), **Gritty McDuff's** (396 Fore Street), or **Three Dollar Dewey's** (241 Commercial Street). For fresh Maine seafood in an upscale setting, **DiMillo's Floating Restaurant** (Long Wharf/Commercial Street) is a solid choice. For casual seafood dining, **Newick's Seafood Restaurant** (740 Broad Street) is just across the bridge in South Portland. You wouldn't expect to find great Italian food in Portland, Maine, but for softball-sized meatballs and delicious homemade pasta, head to **Espo's Trattoria** (1335 Congress Street), which is less than a mile from the ballpark.

The original **LL Bean** store in Freeport is just a half-hour drive north of Portland along I-295. Meanwhile, just a short drive to the south Maine's white sand beaches attract tourists from all over the East Coast and Canada. **Old Orchard Beach** offers a carnival type atmosphere on its trademark pier, bars, restaurants, and glimpses of **Old Orchard Park**, the former home of the Maine Guides. The ballpark sits in ruin behind a wall of trees, located between the Old Orchard Beach police station and Old Orchard Beach High School on East Emerson Cummings Boulevard.

MERCHANTSAUTO.COM STADIUM

New Hampshire Fisher Cats

Class AA, Eastern League
(TORONTO BLUE JAYS)

Merchantsauto.com Stadium
One Line Drive/South Commercial Street
Manchester, New Hampshire
603–641–2005

Before I tell you about Merchantsauto.com Stadium, let me briefly weigh in on the stadium naming-rights craze currently sweeping across the minor league landscape. The stadium formerly known as Fisher Cats Ballpark is just one of many ballparks this book will discuss that unfortunately bears a completely ridiculous corporate name. These days more and more parks are being named in "honor" of Web site addresses, soda pop flavors, and Fortune 500 companies. I realize that the easy money teams and cities get for selling their stadiums' souls is too tempting to pass up. What I don't understand is why these companies continue to fork over hundreds of thousands of dollars, and sometimes millions, to smack their names on baseball parks, when all their gestures serve to do is irritate any baseball fan with any sense of taste whatsoever. I, for one, have vowed never to visit any Web site that has appropriated the name of a baseball park, and I quit drinking Dr Pepper when the new ballpark in Frisco, Texas, opened, and I closed my account at Fifth Third Bank the day it launched its campaign to claim the name of every ballpark in the Midwest. Hey, it's easier to boycott the brands than the ballparks, right?

Merchantsauto.com Stadium opened on the banks of the Merrimack River in 2005 to replace Gill Stadium, a converted football field that had served as the temporary home of the Fisher Cats during their inaugural 2004 campaign. The new 6,500-seat ballpark follows the same template as many of the recently constructed minor league yards. The seating bowl is low to the field and extends all the way out to the foul poles. The concourse runs atop the last row of seats, allowing those fans wandering around the concessions to keep an eye on the game. And the upper deck shelters the concourse while housing thirty-two indoor/outdoor luxury boxes.

The ballpark in Manchester also offers a couple of eccentricities. First, there is the six-story Hilton Garden Inn hotel, which looms over the field in left. The redbrick façade of the hotel and its tall brick clock tower match the brick atop the ballpark's outfield fences, contributing to a nice unified effect. Although the hotel opened a year after the ballpark, it looks like it has always been there. Because the Hilton is just 425 feet from home plate, all of its field-side windows are made of shatterproof glass, just like the windows of the hotel overlooking the field at the Rogers Centre in Toronto, where the big league parents of the Fisher Cats play. Another interesting feature of this park is the retractable batter's eye in center field. So hitters can get a good read on the baseball, a big green curtain rises above the outfield fence during games. Then, once the game ends, the curtain is lowered so that guests in the hotel courtyard can enjoy an unobstructed view of the baseball field. This reminded me a bit of the retractable green batter's eye that existed at old Yankee Stadium in the 1940s through 1960s. The Yankees would raise it when they were batting, then lower it when the visitors were at the plate, forcing opposing hitters to contend with a backdrop of bleacher fans wearing white T-shirts. And you probably supposed the Yankees were a classy

Merchantsauto.com Stadium

organization until George Steinbrenner arrived in the Bronx!

The outfield skyline also offers a view of the Verizon Wireless Arena off in the distance in center field. The arena is home to the American Hockey League's Manchester Monarchs and the Arena Football League 2's Manchester Wolves. The Merrimack River is not in view from the seats, but fans on the left field side of the concourse can peer down at the dirty water. The ballpark's upper deck is adorned with the colorful logos of all twelve Eastern League teams. These appear above the windows of the luxury boxes on the aluminum interior façade. If I have one complaint about this ballpark (besides the name), it's that alu-

minum is featured rather prominently in the design, both on the face of the second level and underfoot on the first level, where the seats are set in vibrating metal instead of sturdy concrete.

On arriving at Gill Stadium in 2004, the Fisher Cats returned affiliated ball to the Granite State for the first time since the Nashua Pirates left the Eastern League in 1986. The Fisher Cats arrived in Manchester via New Haven, Connecticut. Initially, the club was to be named the New Hampshire Primaries, but when locals bristled at the proposed name, the team ran a fan contest that resulted in the Fisher Cats moniker. A fisher or "fisher cat" is a carnivorous water-dwelling mammal that's something like a weasel. I doubt there are any of these creatures in the stretch of the Merrimack that flows behind the ballpark, since the postindustrial landscape doesn't look too conducive to animal life. I do agree with local fans, however, that a fisher is more tangible and easier to root for than a once-every-four-years political process.

During their first few seasons, several former Fisher Cats made it to the major leagues, most notably Gustavo Chacín, who went 16–2 with a 2.86 ERA for the Fisher Cats in 2004, then posted a 13–9 record with a 3.72 ERA for the Blue Jays in 2005.

Game Day

Getting to the Park

Manchester is located in southern New Hampshire about 60 miles from Boston and 90 miles from the nearest Eastern League rival in Portland. The ballpark sits between the Merrimack and a set of railroad tracks. Those coming from the north and south should follow I–93 to I–293 South, and then take exit 6 and bear right onto Canal Street. Turn right onto Granite Street, and then left onto South Commercial Street and the ballpark will appear directly ahead. From the east and west, follow Route 101 to I–93 South to I–293 North, and then take exit 5. Turn right onto Granite Street, and then right onto South Commercial Street.

Unfortunately, the parking situation in Manchester is not good. The team lot at the stadium is reserved for luxury suite ticket holders, and common fans are left to park in privately run lots that charge as much as $10 per car. These lots are on South Commercial Street and east of the park on Old Granite Street and Elm Street. The public parking garage at the corner of Granite Street and Canal Street is a ten-minute walk away, but it is the most affordable option, charging only a dollar an hour.

Inside the Park

Good tickets are usually available on game day in Manchester, except when the Portland Sea Dogs are the visitors, in which case the ballpark usually sells out. Folks in these parts love their Red Sox, even their minor league Red Sox.

The main entrance to Merchantsauto.com Stadium is in left field. On passing through the understated entrance gates, fans pass the clubhouse store, and then ascend a steep set of stairs, which leads to a large plaza on the concourse level. Part of this plaza provides standing room just 330 feet from home plate, and part houses a two-tiered group picnic terrace. All of the ballpark seats consist of green plastic stadium chairs with drink holders, except for one section of Bleachers in foul territory out in deep right field. There are seventeen rows in most sections, and those lucky fans in Row A have their feet right down at field level, which is the way it should be at all parks. The nine sections between the dugouts (105–113) consist of Premium Box Seats, while the three sections just past third base (102–104) and the two sections just past first (114 and 115) contain the Box Seats. Sections 100 and 101 in left field and Section 116 in right field house the Grandstand Seats. Section 117 in deep right field offers plastic benches that sell as Bleachers. The right field foul pole is only 306 feet from home plate, and the left field pole is only 326 feet away, so even the deepest outfield seats provide decent views of the game.

The concession stands in Manchester offer grilled Italian sausages, soggy pulled pork sandwiches that are best to be avoided, and cups of milk for the kids. The pizza at the specialty stand behind home plate that is operated by Sal's Pizza of South Willow Street is excellent. Another solid choice is the Chowda House, which serves New England–style clam chowder, lobster rolls, fried shrimp, and fried fish. The ballpark brews include Sam Adams, Guinness, Bass, Labatts, Red Hook, and Smuttynose.

Young fans will want to visit Fungo's Playland, which is accessible via a stairway behind Section 110. This larger-than-usual ballpark playground features a bouncy house, a slide, an obstacle course, and other games.

The Merchantsauto.com Stadium Experience

The Fisher Cats have a brand new Diamond Vision scoreboard in right field and a top-notch PA system, and they seem intent on getting their money's worth out of both. The team plays loud sound bites and song rifts between every pitch, and in between innings a roving MC named "Jackie B" engages fans in a range of promotions while a camera captures the festivities for broadcast on the video board. Most of the promotions are basic minor league stunts like the ubiquitous dizzy bat race and sumo suit wrestling, but one unique event is the game of musical chairs sponsored by the New Hampshire State Highway Department. The team drives a four-seat golf cart onto the field, and then four select fans race around the cart while "I Can't Drive 55," blares through the ballpark speakers. When the song stops, the contestants jump onto the cart and buckle their seat belts as fast as they can. The last fan to buckle up is eliminated, and then the strange maypole dance continues until only one fan remains. The most proficient buckler wins a free T-shirt.

Fungo the Fisher Cat is the local mascot. He seemed a bit sluggish on the sunny summer day that I visited Manchester, probably because he was sweating up a storm inside his brown fur and black Fisher Cats jersey.

On the Town

New Hampshire's largest city has a population of just over 100,000 people. The state's one television station, WMUR-TV Channel 9, is located right beside the ballpark on South Commercial Street, while the neighborhood also includes a beauty salon, a dance studio, and some converted riverside millhouses that now serve as office and retail space. Fisher Cats fans are still waiting for a festive sports bar to open in one of these old brick buildings, but for now they have to trek a few blocks to **Johnny Bad's Sports Bar and Grille** (542 Elm Street) for their pregame revelry. The ballpark neighborhood does offer a solid choice for a pregame seafood meal, as the **Starfish Grille** (33 South Commercial Street) inhabits one of the old mill buildings.

Just 30 miles east of Manchester via Route 101, travelers find a New Hampshire landmark at **Hampton Beach**. Hampton offers a large sand beach, good-sized waves, deep-sea fishing excursions, waterslides, a festive boardwalk, a rowdy nightlife scene, tattoo parlors, and lots of fireworks stores.

Meanwhile, 20 miles south of Manchester via Route 3, hardcore baseball fans will be happy to find an independent league baseball venue. The Nashua Pride of the Can-Am League plays at **Historic Holman Stadium** (67 Amherst Street). The ballpark originally served as the home of a Brooklyn Dodgers affiliate in the New England League in the 1940s. It has hosted indy ball since 1995 and was renovated in 2002. Former Boston Red Sox manager and third baseman Butch Hobson has spent the last several years at the Pride's helm.

MCCOY STADIUM

Pawtucket Red Sox

Class AAA, International League
(BOSTON RED SOX)

McCoy Stadium
1 Ben Mondor Way
Pawtucket, Rhode Island
401–724–7300

If you take your family to Fenway Park—where tickets cost more than at any other major league ballpark and where a parking space within walking distance of the turnstiles costs upward of $50—your night at the old ball game is apt to cost you somewhere in the neighborhood of a week's pay, after you factor in hot dogs, sodas, beers, and souvenirs, of course. Take the wife and kids to a game at McCoy Stadium, just 50 miles south of Boston, where the Old Towne Team's Triple-A club plays in Pawtucket, Rhode Island, though, and it's a whole different story. At McCoy Stadium, box seats still sell for less than $10 and parking in the stadium lot is still free. But affordability is just one of several reasons why the "PawSox" perennially vie for, and usually win, the International League attendance title. The old-time ballpark experience found at McCoy, and the insatiable appetite for all things Red Sox that New Englanders seem to possess, also factor into the equation.

McCoy Stadium was built in 1942 as a Works Progress Administration project and named after former Pawtucket mayor, Thomas J. McCoy. Presidents Roosevelt and Truman both visited during the 1940s to see the product of the federal funding they'd provided. Despite two renovations to McCoy in the 1990s, the main seating bowl has changed very little in the six-plus decades since the park originally opened. The renovations, which took place in 1992 and 1999, expanded the seating bowl down the left field line, added a grass berm in left field home run territory and bleachers in right field home run territory, and added a new three-story main entrance in left field foul territory.

The seating bowl rises steeply around the infield, and a steel-framed wooden roof covers all of the seats behind home plate and the back two-thirds of the seats down the baselines, except for those in the three new sections in left field foul territory, which are not covered. Gray steel pillars rise between the grandstand seats to support the roof, while the press box, suspended beneath the roof, makes for comically obstructed views from the General Admission seats in the two sections directly behind it. The stadium is rounded so that the seats are fairly close to the action behind home plate but rather far from fair territory along the baselines. Indeed, there is more foul territory in Pawtucket than at most minor league or major league ballparks.

The dugouts are not dug out but located at field level, tucked beneath the first row of box seats, which is raised about 10 feet above the field. A handful of luxury boxes appear on the outfield sides of both dugouts, also tucked below the first rows of seats. If this doesn't sound like the type of fan-friendly seating bowl you've grown accustomed to in recent years, you're right, it's not. And yet, here's betting that the old-time ambience of McCoy Stadium will enchant you so thoroughly that you really won't find yourself pining for your usual seat so close to the first base bag that you can spit sunflower seeds at the first base coach when the mood strikes you.

The entrance tower in left field foul territory, the narrow berm atop the left field home run fence, and the bleachers and party tent in right field home run territory combine to seal in the stadium from the parking lot just beyond the outfield fences, while the track around the schoolboy football field just beyond the stadium in right field foul territory sees steady action all night long as local fitness buffs circle it and occasionally stop to pick up any stray foul balls that come their way.

Just how popular are the Pawtucket Red Sox these days? In 2005 they ranked first in the International League and fourth in all of minor league baseball when they drew 688,421 fans. That tally established a new franchise attendance record and bested other New England teams like the Boston Celtics (656,081) and New England Patriots (550,048). Among the many pro teams in New England, only the Boston Red Sox, who drew 2,847,888 fans to Fenway Park, attracted more visitors than the "PawSox" in 2005.

Pawtucket has been a Red Sox outpost since 1970 when it fielded a Boston affiliate in the Eastern League. After the Double-A team moved to Bristol, Connecticut, following the 1972 season, the woebegone Louisville Colonels moved to McCoy Stadium to become the International League Pawtucket Red Sox in 1973. The PawSox got off to a smashing start in Triple-A, winning the IL's coveted Governor's Cup in that first season. In 1977 local businessman Ben Mondor bought the team and he continues to own it to this day. Throughout his tenure Mr. Mondor has kept prices low and cultivated a family friendly environment where the game on the field is more important than goofy promotions and other distracting forms of ballpark entertainment.

The relationship between Boston and Pawtucket has offered Rhode Islanders the chance

McCoy Stadium

to witness the development of nearly every home-grown prospect to come up through the Boston system during the past three decades—including future stars like Wade Boggs, Roger Clemens, Cecil Cooper, Nomar Garciaparra, Bruce Hurst, Jon Lester, Trot Nixon, Jonathan Papelbon, Jim Rice, and Mo Vaughn.

Rice won the International League Triple Crown in 1974, and Boggs won a batting title in 1981. Bronson Arroyo and Tomo Ohka both pitched nine-inning perfect games at McCoy Stadium in the early 2000s. Yankee prospect Dave Righetti and native New Englander Mark Fidrych hooked up for a classic pitchers duel before a then-record crowd of more than 9,000 fans in 1982, and Fidrych prevailed. Dom DiMaggio, Johnny Pesky, and Bobby Doerr turned out at McCoy to watch the 2004 Triple-A All-Star Game, and the International League beat the Pacific Coast League in dramatic fashion, winning on a walk-off homer by Columbus slugger Andy Phillips.

From 1977 through 1999, the Boston Red Sox traveled to McCoy once a year to play an exhibition game. And stars like Clemens, Manny Ramírez, Dennis Eckersley, and Jose Canseco all stopped by McCoy Stadium on rehab assignments. But McCoy's claim to fame continues to be that it hosted the longest professional baseball game ever played. On a chilly Saturday night in 1981, the PawSox and Rochester Red Wings began play at 8:00 P.M. The Red Wings had a 1–0 lead heading to the bottom of the ninth inning, but Rochester starter Larry Jones bounced a pitch in the dirt that allowed Pawtucket to send the game into extra innings tied 1–1. Well after midnight in the wee hours of Easter morning, the Red Wings took a 2–1 lead in the top of the twenty-first. In the bottom of the inning, though, the PawSox tied the score on a double by Boggs. Afterward, Wade's wife Debbie—one of just nineteen frozen fans still roaming the McCoy Stadium stands when the game was suspended at 4:07 A.M., after thirty-two innings and four seventh-inning stretches, said, "I didn't known whether to boo him, kiss him, or kill him."

After International League commissioner Harold Cooper ruled that the game should be completed (hopefully) on June 23, it took just one inning for the two teams to settle the matter before 5,756 fans and an international media contingent. Pawtucket's Dave Koza blooped a bases-loaded single into left field in the bottom of the thirty-third inning to plate Marty Barrett and give the home team a 3–2 win. Boggs went 4 for 12 in the game, while Rochester's Cal Ripken Jr. went 2 for 13. Bob Ojeda pitched one inning and got credit for the win. In all, twenty-five future major leaguers played in the game.

The longest game's 33 innings, 219 at bats, 882 pitches, and 60 strikeouts still rank as the most ever in a pro game, while no contest has surpassed the game's 8:25 duration either. In 2006 the PawSox invited several members of the 1981 club back to Pawtucket, along with manager Joe Morgan, to celebrate the twenty-fifth anniversary of the longest game. And fans today find a special exhibit behind Section 13 on the McCoy Stadium concourse where the team displays a line score from the game, a box score, photos, and several newspaper articles.

Game Day

Getting to the Park

Pawtucket is located a few miles east of Providence along the Massachusetts state line. McCoy Stadium is less than a mile from I–95. From the north, take I–95 South to exit 2A in Massachusetts and follow Newport Avenue for 2 miles and then turn right onto Columbus Avenue. Follow Columbus for ½ mile, then turn right onto the George Bennett Highway and follow it for ³⁄₁₀ mile before turning left onto Division Street, which leads to the ballpark. From the south, take I–95 North to exit 27, 28, or 29 in Rhode Island and follow the many signs to McCoy Stadium. As mentioned earlier, parking is free in the stadium lot, but the lot usually fills up about half an hour before the game. For those who arrive late, the lot at Jenks Junior High on the corner of Division and Ashton Streets is also free.

Inside the Park

McCoy Stadium offers just over 10,000 comfortable stadium chairs. There are also bleachers in right field foul territory and right field home run territory. And there is standing room above the home bullpen in deep left field and at field level in right field foul territory. The stadium fills up during the summer months, especially when the archrivals from Columbus are in town. Yes, the Red Sox–Yankees rivalry extends to the Triple-A level. So, be sure to order your tickets in advance if possible.

The runways off the main concourse lead to an interior walkway a third of the way up the seating bowl. Below the walkway are eight rows of Green Box Seats, while just above the walkway are ten rows of Red Box Seats. Section 1 is located near first base, while Sections 6 and 7 are behind home plate, Section 12 is at third, and Section 15 is in medium-depth left field.

Above the red seats are another ten rows of blue seats, which sell as General Admission. A general admission ticket is good for a spot in any of these seats or for a spot on the Bleachers or berm. The sun sets behind the left field foul pole, so if you mind an early inning glare, shoot for seats along the third base side where the sun will be at your back.

Most of the concession stands are located on the concourse behind the seats, while there are a limited number of stands inside the seating bowl atop the very last row of seats. The ballpark treats include the strip steak sandwich, sausages, bratwurst, and burgers at the grill on the left field side of the concourse, along with a delicious chicken Parmesan sandwich, popcorn chicken, a taco salad, vegetarian burgers, fast-food-style french fries, giant Freeze Pops, Papa Gino's pizza, Hershey's ice cream, and Hebrew National hot dogs. The wide selection of ballpark brews includes Amstel Light and Guinness, while there is also a wine bar on the third base side of the concourse.

There are several exhibits on the concourse worth checking out in addition to the display commemorating the longest game. Black-and-white plaques on the pillars that support the roof over the concourse remember special moments in McCoy Stadium history. Most of these concern the PawSox, but a few pay tribute to the exploits of Team USA, which has used the stadium periodically through the years. In addition there are dozens of pictures of former PawSox who went on to play in the major leagues, ranging from Don Aase to Bob Zupcic, on the spiraling entrance ramp behind home plate. Some of the pictures that made me chuckle were ones of Lou Merloni, Oil Can Boyd, Butch Hobson, Sam Horn, Chico Walker, Rich Garcés, Luis Rivera, Steve Crawford, John Marzano, Steve Lyons, Scott Cooper, Carlos Quintana, and Phil Plantier (crouched, of course, in his crazy "toilet bowl" batting stance). At the very bottom of the ramp, there is a "Wall of Legends" photo exhibit that captures the history of baseball through the decades.

The large team store is located at ground level just inside the left field entrance. Blue-and-red foam paws are hot sellers among the all-important eight-year-old and younger demographic group.

The McCoy Stadium Experience

At McCoy Stadium the focus is on the game, not on commercial advertisements disguised as between-innings competitions or on loud and annoying sound bites that blare through the stadium speakers. This is a baseball park for baseball fans. Even the two bears that serve as the PawSox mascots—Paws, the male, and Sox, the female—barely make their presence known, emerging from their left field den just long enough to toss soft baseballs into the stands while they walk the warning track midway through the fifth inning.

Because the seats are elevated well above the field, fishing for autographs is the pregame activity of choice among young fans. After batting practice a contingent of industrious youngsters casts down cutout milk cartons—each with a baseball and Sharpie inside—from the seats above the home dugout. The cartons hang on strings and when the players emerge from the clubhouse, they reach into the cartons and sign the balls, then the young fans reel in their cartons to see which players signed for them. It is quite a sight to see, and one that's sure to put a smile on the face of the kid in all

of us. And for the record, I hauled in my carton to discover that Abe Alvarez and Adam Stern had both signed my ball.

On the Town

Pawtucket is a hardscrabble town that is worth visiting for a ball game, but it's not worth staying in much longer than that. For nightlife and overnight accommodations, I recommend heading to Providence just 5 miles away.

Those intent on having a pregame brew at a local establishment will find the **Left Field Pub** (South Bend Street and Meadow Street) and **Mei King** (South Bend Street) within easy walking distance of the stadium parking lot.

Old ballpark buffs can head south to **Cardines Field** (20 America's Cup Avenue) in Newport, where the Newport Gulls of the New England Collegiate Baseball League (NECBL) play their home games. The original seats at this ancient yard were replaced in the 1980s, but the distinctive green façade behind home plate remains. Back in the late 1800s, the Newport Colts of the old New England League played here, then in the early 1900s, the George S. Donnelly Sunset League began using the field. Several barnstorming Negro League teams stopped by Newport during the 1930s and 1940s, including squads featuring Satchel Paige and Larry Doby. After the NECBL came to Cardines Field in 2001, the 3,000-seat stadium was ranked the fourth-best collegiate summer league facility in the country by *Baseball America*.

NEW BRITAIN STADIUM
New Britain Rock Cats

Class AA, Eastern League
(MINNESOTA TWINS)

New Britain Stadium
Willow Brook Park/South Main Street
New Britain, Connecticut
860–224–8383

Whenever a community replaces an aging ballpark with a new one, a certain percentage of the local fan base waxes nostalgic and laments the break from tradition. Sometimes fans are justified in pining for the good old days when the local yard was quaint and cozy and everything else it needed to be, even if it didn't offer the bells and whistles found at its all too spacious, all too modern replacement. Other times, though, Father Time sweetens the memories of fans. They remember all of the special moments they shared at the old park with their family and friends, but they forget about the splinters they used to pick out of their legs after nights spent on its wooden bleachers or about the ungodly stench that emanated from the cattle-trough urinals on warm nights. To guard against such selective remembering, the city of New Britain did a smart thing. When it came time to build a new ballpark for the local nine, the city built it right next to the old one . . . and left old Beehive Field standing, to serve as home to New Britain High School's baseball team. True, the new ballpark, New Britain Stadium, could offer more personality. And true, it could have been designed more like the many other 1990s-era ballparks that have open concourses and family friendly seating berms in the outfield. But if anyone should ever entertain the delusion that the stadium isn't a tremendous upgrade over

the city's previous one, the rather convincing evidence to the contrary sits right next door. The two stadiums are located within Willow Brook Park.

Beehive Field was home to the New Britain Red Sox from the time they arrived in 1983— after moving from Bristol—through the 1994 season. With wooden bleachers that could accommodate only about 4,000 people, tiny dugouts, and a Spartan press box, "The Hive" quickly became obsolete as the minor leagues established new stadium standards in the early 1990s.

New Britain Stadium was designed and built entirely by Connecticut companies. It went up during the summer of 1995 while the "Hardware City Rock Cats," a Twins affiliate, played their first season in New Britain at Beehive Field. The Red Sox affiliation had ended after the previous season when Boston decided to move its Double-A squad to Trenton. New Britain's new ballpark opened on April 12, 1996, and the Rock Cats (who would drop the "Hardware City" from their nickname in 1997) have posted healthy attendance totals ever since. Today, the Rock Cats are more popular than ever. They set a franchise attendance record in 2005, drawing 337,687 fans, and then signed a new five-year lease agreement with the city that guarantees they will stay in New Britain through 2011 and contains extensions that could continue the relationship through 2026.

New Britain Stadium's redbrick façade is adorned by green iron arches, while a green roof extends over the main entranceway. Inside, the grandstand rises sharply, to be topped by a small roof that covers the press box and outdoor portions of the twelve luxury suites. The outfield fence is 16 feet high all the way across, which causes the field to play "big," just as its predecessor used to.

Among the most memorable nights during the stadium's first decade were two exhibition games between the Rock Cats and Minnesota Twins, one in 1997 and one in 2001. The bush leaguers beat the big leaguers on both occasions. In the first contest Benji Sampson tossed a five-hitter en route to a 3–0 shutout against a lineup that included Chuck Knoblauch, Paul Molitor, and Terry Steinbach. In the second meeting the Rock Cats prevailed 4–2 against a Twins team that featured former Rock Cats Torii Hunter, Jacque Jones, Corey Koskie, Cristian Guzmán, and David Ortiz.

Although New Britain's team has featured heavy hitters like Ortiz, Hunter, Dustan Mohr, Mo Vaughn, Jeff Bagwell, and Ellis Burks through the years, an unlikely candidate holds the city's single season home run record— Michael Cuddyer, who belted 30 dingers in 2001. As for the great pitchers in franchise history, the list is topped by hard throwers like Roger Clemens, who helped guide New Britain to the 1983 Eastern League championship, Curt Schilling, and Francisco Liriano.

Prior to the arrival of the New Britain Red Sox in 1983, the city had not fielded a minor league team since the Eastern Association's New Britain Sinks went 27–97 in 1914. Hmm . . . with a record like that maybe they should have been called the Stinks!

Game Day

Getting to the Park

New Britain is a small city 20 miles southwest of Hartford. Those arriving from the west should take I-84 East to Route 72 East to Route 9 South, then take exit 25 and turn left onto Ellis Street. Turn left onto South Main Street, and after a mile Willow Brook Park will appear on your right. Those coming from the east should take I-84 West to Route 9 South and then follow the directions as above. The city manages the parking operations, charging $3.00 for a standard spot, and $5.00 for a spot closer to the stadium. The situation is less than ideal, as getting in and out of the lot takes much longer than at most parks. Those looking to avoid the traffic jam should park at New Britain High School. The cost is the same, and it's not a bad walk down the hill to get to the stadium.

Inside the Park

With a seating capacity of 6,146, New Britain Stadium is just large enough to accommodate a growing fan base that seems to become a little more avid each season. The seats extend only about 25 feet into outfield foul territory down either baseline. Seating is divided between a lower bowl at field level and an upper bowl that rises steeply behind the walkway that bisects the seating bowl.

The lower level begins with Section 101 in shallow right field, continues down the first baseline to Sections 109 and 110 behind home plate, and finishes with Section 118 in shallow left field. The green stadium chairs all sell as Field Box Seats, whether they're in the front row behind home plate, or in the tenth row down the first baseline. So order your tickets in advance if you want a primo seat that will be better than, but priced the same as, the seat you're likely to get at the box office on game day.

The wide walkway behind the field boxes offers several cement stairways leading up to the second level. The second level is raised about 6 feet, allowing fans in the first row to look easily over the aisle traffic below. On this level the nine sections between the dugouts— Sections 204 through 212—contain molded green bucket chairs that sell as Reserved Seats. The three sections farther down the baselines on either side house Bleachers with backs that sell as General Admission. If you're going to be in New Britain for a night game, shoot for a seat on the third base side, since the ones on the first baseline face the setting sun for the first hour.

The press box rises right behind Section 208, while six indoor/outdoor luxury suites appear on either side of it. The group picnic area is at field level down the right field line, while there is a Standing Room Only (SRO) area down the left field line. Also down the left field line is a playground that contains an inflatable slide, bouncy pen, speed pitch booth, video games, and a spot for kids to have their picture taken in a Rock Cats jersey.

The main concourse is tucked beneath the grandstand down at ground level. Here fans find a wide menu that includes seasoned french fries, Rocky's pizza, hot and cold subs, Italian sausages, kielbasa with sauerkraut, clam chowder, vegetable chili, and more. The stands offer several different macrobrews on tap, as well as Sam Adams. For the grape fans glasses of chardonnay and white zinfandel are also available.

While on the concourse, check out the New Britain Sports Hall of Fame, which features plaques honoring each member. If you're like me, you won't recognize most of the names here. The few notables include current NFL player Tebucky Jones, former National League president Thomas J. Lynch, former NCAA president John Toner, and Nick Tronsky, widely considered the best duckpin bowler ever.

Overlooking the third base grandstands, the Sam Adams Bar and Grill offers a mahogany counter and several picnic tables covered by sun umbrellas. Before the game starts, the bar offers a "happy hour" with music, contests, and drink specials. The grill features marinated chicken sandwiches, half-pound steak burgers, sausages with peppers and onions, and other specialty items.

The New Britain Stadium Experience

Not surprisingly, the New Britain mascot is a Rock Cat. Wondering what exactly a Rock Cat is? Well, judging from the looks of Rocky, a Rock Cat is some sort of a hybrid between a human being and a large flea-ridden feline. Rocky's outfit is pretty lame, barely more than a cat's head plopped atop a teenager in a baseball uniform, really. Oh well, the kids didn't seem to mind.

As for the between innings promotions, they occur in rapid fire succession throughout the game, catering mostly to younger fans who venture onto the field to partake in activities involving pizza paddles, Frisbees, oversized shoes, and other props that have little to do with baseball.

On the Town

The "Hardware City" has a population of about 70,000 people. While Hartford is just twenty minutes away, most fans should find enough to keep them entertained in New Britain for an evening. Those looking for a pregame meal will find several fast-food joints a few blocks south of the park on New Britain Road. For some hearty local cuisine, **Fatherland Polish Restaurant** (450 South Main Street)—which makes delicious strawberry pirogues—and **Guy's Place** (224 South Main Street) are popular.

New Britain offers easy access to a couple of independent league teams that play in the Constitution State. Just 20 miles south of New Britain in West Haven, the Can-Am League's New Haven County Cutters play at **Yale Field** (250 Derby Avenue), which dates back to 1928. Another 20 miles south, the Atlantic League's Bridgeport Bluefish play at **The Ballpark at Harbor Yard** (500 Main Street), which opened in 1998.

DODD STADIUM

Connecticut Defenders

Class AA, Eastern League
(SAN FRANCISCO GIANTS)

Thomas J. Dodd Memorial Stadium
14 Stott Avenue
Norwich, Connecticut
860–887–7962

The 2006 season signaled the dawning of a new era for the Eastern League team in Norwich, Connecticut. Prior to the season new owner Lou DiBella decided to rename the club in an effort to inject some life into a floundering franchise. So long, Norwich Navigators. Hello, Connecticut Defenders. The new moniker isn't so different from the old one, as both acknowledge Southeastern Connecticut's proud military heritage. The New London Submarine Base is 25 miles south of Norwich along the Thames River, and the U.S. Coast Guard Academy is just a couple of miles farther south. As for trying to market the club as Connecticut's team instead of Norwich's, only time will tell if the ploy is successful. One team that took offense to the name change was the New Britain Rock Cats, who thought it inappropriate for DiBella to label his club "Connecticut's team." Throughout the 2006 season, the Rock Cats referred to their Constitution State rivals simply as the "Defenders" on their pocket schedule, in their media guide, in their press releases, in their PA announcements, and in their radio broadcasts, refusing to acknowledge the "Connecticut" half of the name. This came after Rock Cats general manager Bill Dowling said it was "disrespectful" for the Defenders to lay claim to the entire state.

Putting matters of semantics and good taste aside, it will obviously take more than a new name to resuscitate a Norwich club that finished last in the Eastern League in attendance in 2005, and twenty-eighth out of thirty Double-A teams nationally, drawing just 170,686 fans. But DiBella proved to be a creative, aggressive marketer during his overlapping careers as an HBO Sports executive and boxing promoter, and he says that he is committed to keeping the Defenders in Norwich, so it will be interesting to see what else he comes up with to generate buzz in Norwich.

The Navigators actually got off to a pretty good start in the mid-1990s, when they returned minor league baseball to Norwich for the first time in more than eight decades. Buoyed by an affiliation with the New York Yankees, who relocated their Double-A prospects from Albany to Norwich, and by a sparkling new ballpark, the Navigators drew more than 280,000 fans in their inaugural 1995 season and kept their attendance in the respectable mid-200,000 range into the early 2000s.

Norwich was dealt a serious blow when it lost its affiliation with the Yankees in 2002, though. After the Boston Red Sox announced they would be abandoning their outpost in Trenton in favor of a new home in Portland, the Yankees jumped at the opportunity to move their prospects closer to home, seizing the Trenton market. Norwich, in turn, inked a deal with another storied franchise, the San Francisco Giants. But the team quickly discovered that an affiliation with a National League team from out west did not carry the same cachet in Connecticut—traditional border territory between Red Sox Country and Yankee Country—as one with the American League East powerhouse from New York.

If the Defenders aren't able to survive in Norwich, it won't be due to any failing on the part of Dodd Stadium. Although it's no longer shiny and new, the ballpark is more than adequate to serve as a Double-A facility. Named after a popular local senator, Dodd Stadium is one of nine ballparks that opened in the twelve-team Eastern League during the 1990s at a time when a wave of stadium construction projects swept across the minor leagues. Only Reading's First Energy Stadium (1950), Harrisburg's Commerce Bank Park (1987), and New Hampshire's Merchantsauto.com Stadium (2005) debuted in decades other than the one that brought baseball interim commissioner Bud Selig, rampant steroid use, and a memorable National Anthem performance by TV star Roseanne.

Like many parks of its era, Dodd Stadium features a seating bowl sunken below street level so that fans enter on a main concourse that overlooks the field, and then descend stairways between sections to access their seats. One thing that makes this park a bit different is its press box, which is placed right behind the last row of seats behind home plate. Because of this placement, fans walking along the concourse lose sight of the field for a moment as they pass behind the media center. From a design standpoint, placing the press box down low like this left more room for luxury suites upstairs on the second deck that covers the concourse. There are eighteen indoor/outdoor luxury suites at Dodd Stadium, and unlike at most ballparks, these continue uninterrupted high above the home plate area, with four appearing in the space that a press box would normally occupy.

The color scheme at Dodd Stadium is also unique. Rather than embracing the dark green "Camden Chairs" that seem to be all the rage these days, the seats are light gray and maroon. The face of the press box is dark blue, the luxury suites are gray, topped by a gray shingled roof, and the steel trusses that stand at the front of the concourse supporting the suite level are alternately red, white, and blue. The outfield offers a three-billboard-high expanse across home run territory and a large scoreboard with replay capability atop the billboards in right-center. Treetops peek over the billboards across the outfield to complete the view.

While some decent prospects passed through Dodd Stadium during its time as a Yankees outpost (Drew Henson, Hideki Irabu, Nick Johnson, Mike Lowell, Andy Pettitte), Norwich fans also got to watch a larger-than-usual contingent of big leaguers play each year. Norwich was a more convenient rehab destination for the Yankees than Columbus, Ohio, where their Triple-A team played. As such, Roger Clemens, David Cone, Chili Davis, Dwight Gooden, Dave Justice, Tim Raines, Darryl Strawberry, and Bernie Williams all wore the Navigators uniform while working their way back into big league shape. The subsequent affiliation with the Giants, for obvious geographic reasons, has seen far fewer big leaguers drop by Norwich, but it has witnessed the emergence of future major leaguers like Boof Bonser, Noah Lowry, and Marcus Thames.

Game Day

Getting to the Park

Norwich is about 50 miles north of Connecticut's Atlantic shore and 50 miles west of the Rhode Island state line. The closest minor league cities—Pawtucket and New Britain—are both about two hours away. Dodd Stadium is located within an industrial park on the eastern edge of the city. From I–95, take I–395 North to exit 81 for Route 2 West. Bear right onto Route 32 North, then turn right onto New Park Avenue. Enter the Norwich Industrial

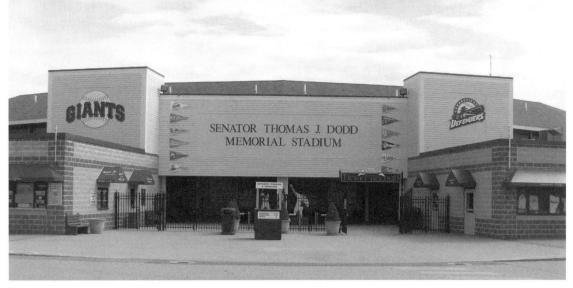

Dodd Stadium

Park and follow the signs to the stadium. The two-way road that runs through the complex is converted into a one-way, two-lane road on game days so that both lanes accommodate traffic heading toward the stadium before the game and then both lanes accommodate traffic heading away from the stadium afterward. Parking is plentiful and free.

Inside the Park

There are three different ticket options in Norwich, all of which provide access to seats that are close to the field and have unobstructed sight lines. The seating bowl extends into medium-depth outfield foul territory down each baseline, offering twenty rows in most sections. In Sections 4–18 around the infield, the first eight rows contain gray stadium chairs that sell as Premium Seats. The twelve rows behind the Premies house maroon plastic bucket chairs that sell as Reserved Seats. The configuration is different in the sections beyond the corner bases—Sections 1–3 in right field and Sections 19–21 in left field—where the first four rows contain Premium Seats, then

the next six rows contain Reserved Seats, and the final ten rows contain aluminum bleachers with backs that sell as Grandstand Seats. The nicely landscaped grass hillsides that fill the spaces between the ends of the seating bowl and the outfield foul poles are merely decorative and do not see use as seating berms. The group picnic areas are above the hills on the concourse level.

The concession stands offer standard ballpark fare, highlighted by Nathan's Famous Hot Dogs. There is also a video arcade for kids on the concourse.

The Dodd Stadium Experience

As part of the effort to establish a new team identity, Connecticut changed mascots before the start of the 2006 season, as well. The team carefully released its slithery old alligator into the Bog Meadow Reservoir, and then welcomed an American bald eagle named "Cutter." Cutter was officially introduced at a press conference held at Fort Trumbull, near the spot where the U.S. Coast Guard's cutter *Eagle* is docked.

Given Norwich's proximity to Connecticut's two popular casinos, it should come as little surprise that the Defenders offer some gambling entertainment for the enjoyment of fans. Midway through the game, the Defenders stage a pony race. Three large horse heads appear above the outfield fence, then make their way along the wall, while fans try to guess which one will reach the edge of the batter's eye first. The heads are supported, of course, by team employees hidden from view behind the wall.

Recent promotional nights in Norwich have included "70s Night," when the concourse was aglow with disco balls and ballpark employees and fans dug their bellbottoms out of storage, and "Don King Night," when the first 1,000 fans to enter the park received frizzy salt-and-pepper wigs styled to look like the mop on top of the legendary boxing promoter's head, and King himself greeted fans at the turnstiles as they entered the park.

As for weekly promotions, on Wednesday afternoons the Defenders fans play baseball bingo all game long, and on Sundays the kids get to run the bases after the game.

On the Town

Visitors will find a concentration of fast-food joints and casual restaurants just 1½ miles south of the stadium on Town Street.

Foxwoods Resort Casino is about 15 miles southeast of Norwich on a Pequot Indian Reservation near the town of Ledyard. The complex boasts the largest casino in the world—with 340,000 square feet of gaming space—as well as shopping, dining, night life, shows, golf, and just about everything else you'd expect to find at a world-class resort.

The **Mohegan Sun**, in Uncasville, is another popular gambling destination. Built to a smaller scale than Foxwoods, it offers restaurants, like Michael Jordan's Steak House and Bubba's Barbecue, and all kinds of entertainment—concerts, comedy shows, and theater. The Mohegan Sun is also home to the WNBA's Connecticut Sun and to a regular schedule of boxing cards.

Connecticut's eastern waterfront is also a popular tourist destination, particularly the town of **Mystic**, which offers fresh seafood, quaint shops, and the Mystic Aquarium.

NYSEG STADIUM

Binghamton Mets

Class AA, Eastern League
(NEW YORK METS)

NYSEG Stadium
211 Henry Street
Binghamton, New York
607-723-6387

The Eastern League returned to one of its founding cities in 1992 with the opening of Binghamton Municipal Stadium and the arrival of a New York Mets farm team. While the stadium has since been renamed after a regional energy supply company, the team that calls it "home" has remained the same. Prior to the debut of the B-Mets, Binghamton had been without a team since 1968 when the Binghamton Triplets left town. Today, Binghamton is the only original Eastern League city still fielding a team in the circuit, which dates back to 1923. The other league founders were Elmira, Scranton, Wilkes-Barre, Williamsport, and York. In the league's second season, Harrisburg and Utica joined the originals, increasing league membership to eight.

Like most of the facilities in today's Eastern League, NYSEG Stadium will never be mistaken for an old-time ballpark, unless it sticks around long enough to see the day forty or fifty years from now when high-rising concrete seating bowls are regarded with the type of nostalgia fans currently reserve for the few remaining covered grandstands on the bush league horizon. Despite its obvious shortcomings in the "charm" department, the stadium is comfortable and well kept and the men and women charged with making the ballpark experience enjoyable carry out their duties with a pleasant and helpful enthusiasm.

Owing to its bright blue seats that rise steeply and its press box and six luxury suites that take up a relatively small area behind home plate, NYSEG Stadium reminded me of the New York Mets Florida State League stadium, Tradition Field, in Port St. Lucie. While the outfield view at Tradition Field is of palm trees, however, the view beyond the fences in Binghamton showcases a stretch of the New York, Susquehanna and Western rail line in left field, and—just in case fans should forget which big league team the B-Mets are married to—a large parking lot beyond the fence in right, just like at Shea Stadium. Off in the distance, the rolling green Catskill Mountains complete the picture.

As for those little eccentricities that make each ballpark unique, NYSEG Stadium offers a couple. The bull pens are hidden practically out of sight deep in the outfield corners, and while they both run parallel to the nearest foul line, the sitting areas for each team's relief corps are in home run territory. The relievers watch the game through cutouts in the advertising signs nearest the foul poles. The field itself is also unique, as the lush green grass on either side of the batter's circle is bisected by dirt paths that connect the on-deck circles to home plate.

A small roof covers the press box, luxury suites, and last few rows of grandstand seats in Sections 200–206. It exists not so much to provide shelter from the rain—which fans find on the main concourse down beneath the seats—as it does to shade the infield and to crown the stadium with a decorative flourish. While the top of the roof, like the façade of the press box and the seats, is bright blue, to match one of the trademark colors of the New York Mets, thankfully the folks in Binghamton resisted the temptation to also feature within the ballpark their parent club's other favorite color, bright orange. The New York Mets logo does, however, hang on the gray cement exterior of NYSEG Stadium.

Prior to moving their Eastern League operation to Binghamton, the Mets had fielded a Double-A team in Williamsport for a single season, in 1991, and before that in Jackson, Mississippi, from 1975 through 1990. The eventual major leaguers who have played for Binghamton include Edgardo Alfonzo, Octavio Dotel, Jason Isringhausen, Lastings Milledge, Rey Ordóñez, Jay Payton, José Reyes, Preston Wilson, and David Wright.

Game Day

Getting to the Park

Binghamton combines with Johnson City and Endicott to form the Triple Cities region, just a few miles north of the Pennsylvania state line. The two full-season minor league towns closest to Binghamton both field teams in the International League, as Scranton–Wilkes-Barre is 65 miles south along I–81 and Syracuse is 75 miles north along the same road. NYSEG Stadium is located in the northern part of Binghamton, just east of the Chenango River and west of the Susquehanna River. The ballpark faces away from downtown, toward the rail yard and rolling green mountains. Those traveling to Binghamton from the north should take I–81 South to exit 4S and then follow Route 7 South for 1 mile. Take the exit for U.S. Route 11 and go straight at the end of the ramp to the stadium. Those arriving from the south, should take I–81 North to exit 2W and follow Route 11 north for 4½ miles before turning right onto Chapman Street, which leads to the stadium. Parking in the city-run lots costs $3.00, but there are also curbside spots available in the streets surrounding the stadium.

Inside the Park

All of the seating is provided in the form of bright blue plastic stadium chairs. There are

NYSEG Stadium

6,012 of them in all, leaving the stadium just twelve seats over the minimum allowable for a facility to meet Double-A specifications. The seating bowl is divided into two levels by a fairly narrow walkway that runs between the tenth and eleventh rows. The lower ten rows sell as Box Seats, which appear in Sections 1 and 2 behind home plate and continue in even-numbered sections down the first baseline and in odd-numbered sections down the third baseline, culminating with Sections 16 and 17 in shallow outfield foul territory. Above the concourse the steep concrete grandstand offers another sixteen rows. Behind home plate and behind the dugouts, the first eight rows of the second level sell as Box Seats, but everywhere else in the park they sell as Reserved Seats. Rows K and L should be avoided, if possible, as the traffic on the walkway can interfere with sight lines.

The concession concourse is tucked beneath the seats. Here fans find hot dogs that cost just $1.00, cotton candy, soft pretzels, and Sponge Bob Square Pants ice-cream bars. But the real treat at NYSEG Stadium is found at the barbecue pit down the right field line where hot spiedie simmers on a charcoal grill all game long. Spiedie is one of those local delicacies that are exceedingly popular in one small corner of the country but virtually impossible to find anywhere else. Spiedie is a Broome County treat that was created and perfected by the region's Italian settlers in the early 1900s. It consists of skewered cubes of marinated chicken or pork grilled over hot coals and served in a long hoagie roll. When the meat is done, the skewer is laid in the roll, then the roll is squeezed together to hold the meat in place while the skewer is extracted. This moist and juicy culinary delight tastes something like shish kabob, but with its own unique zing. While numerous establishments in and around New York's Southern Tier serve

spiedie, Lupo's Char-Pit is generally considered the master, and fittingly Lupo's operates the spiedie stand at NYSEG Stadium.

If you fall in love with spiedie during your trip to Binghamton and want to grill up your own batch at home, here's the recipe for a marinade to get you started. Combine 1 small minced onion, 2 cups olive oil, ½ cup dry red wine, ½ cup balsamic vinegar, ½ cup chopped mint leaves, 1 tablespoon salt, 2 teaspoons black pepper, 5 cloves minced garlic, 1 tablespoon lemon juice, 1 teaspoon crushed rosemary leaves, 1 teaspoon dried basil leaves, and 1 teaspoon dried oregano leaves. Marinade up to four pounds of chicken, pork, or lamb for at least two days, then cook the meat slowly over hot coals.

The NYSEG Stadium Experience

Binghamton fans enjoy the antics of two colorful mascots. Ballwinkle is the chief rabble-rouser, while Buddy Bee buzzes about the park as his bubbly sidekick. Ballwinkle is a blue moose with an oversized baseball for a nose. Buddy Bee is a lanky bumblebee who wears a B-Mets uniform.

The B-Mets offer fans the delightful melodies of a ballpark organist who sets up on the midlevel walkway behind home plate and tickles the ivory all game long. Listening to the old-time tunes in Binghamton recalls a simpler time for the minor leagues, a time when "YMCA" and "Sponge Bob Square Pants" were not yet considered ballpark classics.

Through the years the B-Mets have demonstrated a willingness to stage the occasional zany promotion to attract some attention to their team. The most interesting happening of the 2006 season occurred on May 21 when the team and its fans set the world record for eating the largest spiedie ever created. Throughout the game brothers Sam and Steve Lupo grilled chicken at their outfield barbecue pit. Then, after the last out was recorded, they assembled a spiedie sandwich that spanned from the left field foul pole all the way down the line to home plate. After the team snapped a few pictures, the 330-foot, 300-pound sandwich was served to the hungry fans who stayed around to have a taste.

On the Town

You've probably noticed the spiedie theme running throughout this chapter, so I would be remiss not to mention at least a few spiedie joints worth visiting in the Triple Cities. **Lupo's Char-Pit** offers three locations in Endicott, including the original restaurant that opened in 1967 at 2710 East Main Street. **Binghamton's Spiedie & Rib Pit** (942 Conklin Road) and **Sharkey's Restaurant** (56 Glenwood Avenue) also draw high marks from local connoisseurs.

As for places to eat in the immediate vicinity of NYSEG Stadium, there are plenty in downtown Binghamton, just a few blocks southwest of the park. *Sopranos* fans will want to visit **Bada Bing Pizza** (122 State Street). Sorry, there aren't any topless girls, but you can get whatever topping you want on your pie.

Fans venturing to this part of New York also have the chance to visit several of the small cities that field teams in the short-season **New York–Penn League**. Auburn, Batavia, and Oneonta are all just short drives from Binghamton. (For more information on the teams and ballparks of the New York–Penn League, see the chapter on that league.)

The **National Baseball Hall of Fame** is also just 80 miles northeast of Binghamton. To reach the museum, take I–88 East to Route 28 North and follow Route 28 to Cooperstown.

DUNN TIRE PARK

Buffalo Bisons

Class AAA, International League
(CLEVELAND INDIANS)

Dunn Tire Park
275 Washington Street
Buffalo, New York
716–846–2000

Dunn Tire Park offers as close an approximation of the major league stadium experience as fans find in the minor leagues. Since opening the 18,150-seat facility in 1988, the Buffalo Bisons have claimed the top three spots in the minor league all-time single-season attendance record book, drawing 1,186,651 fans in 1988, 1,174,358 in 1990, and 1,240,951 in 1991. As hard to believe as it may seem, Buffalo actually outdrew several major league teams during those years. In 1988 the Bisons drew more fans than the Atlanta Braves, Chicago White Sox, and Seattle Mariners; in 1990 they finished ahead of the Braves again; and in 1991 they outdrew the Houston Astros, Montreal Expos, and Cleveland Indians. It is important to also keep in mind that the Bisons played just seventy-two home dates in each of those campaigns, not eighty-one like the big league clubs, otherwise they would have surely embarrassed a few more major league operations. The largest crowd ever to fill the park in Buffalo turned out on June 3, 1990, when 21,050 fans enjoyed a game and then a Beach Boys concert afterward.

The Bisons belonged to the old American Association when they forever redefined the idea of a "big crowd" in the bush leagues, then they joined the International League in 1998 and promptly set that circuit's all-time attendance mark, drawing 768,749 fans.

While the days of attracting a million fans or more each year appear to be over in Buffalo, the Bisons still draw quite well, usually finishing near the 600,000 mark.

Dunn Tire Park originally opened as Pilot Field, then later was known simply as the Downtown Ballpark, then later still as North Americare Park. In 1999 the Dunn Tire Company bought the naming rights.

The stadium was designed by HOK, the firm soon to be made famous by Camden Yards, and constructed at a time when Buffalo was dreaming big. The city had aspirations of rejoining the major leagues for the first time since the Federal League folded in 1915. Buffalo's $42 million stadium was especially constructed so that a third deck could be easily plopped atop its club level should the National League Expansion Committee choose Buffalo as the site for one of the two teams to join the major leagues in 1993. As it turned out, Buffalo was one of the six cities that made the committee's short list, but Denver and Miami won out.

Dunn Tire Park offers an attractive white façade that is decorated by green metal arches. Both the United States and Canadian flags fly outside and inside. Inside, the large first-level seating bowl and smaller club level both offer bright red seats. The outfield view looks away from the downtown skyline, toward an on-ramp for I–190. A large net extends atop the left field wall to protect cars from incoming, or more accurately, outgoing, baseballs. The park's 20-by-40-foot video board is unusual in that it is placed in center field rather than in left or right. The board sits high atop the dark wall that serves as a backdrop for the hitters.

Prior to the construction of Dunn Tire Park, the Bisons played at War Memorial Stadium, a Works Progress Administration facility built primarily for football. The stadium was home to the NFL's Buffalo Bills from 1960 until 1972. It was originally named Roesch Stadium, then

Grover Cleveland Stadium, then Civic Stadium, then finally it was renamed War Memorial Stadium in 1960. The seating capacity was gradually expanded over the years, leaving it with room for more than 46,000 people by the 1980s.

Buffalo's baseball history dates back all the way to the 1880s, when the local team bounced back and forth between the International League and National League while playing at Olympic Park at the corner of Richmond Avenue and Summer Street. In 1914 and 1915, the Buffalo Buffeds played in the Federal League, a renegade major league circuit that was eventually bought out by the American and National Leagues.

The Bisons were members of the International League from 1912 through 1970, before spending twenty-seven seasons in the American Association and then returning to the International League. Fifteen former Bisons are enshrined in the National Baseball Hall of Fame, including Connie Mack, Jimmy Collins, Joe Tinker, Herb Pennock, Gabby Hartnett, Ray Schalk, Joe McCarthy, Lou Boudreau, Bucky Harris, and Johnny Bench.

Game Day

Getting to the Park

Buffalo is on the northern shore of Lake Erie. The closest International League rival is the team in Rochester, 80 miles to the northeast. Dunn Tire Park is located downtown, alongside I–190. From I–190 take exit 6 (Elm Street) and turn left at the first light onto Swan Street, which leads to the park. There is a large parking garage just behind the ballpark's right field wall, near the Swan Street entrance, as well as several public and private lots in the neighborhood. Another option for those staying in the city is to take the Buffalo Metro Rail to the Seneca station, which is right near the park.

Inside the Park

The sea of red seats continues all the way out to the foul poles on the first level but only a little way beyond the lip of the outfield grass on the club level. In addition to the 18,150 seats, there is room for a few thousand fans in the party areas, luxury suites, and standing room areas on the concourse. The Special Reserved Seats are between the corner bases on both the first level and club level. Section 100 is behind the plate, while the sections continue in even numbers down the right field line to Section 114 at first base, and in odd numbers down the left field line to Section 113 at third base. Upstairs, Section 201 is behind the plate, while Section 214 is at first and Section 213 is at third. A walkway runs behind the first twenty rows or so of first-level seats, and the seats behind the walkway, as well as those past the corner bases, are the Reserved Seats. The overhang of the upper level covers the back several rows of these seats. Upstairs, there are three sections of Reserved Seats on either side of the Special Reserved. The three sections of bleachers in deep left field (Sections 121, 123, and 125) sell as General Admission. There is a tiered party deck in straightaway right field, while a bit farther toward center field, a grassy hill offers room for fans to stand and watch the game. Closer still to center is a tent-covered party patio.

The main concourse is hidden from view behind and beneath the first-level seats. The concessions stands offer a wider variety of treats than at most minor league parks, and not surprisingly Buffalo wings appear at the top of the menu. Other favorite items include the fried onion chips, fried bologna sandwich, bratwurst, and shaved Italian ice. A large food court behind home plate offers a Red Osier stand, Bigger Burger stand, Russer Deli Shop, Battistoni Italian stand, and a specialty hot dog stand. I recommend the Tex-Mex Dog, which comes topped with chili, salsa, nacho cheese, and jalapeños. As for the ballpark brews, the local favorite is Labatt . . . this is practically Canada, eh?

Pettibones Grille offers upstairs patio seating on the first base side. It is open Monday through Friday for lunch and on game days stays open until the last out is recorded. There are two gift shops, the Batter's Box, on the third base side, which is open daily from 11:00 A.M. until 3:00 P.M. and during games, and the New Era shop on the first base side, which is only open during games.

The Dunn Tire Park Experience

Although the ballpark in Buffalo lacks the intimacy and small-time feel that make the minor leagues the destination of choice for many families these days, the flip side is that it provides the setting of a big league stadium at a fraction of the cost. When 15,000-plus are in the seats, the crowd buzzes with the type of energy and excitement that you won't find at too many other minor league parks.

There are always plenty of seagulls at Dunn Tire Park. They like to congregate on the tarp during rain delays and to forage for leftover onion chips when the crowd thins out in the later innings. On June 4, 2006, a seagull swooped down toward the field in the eleventh inning of a game between the Bisons and Durham Bulls, and the poor bird was accidentally struck by a pitch from Durham reliever Jason Childers. Although the ball and bird collided about 10 feet in front of home plate, sending the ball careening toward the Bulls dugout, Buffalo batter Rámon Vázquez swung at the pitch (and missed). Vázquez then tried to run to first base, but Bulls catcher Kevin Cash chased down the ball and fired to first for the out. Meanwhile, Bisons catcher Einar Díaz raced onto the field and cradled the wounded bird in his mitt. After the gull was carted off the

field, the umpires decided that the play should not count, so Vázquez got another chance and grounded out. As for the gull, after spending some time at the Dunn Tire Park infirmary, it reportedly flew away under its own power. And somewhere, Dave Winfield was smiling.

The mascots in Buffalo are Buster T. Bison and Chip T. Bison, a couple of wild and crazy guys who like to get the fans riled. These two characters, like the rest of the Buffalo faithful, particularly enjoy Friday nights when the team welcomes all fans to a pregame bash at the party tent behind the right field wall.

There is an autograph booth on the concourse behind Section 122 in right field where forty-five minutes before every game a couple of Bisons appear to sign autographs and mingle with fans. They typically stay for twenty minutes, or until they run out of ink.

In the spring of 2006, local fans turned out at the ballpark to watch hockey of all things. Bisons management opened Dunn Tire Park and its concession stands to fans and broadcast the Buffalo Sabres road play-off games on the big board in center field.

On the Town

Baseball fans will find a slew of restaurants and bars to choose from in the downtown streets just a few blocks north of Dunn Tire Park. Visitors will notice that just about every bar, restaurant, pizza joint, and gas station in Greater Buffalo serves wings, or "Buffalo wings" as we call them in the rest of the country. Most folks agree that for the best Buffalo wings you need to head straight to the source, the **Anchor Bar** (Main Street and North Street). Frank and Teressa Bellissimo invented Buffalo wings at the Anchor in 1964. Today, the Bellissimo's hot and buttery concoction can be found at pubs nationwide. As for the Anchor, it offers a full dinner menu and serves about

36,000 pounds of wings per month, both at the restaurant and through mail order.

A couple blocks north of Dunn Tire Park, ballpark junkies will find the remains of **War Memorial Stadium** (Best Street and Jefferson Avenue), which stood from 1937 until 1988. There isn't much left of the park that starred alongside Robert Redford in the film *The Natural*. Today, a youth sports complex resides on the stadium grounds, but two of the stadium's concrete pillars still stand, topped by posturing bison.

A few blocks south of Dunn Tire Park, visitors will find the **Greater Buffalo Sports Hall of Fame** (One Seymour H. Knox III Plaza), located on the lower level of the HSBC Arena. This free museum displays memorabilia related to baseballers like Ollie Carnegie, Luke Easter, Sal Maglie, and Warren Spahn, among other athletes with ties to the Buffalo area.

Finally, a popular tourist attraction in these parts that you've no doubt heard of and seen pictured on TV and in the movies is **Niagara Falls**. The most famous waterfall on the continent is 20 miles north of Buffalo and easy to reach via I–90. The twin cities of Niagara Falls, New York, and Niagara Falls, Ontario, both offer viewing locations, but if you want to play the slots, you'll have to cross the border into the Great White North.

FRONTIER FIELD

Rochester Red Wings

Class AAA, International League

(MINNESOTA TWINS)

Frontier Field
One Morrie Silver Way
Rochester, New York
585–454–1001

Tradition counts for something in the International League, where they've been playing baseball continuously since 1884, and where five current teams can trace their league membership back to before 1900. If one city in the league epitomizes the role continuity can play in the life of a minor league baseball team, that city is Rochester. After joining the International League in 1885, Rochester fielded clubs during seven of the next ten seasons, then it settled into an uninterrupted stretch of play that continues to this day. Rochester has fielded a team in the International League every season since 1895.

Just as they've been loyal to their league, the Red Wings have been unusually loyal to their big league parent clubs. They were a St. Louis Cardinals farm club from 1929 through 1961, then a Baltimore Orioles affiliate from 1962 through 2002, before the O's sent their Triple-A players to Ottawa of all places. Here's guessing that the Red Wings' new affiliation with the Minnesota Twins, which began in 2003, will run a good long time.

Much of the Rochester franchise's stability—at least during the past half century—can be attributed to Rochester Community Baseball, Inc., a public ownership group that bought the Red Wings from the Cardinals in 1956, and which still owns the team today.

When the Cardinals put the Red Wings up for sale, local businessman and baseball enthusiast Morrie Silver rallied more than 8,000 members of the Rochester community to pool their money and buy shares in the team. To show its appreciation of Silver's efforts, Rochester renamed Red Wing Stadium—built in 1929 for $415,000—Silver Stadium in the 1960s.

During the park's seven decades of use, the Red Wings competed in nineteen different International League Championship Series and won the coveted Governor's Cup nine times. Through the years the local fans filled the park to watch Hall of Famers in the making like George Sisler, Rabbit Maranville, Stan Musial, Bob Gibson, Frank Robinson, Cal Ripken Jr., and Eddie Murray. But the old park on Norton Street was showing its age by the early 1990s and rather than embarking on an extensive renovation project to bring Silver Stadium up to current Triple-A code, Rochester opted to build a new ballpark in the heart of downtown. Like it or not, in today's game teams need luxury boxes to survive, and the old ballpark didn't have any. There was also insufficient room for parking in the residential neighborhood around the park.

In the mid-1990s Rochester got to work on a new $35 million stadium that would house not only the Red Wings but the Rochester Rattlers professional lacrosse team and the Rochester Rhinos professional soccer team as well. As far as multipurpose stadiums go, Frontier Field is a pretty good one for baseball, even if it is more visually appealing outside than in. The exterior features a three-story redbrick façade with windows on all three levels. The exposed green steel on the third level matches the dark green roof that covers the thirty-six luxury boxes.

Inside, Frontier Field offers a low field-level seating bowl, then a walkway, then a high second bowl—most of which is uncovered—that rises steeply to meet the bottoms of the luxury boxes. If the stadium had been developed as a baseball-only facility, I'm guessing the seats on the second level would not have risen as high above the field. I'm also guessing that there wouldn't be quite so much foul territory on the infield, where the supposed best seats in the house are pretty far from the diamond. The field has a few unusual nooks and crannies too, especially in left-center where there is a funny triangle on the warning track.

The outfield view features vertical billboards that climb four signs high above the green home run fence. The backs of these signs are decorated with pictures of famous Red Wings players, but unfortunately they are only visible from outside the stadium. Off in the distance fans enjoy a good look at the tall buildings of downtown, including the impressive Eastman Kodak Tower beyond the right field fence.

The good news for baseball purists is that Rochester recently opened Paetec Park, the new home of the Rattlers and the Rhinos, a few blocks west of Frontier Field, signaling the end of Frontier Field's days as a multiuse facility. No, Rochester can't slice off the top several rows of Frontier Field's high seating bowl and plop them across the outfield, but at least the outfield grass won't be torn up by those lacrosse and soccer cleats anymore, and maybe the city will think of some creative way to eliminate some foul territory, either by bringing the seats closer to the field or by bringing the field closer to the seats.

Game Day

Getting to the Park

Rochester is on the shores of Lake Ontario's Irondequoit Bay. The International League rivals from Buffalo play 80 miles southwest of Rochester, while the Syracuse SkyChiefs play 90 miles east. Frontier Field is located right off of I–490. From the south, take I-390 to I-490 East to exit 12 (Brown/Broad). Go straight off the ramp onto Allen Street and the ballpark will be on the right. From the west, take I–90 to I–490 to exit 12, and follow Allen Street to the ballpark. From the east, take I–90 to I–490 and then take exit 14 (Plymouth Avenue). Continue straight off the ramp, then turn right onto Broad Street. Turn left onto Plymouth Avenue and Frontier Field will appear on the left. General parking is available at either the C Lot on Plymouth Avenue or the D Lot on Allen Street.

Inside the Park

Frontier Field offers two seating bowls, separated by a walkway, that combined offer 10,840 seats. There is also standing room for a few thousand more, and sitting room on the small grass berms in the outfield corners. The first bowl offers a gradual incline, while the second bowl rises steeply. All of the seats in the lower bowl sell as Premium Box Seats. These begin with Section 101 in right field, where the seats are angled nicely back toward the infield, and continue down the line to Section 107 at first base and Section 115 behind home plate. After making the turn, the seats continue down the third baseline to Section 125 at third, and then finish at Section 130 near the foul line in relatively deep left. Throughout most of the upper bowl, the first fifteen rows sell as Upper Box Seats and the last six rows sell as Reserved Seats, but the two outfield-most sections on either side—Sections 201 and 202 in right field and Sections 226 and 227 in left—contain only Reserved Seats from Rows A through U.

The luxury box level atop the high grandstand is not symmetrical but extends farther down the third baseline than it does across the diamond, owing to the stadium's previous double . . . nay . . . triple . . . life, as a soccer and lacrosse venue as well.

On the concourse beneath the stands, the Red Wings offer a remarkably diverse sampling of ballpark treats. Honestly, it is worth a trip to Rochester, or maybe several, just to see and taste all of the great food they serve at Frontier Field. You could go to the park every night during a twelve-game home stand and eat something different for dinner each day, and you'd still have several items left to try. For an appetizer every fan should sample at least one of Frontier Field's two unique local hot dogs. The Red Hots are a blend of beef and pork, while the White Hots combine veal, ham, beef, and milk within their firm casing. After sampling these signature wieners, fans can select from a list of entrees that includes grilled Black Angus rib-eyes, Philly cheesesteaks, burritos, quesadillas, Red Osier beef sandwiches, Mama Mittsy's pizza, meatball subs at the Altobelli Deli, blooming onions, pork and chicken barbecue at the Big Red BBQ, Starbucks coffee and sweets, fresh crepes, funnel cakes, flowering deep-fried onions, ice-cream sundaes, chili cheese fries, and more. There are even two additional types of hot dogs for those who are too timid to try the local franks: Black Angus dogs and Hebrew National dogs. Genesee beer is the regional favorite—what else would you expect with the Genesee River just a few blocks east of the ballpark—while the Beer Pen on the third base side offers a wide selection of bottled brews.

In between trips to the concession stands, check out the Frontier Field Walk of Fame on the left field side of the concourse. Here, more than 18,000 engraved bricks honor the local men and women who have chipped in with donations over the years to support the home team and park. A special section of the Walk honors Rochester Sports Legends who represent a variety of sports. Among the notables remembered here is Joe Altobelli, who played for the Red Wings in the 1960s, managed them in the 1970s, then, after guiding the Orioles to a World Series title during his stint as a big league manager in the 1980s, returned to Rochester to serve as Red Wings general manager and president in the 1990s. Today, in addition to honoring Altobelli on the Walk of Fame, and at the ballpark deli that bears his name, the Red Wings hang his number 26 on the outfield wall.

The Frontier Field Experience

The Red Wings don't take seriously the persistent claims by a local group called "Rochester Paranormal Investigations" that Frontier Field is haunted. Likewise, a 2005 visit by ESPN reporter Don Barone uncovered nothing to suggest a link between Rochester's ballpark and the spiritual world.

Even if some of the folks in Rochester have been watching a few too many *X-Files* reruns, for one month a year everyone associated with the ballpark and team plays along. During October, Frontier Field is a field of screams during "Fear at Frontier," when it becomes a Halloween-themed fright park.

During the summer months, when fans turn out at the ballpark and root for the home team to score, not scare, the popular Rochester mascot is Spikes, a big-beaked, red-winged bird who wears a Rochester uniform and high-top baseball cleats just like the ones that Bill Buckner used to don after both of his ankles exploded in the 1980s.

Spikes gets particularly excited on Friday and Saturday nights when the Red Wings shoot fireworks into the air, and he likes Sundays too, when he races around the bases with all of the kids in attendance after the last out of the game.

Rochester has had the same stadium organist for three decades, which is quite an accomplishment when you consider that most teams don't even have a stadium organist anymore.

Fred Costello has been tickling the keyboard in Rochester since 1977. He plays all of the ballpark classics, while mixing in some witty ditties to subtly comment on the progress of the game down on the field.

On the Town

Visiting fans find plenty of places to eat and drink in the streets around the ballpark, especially on State Street just south of the intersection of Allen Street. Just be sure to leave room in your belly for some of the exceptional ballpark food.

A few blocks north of the ballpark is **High Falls**, the city's signature waterfall on the Genesee River. Once upon a time, the river fueled lucrative brewing and flour-milling industries. More recently, Rochester has tried to convert the old mill area into an entertainment district, an effort that has been met with limited success.

Don't bother visiting the corner of Seneca and Clinton Avenues where Silver Stadium once stood. The longtime Red Wings home was demolished in 1998 to make way for an office park.

ALLIANCE BANK STADIUM

Syracuse SkyChiefs

Class AAA, International League
(TORONTO BLUE JAYS)

Alliance Bank Stadium
One Tex Simone Drive
Syracuse, New York
315–474–7833

The similarities between the Syracuse SkyChiefs and their rivals to the west, the Rochester Red Wings, are numerous. Like the Rochester club, the SkyChiefs are a community-owned and community-operated organization. And like Rochester, Syracuse possesses a relationship with the International League that dates back to before the turn of the last century. The two teams also both replaced historic ballparks with new ones in 1997. And both franchises have demonstrated a commitment to maintaining long-term relationships with their big league parents. All of this combines to send the message that although the minor league game has changed quite a bit through the years, and American life has too, baseball remains very much a part of the civic fabric in upstate New York. In these parts the local team is more than just a pleasant diversion to enjoy a few times each summer, but rather a local institution in which residents are willing to invest their own time, effort, and money.

Syracuse originally joined the International League in 1885, and although the city has not fielded a team continuously decade-after-decade like Rochester, it has been a regular presence in the league, especially during the past half century. After a three-year stint in the Eastern League ended for the Syracuse Chiefs in 1957, Syracuse went without a team for two years, and then rejoined the International

League in 1960. Syracuse has been a member of the IL ever since, and it has been affiliated with only two major league teams since 1967. The Chiefs were a New York Yankees farm club from 1967 through 1977; they then switched to a player development contract with the expansion Toronto Blue Jays in 1978.

For six decades MacArthur Stadium was the hub of baseball activities in Syracuse, but when the minor leagues started cracking down on teams with antiquated facilities in the 1990s, the Mac's days were numbered. And so, with help from the ballpark designers at HOK of Kansas City, Onondaga County got to work on a new stadium, opting to build it right next door to the old one. The $16 million project culminated in the opening of P&C Stadium in April of 1997. In conjunction with the move, the local nine changed its name from the Chiefs to the SkyChiefs. The new nickname stuck, but the ballpark name did not. After the local grocery chain that originally named the stadium filed for bankruptcy, the yard was rededicated Alliance Bank Stadium in 2005.

Although Alliance Bank Stadium was designed to serve the local soccer and lacrosse interests as well as the city's baseball team, it sets up pretty well for hardball, even if it offers one of the few artificial turf playing surfaces in the minors today. It resembles Harbor Park, which opened a few years earlier in Norfolk, Virginia. The exterior façade offers the red brick and exposed steel we've come to expect of HOK designs, together with the stadium's architectural trademark—a three-story brick rotunda just to the left of the main entrance. Atop this regal tower flies an American flag. Don't worry, Syracuse hasn't forgotten its big league roots. Inside the stadium, the Canadian flag flies beside the Stars and Stripes behind the fence in right-center.

Outside, the stadium reaches four stories above street level. The first level consists of brick; the upper levels of cream-colored cement and metal. On passing through the turnstiles, fans scale a rather steep set of stairs to reach the main concourse that runs behind the last row of seats in the lower bowl. The concourse is open to a view of the field, yet sheltered from the elements by the overhanging second deck. Behind home plate on the second deck, a two-level structure houses the skyboxes. On either side of this larger-than-usual cream-colored façade, second-level seats continue into outfield foul territory.

All of the seats in the upper and lower bowls are a pleasing dark blue color. Lush green trees grow behind the outfield fence, which is only 10 feet high and largely devoid of signage. There is one retired number in team history, and it hangs on the outfield wall. Number 9 belonged to Hank Sauer, who played for the Chiefs in the late 1930s, before beginning a fifteen-year big league career, during which he hit .269, with 288 home runs and 876 RBI for five different National League teams.

Although MacArthur Stadium was demolished and turned into a parking lot, its light towers live on, relocated to Alliance Bank Stadium. The old-time towers fan across the outfield, perching small banks of lights atop columns of intricate scaffolding.

As aesthetically unsettling as it is for me to admit as much, it does make sense for the SkyChiefs to play their home games on artificial turf. Doing so would seem useful in preparing future Blue Jays for the type of surface that awaits them at Rogers Centre in Toronto. There's only one problem with this logic. Although the Blue Jays ripped out their Astroturf a few years ago and switched to FieldTurf, the SkyChiefs still play on the thinner, harder, brand of plastic. The team wants to upgrade to FieldTurf, and the Blue Jays would like to see that happen. But the proposed field renovation has become one of several sticking points between the community group that owns the team and Onondaga County, which owns the stadium. In addition to FieldTurf, the SkyChiefs' current wish list includes a new scoreboard and improvements to Alliance Bank Stadium's group picnic areas. As a rank-and-file fan, I don't care much about scoreboards and party decks, but I think I speak for all fans when I say that FieldTurf is the lesser of two evils when it comes to plastic grass. The ball bounces a little truer on it, allowing fans to at least pretend it's real turf.

Syracuse has competed in seventeen Governors Cup finals since 1935 and has won the IL championship eight times, most recently in 1976. In addition to Sauer the notable former Chiefs/SkyChiefs include Danny Ainge (who went on to achieve NBA stardom after a short stint with the Blue Jays), George Bell, Chris Carpenter, Bobby Cox, Carlos Delgado, Rick Dempsey, Tony Fernandez, Cecil Fielder, Ron Guidry, Roy Halladay, Jimmy Key, Fred McGriff, Denny McLain, Thurman Munson, and Vernon Wells.

Game Day

Getting to the Park

Syracuse is less than a two-hour drive from Rochester and Binghamton. Buffalo is also reachable in just a couple hours, 150 miles to the west. These four cities combine with several short-season New York–Penn League outposts to make upstate New York a hotbed of hardball activity during the summer months. Alliance Bank Stadium is located just east of Onondaga Lake in the northern part of Syracuse. From the north, take I–81 to exit 25 (7th North Street), turn left onto Hiawatha Boulevard and follow the signs to the stadium. From the south, take I–81 to exit 23 (Hiawatha Boulevard). Parking costs $3.00 at the stadium lot.

Inside the Park

Alliance Bank Stadium has a seating capacity of 11,671, but the typical gameday crowd is only about half that size. There are three ticket levels—the 100 and 200 Level seats are down in the lower bowl, and the 300 Level seats are upstairs on either side of the luxury suites. In the lower bowl, the seats continue out to the foul poles. In the upper bowl, they extend quite a bit farther into left field than they do into right. All of the seats are comfortable blue stadium chairs.

The lower bowl is divided in half by a mid-level walkway that separates seats on the 100 Level from those on the 200 Level. Section 100 is right behind home plate, while the odd-numbered sections continue down the right field line, finally finishing at Section 123, and the even-numbered sections continue down the left field line, culminating at Section 124. Directly behind these field-level sections, the corresponding sections on the 200 Level follow the same number scheme. All of the seats in this lower bowl are close to the field and offer excellent views of the game.

Upstairs, the luxury suites are stacked in two levels behind home plate. The seats on the 300 Level on either side sell as General Admission. There are four sections along the right field line and seven sections along the left field line. Because these upper-level seats hang out over the lower level, they are relatively close to the field and not too high. I recommend buying a General Admission ticket, and then if you don't like the view for whatever reason, you can always sneak down into the first level once the second or third inning rolls around. The SkyChiefs, who already have reasonable ticket prices, offer a discount to children twelve and under and to adults sixty-two and over.

At the group party tents in the outfield, folks enjoy a view of the game through the chain-link outfield fence. A blocky looking building on the right field concourse hosts upscale group functions at the Hank Sauer Room.

On the open concourse behind the first-level seats, the concession stands feature Hofmann hot dogs, hamburgers, Italian sausages, brats, barbeque pork sandwiches, and salt potatoes —which are small spuds boiled in salty water and served with butter.

The Alliance Bank Stadium Experience

The Syracuse mascot is an androgynous, amorphous, orange fellow known as Scooch. I'm guessing he's a distant cousin of Otto the Orange, the goofy puffball who haunts the sidelines at Syracuse University.

Once a summer, the SkyChiefs continue an annual tradition that speaks to the role community plays in the life of the local team. On "Third Base Night" the team invites the many independent businesses in the area that support the team to the park, and the businesses bring their employees to the game en masse. The tradition began all the way back in 1970.

On select nights fans eighteen and older receive coupons for New York State Lottery tickets as they pass through the turnstiles. On Thursday nights fans can present their Price Chopper advantage card at the box office to receive a discount on tickets.

On the Town

There are several fast-food options east of the stadium on Wolf Street, while a few blocks south the **Carousel Center** mall offers familiar chains like Hooters and Ruby Tuesday. Those looking for a local bar can try the **Locker Room** (528 Hiawatha Boulevard East) right near the stadium.

If you're a college football fanatic or college hoops junkie, stop by Syracuse University to check out the largest domed stadium on a college campus in the United States. In additional to hosting Big East athletics, the **Carrier Dome**, which opened in 1970, has welcomed musical acts like the Grateful Dead, Billy Joel, Elton John, the Police, the Rolling Stones, Frank Sinatra, Bruce Springsteen, U2, and, The Who. The dome is about 3 miles south of Alliance Bank Stadium.

LYNX STADIUM

Ottawa Lynx

Class AAA, International League

(PHILADELPHIA PHILLIES)

Lynx Stadium
300 Coventry Road
Ottawa, Ontario
613–747–5969

While minor league baseball has boomed in the United States during the past decade, surging to levels of popularity not seen since the 1940s, the bush league resurgence has not extended into Canada, where affiliated ball is just barely hanging on these days. Once upon a time—and not so long ago—there were major league outposts in Calgary, Edmonton, Lethbridge, Medicine Hat, Quebec City, St. Catherines, and Winnipeg. But today, the only affiliated teams continuing to play north of the border are the Vancouver Canadians of the short-season Northwest League, and the Ottawa Lynx of the International League. The game's future in the Great White North would seem rosier in Vancouver, where the Canadians average close to 3,500 fans per game at Nat Bailey Stadium, than in Ottawa, where the Lynx struggle to attract 2,000 fans per home date at Lynx Stadium.

In 2006 the Lynx sold just 122,574 tickets, placing them dead last among the thirty Triple-A teams, and more than 180,000 ticket sales behind the next worst draw in the International League. Needless to say, if fan interest does not pick up soon in Ottawa, the Lynx will be heading south for greener financial pastures. In fact it may already be too late for the franchise to revive itself in Canada. According to widely circulated rumors, the Lynx will be moving to Allentown, Pennsylvania, in 2008. If such a move occurs, it will be time for the International League to rename itself the *Intra-National League*, since all of its teams will be within U.S. borders.

Hard to believe though it may be, the Lynx actually broke a forty-seven-year-old International League attendance record in their inaugural season. No lie. They drew 693,000 fans in 1993, at a time when baseball was thriving in Canada. The Toronto Blue Jays had just won back-to-back World Series, and Ottawa's big league parents in Montreal were drawing 1.6 million fans a year and cultivating a seemingly endless stream of exciting young players who passed through Ottawa on their way to the big leagues. When the Major League Players Association went on strike in August of 1994, Montreal had the best record in baseball and seemed poised to make its first extended play-off run, and possibly give Canada its third straight World Series title. Of course the season never resumed, so the Expos never got their chance. It would take a few years for the game to bounce back in the Lower 48. In Canada, though, where baseball has always been a pleasant summer diversion but no rival for the country's true passions, ice hockey and curling, fan interest never returned.

You can't blame the fans in Ottawa for being more interested in the local team when it featured up-and-coming Expos on their way to the big league park 130 miles away, than today, when the Lynx serve as a Philadelphia Phillies affiliate. After losing their connection to the local National League team in 2003, Ottawa's baseball fans actually lost the National League team entirely. So it's not hard to figure out why they're turned off to Major League Baseball and by extension to the minor leagues as well.

Lynx Stadium was built at a cost of $17 million CAN to bring the International League back to Ottawa for the first time since the Ottawa Senators left in 1954. While stadium quality is not the problem in Ottawa today, it won't be the local team's salvation either. The facility, which was originally known as Jetform Park, is clean and functional, which is more than could be said of Montreal's Olympic Stadium in its later years. The sightlines are unobstructed and the seats are all comfortable stadium chairs. Lynx Stadium is a suitable venue for the Triple-A game, but it doesn't offer a reason in and of itself for fans to head out to the ballpark like some of the festive new creations down in the States do.

Inside, there is gray cement everywhere you look—on the two-level façade above the top row of seats behind home plate where the luxury boxes are, in the aisles, on the interior concourse walls, around the dugouts, and even on the low wall that separates the stands from the field. All of this concrete would be less visible, of course, if there were 10,000 or 6,000 or even 4,000 fans in the stands, instead of 2,000 or 1,500 or 1,000, and certainly a few more bodies would warm up the joint and make it feel less sterile. The outfield view is unspectacular, featuring passing traffic and a large office building beyond the fence in left.

Game Day

Getting to the Park

Ottawa is located in the westernmost corner of Ontario, along the Ottawa River, which separates Ontario from Quebec. The stadium is on the east side of town, not far from the river. From the south, take Highway 401 East to Highway 416 North to the Queensway East (Highway 417). Take the Vanier Parkway exit (117), turn left at the lights, and then turn right onto Coventry Road. Parking in the stadium lot costs $3.00.

Inside the Park

The two-level seating bowl extends into medium depth outfield foul territory along either baseline and is large enough to accommodate 10,332 fans. Neither level is terribly steep. The twenty-two rows of Lower Seats are below the midlevel walkway, while the fifteen rows of Upper Seats are above the walkway. There's really no sense buying a Lower Seat, since the ballpark is sparsely populated enough to allow for easy seat hopping. The seats begin with Section AA out in right field, and then continue down the first baseline to Sections CC and DD behind the visitors dugout, and on to Section HH directly behind the plate. Sections MM and NN are behind the home team's dugout, and the seating bowl ends at Section PP behind the home bullpen in left field. The thirty-two luxury suites are stacked in two levels behind home plate.

The concourse is hidden beneath the upper-level seats. It offers standard ballpark fare as well as cups of *poutine,* a popular Canadian dish consisting of french fries topped with gravy and cheese curds. The menu also includes beaver tails, pieces of fried dough shaped like, you guessed it, beaver tails. The best bet for a fresh burger or hot dog is at the grill down the left field line. There is a large sports bar on the third level that offers lots of TVs, pool tables, a standard pub menu, and a view of the field.

Be sure to exchange your greenbacks for the Queen's currency before you arrive at the ballpark, where the concession stands treat Canadian and U.S. dollars the same despite the favorable U.S. exchange rate.

The Lynx Stadium Experience

Lynx management certainly tries to make the ballpark experience entertaining and stimulating for fans. In addition to the antics of a krazy kat named "Skratch," the team has staged recent promotions like "Cupid Night," when singles mingled at a mixer in the stadium restaurant, and "The Night of the Dog," when dog owners were encouraged to bring their four-legged friends to the park and allowed to parade them around on the field before the first pitch.

On a nightly basis the team integrates familiar bush league stunts like the Dirtiest Car in the Lot contest with creative promotions like allowing three kids per game to serve as public address announcers for an inning each, staging a nightly 50/50 drawing in the fifth inning that awards half of the money collected to a lucky fan and half to a local charity, and letting kids stand next to their favorite Lynx players during the singing of the National Anthems. Yes, there are two anthems before every game in Ottawa, and all of the public address announcements are read in English as well as French.

There is an autograph booth on the concourse where a player or two signs before every game, and kids get to run the bases after every Sunday game. If you want to put a message to a friend on the right field scoreboard—like "Happy Anniversary," "Happy Birthday," or "Hope You Enjoy the Beaver Tail," the cost is only $10.

On the Town

The Canadian capital has a population of 800,000 people, making Ottawa the country's fourth-largest city. About half of the residents speak English, so it isn't too difficult for non-French-speaking visitors to order their *poutine* without cheese or to make sense of the local bus schedule.

Parliament Hill is located in Uppertown, on the western banks of the Ottawa River. During the summer months the changing of the guard takes place outside the House of Commons daily at 10:00 A.M. The portion of the city east of the river is known as Lowertown. For the best concentration of restaurants and bars, head to the By Ward Market area, Elgin Street, or Hull. For a bite to eat before or after the game, **Perkins Family Restaurant** (Coventry Road and St. Laurent Boulevard) is right near the stadium.

FIRSTENERGY PARK
Lakewood BlueClaws

Class A, South Atlantic League
(PHILADELPHIA PHILLIES)

FirstEnergy Park
2 Stadium Way
Lakewood, New Jersey
732–901–7000

Apparently, the Lakewood BlueClaws are not content to merely lead the South Atlantic League in attendance every year, with nightly crowds that exceed 6,500 people and seasonal crowds that top the 400,000 mark. While the team specializes in providing a first-rate ballpark experience, it also markets itself as a one-stop shopping spot for virtually any other type of community event. The BlueClaws use their ballpark to host scores of peripheral events each year that occur both during and outside of the baseball season, making FirstEnergy Park a year-round hub of activity in its Jersey Shore community.

The extensive level of luxury suites at FirstEnergy Park sees steady use as an executive conference center year-round, sometimes hosting three or four different groups in a single day. Meanwhile, the parking lot outside the stadium offers Sunday afternoon bargain shoppers a festive flea market during the summer months. Also during the summer, First-Energy Park doubles as an outdoor concert venue, attracting national headliners like Bob Dylan, Willie Nelson, Def Leppard, and Bryan Adams. In the spring, summer, and fall, the ballpark is used for various youth baseball and coaches clinics. The BlueClaws also host the annual Jersey Shore Shootout, a three-on-three basketball tournament that takes place

on twenty different basketball courts in the stadium parking lot. During the fall and winter, Pinchy's Pub, the bar on the ballpark's second level, opens its doors to football fans on Sunday afternoons, showing all of the games from around the NFL and serving a tasty buffet. To pull off all this and more, while still offering a top-notch baseball experience, the BlueClaws maintain a year-round staff of more than 20 full-time employees and hire about 200 part-timers and interns for the baseball season.

FirstEnergy Park was designed with the average fan's interests in mind, while a priority was also obviously made of maximizing luxury-suite and group-party revenue potential. The ballpark does a nice job of balancing these two concerns, which do not need to be mutually exclusive, but sometimes are at other parks. Lakewood's ballpark features a sunken playing field with an open concourse that runs behind the last row of seats. All of the seats are comfortable stadium chairs with unobstructed views of the field. The seats extend only a little way past the corner bases, leaving the outfield corners free to provide tiered group picnic areas. Home run territory offers nicely sloped grass lawns where families can spread out blankets and let the kids run wild. The ballpark's upper level houses luxury suites around the infield, while providing shelter to the fans on the concourse below.

The ballpark succeeds aesthetically, featuring a tan-and-red brick exterior, a brown veranda that extends off the first level over the ticket windows, and a larger brown roof atop the second-level luxury boxes. An attractive redbrick elevator tower rises on the third base side of the home plate entrance. Inside the park the dark green seats and green façade of the upper level combine to create a subtle earthy effect. Meanwhile, the color scheme in the outfield is more in line with the usual minor league decor, as gaudy advertising signs plaster the

8-foot high outfield fence, and several three-level billboards rise at the back of the outfield lawns. The billboards, which feature as many as six different signs and logos apiece, are spaced out to allow fans to peer between them into the forest of scraggly trees growing beyond the stadium grounds. The scoreboard that rises at the back of the lawn in left-center is similarly plastered with colorful ads, while off in the distance in straight-away left a water tower, which has not yet been wallpapered with ads, rises amidst the trees.

FirstEnergy Park opened in 2001 to accommodate the BlueClaws, who arrived in town via Fayetteville, North Carolina, where they had been known as the Cape Fear Crocs. With the relocation the franchise began a new relationship with the Philadelphia Phillies, who had previously been sending their South Atlantic League prospects to Kannapolis, North Carolina. The BlueClaws have been a popular draw from the very start. Despite finishing with a losing record in four of their first five seasons, they have led the South Atlantic League in attendance in every year of their existence. The team had its best season ever in 2005 when 444,607 people passed through the ballpark gates. And those were just the folks who turned out at FirstEnergy Park to watch the baseball games!

The BlueClaws' first alum to ascend to the big league ballpark 50 miles west was Ryan Howard. The slugging first baseman was a September call-up to the Phillies in 2004, then won the National League Rookie of the Year Award in 2005 and then posted the most prolific offensive numbers of any major league slugger in 2006. Howard spent the entire 2002 season in Lakewood, batting .280 with 19 home runs and 87 RBIs in his first full minor league season. In 2006 an entire roster's worth of BlueClaws players made their Citizens Bank Park debut in Philly when the BlueClaws played a regular season South Atlantic League game at the stadium against the Delmarva Shorebirds.

Game Day

Getting to the Park

Lakewood is conveniently situated an hour's drive from both New York City and Philadelphia and just forty minutes from Atlantic City. FirstEnergy Park sits 3 miles from the Jersey Shore at the intersection of New Hampshire Avenue (Route 623) and Cedar Bridge Avenue (Route 528). From Philadelphia, follow Route 70 East to Lakewood, and then turn left onto New Hampshire Avenue. Continue through two traffic lights and the ballpark will appear on your left. From the north or south, take the Garden State Parkway to exit 89 and bear right off the exit toward Brick and Lakewood. Turn left onto Cedar Bridge Avenue. There is a large paved parking lot at the ballpark.

Inside the Park

FirstEnergy Park offers room for 6,588 fans between its main seating bowl, picnic areas, and luxury suites. It also has room for another 3,000 on its outfield lawns. The seating bowl offers fifteen sections of comfortable stadium chairs, beginning with Section 101 in shallow right field, continuing down the first baseline to Section 108 behind home plate, and extending out to Section 115 in shallow left field. Most of the time, the Reserved Seats in these sections are only available to fans who order tickets well in advance. The average road tripper buys a General Admission ticket and sits on one of the lawns, either in deep left field foul territory, in left field home run territory, or in right field home run territory. The BlueClaws call the contingent of fans who sit on the lawns the "Sod Squad." Personally, I think the terms "Lawn Pawns," "Green Jeans," or "Grassy Assies" have catchier rings to them, but "Sod Squad" is okay too, I guess. Families with small children may want to stake out a spot on the left field sod, since this will provide easy access to Pinchy's Playground, which has its own minigolf course as well as other attractions. Meanwhile, big eaters may prefer a spot on the right field sod, close to Pinchy's Food Court, and mingling singles may prefer a spot in right field, close to the bar area. The bar is in right-center and is called the WRAT Trap, in homage to a local radio station.

The ballpark concessions are managed by the team, not by an outside company. The menu includes crab cakes, Philly cheesesteaks, grilled sausage sandwiches, barbecued pork sandwiches, chili, candied apples, and other traditional favorites.

Unfortunately, the steamed blue shell crabs that are the team's namesake creature are not on the menu. Maybe they thought it would be inappropriate—dare I say, *sacri-licious*—to eat the animal the team is named after. But then again, fans of the Modesto Nuts have no problem chomping on fresh roasted almonds at Thurman Field, and fans of the Winston-Salem Warthogs have no problem devouring hot dogs at Shore Field. In any case, to enjoy crabs and minor league baseball simultaneously, you'll have to head south to Aberdeen, Maryland, where Ripken Stadium, home of the New York-Penn League's Aberdeen IronBirds, specializes in steamed blue shells.

The FirstEnergy Park Experience

The BlueClaws pride themselves in providing quality entertainment between innings. A popular promotion that debuted in 2006 was called "The Roll for Dough." To participate fans would don sticky suits and then roll around in a mess of dollar bills to see how many bills they could stick to their outfit.

The ballpark staffers dress in colorful flowered shirts, while the team mascot is not a big blue crab as you might expect, but a big yellow mess of fur named "Buster." Popular annual theme nights include Grandparents Day, All Faith's Night, Irish Night, Italian Night, Fire Fighter Night, Company Truck Night, and College Fair Night.

On the Town

A visit to Lakewood offers fans the chance to catch some sun and ride some waves at the nearby beaches of the Jersey Shore. From the ballpark, Cedar Bridge Avenue leads to the Atlantic. The boardwalks at **Seaside Heights** (Route 35) and **Point Pleasant** (Route 34) are popular tourist spots, each offering attractions and activities for the entire family.

For fresh water fun right in Lakewood, weary travelers can stretch their legs at **Lake Shenandoah Park** (Ocean Avenue). The 143-acre park offers wooded hiking and biking trails, picnicking, and fishing. The park's 100-acre lake is stocked with trout, and visitors can rent boats and rods and reels at an on-site bait and tackle shop.

A trip to the boardwalk farther south in Atlantic City offers the chance to visit a ballpark known as **The Sandcastle** (Routes 40/322), home of the Atlantic City Surf of the independent Atlantic League.

MERCER COUNTY WATERFRONT PARK

Trenton Thunder

Class AA, Eastern League
(NEW YORK YANKEES)

Samuel J. Plumeri Sr. Field at
Mercer County Waterfront Park
One Thunder Road
Trenton, New Jersey
609–394–3300

Mercer County Waterfront Park sits beside the Delaware River, where it welcomes a steady flow of Trenton Thunder fans each summer. Because the ballpark is on the eastern banks of the river, along with the rest of Trenton, it could not have been situated to showcase a full outfield view of the water because that would have meant orienting the field so batters would be looking directly into the setting sun. As such, only a small stretch of the river is visible from within the park. Fans seated on the third base side can spot the water beyond right field foul territory through a gap between the end of the home run fence and the start of the seating bowl. To enhance the view and make it easier for left-handed sluggers to deposit long balls into the current, there is only one level of advertising signs on the fence in right, as opposed to the three or four levels across the rest of the outfield.

While the river makes an understated impression on the game day crowd, and while Waterfront Park is a fairly basic facility inside, the ballpark offers an exterior façade that immediately demands the attention and respect of visitors. I'm not sure exactly what percentage of the facility's $18.3 million price

tag went toward its brick exterior, but I'd be willing to guess it was a hefty amount.

Because the main concourse runs atop the seating bowl, and because the field is not sunken below street level like it is at some of the recently built minor league parks, after entering the park fans must climb a set of steps or a ramp to access the concourse. And because the concourse is farther above ground level than at most similarly designed parks, and because the luxury suites over the concourse are therefore also higher, the brick façade outside is larger and higher than at the typical 6,000-seat stadium.

The main entrance behind home plate features a curved canopy that extends over a large plaza. Above the canopy there are three large windows. A pointed metal crown sits atop the ballpark roof as a decorative flourish. The façade also features letters spelling out the stadium's name and the name of the field, which honors Samuel J. Plumeri Sr. Mr. Plumeri, whose father owned the last minor league team to call Trenton home before the game returned in 1994—the Trenton Giants who left in 1950—was one of the driving forces behind the movement to bring baseball back to Trenton. Bob Prunetti, Mercer County executive, was also instrumental in finagling the deal that transferred the Detroit Tigers' Double-A player development contract from London, Ontario, to Trenton following the 1993 season.

Although it has a relatively low seating capacity, Waterfront Park puts to good use the 6,341 seats it has. Trenton has set a number of attendance records since joining the Eastern League, including the mark for the most consecutive seasons with an attendance total greater than 400,000 at the Double-A level or lower. The Thunder attracted more than 400,000 fans for the twelfth straight time in 2006.

The Thunder and Waterfront Park didn't get off to such a smooth start, though. In fact everything that could have gone wrong seemingly did in the weeks leading up to what was supposed to be a glorious new beginning for Trenton baseball. Waterfront Park was supposed to open in time for the beginning of the 1994 season, but construction delays caused by an unseasonably wet spring made an early April unveiling impossible. The Thunder played their "home" games at Veterans Stadium in Philadelphia, Frawley Stadium in Wilmington, and Memorial Municipal Stadium in Reading. Finally, on April 27, the Trenton fans turned out at Waterfront Park expecting to watch the Thunder play the Albany-Colonie Yankees, but the Yankees refused to take the field due to the still-soggy conditions and swaths of loose sod in the outfield. The players signed autographs, the Thunder apologized for the inconvenience, and the fans went home unhappy. At long last, baseball returned to Trenton on May 9, as the Binghamton Mets defeated the home team 5–3.

In Trenton's only season as a Tigers affiliate, Mo-Town prospect Tony Clark became the first player ever to hit a ball into the Delaware River and swatted 21 dingers in total before earning a promotion to Triple-A. The team has since retired Clark's old uniform jersey, number 33. The Thunder drew 318,252 fans to just fifty-one home dates in that first season, even though they went a dismal 55–85 between the lines.

The next year brought a new drainage system to Waterfront Park and a new affiliation with the Boston Red Sox. Brash Thunder shortstop Nomar Garciaparra caused a flap in Trenton when he criticized the local fans in a newspaper story, saying they didn't cheer loudly enough when he made a nice play in the field. But the fans forgave and forgot. When Garciaparra returned to Trenton with the Red Sox in 1998 for an exhibition game, more than 8,000 Trentonians jammed into Waterfront Park to watch as the Thunder retired Garciaparra's number 5.

The Thunder switched to a PDC with the New York Yankees in 2003, after the Red Sox announced they would be moving their Eastern League prospects to Portland, Maine. Given the geographic proximity of Trenton to the Big Apple, this latest affiliation has worked out superbly for the Thunder. The team has welcomed big leaguers like Kevin Brown, José Contreras, Derek Jeter, Kenny Lofton, Gary Sheffield, and Bernie Williams to town on rehab assignments, and local interest in the Yankees has heightened interest in the Thunder.

Game Day

Getting to the Park

Trenton is 35 miles northeast of Philadelphia, 70 miles southwest of New York City, 80 miles north of Atlantic City, and 35 miles west of Lakewood—the closest minor league town. Waterfront Park is wedged between the eastern banks of the Delaware and Route 29. From the New Jersey Turnpike, take exit 7A and follow I–195 West to Route 29 North. The general stadium lot is at the front of the ballpark, while there is also a parking garage across the street from the park on Route 29. The overflow lot at the corner of Cass Street and Route 129 is serviced by free shuttle buses. The cost is $2.00 per car at all locations.

Inside the Park

The seating bowl is low to the field and extends just a short distance into the outfield on either side. Trenton opted to include a walkway in the middle of the bowl—a feature not found at most other parks that have a main concourse atop the last row of seats. I'm not sure what purpose this interior aisle serves. The whole benefit of placing the main concourse behind the seats is that doing so eliminates much of the view-blocking pedestrian traffic within the park, limiting it to the stairways between the sections. In any case the ten rows or so (depending on the section) below the walkway sell as Club Seats, while the rows above the walkway sell as Pavilion or Terrace Seats. The Club level starts with Section 1 in shallow right field, continues down the first baseline to Sections 11 and 12 behind home plate, and ends at Section 22 in shallow left. A tiered group picnic area sits on the Club level down the left field line.

The second-level sections are marked with letters instead of numbers. The two outermost sections on either side—A and B in right field, and R and Q in left field—offer bleachers with backs. These are the Terrace Seats. The rest of the second level offers the same green stadium chairs as in the lower level. These are the Pavilion Seats. Sections C and D are behind the Thunder dugout on the first baseline, Sections I and J are behind home plate, and Sections O and P are behind the visitors dugout.

The sixteen indoor/outdoor luxury suites are topped by a large concrete façade, and there is a glassed-in restaurant high above home plate. I did not visit the Yankee Club, but I was told that it serves a gourmet menu and is decorated with Babe Ruth and Willie Mays jerseys, Mickey Mantle memorabilia, and a ball from David Wells's perfect game. The restaurant is available for group functions only on most nights.

On the concourse the ballpark fare includes pizza, barbecued beef and pork sandwiches, Italian sausages, Italian ice, Philly cheesesteaks, funnel cakes, and a reduced-price, reduced-portion kids stand on the first base side.

The Waterfront Park Experience

There must be a lot of people in Trenton with impressive bobblehead collections, because the local team gives away plenty of dolls. Each year, there are seven or eight bobblehead nights that honor past and present Trenton players, opposing Eastern League players, past and present New York Yankees, and occasionally one of the nonuniformed characters that make a trip to Waterfront Park special. Recent bobbleheads have depicted Babe Ruth, Lou Gehrig, Phil Rizzuto, Joe Torre, Stump Merrill, Don Mattingly, Chien-Ming Wang, Alfonso Soriano, Bernie Williams, Derek Jeter, Randy Johnson, David Eckstein, Trot Nixon, Robinson Canó, Shea Hillenbrand, Garciaparra, Alex Rodríguez, Carl Pavano, Pat Burrell, Thunder groundskeeper Nicole Sherry, and Thunder mascot Chase.

Cut from the same cloth as "Jake the Diamond Dog" and "Digger the Home Run Dog," the loveable pups who entertain fans at points elsewhere in the minor league universe, "Chase that Golden Thunder" is a handsome golden retriever who dutifully delivers bats, balls, water bottles, Frisbees, and whatever other props the players and umpires may need in the course of a game. In addition to entertaining Thunder fans, Chase has appeared at FirstEnergy Park in Lakewood, Citizen's Bank Park in Philadelphia, and Sovereign Bank Arena, where Trenton's minor league hockey team plays.

One of Chase's buddies at Waterfront Park is a 300-pound thunderbird, named "Boomer," who shares the mascot responsibilities. Hey, not everyone's a dog lover, right? Boomer has blue feathers, a wide-open beak, and one white tooth stuck in the middle of his mouth—which causes me to wonder if he really is a bird or if I need to recheck my species chart and reclassify him.

As you might expect, the Thunder offers more than the usual number of fireworks displays each season. The team sets the sky ablaze with color and fills it with noise on most

Campbell's Field

Thursday and Saturday evenings during the summer months.

On the Town

The ballpark neighborhood offers an eclectic mix of eating and drinking spots, including **Jazzy G's Ice Cream & Water Ice** (802 Lamberton Street), **Nino's Waterfront Grill** (802 Lamberton Street), and **Katmandu** (50 River View Plaza). The latter listing is a waterfront restaurant/nightclub with a full dinner menu, indoor and outdoor seating, deejays, live bands, dancing, and more. For those looking to venture a bit farther into Trenton, a few blocks east of the ballpark there are familiar fast-food franchises, pizza shops, and Chinese joints.

Ballpark junkies may find it worthwhile to visit **Clarke Field** on the campus of nearby Princeton University, about 12 miles north of Trenton via Lawrenceville Road. The ballpark, which was renovated prior to the start of the 2006 season, is the largest and finest one in the Ivy League. It has hosted NCAA regional tournaments and New Jersey high school play-off and all-star games. It is named after William "Boileryard" Clarke, who played for Princeton in the early 1890s, then for the early National

League teams in Baltimore (1893–1898) and Boston (1899–1900), and for the American League's Washington Senators (1901–1904) and New York Highlanders (1905). After his playing career ended, Clarke returned to his alma mater to coach and made Princeton his home until the time of his passing in 1959.

For an independent league road trip, fans can venture 25 miles south to Camden, where the Camden Riversharks are one of the most popular draws in the Atlantic League. The team plays at **Campbell's Field** (401 North Delaware Avenue), which offers an amazing outfield view of the Ben Franklin Bridge.

BLAIR COUNTY BALLPARK
Altoona Curve

Class AA, Eastern League
(PITTSBURGH PIRATES)

Blair County Ballpark
1000 Park Avenue
Altoona, Pennsylvania
814–943–5400

It seems like minor league cities are getting more creative and at the same time more random in selecting their team names these days. That being the case, if you guessed that the Altoona Curve was named after the curve ball, it wouldn't be such an outrageous conjecture. After all, the minor leagues already have mascots with names like Slider and Cutter, so why not a whole team named after a pitch? However plausible it may seem, the Altoona Curve are not, in fact, named after the funny pitch also referred to as Old Uncle Charlie, the yacker, or the hammer.

Another logical conclusion for out-of-towners to draw might be that the Altoona team derives its nickname from the 70-foot-tall roller coaster that rises just behind the right field fence at Blair County Ballpark. But that guess too would be incorrect. Altoona's local nine doesn't derive its name from the twists and curves of the coaster at Lakemont Park.

The Altoona franchise *is* named after a famous stretch of railroad located just west of downtown called the Horseshoe Curve. The unusual set of tracks makes a horseshoe shape to allow trains passage through a wooded valley in the Allegheny Mountain range. The Curve was laid in 1854 by Irish immigrants, turned into a public park in 1879, designated a National Historic Landmark in 1966, and today welcomes railroad enthusiasts who come to

watch some 500 trains per week navigate the seemingly impossible bend in the rails.

As far as team names go, I rate this one pretty high. To those familiar with Altoona, the Curve moniker pays homage to a unique historic landmark. To those who know nothing about Altoona aside from the fact that it hosts a team in the Eastern League, the name leaves room for a baseball-centric interpretation too.

Altoona, which entered the minor leagues in 1999, deserves credit for more than just coming up with a catchy team name. Blair County Ballpark is impressive too. The 7,200-seat stadium offers two full seating decks. Rather than following the modern trend of providing one low main bowl around the entire field and a luxury level only up above, the architects at Pittsburgh-based L. D. Astorino Company created what feels like a miniature version of a major league park. If you saw a picture of this ballpark that showed only the grandstands between the corner bases and home plate, you could almost mistake it for a big league facility. View the park through a wider lens, however, and you'll see that both the lower and upper decks extend just barely to where the infield dirt meets the outfield grass along either baseline. There are also bleachers—separate from the main seating bowls, down the right field line and in left field home run territory—that were added in 2003 to keep up with increasing ticket demand.

The upper deck is deeper than the lower one and hangs down over the lower concourse so that its first few rows are not very high above the field. Then it rises gradually, eventually to be topped by twenty-one skyboxes, 70 feet above the field. The seats are dark green, while the press box and skyboxes are cream colored.

The outfield view features the roller coaster just beyond the fence in right. The cars rattling along the elevated rails sport letters spelling out "Go Curve." This outfield attraction reminds me of Brooklyn's Keyspan Park, home of the New York-Penn League's Brooklyn Cyclones, which provides glimpses of the amusement rides of Coney Island beyond its own right field fence. The coaster in Altoona is closer to the field than the rides in Brooklyn, though.

Beyond the fence in left, there rises a grass hillside, then a parking garage that serves patrons of the amusement park, ballpark, and nearby Galactic Ice Arena. From the ballpark seats, the view of the garage is largely obscured by a massive video scoreboard that the Curve installed prior to the 2006 season. The 1,000-square-foot LED screen cost $1 million and is four times larger than the board that preceded it, which, as part of the same project, was moved from left-center field to the right field corner, where it now serves as an auxiliary video board. Don't worry, the old board doesn't block the view of the roller coaster.

The ballpark's exterior also deserves mention. Because the seats rise quite a bit higher than at most minor league facilities, the façade is also higher. With its classy red brick, large rectangular portals, and green iron arches, the building is quite regal; it has drawn favorable comparisons with Oriole Park at Camden Yards.

The Curve came into existence in 1999 when the addition of the Tampa Bay Devil Rays and Arizona Diamondbacks to the major leagues necessitated the creation of two new Double-A clubs. The other city to join the Eastern League in 1999 was Erie. Both Altoona and Erie vied for the coveted affiliation with the home-state Pittsburgh Pirates, and Altoona prevailed.

From the very start minor league baseball has been a smashing success in Altoona. The Curve set one attendance record after another during their first six seasons—as future big leaguers like Bronson Arroyo, Kris Benson, Zach Duke, Rob Mackowiak, Jason Schmidt, and Jack Wilson honed their skills at Blair County Ballpark. The season tally dipped for the first time between 2004 and 2005—from 394,062 tickets sold to 390,239, but the franchise is still in great shape. The team has a top-notch ballpark, a loyal fan base, a stable ownership group that includes Steel City icons Jerome Bettis and Mario Lemieux, and a player development contract with the Pirates that runs through 2010.

Game Day

Getting to the Park

Altoona is 95 miles east of Pittsburgh along U.S. Highway 22. Blair County Ballpark is on the east side of the city, just off I-99, which bisects Altoona from north to south. From I-99, take the exit for Frankstown Road, which leads right to the ballpark. The surface lots around the ballpark charge $3.00 to $5.00 per

Blair County Ballpark

car, while the parking garage beyond the field in left charges just $1.00.

Inside the Park

While the two main seating bowls offer unobstructed sight lines around the infield, the most expensive seats in the house are actually located way out in left field where the first row of the Party Deck provides Rail Kings Seats that come with wait service and cable television monitors positioned every few feet. Around the infield the lower deck houses ten rows of 100-level seats, beginning with Section 101, just beyond third base, continuing down the line to Sections 111 and 112 behind home plate, and extending down the first baseline to Section 122, just past first. The first-level concourse runs right behind these Diamond Club Seats, where it is sheltered by the overhang of the second level but open to a view of the field. The upper deck houses 200-level and 300-level seats. The Terrace Seats are akin to the upper boxes found at many big league stadiums, only much closer to the field. These appear in five rows set below the second deck's midlevel walkway. The Grandstand Seats are above the walkway. There are assigned Bleacher Seats in left field home run territory, while the bleachers along the right field line sell as General Admission. For groups the park offers picnic areas down the right field and left field lines. The concession stands have hot dogs, hamburgers, sausages, pizza, and the rest of the ballpark staples.

The Blair County Ballpark Experience

Altoona's owners aren't as wacky as the bush leagues' notorious Goldklang Group—which owns the St. Paul Saints, Fort Myers Miracle, and Charleston RiverDogs in the Bill Veeck tradition—but they're pretty close, judging from some of the recent promotional nights they've orchestrated. Sure, the Curve have offered the usual promos designed to engage the local community, like "Scouts Sleepover Night," "Most Improved Students Night," "Irish Heritage Night," and "Military Appreciation Night," but they've also shown a willingness to venture into the theater of the absurd. In 2003 the team hosted "Awful Night," during which ballpark employees endeavored to create the worst possible atmosphere for a game. The team gave away twelve-inch squares of bubble wrap to the first 5,000 fans, the PA system blared tunes by Milli Vanilli and William Shatner, and the team did whatever else it could to make the ballpark experience unpleasant. In 2006 the team staged a season-long "Retro Celebrity Series," periodically trotting out has-been actors for the amusement of the fans. The motley cast included Erik Estrada, typecast forever as Ponch from the *CHiPs* series; Barry Williams, who played Greg Brady on *The Brady Bunch*; Jamie Farr, who played Klingler on *M*A*S*H*; and Sherman Hemsley, who played George Jefferson on *The Jeffersons*. I have to think that when your talent agent calls and says he has a gig lined up for you at a minor league ballpark in Altoona, the offer rates slightly higher than one from *Celebrity Boxing,* but not quite as high as one for a toothpaste infomercial.

No, Altoona does not employ a giant bloated tuna named Al as its mascot. That would make too much sense. Rather, the Curve's rabble-rousers are Steamer, a green steam engine with a 7-foot-tall smokestack, and Diesel Dog, an energetic pup who likes to dance on the dugout roofs.

On the Town

Those traveling with children and cotton candy connoisseurs will no doubt find themselves paying the obligatory visit to **Lakemont Park,** right beside the ballpark. The amusement park features thirty rides, as well as a water park, go-kart track, train-themed miniature golf course, and video arcade. The park opened in 1902, which makes it the eighth-oldest amusement park in America. The Leap-the-Dips roller coaster is a National Historic Landmark, widely considered the oldest wooden roller coaster in the world, while the Skyliner coaster, which overlooks the baseball field, is also a scream. The park is open from 11:00 A.M. until 9:00 P.M. during the summer months. An all-day "Ride and Slide" pass costs $7.95 per person, or $5.95 after 5:00 P.M.

The **Horseshoe Curve** (40th Street/Veterans Memorial Highway) makes for a scenic picnic locale on a seasonal summer day. From the visitor center, tourists can traverse the 194 steps that lead to a viewing area or hitch a ride on the Funicular, an incline plane that ferries folks up and down between the center and the viewing spot. As a sidelight folks may also want to visit the **Railroaders Memorial Museum** (1300 Ninth Avenue) in downtown Altoona to learn more about the city's railroading history.

JERRY UHT PARK

Erie SeaWolves

Class AA, Eastern League
(DETROIT TIGERS)

Jerry Uht Park
110 East 10th Street
Erie, Pennsylvania
814–456–1300

Every bush league ballpark offers something to distinguish itself from the many others spread across minor league nation, but it isn't often these days that you happen upon a park that is completely unique. Erie's Jerry Uht Park is one such ballpark, though. Because they needed to fit "The Uht" into the confines of a preexisting city block, the architects who designed it had to get creative . . . very creative. As a result the grandstands on the first base and third base sides bear no resemblance to one another whatsoever. The stadium appears to be two half stadiums spliced together into one whole at home plate. On the first base side, 10th Street runs parallel to the foul line just behind the field-level seats. Because the street left no room to build a normal grandstand, the second deck is stacked high above the concourse and above the back rows of lower seats. Across the diamond though, where the plot offered more room, the grandstand takes a more traditional approach, beginning right behind the walkway atop the field-level seats and continuing up to the press box and six luxury boxes high above the third baseline. That's right, the press box is along the third baseline, not behind home plate. That's because the two unique grandstands never connect, leaving a wide gap without any second-level seats immediately behind the plate. How many parks can you say that about?

If all of the above sounds like the description of a disjointed stadium that lacks a unified personality or cohesive design approach, well, it may sound that way, but the Uht feels a lot more "together" than you'd think. Its quirks were created out of necessity rather than for the sake of eccentricity and somehow it manages to pull them all together into a cozy little ballpark.

The outfield is also a two-of-a-kind phenomenon, owing to the stadium's location half inside and half outside of a mini sports complex. In left field the city's 50-foot-high hockey arena towers over the field. The home run fence measures just 312 feet from home to the left field foul pole and not much more than that as it continues into left-center. The arena serves as a giant billboard, featuring colorful ads for soda brands, cars, insurance companies, and so on. When the arena ends in left-center, the outfield wall continues along the same path, finally reaching its deepest point in right-center. Behind the fence in this part of the park, the view provides glimpses into the backyards of a residential neighborhood.

Jerry Uht Park opened in 1995. It was originally home to the Pittsburgh Pirates short-season team in the New York-Penn League. In 1999 Erie made the jump to Double-A, as the short-season SeaWolves moved to Niles, Ohio, to make way for the Eastern League SeaWolves. The team was an affiliate of the Anaheim Angels (as they were then known) for its first two seasons, and then switched to a PDC with the Detroit Tigers in 2001.

Built for $8.7 million, Jerry Uht Park was the product of a public/private partnership formed to return affiliated ball to Erie. Prior to the Uht's construction, Ainsworth Field had served as the city's hardball hub. Although Erie's connection to the New York-Penn League dated back to the 1940s, the city had difficulty maintaining a steady affiliation with any one big league team through the decades, due in part, no doubt, to the lackluster conditions at its old ballpark. Ainsworth Field was originally built in 1938 and then rebuilt in 1981, but within a decade of the reconstruction it had grown obsolete again. It was originally home to a Mid Atlantic League team named the Sailors in the early 1940s, then when the Mid Atlantic League shut down during World War II, the Sailors switched to the New York-Penn League. The Sailors rejoined the Mid Atlantic League when it resumed play in 1945, then switched back to the New York-Penn League in 1954 when the Mid Atlantic League folded.

Erie was affiliated with the New York Giants, Washington Senators, and Tigers in the 1950s, then with the Senators and Minnesota Twins in the 1960s. Erie was without a team from 1967 through 1980, then the rebuilt park led to a PDC with the St. Louis Cardinals that began in 1981 and lasted through 1987. The late 1980s and early 1990s saw the city run through brief affiliations with the Baltimore Orioles, Florida Marlins, and Texas Rangers, none lasting more than two seasons. After the Rangers jumped town following the 1993 season, the best Erie could do in 1994 was to field a team in the independent Frontier League.

Although Jerry Uht Park is on the small side for a Double-A facility—it holds the classification minimum 6,000 people—it is well built and well maintained. Rumors have circulated in recent years that Mandalay Baseball Properties, which owns the SeaWolves, may be interested in moving the team to a larger market, but even if that happens, some team will surely be calling Erie "home" for a good long time, thanks to the city's unique and inviting ballpark.

Game Day

Getting to the Park

Erie is about as far north and as far west as you can go in the Keystone State. It sits in the little wedge of Pennsylvania between New York State to the east, Lake Erie to the north, and Ohio to the west. Follow I–90 or I–86 to I–79 North, then follow I–79 into downtown Erie. Take the exit for East 12th Street, turn left onto State Street, and then right onto 10th Street. A number of privately operated lots handle the parking detail. There are also curbside spots in the ballpark neighborhood where parking is free after 5:00 P.M. on weekdays and all day long on weekends.

Inside the Park

As mentioned earlier the seating bowl in Erie is entirely unique, but not in a bad way, as the seats are all comfortable green plastic stadium chairs, are all close to the field, and all offer excellent sight lines. The nice thing about this ballpark is that you could go to three games in a row and have a very different experience each night depending on where you sat. You can say that about most major league stadiums, but not about too many minor league parks.

The 100 Level continues uninterrupted from where it begins in shallow right field with Section 101, to Section 109 behind home plate, to Section 117 in shallow left field. There are eight rows of Box Seats in most of these sections. The stadium designers deserve credit for angling the outfield sections back toward the infield. The four sections past the corner bases on either side extend back toward fair territory so that the fans in Sections 101 and 117 are sitting right next to the foul line. The effect reminds me of the seats behind third base at Fenway Park that jut out toward the foul line. Needless to say, for those looking to claim a souvenir, this is great foul ball territory.

As for the 200 Level, it's completely asymmetrical and a bit more complicated to describe. Along the first baseline are six sections of Reserved Seats. These are raised about 20 feet above the first level and are accessible by stairways on the concourse that runs along 10th Street. Section 201 is high above first base, while at the other end, Section 206 hovers just to the right of home plate. A small sunroof covers the back rows and upper concourse. While the first level offers seats directly behind home plate, the second level does not. There is a gap of about 20 feet directly behind the dish, where the covered concourse from the first base side joins up with both the interior walkway that runs between the 100 Level and the 200 Level on the third base side and the concourse that runs behind the third base grandstand. The Reserved Seats along the third baseline begin with Section 207—a bit to the left of home plate—and finish with 201, behind third base. These sections are much larger than the ones across the diamond, and they rise more steeply. At the top of these sections, a small roof covers the press box and luxury suites.

There used to be large banks of bleachers down the outfield lines where the second-level seats end. With the Wolves averaging only about 3,500 fans per game in recent years, though, the bleachers were removed prior to the 2006 season. In their place fans now find matching group picnic areas.

From the main concourse beneath the upper level on the first base side, fans can watch the game while they walk around or wait in line, but there is no view of the field from the concourse on the third base side. The concession menu features standard fare, with the exceptions of the juicy roast beef sandwiches from Red Osier and the saucy meatball subs. The Uht features Smith's hot dogs, which rate in the middle of the pack on my sliding scale of stadium dogs.

The Jerry Uht Park Experience

The local mascot is a salty dog named C. Wolf. With his menacing inch-long canines, black buccaneer's patch covering his left eye, and red bandana atop his head, C. Wolf is about as fearsome as a mascot can be while still being sufficiently warm and fuzzy for the kids. No, this creature doesn't pay tribute to some long ago time in history when pirates pillaged the shores of Lake Erie. Rather, he was created when Erie was home to the Pirates short-season affiliate. *Sea wolf* is a term sometimes used to describe a pirate.

As for the weekly promotions in Erie, thrifty fans enjoy Mondays when hot dogs, soda, beer, and popcorn cost just $1.00 each; seniors enjoy Wednesdays when the team runs Baseball Bingo all game long; gambling degenerates enjoy Thursdays when the team hands out scratch tickets to the first 1,000 fans and one fan wins $5,000; and the party crowd enjoys Fridays when Happy Hour begins two hours before the first pitch at the beer garden on the third base side.

On the Town

The streets around the ballpark offer familiar fast-food chains, local sandwich shops, family restaurants, and pubs. Popular pregame destinations include **Fat Boys Deli and Pub** (1201 State Street), **Dominick's 24 Hour Eatery** (123 East 12th Street), **Bleachers Sports Bar and Grill** (723 French Street), and **Molly Brannigan's Irish Pub** (506 State Street).

Old ballpark buffs will find **Ainsworth Field** (24th Street at Washington Place) still standing and looking very much as it did during its final season of use as a Frontier League venue. It features a small covered grandstand behind home plate and wooden bleachers down the lines. It is owned and used by the Erie School Department. The brick Roosevelt school towers over right field with a distinctive chimney that reaches nearly as high as the ballpark light towers. The face of the school used to be in play before the city erected a high chain-link fence to protect it from home run balls.

COMMERCE BANK PARK

Harrisburg Senators

Class AA, Eastern League
(WASHINGTON NATIONALS)

Commerce Bank Park
City Island
Harrisburg, Pennsylvania
717–231–4444

Not to be confused with Commerce Bank Ballpark, the home of the independent Atlantic League's Somerset Patriots in Bridgewater, Commerce Bank Park sits on a scenic island in the midst of the Susquehanna River. This small Harrisburg stadium has served as the home of the Eastern League's Senators since 1987. Commerce Bank Park was built prior to the team's arrival on the same plot of land where the Class B Interstate League's Harrisburg Senators had played from 1940 to 1952 as a farm team for the Pittsburgh Pirates. After the 1952 season, minor league baseball left Harrisburg for thirty-five years before the current ballpark opened and welcomed the new Senators.

The stadium was known as Riverfront Stadium until 2004 when the city decided to adopt a more-lucrative, though less-descriptive and less-romantic, handle for its ball yard. It's hard to blame the city for going corporate in this instance. Harrisburg stepped up to the plate and bought the Senators in 1996 to prevent the team from moving to a proposed site in Springfield, Massachusetts. Since then, the city has been scraping together whatever money it can to keep the local stadium up to date.

On Opening Day 2005, Harrisburg mayor Steven R. Reed announced plans to give Commerce Bank Park a $30 million makeover in time for the start of the 2006 season. Reed presented fans with renderings of a completely rebuilt stadium that had been designed by the renowned ballpark architects at HOK. The blueprints called for a brand new seating bowl full of comfortable stadium chairs that would increase the stadium's capacity from 6,300 to 8,000 fans. The designs also depicted a second level above the grandstand that would house twenty luxury boxes. Additionally, the project would add a new press box, new clubhouses, a ballpark restaurant, a play area for kids, outfield picnic areas, an expanded concession area, and a classic redbrick exterior. In other words, the work would result in a brand new ballpark where the old one stood. The city floated $18 million in municipal bonds to cover its share of the projected demolition and construction costs and then turned to the state to provide the rest of the funding. That's when the project came to a screeching halt. Pennsylvania didn't ante up as it was expected to, and the project that was supposed to begin midway through 2005 never got under way. As of this book's print date, the team was still hopeful that eventually the state legislature would free up money for the project.

Clearly, this project must take place if Harrisburg is to remain in the Eastern League. Otherwise, the ballpark will not be able to support Double-A baseball much longer. The majority of the seats at Commerce Bank Park are bleachers. There are no luxury boxes. There are no group areas. The concourse beneath the stadium is small and cramped. The ballpark may have been functional, although unspectacular, at the time of its opening, but it is rapidly becoming a dinosaur. Over the past twenty years, the expectations of fans and the revenue-generating needs of teams have evolved to the point where Commerce Bank Park will be teetering on the brink of extinction if the reconstruction initiative fails.

It would be a shame to see Harrisburg lose its team. After all, more than 260,000 fans per year turn out at the city's rundown ballpark, and surely that total would jump if the stadium were raised to modern Double-A standards. Additionally, City Island offers a beautiful location for a ballpark. The field sits in a sixty-two-acre waterfront sports complex that is just a short walk from downtown Harrisburg. The complex offers batting cages, horses, train rides, riverboat rides, shops and restaurants, miniature golf, and walking and biking trails. Fans inside the ballpark do not enjoy a view of the river but of the lush trees behind the outfield fence that provide a rustic setting for a game.

Harrisburg's long history as a minor league town also seems to warrant a renewed investment in the city's baseball grounds. Professional baseball has been played on the site where Commerce Bank Park sits dating back to the early 1900s. An old wooden ballpark housed a number of different minor league teams from 1907 through 1952, including a team affiliated with the Washington Senators, which explains how the Harrisburg team got its name. And you probably thought the team was honoring its generous state politicians, right?

In 1952, after the City Island ballpark flooded for the umpteenth time, the Senators left town, but not before they created a flap by signing a twenty-four-year-old female stenographer to play shortstop. Eleanor Engle suited up for the Senators for four games in June of 1952, but she never got to play in a game. Eventually, the president of the National Association of Professional Baseball Leagues voided the young lady's contract, deriding her signing as a publicity stunt.

Thirty-five years later, the island's current ballpark was built for $1.9 million. It was reinforced with new flood control technology that reassured the Pittsburgh Pirates that

their Eastern Leaguers wouldn't float down the Susquehanna River during rain delays. The team won the Eastern League championship in its first season. Then, in 1991 it signed a player development contract with the Montreal Expos.

The Senators gave the local fans plenty to cheer about during the 1990s, becoming the first Eastern League team to win four straight championships when they accomplished the feat between 1996 and 1999. The 1999 championship finale was the most dramatic, as future big leaguer Milton Bradley blasted a walk-off grand slam with two outs in the bottom of the ninth inning of the fifth and deciding game, to lead the Senators past the Norwich Navigators 12–11.

In addition to Bradley, the list of future major leaguers to pass through Harrisburg during the Senators second incarnation includes Vladimir Guerrero, Rondell White, Mark Grudzielanek, Tony Armas Jr., Brad Wilkerson, Brian Schneider, José Vidro, and Ryan Zimmerman. Here's hoping that with a new ballpark soon in place, the city will continue to serve as a proving ground for future big league stars for years to come.

Game Day

Getting to the Park

Harrisburg is located 90 miles north of Baltimore and 115 miles west of Philadelphia. City Island is accessible via Market Street from either side of the Susquehanna River. From I-83, take the Second Street exit and turn left onto Market at the fourth light. The exit to City Island is halfway across the Market Street Bridge. Parking is available on City Island for $2.00 per car, or fans can park for free in the streets of downtown Harrisburg on the eastern banks of the river and walk across the bridge to the stadium.

Inside the Park

Commerce Bank Park frequently sells out weekend games in June, July, and August. The small seating bowl offers fifteen sections of Box Seats at field level, beginning with Section 2 in shallow right field, continuing to Section 9 behind home plate, and finishing with Section 16 in shallow left. The Boxes offer five rows of comfortable red stadium chairs with drink holders. The rest of the park, unfortunately, is outfitted with metal bleachers. The Reserved Seats are located behind the Boxes on the infield and in shallow right field. These are blue bleachers with back supports. A large General Admission section in left field foul territory, meanwhile, offers aluminum bleachers without backs. Making these left field seats even worse, the setting sun creates a glare for fans during the early innings.

The concession stands are beneath the grandstand at ground level. The barbecue chicken sandwiches and funnel cakes are popular items. There is a small team store on the concourse behind first base and a small entertainment area for kids as well.

The Commerce Bank Park Experience

The team mascot is a rascal called "Rascot." He is a red-nosed river monster that was dredged up from the Susquehanna a few years back. In addition to Rascot's antics, the Senators keep fans entertained with dizzy bat races, sumo suit wrestling, potato sack races, and tricycle races.

Since Harrisburg is the capital of Pennsylvania, it is not uncommon for the governor and local legislators to turn out at the ballpark on warm summer nights. You'd think this would give the team a leg up on getting its new stadium plan financed, but it hasn't worked out that way.

Since there is no indoor luxury seating at the ballpark, and since the park is located on a river, savvy politicians and their knowing constituents spray themselves with insect repellant before heading to the ballpark. If you're visiting during a particularly wet spring, you'd be wise to do the same. You may also want to bring an umbrella, as the mayflies swarm around the light banks, and when they inevitably fly too close to the hot bulbs, their singed carcasses fall onto the fans below.

On the Town

Harrisburg may be the capital of Pennsylvania, but with a population of barely 50,000 residents, it's just one-thirtieth the size of Philadelphia. Harrisburg is 20 miles west of Hershey, known for its chocolate, and even closer to Hummelstown, known for its decorative figurines. Don't worry, I'll spare you the details of the Hummel scene in case you've brought your wife or girlfriend or mother-in-law along with you on your road trip and are as terrified as I would be of getting dragged to a bunch of quaint little Hummel shops. I can tell you and your girlfriend and mother-in-law this: I have heard these shops are very hard, nay, impossible, to locate, so don't dare try finding them on your own.

Candy freaks and amusement park aficionados will have an easier go of it. They can conveniently follow Route 322 east from Harrisburg to Hershey, where **Hershey's Chocolate World** (800 Park Boulevard) offers free tours of its factory, casual restaurants, and a massive factory store. Meanwhile, **Hershey Park** (300 Park Boulevard) is an amusement park with more than sixty rides, including eight roller coasters. I suggest gorging yourself with chocolate *after* you ride the coasters, but as always, the ultimate sequencing of your tourist excursions is left to your best judgment.

Fans looking for a bite to eat or a pint to sip near the ballpark will find an array of options on

Second Street in downtown Harrisburg. **Zembies**, **Molly Brannigan's**, **Cragan Brickhaus**, **Stock's on Second**, **Kokomos**, **Dukes**, and the **Firehouse** are part of a lively entertainment district.

For an independent league road trip, follow I–76 to Lancaster where the Atlantic League's Barnstormers play. **Clipper Magazine Stadium** (650 North Prince Street), which opened in 2005, has a seating capacity of 7,500, counting the space on the left field berm. The park seems more suited for Double-A baseball than Commerce Bank Park is, but it's doing just fine as an indy facility, drawing more than 300,000 visitors a year.

LACKAWANNA COUNTY STADIUM

Scranton/Wilkes-Barre Red Barons

Class AAA, International League
(NEW YORK YANKEES)

Lackawanna County Stadium
235 Montage Mountain Road
Moosic, Pennsylvania
570–969–2255

Lackawanna County Stadium sits at the foot of a wooded, rock-strewn mountainside in Pennsylvania coal country, between the cities of Scranton and Wilkes-Barre. To the first time visitor, the rural surroundings seem to hint at a rustic ballpark experience to follow, one that will surely hearken them pleasantly back to a simpler time in the evolution of the Grand Old Game. The first chink in the armor of this romantic fantasy occurs to such a daydreamer at the end of Montage Mountain Road where the stadium parking lot gives rise to the massive concrete underbelly of the stadium. Surely, this sight brings warm smiles to the faces of any Cement Mixers of America union members who visit, but for most baseball fans the first impulse is to cringe. Yes, it's true. While baseball's cookie-cutter era has thankfully gone the way of the spitball in cities like Cincinnati, Philadelphia, and Pittsburgh, it is still alive and well (sort of) in Lackawanna County, PA.

Lackawanna County Stadium is a multipurpose facility that opened in 1989. It is two hours north of Philadelphia and served as the home of the Phillies' top prospects from the time of its opening until 2007 when the Red Barons switched to a PDC with the Yankees. If imitation is the highest form of flattery, the folks who designed Lackawanna County

Stadium sure sent plenty of love Philly's way. The field dimensions at "The Lack" replicate exactly those that once existed at Veteran's Stadium—a perfectly symmetrical 330 feet down the lines, 371 feet to the power alleys, and 408 feet to center. Likewise, the blue outfield fence is 12 feet high, just like the one that used to stand at "The Vet." And the playing surface is the same type of Astroturf that they had in Philadelphia for years—you know, the early generation kind that was a little too blue to be mistaken for natural grass even by someone with really bad cataracts, hard enough to ignite rug burns whenever an outfielder laid out for a ball, and hot enough to fry an egg on in July and August.

Like any cookie-cutter worth its sugar, The Lack also features a first-level seating bowl situated a bit too far from the field, owing to the spacious foul territory along both baselines. This space must come in handy when the field is converted into a gridiron to accommodate high school and college football games. Also, true to form, Lackawanna County Stadium's upper deck rises more steeply than Jon Miller's forehead. This is a minor league facility with a seating capacity of only about 11,000, so obviously its upper level is not as vast as the one that once existed in the airspace somewhere above the Phillies' plastic field on Broad Street. But make no mistake, the upper-level seats in Scranton/Wilkes-Barre are as *altitudinous* as any you'll find in the bush leagues. Just like at the old Vet, the luxury suites come first, then the upper-deck seats are stacked on top of them. Thus, the interests of a few high rollers trump those of the masses. I know, that's life. I should be used to it by now. But this isn't life, it's baseball, and baseball is supposed to adhere to a higher moral code, especially in the minor leagues.

Before any masochistic fans who were sad to miss out on the chance to see a game at The

Vet cease their self-flagellation and go running to their computer to order tickets to The Lack, I should offer this disclaimer. As hard as I've been on The Lack, it actually offers a game day experience that is much better than the one fans used to find at The Vet. The saving grace at Lackawanna County Stadium is the outfield view, which really is impressive. While the outfield in Philly was pretty much the same as the infield—seats, seats, and more seats . . . oh yeah, and concrete too—at this minor league yard, Montage Mountain rises just beyond the outfield fence, offering distinctive boulders and resilient trees on its craggy face. This otherworldly setting makes the stadium worth a visit, despite the artificial turf and nosebleed seats.

Lackawanna County Stadium was built for $11 million to bring baseball back to a region that once fielded two teams, before the Scranton Red Sox and Wilkes-Barre Barons, both of the Eastern League, closed up shop in the 1950s. The longtime rival cities merged their baseball interests into one entity in the mid-1980s and embarked on the arduous process of finding funding for a stadium and a team to play in it. Lackawanna County commissioners Ray Alberigi and Joe Corcoran led the effort, while Pennsylvania governor Bob Casey was instrumental in providing state money, and local businessman Bill Gilchrist offered the fifty acres upon which the stadium was built.

The effort hit a few snags along the way. First, the owners of the Maine Guides tried to renege on an agreement to sell their team to the newly formed Lackawanna County Stadium Authority, which planned to move the team to Lackawanna County. The matter was not resolved until a protracted court battle resulted in a favorable ruling for Lackawanna County. Then the stadium construction exceeded its budget and was completed later than expected, a month into the 1989 season. Then the state funding that Governor Casey had promised was withheld while state auditors launched a highly publicized investigation into whether the Stadium Authority had allocated funds improperly. In the end the investigation revealed that only a small percentage of the work had been awarded without the necessary public bidding process and that no laws had been broken. Nearly a year after the stadium opened, the state released the money for the ballpark.

Before the Red Barons signed their recent PDC with the Yankees, Scranton/Wilkes-Barre offered local Phillies fans the chance to see such rising stars as Pat Burrell, Darren Daulton, Ryan Howard, John Kruk,

Lackawanna County Stadium

Von Hayes, Chase Utley, Cole Hamels, Vicente Padilla, and Curt Schilling strut their stuff while on their way to the majors. In 2007, the Phillies moved their Triple-A prospects to Ottawa for a one-year layover that seems sure to be followed by a switch to a new park in Allentown, Pennsylvania in 2008.

Game Day

Getting to the Park

Scranton and Wilkes-Barre are separated by a 15-mile stretch of I–81 in northeastern Pennsylvania. Lackawanna County Stadium is right between the two cities in the town of Moosic. From the northeast extension of the Pennsylvania Turnpike (I–476), take the Wyoming Valley exit and then take I–81 North to exit 182. Turn right at the light and follow Montage Mountain Road to the stadium. Montage Mountain Road is the only way into or out of the stadium parking lot, so it backs up on days when large crowds turn out.

Inside the Park

The lower deck extends nearly to the foul poles on either side of the diamond, offering sixteen steeply ascending rows. The outfield-most three sections on either side house Bleachers, while the rest of the lower sections provide green stadium chairs that sell as Lower Boxes. Sections 119 and 120 are directly behind home plate, Sections 126 through 129 are behind the home dugout on the first baseline, Sections 110 through 113 are behind the visitors dugout, and the Bleacher sections are 100 through 102 in left and Sections 137 through 139 in right. Party decks in deep outfield foul territory overlook the home bullpen in right, and the visitors pen in left.

The second deck continues not quite as far as the lower one, but stops where the bleachers begin on the deck down below. The luxury suites and glassed-in restaurant appear first, while above them sixteen rows of red Upper Reserved Seats rise so steeply that when fans sit down their feet are near the top of the chair in front of them. The incline reminded me of the upper deck at Rogers Centre in Toronto, only in Canada every row comes with its own railing, adding something of a security blanket for *acrophobiacs*. The Upper Reserved Seats begin with Section 301 in deep left field, continue down the third baseline to Sections 317 and 318 behind the plate, and finish at Section 334 in deep right.

Philly favorites like cheesesteaks and pirogues highlight the concession menu, while the ballpark pizza is also good. The Stadium Club is on the second deck in deep right field and is open to all fans.

The Lackawanna County Stadium Experience

At a stadium this large, it's really difficult for a mascot to work the crowd with any degree of success, but the grouchy green monster known as "The Grump" deserves points for trying.

The Red Barons offer familiar minor league promotions like fireworks on Fridays, 50-cent hot dogs on Tuesdays, baseball bingo on Wednesdays, and a race around the bases for kids after Sunday games.

In 2006 the team drew a large crowd to a "Christmas in July" celebration that looks like it will become an annual event. And you probably thought The Grump was a grinch? Think again. He was the life of the party.

On the Town

Let's just say that Stark Reservoir, which is right near the ballpark, is aptly named. Other than the ski resort at the top of the mountain and the **Ruby Tuesday** (15 Radcliffe Drive) and **Johnny Rockets** (5 Radcliffe Drive) a mile away, the area around the park is rather desolate.

I would encourage all fans, especially those traveling with kids, to head 70 miles west to Williamsport, where the Little League World Series takes place each August. There are three different ballparks to see at the Little League complex (100 West Fourth Street). **Lamade Field** is the 10,000-seat stadium that has hosted the Little League World Series since 1959, **Carl E. Stotz Field** is the park that hosted the Series from 1947 through 1958, and **Memorial Park** is where the first Little League game ever was played in 1939. Not far away, fans find eight-decade-old **Bowman Field** (1700 West Fourth Street), a pro diamond that serves as home to the New York-Penn League's Williamsport Crosscutters. The **Peter J. McGovern Little League Baseball Museum** (525 Route 15 Highway, South Williamsport) is also worth a visit. The Hall of Excellence pays tribute to former Little Leaguers who grew up to achieve big-time success in different walks of life. The honorees include politicians George W. Bush and Rudolph Giuliani, actors Kevin Costner and Tom Selleck, newspaper columnists Dave Barry and George Will, basketball players Bill Bradley and Kareem Abdul-Jabbar, singer Bruce Springsteen, and major league baseball players Mike Schmidt, Cal Ripken Jr., Dale Murphy, Jim Palmer, Nolan Ryan, and Tom Seaver. Between Memorial Day and Labor Day, the museum is open Monday through Saturday from 10:00 A.M. until 7:00 P.M., and Sunday from noon until 7:00 P.M. Admission costs $5.00 for adults and $1.50 for children.

FIRSTENERGY STADIUM

Reading Phillies

Class AA, Eastern League
(PHILADELPHIA PHILLIES)

FirstEnergy Stadium
Route 61 South/1900 Centre Avenue
Reading, Pennsylvania
610–375–8469

Reading bills itself as "Baseballtown, USA" and for good reason. Watching a game at First-Energy Stadium—previously known as Reading Memorial Municipal Stadium—provides an experience that is about as enjoyable as minor league baseball can get. The old ballpark reflects Reading's baseball history, while it also provides a comfortable, fan-friendly, gameday experience.

With a history that dates back to its debut as home to a Cleveland Indians farm club in 1952, FirstEnergy Stadium is the oldest ballpark in the Eastern League. To put that in perspective, the circuit's next oldest facility is Commerce Bank Park in Harrisburg, which opened twenty-five years later in 1987.

The ballpark experience in Reading is full of delightful quirks, characters, and traditions that the local fans cherish. The relationship between the fans and team seems to work both ways too. Since the early 1990s, ownership has implemented a steady stream of expensive renovations to the ballpark while keeping ticket prices low, parking free, and hot dogs at $1.50 apiece.

The stadium was dreamed up in 1945 when the Reading City Council voted unanimously to purchase twenty-seven acres of land in a part of town known as Cathedral Heights. Construction began in 1949, and two years later the stadium was completed. The Reading Indians called the park "home" from 1952 through 1961, then the Boston Red Sox fielded a farm team in Reading in 1963 and 1964, before the Indians returned for a one-year stint in 1965. After sitting out the 1966 season, Reading got back into the game in 1967, attracting the Philadelphia Phillies Eastern League affiliate to town. And the team has played in Reading ever since.

Today, the original brick wall around the stadium still stands, offering classy arches that fans pass through on their way inside. Just outside these arches giant metal dog tags adorn the ballpark plaza, paying tribute to U.S. veterans and fallen military personnel. Inside the gates on the third base side, bronze plaques honor past owners of the Reading Phillies and community leaders who have played important roles in the life of the local team. A "Baseballtown to the Majors" exhibit on the concourse behind home plate lists all 251 (and counting) Reading Phillies who have played in the majors. Every Reading team picture since 1967 is also on display here. A "Reading Baseball Hall of Fame" exhibit on the first base side provides brief biographies of famous Reading players from before and during the Phillies era. These include such notables as Frank "Home Run" Baker and Roger Maris, home run kings who played at old Lauer's Park, and more recent Reading stars like Mike Schmidt, Bob Boone, Greg Luzinski, Ryne Sandberg, George Bell, Juan Samuel, and Julio Franco.

Distinctive features adorning the field include the team's retired numbers (Schmidt's 24, Sandberg's 26, and Jackie Robinson's 42), which hang in center field, a 1,000-square-foot heated pool behind the right field fence that provides a nice target for left-handed pull hitters, a miniature train with an exploding smokestack that runs atop the right field fence, a red-and-white bull's-eye painted atop the Power Alley Pub in left field home run territory, and a state of the art video board in left-center.

The outfield sightlines provide gorgeous views of Mount Penn and several other rolling green mountains. Mount Penn rises beyond the right field fence, offering the highest peak. The fire tower and Japanese pagoda atop the mountain are the city's most recognizable symbols. Beyond the left field fence, trains can often be spotted chugging along the Norfolk Southern line. A water tower rises over the picnic area on the third base side and is visible to fans seated on the first base side of the park. The panoramic outfield view also includes church steeples, smoke stacks, and plenty of trees.

As you might guess, the Reading Phillies have treated their fans to many magical moments over the years. Some recent highlights

that local fans still talk about are Carmine Cappuccio's walk-off grand slam in Game One of the 2000 Eastern League Championship semifinals against four-time defending champion Harrisburg, which ignited a three-game Reading sweep; Adam Walker's 2001 no-hitter against New Haven; and the mammoth home run that Ryan Howard hit in 2004 that landed atop the grass embankment in center field, an estimated 480 feet from home plate.

Reading's baseball history actually predates the existence of Memorial Municipal Stadium by several decades. The Reading Actives were members of the Interstate Association back in the 1880s. The first woman to play for a minor league team was Lizzie Arlington, who pitched a scoreless inning for the Reading Coal Heavers (what a great name) in 1898. The Reading Keystones of the Inter-

FirstEnergy Stadium

national League were known for fielding some of the worst minor league squads ever. The 1926 edition went 31–129 and the 1927 team lost thirty-one straight games on the way to a 43–123 mark. Other teams to play in Reading included the Pretzels, Dutchmen, Marines, and Coal Barons.

Reading's minor league teams played at Lauer's Park from 1907 through 1941, until the city decided to raze the field and build a municipal parking lot and elementary school on the site. In 2006 the Reading Phillies and the city teamed up to build a new youth baseball field and children's playground where the old field once stood.

Game Day

Getting to the Park

Reading is 65 miles northwest of Philadelphia. From the City of Great Cheesesteaks, follow Route 76 West to Route 422 West, then to Route 12 East and Route 61 South. There is plenty of free parking at various lots around the stadium and along Centre Avenue and Front Street. For those who want to park as close to the stadium as possible, the community pool beyond the left field fence offers parking for a small fee.

Inside the Park

FirstEnergy Stadium offers seating for 9,000 fans. Good tickets are usually available on game day, although the team attracts large crowds on Fridays and Saturdays during the summer.

The original seating bowl still stands around the infield, featuring new seats that were installed in the late 1980s. Section 1 is on the first base side of home plate, while Sections 4 and 5 are behind the plate, and Section 9 is on the third base side. The blue Field Box Seats are followed by a ring of yellow Box Seats, and then a ring of red seats in the General Admission section. A small roof covers the red seats behind the plate.

New seating areas were constructed in the 1990s between the ends of the original bowl and the foul poles. The Blue Box Seats along the right field line provide good views of the game but don't showcase the pastoral outfield view like the seats in the main bowl do. These seats begin with Box 1 in medium-depth right and end at Box 4 at first base. There are also three sections of Green Reserved Seats behind the Boxes on the right field line, while across the diamond there are four Green Reserved sections just past third base. General Admission sections fill the ends of the stadium in right and left.

The stadium does not offer any luxury boxes. The group picnic areas are behind third base and behind the home run fence in right and left.

The menu at the concession stands behind the stadium offers the ballpark basics, while a food court on the first base side provides more choices. The cheesesteaks and chicken steaks are popular, as are the loaded meatball sandwiches and the homemade soft pretzels. The Grand Slammer is a double burger with fries and a special mystery sauce. There is a bar in left field and the private Power Alley Pub in left-center. Both serve Yuengling, brewed in nearby Pottsville.

The FirstEnergy Stadium Experience

The Reading Phillies offer five different mascots: Screwball the Seam-Head, Change-Up the Turtle, Bucky the Beaver, Blooper the Hound Dog, and Quack the Rubber Ducky. The quintet forms the Reading Phillies Mascot Band, which puts on concerts following Saturday night games during the summer. This is not a prerecorded Ashlee Simpson lip-synch job either. The Reading mascots play guitars, drums, bongos, and keyboards, while Quack sings favorite children's songs, as well as a few originals.

The Crazy Hotdog Vendor is also a mascot of sorts. This unique bespectacled individual dresses in red-and-white-striped garb and rides a fake ostrich up and down the aisles, doling out ballpark wieners.

The big league Phillie Phanatic also makes his share of appearances in Reading each year.

Another fan favorite is Dave "Frenchy" Bauman, who has sat behind the public address microphone in the press box for every Reading home game since 1975.

The kiddies love the miniature Viking ship that rises behind the third base dugout at the end of each game while a short operatic tune indicates it's time to head home. Many fans reach down from the first base grandstands to give members of the Phillies high-fives as they come off the field after games. Fans also line up outside the home clubhouse on the first base side to get autographs, as the players have to walk through a gauntlet of fans to get from the dugout to the clubhouse.

On the Town

Located in Pennsylvania Dutch Country, Reading is known worldwide for the Reading Railroad line, which is featured on the original Monopoly game board. The railroad was once used to transport coal from the northern part of the state to points south.

Mount Penn is a popular tourist destination. Visitors follow Duryea Drive up the side of the mountain to the pagoda at the top, then look down at the city and at Neversink Mountain. Drive carefully on Duryea Drive. This road was once used to test-drive early automobiles due to its many twists and turns. Either a new model handled the curves, or it went crashing off the side of the mountain.

The new youth baseball facility that stands on the former site of Lauer's Park is called **Gordon Hoodak Stadium at Lauer's Park** (251 North Second Street). The field is lighted at night and provides a roof over its grandstand. It is named after the principal of Lauer's Park Elementary School. Frederick Lauer, in case you're wondering, was a Civil War–era brewer who made Reading his home.

FRAWLEY STADIUM
Wilmington Blue Rocks

Class A, Carolina League
(KANSAS CITY ROYALS)

Judy Johnson Field at Daniel S. Frawley Stadium
801 South Madison Street
Wilmington, Delaware
302–888–2583

The home of the Wilmington Blue Rocks goes by the name "Frawley Stadium" for short, but its full name is "Judy Johnson Field at Daniel S. Frawley Stadium." Talk about a mouthful. The long-winded handle pays tribute to both Mr. Frawley, the Wilmington mayor who championed the construction of the ballpark that returned professional baseball to Wilmington in 1993 after a forty-year hiatus, and Mr. Johnson, a Negro League star who was inducted into the National Baseball Hall of Fame in 1975.

William Julius Johnson was born in Snow Hill, Maryland, but lived most of his life in Wilmington, until the time of his passing in 1989. During his eighteen-year playing career, Johnson starred as a third baseman for the Philadelphia Hilldales, the Homestead Grays, the Darby Daisies, and the Pittsburgh Crawfords. He played alongside such fellow Hall of Famers as Satchel Paige, Josh Gibson, and Cool Papa Bell. After his playing days, Johnson served as a scout for the Philadelphia A's, Philadelphia Phillies, and Milwaukee Braves.

The Blue Rocks honor Johnson with a life-sized statue outside the stadium that depicts him crouched in his fielder's position, ready to pounce on a hot grounder. Additionally, the team hosts a special "Judy Johnson Night" each year, during which it honors former Negro League stars in a pregame ceremony. The

honorees have included Buck Leonard, Buck O'Neil, Gene Benson, Jackie Robinson, Leroy Ferrell, and Gibson. Once the game begins, the Blue Rocks and their opponents take the field in throwback uniforms designed to replicate those worn by Negro League teams. This classy Wilmington tradition is a great way to educate the general public about the contributions Negro Leaguers made to the game's history at a time when racism pervaded the nation and National Pastime.

The ballpark that bears Johnson's name sits between I–95 and the Delaware River within an entertainment district known as Riverfront Wilmington. The park's redbrick façade is topped, appropriately, by a blue roof. Inside, a large second level hovers over the infield grandstand, housing eighteen luxury boxes. Snazzy white cursive letters appear atop the blue interior façade, spelling out "Blue Rocks." From the ballpark seats, the elevated interstate dominates the industrial outfield view in left and center, while the buildings of downtown Wilmington rise beyond the fence in right. A large video board sits in right-center atop the two levels of signage on the outfield fence.

As Delaware's only professional baseball team, the Blue Rocks draw more than 300,000 fans per season, placing them atop the high-A Carolina League's attendance ledger and even ahead of many Double-A teams. The club is named after the original Wilmington Blue Rocks franchise, which left the city four decades before the Peninsula Pilots of Hampton, Virginia, agreed to relocate to Wilmington in 1993. Today, as it did in the 1940s and 1950s, the nickname references the blue granite stones found along the banks of the Brandywine River.

The original Blue Rocks played in the Interstate League from 1940 through 1952, making their home at Wilmington Park, at the corner of 30th Street and Governor Printz Boulevard. The Blue Rocks were a Philadelphia A's affiliate from 1940 through 1943, then switched to an affiliation with the Phillies in 1944. Notable old-time Blue Rocks players included future major leaguers Robin Roberts, Curt Simmons, and Elmer Valo. After the 1952 season the Interstate League disbanded though, and minor league baseball left Wilmington. After a decade of neglect, in 1963 Wilmington Park was demolished.

At the time of its opening, Frawley Stadium was called Legends Stadium, but the name was soon changed to honor Frawley and Johnson. The Blue Rocks served as a Kansas City Royals affiliate from 1993 through 2004, then switched to a PDC with the Boston Red Sox in 2005, then rejoined the Royals system in 2007. The team's alumni roster includes Carlos Beltrán, David DeJesús, Jon Lieber, Mike Sweeney, Johnny Damon, and more than eighty others who have reached the major leagues. These future big leaguers are honored on boards that hang from the ceiling of the Frawley Stadium concourse.

In addition to doing well at the box office, the Blue Rocks have done well on the field. The team won eight Northern Division titles in its first twelve seasons, on the way to four Carolina League championships. Highlights have included the team's first no-hitter, which José Rosado and Pat Flurry combined on against the Winston-Salem Warthogs in 1993, a 20–3 win over the Myrtle Beach Pelicans in 1999, and a Brian Sanchez no-hitter in 2000.

Game Day

Getting to the Park
Wilmington is 45 miles south of Philadelphia along I-95. From the north, take I-95 South to exit 6 and turn left onto Martin Luther King Boulevard, then right onto South Madison Street, which leads to the stadium. From the south, take I–95 North to the Maryland Avenue exit and turn right onto Read Street, then right onto South Madison Street. Parking at the ballpark is free.

Inside the Park
Frawley Stadium can seat more than 6,500 fans, and even when the seats are sold out, standing room is available on game day. The seating bowl extends nearly to the foul poles on either side, offering eight rows of blue Box Seats at field level and bleachers with backs in most of the sections above the midlevel walkway. The Box Seats begin with Section 1 in right field, continue to Sections 7 through 9 behind the home dugout on the first baseline, make the turn at Sections 14 and 15 behind the plate, and finish at Section 28 in left field. The second level offers six sections of Reserved Box Seats behind home plate (Sections E through J) and Reserved Bleachers along either baseline. A large bank of bleachers, added during a 2001 renovation, sits atop the regular seating bowl on the third base side, serving as a General Admission section.

The concourse runs above the grandstands and offers basic concessions—sorry, no rock candy and no rock crabs—and macrobrews from Budweiser, Miller, and Coors—no whiskey on the rocks. The Blue Rocks Cafe behind home plate offers a slightly more expansive beverage list.

The Frawley Stadium Experience
The Blue Rocks feature different kid-friendly events and activities during each game, as well as a kids area on the concourse with the ubiquitous bouncy pen and speed pitch booth. The team usually welcomes a lucky child into the public address announcer's booth to introduce the players for an inning. Nightly baby races take place down on the field between innings, putting smiles on the faces of parents

and giving degenerate gamblers something to wager on.

The Blue Rocks offer fans a trio of eclectic mascots. Rocky Bluewinkle is a 7-foot-tall blue moose that wears a Blue Rocks uniform with the number 0 on it. Mr. Celery is a 7½-foot-tall stalk of celery that runs onto the field whenever the Blue Rocks score a run and dances. Rubble is a 6½-foot-tall inflatable rock.

On the Town

Before and after games fans often congregate at several restaurants within a five-minute walk of the park, including **Timothy's on the Waterfront** (930 Pettinaro Park Drive), **Kahunaville** (500 South Madison Street), the **Iron Hill Brewery** (620 South Madison Street), and **Joe's Crab Shack** (600 South Madison Street).

The **Delaware Sports Hall of Fame** resides outside Frawley Stadium on the first base side. It is open Tuesday through Saturday from noon until 5:00 P.M. and admission costs $4.00. The museum honors scores of Delawareans, the names of whom most out-of-state visitors will not recognize. Among the inductees visitors are likely to have heard of are Michael Neill, who played on the United States 2000 Olympic baseball team that won gold in Sydney; *USA*

Today sports columnist Hal Bodley; and NBA star A. J. English.

On the Judy Johnson trail, baseball pilgrims can visit the Hall of Famer's gravesite at **Silverbrook Cemetery** in Wilmington, and the **Judy Johnson House** (Newport Road and Kiamensi Street, Marshallton) where Johnson and his wife Anita lived for fifty-five years.

Also located conveniently along this stretch of I–95 is the **Cal Ripken Museum** in Aberdeen, Maryland. The museum originally opened inside the Aberdeen City Hall in 1996, then in 2006 it relocated to **Ripken Stadium** (873 Long Drive), home of the short-season Aberdeen Ironbirds of the New York-Penn League. The museum houses memorabilia from Ripken's record-breaking consecutive games streak and a gift shop with plenty of autographed merchandise. Across the street from the stadium and museum, the multi-field **Ripken Youth Baseball Academy** is home to the Ripken World Series. The tournament welcomes the best Babe Ruth League teams in the world—in the eleven- and twelve-year-old division—to the Ripken campus each August. The championship game is played at a ballpark called "Cal Senior's Yard," a 600-seat miniature version of Oriole Park at Camden Yards.

PRINCE GEORGE'S STADIUM

Bowie Baysox

Class AA, Eastern League
(BALTIMORE ORIOLES)

Prince George's Stadium
4101 NE Crain Highway
Bowie, Maryland
301–464–4865

No major league organization does a better job of keeping an eye on its prospects than the Baltimore Orioles. The O's keep their hatchlings close to the nest, as four of their six minor league teams play in the state of Maryland: the Double-A Bowie Baysox, high-A Frederick Keys, low-A Delmarva Shorebirds, and short-season Aberdeen Ironbirds.

The Baysox play their home games closer to Camden Yards than any other affiliate in the Orioles system, as their Prince George's Stadium is just a half-hour drive south of Baltimore. For this reason Bowie is a convenient rehab destination for Orioles big leaguers, and the Baysox roster usually features at least a couple of former major leaguers who are available at a moment's notice to join the Orioles.

In addition to their close geographic proximity to one another, the Baysox and Orioles share something else in common: both once played their home games at Memorial Stadium in Baltimore. The Orioles played there from 1954 until 1992 when Oriole Park at Camden Yards opened. The Baysox played there during their inaugural 1993 season while Prince George's Stadium was being built. Imagine that, a minor league team playing a full season at a 48,000-seat stadium.

When construction delays postponed the opening of Prince George's Stadium, the Baysox were forced to play the first half of the 1994 season at four different locations. The team borrowed the minor league fields in Frederick and Wilmington and the college diamonds at the University of Maryland and the U.S. Naval Academy. Incidentally, Memorial Stadium was demolished in 2001, lest any road-tripping fans decide to make a pilgrimage to all six fields the Baysox have called "home."

Since opening on July 16, 1994, Prince George's Stadium has averaged crowds of 4,000 to 5,000 fans per game. However, it usually seems empty due to its sheer size. The stadium can seat 10,000 fans. The extra seats may come in handy when Willie Nelson or Bob Dylan stop by for a summer concert or when Allen Iverson borrows the field for his annual celebrity softball game, but during baseball season the effect is similar to the one that plagued old Municipal Stadium in Cleveland for decades. Those who remember the "Mistake by the Lake" will recall that even when the Indians drew 40,000 fans, their cavernous ballpark seemed empty. I don't mean to say that Prince George's Stadium is a "mistake" to the degree that the monstrosity in Cleveland was, but the ballpark atmosphere would be livelier if there were a few thousand fewer seats.

The ballpark's most endearing feature is its outfield view, which looks into a rich green forest. The trees behind the two levels of advertising signs on the outfield wall combine to create a cozy green backdrop for a game. Around the infield the overhang of the skybox level shelters the main concourse atop the last row of seats, while fans enjoy a nice view of the field from the concession lines on the concourse. While it hadn't been installed in time for my visit to Bowie, the Baysox were planning to install an outfield lighthouse similar to the one at Hadlock Field in Portland, which will be in place for the 2007 season.

More than ninety former Baysox have found their way to the major leagues, including Jeffrey Hammonds, Armando Benítez, Sidney Ponson, David Dellucci, Jorge Julio, Josh Towers, Brian Roberts, Daniel Cabrera, and Jerry Hairston Jr.

In addition to housing the Baysox, summer concerts and an annual gathering of AI's NBA friends (Vince Carter, Gilbert Arenas, Steve Francis, Antawn Jamison, Larry Hughes, etc.), Prince George's Stadium is also used twice a year for Central Maryland Career Fairs, and once hosted a live boxing card that featured foxy boxer Layla Ali (daughter of Muhammad Ali). During October the ballpark is converted into the "Boooowie Baysox Haunted House" for the enjoyment of area youngsters. Additionally, one of the stadium's parking lots doubles as a drive-in movie theater when the Baysox are on the road.

In case you're wondering who Prince George was, I can tell you that he was not the stadium architect, nor was he the mayor of Bowie when the stadium was constructed, nor is Prince George the name of a local savings bank that bought the naming rights. The stadium's name recognizes its place within Prince George's County. The county is named after Prince George of Denmark, the brother of King Christian V of Denmark and Norway, and husband of Queen Anne of Great Britain.

As for the home team's name, the Bowie club plays about 15 miles west of Chesapeake Bay.

Game Day

Getting to the Park

From the Baltimore Beltway/I–695, take the exit for Route 97 South toward Annapolis. Take exit 7 and follow Route 3 South toward Bowie. After passing under the Route 50 overpass, Route 3 turns into Route 301 South. Go through one traffic light and then turn left at the next light onto Ballpark Drive. Parking is free in the two large stadium lots. The entrance to the main lot is on Ballpark Drive, and the entrance to the north lot is on Governor's Bridge Road.

Inside the Park

The seating bowl extends into medium-depth outfield foul territory on either side of the diamond. Sections 101 and 102 are behind the plate, and the odd-numbered sections continue down the right field line, while the even-numbered sections continue down the left field line. The bowl ends at Section 123 in right and Section 124 in left.

The first five rows of stadium chairs are the Field Box Seats, while the next eight rows are Reserved Box Seats. After a midlevel walkway, the remaining seats take the form of red aluminum bleachers with backs that sell as General Admission. The good news is that a General Admission ticket will score you a pretty good view of the game right behind home plate or wherever else you choose to sit. The bad news is that you'll probably get a sore rump from sitting on an uncomfortable metal bench all night.

The main concourse runs above the top row of bleachers and beneath the luxury boxes. The highlight of the right field kids park is a beautiful carousel, similar to the one at Frederick's Harry Grove Stadium. If you notice similarities between Price George's Stadium and Harry Grove—like the carousel and the sloped outfield berms between the ends of the seating bowl and the foul poles—that's because both stadium projects were overseen by Peter Kirk, who once owned both teams.

The favorite concession item in Bowie only appears at the concession stands one day a week. On Rock Fish Fry-days fans chow down on deep-fried fish. The Diamond View Restaurant behind home plate is usually reserved for private parties, but its buffet dinner is some-times made available to the general public.

The Prince George's Stadium Experience

The local mascot is Louie, a furry green mon-ster who lives in the woods behind the outfield fence and comes out of hiding on game days to entertain fans with his wry sense of humor and flair for melodrama. This pear-shaped fel-low wears a Baysox jersey that is a few sizes too small for his robust upper body and has a bright red tuft of hair atop his head. If I had to guess, I'd classify him as some sort of dino-saur/bullfrog hybrid. I'm pretty sure there was an *X-Files* episode that investigated this type of creature.

Louie was never more in his element than on July 1, 2004, when he and his fellow Baysox fans etched their names in the annals of the *Guinness Book of World Records* with a group whoopee cushion flatulence that included 4,438 people and one gassy green monster.

On the Town

Suburban Bowie is conveniently located a short drive from the major league stadiums in Baltimore and Washington, D.C., and fans may want to check out these big league digs while they're in the area. A trip to scenic Anna-polis is also worthwhile. If you make the trip to Baltimore, I recommend visiting the **Babe Ruth Birthplace and Museum** (216 Emory Street), which is located in the brick row house where the Bambino was born in 1895. In addition to displaying memorabilia related to Ruth's childhood and career, a special exhibit honors the other great long-ball hitters in the game's history.

As for the best place to grab a bite and enjoy a few drinks before the ball game in Bowie, I suggest **Rip's Country Inn** (3809 Crain Highway), which is right on the way to the ballpark. Rip's offers local seafood and juicy steaks.

HARRY GROVE STADIUM

Frederick Keys

Class A, Carolina League
(BALTIMORE ORIOLES)

Harry Grove Stadium
21 Stadium Drive
Frederick, Maryland
877–846–5397

The Frederick Keys are named after Francis Scott Key, the man credited for writing the lyrics to "The Star Spangled Banner." It seems fitting that a minor league baseball team bears Mr. Key's name since the National Anthem and the National Pastime have been inextricably linked for decades. Key was born in 1779 and grew up on his family's plantation in Frederick. In 1814, when he wrote the lyrics to the song that would one day become the National Anthem, Key was a lawyer, practicing in downtown Frederick. He set the song to the melody of the popular drinking song, "To Anacreon in Heaven," then lived another twenty-nine years before being laid to rest in Frederick's Mount Olivet Cemetery.

"The Star Spangled Banner" was first played at a professional baseball game during the 1918 World Series when a military band performed the song during the seventh-inning stretch of the first game between the Red Sox and Cubs at Chicago's Comiskey Park. No, that's not a typo—the Cubs were using the American League field as their World Series home away from home because it could seat more fans than their tiny North Side ballpark. Because the United States had just entered World War I, the fans at the ballpark were unusually moved by the song, and in a show of patriotism, they sang along boisterously with the latter verses.

In the decades to follow, the song became a staple at every World Series and Opening Day game. Later, during World War II, baseball teams began the custom of playing it before every game. "The Star Spangled Banner" officially became the country's National Anthem in 1931. Today, just as the fans do at Oriole Park in Baltimore, fans in Frederick shout "O" when the anthem singer gets to the final line, "Oh, say does that star spangled banner yet wave?" as a way of honoring the hometown team. Get it? "O" is for Orioles.

When Frederick was awarded a Carolina League franchise prior to the 1989 season, the city announced that it would play its first season at Frederick's venerable McCurdy Field, while a new stadium was constructed across the street from the Mount Olivet Cemetery. The team would be named after the most famous person buried in the cemetery, and the new ballpark would be named after Harry Grove, the man who brought a Class D Blue Ridge League team to Frederick in 1915.

The Frederick Hustlers played in Frederick from 1915 until 1930, then the city went without a minor league team until the Keys arrived. The team that would become the Keys arrived via Hagerstown, a city 28 miles south. When the Hagerstown Suns switched from the Single-A Carolina League to the Double-A Eastern League in 1989, the Carolina League needed to fill the void and Frederick got the nod. The Keys have been an Orioles affiliate since their inception, which makes sense, given Baltimore's proximity to and popularity in the local market.

Prior to playing their inaugural season at McCurdy Field, the Keys made some minor renovations to their temporary home, outfitting the 1920s-era park with new dugouts, a new press box, and new lights. While the Keys were opening a new era in Frederick baseball history at the old park, the city unlocked its bank vaults to the tune of $5.5 million to build Harry Grove Stadium. Harry Grove's son, M. J. Grove, also contributed to the project, donating $250,000.

The ballpark is not terribly unique, but a renovation scheduled to take place between the 2006 and 2007 seasons figures to spiff it up a bit. The work will provide a complete overhaul of the playing surface, add more concession stands, build new space for the front office, and turn the old team offices into a souvenir store.

From the outside the stadium features beige bricks and a tan aluminum roof. Inside, the press box sits behind the last row of seats, while a second level houses eighteen luxury boxes and the Keys Cafe. The outfield view offers a glimpse of the downtown skyline in left and a view of Route 70 in center.

As for memorable moments, Harry Grove Stadium has enjoyed a few during its first two decades. On August 1, 1996, the Keys hosted the Salem Avalanche for the first triple-header in Carolina League history. The longest day of baseball Frederick has ever witnessed came about this way: On July 30, the Keys and Avalanche played to a 0–0 tie before their game was suspended because of rain. Then rain wiped out the conclusion of the series opener and the regularly scheduled game on July 31. Because the Avalanche were not scheduled to return to Frederick again in 1996, all three games had to be played on August 1, when the skies finally cleared. The Keys won the completion of the first game 1–0, then won the makeup of the rainout from the night before 5–3. In the third game the Avalanche won 11–5 in eleven innings. And yes, somewhere Ernie Banks was smiling.

In 2003 Keys right-hander John Maine pitched a seven-inning no-hitter at Harry Grove Stadium against the Winston-Salem Warthogs.

The game was just Maine's second start for the team.

In 2005 the Keys hosted the All-Star Game between the Carolina League and California League and one of Frederick's players seized the moment. Top Orioles prospect Nick Markakis won the home run hitting contest before the main event, then smacked two homers in the game. Frederick fans had reason to celebrate again two months later when the Keys won the Carolina League championship.

Due to Frederick's proximity to Camp David, many famous politicians have visited Harry Grove Stadium through the years, including President George H. W. Bush and Attorney General John Ashcroft.

In addition to housing the Keys, Harry Grove Stadium hosts a WWE Smack Down wrestling event each summer and the annual "Taste of Frederick" that promotes fine dining in Frederick County. Local colleges, including the University of Maryland and Mount St. Mary's, have played exhibition games against the Keys.

Game Day

Getting to the Park

Frederick is about a one-hour drive west of Baltimore and northwest of Washington. From the nation's capital, take I–270 North to Route 70 East, then turn right at the second light onto Market Street. At the second left, turn onto Stadium Drive. From Baltimore, take Route 70 West to exit 54. Turn left at the first traffic light and then right onto Stadium Drive. Parking is free at the stadium.

Inside the Park

The low seating bowl offers clear sight lines from all of its 5,400 seats, ending where the infield dirt meets the outfield grass on both sides. Lawn seating extends into outfield foul territory on both sides. Six rows of orange Box Seats appear below the midlevel walkway, while blue Reserved Seats appear above the walkway between the dugouts. On the second level past the dugouts, bleachers offer General Admission seating. The grass seating areas begin immediately where the General Admission seats end.

A group picnic area sits on the left field side and a playground with a carousel sits in right. The concession areas on either side of the concourse allow for a view of the field below. The barbecued pork sandwich is a popular seller, as are the microbrews poured by the Brewer's Alley Pub on the first base side. The Keys Cafe, located above the press box on the second level behind home plate, serves a nightly buffet dinner that is open to the public on most nights and also provides a bar area.

The Harry Grove Stadium Experience

The Keys offer a different concourse entertainment package for every game. Sometimes there are live musical acts, other times stilt-walkers or magicians or balloon benders.

The best places to get autographs are on the outfield lawns just past the end of the seating bowl. Here, fans are just a few feet away from where the players come out of the clubhouses when they take the field.

The Keys play a few early games each year—and I mean *really* early, as in 9:30 in the morning—when they invite fans to the ballpark for breakfast and a ball game. The Keys also host a few beer-tasting nights each season, when they invite fans to sample an array of brews from the Brewer's Alley Pub before the game.

The team's popular mascot is Keyote, a tall coyote who wears a baseball uniform and leads the crowd in the traditional singing of "Shake Your Keys," during the seventh-inning stretch. Two fans wrote this unique ballpark ditty in 1989. The fans shake their car keys while they sing along. The song begins:

> *We're the Frederick Keys*
> *Come on out support your team*
> *Baseball is back in town*
> *You can hear the shaking sound*
> *Bring the family—Go Keys*

On the Town

In addition to offering easy access to Francis Scott Key's gravesite, Harry Grove Stadium provides the opportunity to visit a couple of other historic sites.

McCurdy Field (209 South Jefferson Street) was home to the minor league Hustlers in the 1920s and to the spring training Philadelphia A's in the 1940s, when World War II travel restrictions prevented big league teams from heading south. It was also home to the Keys, of course, in 1989. Today, the ballpark hosts Frederick's Babe Ruth League games. McCurdy Field can seat 4,000 people in its covered metal bleachers, thanks to a 1980 renovation that replaced the old wooden grandstand with concrete and steel.

Frederick is also home to Charlie Keller's horse farm, **Yankeeland Farms** (8423 Yellow Springs Road). Keller played twelve of his thirteen big league seasons with the New York Yankees, and then opened this one-hundred-acre breeding facility in 1955. Although Keller died in 1990, his family continues to operate Yankeeland. The farm has bred such champions as Fresh Yankee, Muscles Yankee, and Yankee Paco.

Finally, fans who enjoy the microbrews at the ballpark can visit the original **Brewer's Alley Pub** (124 North Market Street) in downtown Frederick.

MUNICIPAL STADIUM

Hagerstown Suns

Class A, South Atlantic League
(WASHINGTON NATIONALS)

Municipal Stadium
274 East Memorial Boulevard
Hagerstown, Maryland
301–791–6266

Hagerstown's Municipal Stadium is one of the three oldest ballparks still in use in the minor leagues. Although it has undergone a couple of substantial renovations since opening in 1930 as home to the Hagerstown Hubs, it retains plenty of old-time charm and offers eccentricities like an uneven outfield lawn that rises dramatically toward the left field fence, a manually operated scoreboard, a tiny four-window press box atop a small grandstand roof, and outfield views that showcase a number of neighborhood homes, backyards, and trees.

The ballpark was originally built to supplant Willow Lane Park, which had hosted minor league baseball in Hagerstown since the debut of the Hubs in the Class D Blue Ridge League in 1915. Constructing a new ballpark became necessary in the late 1920s when Hagerstown decided to build the Bester Elementary School on the site of Willow Lane Park. After Hagerstown created a Field and Athletic Association to find a new home for the Hubs, the association wound up leasing a plot of land from the city at a cost of $1.00 per year, for a term of ninety-nine years, and Municipal Stadium was hastily built in just six weeks. It was ready for the start of the Hubs home schedule season on May 8, 1930.

The Hubs stayed in town for two years after the new ballpark opened, before departing for Parkersburg, West Virginia, after the 1931 season. Thus began a ten-year drought for pro ball in Hagerstown, before the Owls of the Class-B Interstate League arrived in 1941. The Owls left in 1949, making way for the Braves, then the Braves gave way to the Packets in 1953. After the Packets left following the 1955 season, Hagerstown was again left without a minor league team, for a long time.

Finally, in 1981 the Suns arrived, as an affiliate of the Baltimore Orioles in the Carolina League. In 1988 the Orioles moved their Class A team a few miles southeast to Frederick and made Hagerstown a member of the Double-A Eastern League. Hagerstown played Double-A ball for five years until the O's moved the local team to Bowie in 1992. Six weeks after the Orioles severed ties with Hagerstown, the city reached a player development agreement with the Toronto Blue Jays, who moved their South Atlantic League team to town. Hagerstown's affiliation switched to the San Francisco Giants in 2000, and to the New York Mets in 2005, and to the Washington Nationals in 2007.

The first renovation of Municipal Stadium, to ready the yard for the return of professional baseball to town, took place in 1981. More than $500,000 was spent on stadium lights, new bleachers, and a public-address system. In 1995 the city spent another half million dollars to install new seats at field level and to add luxury suites and a beer garden. In addition to hosting the Suns, a number of high school games are played at Municipal Stadium each spring, and the Suns host an annual exhibition game against the Hagerstown Community College Hawks in April. Country music acts like Hank Williams Jr. and John Michael Montgomery have held concerts at the ballpark.

Game Day

Getting to the Park

Hagerstown sits on the thin sliver of Maryland that extends west between Pennsylvania to the north and Virginia and West Virginia to the south. I–81 bisects the city from north to south, while I–70 runs laterally across the south side of town. The ballpark is just east of downtown. From I–81, take the exit for US 40 East and follow US 40 through downtown. Take a right onto Cleveland Avenue and follow it to the ballpark. From I–70, take the exit for US 40 West, then take a left onto Eastern Boulevard, which leads to the ballpark. Parking in the large lot beside the ballpark is free.

Inside the Park

This is a small stadium that seats just 4,200 fans. All of the seats are on the infield, and almost all come in the form of bleachers that sell as General Admission, except the three or four rows (depending on the section) of Box Seats below the interior walkway at field level. The Box Seats are comfortable stadium chairs, while the bleachers are aluminum benches. Section B is at first base, Sections E and F are behind the Suns dugout on the first baseline, Section F is behind the plate, Section H is behind the visitors dugout, and Section L, just past third base, completes the seating bowl.

There are two field-level luxury suites just beyond the first base bag, while across the diamond there is a beer garden just past third that offers a great place to view the game while mingling. The beer garden has stand-up cocktail tables for those looking to have a bite to eat while drinking, talking, and watching the game.

Plaques and photographs on the concourse behind the seats pay tribute to Municipal Stadium's historic moments. Visitors will learn about Babe Phelps, considered the greatest player in Hagerstown hardball history; about Fred "Dutch" Dorman, considered the greatest manager; about the day 8,444 fans crammed into Municipal Stadium to watch Jim Palmer make a rehab start; about the day Clay Hensley pitched the first perfect game in Suns history; and about the day Willie Mays made his professional debut at Municipal Stadium as a member of the visiting Trenton Giants.

In addition to the usual ballpark treats, Municipal Stadium serves Italian sausages and cheesesteak sandwiches.

The Municipal Stadium Experience

The local mascot is Woolie, an orange-and-black caterpillar, who has a bloated belly and a perpetual leaf-eating grin on his face. Woolie performs skits on the field between innings and can sometimes be spotted in the trees beyond the outfield fence devouring leaves and reeking havoc on the local ecosystem. Fans hold out hope that he will one day morph into a bright yellow butterfly and fly away.

The Scoreboard Cowboy was a long-standing ballpark favorite at Municipal Stadium until he rode off into the sunset in 2006. This charismatic figure used to hang out on the platform behind the left field fence, changing the slates on the manually operated scoreboard and inciting the fans to root for the home team. The Suns were still searching for an equally enthusiastic individual to man the board in 2007.

One interesting recent promotion in Hagerstown was "George Washington Bobblehead Night." No, the Suns weren't honoring the outfielder by that name who played for the Chicago White Sox in the early 1930s. They were honoring the first U.S. president, with his silly white wig and all.

The most bizarre promotion in team history occurred in 2003 when the team offered fans the chance to win a prepaid funeral from a local funeral home. The $6,500 grand prize included complimentary embalming, a casket, calling hours, and a death certificate for the winner.

The team's special weekly promotion is "Feed Your Face Monday," when fans get all-they-can-eat privileges at the concession stands for a fixed rate of $10 with a General Admission ticket or $13 with a Box Seat.

On the Town

On game days fans tend to congregate at the **Corner Pub** (Mulberry Street and Frederick Street), half a mile from the ballpark. This is a good place to stretch your stomach before attending a game on "Feed Your Face Monday."

About 15 miles south of Hagerstown, travelers will find the **Antietam Battlefield** (5831 Dunker Church Road, Sharpsburg). This Civil War site commemorates the end of General Robert E. Lee's first invasion of the North. The battle took place on September 17, 1862, claiming more than 23,000 lives and led to President Lincoln's eventually issuing the Emancipation Proclamation. A self-guided driving tour of the battlefield offers eleven stops over 8½ miles of scenic cannon-filled countryside.

A few miles west of the battlefield, in Martinsburg, West Virginia, **Rosedale Cemetery** (2060 Rosedale Road) serves as the burial ground of Lewis "Hack" Wilson, the Hall of Fame slugger who still holds the major league record for the most RBIs in a single season. Wilson smashed 56 homers and knocked in 190 runs for the Chicago Cubs in 1930. Making the RBI record even more impressive, baseball historians are pretty sure there was no bottle of andro in Wilson's locker and no shot of B-12 in his carry-on luggage. Most agree that he probably didn't take a daily multivitamin either. It was often said of Wilson that he was "a lowball hitter and a highball drinker." He succumbed to alcoholism after his playing career ended prematurely in 1934, and was buried in Martinsburg in 1948.

PERDUE STADIUM

Delmarva Shorebirds

Class A, South Atlantic League
(BALTIMORE ORIOLES)

Arthur W. Perdue Stadium
6400 Hobbs Road
Salisbury, Maryland
410–219–3112

If you're like me, when you come across a ballpark that bears the name of some random multinational conglomerate, you bristle at yet another example of how the business world has hijacked our National Pastime. You may remember I went on a lengthy rant about this unfortunate stadium-naming-rights trend while discussing Merchantsauto.com Stadium. In short I believe that when a ballpark is named after a credit union, communications company, restaurant chain, or brand of soda pop, it loses the opportunity to establish its own identity with a name reflective of its resident team or surrounding community.

Well, you'll be happy to hear that Perdue Stadium's nametag is more than just a random chicken advertisement. In fact Salisbury's ballpark represents a case of a local business actually giving something back to its baseball community. The story of how baseball once flourished on the Delmarva Peninsula, and now flourishes again—thanks in part to the generosity of the Perdue Company—goes something like this: Back in the 1920s, 1930s, and 1940s, the large peninsula between Chesapeake Bay and the Atlantic Ocean, which includes towns in Delaware, Maryland, and Virginia, treated residents to minor league games between several local Class D Eastern Shore League teams, including clubs representing Cambridge, Chestertown, Crisfield, Easton, Federalsburg, Poco-

moke City, and Salisbury. The rise of the Eastern Shore League coincided with the rise of Perdue Farms—which Arthur W. Perdue founded in 1920. The company began as a regional egg producer then blossomed into a national leader in the poultry distribution business. As the Salisbury Cardinals were treating local baseball fans to ball games at Gordy Park, Arthur Perdue and his son Frank were filling people's bellies with delicious chicken and making a name for themselves. The Perdue brand, as it turned out, would have more staying power than the Salisbury Cardinals and their opponents. The Eastern Shore League disbanded after the 1949 season, and thus began a long dearth of professional baseball on the Delmarva Peninsula.

When minor league baseball finally returned to the region nearly half a century later, the Perdue family led the way, donating a parcel of land in Salisbury that once housed its chicken coops to serve as home to a new stadium, and donating money to help fund the construction of an $11.5 million stadium that would open its doors to the Delmarva Shorebirds in 1996. Appropriately then, the stadium was named to honor the memory of Arthur W. Perdue. Also appropriately, the stadium houses the Eastern Shore Hall of Fame Museum, which is open to ticket-holders on game day.

Perdue Stadium is a good-looking facility, both inside and out. The only real knock on it is that a large percentage of its seating consists of metal bleachers with backs, rather than stadium chairs. But stadium comfort, like all things, is a relative commodity. I'm sure that the baseball fans who turned out at the ballparks of the Eastern Shore League six decades ago sat on wooden benches and would find Perdue Stadium's bleachers more than comfortable enough to accommodate their rumps for nine innings.

The ballpark design offers a distinctive main entrance behind home plate, consisting of yellow cinderblock-sized bricks at ground level and jumbo mauve bricks on the second level, topped by a dark green roof. Fans entering the stadium must walk up a flight of stairs to access the main concourse that runs atop the seating bowl. A small second level hovers over the concourse behind home plate, housing the press box, six luxury boxes, and 120 Club Seats. The outfield view showcases three levels of advertising signs, large scoreboards above the signs in left-center and right-center, and the tops of nearby trees. From the seats on the first base side, a stretch of Route 50 is visible beyond the left field wall.

The Shorebirds were originally affiliated with the Montreal Expos, before becoming an outpost of the Baltimore Orioles in 1997. They led the South Atlantic League in attendance for five straight seasons between 1996 and 2000, and claimed league championship honors in 1997 and 2000. Delmarva has seen such former Shorebirds as Javier Vázquez, Orlando Cabrera, Erik Bedard, and Ryan Minor reach the major leagues. It was Minor, of course, who started at third base for the Orioles on the day that Cal Ripken Jr.'s record consecutive games streak ended.

In addition to serving as the home nest of the Shorebirds, Perdue Stadium also hosts high school and college baseball tournaments, local charity events, and summer concerts that typically have a country beat. Headliners who have performed at the ballpark include Lynyrd Skynyrd, Kenny Chesney, the Beach Boys, Travis Tritt, Martina McBride, and Daryl Worley.

Game Day

Getting to the Park

The team and peninsula may be named after *Del*aware, *Mary*land and *V*irginia, but make no mistake the ballpark is in Salisbury, Maryland. Salisbury is just south of the Delaware state line and just north of Virginia. From the north or south, take Route 13 to the Route 13 Bypass, to Route 50 East, and then take the first right onto Hobbs Road. Parking is free at Perdue Stadium.

Inside the Park

The ballpark can hold 5,500 fans, and although crowds are usually in the 3,000 range, they swell to near capacity on nights when the team offers postgame fireworks. In 2006 the Shorebirds lit up the night sky some eighteen times.

The seating bowl extends just a bit past the corner bases, offering nine rows of green stadium chairs that sell as Box Seats, then an interior walkway, and then red metal bleachers with backs that sell as General Admission. Sections 101 and 102 are behind home plate. Then even-numbered sections continue down the right field line to Section 120, and odd-numbered sections continue down the left field line to Section 119.

Above the lower bowl, the second deck offers Club Seats, three luxury boxes on either side, and an enclosed Executive Club on the first base side. A picnic pavilion in right field has room for 400 fans in a multitiered area. Behind the home bullpen in left, a grassy hill opens up on nights when large crowds are expected.

The concourse in left field features a carousel—a unique ballpark feature nationally, but one that is in danger of becoming a collective cliché at the bush league parks in Maryland. There is also a speed-pitch booth and playground.

The Eastern Shore Museum displays old uniforms, equipment, team photos, and ballpark photos related to the long extinct league. The concession stands provide a view of the game and favorite items like the shrimp salad, fried chicken strips, and grilled chicken sandwiches.

The Perdue Stadium Experience

The local mascot is a big orange shorebird named "Sherman." This oversized oven-stuffer stands 7 feet tall, counting the 3 or 4 inches that the rainbow feathers atop his head add. Sherman likes to ride his four-wheeler on the warning track and lead fans in the traditional seventh-inning chicken dance. Sherman also runs the bases with young fans after every Sunday home game.

Though not an official mascot, another unique ballpark presence comes in the form of a fan who sits behind home plate wearing oversized glasses, heckling the home plate ump whenever a call goes against the home team.

On the Town

Salisbury is one of the smallest minor league towns that baseball fans will visit as they traipse around the country. While it may not present the wealth of tourist activities that many cities do, it is conveniently located just a half-hour drive west of **Ocean City,** which is accessible via Route 50 East. This popular resort town is famous for its white sand beaches, festive boardwalk, amusement parks, minigolf, crab shacks, and waterfront bars and restaurants. The Ocean City Fishing Center sponsors the longest-running tuna tournament on the East Coast, an event that has taken place every July dating back to 1987, and that awards more than half a million dollars in prize money.

APPALACHIAN POWER PARK

West Virginia Power

Class A, South Atlantic League
(MILWAUKEE BREWERS)

Appalachian Power Park
601 Morris Street
Charleston, West Virginia
304–344–2287

When it came time for Charleston to build a new ballpark, the city followed the examples set by the Baltimore Orioles and San Diego Padres and integrated part of the preexisting ballpark neighborhood into the ballpark design. Just as the Orioles and Padres refurbished the B & O Warehouse and Western Metal Supplies Building, respectively, in their cities, the Power renovated a four-story redbrick building that had previously served as a produce warehouse before falling into disrepair. This savvy design choice contributes to Appalachian Power Park's retro quality and is helping to revitalize one small part of the "East End" warehouse district where the park opened in 2005. The city hopes developers will follow its lead and help transform the other old warehouses of this once blighted neighborhood into a thriving entertainment district.

The circa-1913 "Warehouse at the Ballpark" sits in deep right field, running parallel to Appalachian Power Park's right field line. The building's storefront, on Morris Street, provides a regal entrance to the Power's front office and ticket office. The building also houses the Power Alley Grill, a restaurant that is open year-round. In addition to serving the Power's brain trust and hungry fans, it also provides

the players with clubhouses, storage space, and indoor batting cages.

Appalachian Power Park is unique in that its most pronounced structure is in deep right field, rather than behind home plate as is the custom at most minor league yards. In addition to the Warehouse, the structure that houses the park's fourteen luxury boxes is along the first base/right field line. The long thin building offers second-story porches for the local suits and stands behind the open concourse that runs atop the lower level seats. Like the Warehouse, this building dwarfs the small one-level press box that sits on the concourse behind home plate.

Despite its uncovered and open urban atmosphere, Appalachian Power Park is cozy and intimate thanks to an exceptionally small seating bowl that places every seat close to the field. Rather than providing a high-rising seating bowl solely around the infield as many Class A parks do, this park provides just twelve rows of seats in most sections, with the seats continuing nearly to the foul poles on either side of the diamond. The concourse atop the seats allows fans ample room to walk all the way around the field, while only losing sight of the game momentarily from the spot directly behind the press box.

As for outfield sight lines, the hope is that the old furniture warehouses beyond the outfield fences will get face-lifts when the wave of urban revitalization that the ballpark catalyses sweeps through the neighborhood. The gold dome of the state capitol can also be seen in the distance beyond the right field wall, while the rolling green hills of the Mountain State are also visible. From the outfield seats in right and left, fans enjoy a view of the downtown skyline behind the humble home plate grandstand.

In a nice tribute to their former ballpark, the Power outfitted Appalachian Power Park

Appalachian Power Park

with two rows of gold seats in left field home run territory directly beneath the scoreboard. These seats were transplanted from Watt Powell Park, the small ball yard that served as home of Charleston's minor league scene for more than five decades. That park opened in 1949, replacing old Kanawha Park, which had burned down a few years earlier. Over the years Powell Park hosted several teams that represented several leagues and major league organizations. At different times Charleston was home to Single-A, Double-A, and Triple-A clubs. The park's last tenant was the South Atlantic League's Charleston Alley Cats. That team changed its name to "the Power" and changed its affiliation from the Toronto Blue Jays to the Milwaukee Brewers when it moved into Appalachian Power Park in 2005.

Recent Charleston lore includes the story of a monstrous home run that Carlos Delgado hit at Powell Park as a member of the visiting Myrtle Beach Pelicans. According to legend, the shot landed in a passing coal car on the CSX railroad tracks that ran behind the outfield fence. Delving back farther into Charleston baseball history, old-timers recall that future Hall of Famer Jim Bunning began the 1956 season at Powell Park as a member of the American Association's Charleston Senators before getting recalled by the Detroit Tigers.

Today, the parcel where Powell Park once stood has been divided and sold in part to the University of Charleston and in part to the Charleston Area Medical Center, both of which are developing the property with new buildings. While it is sad that Charleston bid adieu to an historic ballpark and couldn't find a use for it as a youth field, the upside to the story is that the city replaced Powell Park with a new ballpark that is as aesthetically unique as it is fan-friendly and one that should provide a home to the local minor league team for decades.

In addition to housing the Power, Appalachian Power Park currently serves as the home of the Division I Marshall University baseball team and the Division II University of Charleston team.

Game Day

Getting to the Park

Charleston is in the western part of West Virginia, 50 miles from the Kentucky and Ohio state lines. From the north or south, take I–77 to the Capital Street/Leon Sullivan Way exit. At the second traffic light, turn left onto Lee Street, then turn left onto Morris Street, and the ballpark will appear on the left. From the east or west, take I–64 to the Capital Street/Leon Sullivan Way exit, then turn left onto Lee Street and follow the directions as above. Parking is managed by the city, which charges $3.00 per car. There are three lots located within a block of the ballpark, as well as a large parking garage on Morris Street.

Inside the Park

With the opening of its new ballpark, Charleston's average attendance jumped from 1,800 fans per game in the final seasons at Powell Park to 3,300 per game in the first seasons at Appalachian Power Park. The new ballpark can seat 5,000.

The Power keeps things simple, offering just two ticket options. Fifteen of the seventeen seating sections are considered Box Seats—from the first row to the last—while the outfield-most section on either side of the diamond contains Reserved Seats, which are actually metal bleachers with backs. The best seats in the house are in Sections 103–112 around the infield. Fans who have purchased General Admission tickets, or who just want to experience the game from a different point of view, can find a spot on the small banks of bleachers in right field home run territory.

The Bullpen Bar and Grill Picnic Garden in the left field corner offers four tiers of group space, while a smaller party area is located beneath the scoreboard in left.

For concession stands, fans find the Coal Car Cafe on the first base side of the concourse and the Mineshaft Grille on the third base side. The grilled offerings—burgers, sausages, and steak sandwiches—are freshly prepared and tasty. For dessert, the deep-fried Twinkies and deep-fried Snickers are local (not to be confused with low-cal) favorites. Fans can also purchase dinner before, during, or after games at the Power Alley Grill in right field. The ballpark offers Budweiser products on draft and domestic and imported bottles.

The Appalachian Power Park Experience

Whenever a member of the Power hits a home run, the team celebrates the occasion by sounding a train horn atop the press box roof. But the real fun occurs when the home team is in the field. That's when superfan Rod "Toast Man" Blackstone works the crowd into a delighted frenzy every time a Power pitcher notches a strikeout. In a truth-is-stranger-than-fiction kind of way, Blackstone sits in Section 107 with a loaf of bread and a four-slice toaster that he plugs into the stadium's electrical grid.

Whenever a visiting player whiffs, Blackstone chants, "You Are Toast," then tosses a slice of crispy bread into the crowd. Hey, I know it's a "different" kind of ballpark tradition, but why not? I'm just thankful Blackstone isn't tossing gobs of strawberry jelly into the crowd every time the visiting pitcher is in a jam, or plugging in an oil-splattering stir-fry wok every time a visiting pitcher runs the count to three balls on a hitter.

As if the Toast Man weren't enough to keep fans entertained, the Charleston team has five different mascots, each of whom pays tribute to the region's geological or *baseballogical* identity. This quintet of superheroes includes Axe, who wears a miner's helmet and carries a pickaxe, representing West Virginia's coal industry; Gusty, who wears a propeller on his head, represents the power of wind; Hydro, who has a teardrop-shaped head, representing hydroelectrical power; Pyro, who has hair made of flames, symbolizing the natural gas industry; and Charley, who wears a derby hat and red suspenders, representing the local team's old-time name, the Charleston Charlies. The Charlies, who played in Charleston from 1971 through 1983, were so named because owner Bob Levine wanted to pay tribute to his father, Charles Levine . . . and because the team played in Charleston.

On the Town

Charleston is West Virginia's largest city with a population just over 50,000 people. Fans interested in visiting the site of Watt Powell Park can head to the intersection of MacCorkle Avenue and 35th Street in the Kanawha City section of the city. The University of Charleston plans to build a new basketball arena there.

The **Clay Center for the Arts and Sciences** (One Clay Square) is a popular destination for road-tripping families, as its Avampato Discovery Museum offers interactive activities that make learning fun for kids and parents alike. The museum is open Wednesday through Saturday, from 10:00 A.M. until 5:00 P.M., and Sunday, from noon until 5:00 P.M.

PFITZNER STADIUM
Potomac Nationals

Class A, Carolina League
(WASHINGTON NATIONALS)

G. Richard Pfitzner Stadium
7 County Complex Court
Woodbridge, Virginia
703–590–2311

To celebrate the announcement of a new player development contract with the Washington Nationals in 2005, the Potomac Cannons changed their name to the Potomac Nationals. The team will certainly benefit from its association with the new National League club that plays just 20 miles away in the nation's capital, but what the Potomac franchise really needs is a new ballpark. The team's current home, Pfitzner Stadium, may have been suitable for Carolina League play when it opened in 1984, but it is not fan-friendly enough to last much longer in the modern era. With a seating capacity of 6,500, the stadium is larger than it needs to be, and it is usually at least two-thirds empty. That's the first strike against it. The second is its less-than-comfortable seating bowl, which relies heavily on aluminum bleachers, while offering just a smattering of metal stadium chairs. The third strike against "The Pfitz" is the absence of a roof overhead. The sun beats down on the metal bleachers and seats, making for a sweltering ballpark experience for fans during the summer time. Additionally, the stadium doesn't offer any luxury boxes, which doesn't make a difference to the average fan but certainly cuts into the home team's bottom line. Finally, with its high-rising grandstands and symmetrical playing field, Pfitzner Stadium draws low grades in the "atmosphere" department, as it is neither

quaint nor cozy in the way that many minor league ballparks are—particularly at the Class A level.

With all of that said, there is reason for optimism among the tight-knit group of fans who make up the Potomac team's loyal booster club. The fans—who continue a long-standing tradition of providing home-cooked meals for the Potomac players after every Saturday home game—have reason to believe that construction will begin soon on a new ballpark for the P-Nats. The team's owner and the Prince William County Board of Supervisors both seem to recognize the importance of replacing Pfitzner Stadium with a fan-friendly modern facility, and although no plans had been finalized by the time this book went to print, local fans were expecting an announcement soon from the team and county detailing a plan to build a new ballpark adjacent to the current one. Pfitzner Stadium will likely be renovated to serve as a multiuse amateur field.

For the time being though, Pfitzner Stadium will continue to serve the Potomac Nationals. Lest there be any confusion in the minds of traveling fans, the stadium is not located in the city of Potomac but in the northern Virginia city of Woodbridge. The stadium's one saving grace is that it is located in a fairly wooded area, away from the commotion of the strip malls a few miles away. The outfield view showcases a thick green forest, which makes for a nice backdrop for a game.

The ballpark sits in the midst of a sports complex, appearing as one petal in a cloverleaf of fields. The other fields are softball diamonds. There is also a BMX bike course on the site. The stadium was originally known as Davis Ford Park. It was built to replace Cora Kelly Field where the Alexandria Dukes had played in Alexandria, Virginia. Because it sat on the grounds of a public school, Cora Kelly Field could not sell beer at its concession stands, hampering the efforts of the Dukes to turn a profit. The team's move to a new stadium in Woodbridge solved that problem, and the beer flowed freely as 2,300 fans turned out in anticipation of the stadium's inaugural game between the Prince Williams Pirates and the Hagerstown Suns on April 19, 1984. Soon the fans were crying in their suds, as the game was delayed when the visiting Suns refused to take the field. Hagerstown management claimed that the field's newly laid sod was too soggy and loose for play. Finally, after a delay of more than an hour, the Suns agreed to take the field on the conditions that no bunting would be allowed and that any ball landing on the outfield warning track would be declared a ground-rule double. Under these unusual circumstances, the home team prevailed 6–2 in a slippery but injury-free contest.

The stadium's original name reflected its location on what was then known as Davis Ford Road. A few years later, the stadium was renamed Prince William County Stadium, then in 1995 it was rechristened G. Richard Pfitzner Stadium to honor the County Board of Supervisors member who led the effort to bring the team to Woodbridge.

Affiliations with the New York Yankees (1987–1993), Chicago White Sox (1994–1996), St. Louis Cardinals (1997–2002), and Cincinnati Reds (2003–2004) followed the team's years as a Pirates farm club, then the club hooked up with the Nationals in 2005. A number of prominent future major leaguers have played for the Potomac club, including Barry Bonds, Bobby Bonilla, Mike Cameron, Albert Pujols, Bernie Williams, Andy Pettitte, Jorge Posada, and Rick Ankiel. Five plaques on the stadium concourse honor the men in the Potomac Baseball Hall of Fame: Bonds, Bonilla, Williams, Pettitte, and team owner Art Silber.

Former big leaguers who have visited Woodbridge to watch a game include Bobby Thomson, Bob Feller, Vida Blue, George Foster, Boog Powell, Graig Nettles, and Luis Tiant. Washington politicians like Al Gore and John Ashcroft have also turned out at the ballpark, as have nationally known baseball enthusiasts like the San Diego Chicken, the Phillies Phanatic, and the busty ballpark babe known far and wide as Morganna the Kissing Bandit. Three-time U.S. National Figure Skating champion and two-time Olympian Michael Weiss also visits the park regularly with his family.

In addition to housing the Nationals, Pfitzner Stadium hosts the Gardziel Fall Classic, a high school baseball tournament that offers schoolboys the chance to showcase their skills for college scouts. In 2006 the Nationals hosted the George Mason University Patriots for a preseason exhibition game, with the preppies from the Colonial Athletic Association using wooden bats, instead of their usual aluminum sticks.

Game Day

Getting to the Park

Woodbridge is 20 miles south of Washington. Take I–95 to the Prince Williams Parkway and follow the Parkway toward Manassas. After about 5 miles, turn right onto County Complex Court. The paved and grass lots at the sports complex charge $3.00 per car. The ballpark gates usually open one hour before game time, but on Saturdays they open half an hour earlier, allowing fans to watch the last thirty minutes of batting practice.

Inside the Park

The main seating bowl surrounds the infield, then there is a 20-foot gap where there are no seats, and then the grandstand sections begin. Although the Field Box seats are the most expensive at Pfitzner Stadium, they are located past the dugouts in front of the grandstands and don't provide as good a view as the Box Seats, which are located between the dugouts. The red metal bleachers behind the Box Seats sell as Reserved Seats, while the silver bleachers behind the Field Boxes sell as Grandstand Seats.

The main concession stand is behind the home plate area at ground level, while smaller stands operate on the first and third base sides. The funnel cake is a fan favorite.

The Pfitzner Stadium Experience

The Nationals keep fans entertained between innings with dugout golf, dizzy sack races, musical chairs, and the always-popular chicken wing toss. Every Monday night is Dollar Night, when fans get grandstand tickets, hot dogs, popcorn, and sodas for only $1.00 apiece.

In 2005 the P-Nats teamed with a local Cosmetics Clinic to run a "Hairiest Back at the Ballpark" contest, eventually awarding the top prize to a forty-seven-year old army sergeant from Fairfax who received $2,500 in free laser hair removal services.

Also, in 2005 the Nationals unveiled a new mascot who quickly won over the hearts of local fans. Uncle Slam is a patriot in the truest sense of the word. This hulking blue fellow wears a red, white, and blue outfit, with a bow tie and a stovepipe hat. He gets very excited when a member of the home team "slams" a long ball.

The P-Nats celebrate home runs by sounding a submarine horn, which serves as a tribute to the large contingent of armed forces members in the area. In another unique local tradition, whenever a member of the home team makes a nice play in the field, superfan Dusty Rhodes leads the crowd in cheers of "hubba-hubba."

On the Town

Woodbridge is a rapidly growing city that offers easy access to the national tourist sites in Washington and to the Washington Nationals big league ballpark.

For hungry baseball fans, there are plenty of restaurants to choose from among the strip malls on Prince William Parkway. Because the menu at the ballpark is rather basic, I recommend taking advantage of these spots on the way to the game. In addition to the usual fast-food chains that appear in suburban anywhere, the options include **Don Pablo's Mexican Kitchen** (2840 Prince William Parkway), **Famous Dave's Barbecue** (2430 Prince William Parkway), the **Old Country Buffet** (2942 Prince William Parkway), **Pizzeria Uno** (2680 Prince William Parkway), **Red Lobster** (2544 Prince William Parkway), the **Red River Barbecue & Grill** (2430 Prince William Parkway), and the **Macaroni Grill** (2641 Prince William Parkway).

LYNCHBURG CITY STADIUM

Lynchburg HillCats

Class A, Carolina League
(PITTSBURGH PIRATES)

Calvin Falwell Field at Lynchburg City Stadium
3180 Fort Avenue
Lynchburg, Virginia
434–528–1144

Nestled amidst the rolling green hills of central Virginia, Lynchburg City Stadium has served minor league baseball and its fans since 1940. The ballpark looks and feels much younger than it actually is, thanks to a $7 million renovation that was completed prior to the 2004 season. The work added comfortable stadium chairs throughout the original seating bowl, replacing the bleachers that had previously occupied all but the first three rows between the dugouts. The work also added a new scoreboard and message board, concession stands, restrooms, picnic decks, luxury suites, and a new press box. In short the work outfitted an antiquated stadium from a simpler time in the game's history with the technological infrastructure and consumer comforts that ballparks need today to survive. Buoyed by these improvements, City Stadium saw its nightly attendance jump from 1,300 fans per game in 2003, to 2,300 in each of the next two years.

The stadium's earth-tone brick exterior features a diamond pattern that projects something akin to a southwestern design flair, even though Virginia is about as far from Arizona and New Mexico as you can get while still keeping your feet planted in the U.S.A. The ballpark is attractive, if unique for its part of the country. Complimenting the multicolored bricks are light-green awnings over the ticket windows and a light-green roof over the press box level.

Inside, luxury boxes cover the grandstand seats behind home plate, which is a nice feature for those seated below on rainy nights, but a not-so-nice feature on a sunny spring days. The sight lines showcase two levels of advertising on the outfield fence, scoreboards in right-center and left-center, and green treetops that peek over the wall of ads. The folks in the luxury boxes enjoy the best views of the Blue Ridge Mountains.

City Stadium was built in the late 1930s on the site of the Lynchburg fairgrounds. The

Lynchburg City Stadium

success of early minor league teams that played at the fairgrounds, like the Tobacconists (1895–1896) and Shoemakers (1906–1917), and of a thriving local industrial league in the 1920s and 1930s convinced city officials that a new stadium would lure an affiliated minor league team to town. And that's exactly how it played out.

City Stadium was designed by a New York ballpark architect named Gavin Hadden, who made sure to orient the field so that the grandstands faced the mountains. The ballpark project began in 1936, after the city purchased twenty-eight acres of land on the outskirts of town from the Interstate Fair Association for $30,000. City Stadium was completed in 1939, thanks in part to a $100,000 grant from the Works Progress Administration. The city contributed the remaining $190,000.

City Stadium hosted its first game on April 11, 1940, when the New York Yankees and Brooklyn Dodgers traveled to Lynchburg for a preseason exhibition. At the time the field had no outfield fence, scoreboard, or lights, but just the same more than 7,000 people crowded into its 4,000-seat bowl for the inaugural game. Once the regular season began, Lynchburg fielded a team in the Class B Piedmont League that was affiliated with the Washington Senators. In the years to follow, Lynchburg hosted a number of teams representing a number of leagues and big league organizations. Since 1995 Lynchburg has been a Pittsburgh Pirates outpost. Something about that seems right: A burgh for a burgh, that's what I always say.

Remarkably, current HillCats president Calvin Falwell has been intimately involved with the inner workings of the local baseball team for seven decades. The man known as "Mr. Baseball" cut his teeth in the minor league business as president of the Lynchburg Cardinals back in the 1940s, when Lynchburg's McKenna family owned the team. As Falwell's stature in the community grew, he played an integral role in keeping baseball in the city through ownership and affiliation changes. In 1966 Falwell teamed with Wallace McKenna to form the Lynchburg Baseball Corporation. The LBC has distinguished itself from the many other minor league ownership groups by consistently putting the best interests of the team ahead of its own financial concerns. The LBC operates more like a community trust than a for-profit ownership group.

On June 28, 1992, Carolina League representatives joined Lynchburg city officials and fans to celebrate Calvin Falwell Day at City Stadium, installing a plaque at the main entrance to honor "Mr. Baseball." In 2004 Lynchburg rededicated the stadium "Calvin Falwell Field at Lynchburg City Stadium." In 2005 Falwell was awarded the prestigious "King of Baseball" title that is given to one influential minor league veteran at baseball's annual winter meetings.

To learn more about Lynchburg baseball history, many fans visit the Lynchburg Area Sports Hall of Fame during their visit to City Stadium. The Hall, located in the ballpark lobby, has plaques that honor inductees, old game programs, baseball cards, bobblehead dolls, trophies, and other artifacts on display. The Hall is open during games and during business hours throughout the baseball season. The most famous member of the Lynchburg Hall is Jim Bibby, the former big league pitcher who served as the pitching coach for Lynchburg for fifteen years, spanning the team's affiliations with three different major league organizations: the Mets, Red Sox, and Pirates. Bibby's number 26 was retired by the HillCats in 2002, shortly after he announced his retirement. Today, Bibby lives just across the James River from Lynchburg in Madison Heights, and he's a regular fixture at City Stadium.

City Stadium has hosted its share of football games, fairs, and other community events through the decades, but these days it serves mainly as a baseball venue. In addition to housing the HillCats, it hosts American Legion games and Old Dominion Athletic Conference tournament games. The HillCats have played exhibition games against Lynchburg College in the past.

Game Day

Getting to the Park

Lynchburg is 120 miles west of Richmond and 50 miles north of the North Carolina state line. Those approaching from the north should take Business Route 29 South (aka the Lynchburg Expressway) to the Lynchburg City Stadium exit, and then follow the signs to the ballpark. From the south, follow Business Route 29 North to the James Street exit, turn left off the ramp, and then follow the signs. Parking is free in the large lot behind the stadium.

Inside the Park

The seating bowl offers room for 4,000 people around the infield. About two-thirds of the seats are green stadium chairs, while bleachers make up the remainder. Other than the first three rows behind the dugouts, all of the seats are sold as General Admission, making it worthwhile for fans to arrive at the park early. Sections 1 through 3 on the first baseline and 9 through 11 on the third baseline offer Reserved Seats and bleachers. Sections 4 through 8 between the dugouts house General Admission chair-backs from the first row to the last, while the stadium's fourteen skyboxes hover overhead. The best views of the Blue Ridge Mountains are to be had from the upper seats on the first base side.

There is one group picnic area beyond the seating bowl in shallow right field and one above the seating bowl on the third base side.

The concession stands are located on the first and third base sides of the concourse atop the seating bowl. The Big Cat, a quarter-pound hotdog, highlights the offerings.

The Lynchburg City Stadium Experience

The HillCats take a conservative approach when it comes to gameday entertainment. Don't expect to see any cat juggling between innings or bring-your-cat-to-the-game nights on your HillCats schedule. Even Southpaw the Cat, the local mascot, seems to enjoy watching the game as much as he enjoys acting like a goofball. I suppose when you've been in the minor league baseball business as long as Calvin Falwell, you've earned the right to present the game as the featured attraction without messing around with the hijinx and hoopla many teams use to boost attendance. In Lynchburg the nightly dizzy-bat-race is about as crazy as things get, and that seems to sit well with the fans who turn out at City Stadium.

Lynchburg always has a home game on the Fourth of July due to its longevity in the Carolina League, and the local fans always make sure the game is a sellout in anticipation of the postgame pyrotechnics.

On the Town

Lynchburg is a relatively small minor league city that has a population of about 65,000. City Stadium shares the immediate neighborhood with the Spring Hill Cemetery, while an array of fast-food joints operate half a mile north of the stadium on Memorial Avenue.

Twenty miles east of the city visitors find the **Appomattox Courthouse National Historic Park**, which marks the site where Robert E. Lee surrendered his army to Ulysses Grant on April 9, 1865, effectively ending the Civil War. From Lynchburg follow Highway 460 East to

Appomattox, then take Route 24 East to the reconstructed courthouse and surrounding park.

Those looking to spend some time in the great outdoors after a few weeks of highway driving between minor league destinations can quench their thirst for fresh air at either the **Jefferson National Forest**, 60 miles west of Lynchburg in the Allegheny Mountain range, or at the **George Washington National Forest**, 40 miles north of Lynchburg. Both are great for hiking and camping and sure to return traveling fans to the road refreshed and ready to tackle another string of stadiums.

HARBOR PARK
Norfolk Tides

Class AAA, International League
(BALTIMORE ORIOLES)

Harbor Park
150 Park Avenue
Norfolk, Virginia
757–622–2222

If you find yourself suddenly overcome by a sense of déjà vu on passing through the ballpark gates at Harbor Park in Norfolk, don't panic. You're not turning into Shirley Maclaine or that creepy kid from *The Shining*. You really haven't been here before. And you don't have the ability to see into the future. In all likelihood you're just remembering a recent visit to Alliance Bank Stadium in Syracuse. Both International League venues—Norfolk's, which opened in 1993, and Syracuse's, which opened in 1997—were designed by HOK, and there was obviously quite a bit of photocopying involved when the latter park's blueprints were assembled. Inside and out, the two stadiums are nearly identical. Both offer exteriors of attractive brick down at street level and tasteful beige cement up above. Both have wide main entrances behind home plate, which lead to staircases that bring fans to open concourses atop the first-level seats. Both have a restaurant in right field foul territory. Both have a lower seating bowl divided by a midlevel walkway. Both have second-deck seats on either side of the press box and luxury suites, and at both parks these upper seats extend farther down into left field than right. The guess here is that Syracuse saw the new facility in Norfolk, liked it, and told HOK, "We'll take one just like that." For the record Harbor Park was constructed for

$16 million while Alliance Bank Stadium was built for . . . you guessed it . . . $16 million.

Despite their many similarities, the ballpark in Virginia makes a better first impression than the one in upstate New York, thanks to its natural grass playing surface and its setting on the Norfolk waterfront. The Elizabeth River runs just beyond the right field fence, making for splash landings off the bats of powerful left-handed hitters, and offering glimpses of the Norfolk and Portsmouth shipyards. A set of rails runs behind the left field fence and the occasional rumble of a freight train compliments the pleasantly industrial ballpark setting.

Other than the tiered party deck in straightaway left field, there is no seating across the outfield, only a low blue fence. The visitors bullpen is behind the fence in left-center, while the Norfolk relievers toil behind the fence near the right field foul pole. For some reason the stadium's large ad-plastered scoreboard is situated in right field, instead of left, so that it blocks much of what would otherwise be an excellent water view.

At the time of its opening, Harbor Park was hailed as one of the finest minor league ballparks in the country by many media outlets and ballpark aficionados, and in fact *Baseball America* ranked it first among all minor league yards in 1995. The bush league landscape has continued to evolve in the intervening years, of course, to the point where today Harbor Park does not merit such lofty praise. The recent trend has been to build lower stadiums that surround the entire field with seating, rather than high-rising stadiums that place many seats well above and well behind the field. Still, Harbor Park is a fine place to watch a game, and it is an important evolutionary link in the life of HOK, a firm that continues to be on the cutting edge of ballpark design.

Harbor Park was financed by the city of Norfolk and has been instrumental in revitalizing the city's downtown district. Prior to the ballpark's opening, the local nine played at Met Park from 1970 though 1992, where they were known as the Tidewater Tides. A 6,200-seat stadium near the Norfolk International Airport, Met Park was demolished to make way for an office park once Harbor Park opened.

The Tides arrived in the Hampton Roads area in 1961, playing their first two seasons in the South Atlantic League, then joining the Carolina League. In those days the Tides played at Lawrence Stadium, across the river from Norfolk in Portsmouth. After signing a Triple-A player development contract with the Mets in 1969, the Tides played one final season at Lawrence Stadium before moving to Met Park. The Tides won two International League championships in the 1970s, then dominated the circuit in the early 1980s, claiming the Governor's Cup in 1982, 1983, and 1985, but they haven't won a league title since. The Tides alumni roster includes Wally Backman, Lenny Dykstra, Carl Everett, Dwight Gooden, Mike Scott, Darryl Strawberry, local favorite David Wright, and the father-(step)son tandem of Mookie and Preston Wilson.

In 2006 washed-up big leaguer José Lima pitched for the Tides, and while he didn't throw the ball particularly well, he did a nice job hitting the high notes when he sang "God Bless America" during the seventh-inning stretch on Opening Day.

Following the 2006 season, the Tides severed their longstanding relationship with the Mets and switched to one with the Baltimore Orioles.

Game Day

Getting to the Park

Norfolk is right beside Virginia Beach in the southeast corner of Virginia. The closest International League rival is Richmond, 95 miles to the northwest. Harbor Park sits on the eastern banks of the Elizabeth River in downtown Norfolk. From the north or south, take I–95 to I–64 East, on to I–264 toward downtown Norfolk. Take exit 9 (Waterside Drive) and at the end of the ramp turn right onto St. Paul's Boulevard. Take the next right, Union Street, and follow the signs to the stadium parking lots. The several different stadium lots all charge $4.00 per car. Meanwhile, additional parking can be found a bit farther away at the Dominion Tower Garage on Water Street, the Downtown Plaza on St. Paul's Boulevard, and the Waterside Garage on Waterside Drive.

Inside the Park

Harbor Park has an official seating capacity of 12,067, which includes 8,867 seats in the lower deck, 2,800 seats in the upper deck, and 400 seats in the twenty-four luxury boxes on the second deck between the dugouts. The tiered party area in left field home run territory can accommodate up to 300 people. The Tides draw well, attracting an average of about 7,500 fans per game. During the summer months crowds often swell to near capacity, so you may want to order tickets in advance.

The lower seating bowl is divided by a mid-level walkway that leaves twelve rows of 100 Level seats closest to the field, and ten rows of 200 Level seats up above. Between the corner bases the sections on both levels sell as Box Seats, while past the corner bases they sell as Lower Reserved. Sections 100 and 200 are directly behind home plate, and then the even-numbered sections continue down the right field line and the odd-numbered sections continue down the left field line. Section 123 is the deepest section in left, while Section 126 is the deepest section in right.

Upstairs, there are four sections of 300 Level seats along the right field line and five along the left field line. These Upper Reserved Seats begin at the ends of either dugout and continue well into outfield foul territory. On either side a roof covers the back several rows. The best views of the river can be had in the 300 Level seats above the left field line in odd Sections 309 through 317.

The main concourse runs atop the lower deck seats and offers views of the field. The concession highlights include grilled Italian sausages, Philly cheesesteaks, Black Angus burgers, and Polish sausages. There are also veggie burgers and veggie dogs for the growing legion of herbivores out there in minor league nation. The Hits restaurant in right field offers tiered window seating and an all-you-can-eat buffet.

While you're on the concourse, check out the plaques that pay tribute to local diamond kings like Yogi Berra, Bob Feller, Catfish Hunter, Ace Parker, Pie Traynor, Ray White, Hack Wilson, and nearly fifty others who played for the Norfolk Tars, Newport News Builders, Portsmouth Merrimacs, Peninsula Pilots, and Tides through the years.

The Harbor Park Experience

A friendly blue sea monster named "Rip," as in Riptide, serves as the Norfolk mascot. Rip especially enjoyed the scenery at the ballpark on a hot and sticky August night in 2006 when the Washington Redskins cheerleaders paid a visit to Harbor Park. The ladies were looking to play a warm-up venue to get their game in shape before the start of the new NFL season, and the Tides were happy to oblige, staging "Washington Redskins Cheerleaders Night." Another popular promotion during the 2006 season was "Camera Night," when the Tides allowed fans to take the field prior to the game and to snap pictures of their favorite players. Now, if only the Tides could combine these two promotions . . . Hopefully there's an intern in

the Norfolk Media Relations department working on the concept right now.

On the Town

Baseball fans find a concentration of bars and restaurants just west of the ballpark at **Waterside Marketplace** (333 Waterside Drive), where the options include the **Outback Steakhouse, Hooters, Joe's Crab Shack, Waterside Hamburgers,** and **Wolfy's Hot Dogs.** There are two Irish pubs west of the ballpark on Granby Street, as well as **A. J. Gator's Sports Bar** (244 Granby Street).

The **Virginia Sports Hall of Fame and Museum** (206 High Street, Portsmouth) is worth a visit if time allows. In addition to honoring baseballers like Al Bumbry, Johnny Oates, and Eppa Rixey, the museum celebrates hoopsters like Moses Malone and Ralph Sampson, gridders like Lawrence Taylor, and nearly 200 other athletes, coaches, team executives, and journalists who have contributed to amateur and professional athletics in the Commonwealth. During the summer months the museum is open Monday through Saturday from 9:00 A.M. until 5:00 P.M. and Sunday from 11:00 A.M. to 5:00 P.M. The $6.00 admission charge includes nine holes of minigolf at the museum's indoor course.

Ballpark junkies will no doubt want to head across the Newport News to Hampton where they'll find **War Memorial Stadium** (1889 West Pembroke Avenue, Hampton) still standing. The simple wooden park dates back to 1948. It currently serves as the home of the Peninsula Pilots of the collegiate Coastal Plains League. The ballpark was originally the field of a Brooklyn Dodgers farm club that played in the Piedmont League from 1948 until 1955, then it served affiliates of the Washington Senators, Philadelphia Phillies, Kansas City Athletics, Cincinnati Reds, and a host of other teams during the 1960s, 1970s, and 1980s. Pro baseball hasn't been played on-site since the Seattle Mariners pulled their Carolina League franchise out of Hampton in 1992, but the local fans still love baseball. The Coastal Plains League offers a schedule that runs from late May though July, and the Pilots regularly draw crowds of 2,000 people or more.

THE DIAMOND

Richmond Braves

Class AAA, International League

(ATLANTA BRAVES)

The Diamond
3001 North Boulevard
Richmond, Virginia
804–359–4444

When the National League's Braves moved from Milwaukee to Atlanta in 1966, they had to find a new home for their Triple-A team, which had previously been playing in Atlanta. The Braves eventually settled on Richmond to serve as their International League outpost, beginning what stands today as the second-longest affiliation between any minor league team and its big league parent. Only the marriage between the short-season Appalachian League's Bluefield Orioles and the Baltimore Orioles, which began in 1958, predates the union between Richmond and Atlanta. While this nugget of baseball trivia may seem to portend a happy, stable relationship sure to last forever, the current state of affairs in Richmond is actually not quite so rosy.

As Richmond's Diamond has become an increasingly less viable home for the "R-Braves" in recent years, the city has been unable to finalize plans for a new ballpark, casting doubt over the long-term future of the team. The Richmond club is owned and operated by the big league Braves, and in recent years rumors have circulated that Atlanta might move its Triple-A squad closer to home. If Richmond can't settle on a site for a new ballpark soon and start digging, that may happen, although one thing in Richmond's favor is that, geographically, there doesn't appear to

be any unoccupied market suitable for Triple-A between Richmond and Atlanta.

The Diamond opened in 1985 on a site where baseball had been played in Richmond since the 1950s. It was built at a time when minor league teams and fans had very different preferences and requirements than they do today. The stadium offers a massive concrete seating bowl that towers over the infield. Nearly two-thirds of the 12,134 seats are located in a steep upper deck, and throughout the stadium the seats take the form of aluminum benches with backs, rather than individual stadium chairs. Both the lower and upper concourses are hidden from view behind the stands, and both are cramped on days when large crowds turn out.

A large slanted roof extends skyward atop the upper deck. Just how high is the roof? Well, it's high enough so that the stadium lights are mounted right on top of it, without needing any poles or extensions to bring them up to Triple-A specs.

The luxury boxes are located on the first deck behind the last row of seats, but the press box is located on the second deck, in front of the first row of seats. The outfield view showcases the large stadium parking lot and I–95. The field, which is notorious for flooding during times of rain, measures a perfectly symmetrical, perfectly boring, 330 feet down the lines and 402 feet to center.

In 2003, realizing that the local yard was quickly outliving its era (yes, there really was an era when concrete behemoths like this were in vogue), Richmond announced plans for an $18.5 million renovation to the Diamond. The work was to be funded by a municipal bond offering. But when many fans and civic leaders raised objections, saying it would make more sense to start from scratch with a brand new ballpark closer to downtown, the project was put on hold. Richmond contracted HKS to draw

The Diamond

up blueprints for a new park, and local fans seemed to have reason for optimism. But when the proposed site for the new park—a plot in the Shockoe Bottom district along the city's Canal Walk—flooded during Tropical Storm Gaston, the plan rapidly lost support.

Since then, one proposed site—a plot beside the former Fulton Gas Works—has lost support due to environmental concerns, while Mayor L. Douglas Wilder's latest proposal—to build the park beside the current one on North Boulevard—has failed to rally widespread support.

As this political hemming and hawing continues in Richmond, the Diamond continues to offer baseball fans a minor league experience unlike any other. Although it doesn't belong at the top of any fan's list of must-see parks, it is unique and for that reason worthy of a visit.

Just about every homegrown prospect who has come through the Braves system since the team moved to Atlanta has played at the Diamond or at its predecessor, Parker Field, which Richmond used from 1966 through 1984. Notable former R-Braves include Steve Avery, Steve Bedrosian, Jim Bouton, Brett Butler, Jermaine Dye, Andruw Jones, Chipper Jones, Dave Justice, Tom Glavine, Dale Murphy, and John Smoltz.

Richmond's history with the International League actually dates back much further than its affiliation with Atlanta, though. The city was one of the IL's founding members in 1884, but left the league after just one season. Richmond rejoined the circuit for the 1915 through 1917 seasons, and then from 1954 through 1964.

Game Day

Getting to the Park

The R-Braves play their home games 95 miles west of the closest International League rival, the Norfolk Tides, and 105 miles south of Washington. The Diamond is conveniently located right off I–95 at the Boulevard exit (exit 78). A large stadium lot offers plenty of parking.

Inside the Park

The seating bowls on both levels continue just a short distance past the corner bases. The red seats on the first level are metal benches with backs and arm rests. All of these seats offer excellent views of the action. Section 101 is in shallow right field, Sections 110 and 111 are behind home plate, and Section 120 is in shallow left field. These seats are all exposed to the elements, so on a rainy night it's best to opt for a seat in the upper deck. The lower one-third of the upper deck offers assigned seating, while the upper two-thirds sells as General Admission. There are no armrests in this level, but the silver-and-gold seats have back supports.

Down on the first level, nine glassed-in luxury boxes rise at the back of the seats along either baseline. The four outfield-most windows on the first base side belong to the in-stadium restaurant. Between the luxury windows behind home plate, a stretch of the first-level concourse is open to a view of the field. The rest of the concourse is enclosed.

The concession highlights include Famous Dave's Barbecue, grilled Italian sausages, and corn dogs. A unique concourse decoration is the 25-foot-wide fiberglass bust of a Native American brave, whose head can actually be seen from outside the stadium. The piece, titled *Connecticut,* was created by a local artist.

The Diamond Experience

The R-Braves don't bombard fans with too many annoying sound bites or commercial promotions, which is refreshing at a time when it seems like every other team has guitar riffs blaring through its PA system and a miked-up deejay working the crowd between innings. The ballpark mascot, Diamond Duck, is also an understated presence.

Tuesday is traditionally "Dollar Dog Night."

On the Town

Right near the stadium, **Bill's Barbecue** (3100 North Boulevard) feeds a hungry flow of fans on game day. If the restaurant across the street from the Diamond is too crowded, head to Bill's other location a few blocks south at 927 Meyers Street.

The best dining and nightlife in Richmond is located along the **Canal Walk**, a scenic stretch that traces the banks of the Haxall Canal, James River, and Kanawha Canal. Trendy spots include the **Richbrau Brewing Company** (1214 East Cary Street), **Buffalo Wings Grill & Bar** (1501 East Cary Street), the **Siné Irish Pub** (1327 East Cary Street), and **Bottoms Up Pizza** (1700 Dock Street).

The **Civil War Center** (Fifth and Tredegar Streets) is a popular Richmond tourist attraction, while racing enthusiasts may want to check out the schedule at **Richmond International Raceway** (Meadowbridge Road), a ¾-mile oval just east of town.

SALEM MEMORIAL BASEBALL STADIUM

Salem Avalanche

Class A, Carolina League
(HOUSTON ASTROS)

Salem Memorial Baseball Stadium
James E. Taliferro Sports & Entertainment Complex
1004 Texas Street
Salem, Virginia
540–389–3333

If you've read this far, you've probably noticed that I usually prefer ballparks that provide all of their seats down close to field level, as opposed to parks that offer large, high-rising seating bowls that hover above the field. You may have also noticed that I am often critical of stadiums that are larger than they need to be, given the size of their local fan base, and their team's classification level. Well, Salem Memorial Baseball Stadium is certainly larger than it needs to be to house a Carolina League team, with its 6,300 seats. It is also a high-riser, with a seating bowl that towers over the infield. And yet, despite my usual biases, I found my visit to Salem utterly enjoyable. Before the game I found a seat in the third and highest tier of seating and sat and marveled at the amazing view of the Blue Ridge Mountains that roll along in a wave of green beyond the outfield fence. Then, when the game began, I stayed put and enjoyed a comfortable ballpark experience.

Salem Memorial Baseball Stadium rates higher than most parks in the consumer comfort department. All of the seats, including those within the large General Admission level, are comfortable plastic stadium chairs; all of the rows provide more than ample leg room;

and the ballpark is configured so that every seat has an unobstructed view of the field at all times, pedestrian traffic be damned!

Although the ballpark was built fairly recently, and at a time when many cities were constructing new yards with classic features like redbrick facades, open concourses, and quirky home run porches and patios, this stadium offers none of these. It fits a mold all its own. Fans arrive at the park to find large brick stairwells flanking the main entrance behind home plate. At street level the 60 feet or so between these towers is wide open, allowing for a large concourse area where fans can congregate either just outside of, or just inside, the park, beneath the two-level cement press box that spans the towers. From this spot fans can enjoy a view of the field without blocking the views of fans in the Reserved and Box Seats down below, or in the General Admission section that rises nearly as high as the second level of the press box along either baseline.

The stadium opened in 1995. It sits in the midst of a sports complex that also houses a civic center, football field, and cloverleaf of multipurpose fields. The baseball portion of the complex was built at a cost of $10.1 million to provide a new home to the local Carolina League outfit. The Salem team signed a new player development contract with the Colorado Rockies at the time that it moved into its new park, and the team celebrated this new affiliation by changing its name from the Buccaneers—a handle that reflected the identity of its previous parent team, the Pittsburgh Pirates—to the Avalanche, a moniker more befitting an affiliate of the mountaineering Rockies. Previously, the team had played at Salem's old Municipal Field.

Salem's history as a minor league town dates back to 1939, when it first fielded a team in the Virginia League. The team moved a few miles east to the town of Roanoke in

1943 though, and the Roanoke Red Sox spent the next ten years playing at Maher Field. One year the team surprised its fans and parent club by beating the big league Red Sox in an exhibition game. The minor league Red Sox left Roanoke in 1953, setting the stage for the return of professional baseball to Salem in 1955, when the unaffiliated Salem Rebels debuted at Municipal Stadium as a member of the Appalachian League. The team featured an up-and-coming slugger named Orlando Cepeda, who would begin his Hall of Fame major league career three years later with the San Francisco Giants. During the 1960s, 1970s and 1980s, the Salem Rebels (also known at various points as the Pirates and Buccaneers) enjoyed a few different stints as a Pittsburgh affiliate, while also representing the Giants, San Diego Pirates, Texas Rangers, and Philadelphia Phillies at different times. The team joined the Carolina League in 1968.

Sadly, one of professional baseball's greatest tragedies occurred at Municipal Stadium on August 22, 1974, when seventeen-year-old Salem right fielder Alfredo Edmead, a Dominican prospect whose skills had been compared with those of Roberto Clemente, died on the field. In a game against Rocky Mount, Edmead raced in from right field to make a diving catch and collided with second baseman Pablo Cruz. His head struck Cruz's knee, and he died from his injury. The official cause of death was listed as a massive skull fracture.

During the 1970s, 1980s and 1990s, notable future major leaguers to play for the team in Salem included Dave Parker, Mitch Williams, Kenny Rogers, John Candelaria, Jeff King, Orlando Merced, Stan Belinda, Moisés Alou, and Tim Wakefield. Wakefield, who spent the 1990 season in Salem as he made the conversion from light-hitting third baseman to knuckleball pitcher, still holds many Avalanche single-season records, including the most games started (28), the most innings (190), the most losses (14), the most hits allowed (187), the most walks allowed (85), and the most earned runs allowed (100).

After moving to their present ballpark, the Avalanche represented the Rockies from 1995 through 2003, when Colorado, opting to bring its prospects closer to home, signed on with the California League's franchise in Visalia. At that time the Avalanche switched to its current affiliation with the Houston Astros and proceeded to set a new franchise attendance record in 2004, attracting more than 225,000 fans to Salem Memorial Baseball Stadium. Since then, the team has increased its attendance every year.

In 2006 the Avalanche got the chance to play in a stadium even bigger than its own yard, one much bigger in fact. The team played an official Carolina League game against the Potomac Nationals at RFK Stadium in Washington. The game followed a major league tilt between the Washington Nationals and Baltimore Orioles.

Game Day

Getting to the Park

Salem is a small town in the western part of Roanoke Valley, nestled between the Brush Mountains to the west, and the Blue Ridge Mountains to the northeast. The ballpark is just 2 miles from I–81. From I–81, take exit 141 and follow Route 419 South into Salem. Bear right onto Texas Street and the ballpark will appear on your left. Parking is free at the sports complex.

Inside the Park

Salem Memorial Baseball Stadium is more than large enough to accommodate the 3,600 fans per game that the home team attracts on average. The stadium offers three tiers of comfortable blue stadium chairs in a seating bowl that extends just barely past the corner bases on either side. Sections 100 and 101 are behind the plate. The odd-numbered sections continue to Section 117 in shallow right and the even-numbered sections continue to Section 116 in shallow left. The first tier offers Diamond Club seats in the first three rows between the dugouts, then several rows of Box Seats. The second tier, which is below the main concourse but above the Boxes, offers Reserved Seats. The third tier, which rises sharply above the open part of the concourse behind home plate and the interior walkway that continues down either line, offers General Admission seats. I recommend sitting high above the field on the third base side, so as to enjoy the best view of the mountains beyond the right field fence. There are Club Seats upstairs in the press box structure, and for groups, there is a picnic patio down the left field line.

Most of the concourse is hidden beneath the General Admission seats, except for the area behind home plate where the opening beneath the press box allows for a view of the game from the concourse. Accordingly, most of the concession stands are located behind the plate so that fans can steal peeks of the field while waiting in line for grilled buffalo burgers and other ballpark treats.

The clubhouse store is located within a separate building behind the stadium on the third base side.

The Memorial Stadium Experience

The local mascot is a 300-pound, 7-foot-tall, shaggy dog named "Mugsy," who wears his Avalanche hat sideways, perhaps copying the style of fellow behemoth C. C. Sabathia, the massive Cleveland Indians pitcher who wears his hat the same way.

Salem offers a special promotion for every day of the week. The best deal is on Wednesday when a $10 pass is good for a General Admission ticket and all-you-can-eat hot dogs, hamburgers, peanuts, and popcorn. Saturday is also fun, as the Avalanche provides live music at the ballpark before the game, thanks to a partnership with a local radio station. On Sunday the kids get to run the bases after the game.

On the Town

Although the Avalanche plays in a large modern facility, a trip to Salem still offers the chance to see a quaint old-time ballpark that is steeped in hardball history. Municipal Stadium still stands, and still sees regular use as an amateur field, even though it goes by a different name these days. **Kiwanis Field** (1000 Union Street) is located just a short drive from Salem Memorial Baseball Stadium. Like its minor league successor, Kiwanis Field treats fans to striking outfield views of the Blue Ridge Mountains. The circa-1932 ballpark provides a small covered grandstand behind home plate and uncovered grandstand sections on either side of the plate area. The park serves the Roanoke College and Salem High School baseball teams.

Another historic ballpark that dates back to the 1930s sits 80 miles west of Salem, just across the state line in Bluefield, West Virginia. **Bowen Field** hosts the short-season Appalachian League's Bluefield Orioles. This charming old park features a tiny covered grandstand and a thick wall of trees behind its outfield fence. The Bluefield franchise has had a player development relationship with the Baltimore Orioles since 1958, making for the longest current relationship between a major league team and minor league affiliate.

(For more about the franchise, see the chapter on the Appalachian League.)

SECTION 2

THE SOUTH

Kentucky, North Carolina, Tennessee, South Carolina,
Georgia, Florida, Alabama, Mississippi, Louisiana,
Arkansas

APPLEBEE'S PARK

Lexington Legends

Class A, South Atlantic League
(HOUSTON ASTROS)

Applebee's Park
207 Legends Lane/North Broadway Street
Lexington, Kentucky
859–252–4487

When the Lexington Legends went on the auction block in 2005, the team fetched a whopping $24 million, which represented the highest figure ever paid for a Class-A franchise and its ballpark. And yet, just five years earlier, Lexington had borne the ignominious distinction of being the largest American city without a minor league team to call its own. So, how did this historic central Kentucky town transform itself from outsider-looking-in to a major player in the minor leagues in the span of five short years? Well, actually, the city itself didn't do much of the transforming. Lexington had several chances to bring minor league baseball within its city limits during the 1990s when a number of teams expressed interest in moving to town. But one publicly funded ballpark initiative after another fell by the wayside in the absence of city and state support. Finally, the fans took matters into their own hands.

After Lexington swung and missed on three different opportunities to get a team, a group of private investors stepped to the plate and delivered the new ballpark that Lexington sorely needed. Led by local businessman Alan Stein, the group purchased a twenty-six-acre plot of land just north of downtown and broke ground on a $13.5 million stadium in February of 2000. Over the next year the group teamed with the *Lexington Herald-Leader* to hold a name-the-team contest, announce a player development

agreement with the Houston Astros, interview 750 applicants for 200 ballpark employment positions, audition 500 prospective National Anthem singers, and try out 125 potential public address announcers. Before playing a game the team sold 2,000 season tickets and 290,000 single game tickets.

The ballpark was completed in time to welcome the Lexington Legends to the South Atlantic League in 2001, and the Legends made their Applebee's Park debut a memorable one. On April 9, 2001, the Legends christened their stadium with a 15–1 romp over the Hagerstown Suns before 8,037 wildly enthusiastic fans and 225 credentialed media members. The game was broadcast on live TV on Lexington's ABC affiliate, WTVQ. Applebee's Park has been jam-packed ever since, making the Legends perennial contenders for the South Atlantic League attendance crown.

Having accomplished its goal of returning minor league baseball to Lexington after a nearly five decade hiatus, Stein's group left the team in good hands in 2005, turning the Legends over to Bill Shea, a former oil company executive who wanted to get into the minor baseball business.

Applebee's Park has a welcoming exterior with a distinctly Kentuckian flair. The regal beige façade rises high above street level, eventually to be topped by a light green roof and four green steeples. Inside the turnstiles the design deviates from the open concourse approach that swept across the minor leagues in the 1990s. In Lexington the concourse is hidden beneath the seats, and rather than offering a low seating bowl that encircles the entire field, Applebee's Park provides a main seating bowl that extends only to the lip of the outfield grass on either side of the diamond. The stands rise sharply around the infield, providing clear sight lines. At the very top of the stadium, twenty-six luxury suites overlook the field. The park offers the obligatory lawn seating areas, but with a unique twist. As opposed to the steeply sloped and expansive lawns found elsewhere, the small left field and right field lawns at Applebee's Park are down nearly at field level in foul territory. What's more, they jut out toward the foul line, angling fans nicely toward the infield. My one complaint about the layout at Applebee's Park is that the field has more foul territory than most minor league parks, leaving fans farther from the action than necessary.

The outfield view offers two interesting features. A seven-story-high video/scoreboard rises in right-center. A green steeple tops the board, displaying a face clock that bears the Applebee's company logo. In left-center, a 26-foot-tall baseball bat rises from behind the fence. The giant bat is topped by a proportionately giant baseball that is covered with dripping red wax. The bat and ball are part of the Maker's Home Run Challenge. If a Legends player hits the faux baseball with a home run, Maker's Mark Whiskey (which tops its bottles with red wax) will donate $100,000 to a central Kentucky charity. Hopefully, the local nonprofit community isn't holding its collective breath, because the money-ball is more than 430 feet from home plate and 30 feet above the field.

Among the players who have left their mark in Lexington are Felix Escalona, who raked 42 doubles for the Legends in the team's debut season and then became the first Legend to reach the major leagues in 2002, and John Buck, who swatted 22 round trippers in the team's first season while on his own fast track to the big leagues. To date the Legends alumni roster includes mostly fringe major leaguers like these players though. The team and its fans are still waiting for the first budding superstar to come through Lexington . . . the first real legend in the making.

A legend did stop by Applebee's Park for a tune-up in 2006, as Roger Clemens started a game against Lake County on June 6, before a packed house. The forty-three-year-old future Hall of Famer had sat out the first two months of the season while deciding if he wanted to continue playing. In the game Clemens's oldest son, Koby—an eighth-round pick by the Astros in the 2005 amateur draft—played third base for the Legends. Clemens allowed 1 run on 3 hits, while striking out 6 in three innings of work, as a national TV audience watched on ESPN.

In addition to housing the Legends all summer long, Applebee's Park sees use as an amateur venue in the spring, hosting a busy slate of high school games that culminates with the Kentucky High School Athletic Association state tournament in June.

Game Day

Getting to the Park

Kentucky's second-largest city is located 75 miles east of Louisville along I–64, and 80 miles south of Cincinnati along I–75. Applebee's Park is about a mile northeast of downtown Lexington in an industrial area just inside New Circle Road, the beltway that encircles the city. The ballpark shares its neighborhood with the North Park Shopping Center. From the north or south, take I–75 to I–64 East to exit 113. Turn right at the end of the exit ramp onto North Broadway and follow North Broadway toward downtown for about 1½ miles. The ballpark will appear on your right. From the east or west, follow I–64 into Lexington and follow the directions as above. There is ample parking adjacent to the stadium, at $3.00 per car.

Inside the Park

The main seating bowl contains only 5,000 seats. There are another 500 bleacher seats in left field home run territory, while the two lawn areas can accommodate about 1,000 fans apiece. This is a case where you may want to order your tickets in advance, since the Legends average more than 5,500 fans per night. From the concourse fans use runways to access the seating bowl, then walk down a set of steps to their seats on the100 Level, or up a set of steps to their seats on the 200 Level. There is no walkway inside the seating bowl, so fans can't walk around it. You must use the appropriate runway to reach your section, then you have no option but to report directly to your seat.

The Super Club seats appear in the three lower sections (106–108) behind home plate, while the Club Seats are in the three upper sections (206–208) behind the plate. If these sections seem sparsely populated during your visit to Applebee's Park, don't assume it's because the team didn't sell the seats or because their ticket holders were no-shows. Rather, fans with Club and Super Club tickets often disappear to visit the Maker's Mark Club inside the stadium. The 145-seat restaurant provides an upscale menu and full bar, while showing the game on television. The restaurant is also open to the fans in the luxury suites.

The Field Box seats appear in the first three rows along the baselines, while the rest of the seats, both in the 100 and 200 Levels, sell as Box Seats. These are all comfortable stadium chairs. Sections 101 and 201 are just past first base at one end of the bowl, while Sections 114 and 214 are just past third at the other end.

A General Admission ticket is good for a spot in the bleachers in home run territory near the left field foul pole. These are basic benches without backs. Meanwhile, a Lawn ticket is good for a spot in deep right field, where fans are allowed to set up their own lawn chairs, or in deep left field, where chairs are not permitted. There is a group party area along the right field foul line, between the end of the seating bowl and the beginning of the Lawn, and another in right field home run territory.

For those who don't have access to the exclusive Maker's Mark Club, the regular concession stands offer rib tips just like the ones at your neighborhood Applebee's, four-bone baby back ribs, three-piece chicken baskets, beef brisket, bratwurst, Italian sausage, chili cheese fries, funnel cakes, and twenty-four-ounce drafts. The picnic area along the third baseline offers a pregame all-you-can-eat buffet that is open to all fans. Behind the picnic area is a Playground for kids, which features a carousel.

The Applebee's Park Experience

The Legends offer a trio of mascots. Big L looks like your average man in a baseball uniform from the neck down. But instead of a regular human head, he has a cartoon style noggin, complete with an ill-kempt handlebar mustache. Until I saw Big L, Louie the LumberKing of the Midwest League had my vote for the creepiest mascot in the minor leagues. Now, I'm not so sure. With his bulbous head and sunken eyes, Big L is a monstrosity. And his girlfriend Elle isn't much better, although her shapely bottom looked kind of cute in a miniskirt. There's something very disturbing about combining regular human bodies with bizarre cartoon heads. I found myself having unsettling nightmares involving L and especially Elle for nearly a week after my visit to Lexington, and I'm betting the kids in Lexington have those dreams all summer long. Fortunately, fans find a less menacing figure in Pee Wee, the giant, walking, talking baseball.

A popular promotion in Lexington is the "diamond dig." Several times a year, the Legends bury a diamond ring or diamond tennis bracelet in the infield dirt and then invite male or female fans onto the field to dig for the treasure.

On a nightly basis fans enjoy playing Cornhole between innings. Cornhole, for those unfamiliar with this popular regional game, involves players tossing beanbags (actually corn bags) at a slanted wooden ramp. Players are awarded points when their bags stay on the ramp or pass through the hole in the ramp.

On the Town

Lexington is known as the "city in the park" due to its many urban green spaces and to the multitude of horse farms around it. Those who want to get up close and personal with some Kentucky thoroughbreds can visit the **Kentucky Horse Farm** (4089 Iron Works Pike), which offers kids and adults the opportunity to ride saddleback or in drawn carriages.

Those visiting Applebee's Park find an assortment of pregame and postgame restaurants on New Circle Road, just east of the stadium, as well as a cluster of bars a few blocks southwest, including the **Phoenix Bar and Grill** (401 West Short Street), **McCarthy's Irish Bar** (117 South Upper Street), and the **North Limestone Bar** (648 North Limestone Street).

LOUISVILLE SLUGGER FIELD

Louisville Bats

Class AAA, International League
(CINCINNATI REDS)

Louisville Slugger Field
401 East Main Street
Louisville, Kentucky
502–212–2287

Professional baseball's history in Louisville dates back to the founding of the National League in 1876. Although the game has changed a bit since the Louisville Grays and seven other teams took the field in that inaugural season, it is as healthy today in Louisville as it's ever been, thanks to gorgeous Louisville Slugger Field, which opened in 2000. The ballpark offers a retro façade and main entrance, outfield views of the Kennedy and Clark Memorial Bridges that span the Ohio River, and a cozy seating bowl that encircles the entire field. Rounding out the gameday experience for fans, two sports bars can be found at the park, as well as a carousel, outfield seating berm, and plenty of delicious treats.

Just how different was the game our great, great, grandfathers watched from the game we enjoy today? Consider that in 1876 Louisville pitcher Jim Devlin started every game but one for the big league Grays. He led the league in games started (68), complete games (66), and innings pitched (622). As for his reason for sitting out the final game of the season—you guessed it, a sore arm. Devlin bounced back the next year though, and was in top form as Louisville carried the NL's best record into mid-August. But suddenly the Grays swooned, dropping seven games in a row to their top competitors in Boston and Hartford. When it later came to light that four of the team's players, including Devlin, had accepted money from bookmakers to throw those games, the Grays kicked them off the team. Missing four key players, Louisville was forced to sit out the 1878 season. The city got back into the game before long though, playing in the American Association from 1882 through 1891, when it was a major league, and then rejoining the National League from 1894 through 1896. Louisville finished in last place in all three of its final big league seasons before merging with the Pittsburgh Pirates.

Fast-forward eight decades or so to 1982, and we arrive at a time when Louisville was the hottest minor league town in the country. More than 800,000 fans turned out at Cardinals Stadium to celebrate the first year of an affiliation between the local Triple-A team and the St. Louis Cardinals. The new minor league attendance record that the Louisville Redbirds set that year didn't last long, though, as the very next season the team beat its own mark, becoming the first bush league club to put more than a million fannies in the seats. Believe it or not, the Redbirds drew more fans than three major league teams—the Cleveland Indians, Minnesota Twins, and Seattle Mariners—in 1983.

When the American Association folded in 1998, the Cardinals moved the Redbirds to Memphis and the team joined the Pacific Coast League, which made a lot of sense geographically, considering Tennessee's proximity to the Pacific Ocean. Louisville, meanwhile, established a new franchise, joining the International League, and finagled a player development contract with the Milwaukee Brewers. The city also began work on a new downtown ballpark on a fifteen-acre plot near the banks of the Ohio. The Riverbats played one season as a Brewers farm club, then switched to an affiliation with the Cincinnati Reds and changed their name simply to the "Bats" in time to open Louisville Slugger Field in 2000.

While providing yet another example of a ballpark revitalizing a previously blighted downtown neighborhood, Louisville Slugger Field combines the charm and intimacy of an old-time yard with the fan-friendliness and consumer comforts made possible by modernity. The $39 million facility makes excellent use of the circa-1889 Brinly-Hardy warehouse building—a redbrick train depot that once served the Chesapeake & Ohio railroad line and now serves as the ballpark's main entrance. The building also houses the Bats front office, gift shop, Hall of Fame, and two restaurants.

Outside the ballpark fans encounter a bronze statue of native son Pee Wee Reese in mid-throwing motion as he comes across the second base bag to turn a double play. On entering the old warehouse, fans are greeted by replicas of the Hall of Fame plaques that hang in Cooperstown for former Louisville players like Carlton Fisk and Honus Wagner, and by photos of other Louisville stars like Vince Coleman, Willie McGee, and Andy Van Slyke. The nostalgic warehouse leads to an open concourse that runs atop the lower-level seats. Between the lower level, which surrounds the entire field with a variety of seating options, and the second level, which offers club seats and thirty-two luxury suites, Louisville Slugger Field can hold about 14,000 fans. And it's a good thing, because Bats games are very well attended. Louisville vies with Pawtucket each year for the International League attendance crown, averaging more than 600,000 fans.

Game Day

Getting to the Park

Louisville is located on the Kentucky-Indiana border where it is easy to reach via I-64, I-65,
and I-71. The only other affiliated team in Kentucky, the Lexington Legends, play 75 miles east, while the closest International League rival, the Indianapolis Indians, plays 150 miles north. Louisville Slugger Field is on the eastern edge of Louisville, right near the Ohio River and right off I-65. From the I-264 beltway, take I-65 to the Jefferson Street/Downtown exit. Off the exit, follow North Brook Street north, then turn left onto East Market Street, then left onto Hancock Street, then left onto Main Street. The ballpark sits at the corner of Main and Preston Streets.

The team-run parking lot, located between the first base side of the stadium and the I-65 overpass, is reserved for season ticket holders until fifteen minutes before the first pitch at which time it opens to members of the general public if spots still remain. Rather than missing the first half inning while you wait for the privilege of parking here, I suggest heading to the privately operated lot across the street on Preston or parking in one of the nearby garages—on Washington Street (2 blocks away) or Witherspoon Street (5 blocks away). You may also find on-street parking west of the stadium after 6:00 P.M. on weekdays and all day on weekends.

Inside the Park

The first level offers seating around the entire field, except in straightaway center where a stretch is left empty and blackened to serve as the hitter's backdrop. The second level offers luxury suites and club seats that extend only so far as the corner bases. The most expensive seats in the house are the Upper Reserved Seats. The upper deck hangs out over the lower deck, positioning these plush upper-level seats close to the field and relatively low. There are only six rows in each section.

In the much larger main bowl down below, the Field Reserved Seats are around the infield and continue just a little way into outfield foul territory. Section 109 is at first base, Sections 115 and 116 are behind home plate, and Section 121 is at third. There are three sections of Outfield Reserved Seats in right field (Sections 104–106), then three sections of field-level Bleachers (101–103) that end out behind the foul pole. In left field the layout is different, as there are eight sections of Outfield Reserved Seats (125–132), including four sections in home run territory, and no Bleachers. When it comes to the outfield seats at this park, I recommend Sections 129 through 132 in left field home run territory, where the view of the infield is best.

A steeply sloped lawn picks up where the seats leave off in left-center, continuing to the batter's eye, while in right there are picnic areas immediately beyond the fence, and a bank of Bleachers behind the picnic tables. The Bleachers in right are far from the field, so if forced to choose between the two penny monger locations, I would opt for a spot on the Lawn over one in the Bleachers.

The concession highlights include barbecued beef, pork and chicken, pork chop sandwiches, smoked turkey legs, baked potatoes, corn on the cob, Italian sausages, brats, and fried bologna sandwiches. If some of these items sound too messy to enjoy while sitting in a stadium chair, don't fret. At Louisville Slugger Field you can have a pulled pork sandwich and still wear your khakis the next day thanks to a three-tiered patio deck just behind the right field fence, where fans can sit at picnic tables and chow down while enjoying a view of the game.

The restaurants are Browning's Brewery, named after Louisville legend Pete Browning, and the Jack Daniels #7 Lounge. All fans can venture into Browning's, but only Upper Reserved ticket holders and luxury suite guests can access JD's, which is on the upper level.

For the kids, a playground in deep right field comes complete with a colorful carousel.

The Louisville Slugger Experience

Once upon a time, the local mascot in Louisville was a Redbird. Now it's a big black bat—as in a winged rodent—named "Buddy." Oh well, times change.

On Sundays, Buddy leads all of the kids onto the field after the last out and they race around the bases. On Mondays, Buddy plays Ballpark Bingo with the gray hairs. On Tuesdays, Buddy and the rest of the fans enjoy $1.00 hot dogs and sodas. On Thursdays, fans toast Buddy while they enjoy $1.00 bottles of Bud and live music before the game at the Overlook Deck in right-center.

On the Town

Traveling fans find plenty of restaurants and watering holes west of the ballpark on the other side of I–65. The largest concentration of these is on Market Street, while there are also several worthwhile spots on Main Street.

There was a day not long ago when you could safely say that just about every American kid who has ever played baseball has held a Louisville Slugger in his hands. Sadly, in recent years shiny aluminum models with Japanese names and hollow pings have made the romantic crack of the bat an all too infrequent phenomenon at sandlots and Little Leagues field across the country. But the company that began lathing bats into Louisville Sluggers more than 120 years ago—Hillerich & Bradsby—is still going strong. When it comes to the bats the pros use, the Louisville Slugger is still the tool of choice. More than 60 percent of current major leaguers swing bats made in Louisville, including stars like Derek Jeter, Ken Griffey Jr., and David Ortiz. Each player is able to design his own model, informing the company of his preferences in such basic areas as weight, length, and color, and such specialized areas as handle width, barrel width, and wood type. The typical player goes through about one hundred bats per season, keeping the lathe-workers in Louisville busy. Using white ash and maple harvested from company-owned land in upstate New York and Pennsylvania, Hill-erich & Bradsby produce upward of one million bats per year. Meanwhile, the **Louisville Slugger Factory and Museum** (800 West Main Street) is a popular tourist attraction. A 120-foot tall steel replica of a Louisville Slugger leans against the company's brick factory at the main entrance. Inside, there is information about how a young woodshop apprentice named Bud Hillerich handmade a spe-cial bat to help Pete "The Old Gladiator" Browning, a star of the American Association's Louisville Eclipse, out of a slump in

Louisville Slugger Museum

1884, as well as info about the whoppers that baseball immortals like Ty Cobb, Babe Ruth, and Ted Williams once swung, and about the company's efforts making M-1 carbine stocks, tank pins, and Billy clubs during World War II. In addition a tour takes visitors through the factory where they can witness the step-by-step process of turning a piece of wood into a precisely designed athletic tool capable of driving a baseball 450 feet . . . that is if you're Albert Pujols. Visitors can even have their own personalized bats made for them while they take the tour. The museum is open Monday through Saturday from 9:00 A.M. until 5:00 P.M.

and Sunday from noon until 5:00 P.M. Admis-sion costs $9.00 for adults and $4.00 for chil-dren under twelve.

A trip to Louisville also offers a couple of historic fields to check out, both of which may not be left standing too much longer. **Cardinal Stadium** (Exposition Center) served as home of the Louisville nine from 1957 through 1999. Known as Fairgrounds Stadium before the city's affiliation with the St. Louis Cardi-nals began, the 33,500-seat stadium was also home to the University of Louisville football team from 1957 through 1997, and to the university's baseball team from 1998 through 2004. Today, Car-dinal Stadium is used for various events during the Kentucky State Fair, but it sits dormant for most of the year. As a minor league baseball facility, the sheer size of Cardinal Stadium's multicolored seating bowl made it unique, as did its Astroturf field and its irregular dimensions that measured 360 feet down the left field line, but just 312 feet to right. The stadium has a covered grandstand and a press box hung from the underside of the roof. Louisville is report-edly exploring the idea of demolishing it to make way for more modern facilities on the Expo grounds.

The other old park in Louisville is the much smaller, much more dilapidated **Parkway Field** (Eastern Parkway and Brook Street). This field was home to the American Association's Louis-ville Colonels from 1923 through 1956, and to Negro League teams like the Louisville Black

Caps and Buckeyes. It also welcomed barn-storming big leaguers to Louisville, including Babe Ruth, Honus Wagner, and Grover Cleveland Alexander. More recently, the field was home to the University of Louisville baseball team, until it left in 1997. While the original stands are long gone—they were torn down in the 1960s—the green outfield wall, which is much taller in left field than in center and right, still stands. The field currently belongs to the University of Louisville and is slated to undergo a renovation that will turn it into an intramural athletics field as part of an ongoing campus beautification initiative.

Finally, racing enthusiasts may want to visit **Churchill Downs** (700 Central Avenue, Gate 1), which offers live racing during May and June on Wednesday through Sunday. The **Kentucky Derby Museum** is open year-round, Monday through Saturday from 9:00 A.M. until 5:00 P.M. and Sunday from noon until 5:00 P.M. and the **Derby Cafe** is open for lunch on weekdays.

MCCORMICK FIELD

Asheville Tourists

Class A, South Atlantic League
(COLORADO ROCKIES)

McCormick Field
30 Buchanan Place
Asheville, North Carolina
828–258–0428

In addition to providing as cozy a setting for a ball game as fans will find anywhere in the minors, Asheville's McCormick Field possesses a colorful history. This tiny ballpark in the farthest-most reaches of the western Carolinas was rebuilt in time for the start of the 1992 season, but it retains its old-time charm. The exterior features regal red brick and inside, a cantilevered roof covers most of the grandstand. The 36-foot-high fence in right field stands just 301 feet from home plate.

McCormick Field opened in 1924 to serve as home to the Asheville Skylanders of the South Atlantic Association. Before long the Skylanders, themselves a descendant of the Mountaineers and Tourists, readopted the Tourists nickname. From the very outset McCormick Field was named after Dr. Lewis McCormick, a resident bacteriologist who famously led a citywide campaign against houseflies in 1905. Apparently, Asheville's many horses were producing mounds of manure, and the mounds were spawning swarms of flies. Through his research McCormick deduced that if the flies did their breeding in horse manure, then landed on freshly baked apple pies cooling on windowsills, the people who ate those pies were apt to get sick. McCormick knew that he couldn't rid Asheville of horse manure,

since that would require getting rid of the horses, which were the city's primary mode of transportation, or pies, which were its favorite dessert. He also knew that attempting to convince his fellow townsfolk to close their kitchen windows would be a losing battle, since ventilation was at a premium during the sweltering summer months. McCormick's solution was an initiative known as the "Swat That Fly Program." He hung posters around the town and hopped up on a pulpit wherever he spotted a crowd to explain that flies bred with other flies and that by killing existing flies Ashevillians could reduce the number of future flies. After tirelessly spreading the gospel of housefly awareness and extermination, McCormick died suddenly in 1922. The flies were no doubt ecstatic, but the people of Asheville missed him greatly. When the city opened a new ballpark two years later, Asheville named it in McCormick's honor. See what I mean about this ballpark having a colorful history?

The first game ever played at McCormick Field was an exhibition between the Skylanders and Detroit Tigers prior to the start of the 1924 season. Ty Cobb hit a home run in the opener. The next season, Asheville welcomed the Brooklyn Dodgers and New York Yankees to town for a preseason game, and this time Asheville found itself thrust into the middle of national news story. As Asheville's welcoming committee cheered, Babe Ruth emerged from a train, stepping onto the platform at Depot Street. The Bambino took two steps then toppled over backward. His teammates hastily carried his limp body to the Battery Park Hotel. Soon, rumors circulated that Ruth had died in Asheville, North Carolina, and several news agencies reported the story as if it were a fact. In reality Ruth had merely fainted due to the onset of a mysterious ailment (alcohol abuse, an intestinal abscess, venereal disease?). The slugger was brought to St. Vincent's Hospital in New York, where he remained for nearly two months. Despite missing April and May, Ruth returned in June and wound up hitting 25 homers over the final ninety-eight games, doing his best to put behind him the "Bellyache Heard Round the World," as *New York Tribune* writer W. O. McGeehan dubbed the incident. Ruth returned to Asheville for exhibitions in 1926 and 1931 and both times made it to the ballpark without incident. The 1926 affair was rained out, but in 1931 Ruth smacked a long ball in an 11–3 Yankee win. The Bambino was impressed by McCormick Field, which he called "a damned delightful place."

In 1948 Jackie Robinson's Brooklyn Dodgers visited Asheville for a preseason matchup with the local nine. The Tourists were playing in the Tri-State League at the time. When that league folded after the 1955 campaign, Asheville was left without a professional team and McCormick Field was converted into a stock car racetrack. Baseball returned to Asheville in 1959 though, as the city joined the South Atlantic League as a Philadelphia Phillies farm club.

Over the next two decades, the Tourists switched big league affiliations and leagues often. When Willie Stargell played for Asheville in 1961, the team batboy was a local kid named Ron McKee. Two decades later, McKee would begin a long tenure as the Tourists general manager. When the Tourists joined the Western Carolinas League in 1976 (the league that would become the modern South Atlantic League), they also had to break in a new batboy. That was because their previous one, Cal Ripken Jr., had moved on to bigger and better things after enjoying a three-year stint with the Tourists.

The 1980s brought a taste of Hollywood to Asheville, as McCormick Field made a cameo appearance in the 1988 movie *Bull Durham*. Fans of the film may recall that after Nuke LaLoosh earned his promotion to the big leagues, the Bulls gave Crash Davis his walking papers, even though he was just one homer shy of the minor league record. In one of the movie's final scenes, Crash, who had signed with the Tourists, hit his record-breaker amidst little fanfare at McCormick Field. The ball soared over the left field fence into the trees.

The wooden bleachers that appeared in *Bull Durham* have since been replaced, the pillars supporting the roof have been removed, the picket fence across the outfield has been replaced by a more modern one, many of the trees beyond the outfield fence have been cut down, and the old light towers have been replaced, but the layout of the diamond remains the same as when Cobb and Ruth took the field.

The Tourists have been a Colorado Rockies affiliate since 1994, making for the longest current association between any South Atlantic League team and its parent club. While more than 500 Asheville players have gone on to reach the major leagues through the decades, some recent Tourists to make The Show are Todd Helton, Jake Westbrook, Shawn Chacón, Jason Jennings, and Juan Uribe.

Game Day

Getting to the Park

Asheville is in the far western reaches of North Carolina, 75 miles from Hickory, and 125 miles from Charlotte. McCormick Field is on the eastern side of downtown, between I–40 and I–240. From I–240, take exit 5B and follow Charlotte Street south for about a mile. Turn left at McCormick Place and the ballpark will be on your left. From I–40, take exit 50 and proceed north on Biltmore Avenue, then turn right at

McCormick Place, and the ballpark will be on your right. There is a small parking lot at the ballpark and another one up the hill at Asheville Municipal Stadium. There is no charge at either location. There is a limited amount of on-street parking in the ballpark neighborhood.

Inside the Park

The smallest ballpark in the fourteen-team South Atlantic League provides room for just 4,000 fans. On most nights the stands are about half full. A small seating bowl around the infield provides six rows of blue stadium chairs down at field level, which sell as Box Seats, followed by an interior walkway, and then eleven rows of metal bleachers with backs, which sell as General Admission. The VIP terrace down the right field line and picnic area down the left field line were added prior to the 2006

season as Palace Sports and Entertainment, which owns the team, spent $600,000 on the renovations. The ballpark offers only a small press box behind home plate, with no traditional luxury boxes, so the two new areas will be important revenue sources for the team in the years to come.

The concession stands are on a covered concourse behind the stadium. Here fans find bratwurst, corn dogs, hamburgers, hot dogs, deli sandwiches, pizza, snow cones, and boiled peanuts. The souvenir store is in a small building just inside the main entrance.

The McCormick Field Experience

While Asheville's team is creatively named after the many tourists who pass through the city en route to the Great Smoky Mountains, it would be rather difficult to conceptualize a

McCormick Field

tourist as a team mascot and even more difficult to sell such a character to the local kids. I'm imagining a mascot wearing old-fashioned driving goggles and weighted down by a suitcase under each arm and maybe his wife's hairdryer around his neck, and well, he just isn't too cuddly. He's haggard and road weary, and not really in the mood to play with a bunch of excited youngsters. Wisely, then, the Tourists feature a loveable teddy bear instead as their resident rabble-rouser. Ted E. Tourist is not your average bear. His many talents include the ability to ride a unicycle along the warning track. And he's also a natural at stealing corn dogs, so keep an eye on him.

On the Town

Asheville's stately downtown features distinctive old buildings. The most popular historic buildings are the **Biltmore Estate** and the **Thomas Wolfe House**. The Biltmore (One North Pack Square) is a 250-room mansion that was built in the late 1800s by railroad heir George Washington Vanderbilt. The Wolfe House (52 North Market Street) is the boarding house once run by the famous author's mother. The building was restored in 2004 after it was badly damaged by a fire in 1998. Wolfe, who was a batboy for the North Carolina State League's Asheville Tourists in 1916, when the team played at Oates Park, is buried at **Riverside Cemetery** (53 Birch Street).

The closest restaurant to McCormick Field is the **Wild Wing Cafe**, which is right across the street from the ballpark on Biltmore Avenue. The popular chain, which specializes in chicken wings of assorted flavors, partners with the Tourists to sponsor Thirsty Thursdays at the ballpark all season long. Just a half mile farther north on Biltmore, visitors find a slew of restaurants and taverns, including **Hot Dog King** (63 Biltmore Avenue), **Hannah Flanagan's Pub** (27 Biltmore Avenue), **Ed Boudreaux's Barbecue** (48 Biltmore Avenue), and **Mamacitas** (77 Biltmore Avenue).

The **Great Smoky Mountains National Park** straddles the North Carolina/Tennessee border. It is home to bear, elk, and all kinds of other creepers and crawlers. More than two million tourists enjoy hiking, fishing, camping, and biking at the park each year. The nearest park entry point to Asheville is about 40 miles away in Cherokee. To reach the park, follow I–40 West, to Route 19 West, to Route 441 North.

DURHAM BULLS ATHLETIC PARK
Durham Bulls

Class AAA, International League
(TAMPA BAY DEVIL RAYS)

Durham Bulls Athletic Park
409 Blackwell Street
Durham, North Carolina
919–687–6500

No movie has captured the ethos of minor league baseball in quite the way the 1988 classic *Bull Durham* did, and by the same token, no movie has ever kindled fan interest in the bush leagues like the film that featured Kevin Costner as a minor league catcher nearing the end of the line, Tim Robbins as an up-and-coming Durham Bulls pitcher, and Susan Sarandon as a ballpark tart/philosopher. Amidst the backdrop of quaint and charming Durham Athletic Park, the movie painted a picture of a game that was silly and romantic and at the same time deadly serious. The public ate it up. And before long, fans were turning out at the old ballpark in Durham in droves—the Bulls became the first Single-A team in the modern era to attract more than 300,000 fans in 1990—and the ripple effect catalyzed a surge in attendance at minor league parks across the country. After the movie got the ball rolling, the minor league renaissance picked up speed when the big leaguers went on strike in 1994, then it gathered more momentum as minor league cities across the country began replacing aging ballparks with new fan-friendly stadiums. The irony, of course, is that the movie's romantic depiction of an old-time bush league ballpark helped bring many fans back to the minor leagues, then those same fans helped convince many towns and teams that they needed bigger, newer ballparks to stay competitive, thus resulting in the closing of many old parks.

You can count Durham Athletic Park among the old-time yards that fell victim to the influence of the movie. The ballpark was replaced in 1995 with Durham Bulls Athletic Park. There is good news in Durham though, and lots of it. For one, Durham built the right kind of new park, constructing a stadium that features many retro design flourishes and has plenty of personality. For two, Durham left the old park intact, not only to serve as a local shrine, but to serve as a venue for amateur games. And last, but not least, the new ballpark helped Durham, a longtime Single-A city, make the jump from the Carolina League to the Triple-A International League. So now the folks in Durham have a higher level of ball to watch and a fabulous throwback ballpark to watch it in.

Durham Bulls Athletic Park was designed by the ballpark outfitters at HOK of Kansas City, and built at a cost of $16 million. It offers a redbrick façade that blends in with the preexisting warehouses of Durham's abutting tobacco district. On entering the park fans find themselves on a concourse that runs behind and beneath the grandstand seats. Here, colorful murals pay tribute to great players in Durham history, and here resides the famous bull that appeared above the outfield fence at the old ballpark in the movie. You remember, the bull that would blow smoke out of its nose every time it got dinged by a home run ball.

Narrow runways lead from the concourse to the seating bowl, depositing fans on a midlevel walkway that separates the Box Seats from the Terrace Seats. Between the dugouts an old-fashioned cantilevered roof covers the terrace level and luxury suites, while a 32-foot-high outfield wall known as the "Blue Monster" rises in left. The wall features a manual score-

Durham Bulls Athletic Park

board on its face and a newer, larger version of the team's trademark snorting bull on top.

Six sections of steeply rising seats appear above the much lower outfield wall in right field, while an equally steep grass hill in right-center gives rise to the scoreboard and provides a place for families to spread out beach blankets and watch the game. A long brick building beyond the ballpark grounds in right combines with the towering home run fence in left to make the ballpark feel like a hardball oasis amidst an otherwise urban setting.

The Bulls' old park was neither as spacious nor as luxurious as the new one, but it was every bit as grandiose in its day. Durham Athletic Park's trademark feature was, and still is, a cylindrical brick building that serves as the gameday ticket office. Inside, a large blue roof covers the bright blue seats. The ballpark originally opened in 1926 as El Toro Park, but it was completely rebuilt following a fire in 1939. The first game at the rebuilt park—an

exhibition between the Boston Red Sox and Cincinnati Reds—was played on April 7, 1940. Ten days later, the Bulls hosted the Winston-Salem Twins in the first Piedmont League game at the reopened park. The Bulls—who were named then, just as they are now, after a popular brand of cigarette that was made in Durham—played their first Carolina League game at Durham Athletic Park in 1945.

The Carolina League maintained a regular presence in Durham until 1968 when the Durham club merged with one from Raleigh to form the Raleigh-Durham Mets. For the next few years, the team played half of its schedule at Durham Athletic Park and half at Raleigh's Devereaux Meadow. Plagued by low attendance at both home locations, the team dropped out of the league after the 1971 season. And professional baseball didn't return to Durham until 1980 when the city rejoined the Carolina League with a team once again named the Bulls.

After the release of *Bull Durham,* and the opening of the new ballpark, the Bulls made the jump from Single-A to Triple-A in 1998, becoming the top minor league club of the expansion Tampa Bay Devil Rays. The parent organization's poor showing at the big league level since then has resulted in more than the usual number of top draft picks passing through Durham on their way to the majors, including players like Rocco Baldelli, Jorge Cantú, Carl Crawford, Jonny Gomes, Toby Hall, and Aubrey Huff. Prior to the connection with the Devil Rays, the Bulls featured budding Atlanta Braves stars like Andruw Jones, Chipper Jones, and Dave Justice.

No season in Durham began amidst higher expectations for the Bulls than the 2006 campaign, and no season resulted in as many embarrassing disappointments. The 2006 Bulls were stocked with budding young stars that, rather than shining on the field, brought one negative news story after another to the team. First, uber-prospect Delmon Young—rated the top minor leaguer in the country by *Baseball America*—drew an unprecedented fifty-game suspension from the International League when he struck an umpire with a thrown bat after being called out on strikes in the first inning of an April game in Pawtucket. Then, fellow top-prospect Elijah Dukes was sent home for ten days by the Bulls after he got into a heated argument with Durham hitting coach Richie Hebner. Next, after the International League suspended Bulls manager John Tamargo for ten games for repeatedly bumping an umpire during an on-field argument, future star B. J. Upton was arrested by Durham police and charged with driving while intoxicated.

At least during one special game of the 2006 season the Bulls and their fans could forget all of their troubles. On a sweltering night in mid-July, Bulls pitchers Jason Hammel and Juan Salas combined to pitch a no-hitter at Durham Bulls Athletic Park, turning the trick against the Columbus Clippers in a 4-1 Bulls win. Hammel pitched the first 8⅓ innings but departed after throwing 125 pitches and watching his fielders commit two errors in the ninth. Salas entered and threw a wild pitch to allow the Columbus run to score, then got the final two outs.

Game Day

Getting to the Park

Durham is part of the Triangle that also includes the cities of Raleigh and Chapel Hill. The city is accessible from both I–40 and I–85. From I–40, take the Durham Freeway to the Mangum/Roxboro Street exit. Go straight on Willard Street and the ballpark will be on the right. From I–85, take the Downtown Durham exit and follow Mangum Street for 2 miles to the ballpark. There is limited on-street parking on Willard Street and there are large lots on Mangum and Blackwell Street.

Inside the Park

Durham's ballpark accommodates 10,000 fans in a comfortable seating bowl composed entirely of stadium chairs. There is room for another 1,000 fans or so on the right field berm. Below the interior walkway, the 100 Level offers Field Box Seats that all offer great views. Section 100 is directly behind home plate. The odd-numbered sections continue down the left field line, culminating in Section 119 by the bull pen in deep left. Across the diamond the even-numbered sections don't stop at Section 122 in deep right, they just take a time-out to leave room for a picnic area, then resume at a much steeper pitch above the right field home run fence. The outfield sections (even Sections 124–134) sell as Diamond View Seats.

The 200 Level begins about 5 feet above the walkway. Sections 200 through 208 are covered by the roof and are the best bet on a rainy night or sunny day.

The ballpark concession treats include the smoked meats of Dillard's Barbecue, a local outfit that has been scintillating palates in the Triangle for more than fifty years with its vinegary sauce, and the spicy offerings at the Flying Burrito, which takes a unique approach to freshening up traditional Mexican fare. The yam and black bean burrito is just one example of the stand's many innovative offerings. The Flying Burrito's main location is on Airport Road in Chapel Hill, hence its unusual name, but the name is appropriate for another reason too. The Flying Burrito stand at the old ballpark in Durham had a tin roof and whenever foul balls would plop down on top of it, there would be a loud clatter that would often cause customers and the counter help to nearly jump out of their shoes. More than one burrito went flying under such conditions.

Durham Bulls Athletic Park also offers several different types of hot dogs, honey-roasted pecans, and jumbo cans of Pabst Blue Ribbon.

The Bulls' lone retired number—number 18—hangs on the left field wall. It belongs to Hall of Famer Joe Morgan who played for Durham in the early 1960s.

The Durham Experience

An old-fashioned organist sets up on the mid-level walkway above the Bulls on-deck circle. This is always a nice touch, and one that I wish more teams would emulate. If what's old is new again in ballpark architecture, why shouldn't the same hold true in ballpark entertainment? In any case it holds true in Durham where the Bulls are kind enough not to bombard fans with too many loud sound bites and shameless corporate promotions. The mascot is a bull named Wool E. Bull. This bull is always friendly and approachable, but such is not the case with the imposing toro atop the left field wall, whose eyes glow, tail wags, and nostrils spout smoke whenever a Durham player sends a long ball into the screen atop the fence.

On the Town

Durham lives a sort of double life. On one hand, it's a college town, owing to the presence of the many students from Duke University and the University of North Carolina. On the other hand, it's a blue-collar city full of working-class people just trying to make a living.

While both Tobacco Road campuses are scenic and worth checking out, Durham is also home to some excellent restaurants, particularly those specializing in North Carolina barbecue. If you like the smoked meat at the ballpark, schedule a follow-up visit to **Dillard's Barbecue** (3921 Fayetteville Street), which offers a classic southern-style cafeteria. Another local favorite is **Bullock's Barbecue** (3330 Quebec Drive), the walls of which are decorated with photos of many ballplayers and celebrities who have stopped in to sample the sauce through the years.

As game time nears, fans find several bars and restaurants north of Durham Bulls Athletic Park on and around Main Street, including the **James Joyce Irish Pub** (912 West Main Street).

The old **Durham Athletic Park** (West Corporation Street and Morris Street), where the movie was filmed and where the Bulls played for decades, is expected to receive a renovation in the next few years so that it can serve as the home of the new college baseball program at Division II North Carolina Central. In the meantime you'll find it looking very much as it did in the movie.

L. P. FRANS STADIUM

Hickory Crawdads

Class A, South Atlantic League
(PITTSBURGH PIRATES)

L. P. Frans Stadium
2500 Clement Boulevard NW
Hickory, North Carolina
828–322–3000

Anyone who has ever bought a house on a quiet country road only to watch in horror over the next few years as that road becomes a lot less quiet and a lot less country will be able to identify with the Hickory Crawdads. When the 'Dads made their South Atlantic League debut back in 1993, returning minor league baseball to Hickory after a thirty-three-year drought, the outfield view at brand new L. P. Frans Stadium featured a vibrant green hillside. A lush forest of pines and hardwoods rose steeply on the hill beyond center field and right field, making for a cozy sealed-in setting for a game. Unfortunately, the forest is no longer. Today, a massive white Pepsi warehouse sits on the leveled hillside beyond the outfield walls. The building was constructed in 2002, a campaign remembered in Hickory as much for the South Atlantic League championship the Crawdads won, as for the constant rumble of heavy machinery just beyond the ballpark grounds, and for the dusty brown film that fans found themselves perpetually wiping off their seats and brows.

While they were certainly not happy to witness the destruction of their quaint little outfield view for the greater good of the ever-expanding Pepsi empire, the Crawdads couldn't exactly complain. After all, their ballpark was named after L. P. Frans, a local Pepsi bottling magnate who donated to Hickory the

land upon which the park was constructed. The ballpark also shares its neighborhood with the Hickory Regional Airport and the surrounding Winkler Park. In addition to the ballpark, the park contains picnic tables, barbecue grills, a playground, walking trails, and horseshoe pits.

Frans Stadium has a fairly distinctive main entrance that features a peaked redbrick facade with three arched doorways through which fans must pass to gain access to the concourse inside. On either side of this impressive two-story entrance, significantly lower brick walls trace the back of the concourse. Brick pillars rise up from these walls to support the large green roof that covers the concourse and back several rows of the seating bowl. The ballpark has a very open look and feel, since the exterior walls don't rise all the way up to the roof. There is plenty of shade, and at the same time, a free and easy airflow. With this "roof on stilts" design, Frans Stadium reminds me a bit of Mavericks Stadium in the California League, although there is even less of a structure to enclose the back of the field in the High Desert.

Inside the turnstiles Frans Stadium doesn't deviate much from the prevailing ballpark design model that dictates an open concourse should run atop the seating bowl so as to allow fans to keep an eye on the game while milling around. The design does, however, offer glassed-in luxury suites immediately behind the last row of seats in the sections behind home plate. These suites block the views from the concourse in this part of the park, but the concourse is open on either side of them.

The folks in Hickory sure hit a home run when it came time to endow their team with a catchy nickname and creative mascot. On making their start in 1993, the Crawdads watched with delight as their merchandise sales rose to the top tier of the minor league marketing charts. Only the Durham Bulls and Carolina Mudcats outsold the Crawdads in their inaugural campaign, as 'Dads fans gobbled up hats, T-shirts, lapel pins, wristwatches, necklaces, and all sorts of other gear depicting the likeness of their cuddly ballpark crustacean, Conrad the Crawdad. For those unfamiliar with the bottom-dwelling freshwater fauna of the South, a crawdad (synonymous with "crawfish" or "crayfish" or "prickly pincher") is essentially a miniature lobster that lives in mucky freshwater ponds and rivers. They are equally popular among bass and Creole chefs. Hickory was initially an affiliate of the Chicago White Sox, before switching in 1999 to its present player development contract with the Pittsburgh Pirates. The fans in Hickory have seen more than their share of budding stars in recent years, as future major leaguers like Joe Crede, Jon Garland, Carlos Lee, Magglio Ordoñez, Aaron Rowand, Chris Shelton, and Zack Duke have all played for the home team.

The arrival of the Crawdads did not mark Hickory's first foray into the South Atlantic League. Back in 1952 and 1960, the city fielded a team known as the Rebels.

Today, in addition to serving as the home park of the Crawdads, Frans Stadium sees occasional use by collegiate teams like Appalachian State University and Lenoir-Ryhne College, and is the site of the annual Greater Hickory Smoke Barbecue Competition and Festival.

Game Day

Getting to the Park

Hickory is located in the western hills of North Carolina where it can be reached via short drives from several of the other minor league towns in the Tar Heel State. This small city is about 75 miles east of Ashville, 65 miles northwest of Charlotte, 75 miles southwest of Winston-Salem, and 50 miles northwest of Kannapolis. The ballpark sits on the western edge of town. From I–40, take Highway 321 North and follow it to the fifth traffic light, then turn onto Clement Boulevard Northwest, which leads to the park. There is a large parking lot behind the grandstand.

Inside the Park

While Frans Stadium can accommodate a shade over 5,000 fans, in recent years the Crawdads have drawn about 2,300 per night. So there is no compelling reason to order tickets in advance, unless you're traveling with an extremely large group of friends. The stadium offers three different ticket options. The Box Seats are the comfortable red stadium chairs that appear in the first twelve rows at field level. After a wide midlevel walkway, the seating bowl's second level offers six sections of comfortable blue Reserved Seats between the dugouts, then midway down the first and third baselines, the second level switches to Grandstand Seats, which are actually bleacher benches. The tri-tiered party deck down the right field line is reserved for groups on most nights, but on Thursdays it is opened up to the public.

The concession concourse runs behind the last row of Reserved/Grandstand Seats. Here, fans find a basic ballpark menu. The most interesting item is the Carolina hot dog, a meaty wiener topped with chili and coleslaw. For the kids there's a funnel cake stand, and for the adults there's the Crawdads Cafe on the first base side, which serves locally brewed Crawdad Red Ale.

The main attraction at the playground is a carousel on the third base side.

The Frans Stadium Experience

Conrad the Crawdad was dredged more than a decade ago from the nearby Catawba River.

Since then, Conrad has grown fat on a steady diet of leftover ballpark hot dogs and flat ballpark Pepsi. Curiously, this gentle crustacean's shell is bright red, even though he insists he's never been steamed, boiled, stewed, or fricasseed. That's funny, because most of the crawfish I've had the misfortune of stepping on during my ventures into freshwater have presented an amalgam of various shell tones of light orange and dark blue. In any case Conrad is a huge hit in Hickory. He's a hugger and loves to wrap his claws around his adoring fans young and old. Conrad is able to wear a Crawdads hat thanks to special holes that the team's director of marketing cut into his cap, allowing for his antennae to poke through the top.

Two popular promotions in Hickory during the 2006 season were "Dukes of Hazard Night," when actor James Best, of Rosco P. Coltrane fame, appeared at Frans Stadium along with the General Lee, and "Mayberry Deputy Night," when Don Knotts impersonator David Browning had the fans in stitches, even those too young to remember the *Andy Griffith Show*.

Also during the 2006 season, the Crawdads hosted "Barry Bonds Bobblehead Night." The figurine depicted Bonds back in his younger days with the Pirates. Strangely, the doll drew more than the usual number of comments that "his head looks too small for his body."

A few annual events help define the Hickory baseball experience. Each spring, the Crawdads stage a 5K road race that takes place on the grounds of Winkler Park. The event is called the "Hickory Crawdads Fleet Feet Home Run Trot." Another popular promotion is "Bring Your Pet to the Ballpark Night," when fans show up at the game with dogs, cats, rats, rabbits, snakes, hermit crabs, and a whole bunch of other creatures.

On the Town

With a population of only 37,000 people, Hickory is the second-smallest city in the South Atlantic League. One of the city's trademark events is the **Greater Hickory Smoke Barbecue Competition and Festival,** which takes place at Frans Stadium over Memorial Day Weekend. The event attracts professional and amateur barbecue chefs from across the South, and area residents turn out to enjoy rib-eating contests, sauce-tasting tests, live music, fireworks, a beauty pageant, a hog run, an art show, and more.

Because Frans Stadium features little more than the ballpark basics at its concession stands on most nights, though, it may not be a bad idea to grab a bite to eat before the game at one of the food joints (Arby's, Taco Bell, McDonalds, Pizza Hut) or local restaurants on Highway 321/13th Avenue, less than a mile from the park.

During the summer, aside from minor league baseball, Hickory offers the chance to check out minor league stock car racing at the **Hickory Motor Speedway** (3130 Highway 70 SE). The .363-mile bullring first opened in 1951. It offers Saturday night races all summer long.

FIELDCREST CANNON STADIUM

Kannapolis Intimidators

Class A, South Atlantic League
(CHICAGO WHITE SOX)

Fieldcrest Cannon Stadium
Stadium Drive
Kannapolis, North Carolina
704–932–3267

In baseball's early days it was not uncommon for teams to name themselves, directly or indirectly, after popular players and managers who wore their uniforms. From the major leagues we find such examples of this once fashionable trend as the Brooklyn Robins, who were named after their colorful manager Wilbert Robinson, and the Cleveland Indians, who were named after slugging outfielder Louis Sockalexis of Maine's Penobscot tribe. This was certainly also the case in the early days of the minor leagues, as local teams often identified themselves by the name or nickname of their best known players. But when, I ask, in the history of the Grand Old Game, has a baseball team ever been named after an athlete from another sport? The answer to this confounding trivia question can be found in the South Atlantic League, where today's Kannapolis Intimidators bear the nickname that once belonged to NASCAR legend Dale Earnhardt.

When professional baseball came to Kannapolis, a small city 20 miles northeast of Charlotte, in 1995, the local team was known as the "Piedmont Phillies." Kannapolis sits in the Piedmont region of North Carolina, hence the first half of the handle. As for the Phillies nickname, it reflected the identity of the team's parent organization. After the first season in Kannapolis, however, management decided that a new nickname reflective of Kannapolis's own identity would be more appropriate. So the team ran a fan contest and eventually settled on the "Piedmont Boll Weevils" as its new name. A boll weevil, for those of you happily unaware of rural southern pestilence, is a type of beetle famous for its unparalleled ability to destroy cotton crops. The name, which ranks right up there with the Savannah Sand Gnats in the tongue-in-cheek department, was a nod to Kannapolis's long history as a leading player in the textile industry. Kannapolis, in fact, derived its name many decades earlier from its long-standing association with the Cannon Manufacturing Company.

The team played under the Boll Weevil banner from 1996 through 2000, even featuring a cotton-shirt-devouring boll weevil as its mascot. Then, following the 2000 season, Earnhardt, a Kannapolis native, bought a stake in the team. The Boll Weevils were promptly renamed the "Intimidators," as the team took the nickname that Earnhardt's aggressive driving style earned him on the NASCAR circuit. Before the legendary racer got the chance to see his namesake team play, however, he perished in a crash at the Daytona 500 in 2001. Ironically, his memorial service in Kannapolis was held at Fieldcrest Cannon Stadium. On a chilly day in late February, more than 4,500 people turned out at the ballpark to pay their last respects to the fallen giant. A year later, the Intimidators retired uniform number 3, the one that once adorned Earnhardt's car. Today, the "I's" continue to serve as one of the many Earnhardt legacies in his hometown.

Fieldcrest Cannon Stadium was designed to resemble the old mill buildings found in downtown Kannapolis. At least the stadium's exterior was, with its pitched roof and brick facade. Inside, the stadium follows the template of so many other minor league facilities designed and built in the 1990s, featuring a sunken playing field and a concourse atop the last row of seats. The ballpark breaks the mold a bit too, as its main structure is actually located along the first baseline, rather than behind home plate, as is usually the case. The mill-like building on the first base side serves as the main entrance outside and houses six indoor-outdoor, second-level luxury boxes at the back of the concourse inside. Meanwhile, only a small one-level press box sits at the front of the concourse behind home plate. In left field a large roof over the third base concourse serves as a group picnic shelter. The overall effect of these three disparate design features is a somewhat disjointed setting for a game. That said, I really can't complain too much about the sight lines. The seating bowl starts down low to the field where it should, and although it rises rather sharply, there are only eighteen rows in most sections, so the views are consistently good, even for those seated in the metal bleachers in deep right field. I also like the view beyond the outfield fence, which is a scenic panorama of trees and pastureland.

The I's switched to an affiliation with Chicago White Sox in 2001, and recently signed on to represent the South Siders through 2010. Among the players to have suited up for Kannapolis are Jimmy Rollins, Jeremy Reed, and Brandon McCarthy. Since the Kannapolis team has crossover appeal, invoking the hero of another sport, fittingly, the team's alumni roster does as well. Future NFL running back Ricky Williams played for the Piedmont Boll Weevils during the 1996 and 1997 South Atlantic League seasons, while also starring on the gridiron for the University of Texas. Williams, a shortstop who was selected in the eighth round of the 1995 amateur draft by the Phillies, batted .187 and .206, respectively in his two seasons in Kannapolis, before abandoning

baseball to concentrate on football and holistic medicine.

Game Day

Getting to the Park

Kannapolis is just a half hour ride north of Charlotte on I–85. Fieldcrest Cannon Stadium is about 1 mile west of the interstate and 1 mile east of downtown. From I–85, take exit 63 and follow Lane Street west. Stadium Drive, which will appear on your right after ½ mile, leads to a large stadium parking lot.

Inside the Park

The ballpark seats 4,700 fans comfortably, with room for more on a grassy area down the left field line. Typically, the I's draw about 1,500 people per night, so there's no reason to order tickets in advance. The Box Seats are the first eight rows or so (depending on the section) at field level. Sections 101 and 102 are behind the plate and the odd-numbered sections continue down the first baseline to Section 117, and the even-numbered sections continue down the left field line to Section 116. These comfortable green stadium chairs appear around the infield and extend into outfield foul territory. The second-level seats appear behind the Boxes and are elevated enough to allow for a clear view over the walkway between the two levels. Between the dugouts the second level features the same comfortable stadium chairs as below and these sell as Reserved Seats. Past the ends of the dugouts, however, the second level offers aluminum bleachers instead of individual seats. A General Admission ticket gains access to any of the five bleacher sections between first base and the right field foul pole or to either of the two bleacher sections across the diamond in shallow left.

The concession stands offer barbecued pork sandwiches (what would a game be in

North Carolina without this local staple?), old-fashioned fountain sodas mixed from syrup and soda water, and jumbo cans of Pabst Blue Ribbon.

The Pit Stop Playground behind the bleachers in right offers inflatable pens and other games for the kids. The souvenir shop on the first base side is called the "Intimidation Stadium," but don't be scared off. The store offers a wide selection of reasonably priced gear.

The Fieldcrest Cannon Stadium Experience

The I's offer recurring theme nights to engage fans belonging to different target groups. "Senior Night" features an ongoing bingo game that plays out between innings. "Guys Night Out" presents activities and attractions that the males in the stands are sure to appreciate. "Thirsty Thursday" caters to the gluttons, lushes, and cheapskates, offering two-for-the-price-of-one sodas, draft beers for $1.25, and buffalo wings for 25 cents. "Business at the Ballpark Night" invites different chambers of commerce to the ballpark, encouraging Kannapolis movers and shakers to exchange business cards and form strategic partnerships. "Church Night" invites different youth groups to the ballpark to hear religious testimony from former ballplayers who have seen the light. And "Hot Dog Night" caters to processed meat lovers of all ages, faiths, professions, and persuasions, offering 50-cent franks all game long.

The Kannapolis team offers another interesting service for fans that I haven't come across anywhere else. Families that wish to celebrate their loved ones' birthdays or other special occasions at the ballpark can contact the team five days in advance and order a handmade cake to be delivered to their seats at a specified time during the game. The cake, which comes complete with frosting that depicts the Intimidators logo, costs $15.

On the Town

Parts of downtown Kannapolis may resemble the cliched American mill town that has fallen on hard times since its jobs went overseas. But that doesn't mean you'll have to go hungry during your visit. Less than a mile west of Fieldcrest Cannon Stadium, you'll find a cluster of restaurants on North Cannon Boulevard and Jackson Parkway. The options range from the usual burger franchises found in suburban anywhere to Chinese, Thai, and Mexican establishments.

Racing fans will surely want to visit the 9-foot-tall, 900-pound statue of the town's most famous native son that stands at **Dale Earnhardt Plaza** on Main Street. The statue, which was erected in 2002, attracts tens of thousands of pilgrims each year. Savvy racing fans will pick up on the subtle imagery and symbolism that influenced the plaza's design. On a rather obvious level, the walkway around the plaza is shaped like a racetrack. Less overtly, the benches along the walkway are arranged in groups of three, paying tribute to racing's most famous number. A bit more subtly, visitors must descend seven steps to reach the plaza from Main Street, with each step representing one of Earnhardt's Winston Cup titles. And for hardcore racing buffs willing to do some serious mental dot connecting, you'll notice there are seventy-six granite sections on the base of the statue, with each section representing one of Earnhardt's career victories. See if you can discover for yourself some of the other allusions to Big E's greatness.

GRAINGER STADIUM
Kinston Indians

Class A, Carolina League
(CLEVELAND INDIANS)

Grainger Stadium
400 East Grainger Avenue
Kinston, North Carolina
252–527–9111

It is rare to find a minor league ballpark that succeeds as well as Grainger Stadium does at offering both an old-time experience and a comfortable experience all in one. The tiny ballpark, which dates back to an opening in 1949, underwent a series of renovations in the late 1990s and early 2000s to bring its playing field and stands up to contemporary standards. For fans this work reseated the covered grandstand sections with comfortable plastic stadium chairs, leaving plenty of legroom between rows. It also added new concession stands and bathrooms. For the players the field was excavated, regraded, and outfitted with brand new sod, and the dugouts were enlarged and modernized. Despite receiving this major overhaul, Grainger Stadium retains the classic charm it has offered fans for decades. Home plate is still just 30 feet from the first row of seats, the outfield fence is still made of painted brick, and the low roof over the small grandstands still makes for a cozy, intimate ballpark experience.

As fans approach the stadium they find attractive brick pillars supporting a wrought-iron fence that separates the interior concourse from the parking lot outside. A small freestanding brick building serves as the ticket office. As for the stadium itself, a skeleton of blue steel girders supports the low seating bowl and the large metal roof that covers most of the seats. Inside, the outfield view features colorful advertising signs, trees growing beyond the wall, and a scoreboard that rises in right-center.

With an official seating capacity of 4,100, Grainger Stadium is the second-smallest facility in the Carolina League, offering about one hundred seats more than Lynchburg's City Stadium. It is also the second-oldest facility in the circuit, having opened its gates nine years after City Stadium debuted.

Minor league baseball has never exactly flourished in Kinston, and yet, admirably, it has persevered. Every time the minor league game has deserted this tight-knit little community along the banks of the Neuse River, it has eventually returned a little stronger and a little healthier than before. In the 1920s the city fielded a team named the Kinston Eagles in the Virginia League. Over the course of the next three decades, the Eagles made on-again, off-again appearances in the Eastern Carolina League and the Coastal Plains League.

In 1956 Kinston fielded a team in the decade-old Carolina League for the first time, serving as the second-highest minor league affiliate in the Pittsburgh Pirates chain. When the Pirates opted not to renew their player development agreement with Kinston after the season, the local nine signed on with the Washington Senators, but the Kinston fans made such a poor showing at Grainger Stadium during the first few weeks of the 1957 season that the team owner abruptly moved the Eagles 40 miles north to Wilson. The Eagles were resurrected five years later to once again serve as a Pirates affiliate in the Carolina League. This time, the team lasted nine years, representing the Pirates, New York Yankees, and Montreal Expos. Yankee lefty Ron Guidry was the most prominent future major leaguer to play for Kinston during this era.

The Eagles renamed themselves the "Expos" in 1974 as a show of loyalty to their new parents. That year, the team endured a miserable thirty-eight-win season and only drew 30,000 fans to Grainger Stadium. Afterward, Montreal told Kinston it would not be sending its minor leaguers back to town in 1975. Another hiatus from the minor league game followed, this one lasting three years, then Kinston bounced back yet again in 1978, fielding an independent club made up of minor leaguers from several different major league organizations. The next year, the expansion Toronto Blue Jays signed on with Kinston, beginning a relationship that would last through 1985. During this time Kinston was the home nest of future Blue Jays like Jesse Barfield and Tony Fernández.

The Blue Jays skipped town in 1986 though, moving their Class-A operation to Dunedin, Florida, and joining the Florida State League. Kinston hung on, going the independent route again, and calling its team the Eagles for the first time in twelve years. In 1987 the Cleveland Indians tabbed Kinston as their new Carolina League affiliate and Cleveland and Kinston have been connected ever since. Kinston still doesn't draw large crowds—it averages about 100,000 per year—but it is surviving. The relationship with Cleveland has witnessed an infusion of talented players, highlighted by future major leaguers like Albert "Joey" Belle, Manny Ramírez, Jim Thome, Sean Casey, Bartolo Colón, Richie Sexson, and Victor Martínez.

Game Day

Getting to the Park

Kinston is in eastern North Carolina, about 40 miles from Raleigh Bay. Durham is the next closest minor league city, about 90 miles to the northwest. Grainger Stadium sits in the midst of a residential neighborhood. From U.S.

Highway 70, take Business Route 70/Vernon Avenue, and then turn left onto East Street. Follow East Street to the ballpark. The stadium lot provides ample free parking.

Inside the Park

Despite the fact that this is a tiny ballpark, traveling fans should have no problem getting good seats on game day. The Indians average smaller crowds than any other team in the Carolina League, drawing fewer than 1,500 fans per game.

Thanks to the renovation that took place between the 2002 and 2003 season, the bulk of the seating comes in the form of comfortable plastic stadium chairs. The covered grandstand extends just barely to the corner bases on either side of the diamond, while down at field level the Box Seats continue past the main seating area, tracing the foul lines into the outfield. The Box Seats are folding metal chairs set within their own railings, making them "box seats" in the truest sense of the term. The Reserved Seats appear in eight sections around the infield where they are nicely shielded from the elements by the large roof. The metal pillars that rise to support the roof interfere with sight lines for some fans in the Reserved Seats, but the plethora of empty seats makes it easy for fans who find themselves peering around a pole to simply relocate to a seat with a better view. Sections 3, 4, and 5 behind home plate are shielded by the protective screen, while Sections 1 and 2 on the first baseline and Sections 6, 7, and 8 on the third baseline offer the chance to score foul balls. A General Admission ticket is good for a spot on the bleachers in left field foul territory. Across the diamond in right, groups enjoy an elevated picnic pavilion. There is no luxury box level, nor is there an elevated press level. The scribes sit in a small brick press box behind the last row of seats in Section 4.

The small concession concourse runs behind the stadium at ground level providing access to an assortment of reasonably priced menu items. Those hungry for a messy but delicious taste of local flavor can chow down on barbecued ribs. Other top choices include the chicken wings, chicken tenders, and Angus beef patties.

The Grainger Stadium Experience

While many sports teams have recently abandoned monikers, logos, and mascots that project stereotypical representations of different ethnic groups, the Kinston Indians still identify themselves with a logo that depicts a red-skinned Native American wearing a headdress, braids, and war paint. In the image, which seems a bit less politically correct than the Cleveland Indians' Chief Wahoo, the Kinston chief is drawing back the string on his bow, preparing to shoot an arrow into the sky. Creatively, the arrow at the end of the bow has already impaled a baseball.

As for the team mascot, the team keeps the kids and grownups entertained with an innocuous floppy-eared dog, Scout, and with the usual array of between innings contests and stunts.

On the Town

Kinston is one of the smallest cities to host a full-season minor league baseball team. The most recent census calculated Kinston's population at just 24,000 people. The city was originally known as "Kingston," in tribute to England's King George III, but after the American colonies won the Revolutionary War, local residents voted to drop the "g" as a sign of their new patriotism.

Today, in addition to offering the chance to experience a delightful ballpark experience, Kinston treats passers-through to the delicious tastes of Carolina barbecue. The most popular rib joint in town is **King's Restaurant** (910 West Vernon Avenue). King's has been serving heaping plates of fall-off-the-bone tenderness for generations. The restaurant's mouth-watering meats and secret sauces are so popular that it operates the "Carolina Oink Express," shipping menu items all over the country. Those not satisfied to sample merely one rib shack's offerings while they're in the heart of East Carolina barbecue country, will find more savory delights at **Chap's Restaurant** (1131 Patterson Road) and at **J & L Bar-B-Q** (1600 North Queen Street).

FIRST HORIZON PARK
Greensboro Grasshoppers

Class A, South Atlantic League
(FLORIDA MARLINS)

First Horizon Park
408 Bellemeade Street
Greensboro, North Carolina
336–268–2255

When it came time for Greensboro to replace its World War Memorial Stadium with a new minor league park, the city didn't cut any corners. First Horizon Park, which opened in 2005, was built to Double-A standards, even though the home team plays in the low-A South Atlantic League. The city's above-and-

beyond commitment to minor league baseball created a sparkling new home for the Greensboro Grasshoppers. First Horizon Park offers a 30-foot-wide open concourse that surrounds the entire stadium above the seating bowl, two grass berms, an outdoor sports bar, a play park for kids, and a truly jumbo JumboTron. The park combines the look and feel of an old-time stadium with a modern design approach.

The team formerly known as the Greensboro Bats was renamed the Grasshoppers after the 2004 season as the finishing touches were made on the new stadium. Then, on April 3, 2005, 8,500 fans crammed into First Horizon Park to watch the Grasshoppers play an opening night exhibition against the Florida Marlins. After watching Carlos Delgado, Mike Lowell, Dontrelle Willis, and Paul LoDuca take the field against the local nine, Greensboro fans kept

First Horizon Park

turning out at the ballpark all summer long. The Grasshoppers shattered the city attendance record before the campaign's midpoint, and went on to attract 407,711 fans to First Horizon Park by season's end.

First Horizon Park's design features red bricks aplenty, both inside and out, while a classic green roof caps the stadium. Plaques on the Eugene Street side pay tribute to the Ferrell brothers, who hailed from Greensboro. Rick and Wes played in the major leagues, while a third brother, George, played for two decades in the minors. Wes, a pitcher, won 193 games and slugged 38 home runs in a big league career that spanned from 1927 until 1941, while Rick, a Hall of Fame catcher, batted .283 and racked up 1,692 hits from 1929 through 1947.

Approaching the main entrance, fans find three-dimensional mason work that depicts the motion of a pitcher throwing a baseball and a batter swinging at the ball. Meanwhile, above the gates fancy metalwork portrays a large wooden baseball bat from its grip to its barrel. The ballpark gates are made of stacked aluminum Little League bats. In addition five large concrete baseballs grace the entrance plaza, along with a bubbling water fountain.

As fans enter the seating bowl, the 66-foot-tall scoreboard in right field dominates the outfield sight lines. The scoreboard features a 17-by-23-foot video screen. Behind the scoreboard the brick buildings of downtown Greensboro loom invitingly over the outfield.

In addition to using First Horizon Park for baseball games, the team and city have opened its gates for concerts and other community events. In 2005 Willie Nelson and Bob Dylan performed at the park.

Prior to the construction of the new park, World War Memorial Stadium had served as the hub of Greensboro's baseball activities for more than seven decades. The stadium was built in 1926 to host football games and track events, and then was converted for baseball in 1930. On July 28, 1930, World War Memorial Stadium hosted its first night game, as the Greensboro Patriots played the Raleigh Caps. The game was played five years before the first major league game would be played under stadium lights and less than three months after the Iowa Cubs became the first minor league team to outfit their ballpark with lights.

Future Hall of Famer Johnny Mize played for the Patriots during that first illuminated season. The next year, the Patriots became part of baseball's first farm system, becoming a Class D affiliate of Branch Rickey's St. Louis Cardinals. In the decades to follow, Greensboro would change leagues and affiliations often, and World War Memorial Stadium would serve as home to such up-and-coming players as Jim Bouton, Roy White, Bobby Murcer, Carl Yastrzemski, Curt Schilling, Don Mattingly, and Derek Jeter.

Game Day

Getting to the Park

Greensboro is in north-central North Carolina, 30 miles east of Winston-Salem and 55 miles west of Durham. From I–85 South, follow I–40 West toward Greensboro, then take the Freeman Mill Road exit and follow Freeman Mill Road until it turns into Edgeworth Street. First Horizon Park is located on the corner of Edgeworth and Bellemeade Streets. From I–85 North, merge onto I–40 West and take the exit for U.S. Highway 220 North toward the Coliseum Area. US–220 North becomes Freeman Mill Road and Freeman Mill Road becomes Edgeworth Street. There are several parking lots around the stadium that charge between $3.00 and $5.00 per car. The city also offers free parking on weekends and after 6:00 P.M. on weekdays at a 1,200-spot garage at 220 North Greene Street.

Inside the Park

First Horizon Park played the 2006 season with an official seating capacity of 7,599 fans, though efforts were underway to expand the lawn seating area in left field. The ballpark offers 5,300 stadium chairs and room for more than 2,000 fans in the luxury boxes, picnic areas, and lawn areas. During the ballpark's inaugural season, games scheduled for Thursdays, Fridays, and Saturdays frequently sold out. While interest in the team and the ballpark should gradually diminish in the years ahead, this is currently one of the hottest markets in minor league baseball, so be sure to call ahead for tickets if you plan to visit on the weekend.

The main seating bowl extends into medium-depth outfield territory. Section 101 is in left field, Sections 103 and 104 are behind the Hoppers dugout along the third baseline, Sections 107 and 108 are behind home plate, Sections 111 and 112 are behind the visitors dugout, and Section 114 is the Family Section, at the end of the seating bowl in right.

The low bowl keeps all of the fans close to the action. The lawn seating areas place fans along the right field foul line and behind the left field home run fence. Lawn tickets are sold as General Admission. Those who like watching a game in style should seek tickets in one of the twenty Club Boxes down the left field line, where in-seat wait service spoils fans who are too lazy to fetch their own hot dogs. Meanwhile, up above the lower bowl, a suite level contains sixteen luxury boxes.

There are three main concession areas on the wide concourse atop the seating bowl, one on the first base side and two on the third base side. Fans enjoy a view of the field from all three locations. Popular offerings are barbe-

cue pork, Philly cheesesteaks, burritos, wraps, chicken wings, and fruit smoothies. There is also a special concession stand for kids on the first base side.

The Grandstand Bar down the left field line is elevated above the playing field, providing drinkers with an amazing view of the game. This unique outdoor area offers a number of televisions, showcasing other games from around the South Atlantic League and major leagues.

In right field a play park offers an inflatable speed pitch booth and all kinds of other activities to keep the youngsters occupied, while fans looking to bone up on their knowledge of Greensboro sports history can visit the Greensboro Sports Hall of Fame.

The First Horizon Park Experience

The stadium features a gameday master of ceremonies named "Spaz," who roams the crowd with a microphone in hand, harassing fans between innings. You'll be able to pick out this goofy character when you see his jester hat bobbing down your aisle. Be careful not to make eye contact, or your ugly mug might wind up on the JumboTron, and you might become the subject of ballpark conversation until the game resumes.

Another fan favorite is Guilford, a cartoon grasshopper who wears a baseball uniform. Guilford is often joined by his devoted mate, GiGi, a female hopper. Timmy the Turtle also makes regular appearances at the ballpark. Correct me if I'm wrong, but don't turtles eat grasshoppers? In the wild world of my backyard in Maine, this may be true, but in the multimascot fantasy world of Greensboro, Timmy and the resident hoppers seem to get along quite well together.

One word of warning for those with sensitive ears: Whenever a member of the home team blasts a long ball, the Hoppers celebrate with an outfield fireworks display. In other words, pyrotechnic fans, this is a ballpark where you should root for a slugfest.

Autograph collectors should stake out a position before the game in Section 105, near the tunnel through which players enter the field.

On the Town

Before and after games Greensboro fans congregate at **The Left Field Tavern** (422 Edgeworth Street) right across the street from the stadium, and at **Natty Greene's Pub and Brewery** (345 South Elm Street).

World War Memorial Stadium (510 Yanceyville Street) still stands and sees use for local college and high school games. It offers bright orange-and-yellow seats, a tiny blue roof over the home plate grandstand, and a chain-link fence that protects fans in the first few rows from foul balls.

Those wishing to visit the gravesites of the Brothers Ferrell can head to **New Garden Friends Cemetery** (801 New Garden Road).

FIVE COUNTY STADIUM

Carolina Mudcats

Class AA, Southern League

(FLORIDA MARLINS)

Five County Stadium
1501 Highway 39
Zebulon, North Carolina
919–269–2287

Five County Stadium is one of the most unique ballparks in all of minor league baseball. It truly presents fans with a seating bowl unlike any other. Or more aptly, with two seating bowls, unlike any others. The stadium, which opened in 1991, underwent an extensive renovation before the start of the 2000 season, accounting for its present appearance. It offers just four rows of seats in a lower seating bowl down at field level, while the majority of the seats are upstairs in a steeply graded upper deck that hangs down over the main concourse and first level. This unique upper deck places fans right on top of the action around the infield. As if it weren't unusual enough to offer an upper deck steeper and closer to field than at any other park, the seats in this part of the park are bright red, rather than the ubiquitous dark green that is in danger of becoming a cliche at ballparks these days.

Usually my advice to traveling fans is to score the best (read: most expensive) tickets they can get their hands on, since at most minor league parks shelling out an extra dollar or two can mean the difference between sitting in the third row behind home plate or the tenth row along the right field line. But in this case, I suggest aiming for a seat in the upper deck. If you're like me, it may take you an inning or two to get used to watching a game from such a strange vantage point, but once you do, and once you learn to live with the fear that you might stand up out of your seat too quickly and go tumbling down onto the field, I think you'll really appreciate the Five County Stadium experience.

As its name suggests, Five County Stadium is conveniently located within easy driving distance of five different counties in central North Carolina. The ballpark sits in Wake County, and is easily accessible to those living in the counties of Franklin, Johnston, Nash, and Wilson. Although the Mudcats are often viewed as Raleigh's team, the stadium is actually located in the sparsely populated town of Zebulon, an eastern suburb of the state's second-largest municipality. This location allows for the necessary geographic separation between the Double-A Mudcats and the Triple-A Durham Bulls, who play just 35 miles away at Durham Bulls Athletic Park.

Five County Stadium was built on the site of a former tobacco field to lure a Southern League team to the Raleigh area from Columbus, Georgia, in 1991. Zebulon's population is only about 4,000 people, while the ballpark seats 6,500. As far as I can tell, this is the only minor league ballpark that has room enough to seat every single member of the town in which it resides.

When the team originally arrived in Zebulon, the ballpark was constructed hastily to claim the Raleigh market that ownership believed would be lucrative for years to come. In the early years the team clubhouses, front offices, and concession stands existed in the form of trailers plopped down around the field. The ballpark grandstands were bleachers and the box seats were folding metal chairs. The stadium and surrounding facilities evolved gradually over the next several years, then in 1999, the team, the town of Zebulon, and Wake County embarked on a two-year, $15 million

Five County Stadium

project to build a new ballpark around the footprint of the field while play continued.

The unique seating design was the result of management's desire to provide a concourse area with a view of the field. Rather than sinking the field below street level and putting the concourse at the top of the seating bowl as has been done at many other minor league parks in recent years, the Mudcats decided to simply build the concourse at street level, place just a few rows below it, and then hang the rest of the seats up above, leaving a giant window through which fans on the concourse can view the game.

Today, Five County Stadium is almost as visually distinctive outside as it is inside. The three-story white-brick façade reminds me a little bit of Churchill Downs and a little bit of a parking garage. I'll leave it up to you to decide for yourself where the stadium falls aesthetically between these two extremes on the architectural spectrum. The structure offers three levels of large windowlike openings between the white grid of support columns framing the

concourse and upper deck. A green roof covers the press box and luxury boxes that sit behind the last row of seats in the upper deck.

At the outset the Mudcats were affiliated with the Pittsburgh Pirates. Then, in 1999 the team began a relationship with the Colorado Rockies that lasted four years. Since 2003 the team has been an affiliate of the Florida Marlins. At various points all three big league organizations sent their major league teams to Zebulon for exhibitions against the home team. For their part the Mudcats have sent plenty of their alumni onward and upward to the majors. The team's all-time roster includes such notables as Dontrelle Willis, Josh Beckett, Miguel Cabrera, Juan Pierre, Jason Kendall, Bob Walk, Don Slaught, Zane Smith, Tim Wakefield, and Andy Van Slyke.

Finally, for those who may be wondering just what in the world a mudcat is, I can tell you that it is a catfish. These prehistoric-looking bottom-dwellers often grow quite large in the warm waters of the Carolinas, so bring your noodling shoes if you're feeling lucky.

Game Day

Getting to the Park

From Raleigh, take the I–440 Beltline to US 64 East, then take US 264 East to U.S. Highway 39. Turn right onto US 39 and the stadium will be on the right. From the north, take I–95 South to US 64 West, to US 39. Turn left onto US 39 and the stadium will be on the right after about 3 ½ miles. From the south, take I–95 North to I–40 West, to US 64 East, and follow the directions above. For a visual point of reference, the first thing you're apt to notice on the horizon as you approach the ballpark is the large water tower painted to look like a baseball along US 39. There is plenty of free parking in the lots around the stadium.

Inside the Park

Instead of selling tickets, the Mudcats sell "fishing licenses." Each fishing license bestows on its holder the authority to "catch" one Mudcats game at Five County Stadium. The first-level sections between the dugouts house the Premium Field Level Seats. Beyond the dugouts on either baseline, the next two sections offer First Level Box Seats. Farther down the lines, seats on the first level in shallow right and left house Reserved Field Level Seats. Ordinarily, I would recommend any of these three options, because they're all affordably priced and they all place fans close to the action. For the sake of something entirely different though, I suggest sitting in the Second Level Box Seats, which loom over the infield. Section 203 is high above first base, Section 210 is directly above home plate, and Section 217 is above third base.

For those afraid of heights and steep pitches, the general admission Grandstand Seats in right field and left field foul may be preferable. In these locations, where the stands are angled nicely toward the infield, the incline of the rows is more gradual than in the main deck of upper-level seating.

Five County Stadium offers a picnic area high above the field on the third baseline. Across the diamond, high above the field on the first base side, fans find Cattails Restaurant. This swank establishment is open year-round. The entrées include braised American red snapper, grilled mahimahi, horseradish-encrusted Australian lamb, beef Wellington, and roasted chicken with Cajun hash browns and grilled andouille sausage.

For simpler tastes the concession stands on the concourse offer the ballpark's trademark fried catfish sandwich, a tasty North Carolina

pork sandwich, and other staples like hot dogs, chicken fingers, and pizza.

The Five County Stadium Experience

Muddy is a human-sized catfish that wears a Mudcats uniform. Fans enjoy yanking on his dangling whiskers and pulling on his long tail. Muddy endures this sort of harassment good-naturedly, but he offered a terse "no comment" when I asked if it upsets him to see fans devouring catfish sandwiches at the ballpark.

New in 2006, the Mudcats unveiled a giant billboard in right field that depicts Muddy holding a digital readout of each pitch's speed.

Mudcats fans enjoy between-inning sack races down on the field and oversized underwear races. In the latter event, teams of three fans must squeeze into giant pairs of underwear—three to a pair—then race against another similarly conjoined threesome. Now, if they could only combine the three-person underwear race with the ubiquitous frozen T-shirt contest, and maybe enlist Snoop Dogg to participate with a video camera, I think they'd really be onto something. Snoop, you reading this?

On the Town

This ballpark is located pretty much in the middle of nowhere. While I suppose it's possible that one day a wave of development will overtake the area, I wouldn't count on it any time soon. The best bet for the traveling fan is to find a hotel 20 miles away in Raleigh. Raleigh offers the chance to visit the **North Carolina Sports Hall of Fame** (5 East Edenton Street). The museum is open Tuesday through Saturday, from 9:00 A.M. until 5:00 P.M., and admission is free. The Hall honors local legends from a wide range of sports, with college basketball, auto racing, and baseball all well represented. To name just a few, the inductees include Duke coaches Eddie Cameron and Mike Krzyzewski, University of North Carolina coach Dean Smith, North Carolina State coach Jim Valvano, Wake Forest guard and CBS analyst Billy Packer, NASCAR stars Dale Earnhardt and Richard Petty, NBA stars Brad Daugherty and Cedric Maxwell, and baseball players like the Ferrell brothers, Perry brothers, Buck Leonard, Ernie Shore, Enos Slaughter, Smokey Burgess, Mike Caldwell, Tony Cloninger, Roger Craig, and perhaps most appropriately of all Jim "Catfish" Hunter.

ERNIE SHORE FIELD
Winston-Salem Warthogs

Class A, Carolina League
(CHICAGO WHITE SOX)

Ernie Shore Field
401 Deacon Boulevard
Winston-Salem, North Carolina
336–759–2233

In the heart of big tobacco country, road-tripping baseball fans find an enjoyable family experience at venerable Ernie Shore Field. Although this Carolina League ballpark dates back to 1956, it has been updated through the years and seems much newer. The stadium offers a classy redbrick façade with several arches through which fans walk to enter it. Flags fly on poles atop this distinctive exterior, while a monument outside serves as the official registry of the Greater Winston-Salem Professional Baseball Hall of Fame. Among those honored here are Earl Weaver, Wade Boggs, Rico Petrocelli, Bill Slack, Don Cardwell, and all three of the famous Ferrell brothers, who seem to keep working their way into all of these North Carolina ballpark chapters.

Bricks also play a prominent role inside the park, creating a low retaining wall that separates the seats from the field. The original seating bowl was built into a hillside, placing the concourse atop the last row of seats. This made the park ahead of its time back in the day, making it up to code with the preferred modern method of presenting baseball games to fans. Recent renovations have included the construction of new clubhouses and concession stands in 1993 as well as an expansion of the seating bowl that same year. In 1997 the Warthogs added a new scoreboard. In 2000 they added new dugouts and light towers. In 2001 they redid the press box and grandstand roof.

The press box certainly is unique, appearing atop the seating bowl in two locations, just to the left of and just to the right of home plate. This leaves the concourse directly behind home plate wide open so that fans can linger there and enjoy a bird's-eye view of the batter's box from behind the catcher. The small roof covers the concourse behind home plate and the last few rows of seats in the home plate grandstand. A larger-than-normal protective screen shields all fans seated between the dugouts from foul balls.

The outfield offers three levels of signage, except in center where a black batter's eye stands. A line of pines grows down the left field line, the treetops peeking above the signs; the large scoreboard rises above the signs in right-center; and the RJR Tobacco plant towers over the field in straightaway right.

Ernie Shore Park opened in 1956 after a fire destroyed old Southside Park, which had hosted Carolina League teams affiliated with the St. Louis Cardinals and the New York Yankees dating back to 1945. Back in those days the local team was known as the Twins, in recognition of the twin cities—Winston and Salem—that merged in 1913 to form one supercity. At the time of the new park's opening, it was named after former Boston Red Sox and New York Yankees pitcher Ernie Shore, who won 65 games in a seven-year big league career, before retiring in 1920. After his playing days Shore returned to Winston-Salem and served as a Forsyth Country sheriff. He was instrumental in raising money to build the new park, so the city showed its appreciation by naming the product of his labors in his honor.

During a rebranding effort in 1995, the Winston-Salem team adopted the name "Warthogs." A warthog is a husky African boar that has two rough warty patches on its face and

Ernie Shore Field

two large husks protruding from either side of its jowls. This is one of the foulest looking creatures that Mother Nature ever created, and the local mascots in Winton-Salem do well to characterize the warthog's unseemliness. Sorry, Wally and Wilbur, but even on your good days you look more haggard and hung over than my Uncle Vit after one of his famous benders.

The Warthogs have been affiliated with the Chicago White Sox since 1997. Previously, the team enjoyed player development contracts with the Red Sox, Chicago Cubs, and Cincinnati Reds. In addition to the Winston-Salem legends mentioned earlier, other members of

the team's alumni association include Dwight Evans, Mike Greenwell, Aaron Boone, Joe Crede, Carlos Lee, Aaron Rowand, Jon Garland, Kip Wells, Josh Fogg and Chad Fox.

Game Day

Getting to the Park

Winston-Salem is in northwest North Carolina, about 80 miles west of Durham via I-40, and 80 miles northeast of Charlotte via I-85 and U.S. Highway 52. Ernie Shore Field sits in the northwest quadrant of town, west of US 52 and north of I-40's business route. From BR I-40, take the Cherry Street exit. Cherry Street turns into University Parkway. Continue north on University Parkway past the Coliseum on your right, then at the traffic light for Deacon Boulevard, turn right. The ballpark will be on your left, across the street from the LJVM Coliseum Annex. From US 52, turn left onto Akron Drive, then turn left onto Reynolds Boulevard, then left onto Shorefair Drive, and finally right onto Deacon Boulevard. The several parking lots around the stadium all charge $2.00.

Inside the Park

The seating bowl can accommodate 6,000 fans. Seats are usually available on game day, although Christian Concert nights and Fireworks nights often sell out.

Ernie Shore Field offers great sight lines thanks to a design that places the concession traffic behind the last row of seats. There is no seating in the outfield behind the home run fence, but the ballpark utilizes almost all of the space between home plate and the foul poles. About half of the seating comes in the form of comfortable stadium chairs, while the other half is seating in the bleachers, on the lawn, and in the picnic area.

The seating-bowl proper extends just past the corner bases. Section A is at first base, Section F is behind the plate, and Section L is at third base. Between the dugouts at field level, the first several rows are red Box Seats. In the three sections behind home plate, E, F and G, the Boxes extend all the way up to the press box, but along the baselines the Boxes are followed by blue Reserved Seats. In the sections past the corner bases, bench-style metal bleachers take the place of the Reserved Seats, offering General Admission seating.

The grass berms begin where the bleachers end, continuing almost all the way to the foul poles. A group party deck occupies the areas atop the berms in deep right field, while the Blue Rhino Deck offers a tiered party area built into the side of the hill. The park does not offer any luxury suites.

There are four large concession stands on the concourse, each offering different menus. Between the four locations, hungry fans find pulled pork, Angus burgers, chicken wings, chicken wraps, brats, and an array of other treats. The ballpark serves a range of macrobrews, as well as Corona, Rolling Rock, Shiner Boc, and Ice House. Margaritas and glasses of wine are also available. The beer garden on the third base side of the concourse provides a fun place to watch the game, listen to music, and mingle with other fans. This area is absolutely packed on Thursday evenings, so arrive early if you want to stake out a spot.

The Ernie Shore Field Experience

For weekday games scheduled to start at 7:00 P.M., the Warthogs open the ballpark gates at 4:00 in the afternoon, allowing fans to watch batting practice. Then the park closes briefly at 5:45 and reopens at 6:00. This early opening allows a great time for young fans to scavenge for souvenir baseballs or autographs before the ballpark gets too crowded.

Until recently, smoking was allowed in the ballpark seats, except for in the six rows of Section E that were designated as a Family Section. Yeah, like the smoke from the rest of the park didn't waft into this miniscule section, right? Anyway, even in this bastion of nicotine country, smoking is now prohibited throughout the seating bowl at Ernie Shore Field. Smokers must report to designated areas on the concourse to get their fix. The good news is that this is an open-air concourse behind the seats, so the smoke really doesn't bother the nonsmokers and asthmatics down below; it just wafts away into the night.

For young fans looking to run off some energy during the game, the concourse offers plenty to amuse them, including a carousel, speed-pitch booth, spin the prize wheel, putting green, clown, and face painters. The kids get excited when the Warthogs hit a home run and the PA system plays a unique celebratory siren, while the ballpark ushers throw softy balls into the crowd as prizes.

Wally the Warthog and his younger brother Wilbur lead the crowd in cheers, dance on the field, do headstands during the nightly singing of "YMCA," ride four-wheelers, and slide off the dugout roofs. Wally has a voracious appetite and eats just about anything he can get his hooves on, so visiting fans would be wise to closely guard their ballpark munchies when he's nearby. According to the local fans, Wilbur is a bit more considerate and less of a moocher, but I suggest holding onto your hot dog extra tight when he ambles into your section just in case.

A gentleman by the name of Homer Crafford is the biggest superfan Winston-Salem has seen since Ernie Shore. Mr. Crafford has been showing up at the ballpark, rain or shine, day or night, for the past five decades. He is the first fan to arrive and the last to leave. Homer sits in the last row of Section F, sings his heart out during the national anthem, cheers when the Warthogs do something worth applauding, and occasionally heckles the home plate ump when calls start going against the home team. Through the decades Homer has been such an ardent supporter of Winston-Salem baseball that he was the first fan inducted into the Greater Winston-Salem Professional Baseball Hall of Fame. Congrats, Homer. You deserve it.

On the Town

Winston-Salem is a college town, as eleven different institutions of higher learning reside within its limits, including Wake Forest, Winston-Salem State University, and Salem College. There are several local taverns near the ballpark where fans congregate, including **Pig Pickins** (613 Deacon Boulevard), **Village Tavern** (102 Reynolds Village), **Elizabeth's** (2824 University Parkway), and **Cactus Jack's** (3001 University Parkway).

Just south of downtown, **Old Salem** offers a restored Moravian Congregation town, where life continues today much as it did in the 1700s.

The **Winston Cup Museum** (236 Industrial Drive) is also a popular tourist destination, as it showcases racecars driven by Dale Earnhardt, Kevin Harvick, Mike Skinner, Richard Childress, and others.

BELLSOUTH PARK

Chattanooga Lookouts

Class AA, Southern League
(CINCINNATI REDS)

BellSouth Park
201 Power Alley
Chattanooga, Tennessee
423–267–2208

The owners of the Chattanooga Lookouts faced an impossible task when the economic realities of the modern game made it necessary for them to replace venerable Engel Stadium, which had been the hub of the city's minor league baseball universe since 1930. The old park was eccentric and quirky, and truly one of a kind. And it had etched seven decades of cherished hardball memories into the hearts and minds of local fans. But with each passing year, the maintenance costs associated with keeping the old yard viable grew larger and larger. What's more, the park offered none of the luxury boxes that minor league teams depend on these days for revenue. And the park's location, a few miles outside of downtown, was not ideal for a team looking to engage a cosmopolitan fan base.

Chattanooga has as rich a minor league baseball history as any city, and its residents possess a keen appreciation of that history, so it is easy to understand why some locals still decry the Lookouts abandonment of Engel Stadium with their move to new BellSouth Park in 2000. At the same time it seems reasonable to cut the team's owners—Frank Burke, Dan Burke, and Charlie Eshbach—some slack. After all, the luxury boxes and downtown setting that the Lookouts sought and found in their new park have proven time and again to

provide teams across the country with the best chance of success. The owners also deserve credit for building BellSouth Park with $10 million of their own money. In an age when many teams hold their home cities hostage by threatening to move unless they get a new publicly funded stadium, the Lookouts anteed up and delivered a privately financed ballpark.

With that said, I think the transition would have been easier for Chattanooga fans had BellSouth Park been cast in the retro mold that has become so popular in ballpark design in recent years. While the stadium offers a brick retaining wall around the base of the field, it does not do much else to encourage an oldtime atmosphere. BellSouth Park provides an unmistakably modern setting for a game. It is clean, functional, comfortable, and a bit on the sterile side. Its location atop Hawk Hill offers a pleasant semirural environment even though it is part of downtown.

The park offers a seating layout that places most fans on the first base side of the field, while leaving room for a highway to run down below the hill on the left field side. The park opened on April 10, 2000, with a 5–4 Lookouts win over the Birmingham Barons. The Lookouts were then, just as they are now, an affiliate of the Cincinnati Reds. The team has operated continuously in the Southern League since 1976, when an affiliation with the Oakland A's returned minor league ball to the city after a ten-year layoff. The affiliation with the A's was followed by a relationship with the Cleveland Indians from 1978 through 1982, then a PDC with the Seattle Mariners from 1983 through 1986. Then Chattanooga hooked up with the Reds in 1987.

Professional baseball debuted in Chattanooga way back in 1885 when the city fielded a team that played at Stanton Field as a member of the fledgling Southern League. After ten seasons that team moved to Mobile, but the Scenic City soon bounced back, placing a team in the newly formed Southern Association in 1901. After that team moved to Montgomery, following the 1902 season, Chattanooga imported a team from Little Rock in 1910, and this time the pro game established lasting roots. Chattanooga played in the Southern Association through 1965, winning league titles in 1932, 1939, 1952, and 1961.

The team was a Washington Senators affiliate in the late 1920s when Senators owner Clark Griffith sent former big league pitcher and vaudeville entertainer Joe Engel to Chattanooga to spearhead the effort to construct a new ballpark. Engel liked the city so much that he decided to stick around and run the team after the new stadium that would bear his name opened in 1930. He was famous for his outlandish publicity stunts, which included signing a seventeen-year-old girl named Jackie Mitchell to a professional contract in 1931. When the New York Yankees visited Chattanooga for an exhibition game against the local team on April 2, 1931, Mitchell struck out Babe Ruth and Lou Gehrig consecutively. Ruth watched a called third strike sail past, then Gehrig went down swinging. While footage of the unbelievable occurrence played at movie theaters across the country, baseball commissioner Kennesaw Mountain Landis voided Mitchell's contract on the grounds that there was no place for a female in professional baseball. More than fifty years later, Mitchell returned to Engel Stadium and threw out the first pitch before the Lookouts played their home opener in 1982. Engel's other stunts included giving away a house to a lucky fan and trading one of his players for a Thanksgiving turkey. With a history as colorful and humorous as that, it's easy to see why some fans still wax nostalgic when they think of Engel Stadium.

Game Day

Getting to the Park

Chattanooga sits on the Tennessee-Georgia state line where it is accessible via I–75, I–24, and I–59. BellSouth Park is on the eastern side of town, alongside U.S. Highway 27 and the Tennessee River. From I–75, take I–24 West and then U.S. 27 North. Take the exit for 4th Street/Downtown, and then turn left onto Chestnut Street. Turn left onto 3rd Street and BellSouth Park is at the top of Hawk Hill. Unfortunately, there isn't much parking for fans at the ballpark. The best bet is to head for the private lot just past the intersection of 3rd and Market Streets, or the garage at the intersection of 3rd and Chestnut. A free trolley runs back and forth between the remote parking locations and ballpark.

Inside the Park

The seating bowl is severely weighted toward the first base side of the diamond. While the seats extend no farther than third base on the left side, they continue almost all the way to the right field foul pole, and a large picnic pavilion extends into right field home run territory high above the right field fence. The sight lines are good throughout the park, but the seating bowl is not quite as intimate as those of most of the newer parks that have opened in recent years.

At field level the twelve rows of green stadium chairs set in the concrete base of the 100 Level contain Box Seats. Behind the Boxes, there runs a midlevel walkway, then the aluminum upper bowl begins, offering six rows of blue stadium chairs that sell as Reserved Seats, and then bleachers with backs that sell as General Admission. At the top of the seating bowl, there are a few final rows of stadium chairs that belong to the indoor/outdoor luxury boxes. A small roof covers these luxury seats and the last few rows of the bleachers. All in all, this design is very similar to that of Hadlock Field, in Portland, Maine. In Chattanooga, Sections 101/201 are in shallow right field, Sections 109/209 are behind home plate, and Sections 113/214 are just past third base.

While it is unfortunate that the seating bowl has as much bleacher seating as it does, I like the fact that BellSouth Park has plenty of General Admission space around the infield, which cannot be said of most parks. One tip: Sit on the third base side if possible, especially if you like to see the entire field at all times. The protrusion of Boxes 101 through 103 in right field foul territory blocks the view of the right field corner for many fans sitting in the Reserved and General Admission sections along the first baseline. Also, the sun sets behind the third base bag, so those on the first base side contend with a glare in the early innings.

BellSouth Park bucks the popular trend in ballpark design by providing its concession concourse beneath the grandstand, thus prohibiting fans from peeking at the game while waiting in line or mingling with friends. Popular menu items include spicy chicken nuggets, bratwurst, grilled chicken sandwiches, and pizza.

The BellSouth Park Experience

BellSouth Park's trademark attraction is a large model train that sits behind the advertising signs in the right field corner, waiting to emerge when a member of the Lookouts hits a home run. The locomotive chugs along the top of the right field fence, puffing out clouds of steam and blowing a whistle while the fans cheer wildly. This exciting ballpark feature was brought over from Engel Stadium, where it first appeared in 1995.

The team's popular mascot is a wide-eyed red puffball named "Louie the Lookout."

On the Town

Right next door to BellSouth Park, the **Tennessee Aquarium** (One Broad Street) makes for a natural side trip. The world's largest freshwater aquarium makes good use of the Tennessee River, while providing a home to more than 12,000 animals, including fish, amphibians, reptiles, birds, and other creatures. The aquarium offers a Riverview Journey and Ocean Journey, and is visible from the ballpark beyond the first base side. Visitor passes are good all day long, allowing folks to leave to catch an afternoon baseball game next door and then reenter later on. The aquarium is open from 10:00 A.M. until 6:00 P.M., seven days a week.

Another trademark Chattanooga tourist destination is **Lookout Mountain**. This peak just southwest of downtown offers sweeping views of the city. No, you don't need to bring your hiking boots. A broad gauge railway that dates back to 1895 hauls visitors up the slope of this historic Civil War battle site. **Incline Number 2** departs from a station located on St. Elmo Avenue. The mountain's features include a mineral spring and unique rock formations like the "Natural Bridge" and "Sunset Rock."

Finally, those looking to embrace Chattanooga's storied baseball past can pay a visit to **Engel Stadium** (East 3rd Street), which sees use today as an amateur field. The seven-decade-old park features a hillside in left-center field that is in play some 471 feet from home plate, an expansive roof supported by a matrix of steel girders, and a press box atop the grandstand roof.

PRINGLES PARK
West Tennessee Diamond Jaxx

Class AA, Southern League
(SEATTLE MARINERS)

Pringles Park
4 Fun Place/Ridgecrest Road
Jackson, Tennessee
731–988–5299

No city's place in the minor league game currently rests on shakier ground than Jackson, Tennessee's. Even so, it's hard to tell if anyone really cares. Of course the city—which still has $5 million of outstanding debt on Pringles Park—cares, but as for the rank and file citizens of Jackson . . . well, they just haven't supported this team. The Diamond Jaxx will likely move to the next attractive Double-A market to open up. Possible destinations for the team include Biloxi, Mississippi; Baton Rouge, Louisiana; or Lafayette, Louisiana.

Jackson is a small city between Nashville and Memphis on I–40 that built Pringles Park during the height of the minor league boom in the late 1990s. For a while the game appeared to be on solid footing in Jackson, but it was a short while. Buoyed by the $8 million stadium and a promising crop of Chicago Cubs prospects, the Diamond Jaxx led the Southern League in attendance in their inaugural 1998 season, drawing 313,775 fans. Nonetheless, within a few years interest in the team declined dramatically.

The team changed hands in 2002 and the incoming owners, Lozinak Baseball Properties, sank $2 million into sprucing up the five-year-old stadium. Renovations replaced many of the stadium's aluminum bleachers with green stadium chairs, added a picnic terrace, redesigned the berm area just past first

base, and covered wide stretches of ugly gray concrete with charming red brick. And yet, attendance continued to trend steadily downward, from 224,698 in 2002, to 197,226 in 2003, to 159,308 in 2004.

This led Lozinak to conclude that residents of Jackson, a city of only about 60,000 people, were unwilling or simply unable to support a minor league team. Looking to get out while the getting was still good, the Diamond Jaxx attempted to claim the Greenville market after the Southern League's Greenville Braves announced they would be moving to Pearl, Mississippi, to start the 2005 season. But the powers that be within minor league baseball eventually decided that the South Atlantic League's Capitol City Bombers should move to Greenville instead. But the damage was done in Jackson, and a bad situation quickly grew worse.

After reading in the newspapers all winter long that the Jaxx were trying to leave Jackson, local residents found themselves with two choices once the 2005 season began. They could either turn out at the ballpark in record numbers to show ownership that their city was indeed a viable market, or they could ruffle their feathers and return the team's off-season snub by pointedly avoiding the ballpark. Unfortunately, the fans chose the latter option, and the Jaxx sold just 105,893 tickets in 2005, easily the worst in all of Double-A.

After the debacle of 2005, Lozinak was ready to cut its losses. And so, Overtime Sports arrived as the Jaxx's third owner in eight years. Overtime's director Tim Bennett said all the right things on arriving in Jackson, stating that he hoped to keep the team in town. Bennett's vision included a partnership with the city that would reenergize the team by developing the rural just-off-the-highway ballpark neighborhood into a residential and retail center. It is worth noting, however, that the three-year lease extension that Overtime signed with the city to use Pringles Park allowed the team an out clause after the 2006 and 2007 seasons.

So, stay tuned to see how this saga in Jackson plays out. While Pringles Park will certainly be standing when your travels take you through West Tennessee, it remains to be seen whether there will be any reason to stop by the park, or if you'll have to continue on to either Nashville or Memphis to see your next game. One thing's for sure, if the Diamond Jaxx do pull up stakes, Jackson will have to host a heck of a lot of concerts and monster truck rallies to pay off the mortgage on Pringles Park.

The park will never be accused of being quaint, charming, or intimate, but it's not the worst place to watch a game either. It is an amalgam of the two prevailing ballpark design approaches—the old one that says a park should provide a steep seating bowl around the infield with a midlevel walkway, and the new one that says a park should offer a sunken field with an open concourse atop a seating bowl that stays low to the field.

Pringles Park's seating bowl is built into the side of a hill so that fans enter on a concourse atop the last row. But oddly, the concourse does not trace the back of a nice low seating bowl that extends into the outfield corners. Rather, the open concourse sits atop a high seating bowl that barely extends past the corner bases. The stadium is made even higher and steeper by a midlevel walkway that divides the bowl in half between field-level and second-level seats. Ordinarily, the benefit of having an open concourse atop the seats is that you no longer need a midlevel walkway. And as a result the sight lines improve for everyone. But in Jackson that really isn't the case. They built up, when they should have built down the baselines. The stadium is made all the more towering by the club seats and luxury suites on the press box level high above the concourse.

If the minor league game does indeed leave Jackson, local fans will be left to live off the memories of the West Tennessee team's short list of franchise highlights. The team won the Southern League championship in 2000 with a roster stacked with future major leaguers like Eric Hinske, Corey Patterson, and Carlos Zambrano. It hosted an exhibition against Sammy Sosa's Chicago Cubs in 2001 that brought 7,777 fans to Pringles Park. And it welcomed Nomar Garciaparra to West Tennessee on a rehab assignment in 2005. Following the 2006 season, the team switched from a relationship with the Cubs to one with the Mariners.

Game Day

Getting to the Park

Jackson is 85 miles northeast of Memphis and 130 miles southwest of Nashville. "The Chip," as Pringles Park is sometimes called, is northeast of downtown. Take I–40 to exit 85 and follow Doctor F. E. Wright Drive south. Turn left onto Ridgecrest Road and after 1/2 mile the stadium will be on your left.

Inside the Park

Pringles Park contains 6,000 seats. Section A is in shallow right field, Section G and H are behind home plate, and Section N is in shallow left field. The nine rows below the midlevel walkway in all sections offer green stadium chairs that sell as Field Box Seats. On the second level Sections D through K contain sixteen rows of stadium chairs that sell as Box Seats, but the three outfield-most sections contain aluminum bleachers with backs that sell as General Admission. The first bleacher section on either side is behind a dugout, the second section is on the outfield side of the nearest corner base, and the third section is in shallow outfield territory.

The three sections of Club seats upstairs on the first baseline make the stadium feel unbalanced, since on the other side of the press box, the second level abruptly ends before reaching the home dugout, leaving the concourse uncovered.

The concession stands atop the seating bowl feature a wide array of offerings. Aside from the obligatory Pringles potato chips, kids enjoy fried bologna sandwiches and grilled ham-and-cheese sandwiches, while adults sink their teeth into pulled pork sandwiches, pork chop sandwiches, Philly cheesesteaks, Chicago-style hot dogs, and chili cheese fries. A covered picnic patio on the concourse over-looks third base, while a tiered group picnic area is built into the hillside past first base. Kids find a playground down the first baseline.

The Pringles Park Experience

If the Diamond Jaxx can't make the game work in Jackson, it won't be for a lack of trying. While the previous owners focused on improving the ballpark, the current ones have tried to bring back the fans with low ticket and concession prices and lots of promotions and giveaways. On Monday nights fans can buy twenty-four-ounce beers for just $2.00. On Tuesday nights General Admission tickets, hot dogs, and pop-corn all sell for $2.00. On "Thirsty Thursdays"

beer and soda sell at buy-one-get-one-free prices. On Fridays the team offers fireworks.

A popular between-innings contest involves team employees tossing catfish high in the air while fans circle underneath and try to catch them in large fishnets. Don't worry fish-huggers, the Jaxx use fake catfish.

On the Town

Although Jackson hopes to develop the area around the stadium into some sort of shopping center, none of the city's plans have come to fruition yet, so when it comes to pregame eats, traveling baseball fans are left with a choice between **Subway** and **Sonic,** which are both at the stadium exit off the interstate.

Jackson's trademark tourist attraction sits on the southwest side of town where U. S. Highway 45 crosses I–40. **Casey Jones Village** (56 Casey Jones Lane) includes a museum dedicated to the life and lore of the Jackson train conductor who died at the switch on April 30, 1900, in a famous wreck. On display are Casey's home and an old-fashioned steam engine like the one he was driving. The site, for obvious reasons, will be a must-see on any Dead Head's tour of the minors.

SMOKIES PARK

Tennessee Smokies

Class AA, Southern League
(CHICAGO CUBS)

Smokies Park
3540 Line Drive
Sevierville, Tennessee
865–286–2300

In 2000 East Tennessee's minor league baseball team retired its old ballpark in Knoxville and moved to new digs in Knoxville's southeastern suburbs. Built by Sevier County for $19.4 million, Smokies Park ushered the Smokies out of a city with 175,000 residents and into a town with barely 12,000 people. But Smokies Park is consumer-friendly and conveniently located off I–40, making it a more appealing destination than old Meyer Stadium had become as its neighborhood deteriorated in the 1990s.

Smokies Park offers a typical design with a field below street level, a low seating bowl that extends well into the outfield corners, lawn seating across the outfield, a concourse that encircles the entire field, and plenty of luxury boxes suspended above the concourse around the infield. While the new stadium brought the Smokies that much closer to the Great Smoky Mountain range after which they are named, unfortunately, Smokies Park does not offer any mountain views. The park is built into the side of a hill, and the view behind the narrow seating berm that rims the outfield fence is of a quick-rising, shrub-covered hill that eventually levels off to be topped by trees. The hillside is part of a KOA campground and ballpark fans can actually see campers stealing peaks at the game while they roast marshmallows and tell their ghost stories at campfires that burn on the hill. While this outfield terrain is brambly,

sunburned, and generally unkempt, it contributes to a rustic ballpark atmosphere that seems befitting a park that sits just outside the gateway to a sprawling national park.

As for the outside of Smokies Park, if it looks like one of the visitor information centers that you see alongside highways, well, that's because it is one. The ballpark lives a double life, also serving as the Sevier County Welcome Center. Think of the many welcome centers you've visited during your trips back and forth across this great land of ours. Don't they all kind of look the same? Well, that's what the exterior of this ballpark looks like: a welcome center. It isn't unpleasant. In fact it's quite welcoming. But at the same time, it doesn't really look like a ballpark. Stone pillars support the pitched roofs on either side of the main entranceway. Behind these decorative overhead peaks, the first level is finished with attractive stone masonry. A green metal roof extends off the top of the stone front, and then the cream-colored second level rises above that roof to be topped by another, similar roof.

At the time of their move, the Knoxville Smokies changed their name to the Tennessee Smokies. The team has a long history. It joined the new Southern League as a charter member—along with Chattanooga, Charlotte, Asheville, Lynchburg, and Macon—in 1964. Prior to that Knoxville's team played in the Southern League's precursor—the South Atlantic League. And before that, it had played in the Tri-State League, Appalachian League, Southeastern League, and Tennessee-Alabama-Georgia League.

The team first began embroidering the name "Smokies" on its jerseys in the 1920s when it moved to a new ballpark on Willow Avenue. The site would be Knoxville's hardball hub for eight decades. The Smokies played at Caswell Park until the Great Depression hit, and then they suspended operations. The Smokies returned in the early 1930s after Smithson Stadium was erected around the footprint of Caswell Park. When that park burned down in 1953, Knoxville shelled out $500,000 to build a 6,700-seat stadium at the same location. The facility, originally called Municipal Stadium, was renamed Bill Meyer Stadium in 1953 to honor a homegrown hero who played his high school ball in Knoxville, then played for the 1910 Knoxville Appalachians—a member of the Southeastern League—on his way to the big leagues. After playing for the Chicago White Sox and Philadelphia A's, Meyer returned to Knoxville and managed the Smokies for many years. When he died unexpectedly in 1957, the city rechristened its baseball stadium in his memory.

Throughout the 1980s and 1990s, Meyer Stadium was one of the two elder statesmen of the Southern League, along with Jacksonville's Sam T. Wolfson Stadium, which was also built in the 1950s. Ironically, the two stadiums were demolished within six months of each other. Wolfson Stadium met the wrecking ball in November of 2002, while Meyer Stadium was destroyed in May of 2003. Meyer Stadium featured a high-rising grandstand full of blue seats around the infield. A large roof covered most of the seats, and the press box actually sat atop the roof. Although the stadium is gone, the field remains, thanks to a donation by major league star Todd Helton. The slugging first baseman grew up in Knoxville watching games at Meyer Stadium. When he heard the stadium was going to be demolished, he wrote a check to preserve the field as a youth baseball venue.

Knoxville's team abandoned the Smokies moniker during the 1960s, instead identifying itself by the nickname of its big league parents. After stints as the Knoxville Reds, Knoxville White Sox, and Knoxville Blue Jays—or K-Jays, as they were often called—the team eventually returned to its roots, becoming the Smokies

again in 1993. Knoxville was a Toronto Blue Jays affiliate from 1980 through 2002, then spent two years as a St. Louis Cardinals farm club, before signing on with the Arizona Diamondbacks in 2005 and then with the Chicago Cubs in 2007.

Game Day

Getting to the Park

Smokies Park is 20 miles southeast of Knoxville in southeastern Tennessee. The closest minor league ballpark is McCormick Field, 60 miles east in Asheville, and the closest Southern League rival is the team in Chattanooga, 115 miles away. From I-40, take exit 407 for Highway 66 North. Smokies Park will appear immediately on your right. Parking in the large stadium lot costs $3.00.

Inside the Park

Smokies Park has 6,000 seats and room for 2,000 people on the lawn that runs atop the outfield fence. And though they're not counted in the team's nightly attendance tally, don't forget about those campers who set up lawn chairs on the craggy hillside just outside the stadium and watch the game for free. The Smokies draw crowds in the 3,500 range, so good tickets are usually plentiful on game day.

The seats are all below the concourse. There are seventeen rows in most sections. About two-thirds of the seats are green plastic stadium chairs, while the rest are aluminum bleachers with backs. The Box Seats begin with Section 103 just past first base, continue down the baseline to Sections 109 and 110 behind home plate, and end at Section 116 just past third base. The Reserved Seats are the bleachers in outfield foul territory. Sections 101 and 102 are in right field; Sections 117 and 118 are in left field. The lawn areas in deep foul territory on either side of the diamond serve as group picnic areas. The general seating lawn stretches from foul pole to foul pole. A parcel is fenced off in straightaway center to serve as a green batter's eye. The sixteen skyboxes offer indoor and outdoor seating and hang out over the open concourse and back rows of infield seats.

Favorite concession items at Smokies Park include pulled pork at Buddy's Barbecue and the barbecued nachos. Fans find a buffet menu that includes everything from burgers, to fried chicken, to mashed potatoes at the Double Play Cafe down the third baseline.

The Smokies Park Experience

The Smokies mascots are a duo of oversized bears, Slugger and Diamond. Diamond has shiny blue fur, while Slugger sports a more traditional brown coat. I kept waiting for one of these big burly bears to stop by my row so I could pull him aside and say, "Remember, only *you* can prevent forest fires," like Smoky the Bear used to say in those public service announcements back in the 1980s. The comment would have been appropriate, given all of the smoke billowing out of the campground in right-center. But the bears—who were busy chasing little kids up and down the ballpark steps—never made their way out to my section, and I was left to keep my 1980s flashback to myself.

In the middle of the fourth inning, the Smokies send a giant chicken named "Clucky Jacobsen" (named after former Smokies player Bucky Jacobsen) onto the field to run full speed across the outfield grass while local kids try to catch him. Usually, at least one member of the visiting team's bull pen corps also joins in the race.

The Smokies offer several weekly promotions, highlighted by postgame fireworks on Fridays, and $1.00 hot dogs on Mondays.

On the Town

Although I don't necessarily recommend watching the game from the potentially snake-ridden and spider-ridden hillside outside the stadium, I do suggest staying at the **Knoxville East, KOA Campground** (241 Koa Way, Kodak) if you have the chance. At game time you can walk next door and buy a ticket, then after the last out, you can walk back to your campsite and make some smoke. For those traveling without a tent or trailer, the campground offers cabins. A stay at the KOA is not really roughing it, as the campground offers a minigolf course, hot tubs, saunas, and cable TV.

Campers and other Comcast subscribers can actually watch the "Smokies Game of the Month" and the Smokies weekly magazine show on demand thanks to a partnership between the Smokies and the local cable company.

Dollywood is a popular tourist attraction in these parts, especially among country music buffs. The 125-acre adventure park, inspired by the life of East Tennessee legend Dolly Parton, is located south of the ballpark off U. S. Highway 66 in Pigeon Forge. It offers more than thirty rides, twenty restaurants, the Southern Gospel Music Hall of Fame, the Dreamland Forest, the Eagle Mountain Sanctuary, and more.

Tourists who follow US 66 a bit farther south into Gatlinburg will find themselves at the entrance of the **Great Smoky Mountain National Park**. The park offers camping, hiking, biking, fishing, and a scenic 11-mile driving loop. For more information about the national park and the wildlife it provides a home to, stop by the Smoky Mountain Visitors Center at the main entrance of Smokies Park.

AUTOZONE PARK
Memphis Redbirds

Class AAA, Pacific Coast League
(ST. LOUIS CARDINALS)

AutoZone Park
200 Union Avenue
Memphis, Tennessee
901–721–6000

When the nonprofit foundation that owns the Memphis Redbirds decided to replace thirty-year-old Tim McCarver Stadium with a new downtown ballpark in 2000, it certainly spared no expense. The Memphis Redbirds Baseball Foundation shelled out $46 million to build AutoZone Park and another $22 million to renovate the historic Moore Building—since renamed the Toyota Center—that stands beside the main entrance of the park where it houses the clubhouse shop and front office and will eventually house a baseball museum.

AutoZone Park opened in 2000 and has been wowing fans ever since with a low-to-the-field main seating bowl that offers great views of the game, a wide concourse that laps the field and leaves plenty of room for mingling, two suite levels that combine to offer more luxury boxes than any other minor league ballpark, a festive outfield boardwalk, major league caliber light banks, and a right field video board that is the largest (23 by 30 feet) and highest (thirteen stories) in all of the minor leagues. From both the infield and out-field seats, the ballpark offers stunning views of the downtown Memphis skyline, including an up-close-and-personal look at the historic Peabody Hotel, which rises right behind the home plate grandstand.

AutoZone Park has the type of retro design that fans have come to expect of urban ball-parks in the post–Camden Yards era and the type of main entrance plaza that fans find at the finer minor league and major league stadiums. It should come as no surprise that AutoZone Park offers a classic exterior of red brick and green steel, since HOK of Kansas City, who designed the groundbreaking Oriole Park at Camden Yards in Baltimore, served as a consultant on a design team led by Memphis-based Looney Ricks Kiss Architects.

Fans arrive at the ballpark to encounter a most unique main entrance. The massive silhouette of a left-handed batter about to take a hack is integrated into the gates that lead from the world outside onto the large plaza between the Toyota Center and stadium con-course. Fans pass between the giant slugger's legs or between one of his legs and one of the tall brick columns on either side of him to enter the park. Inside, all of the seats are attrac-tive Camden-green, as are the facings of the double-decked suite level, the light stanchions atop the ballpark roof, and the roof itself. Atop the scoreboard in right, an old-fashioned face clock displays a bright red cardinal. Green trees grow behind the outfield fence in center, composing an organic hitter's backdrop. The bull pens run behind the fence in left-center. A grassy bluff looms high above field level in left, offering a unique perch from which to watch the game. The ballpark is cozy without feeling cluttered.

The Redbirds have been affiliated with the St. Louis Cardinals since they entered the Pacific Coast League as an expansion team in 1998. During their first decade, they show-cased the talents of future big leaguers like Rick Ankiel—who pitched for the Redbirds before his control went haywire, Albert Pujols—who played only three games for Memphis at the tail end of the 2000 season before essentially making the jump from high-A to the majors the next spring, Dan Haren—who was traded to the Oakland A's in the Mark Mulder deal, and J. D. Drew—who began his minor league career with the independent St. Paul Saints of the Northern League during a contract holdout in 1997 and ended it with the Redbirds in 1999 before earning a promotion to St. Louis.

Before moving to AutoZone Park, the Redbirds played at McCarver Stadium, a converted American Legion field at the Mid-South Fairgrounds. The ballpark had an artificial turf infield and real grass outfield. It could accommodate 8,800 fans.

Prior to the arrival of the Redbirds, McCarver Stadium was home to the Memphis Chicks, who represented the city in the Southern League from 1978 through 1997, and before that the Memphis Blues, who played in the Texas League from 1968 through 1973, and in the International League from 1974 through 1976.

Delving back further into the annals of Memphis baseball history, the Blues City fielded a team in the Southern Association from 1902 through 1960. The original Memphis Chicks, named after the Chickasaw tribe, played at Russwood Park.

Don't bother looking for either old field when you're in Memphis. Russwood Park burned down in 1960, and McCarver Stadium was demolished in 2005.

Game Day

Getting to the Park

Memphis is tucked in the southwest corner of Tennessee, just north of Mississippi and just east of Arkansas. The Redbirds play 200 miles southwest of Tennessee's other Pacific Coast League franchise, the Nashville Sounds. In less than three hours, fans can shuttle between the two PCL cities via I–40. And you probably thought the Pacific Coast was located somewhere out west! Oh well, the International League isn't going to be very international once the Ottawa club moves to Pennsylvania in 2008.

AutoZone Park is just a few blocks from the Mississippi River in downtown Memphis, at the corner of Union Avenue and Third Street. From the east, follow I–40 West to exit 10B and stay right, following the signs for Little Rock. After 9 miles, turn right at exit 1E, then take exit 1C and turn right onto Madison Street and follow it to Union. From the west, take I–40 to exit 1 and follow Riverside Drive to Union. There are several privately operated parking lots and garages in the ballpark neighborhood, including three at Peabody Place.

Inside the Park

AutoZone Park has 12,500 seats and room for nearly 2,000 fans on its left field bluff. The Redbirds have averaged more than 10,000 fans per game since opening the Zone, so fans would be wise to order tickets in advance. And besides, the Redbirds offer a $1.00 discount on tickets purchased before game day, or to put it another way, impose a $1.00 surcharge on walk-up ticket sales. In either case it pays to order ahead of time.

The large main seating bowl houses nothing but comfortable green stadium chairs—no bleachers—divided into five ticket categories. The seats extend only so far as the outfield corner in left, but wrap around the foul pole and continue into home run territory in right. Section 100 is behind home plate, and the odd-numbered sections continue on the right side and the even-numbered sections continue on the left. The first several rows of Sections 100 through 112 around the infield house the

Lower Dugout Boxes, while the rows behind them house the Dugout Boxes. Next come three sections of Field Boxes in left (Sections 114, 116, 118), and four in right (113, 115, 117, 119), then two sections of Outfield Boxes in left (120, 122) and four in right (121, 123, 125, 127), and three sections of Pavilion Box seats in right field home run territory (129, 131, 133). Generally speaking, the seating bowl offers excellent views throughout, but I prefer the Pavilion Boxes to the more expensive Outfield Boxes. The straight-on vantage point from behind the right field fence is superior to the view from deep right field foul territory.

Instead of home run territory seats in left field, there is a grassy bluff where fans spread out blankets, plop down, and watch the game. The asymmetrical playing field places the Bluff closer to home plate than the seats in right field, and the hill is nicely elevated, rising atop a left field fence that stands 15-feet, 8-inches tall, or nearly twice the height of the fence across the rest of the outfield.

Upstairs, the Diamond Club Seats hang down over the first-level concourse and extend over the last several rows of first-level seats. Sections 201 and 202 are behind the plate, while the odd sections continue to Section 219 in fairly deep right field and the even sections continue to Section 216 in medium-depth left. The forty-eight indoor/outdoor luxury suites—yes that is not a misprint, there are actually *forty-eight* of them—appear on two levels behind the Club Seats.

The Zone's trademark food is the pulled pork at the Rendezvous barbecue stand. This dry rubbed pork shoulder is cooked over charcoal at the nearby Rendezvous restaurant and served to fans in sandwich form or over nachos, piled high with jalapeños and cheese. Also popular are the deep fried skewers of onions, pickles, and potatoes. Memphis also scores high in the ballpark hot dog category, offer-

ing the Big Dog—a half-pound frankfurter that comes topped with cheddar cheese, chili, and onion rings. This may be the only hot dog in the minors that you'll need a fork and knife to eat. Redbirds fans also enjoy fried shrimp, fried oysters, and fried chicken at the ballpark.

The Boardwalk in left field offers youngsters the chance to burn off some energy at a 24-foot-high rock-climbing wall, pop-shot basketball hoops, batting cages, speed-pitch booths, and at P. D. Parrot's Playhouse Perch.

The AutoZone Park Experience

The local mascot is Rockey the Rockin' Redbird, a big red cardinal who likes to ride around the warning track on a four-wheeler, sing happy birthday to fans (whether its their birthday or not), and sign autographs on the Boardwalk.

Rockey gets help in entertaining the crowd from the Redbirds RedHots. This troop of foxy dancers takes the field several times a game to perform choreographed dance routines. Ah, if the sight of young ladies bumping and grinding to blaring tunes doesn't say "baseball," I don't know what else does.

On the Town

Just a few blocks from AutoZone Park, historic **Beale Street** is the center of the Memphis entertainment district. Here, visitors find blues clubs and barbecue joints galore. This is where musicians like Muddy Waters, Robert Johnson, and B. B. King made their names . . . literally in B. B.'s case. Mr. King got his nickname from Beale Street, as he was originally known as the Beal Street Blues Boy, before the moniker was abbreviated to simply B. B.

The best time to visit Memphis is in May, when a month-long festival rages on Beale Street that has been called "the Mardi Gras of the Mid-South." **Memphis in May**, an annual event since 1976, features the World

Championship Barbecue Cooking Contest, and the Beale Street Music Festival, which through the years has showcased acts like B. B. King, the B-52s, Sheryl Crow, the Foo Fighters, L. L. Cool J, George Thorogood, ZZ Top, and lots of other famous acts.

The scores of barbecue joints in Memphis distinguish their product from the other regional varieties of "Q" by smoking pork exclusively, never beef, and by rubbing their ribs and shoulder meat with seasoning before cooking, rather than using a basting or finishing sauce. If you like the barbecue at the ball-park and want more of the same, head to **Charlie Vergos' Rendezvous** (52 South Second Street), or for something different, try **Corky's** (5259 Poplar Avenue), which has both dry-rubbed and wet ribs, as well as delicious tamales, or the **Big S Grill** (1179 Dunnavant Street), which specializes in smoked shoulder sandwiches topped with coleslaw.

The **Graceland Mansion** (3734 Elvis Presley Boulevard) is southwest of downtown, near the Memphis International Airport. Elvis pilgrims enjoy daily tours of the King's home, autos, jets, and gravesite.

GREER STADIUM
Nashville Sounds

Class AAA, Pacific Coast League
(MILWAUKEE BREWERS)

Greer Stadium
534 Chestnut Street
Nashville, Tennessee
615–242–4371

In 2008 the Nashville Sounds will open a beautiful new downtown ballpark on the banks of the Cumberland River. The $43 million facility, which was designed by HOK, will be called First Tennessee Field. It will lie at the corner of Gateway Boulevard and First Avenue, on the former site of the Nashville Thermal

Transfer Plant. First Tennessee Field is being constructed as part of a larger project that includes a 175-room luxury hotel beyond the ballpark in left field and a twenty-story-high condominium tower overlooking the first base grandstand. In addition the project will create a slender park with walking and biking trails along the river.

The ballpark will be oriented so that the river runs behind its right field fence, and the water will be reachable, perhaps, for the strongest of left-handed pull hitters. To "splash down" balls will have to clear the outfield fence 330 feet away, a 30-foot-high rocky bluff that will rise behind the fence, and the green space outside. The distance from home plate to the river will be about 490 feet.

The ballpark will have approximately 12,500 seats in a large lower bowl and small club

Greer Stadium

level, and room for as many as 5,000 people on an expansive outfield berm. Fans on the third base side will enjoy views of the Gateway Bridge to the south, and fans on the first base side will enjoy views of the Shelby Avenue Bridge to the north.

After years of lobbying for a new ballpark to replace aging Greer Stadium, the Sounds finally got their wish when the local Metro Council voted 28–9 in favor of the ballpark proposal on February 7, 2006. A consortium of twelve regional banks, led by First Tennessee, will fund $23 million of the construction costs, while tax revenues will cover another $17 million. The project's balance will be funded by Struever Bros. Eccles & Rouse, the developer of the abutting residential and commercial buildings. The Metro government will own First Tennessee Field, and the Sounds will manage it.

Nashville's baseball fans will be happy to bid adieu to Greer Stadium, a rather basic ballpark from the late 1970s that has never offered much to distinguish itself, aside from the guitar-shaped scoreboard that has extended horizontally above its left field fence since 1993. The 60-foot-long, six-string guitar displays the game's line score on its frets, a face-clock where the soundhole should be, and advertisements on its body and tuning knobs. Strummers who read tablature will note that the guitar displays a D chord whenever the visiting team has 1 run, 0 hits, and 1 error, and the home team has 0 runs, 1 hit, and 0 errors.

Greer Stadium debuted as a Southern League facility in 1978 and remained an outpost of that circuit through 1984. It is named after local businessman Herschel Lynn Greer, an avid baseball fan who earned his place in the hearts of local fans in the early 1960s when he spearheaded an effort to bring a South Atlantic League team to town. Greer sold stock in Vols, Inc., and he created a publicly

owned company that was awarded an expansion team. But after a disappointing showing at the turnstiles in their inaugural 1963 season, the Nashville Vols disbanded, and the city's longtime hardball home, Sulphur Dell, was demolished and turned into a parking lot. It would be fifteen years before professional baseball would return to the Music City at a new stadium just south of downtown.

Greer Stadium initially offered more than 17,000 seats, but in the late 1990s, the outfield bleachers were removed, reducing its capacity to a cozier 10,700 seats.

After serving as the Southern League home of the Cincinnati Reds and then the New York Yankees—who brought to town a prospect named Don Mattingly whose number 18 has since been retired by the Sounds—Nashville made the jump to Triple-A in 1985 when it joined the American Association as a Detroit Tigers farm club. The match with Detroit did not last long though, and Nashville renewed its relationship with Cincinnati in 1987. In August of 1988, Greer Stadium treated fans to no-hitters on back-to-back nights. First Jack Armstrong tossed a no-no for the local nine, and then the next day Randy Johnson turned the trick for the visiting Indianapolis Indians. Nashville won both games, thanks to some sloppy Indianapolis fielding that led to the game's only run in the second game.

Nashville set an American Association attendance record in 1990, drawing 605,122 fans. Three years later, the Sounds switched to an affiliation with the Chicago White Sox and welcomed a second team to town. That's right, in 1993 and 1994 Nashville was home to two different minor league teams. The Nashville Xpress, a Southern League affiliate of the Minnesota Twins, used Greer Stadium when the Sounds were on the road. The Xpress had previously played in Charlotte, but when that city jumped to Triple-A and a planned move to New Orleans fell through, the team was left without a home. The vagabond club eventually found a permanent home in Wilmington, North Carolina, in 1995, but not before Michael Jordan's Birmingham Barons stopped by Greer Stadium for a few visits during the 1994 season.

The Sounds switched to an affiliation with the Pittsburgh Pirates in 1998, joining the Pacific Coast League at that time as well. They switched to their present affiliation with Milwaukee in 2005 and made their first season with the Brewers memorable, sweeping Tacoma in three games to win the Pacific Coast League championship. The title represented Nashville's first league crown since 1982.

In addition to housing the Sounds, Greer Stadium sees springtime use as the home field of the Belmont University Bruins. It remains to be seen where the Bruins will play once Nashville begins a new baseball era in 2008, although it would seem likely that Greer Stadium will meet the wrecking ball at some point in the near future.

Game Day

Getting to the Park

Nashville is in the north-central part of Tennessee, at the junctions of I–24, I–40, and I–65. Greer Stadium is a couple of miles south of downtown on the former site of a Civil War fort. Take I–24 or I–40 to I–65, then take exit 81 and turn right onto Wedgewood Avenue if you're coming off the I–65 South ramp, or left onto Wedgewood if you're coming off the I–65 North ramp. Turn right onto 8th Avenue and then right onto Chestnut Street, and Greer Stadium will appear on your left. Parking is free.

Inside the Park

The Greer Stadium seating bowl extends farther down the right field line than it does in left. The first twenty rows are below a mid-level walkway, and the rest are above it. There are nine glassed-in skyboxes on either side of the press box, and Slugger's Sports Bar sits atop the press box. The main concourse runs at ground level behind the stadium.

All of the blue stadium chairs sell as Reserved Seats, while the bleachers above the walkway in the outfield sell as General Admission. Section A is in deep right field, Section H is at first base, Sections M and N are behind home plate, Section S is at third base, and Section V is in left field. Above the walkway Section HH is at first base, Sections MM and NN are behind the plate, and Section SS is at third base. The bleachers are on the outfield sides of HH and SS.

A party deck rises above the right field fence, along with a Hot Tub for the really hardcore fans. Left field foul territory offers a large picnic area and playground.

The concessions are sold at stands named after famous players in Nashville history, like Rob Dibble, Don Mattingly, and Magglio Ordoñez. Behind the home plate grandstand, Dibble's Den serves Black Angus burgers, Chick-fil-A sandwiches, and sweet tea. Not far away, Magglio's specializes in pepperoni and sausage pizza, offering slices or whole pies. On the first base side, Donnie's Delights features an array of deep fried foods, including chicken wings, chicken fingers, catfish nuggets, French fries, foot-long corn dogs, and fried cheesecake. Elsewhere on the concourse, fans find smoked turkey legs, bratwurst, barbecue nachos, deli sandwiches, and Chicago-style kosher dogs. Blackstone beer is the local brew of choice.

The Greer Stadium Experience

The Nashville mascot is Ozzie, an energetic red-nosed cougar who wears a pinstriped Sounds uniform and baseball cleats. His long tail pokes through the back of his pants. Ozzie enjoys throwing balled-up T-shirts to the crowd and dancing with fans on the roof of the Sounds first base dugout. He's been known to steal peanuts and popcorn from unsuspecting children, so keep an eye on him.

While Ozzie seems a safe bet to accompany the Sounds to First Tennessee Field, it remains to be seen whether Greer Stadium's trademark scoreboard will survive the move. At press time Nashville still had not decided whether it would be moving the big blue guitar to its new yard. For the time being, though, the guitar will continue to send colorful fireworks into the sky whenever a member of the Sounds hits a home run and whenever a Sounds fielder records the final out of the game.

On the Town

As its reputation suggests, Nashville offers an exceptional live music scene, with the center of the entertainment district located on Broadway.

One of the city's most popular tourist destinations is the **Country Music Hall of Fame & Museum** (222 Fifth Avenue South). Since 2001 the museum has resided in an architecturally stunning building with long, tall windows on its façade that look like the black keys on a piano. The museum offers original recordings, instruments, costumes, photographs, and bronze plaques that honor all of the genre's greatest stars. It is open daily from 9:00 A.M. until 5:00 P.M., and admission costs $16.95 for adults, and $8.95 for children ages six through seventeen.

The **Grand Ole Opry House** (2808 Opryland Drive) is another Nashville landmark. The theater offers weekly radio shows and is one of the venues used during the annual CMA Music Festival, which takes place over four days in June.

JOSEPH P. RILEY, JR. PARK

Charleston RiverDogs

Class A, South Atlantic League

(NEW YORK YANKEES)

Joseph P. Riley, Jr. Park
60 Fishburne Street
Charleston, South Carolina
843–577–3647

A visit to Charleston offers baseball fans the chance to enjoy the ever-interesting ballpark experience that Mike Veeck and his Gold-klang Group have perfected at minor league ballparks across the country during the past decade. Veeck, of course, is the son of Hall of Fame ballpark promoter Bill Veeck, the man credited with installing the exploding score-board at Comiskey Park, allowing fans to manage a major league game by holding cue cards for a manager behind the home dugout, and sending the 3-foot 7-inch Eddie Gaedel to the plate to work a walk. Well, as the saying goes, the apple doesn't fall far from the tree. Mike Veeck has the same innovative imagi-nation that his father had. Sometimes he hits a home run—like when his Saint Paul Saints hired a highly trained potbellied pig to deliver baseballs to the home plate umpire, and the pig became a favorite ballpark attraction. Other times, Veeck strikes out—like when his Charleston RiverDogs had to cancel a Father's Day promotion dubbed "Vasectomy Night" when the local Catholic diocese raised a stink. But when Veeck is involved—be it with the Fort Myers Miracle, Brockton Rocks, Saints, RiverDogs, or any other team that his group owns—you can bet the ballpark experience is going to be zany.

Although minor league baseball had enjoyed a home in Charleston for more than a century, the Veeck effect, coupled with a new ballpark that opened in 1997, breathed new life into the local franchise. Located just out-side of town, Joseph P. Riley, Jr. Park sits on the site of a former city dump near the banks of the Ashley River. The $19.5 million facility was designed by HOK. It is named after Mayor Joseph P. Riley Jr., a Charleston icon who was serving an unprecedented eighth term in office at the time of this book's publication and has been running the show in Charleston since 1975.

The local fans responded to the opening of "The Joe" with enthusiastic support. The attendance figures tell the story. Between 1947 and 1996 Charleston fielded a minor league team in thirty-three seasons at the city's pre-vious hardball hub, College Park. During that time 2.8 million fans turned out to watch the local nine play. Charleston's new park is on pace to eclipse that attendance total in just its eleventh year of operation, midway through the 2007 season.

In addition to housing the RiverDogs, "The Joe" is home to the Division I Citadel Bulldogs, and it is the site of the annual Southern Confer-ence Baseball Tournament. Each spring, the RiverDogs and Bulldogs play several double-headers, allowing fans to watch both resident teams in one sitting. The ballpark has also hosted concerts by Willie Nelson, Bob Dylan, Hootie & the Blowfish, Big Head Todd & the Monsters, and Jack Johnson.

"The Joe" offers a backward J-shaped seat-ing bowl, similar to the one at Hadlock Field in Portland, Maine. At both stadiums the seats extend much farther down the left field line than the right field line. It makes sense that Riley Park was designed this way since the best outfield view is beyond the right field fence

Joseph P. Riley, Jr. Park

where the Ashley River wends its way through town. The new Ravenel Bridge and several bridges to West Ashley and James Island are visible from the ballpark seats. Instead of offering deep outfield seats on the right field side, the park offers a small grassy knoll, known as "Shoeless Joe Hill," where kids like to hang out and wait for foul balls. The stadium offers a low roof that covers the last several rows of seats along both baselines, and a covered press box level behind home plate that is a story higher than the roof on either side of it. The playing field is unique in that the left field foul pole rises just 305 feet from home plate, then the left field wall shoots straight back for 25 feet before it begins its expanse across the outfield. Although the center field fence is just 386 feet from home plate, "The Joe" is known

as a pitcher's park due to the stiff breeze that blows in off the river on most nights.

Charleston's long history as a minor league town dates back to the debut of the Charleston Sea Gulls in 1886 as a member of the Southern League. The team played for eight seasons before taking a decade off and returning in 1904 as a member of the South Atlantic League. The Gulls changed their name to the Palmettos, then the Pals, then the Rebels, then the White Sox, but maintained a relationship with the old Sally League until it disbanded in 1963. After Charleston fans endured a ten-year hardball hiatus, minor league ball returned to the city in 1973 with the arrival of the Western Carolina League's Charleston Pirates. The Pirates left after the 1978 season, but in 1980 the Charleston Royals arrived, joining the resurrected South Atlantic League. The team became known as the Charleston Rainbows in 1985. When the Goldklang gang arrived in 1993, the team sponsored a fan contest to rename the Rainbows, resulting in the current RiverDogs moniker.

The RiverDogs began a player development relationship with the New York Yankees in 2005. Before that they were a Tampa Bay Devil Rays affiliate. The Rays sent future stars like Toby Hall, Aubrey Huff, Brandon Backe, Rocco Baldelli, Carl Crawford, Jorge Cantú, Delmon Young, and B. J. Upton to Riley Park.

The many memorable nights at "The Joe" include July 4, 2003, when a Charleston-record 8,116 fans turned out to watch the ball game and enjoy a postgame fireworks extravaganza, and July 8, 2002, when an official crowd of 0 fans watched the RiverDogs lose to the Columbus River Stixx. The previous record for the smallest crowd to watch a professional game was set on September 17, 1881, when just twelve fans braved a rainstorm to watch a National League game in Troy, New York. No, it didn't rain in Charleston on the day the players played before empty stands in 2002, and no, Veeck hadn't turned off the local fans with an offensive stunt. "Nobody Night" was a planned promotion. Fans arrived at the park expecting to find the gates padlocked and that's exactly what they found. After the ceremonial first pitch was delivered in the parking lot, the game began inside while Veeck and hundreds of fans waited outside until the gates opened after the game became official in the sixth inning.

Game Day

Getting to the Park

Charleston is located on the South Carolina waterfront, 100 miles south of Myrtle Beach and 80 miles north of Hilton Head. Riley Park is near the Citadel campus and adjacent to Brittlebank Park. From I–26, take the exit for Highway 17 South and then turn right onto Lockwood Boulevard, which leads to the ballpark. The parking lots next to and across the street from the stadium charge $4.00 per car.

Inside the Park

Riley Park can seat nearly 6,000 fans and provides additional standing room on the outfield wings. Tickets are usually available on game day, unless a particularly wacky promotion has captivated the attention of local fans. The seating bowl offers Box Seats, which appear in the form of comfortable green stadium chairs below a midlevel walkway, and Reserved Seats, which are bleachers with backs, located above the walkway. The seating bowl begins with Section 101 in medium-depth right field, continues down the line to Section 110 behind home plate, and ends at Section 112 in deep left. A General Admission ticket is good for a spot on the berm in right field foul territory or on the upper patio left field foul territory.

The main concourse runs behind the stadium at ground level. Here fans find plenty of old ballpark photos and an eclectic array of concession offerings. There are six different stands and they all serve different specialty items as well as different types of hot dogs, so be sure to shop around before settling on your meal. Popular items include the hummus and tortilla chips, Garden Burgers, trail mix, turkey legs, fried dill pickles, The Elvis—a peanut butter, honey, and banana sandwich in a hot dog roll, churros, taco sticks, and sliders—miniburgers with ketchup and onions. Hot dog lovers can sample them all or choose from the turkey dog, Jailhouse Dog (sauerkraut), Bull Dog (chili and cheese), Smokehouse Dog (barbecue sauce, bacon, and onions), and River Dog (mustard, barbecue sauce, coleslaw, and pickled okra). For beer lovers the Ashley View Pub beneath the third base grandstand offers more than fifty varieties of frosties.

The Riley Park Experience

Riley Park presents many traditional promotions, like frozen T-shirt contests and sumo-suit wrestling, as well as an ever-changing array of Mike Veeck specials. You may arrive at the ballpark to find that you qualify for a ticket discount because you've recently had a vasectomy, or you may find that you have to pay double for your ticket because you haven't brought your mother-in-law to the game. It's always an adventure.

Actor Bill Murray is a part owner of the team and makes sporadic summer appearances at the ballpark, as does national newspaper columnist and devoted baseball fan George Will.

Charlie the RiverDog is a big furry mascot who likes to sniff around for sliders. Feed him one and he'll be your friend for life.

"Tony the Peanut Man" is a local legend, who has been tossing roasted salties to fans since before Riley Park opened.

On the Town

Known as "The Holy City," owing to its many prominent church steeples, Charleston features art and culture, fine dining, golf courses, fishing excursions, more than a dozen museums, carriage tours and more. Although the ballpark's immediate neighborhood doesn't offer much more than the opportunity to watch a ball game, there's something for everyone at points elsewhere in town, so take some time to explore.

For traveling baseball fans, old **College Park** (Rutledge Avenue) is worth a visit. It stands at the entrance of Hampton Park where it serves as a multisport Citadel practice field. The park, which was built in 1939, features box seats that are sunken below the playing surface and an unusual outfield configuration that places the home run fence just 290 feet from home plate in right, 435 feet away in center, and 315 feet away in left.

KNIGHTS STADIUM

Charlotte Knights

Class AAA, International League
(CHICAGO WHITE SOX)

Knights Stadium
2280 Deerfield Drive
Fort Mill, South Carolina
704–357–8071

Not only do the Charlotte Knights play their home games at a stadium 15 miles from downtown Charlotte, but they play across the state line in rural South Carolina. Their ballpark sits just off the interstate, sharing the neighborhood with an abandoned Charlotte Hornets practice facility and a vast parking lot. When the "Castle" opened in 1990, the prevailing school of thought in stadium construction prized convenient street access and plentiful parking above most other considerations. Then a couple of years later Oriole Park at Camden Yards opened in downtown Baltimore, and well, we all know what's happened in ballpark design and construction since then. Nowadays, downtown ballparks are all the rage, and out-of-the-way suburban ones like Knights Stadium have lost their allure.

The good news for Charlotte baseball fans—and the bad news, I suppose, for the 8,000 people who live in Fort Mill—is that plans are currently taking shape to build a new ballpark in uptown Charlotte that will return the Knights to their rightful kingdom, possibly as soon as 2008. The initiative that would build the team a new ballpark in Charlotte's Third Ward is being led by a group of private investors who have already committed up to $34 million toward the project. At press time the group was negotiating a land swap between the county and a couple of private businesses—Wachovia and Mass Mutual—to create a footprint for the new ballpark near the home stadium of the NFL's Carolina Panthers.

The Knights are certainly enthusiastic about the move, as they have perennially finished thirteenth in the fourteen-team International League in attendance in recent years, ranking ahead of only the hapless Ottawa Lynx. Typical crowds in Fort Mill consist of about 4,000 people.

The team actually got off to a good start at Knights Stadium—then called Knights Castle—in the 1990s. As members of the Southern League, the Knights led all of Double-A in attendance in 1991 (313,791) and 1992 (338,047), before jumping to Triple-A the next season. When the Knights joined the International League, surely the folks in Charlotte were thinking: next stop . . . the major leagues. Knights Stadium was built at a time when Charlotte was first beginning to think of itself as a major league city. As those aspirations gradually panned out on the hardwood (for a little while at least), on the ice, and on the gridiron, the hope was that they would come to pass on the diamond as well. For that reason the Castle was designed so that it could be easily expanded into a larger stadium should the time come when a major league expansion team set its sights on the Queen City—or, more aptly, when a big league team set its sights about 15 miles south of the Queen City.

Knights Stadium places all of its 10,002 seats in two decks that extend only so far as the corner bases. Berms that are larger than usual occupy the spaces between the ends of the first level bowl and the outfield fences, and it is easy to envision these lawns overlaid with seats to create a first level that is big league caliber. If you stand at either end of the wide first level concourse and look up at the concrete frame of the upper deck, it is likewise easy to imagine an extension that also would bring that level up to big league specifications. In addition the stadium lights—although José Canseco complained about them while attempting a comeback with the Knights in 2002—rise higher and shine more brightly than the lights at most minor league parks. It will never happen now, of course—Knights Stadium is exponentially more likely to meet a wrecking ball than a big league game—but once upon a time the folks in Charlotte were dreaming big. Now that they're resigned to being a Triple-A town, hopefully, they'll get it right. Placing the new ballpark in Charlotte, as planned, will certainly be a good first step.

Minor league baseball actually thrived within the Charlotte city limits for decades, so there is every reason to think that it will again. Between 1901 and 1989, the city fielded teams at one point or another in the North Carolina League, South Atlantic League, Piedmont League, Tri-State League, Southern League, and International League. The future big leaguers to call the city "home" included Early Wynn, Harmon Killebrew, Tony Oliva, Minnie Mendoza, Cal Ripken Jr., Eddie Murray, Curt Schilling, Steve Finley, and scores of others.

Prior to the construction of Knights Stadium, the local nine played at a ballpark on Magnolia Avenue that dated to 1940. Back then, the Charlotte Hornets were owned by the Washington Senators and the stadium was originally called Griffith Park, in honor of the Senators owner. The stadium was later renamed Crockett Park, in honor of Francis Crockett, who ended a three-year hardball hiatus in Charlotte when he created the Charlotte Orioles in 1976. Crockett Park burned down though in March of 1985, setting in motion a chain of events that would eventually result in the construction of Knights Stadium.

After a thirteen-year affiliation with the Baltimore Orioles ended in 1989, the local team was renamed the Knights, as a play on Charlotte's "Queen City" nickname. The city got its proper name in the 1760s when it was bequeathed in honor of England's Queen Charlotte, the wife of King George III. During their brief Double-A stint, the Knights were an affiliate of the Chicago Cubs. Since joining the International League, they have been affiliated with the Cleveland Indians (1993–1994), Florida Marlins (1995–1998), and Chicago White Sox (1999–present). While the team's alumni roster includes notables like Jim Thome, Manny Ramírez, Livan Hernández, Joe Crede, Jon Garland, and Aaron Rowand, an unlikely suspect accounted for the most memorable evening in Knights history—Tetsu Yofu, who pitched a no-hitter against the rival Durham Bulls on August 1, 2004.

Game Day

Getting to the Park

A quartet of South Atlantic League teams— the Asheville Tourists, Hickory Crawdads, Kannapolis Intimidators, and Greensboro Grasshoppers—play within a two-hour drive of Charlotte. Knights Stadium is located off I–77, 15 miles south of Charlotte. Look for the water tower painted to look like a giant baseball as you approach the stadium. Those arriving from the north should take exit 88 (Gold Hill Road) and make a left at the end of the ramp. Those arriving from the south, should take the same exit, but make a right at the end of the ramp. Parking costs $2.00 in the spacious stadium lot.

Inside the Park

All of the seats at Knights Stadium are fold-down stadium chairs. Oddly, the seats appear in many different colors. Most of the seats in the first level are black, except for the two seats along the aisle in each section. These are gold, blue, green, red, and an assortment of other colors that create vertical stripes throughout the seating bowl. This decorative flourish is distinctive but only apparent when the stadium is largely empty, which, sadly, Knights Stadium has been all too frequently in recent years. The first sixteen rows in the lower bowl are the Field Box Seats, then after a narrow cement walkway the back twenty rows are the Lower Reserved Seats. Section 102 is at first base, Section 108 is directly behind home plate, and Section 114 is at third base. The upper deck offers ten rows of multicolored General Admission seats that allow fans to experience the type of upper-level views normally reserved for skybox ticket holders. The twenty-two skyboxes sit behind these upper-level seats. On a sunny day or rainy night, General Admission seating may be preferable to the seats down below, owing to the matching roofs that cover the second level on either side of the press box. As for the press box, it offers one level for the media and the glassed-in Home Run Cafe up above. The berms lining outfield foul territory are only opened on fireworks nights or when large crowds are expected.

The Fun Zone in right field offers a merry-go-round, rock-climbing wall, and inflatable pens for the kids, while across the diamond in shallow left fans find a beer garden and picnic area. The concourse runs behind the last row of first-level seats. It is decorated with banners that pay tribute to great figures in Charlotte baseball history and offers stands for Subway, Wendy's, Papa John's and Chick-fil-A. The regular concession stands offer brats, Carolina Pride hot dogs, North Carolina barbecue, and the usual ballpark staples. The Home Run Cafe is usually open to the public and on select days it offers an all-you-can-eat buffet.

The Knights Stadium Experience

The team mascot is Homer the Dragon. This loveable green fellow likes to ride his four-wheeler around the warning track to throw T-shirts into the stands and to whack people with his long tail. Homer wears a Knights jersey with the number 0 on it. It remains to be seen if Homer will move north with the Knights when they move to Charlotte, or if he will stay behind in the concrete castle that has been his home since 1990. For his sake I hope the team brings him along.

The weekly promotions in Fort Mill include "Thirsty Thursday" when beers are just $2.00 and "Wiener Wednesday" when hot dogs are $1.00.

As for annual events Knights fans traditionally ride the rails en masse once a season to watch a game between their team and its top rival, the Durham Bulls. The trip takes about two hours.

On the Town

If you're looking for a place to eat in the ballpark neighborhood, your best bet is the **Red Bowl Asian Bistro** (845 Stockbridge Drive) located right off the interstate at exit 88. There are also a couple of fast-food joints on Gold Hill Road. **Stir Crazy Sports Bar** (2150 Gold Hill Road) and **Hoopers Bar & Grill** (900 Crossroads Plaza) are about 2 miles northwest of the park and easy to reach from exit 88.

Carowinds (Rock Hill, South Carolina), a 105-acre theme park, is located a few miles north of the ballpark where it is accessible from exit 90 off I–77. It features forty-nine different rides, including Thunder Road, a wooden roller coaster that crosses the North Carolina/South Carolina border. The park is open from 10:00 A.M. until 8:00 P.M. daily and admission costs $49.99 per person.

WEST END FIELD

Greenville Drive

Class A, South Atlantic League
(BOSTON RED SOX)

West End Field
945 South Main Street
Greenville, South Carolina
864–240–4500

When the Boston Red Sox decided to sever ties with the Augusta Green Jackets and sign on with the Capitol City Bombers in November of 2004, they did so with the understanding that the Bombers would move from Columbia to Greenville before the start of their inaugural season as Boston's low-A affiliate. The deal also presupposed that the Bombers would work with Greenville to replace the city's aging Municipal Stadium with a new downtown ballpark in the heart of South Carolina's largest metropolitan region. Well, the Bombers—soon to become the Greenville Drive—delivered everything they promised and then some. The team not only financed and built a new downtown stadium, but it designed the stadium to look a lot like Fenway Park. The ballpark—known as West End Field—features a 30-foot-high Green Monster in left field, complete with a manually operated scoreboard; a triangle in right-center; and a Pesky Pole in right that stands just 302 feet from home plate. Visitors familiar with the old-time yard in Boston will be amazed by how similar the two fields look, even if the left field wall in Greenville isn't quite as high as the one in Boston and even if the center field triangle isn't quite as far from home plate.

While Fenway Park offers outfield views of Boston's downtown skyline, West End Field showcases downtown Greenville. The city's famous Paris Mountain is also visible from the ballpark seats. West End Field blends in seamlessly with its downtown neighborhood thanks to a façade constructed of 500,000 bricks that were reclaimed from local mills that had been recently razed. As another nod to the local landscape, the Drive renovated an old firehouse to serve as the team's ticket office.

Prior to the arrival of the erstwhile Bombers, Greenville had been home to the Greenville Braves, a Southern League affiliate of the Atlanta Braves that played at Municipal Stadium from 1984 through 2004. When the Braves moved to Pearl, Mississippi, after the 2004 season, that created an opening for the Bombers to claim the Greenville market. Before signing on with the Red Sox and making the move up I–26, the Bombers had been affiliated with the New York Mets for twenty-two seasons.

After arriving in Greenville, the Bombers committed more than $10 million to build the stadium, while the city offered $7 million for the land procurement and neighborhood infrastructure improvements. Construction on the ballpark began in February of 2005 and continued steadily through the next year, while the Bombers played their first season in Greenville at lame-duck Municipal Stadium, and while other downtown construction projects—including two new commercial buildings that now stand behind the new park's left field wall—took place.

Greenville's baseball history dates back to well before Municipal Stadium was built south of downtown in 1984. A West End field now known as Shoeless Joe Memorial Park served as home to the Greenville Eskimos, the city's first minor league team, in 1907. The team changed its name to the Spinners the next year and played the next several decades in a variety of leagues that ranged from the South Carolina State League, to the Carolina Baseball Association, to the South Atlantic Association, to the Palmetto League. Greenville fielded its first South Atlantic League team in 1938.

At various points during the 1960s, Greenville was a Western Carolina League affiliate of the Milwaukee Braves, New York Mets, and Red Sox. Nolan Ryan, a Mets prospect, was the most notable future big leaguer to suit up for Greenville during this era. Ryan was named Most Outstanding Pitcher of the Western Carolina League All-Star Game in 1966. After spending the 1972 season as a Texas Rangers farm club, minor league ball left Greenville and did not return until 1984. It would still be twenty-two more years before baseball would return to downtown Greenville, though, with the construction of beautiful West End Field.

Game Day

Getting to the Park

Greenville is in the northwest corner of South Carolina, just 20 miles from the North Carolina border and 40 miles from the Georgia border. West End Field is bordered by Main Street, Field Street, and Markley Street and is easily accessible from I–185, which becomes Mills Avenue in Greenville. From I–185 North, turn left onto Augusta Street, then turn right onto Harris Street, which leads to the County Square Parking Center, a block away from the ballpark. For those unwilling or unable to walk a short distance to the game, another option is to park at the privately owned lots on either side of the Markley and Main Street intersection.

Inside the Park

West End Field offers a low seating bowl that extends from foul pole to foul pole. Sellouts were common occurrences during the ballpark's first season and should continue to be, as local fans and traveling pilgrims flock to this gem in Greenville. The crowds are particularly large when the Charleston RiverDogs

come to town, proving yet again that the Red Sox-Yankees rivalry extends even to the low minors.

The stadium offers 5,000 seats, as well as a grass berm in left field foul territory that is nicely angled toward the infield a la the left field loge boxes at Fenway. The farthest seats are just thirteen rows from the field, and the covered concourse atop the seating bowl is just 50 feet from the field.

The eleven infield sections house Box Seats, all of which appear behind protective netting. The next two sections along either baseline house the Reserved Seats. A large General Admission bleacher area come next in right field foul territory, while the berm begins in left after the last Reserved section. There are eighteen luxury boxes on the press box level above the infield, and there is a patio deck on the concourse in deep right.

The most unique item at the concession stands is the deep-fried cheesecake.

The West End Field Experience

The ballpark in Greenville features a mascot that was created for the fans, by the fans, or more precisely for the kids, by the kids. Unfortunately, what began as an innocent figment of some kids' imaginations turned into a real-life adult horror story. Here's what happened: Prior to moving to West End Field, the Drive solicited mascot suggestions from local schoolchildren. After receiving hundreds of entries from more than fifty upstate South Carolina schools, the Drive selected a friendly frog named "Reedy Rip It" to be the public face of the team. A group of fifth-graders from Wren Elementary School in Piedmont got credit for the winning idea. A big green frog with a perpetually goofy smile on his face, Reedy made his debut during an April game between the Drive and the Savannah Sand Gnats. Unfortunately, before long the man who was portraying Reedy was arrested by Greenville police and charged with groping a woman's breasts while in costume during a game at West End Field. Compounding the embarrassment for the Drive, the incident wound up splashed in the pages of *Sports Illustrated*.

On the Town

Greenville chooses to celebrate the life of controversial native son Joseph Jefferson Jackson, the legendary slugger who refused to "say it wasn't so" on a sad day outside a Chicago courthouse in 1921. Before achieving major league stardom and then allegedly accepting a bribe to fix the 1919 World Series, Jackson played for a semipro textile league team in Greenville, then for the Greenville Spinners in the Class-D South Carolina State League. After being banned from the game by baseball's first commissioner, Kennesaw Mountain Landis, Jackson played outlaw ball under an assumed name for several years, then returned to Greenville to run a liquor store in the West End.

A bronze statue of Jackson stands today at **West End Park** (West Avenue), where Jackson developed his legendary batting eye and first wielded the famous forty-eight-ounce bat that he coated with chewing tobacco spit and called "Black Betsy." This field is also where Connie Mack discovered Jackson and persuaded him to sign his first big league contract with the Philadelphia A's. In addition to the statue, the park offers a plaque that reads: "As a thirteen-year-old, Joe Jackson earned a position on the Brandon Mill team. He possessed a talent so uncommon that legends grew from his deeds. His home runs were known as 'Saturday Specials,' his line drives as 'blue darters.' His glove 'a place where triples die.' Shoeless Joe was the greatest natural hitter

ever to grace the diamond, and was such an inspiration that Babe Ruth chose to copy his swing. He was banished from baseball for his complicity in the 1919 Black Socks scandal, yet his memory still moves across the conscience of America."

After visiting this city park, which offers **Shoeless Joe Memorial Ballpark**, other ball fields, and playgrounds, fans can walk along nearby Pendleton Street to see the building at 1262 Pendleton where **Jackson's liquor store** was located. According to Ken Burns's documentary, *Baseball*, Ty Cobb once stopped at the store to buy a pint of whiskey while he was passing through town and was saddened to see a broken-down Jackson working behind the counter.

The **Jackson home** (119 East Wilburn Avenue), where Jackson lived with his wife Katie until the time of his death in 1951, is another stop on the unofficial Joe Jackson tour. Finally, fans can visit Jackson's grave at **Woodland Memorial Park** (Wade Hampton Boulevard). The slugger's tombstone is nothing grand or fancy, but it is recognizable due to the baseballs, bats, white socks, and other mementos that traveling fans leave behind.

Those wishing to visit **Municipal Stadium** (Mauldin Road) where the Greenville Braves played from 1984 through 2004, and where the city's current team played during its inaugural season, will find the ballpark south of downtown. The uncovered grandstands, which offered mostly bleacher seating, had room for more than 7,000 fans. The playing field was sunken below street level and the main concourse ran around the top of the seating bowl. While this type of ballpark design is practically standard issue these days, at the time of Municipal Stadium's opening, it was unique.

COASTAL FEDERAL FIELD

Myrtle Beach Pelicans

Class A, Carolina League
(ATLANTA BRAVES)

Coastal Federal Field
1251 21st Avenue North
Myrtle Beach, South Carolina
843–918–6002

The Carolina League's newest ballpark sits in the tourist mecca of Myrtle Beach. When Coastal Federal Field opened in 1999, its arrival stretched the boundaries of this half-century-old league farther south than ever before. Although minor league baseball has historically struggled to establish viable fan bases in tourist havens like Hawaii, Old Orchard Beach, Atlantic City, Orlando, and vacation destinations elsewhere, the Myrtle Beach experiment has been a success. The Pelicans have proven over the past several years that a minor league team can survive and flourish in a tourist town. The Pelicans attract upward of 200,000 fans per season, which is respectable for a Class-A outfit.

The ballpark's central location and overall quality certainly contribute to its success at drawing tourists and locals alike. Coastal Federal Field projects a uniquely open two-level exterior façade that consists of brick pillars that support an arched sunroof covering the back one-third of the grandstand inside. A large water tower rises behind the stadium on the first base side, while the outfield view looks out into a lush tropical garden of palm trees and other vegetation. The seating bowl is cozy and the sight lines are unobstructed. The Pelicans logo is painted onto the grass behind home plate, and a large Diamond Vision board rises above the fence in left. The Atlantic coast is only about a mile from the park, and it usu-ally provides a refreshing breeze that blows in off the water.

Since their debut the Pelicans have treated fans to many memorable moments and to glimpses of future big leaguers. The Pelicans won the Carolina League's Southern Division second half title in their inaugural season but had to settle for being declared a league co champion, along with the Wilmington Blue Rocks, when Hurricane Floyd wiped out the conclusion of the best-of-five league championship series. The Pelicans were leading two games to one in the series before Floyd unleashed his fury. Future Brave Rafael Furcal joined the Pelicans midway through that first season after beginning the year in Macon. Between the two stops the speedy shortstop stole 96 bases to lead all professional players. Meanwhile, Furcal's double-play partner in Myrtle Beach, Marcus Giles, won the Carolina League MVP while blazing his own path to the big leagues. Other future major leaguers to play for the Pelicans include Jason Marquis, Adam Stern, Jeff Francoeur, Adam LaRoche, Andy Marte, and Brian McCann.

In 2000 Braves lefty Steve Avery made seven rehab starts for the Pelicans, posting a 3–3 record and a 1.53 ERA in forty-seven innings. And on September 6, 2004, Kinston pitcher Keith Ramsey spun the ninth perfect game in Carolina League history at Coastal Federal Field. In addition to housing the Pelicans, Coastal Federal Field is the annual site of a high school tournament known as the "Pelicans High School Baseball Showcase." The event takes place in March and features fourteen different South Carolina teams.

Game Day

Getting to the Park

Myrtle Beach is in the northeastern part of the Palmetto State. Coastal Federal Field is located across the street from Broadway at the Beach, a shopping, dining, and entertainment complex. Take U.S. Highway 17 to Myrtle Beach, then turn onto 21st Avenue North and follow it to the ballpark, which sits at the intersection of 21st and Robert Grissom Parkway. There is not usually enough space in the small parking lot behind the right field fence to accommodate the entire ballpark crowd, so some fans park at Broadway at the Beach. Parking is free at both locations.

Inside the Park

The seats at Coastal Federal Field used to reside at Fulton County Stadium in Atlanta, the former home of the big league Braves. The small seating bowl stretches just to the skin of the infield dirt on either side of the diamond, offering 4,324 seats. There is also room for another 1,700 fans in the general admission and group areas in outfield foul territory.

The Box Seats extend farther down the baselines than the Reserved Seats behind them, as the upper bowl extends only halfway down the first and third baselines. The Reserved sections rise more sharply than at most minor league parks, but since there aren't too many rows, fans don't wind up too high above the field. Section 103 is just past first base, Section 110 is behind home plate, and Section 116 is just past third.

Second-level Sections 208 through 212 contain individual seats, while 206 and 207, on the first base side, and 213 and 214, on the third base side, contain bleachers. The General Admission lawn is in left field foul territory, while there is a patio pavilion in right field foul territory.

The ballpark also offers nine indoor/outdoor luxury suites on either side of the press box, a group area on the pavilion in right, and a small lounge area in right field above the Pelicans bull pen. There are group areas along the third

baseline between the end of the seats and the start of the berm.

The concession stands behind the seating area offer the Bird Dog (chili, coleslaw, sauerkraut), the Ole Dog (hot dog, salsa, guacamole, nacho cheese, lettuce), and Frankie's Frank (fries, chili, cheese), as well as Philly cheesesteaks, Italian sausages, pork sandwiches, boiled peanuts, and several different types of sweets and frozen treats.

While on the concourse check out the unique plaza behind the third base seats where a miniature baseball diamond lies in the ground made of brick and marble. Fans looking to leave their mark on Myrtle Beach can purchase their own brick for $50 and inscribe it with as creative and thoughtful a message as they can come up with using twelve characters or less. Otherwise, it's $5.00 for each extra line of text. For the kids the third base side of the concourse also offers a bouncy pen and speed-pitch booth, while the first base side offers a playground.

The Coastal Federal Field Experience

The Pelicans keep fans entertained with a continuous stream of between-inning promotions. The star attraction is Dinger, The Home Run Dog, an adorable yellow lab that runs the bases after every game and carries a basket of baseballs to the home plate whenever necessary. Dinger has some canine company at the ballpark five times per season when the Pelicans open their gates to dog-lovers and dogs alike and hand out special toys and treats to their four-legged friends who pass through the turnstiles.

The Pelicans Pro Shop is on the first base side of the concourse. Buy a T-shirt and hat if you like, but be forewarned, when your roadtrip car rolls into Beloit for a Midwest League game three weeks later, chances are the locals in Wisconsin won't bat an eye at your snazzy

Pelicans gear. After all, on joining the Carolina League at the start of the 1999 season, the Pelicans finished their inaugural campaign ranked first among the 160 affiliated minor league teams in merchandise sales. They may not be at the very top of the list anymore, but the Pelicans still move plenty of apparel. While the team's main logo, which depicts a pelican in baseball spikes taking a swing for the fences, is admittedly a unique and creative image, I have to think Myrtle Beach's status as a vacation town also contributes to its high sales numbers. When folks are on vacation, they buy souvenirs and T-shirts. I should know, my wife has a closet full of T-shirts she never wears, and I've got a rack of hats from places like the Spam Museum and the International Bowling Hall of Fame.

On the Town

Obviously, there is plenty to do in Myrtle Beach besides watching minor league baseball games. The fourteen million tourists who visit the city and the "Grand Strand" annually enjoy 60 miles of white sand beaches, more than 120 golf courses, scores of minigolf courses, delicious seafood, trendy shops, and a hopping club scene.

For baseball fans just rolling into town, **Broadway at the Beach** (Highway 17 between 21st and 29th Avenues North) is a good place to gear up for the ball game, and not just because it's located right across the street from the park. This massive resort complex offers everything a weary traveler might need, from hotels to theaters, restaurants, nightclubs, and all kinds of shops. Heck, there's even a man-made lake. For those in search of a pregame or postgame plate of seafood, the complex offers **Shucker's Raw Bar**, **Malibu's Surf Bar,** and the **Crab House**. Don't worry, you meat-and-potatoes folks, there are also restaurants that don't feature raw fish, including American, Irish, and Mexican places. The nightlife scene includes spots for every taste, catering to Gen-X headbangers, classic rockers, golden oldies, Jimmy Buffett types, and fans of every genre in between.

LAKE OLMSTEAD STADIUM
Augusta GreenJackets

Class A, South Atlantic League
(SAN FRANCISCO GIANTS)

Lake Olmstead Stadium
78 Milledge Road
Augusta, Georgia
706–736–7889

When Georgia's second-largest city decided to build a new ballpark in the mid-1990s, there was much debate as to what the yard should be called. Initially, some Augusta residents and politicians favored naming the park after baseball legend Ty Cobb, but the dissenters, who pointed out that the city might send the wrong message by naming its ballpark after an avowed racist, eventually shot down the notion. And so the ballpark was named instead after a nearby man-made lake, which bears the name of the civil engineer who created it more than one hundred years ago. See why it's far too boring to simply slap corporate nametags on these ballparks? Leave cities and teams to their own devices, and you never know what they'll come up with.

More on Lake Olmstead in a minute, but first I think you'll be interested to learn a bit about Cobb's connection with Augusta, which came at a very formative time for him, both on and off the field. The Georgia Peach made his professional debut with the South Atlantic League's Augusta Tourists in 1904. The seventeen-year-old batted just .237 in thirty-seven games, but the next year he returned to Augusta and won the batting crown with a .326 average. When Cobb returned to Augusta for the third straight spring in 1906, he did so as a member of the Detroit Tigers. The Tourists had sold Cobb's contract to the big league club for $700 at the

end of the 1905 season, but Cobb and the rest of his Detroit teammates traveled to Augusta for spring training in 1906 and 1907.

During these early years Cobb fell in love not only with Augusta, which was at the time a booming resort town, but also with one of its Southern Belles. Cobb married Charlotte "Charlie" Lombard in 1908, and the couple bought a home on Williams Street, near the present site of Augusta College. Cobb and his wife would eventually move to California and then divorce, but he did own a home in Augusta for more than two decades, and he did qualify as one of the five original inductees into the National Baseball Hall of Fame. So Augusta's decision not to name its new ballpark after him speaks volumes about what a scoundrel he was off the field.

So what to name the new park? Some suggested naming it Augusta-Richmond County Ballpark, but others said that was too plain. Others suggested naming it after prominent local baseball coach A. L. Williams, after whom another city park is already named. But eventually, Augusta decided to name the new yard Lake Olmstead Stadium, as a nod to the large lake that lies just west and north of the stadium. Lake Olmstead came to be in 1872 when Augusta mayor Charles Estes hired engineer Charles Olmstead to lead a $371,000 construction project to enlarge the Augusta Canal and dam up Rae's Creek. Olmstead, who had previously worked on the Erie Canal, arrived in Augusta and flooded 113 acres of swampy woodland, transforming it into a glistening lake. Within a few years boaters were flocking to Augusta, and boathouses and cottages were springing up around the lake. Augusta had officially become a tourist town. Hence, by the time Cobb arrived three decades later, the local team was called the Augusta Tourists.

Today's Augusta team is not a direct descendent of the Tourists. The GreenJackets date back only to 1988. The team that returned professional baseball to Augusta after a two-decade-long drought did so as a Pittsburgh Pirates affiliate. After future major leaguers like Tim Wakefield, Jason Kendall, Orlando Merced, and Moisés Alou cut their teeth with Augusta in the late 1980s and early 1990s, the team switched to an affiliation with the Boston Red Sox in 1999, and then to one with the San Francisco Giants in 2005.

Yes, the team is named after the most coveted green jacket in sports, the one that the Augusta National Golf Club bestows upon its Masters champion each April, as the azaleas and dogwoods bloom and Augusta becomes the hub of the sports universe for a weekend. Lake Olmstead Stadium, which sits less than a mile east of the golf course, plays a role in the Masters festivities, hosting the annual Beach Blast concert that the golfers enjoy.

On joining the South Atlantic League in 1988, Augusta played at Heaton Stadium, which wasn't much more than a few banks of rickety wooden bleachers plopped down around a field. After the 1994 season that "ballpark" was torn down and Lake Olmstead Stadium was built in its place. Though Lake Olmstead Stadium was built for the thrifty sum of $3 million, it is a delightful place to watch a baseball game. It is *cozy, quaint, charming, intimate,* and all of those other cliched words that we fans use to describe ballparks that just *feel* right, parks that feel as though they offer us the game in its very best light. There is nothing pretentious or gaudy about Lake Olmstead Stadium. It is a minor league ballpark the exact way a minor league park should be. All of the seats are close to the field and around the infield. And nearly half of the seats are sheltered from the sun and rain by the three ballpark roofs. You read that right. There are three roofs at this ballpark. That's because there are three separate seating structures. Rather than

offering one large continuous seating bowl as most parks do, Lake Olmstead Stadium features three distinct grandstands: one behind home plate, one along the first baseline, and one along the third baseline. There are gaps of about 30 feet between the home plate grandstand and the baseline grandstands, contributing to a nice open effect that reminds me of McKechnie Field—the spring training home of the Pittsburgh Pirates—in Bradenton, Florida.

Lake Olmstead Stadium is set in a quiet part of town near the lake. Fans arrive to encounter a handsome black iron fence separating the parking lot from the interior concourse. Inside the fence, the back of the home plate grandstand features an understated brick façade at ground level, while the underbelly of the seating bowl is exposed above. A small brick press box sits behind the last row of seats atop the home plate grandstand, while there are no luxury boxes. The outfield view consists of pleasant green trees that rise above the fence.

Game Day

Getting to the Park

Augusta is in northeast Georgia, along the Savannah River. On the other side of the river is South Carolina. The closest big league city is Atlanta, 150 miles to the west, and the closest minor league towns—Savannah and Charleston—are both about 125 miles away. Interstate 20 passes through Augusta on the north side of town. From I–20, take exit 199 and bear left onto Broad Street. At the first traffic light, turn left onto Milledge Road, and the stadium will be on the right. There is an ample parking lot behind the grandstand.

Inside the Park

Lake Olmstead Stadium provides only 4,322 seats, but the crowds in Augusta average fewer than 2,000 fans per game, so good tickets are usually plentiful on game day. Six rows of Box Seats ring the infield without interruption at field level. Section A is at first base, Section F is directly behind home plate, and Section K is at third base. Behind these prime seats runs an interior walkway, and behind the walkway sit the three separate grandstands. The home plate grandstand houses Sections 5 through 8, offering comfortable stadium chairs that sell as Reserved Seats. The first base and third base grandstands offer metal bleachers with backs that sell as General Admission. In all three grandstands fans find their views obstructed slightly by old-fashioned steel girders that rise to support the roofs. On hot days or rainy nights, most fans will gladly take the tradeoff.

There is a group picnic pavilion big enough to hold 500 people down the left field line, while across the diamond there is a raised outdoor bar and grill above the right field bull pen. As for concessions fans find traditional ballpark favorites on the concourse behind the seating areas.

The Lake Olmstead Stadium Experience

The mascot formerly known as "Sting" officially received a new identity and a new outlook on life prior to the start of the 2006 season. The big yellow hornet with the green lounge coat was known for his rock-star persona during his days as Sting. He had a sardonic wit, biting edge to him, and had no problem telling folks to buzz off when they got on his nerves. He was frequently overheard telling fans not to stand so close to him, and when a female fan once refused to share her ballpark hot dog with him, Sting reportedly spooked the bee-jesus out of her, stalking her for the rest of the game, and muttering, "I'll be watching you." But all of those shenanigans are in the past. After a mascot-naming contest garnered more

than 2,000 submissions during the winter of 2005–2006, "Auggie" was selected, and with the name change the mascot formerly known as Sting has been transformed into a loveable, huggable, well bee-haved fellow.

A popular promotion in Augusta is the "Dash for Cash." After the team dumps a sack full of money at home plate, a contestant races from third base to the batters box to scoop up as much dough as he or she can with a shovel. The fan dumps the money into a wheelbarrow and motors back to third base to dump the loot. If time allows, the contestant can make a return trip to the plate to load up again, but he or she only gets to keep the money safely deposited back at third base by the end of the 30-second time frame.

The weekly promotions in Augusta include $1.00 hot dogs on Sundays, reduced beverage prices on Thursdays, and postgame fireworks on most Fridays.

On the Town

There aren't too many places to eat or drink in the immediate vicinity of Lake Olmstead Stadium, but there are two excellent hamburger joints a few blocks south of the ballpark. Fans enjoy **Broad Street Burger** (1805 Broad Street) and **Ellis Street Burgers** (1831 Ellis Street), which sit on opposite sides of A. L. Williams Park. I suggest conducting your own taste test to see which juicy patty you prefer.

No visit to Augusta would be complete without doing a drive-by along West Vineland Road to see which flowers are in bloom at **Augusta National Golf Course**, and to steal a few peeks at the links. Just don't get any ideas about joining. This is an "old-boy's club" in every sense of the term. Not only do you need to be a male to gain entry into this club of 300 members, but you need to know someone, and that someone had better be club chairman

Billy Payne or one of his close buddies. There is no formal application process. Membership is by invitation only.

Among the many family-friendly attractions in Augusta is the nicely landscaped, two-tiered **River Walk** that traces the banks of the Savannah. For the kids the city offers access to the **Funsville Amusement Park** (4350 Wheeler Road) and the **Krystal River Water Park** (799 Industrial Park Drive, Evans, Georgia).

GOLDEN PARK
Columbus Catfish

Class A, South Atlantic League
(TAMPA BAY DEVIL RAYS)

Golden Park
100 Fourth Street
Columbus, Georgia
706–571–8866

Minor league baseball is hardly flourishing these days in Columbus, Georgia, where the Catfish typically play before fewer than 1,000 fans per game and rank last in the South Atlantic League in average home attendance. That doesn't mean you should skip Columbus on your tour of the minors, though. The lack of a local fan base can't be traced to a run-down ballpark that has outlived its prime, as is often the case when minor league fans eschew the local team. Nor can the lack of support be attributed to the presence of a generic new stadium that was plopped down too hastily amidst a swirl of concrete and aluminum, which is another reason why fans sometimes decide to stay home and watch TV on gorgeous summer nights instead of heading to the ballpark.

Golden Park, which is endowed with both a rich history and enough amenities to satisfy the expectations of the modern fan, sits on the banks of the Chattahoochee River in downtown Columbus. Why this city of more than 180,000 people can't drum up more than 1,000 fans per night to watch the local team play is a mystery to me. Perhaps the constant rumors that the team will move to another city have dampened the spirit of the local fan base to the point that folks no longer care. Owner David Heller moved the South Georgia Waves from Albany to Columbus in 2003 as the erstwhile Waves replaced the Columbus River Stixx, an affiliate of the Cleveland Indians that had played twelve years in the city. Since the arrival of the Catfish, rumors have persisted that they will move to another city. The possibilities have included Columbia, South Carolina; Evansville, Indiana; Mansfield, Ohio; Bay City, Michigan; and Jackson, Tennessee. Heller snuffed those rumors, at least for the time being, in July of 2005 when he signed a three-year lease extension to keep the Catfish in Columbus through 2008. The owner said, "Over the past year, I have received more than a dozen proposals from groups or individuals seeking to buy the Catfish, as well as invitations from other communities to consider relocation. We have turned down every one. We are in this for the long haul."

As a fan of minor league ballparks, here's hoping that Heller is indeed committed to making baseball work in Columbus and that the Catfish fans eventually start turning out at the ballpark in greater numbers. Golden Park deserves a place in the minor league game. The well-landscaped main entrance offers a classic redbrick façade and an orange-and-green tower that was built in 1995 in preparation for the 1996 Summer Olympic Games. In fact the whole stadium and its surrounding area got a makeover before hosting the Olympic softball tournament. In addition to remodeling the stadium and temporarily converting the field into a softball diamond, the $3.5 million project built several auxiliary softball fields within the South Commons Complex. After the United States won the gold medal, defeating China 3–1 in the championship game, work began to return the Golden Park field to baseball dimensions and build a new softball stadium within the complex for future use. While all this work took place, the River Stixx spent the 1996 season at Columbus State University's Ragsdale Field.

Golden Park offers a small grandstand behind home plate. In left field there's a wall of billboards behind the home run fence, sealing in the park from the traffic and commotion on Victory Drive. Beyond the batter's eye in center, Georgia pines grow tall and true. On the first base side of the stadium, the Chattahoochee, visible from the top of the seating bowl, meanders past. The stadium's most unique feature is its unpadded brick outfield fence. Undeniably, the wall provides a classy backdrop for a game, but if a highly touted prospect ever runs into it and breaks an arm, you can bet there will be plenty of irate fans questioning the logic of this ballpark quirk.

The original Golden Park stood where the current park stands. It was built in 1926 and saw steady use until 1951 when the city rebuilt it entirely. The parks were both named in honor of T. E. Golden, a local businessman who was a prominent supporter of minor league baseball back when the game was struggling to lay down permanent roots in the city. Columbus fielded its first minor league team in 1885, when the Southern League's Columbus Stars played at Stars' Park. After an eleven-year hiatus, a Southern Association team played at Stars' Park in 1896 and 1897. Then, after another lengthy drought, the city fielded a team in the Georgia State League in 1906. Columbus played in the South Atlantic League from 1909 through 1917, then went without a team until the first Golden Park opened in 1926. Since then, the city has never gone more than five years without a professional team. Minor league baseball has been played in Columbus every year since 1969 without interruption. The local team was affiliated mainly with the St. Louis Cardinals in the 1930s, 1940s, and 1950s; then with the New York Yankees in the 1960s; the Houston Astros from 1970 through 1990; the Indians from 1991 through 2002; and the Los Angeles Dodgers from 2003 through 2006.

Prior to the 2007 season, the team switched to its current affiliation with the Tampa Bay Devil Rays.

Among the hundreds of big leaguers that have played minor league ball in Columbus are such Hall of Famers as Babe Ruth, Hank Aaron, Willie Mays, and Ernie Banks, who visited as opposing players. A wall of fame at the stadium honors these and other legends. As for Columbus players who went on to star in the major leagues, the list includes Bob Gibson, Roy White, Mike Easler, Floyd Bannister, Fritz Peterson, Bill Doran, Glenn Davis, Luis González, Ken Caminiti, Darryl Kile, and Richie Sexson.

Game Day

Getting to the Park

Columbus is 100 miles southwest of Atlanta, just across the river from Alabama. Golden Park lies within the South Commons Sports Complex, which also includes eight softball fields, a football stadium, and a civic center. The complex is south of the downtown historic district, along the city's Riverwalk. From I–185, take the Manchester Expressway exit and follow the expressway to Veterans Parkway. Turn left onto Veterans Parkway and follow it to the ballpark. From Route 431, take 280 East and Golden Park will appear on the right shortly after you cross the river. Parking is free in the large lot that Golden Park shares with the Columbus Civic Center.

Inside the Park

The seating bowl can hold 5,000 people. It extends only to the corner bases on either side. The original bowl offers six rows of red Field Box Seats, then a midlevel concourse, and then blue Reserved Seats beneath the grandstand roof. Along either baseline there are four rows of Reserved Seats, then bleachers that sell as

General Admission. Section A is at first base, Section G is behind the plate, and Section M is at third base.

There are climate-controlled luxury suites on either side of the press box, and there is a picnic area in left field foul territory. The members-only Catfish Club is located above the front office in right field foul territory. The club serves beer and wine, while also offering restrooms, balconies, and air-conditioned viewing locations.

For regular fans the concession stands behind the seating bowl serve spicy brats, foot-long hot dogs, quesadillas, chicken sandwiches, funnel cakes, dill pickles, and reduced-price items for kids.

The Golden Park Experience

The mascot is Hook, a fuzzy blue creature who got dredged up from the bottom of the Chattahoochee shortly after Columbus became a Dodgers affiliate and ditched Fred Stixx, the fox that had served as the old mascot.

The Catfish offer "Thirsty Thursday" drink promotions all season long, as well as Military Appreciation Nights that cater to the servicemen and -women at nearby Fort Benning.

Golden Park

How's this for an interesting promotion? As the 2005 season wound down, the Catfish put a season's worth of game-used uniforms to good use, auctioning them off to fans through an online bidding process. The minimum bid allowable was $100. Among the home and away jerseys scoffed up by fans were those that had belonged to 2004 first-round draft picks Scott Elbert and Blake DeWitt, and 2005 South Atlantic League all-stars Blake Johnson and Travis Denker. Johnson's number 45 and Chad Bailey's number 14 fetched the most, garnering $200 each, while sixteen other jerseys were claimed by fans.

On the Town

Columbus is located on the eastern bank of the Chattahoochee River, which separates it from Phenix City, Alabama. Fort Benning, a 182,000-acre U.S. Army Training and Doctrine Command installation, lies south and west of Columbus.

The **Columbus Riverwalk** was conceived by city planners in the late 1980s and has been a work in progress ever since. When completed, the Riverwalk will span 20 miles from Lake Oliver Marina in the north to the Fort Benning Infantry Museum in the south. There is an access point on the right field side of Golden Park where a set of stairs leads to the river.

A visit to Columbus State University in the northeast quadrant of the city allows fans to check out **Charles F. Ragsdale Field**, the 1,000-seat stadium that the River Stixx called "home" in 1996 while their field hosted the Olympic Softball competition. The CSU Cougars play in the NCAA Division II Peach Belt Conference. The Cougars enjoy one of the finest clubhouses in all of college baseball, thanks to late River Stixx owner Charles B. Morrow, who built the facility to minor league specs during his team's stay on campus.

STATE MUTUAL STADIUM

Rome Braves

Class A, South Atlantic League
(ATLANTA BRAVES)

State Mutual Stadium
755 Braves Boulevard
Rome, Georgia
706–378–5144

Although it's somewhat of a stretch to compare any 5,000-seat minor league ballpark with a 50,000-seat major league stadium, the similarities between the home parks of the South Atlantic League's Rome Braves and National League's Atlanta Braves are apparent. To begin both parks honor baseball's all-time, non-steroid-aided home run king, Hank Aaron, with street addresses that reference his 755 dingers. Rome's State Mutual Stadium sits at 755 Braves Boulevard, while Atlanta's Turner Field sits at 755 Hank Aaron Drive. The ballparks also make similar first impressions on fans. Visitors arriving at the ballpark in Rome find a large plaza just outside the main gates. This popular pregame meeting place features multicolored bricks laid in concrete, decorative trees, and sculptures that depict one child standing in the batter's box staring out at an imaginary pitcher and another squatting behind the plate in a catcher's stance. Similarly, Turner Field offers an expansive brick plaza where fans find sculptures honoring Aaron, Ty Cobb, and Phil Niekro. The stadium façades are also similar, as they both feature classy redbrick columns. State Mutual Stadium offers several brick pillars connected by green steel beams that form inviting arches. The upper level consists entirely of brick, while the lower level offers a cream-colored base between the pillars.

Inside the seating bowl State Mutual Stadium offers dark blue stadium chairs, reminiscent of the ones at Turner Field. Like Turner, State Mutual prides itself on offering a technologically sophisticated environment. The minor league yard features more than one hundred television monitors so that fans don't have to miss a single pitch while waiting in line for concessions or walking to the restrooms.

As for the fields themselves, the outfield dimensions in Rome mimic those in Atlanta, measuring 330 feet down the left field line, 380 feet in left-center, 401 feet in straightaway center, 390 feet in right-center, and 335 feet down the right field line.

That's about where the similarities end. Turner Field was built at a cost of $235 million, funded mostly by the 1996 Olympic Committee, while State Mutual Stadium was built for less than $15 million, funded mostly by Floyd County. Turner Field offers multiple seating levels, even in the outfield, while State Mutual Stadium offers a one-deck seating bowl around the infield. There is some outfield seating in Rome, though, as seating berms wrap around the foul poles and continue into home run territory.

State Mutual Stadium was completed in time for the 2003 season. Its opening marked the debut of minor league baseball in Rome, a small city 70 miles northwest of Atlanta. Previously, Atlanta's affiliate in the South Atlantic League had played in Macon, at Luther Williams Field, a historic ballpark that has stood since 1929.

Today's Rome Braves average crowds in the area of 3,500. They won the South Atlantic League championship in their inaugural season buoyed by many of the players who would later emerge on the major league level just in time to lead the Atlanta Braves to the 2005 National League East title when many pundits thought the team might be finally losing its edge. Among the former Rome Braves to reach the big leagues are Jeff Francoeur, Brian McCann, Kyle Davies, Chuck James, Blaine Boyer, Dan Meyer, and José Capellan.

In addition to hosting the Braves, State Mutual Stadium is also the site of an annual college baseball game called the "Rome Braves Invitational." The game pits two different Georgia college teams against one another to raise money for charity. State Mutual Stadium is also used as a concert venue, as Mark Willis, Marty Stewart, and Lorrie Morgan have all played the field.

Game Day

Getting to the Park

From Atlanta, take I–75 North to exit 290 (Rome/Canton) and then take a left off the exit onto Highway 411. Follow Highway 411 into Rome, then turn right onto the Highway 1 loop (Veterans Memorial Highway). The stadium will be on the right at the intersection of Veterans Memorial and Riverside Parkway. Parking in the stadium lot costs $3.00.

Inside the Park

State Mutual Stadium lists an official seating capacity at 5,105. The seating bowl rises rather steeply around the infield, offering six rows below an interior walkway and then twelve rows above the walkway. All of the seats are comfortable stadium chairs and every one provides a personal cup holder on the back of the chair in front of it. On the left field side of the diamond, the lower-level seats extend only to where the infield dirt meets the outfield grass. On the right field side, the seats continue into medium-depth right field foul territory. Section 100 is behind the plate. Sections with odd numbers continue down the right field line, ending at Section 117. Sections with even numbers continue down the left field line, ending at Section 112.

The five sections of lower seats between the dugouts—100 through 104—sell as Club Seats, while the lower seats along the baselines—105 through 117—sell as Field Level Seats. Above the narrow midlevel walkway, the second-level seats are elevated to allow for a view over the pedestrian traffic. Here, fans find three sections of Club Seats behind home plate—Sections 200 through 202—and four sections of Box Seats along either baseline. A General Admission ticket provides access to lawn seating and a limited number of outfield picnic tables.

The fourteen luxury boxes sit on either side of the press box, offering outdoor seats right behind the last row of Boxes. A small roof extends over these outdoor seats.

The stadium's Three Rivers Club is open to club members only during games but is open to the public for lunch each day.

The main concourse runs beneath the seating bowl, offering a Kids Zone and several history boards that tell the story of how professional baseball came to Rome. These boards also commemorate the 2003 championship team. The concession stands feature boiled peanuts, which I found to be just as disgusting as the ones served at Turner Field, as well as tasty Mexican offerings and delicious hand-dipped roast beef sandwiches.

The State Mutual Stadium Experience

The superfans in Rome sit behind the Braves dugout on the third base side where they keep track of the home pitcher's strikeouts. These loyal diehards refer to themselves collectively as the K-Club.

The Rome mascots are not Romulus and Remus, but Romey and Roxie, two friendly blue creatures that reportedly spend their winters swimming in the three rivers that surround downtown Rome, the Etowah, Oostanaula, and Coosa. Romey is a male creature and Roxie is a female. Think Grover, the Muppet, only bigger, with yellow hair, and wearing a baseball jersey.

On Thursdays the gates open at 5:00 P.M., allowing fans to watch batting practice and enjoy live music and drink specials at the Budweiser beach party area in left field.

On the Town

A visit to Rome offers plenty of opportunities for outdoor recreation, thanks to its three rivers and its proximity to the **Chattahoochee National Forest,** which is just north of town. Directly behind the outfield fence at State Mutual Stadium, a scenic path along the Oostanaula River connects the stadium to Rome's historic downtown. Just remember to apply lots of bug spray before setting out on your hike.

Sports history buffs can venture to Macon and/or Royston, during their time in Georgia. In Macon the **Georgia Sports Hall of Fame** (301 Cherry Street) honors baseball legends like Cobb and Aaron, while also celebrating the accomplishments of Georgia natives in a variety of other sports. An interactive area allows visitors to kick field goals, slam-dunk basketballs on lowered hoops, and ride in a NASCAR simulator. The Hall is open Monday through Saturday from 9:00 A.M. until 5:00 P.M. and on Sundays from 1:00 until 5:00 P.M.

Royston, meanwhile, offers two sites related to the life and death of "the Georgia Peach." **The Ty Cobb Museum** (461 Cook Street) is located inside the Joe A. Adams Professional Building of the Ty Cobb Healthcare System. The museum offers some of Cobb's old baseball equipment, some old photos, Cobb's childhood Bible, his dentures, and one of his favorite shotguns. No word on whether this is the same shotgun that Cobb's mother famously used to shoot his father to death as he sneaked through the bedroom window one night. Cobb, his mother, father, and sister all rest at **Rose Hill Cemetery** (Route 17).

GRAYSON STADIUM

Savannah Sand Gnats

Class A, South Atlantic League
(NEW YORK METS)

Grayson Stadium
1401 East Victory Drive
Savannah, Georgia
912–351–9150

With a history that dates back to 1926, when it opened as "Municipal Stadium," Grayson Stadium is one of the oldest minor league parks in the country. It also happens to be one of the largest in low-A, with room for more than 8,000 people. The park's old-time charm has not, unfortunately, translated into success at the box office in recent years. The Sand Gnats average barely 1,000 fans per game and finish ahead of only a handful of teams in the annual full-season minor league attendance ledger.

Hopefully a much-needed renovation of this historic ballpark is on the way, one that will increase the number of stadium chairs, while subtracting some of the bleachers, and one that will add the luxury boxes and party areas the home team needs to survive in the modern era. When the Gnats signed a three-year lease extension with Savannah to stay at Grayson Stadium through 2008, it was with the understanding that the city would renovate the ballpark. I for one will be keeping my fingers crossed, because it would be a shame to see this wonderful old park lose its team, but at the same time, I can see that the park, as it currently stands, has nearly outlived its era.

The stadium sits within Daffin Park. As fans approach, they encounter tree branches laden with hanging Spanish moss and a faded redbrick façade with arched entranceways. Inside, the majority of seating consists of bleacher benches beneath a large grandstand roof. A tiny press box hangs down from the roof. Tall oaks rise behind the outfield fence. A massive bank of wooden bleachers runs across left field home run territory. The bleachers saw steady use when the facility housed high school football games between Savannah High and Benedictine High back in the 1940s, 1950s, and 1960s, but these days they serve no purpose other than to rattle and clank whenever a home run to left crashes onto their planks.

In 1927 and 1928 Municipal Stadium was home to the Savannah Indians, an unaffiliated team in the old Southeastern League. Prior to the stadium's official opening as a minor league venue, it hosted an exhibition between the defending World Series champion St. Louis Cardinals and the defending American League champion New York Yankees in the spring of 1927. Babe Ruth and Lou Gehrig both played in the game, which the Cardinals won 20–10 (yes, they played baseball, not football), then Ruth headed north and hit a record 60 dingers during the regular season.

In 1932 the Boston Red Sox used Municipal Stadium for spring training, then headed north and posted an all-time franchise-worst 43–111 record. The next spring, the Red Sox opted to train in Sarasota, Florida, instead.

Savannah fielded a team in the South Atlantic League for the first time in 1936; it then became an affiliate of a major league team for the first time in 1937 when it hooked on with the Pittsburgh Pirates. Baseball came to a halt in Savannah during the war years but bounced back in 1946 when the Indians drew more than 200,000 fans to a ballpark that had been rebuilt and renamed during the wartime layoff. William L. Grayson was a Savannah resident and hero of the Spanish-American War who led the effort to rebuild Municipal Stadium after its wooden grandstand was destroyed by a hurricane in the late-1930s. The structure that we find in Daffin Park today was actually built between 1940 and 1946. The project took such a long time to complete due to delays and complications brought about by World War II.

In 1957 the Yankees stopped by Savannah again, this time to play the Redlegs, a Cincinnati Reds affiliate, in an exhibition game. Mickey Mantle hit a long home run in an 8–4 New York win.

From 1971 through 1983 the Savannah Braves played Double-A ball at Grayson Stadium, then in 1984 Savannah became a South Atlantic League outpost again as the city began an affiliation with the St. Louis Cardinals. The Savannah Cardinals won back-to-back league championships in 1993 and 1994, then left town.

The Sand Gnats debuted in 1996 as an affiliate of the Dodgers and won the South Atlantic League crown in their first season. In 1998 they switched to a player development contract with the Texas Rangers. The Gnats became a Montreal Expos affiliate in 2003 and continued to serve the team when it became the Washington Nationals. This seemed like a match made in heaven. It made perfect sense for a farm team known as the "Gnats" to serve a big league team known as the "Nats." But in 2007 the Savannah club switched from a relationship with the Nationals to one with the New York Mets. Oh well.

The Gnats have sent a higher-than-usual number of alumni north toward the bigs during their first decade of existence, including Adrián Béltre, Hank Blalock, Eric Gagne, Travis Hafner, Kevin Mench, Laynce Nix, Carlos Peña, and Ryan Zimmerman.

Game Day

Getting to the Park

Savannah is in eastern Georgia, just south and west of South Carolina. From I–95, take I–16

East to the 37th Street exit. Turn left at the end of the ramp and follow 37th Street to Abercorn Street. Turn right onto Abercorn and then left onto Victory Drive; the ballpark will be on the right at Daffin Park. There is free parking at the stadium.

Inside the Park

While Grayson Stadium is a massive facility by South Atlantic League standards, its seating options are rather limited. Four rows of Box Seats span from dugout to dugout. Other than these comfortable stadium chairs, the rest of the seats are General Admission bleachers. The good news is the bleachers have back supports, both underneath the roof in the main grandstand and down the right field line where there is no covering. The fact that Grayson Stadium has about 500 Reserved Seats, however, combined with the stadium's sheer size, surely contributes to the difficulty Savannah has in attracting crowds. Currently, there is no reason for local fans to order tickets in advance because there are always plenty available on game day and one ticket is as good as the next. Fans have no reason to plan ahead, and the Gnats are often forgotten as other summer activities consume the Savannah fans.

The concession counters are located beneath the main grandstand. The menu includes grilled sausages, grilled bratwurst, and boiled peanuts. A photo exhibit on the concourse is called "Farm Team: A Season in the Minors." It was created by a local photographer, Joseph Gamble, who spent the 2004 season shadowing the Gnats and snapping pictures that capture the essence of the minor league game.

Along the right field line, an old football press box has been converted into a festive rooftop-style bar. This is a great place to mingle, sip a beer, eat a burger, and peer down at the field over the top of the two levels of chain-link fence protecting the fans down in the bleachers from foul balls.

The Grayson Stadium Experience

In order for a city to willingly identify its baseball team with a biting pest like a sand gnat, you've got to figure its residents have a good sense of humor and a major insect problem on their hands. Indeed, the folks in Savannah have both. During the spring and fall, folks who venture outdoors at night are besieged by sand gnats—tiny bugs that leave itchy red dots on any exposed skin they can sink their suckers into. When the gnats retreat during the heat of summer, bloodthirsty mosquitoes take their place as the city's resident nuisances.

The Savannah club adopted its unusual nickname in 1996 when the Dodgers brought South Atlantic League baseball back to town after the city went without a team in 1995. Before the 1996 season, the team's general manager polled local residents for name suggestions, then whittled the list down to five finalists: the Hammerheads, Sea Turtles, Shadow, Thrashers, and Sand Gnats. After a subsequent fan poll revealed that more than two-thirds of local baseball fans liked "Sand Gnats" the best, the team designed a logo and started producing merchandise that reflected Savannah's new baseball identity.

Ironically, what began as a cross between a joke and a cry for help turned into a major marketing boon for the Sand Gnats. While Savannah's players were winning ball game after ball game en route to the South Atlantic League championship in 1996, fans across the baseball universe were scarfing up Sand Gnats gear. The team's popular logo, which depicts a cartoon gnat swinging an oversized baseball bat, helped Savannah sell more than $100,000 worth of hats, T-shirts, miniature bats, vanity plates, key rings, bracelets, lapel pins, and other novelties during the course of that magical, if itchy, first season. The team ranked among the top-ten minor league teams in merchandise revenue in 1996, and while sales have leveled off since then, the Gnats continue to sell more logo-bearing merchandise than most teams. So make like a Savannahan and embrace this winged pest if you can. Visit the clubhouse shop at the stadium and buy some gear. Just be sure to bring a bottle of bug spray to the game.

On the Town

Savannah is a historic city that offers downtown carriage rides and trolley tours through charming tree-lined streets. Visitors marvel at the widely divergent Colonial, Georgian, Greek Revival, and Gothic architecture of the city's landmark buildings. But this is also a modern city with fine dining and lively nightlife at scenic **Riverfront Plaza,** just a block north of the historic district.

Fans rolling into town after a long car ride can stretch their legs in **Daffin Park**, which houses ball fields, basketball courts, and walking trails, in addition to Grayson Stadium. For those seeking a quick pregame or postgame meal, there are a slew of restaurants a few blocks east of Daffin Park on Victory Drive and a few blocks north on Waters Avenue. The options within walking distance include fast-food chains, pizza joints, subs shops, and casual Chinese and Japanese restaurants.

BRIGHT HOUSE NETWORKS FIELD

Clearwater Threshers

Class A, Florida State League
(PHILADELPHIA PHILLIES)

Bright House Networks Field
601 Old Coachman Road
Clearwater, Florida
727–442–8496

Although Bright House Networks Field is located in one of professional baseball's most saturated markets, it does much to distinguish itself from its peers. The Tampa Yankees, Dunedin Blue Jays, Sarasota Reds, and Lakeland Tigers are all located within a short drive of Clearwater, as are many short-season Gulf Coast League teams. Yet the home of the Threshers offers an atmosphere and gameday experience unlike any other in these parts. Consequently, a steady flow of fans has passed through the Clearwater turnstiles since Bright House opened in 2004 as the spring training home of the Phillies and Florida State League home of the Threshers.

Bright House meshes well with the region's architectural heritage, projecting a Mediterranean affect common among Gulf Coast edifices. The tan stucco exterior offers an array of visually appealing towers and arches and is adorned with decorative tiles depicting palm fronds and the four different fonts of the letter *P* that have served as the Phillies logo since 1883. A thatch-roofed tiki bar inside the stadium also embraces the Gulf Coast ethos.

As fans approach the stadium, they encounter a wishing well, at the center of which stands a life-sized statue of Phillies great Steve Carlton in mid-delivery. If you have a nickel to spare, toss it into the fountain and wish for the home team to win, or if you're running low on cash, roll up those sleeves, reach into the tepid waters, and fish out enough pocket change to buy yourself a cheesesteak and soda inside.

Aside from presenting as warm and inviting a first impression as any ballpark in Florida, Bright House is unique in another way. Unlike most of Florida's minor league yards, Bright House offers seating around the entire field, not just along the baselines. Following the example set by many of the ballparks constructed in the 1990s, Bright House offers a sloped seating lawn behind the outfield fence where fans can plop down on blankets and watch the game in comfort. The field is sunken below street level, allowing for the grassy berm to begin right at the top of the outfield fence. On a hot summer night, the lawn offers a laid-back and breezy atmosphere from which to watch a game.

HOK, the same firm that designed the regular season home of the Phillies, Citizens Bank Park, drew up the blueprints for Bright House Field. The Clearwater project cost $30 million, which was funded by the Phillies, the City of Clearwater, Pinellas County, and the State of Florida. Previously, the spring Phillies and their Florida State League team played at Jack Russell Stadium, about 4 miles from where Bright House now lies.

The regular season team that called Jack Russell "home" was known as the Clearwater Phillies. The team was renamed the Threshers in 2004 as part of a rebranding effort conducted in conjunction with the opening of the new ballpark. A thresher is a type of shark found in abundance in the warm Gulf waters.

Clearwater fans seem to agree that Bright House is a marked improvement over Jack Russell Stadium. They do miss some things about the old yard, though, like its warning track made of crushed seashells, its delightful palm garden beyond the outfield fence, and its old-fashioned pipe organist. Organist Wilbur Snapp was ejected from a Florida State League game in 1985 for playing "Three Blind Mice" after a first base ump made a call against the home team. Jack Russell, in case you're wondering, was a Clearwater resident and former big league pitcher who led the charge to construct a minor league ballpark in Clearwater back in 1954.

The old ballpark, like the neighborhood surrounding it, had fallen into disrepair in its later years, making the construction of a new park necessary for the survival of spring and summer baseball in this coastal community.

Game Day

Getting to the Park

Clearwater is 15 miles west of Tampa, located on the Gulf of Mexico. Bright House Field is on Old Coachman Road, which runs parallel to U.S. Route 19. The ballpark is 1 block west of the highway. Take the Drew Street exit off Route 19 and follow Drew to the parking lot at the corner of Old Coachman. There is ample parking on Joe DiMaggio Field, across the street from the stadium.

Inside the Park

Because the seating bowl surrounds the entire field, every seat is close to the action. There is nothing even close to resembling a nosebleed seat, as the farthest row from the field is Row 23. The 7,000 fixed seats are all angled nicely toward the infield, and the placement of the main concourse behind the last row of seats results in minimal view-blocking pedestrian traffic.

The seating bowl begins at Section 101 in deep right field and continues down the line to Section 111 behind the plate, then ends at Section 120 in medium-depth left. Sections 108 through 114, between the dugouts, offer Pre-mium Box Seats, while the rest of the stadium offers Box Seats.

The General Admission lawn has room for 1,500 people in home run territory. The most coveted spot is in right field, where folks can see the game as well as the scoreboard atop the lawn in left. Three picnic terraces along the line in deep left offer metal tables and benches from which fans can watch the game while eating dinner.

Frenchy's Tiki Bar in left field home run territory situates fans above the outfield fence in five tiered rows near the foul pole. The effect is similar to the one offered by the Green Monster seats at Fenway Park. Fans looking for a truly unique viewing area and for easy access to fruity frozen drinks all game long should arrive early and stake out their bar stools.

Bright House offers four food courts. The Shortstop Grill serves a kids menu on the concourse above third base. The Strike Out Cafe in right, and Bullpen Grill in left, serve standard ballpark fare. The Home Run Grill behind home plate serves LaSpada Steaks. South of Philadelphia, this is the best cheesesteak you'll find at a professional baseball game. Served on a fresh hoagie roll, the sandwich is piled high with sliced rib eye and gooey cheese. Order a pint of Yuengling to wash it down.

After you stain your favorite road-trip shirt with steak juice and cheese runoff, head to the expansive clubhouse store in left field to freshen up your wardrobe. A month or two later, when you're making a swing through the Midwest League, your Thresher T-shirt will make for a great conversation starter. "The thresher is only the *third* most common species of shark in the Gulf waters," you can authoritatively tell dumbstruck Midwesterners who have never even seen the ocean before. Then extricate yourself from the conversation before they ask you what the two most common species are.

The tiki seats at Bright House

The Bright House Experience

The quintessential Bright House experience is found on the outfield lawn and at the Tiki Bar where a block-party atmosphere often prevails. Mingle with other fans. Sip a few frosties. Check out the sun-bathing young ladies. Make plans for after the game. Scamper after a home run ball. Heckle the opposing outfielders. Lay back and listen to some tunes.

On the Town

Clearwater Beach sits on a barrier island just off the coast. Gulf to Bay Boulevard (Route 60) can be a nightmare to navigate during weekends and picture-perfect beach days, but once you manage to get across the bridge and find a parking spot, the beach is beautiful. **Frenchy's Saltwater Cafe** (416 East Shore Drive) is one of several popular beachside nightclubs worth a visit.

If you find your appetite for scrapple and other fine Philadelphia delicacies whetted by your steak sandwich at the game, satisfy your stomach's urgings with a trip to **Capogna's Dugout** (1653 Gulf to Bay Boulevard), **Philly's Famous Cheese Steaks** (4375 East Bay Drive), or **Lenny's Diner** (21220 Route 19 North). All three establishments cater to Phillies fans in March and Threshers fans in the summer.

JACKIE ROBINSON BALLPARK

Daytona Cubs

Class A, Florida State League
(CHICAGO CUBS)

Jackie Robinson Ballpark
105 East Orange Avenue
Daytona Beach, Florida
386–257–3172

The Daytona Cubs play their home games at one of the most historic sites in minor league baseball. Not only has the hardball been tossed and swatted on this tiny island in the midst of Florida's Intracoastal Waterway since 1914, but the field hosted an important event in the dissolution of the National Pastime's color barrier. And three decades before that, the field played a humorous role in the evolution of Florida as baseball's premiere spring training destination. Additionally, baseball in Daytona has weathered several major hurricanes, including two that nearly spelled an end to the game's presence on the Daytona City Island.

All of this history helped Jackie Robinson Ballpark earn a place in the National Register of Historic Places, but certainly the most important aspect of the ballpark's long life relates to its role in ending segregation in the game. In 1946 the International League's Montreal Royales, a Brooklyn Dodgers affiliate, brought Jackie Robinson south to training camp. But the second baseman was promptly barred from exhibitions in many Florida cities due to laws prohibiting blacks from participating in sporting events against whites. In Sanford a police chief threatened to stop a game if Robinson didn't leave the field. In Jacksonville a stadium

was padlocked an hour before a scheduled start to prevent the Royales from entering. And so on. But at Daytona's City Island Ballpark, Robinson was allowed to take the field for the first time in an exhibition against the Dodgers on March 17, 1946. Robinson went on to make the Royales roster and win the International League MVP award. The next year, he broke the major league color barrier.

Back in the ballpark's second year of existence, in 1915, it earned the attention of the baseball world when another, lighter, event played out on its lawn. Toward the end of spring training, so the story goes, young Brooklyn right fielder Casey Stengel bet manager Wilbert Robinson that Robinson couldn't catch a baseball dropped out of an airplane. Robinson, a former catcher, took the challenge and told Stengel to find a plane, find a pilot, and make the drop. He'd show the entire team he could indeed pull off the feat. During practice the next day, Stengel told his manager that a plane would be arriving soon and that the pilot had been instructed to drop a ball from an altitude of 500 feet. Then Stengel warned his manager that the pilot had told him a falling ball would be traveling at such a velocity that it might rip right through Robinson's catcher's mitt and bore a hole through his head. "Hogwash," Robinson said. Soon the plane flew into view, and when it was directly over the infield, the pilot ejected a small sphere from the cockpit. Robinson staggered under the falling object, waited, waited, and . . . splat. The manager began screaming uncontrollably when he realized that he was covered by what appeared to be chunks of his own pulpy flesh. But then he realized he was only covered with the pulp of a grapefruit. Stengel had substituted a piece of citrus fruit for a ball. The Dodgers had a good laugh over the practical joke, except for Stengel, who was sentenced to run laps around the field for the rest of the afternoon, and Robinson, who fretted over his impending laundry bill. Soon word of the gag spread throughout baseball, and players began referring to the Sunshine State's spring training circuit as the Grapefruit League. The nickname has stuck ever since.

One of the Daytona ballpark's darkest days occurred in 1960 when Hurricane Donna blew across the state and did $75,000 worth of damage to its wooden bleachers and grandstands. Some people lobbied to tear down the park, but eventually the city commission voted to restore it. In 1962 the current grandstands and press box were built. The home clubhouse that sits in left field was built in 1972 to serve the Montreal Expos who used the site as their spring training base at the time. The next year, the left field bleachers were built. The ballpark was renamed in honor of Robinson in 1990, and the statue of Robinson with two small children that appears outside the ballpark was installed a year later. In 1999 Hurricane Floyd destroyed much of the metal roof above the home plate grandstand. Later, the roof was restored as part of a project that also renovated the right field grandstands.

In December of 2004, the Daytona Cubs and the Daytona Beach broke ground on a renovation project that at the cost of one and one-half million dollars added a scenic riverwalk outside the stadium, a new lighting system, and an old-fashioned manually operated scoreboard modeled after the one at Wrigley Field in Chicago.

Jackie Robinson Ballpark

Prior to the arrival of the Florida State League's Cubs in 1993, Daytona's team had served as an affiliate of eleven other major league teams.

Game Day

Getting to the Park

Daytona Beach is on Florida's Atlantic Coast, 55 miles northeast of Orlando. The ballpark is 3 miles east of I–95 and 2 miles east of Daytona International Speedway. Exit I–95 at International Speedway Boulevard and follow Speedway Boulevard to the stadium's free parking lot.

Inside the Park

This cozy ballpark can accommodate 4,200 fans in a seating bowl around the infield. All of the seats sell as General Admission. The home plate grandstand and first base grandstand offer stadium seats, while the third base grandstand offers bleachers. Although the first base side is more comfortable, the third base area offers sparkling views of the Halifax River and International Speedway Bridge.

The picnic area is down the right field line. The concession stands beneath the third base bleachers offer a delicious smoked barbecue plate.

The Jackie Robinson Ballpark Experience

Before the game fans looking to stretch their legs can take a walk along the river to enjoy the scenic Intracoastal Waterways. This is a unique setting, so breathe it in during a pregame stroll, then stop by the outside bar and have a beverage or two.

Also worth checking out is the Jackie Robinson Museum, located on the premises. The museum, which opened in 2005, offers information and artifacts related to Robinson's remarkable and courageous contributions to the game.

Once the game begins keep an eye out for the big fuzzy bear known as Cubby, and see if you can pick out "Front Row Joe," a local superfan who hadn't missed a game in more than ten years.

On the Town

As motor-sports enthusiasts know, the **Daytona International Speedway** is one of the most famous venues in the racing world. The 2½-mile track, which opened in 1959, offers events throughout the summer, serving the Rolex Sports Car Series, the NASCAR Busch Series, and the NASCAR NEXTEL Cup Series. More than just offering racing, the 480-acre complex houses Daytona USA, an interactive tourist destination billed as the "ultimate motor-sports attraction." Here, daily visitors find "Acceleration Alley," where they can compete against one another in 80-percent-scale stock cars; "Daytona Dream Laps," where they can simulate racing in the Daytona 500; and "Thunder Road," where a motion simulator takes them on a high-speed, 360-degree fantasy lap around the racetrack. Daytona USA is open daily from 9:00 A.M. until 7:00 P.M. I suggest visiting before lunchtime, not after, lest you make the same mistake I did and soil a perfectly good road-trip shirt in the simulator.

A trip to **Daytona Beach** is also part of the Daytona experience. College students on spring break have been flocking to the beach for decades. It is located on the long barrier island just east of Jackie Robinson Ballpark. To access the beach follow Speedway Boulevard to the Main Street Bridge, which crosses the Halifax 1/4 mile north of the park. In addition to the 500-foot-wide beach, visitors enjoy a festive boardwalk and the Ocean Pier Casino.

KNOLOGY PARK

Dunedin Blue Jays

Class A, Florida State League
(TORONTO BLUE JAYS)

Knology Park
373 Douglas Avenue
Dunedin, Florida
727–733–9302

Nestled in the quaint coastal Florida town of Dunedin, Knology Park offers baseball fans a delightfully cozy ballpark experience. The park sits on a quiet two-lane road that leads to Dunedin's charming little Main Street district. It blends in perfectly with its small-town surroundings, meshing with the local library, school buildings, VFW post, churches, and homes. The ballpark exterior features beige bricks, a pale blue sunroof, and a small brick decorative tower that rises above the ticket windows. Iron gates and brick pillars divide the concourse behind the stadium at ground level from the sidewalk outside.

Knology Park is small by Florida State League standards, and smaller still by Grapefruit League standards. Although it is the home of the spring training Toronto Blue Jays as well as the Dunedin Blue Jays, the park seats just 6,100 fans, making it the smallest facility in the Florida State League and second-smallest spring training venue. Only Kissimmee's Osceola County Stadium, which hosts the Houston Astros in March, is smaller than Knology Park.

The Dunedin High School baseball team also plays its home games at Knology Park. In addition to their regular home schedule, the Falcons host a sixteen-team single-elimination

tournament called the Dunedin Spring Classic at Knology Park each March. Imagine that, high school kids getting to play regularly on the same diamond as big league stars like B. J. Ryan and Roy Halladay.

On entering Knology Park fans find cramped concourses, narrow aisles, small bathrooms, and minimal legroom between the rows of blue seats. But the proximity of the seats to the field makes it easy to overlook these inconveniences. And the crowds here are generally on the small side, so the ballpark doesn't feel as cluttered as it would if it ever actually sold out. The field offers barely any foul territory, making for great views from anywhere in the seating bowl that surrounds the infield and stretches just a short distance into the outfield on the right side. Appropriately, the outfield dimensions are also cozy. It takes a poke of just 325 feet to reach the clubhouse facility that sits beyond the fence in right, while the distance to reach the lush green trees that grow behind the fence in left field is just 335 feet. The power alleys measure 363 feet, and it's just 380 feet to dead-center. The press box behind home plate is fittingly tiny. The light banks across the outfield have just two rows of bulbs on them. Until recently, the ballpark featured a manual scoreboard, but that was replaced in the latest round of renovations by a small electronic board in left-center.

If Knology Park sounds like it offers fans a chance to hearken back to a simpler era and enjoy the game without the modern array of distractions, it's no wonder. It is endowed with as much history as any yard in Florida. The ballpark, which for years was known as "Grant Field," was built in 1930 when Dunedin mayor Albert Grant oversaw its development. A federal grant in the amount of a whopping $250 in 1933 enabled Dunedin to clear additional land and enlarge the outfield. After four decades as an amateur field, the expansion Toronto Blue Jays arrived in Dunedin in 1977 and christened the field with a 3–1 Grapefruit League victory over the Mets. At the time the stadium offered metal bleachers that could seat just 3,400 fans.

In 1990 Dunedin spent $2.5 million to strip away the old bleachers and install seats throughout the stadium, add two new sections of seats in right field, and weatherproof the press box behind home plate. On March 3, 1990, the stadium was renamed, "Dunedin Stadium at Grant Field."

In 2000 Dunedin, the Blue Jays, and Pinellas County pooled their resources to embark on another round of ballpark renovations, highlighted by the construction of the two-story clubhouse in right field and the remodeling of the exterior façade. As part of the $13.5 million project, Dunedin built a new five-field practice complex for the spring training Blue Jays a few miles north of the stadium.

In 2004 Dunedin finally abandoned the memory of old Albert Grant, renaming the field that had used his name for seven decades after Knology Incorporated, a Georgia-based communications company that provides cable television service throughout Florida. Score another one for Big Business, even in small-town America, where history and tradition still seem to mean something.

Game Day

Getting to the Park

Dunedin is 5 miles north of Clearwater. From U.S. Route 19, follow Sunset Point West, and then turn right onto Douglas Avenue, which leads to the stadium. If the small parking lot behind the grandstand is full, steer your road-trip car into one of the small lots beside or across the street from the stadium. There is also a limited amount of on-street parking along Douglas Avenue between Knology Park and Main Street.

Inside the Park

Knology Park offers just two different seating options: Reserved Seats, which appear in seven rows below the midlevel walkway, or General Admission Seats, above the walkway. You really can't go wrong with either option. Both locations have comfortable plastic seats and both are available at dirt-cheap prices. At the time of this book's publication, a front row Reserved Seat right down on the field cost just $5.00, while a General Admission ticket cost just $3.00. Where else in the world can you find three hours of decent family entertainment for such a pittance? Section 103 is behind the home dugout on the first baseline, Section 106 is directly behind the plate, and Section 109 is behind the visitors dugout.

Take the money you save at the ticket window and treat yourself to a frozen margarita or a bottle of Corona at the small tiki bar on the first base side of the concourse, or load up a plate full of pulled pork at the Bullpen Barbecue on the third base side.

While milling around beneath the stadium, check out the "Dunedin to the Show" exhibit on the third base side that pays tribute to all of the former Dunedin Blue Jays who eventually played in the major leagues, either with Toronto or another big league team. The wall of fame offers baseball-shaped blue plaques that display the name of each player and the year or years he spent playing A-ball in Dunedin. Lloyd Moseby, Mike Timlin, and Vernon Wells are just a few of the players honored here. The concourse is also decorated with large colorful banners that depict many Toronto Blue Jay stars who spent time in Dunedin during spring training. These baseball-card-style banners honor such former Torontonians as Devon White, George Bell, Dave Stieb, Tom Henke, Shawn Green, Joe Carter, Carlos Delgado, Tony Fernández, and manager Cito Gaston.

The Knology Park Experience

If you're a sucker for campy promotions and intra-inning sideshows, you might find your trip to Dunedin a bit of a letdown. Dunedin doesn't have rock 'n' roll riffs blaring through the loudspeakers or a JumboTron, or a roller coaster for the kids to enjoy on the concourse. There's no balloon-bending clowns and no scantily clad dance team. "Schedule Magnet Give-Away Night" is about as wild and wacky as things get in Dunedin. On the other hand, if you enjoy a friendly atmosphere that puts the focus on the field where the greatest game on earth is being played, you'll be happy you made the trip to this little community.

On the Town

Dunedin is the oldest town on Florida's Gulf Coast, dating back to a founding in 1870. Follow Douglas Avenue past the ballpark and turn left onto Main Street and you'll soon find yourself in the heart of the town's charming business and entertainment district. The Dunedin strip features colorful buildings in the Mediterranean tradition that house boutiques and specialty restaurants. **Skip's Bar and Grill** and **La Cantina Mexican Grill** are both safe bets for a pregame bite to eat. If you're looking to take a stroll, follow Main Street to its end and you'll find a scenic marina.

WILLIAM HAMMOND STADIUM

Fort Myers Miracle

Class A, Florida State League
(MINNESOTA TWINS)

William Hammond Stadium
14400 Six Mile Cypress Parkway
Fort Myers, Florida
239–768–4210

A circle completed itself when Fort Myers opened William Hammond Stadium in 1992 and lured the former Miami Marlins to town to become the Fort Myers Miracle. The Miami franchise had roots that traced all the way back to a debut season as the Fort Myers Palms in 1926. After enjoying a successful first season in Fort Myers as a Class D, Florida State League franchise, the Palms departed for greener pastures in Miami. Nearly seven decades later, the arrival of the Florida Marlins as a big league expansion team in the Miami area served as the catalyst for bringing the franchise home. That's not to say Fort Myers had been without professional baseball for all of the years in between. Quite the contrary, a number of different minor league teams played hardball in this Gulf Coast resort town through the decades. Those teams played at Terry Park, which, while historic, had grown too small and rundown to serve as a viable home for minor league baseball much longer. For that reason the opening of Hammond Stadium was seen as a major coup for the city. The ballpark was named after the assistant county administrator who championed the effort to build it. A plaque honoring Mr. Hammond is located on the veranda atop the ballpark's main entrance ramp.

The new stadium harkened not only the arrival of the Miracle, but also the return of big league spring training to the "City of Palms." Fort Myers welcomed the Minnesota Twins to town during the 1992 spring season, and fans have made the Twins one of the top draws in the Grapefruit League ever since. Fort Myers baseball fans have enjoyed watching highly touted youngsters like Brad Radke, Torii Hunter, Jacque Jones, Justin Morneau, and Joe Mauer cut their teeth at Hammond Stadium as minor leaguers, then return for spring training in future years as big leaguers. The stadium has also hosted a number of concerts through the years, including appearances by headliners like Willie Nelson, Bob Dylan, Carlos Santana, and the Beach Boys.

The success of the Twins in Fort Myers prompted a second major league team to move its spring training base to the city, as well. The Red Sox play their Grapefruit League games at nearby City of Palms Park. Each March, the Twins and Red Sox vie for the coveted mayor's cup, awarded to whichever teams wins the season series between the two teams.

The exterior of Hammond Stadium is more appealing than the inside. As fans approach on Six Mile Cypress Parkway, they are welcomed to the ballpark grounds by a nicely landscaped pond beyond the right field fence. Long home runs by left-handed batters occasionally splash down here, as evidenced by the ball or two that can usually be spotted floating along the shoreline. After leaving their road-trip cars in sections of the parking lot with names like Puckett Avenue and Carew Court, fans confront a spectacular main entrance. A 200-foot-long palm-tree-lined path leads to a three-level stadium façade designed in the Old Florida tradition. This beige front has been favorably compared with Churchill Downs, the Kentucky Derby racetrack. An expansive waterfall built into the front of the stadium serves as a pregame meeting spot for fans and as a unique place to snap a picture or two. On passing through the turnstiles, fans climb a staircase to access the concourse that runs behind the stadium, midway up the seating bowl. Inside, the sight lines are adequate, but unless you have a soft spot for concrete and aluminum, the design probably won't do much for you.

Game Day

Getting to the Park

Fort Myers is in southwest Florida on the Gulf of Mexico. From I–75, take exit 131 and follow Daniels Parkway West. Turn left onto Six Mile Cypress Parkway, which leads directly to the Lee County Sports Complex.

After parking, early arrivals can watch the two teams take batting practice on the practice fields adjacent to the stadium. There are also batting cages tucked beneath the left side of the stadium where players sometimes take pregame swings.

Inside the Park

Hammond Stadium can hold 7,500 fans. All of the seats appear around the infield in a sharply rising seating bowl. There are sixteen rows of Box Seats below the midlevel walkway, sixteen rows of Reserved Bleachers above the walkway. Sections 101 and 201 are located just beyond first base, Sections 108 and 208 are directly behind home plate, and Sections 115 and 215 are located just beyond third base. A larger-than-usual protective net covers the seats behind home plate, so fans hoping to catch a foul ball should sit down the baselines.

The concourse behind the seating bowl is decorated with posters of current Twins players and photos of baseball greats like Babe Ruth and Sandy Koufax. The concession stands use real charcoal to cook Johnsonville brats and turkey legs. The ballpark pickle is also popular. The beer garden on the third base side of the concourse sells Black and Tans, and other drafts.

The souvenir stand on the first base side offers Miracle garb and plenty of Red Sox and Yankees gear.

The Hammond Stadium Experience

Owing to a lively ownership consortium that includes Mike Veeck and entertainers Bill Murray and Jimmy Buffet, the Miracle offers an array of innovative promotions each season. One hilarious promo was "Cork Night," when the team handed out sheets of cork to the first 505 fans to enter Hammond Stadium in honor of Sammy Sosa, who had just been caught using an illegally corked bat during a game. Sosa had 505 career homers at the time. I wonder if the team contemplated handing out syringes when accusations later swirled that Sosa had used anabolic steroids. Another quirky promotion was "Costanza Night," in honor of the loveable loser played by Jason Alexander on *Seinfeld*. George Constanza had recently figured out that his life would progress more smoothly if he consistently did the opposite of what his gut instincts said he should do. So the Miracle did everything backward, paying fans to park, charging less for Box Seats than for Reserved Seats, and running the scoreboard's line score from the ninth inning to the first. After the game the players even asked the fans for autographs. Another time, Hammond Stadium celebrated actor Al Pacino's birthday, April 25, with "Godfather Night," when fans and ushers dressed up like gangsters and bloody horse's heads were handed out to fans as souvenirs.

A live dog roamed Hammond Stadium's foul ground from 1992 until 2004, occasionally peeing on the field. After the aged pup took off for that big happy farm in the sky, Miss A-Miracle arrived to replace him as the new

William Hammond Stadium

Miracle mascot. She's a big orange hound who loves to dance and shoot water guns into the crowd. For a glimpse at another dog, fans should check out the superfan named Dianna, who sits in the third base Boxes. This ardent Miracle booster brings a stuffed pup to the ballpark in honor of the team's original four-legged friend.

On the Town

The spring training home of the Boston Red Sox is just 5 miles from Hammond Stadium. With gorgeous royal palm trees lining the out-field fence, a low seating bowl, and a colorful press box that displays the logos of all twenty-nine major league teams and the Kansas City Royals, City of Palms Park (2201 Edison Avenue) is a nicer place to watch a game than Hammond Stadium. Unfortunately, it only sees action for fifteen games a year during spring training, then, sadly, sits dormant throughout the summer when the Miracle has Florida State League territorial rights.

Another ballpark worth visiting in Fort Myers is venerable **Terry Park**, located on Palm Beach Boulevard between Terry Avenue and Palmetto Avenue. This is where the franchise that would become the Miracle played its debut season in 1926. The ancient field was awarded National Historic Landmark status in 1995. It is part of a community sports complex. Terry Park was built in 1906 and named after Tootie McGregor Terry, a local woman who donated the land for the facility. In addition to hosting the Palms for one season, the ballpark was also home to a number of other minor league teams and to the spring training Philadelphia Athletics (1925–1936), Cleveland Indians (1939–1941), Pittsburgh Pirates (1955–1968), and Kansas City Royals (1968–1987). During the Royals tenure, the field was renovated to offer an artificial playing surface just like the one that used to exist in Kansas City. Thankfully, the carpet was ripped up and real grass was planted when the Royals left town.

The practice fields around Terry Park are great places to take some batting practice if you have a bucket of balls and a few shaggers. But if you lack these road-trip essentials and still want to take a few hacks, don't despair. **Mike Greenwell's Family Fun Park** (35 Pine Island Road) is located in nearby Cape Coral. Yes, the park is owned by the same hard-nosed left fielder who used to collide regularly with Ellis Burks in the Boston Red Sox outfield. In addition to batting cages, the amusement park houses a miniature golf course, four go-cart tracks, an arcade, a kiddy maze, and an ever-popular fish feeding dock. It is open from 10:00 A.M. until 10:00 P.M., Sunday through Thursday, and until midnight on Friday and Saturday.

THE BASEBALL GROUNDS
OF JACKSONVILLE

Jacksonville Suns

Class AA, Southern League
(LOS ANGELES DODGERS)

The Baseball Grounds of Jacksonville
301 A. Philip Randolph Boulevard
Jacksonville, Florida
904–358–2846

The Jacksonville Suns currently enjoy the longest-running relationship between any team and the Southern League. Jacksonville has been a member of the Double-A circuit since 1970, and before that it was a stalwart in the old South Atlantic League, which eventually became the Southern League in 1966. These days, Jacksonville is not only the ranking member of the league, but it's also the league's top draw, thanks to the Baseball Grounds, a sparkling $34 million ballpark that opened in 2003. Built by the city as part of the Better Jacksonville Plan, the new park replaced Sam T. Wolfson Stadium, a 1950s-era facility that had served the city well for five decades but had outlived its era.

Buoyed by their new digs, the Suns easily surpassed their all-time single-season attendance record in their first season at the Baseball Grounds, drawing a league-best 359,979 fans in 2003. The previous high for the franchise was set in 1998 when 254,882 fans turned out at Wolfson Stadium. The Suns led the Southern League in attendance again in 2004 and 2005, and soon whispers began to swirl that Jacksonville was a top candidate to make the jump from Double-A to Triple-A should any club in the International League look to relocate. Per-

haps because the city of Jacksonville foresaw just such an opportunity someday presenting itself, the Baseball Grounds is built to Triple-A specifications. So, who knows? The Durham Bulls made the jump from Class A to Triple-A recently, and the Round Rock Express jumped from Double-A to Triple-A, so it could certainly happen in Jacksonville, a city that already has an NFL team, and that has a population of nearly a million people.

The Baseball Grounds is part of the same sports complex that included Wolfson Stadium until it was demolished in November of 2002. The ballpark is just a few blocks east of the St. Johns River—which runs behind the first base side—nestled between Alltel Stadium and Veterans Memorial Arena. The main entrance at the corner of A. Philip Randolph Boulevard and East Adams Street projects an urban retro design, rather than the type of Floridian façade prevalent among Sunshine State parks. Regal brick columns rise to support wrought-iron decorative arches beneath the exposed steel trusses of the roof. With all of the large open spaces between the pillars at ground level and up on the second level where the openings allow air to flow freely into the back of the main concourse, I couldn't help but think that the stadium exterior looked a little like a parking garage.

After walking up a set of steps inside the ballpark gates, fans arrive at a concourse that runs atop the last row of seats and behind the left field berm and right field bleachers. Around the infield twelve indoor/outdoor luxury boxes cover the concourse, supported by green steel girders. The back wall of the concourse is laid with brick. Such design flourishes contribute to the type of old-time atmosphere we've come to expect from the ballpark's architect, HOK.

The playing field offers a few quirks to make it unique. The distance from home plate to the left field foul pole is just 321 feet, while the distance to the right field pole is only 317 feet. The fence in right-center measures 420 feet, however, making it the deepest center field in Double-A. The fence in front of the bleachers in right is only 4 feet high near the foul pole, but grows increasingly higher as it extends toward center, eventually maxing out at 15 feet high. Then it abruptly drops down to a more conventional 8 feet in deep right-center. As a result left-handed pull hitters enjoy the double benefit of a close fence and a low fence down the right field line, while gap hitters have to hit the ball a very long way to clear a very tall fence.

As for the peripheral sight lines, those seated on the right field side can see the roof of the football stadium hovering high above the third base grandstand and the brick steeple of St. Andrews Church protruding sharply into the sky a bit farther down the left field line.

The Suns have been affiliated with the Los Angeles Dodgers since 2000. Before that, they enjoyed a six-year relationship with the Detroit Tigers, and before that, they spent four years as a Seattle Mariners farm club. The team had a PDC with the Montreal Expos from 1984 through 1990, and one with the Kansas City Royals from 1972 through 1984. Among the many Jacksonville alumni are such household names as Randy Johnson, Andres Galarraga, Brett Boone, and Mike Hampton.

In the nine years before they joined the Southern League in 1970, the Suns belonged to the International League, and were affiliated with the Cleveland Indians, St. Louis Cardinals, and New York Mets. Tommy John, Nolan Ryan, and Tom Seaver were just three of many future major leaguers to hone their skills in Jacksonville during this time. Before that, Jacksonville spent more than half a century in the old South Atlantic League, starting with the debut of the Jacksonville Jays in 1904, and continuing with

just a few interruptions through the final season for the Jacksonville Braves in 1961. Future Hall of Famers Hoyt Wilhelm, Hank Aaron, and Phil Niekro all played for Jacksonville.

Game Day

Getting to the Park

Jacksonville is located in northeast Florida along the Atlantic coast. The next closest Southern League team is nearly 300 miles away in Mobile, but if you follow I-95 South for a couple of hours, there are plenty of Florida State League ballparks to visit. The Baseball Grounds is part of the Jacksonville Sports Complex, situated a couple of miles east of downtown on the banks of the St. Johns River. From I-95 South, take the Martin Luther King Parkway exit and then follow Gator Bowl Boulevard around Alltel Stadium to the ballpark. From I-95 North, take the Emerson Street exit and then follow the Hart Bridge Expressway to the Sports Complex exit and follow the signs to the ballpark. The city charges $5.00 for parking.

Inside the Park

The Baseball Grounds offers 6,000 stadium chairs in the main seating bowl and 5,000 bleacher/berm seats in the outfield. Unless the popular Christian rock group Avalon is putting on a show after the game, you should have no problem scoring at least a berm ticket when you visit Jacksonville, and the berm at this park is pretty good.

The seating bowl is anything but symmetrical. The seats extend all the way out to the foul pole in right field, appearing in twenty-two neat rows in sections all angled nicely toward the infield. On the other side of the diamond, the seats extend only halfway down the line before ending in shallow left. Section 101 is just past third base, Section 107 is behind home plate, and Section 120 is deep in the right field corner. Instead of appearing in large sections like on the right field side, the seats on the third baseline are broken up into lower boxes and upper boxes consisting of eight rows each. The only reason I can imagine for setting up a park this way is to make it easier for the hardcore fans behind the Suns dugout to get in and out of their seats for concessions. In any case the first couple of rows between the dugouts contain the Dugout Box Seats, while the remainder of the seats in Sections 102 through 113, between home plate and the corner bases, sell as Home Plate Boxes. Section 101 in left and Sections 114 through 120 in right sell as Reserved Seats.

The berm begins in left field foul territory where the seating bowl ends. This raised lawn juts out into foul territory, bringing fans quite close to the left foul line, then it rises to form a big round mound behind the foul pole. This unique perch is known as the "knuckle." The mound then abruptly levels off into a more traditional berm that spans from left to center field. The bleachers extend from deep right-center to the right field foul pole.

The Suns offer an impressive array of ballpark treats, highlighted by pulled pork sandwiches, smoked sausages, Philly cheesesteaks, Pete's Famous Hot Dogs, Cuban sandwiches, Bubba Burgers, chef's salads, and fruit salads. Fans can also visit the air-conditioned Sundowner Lounge on the upper level to have a drink and watch the game.

The team store is on the concourse behind home plate. The outfield playground has an inflatable obstacle course and a practice putting green.

The Baseball Grounds Experience

Any time a Suns player hits a home run listen for the ding of the ballpark's trademark railroad bell. The person who rings the bell is none other than Suns owner Peter D. Bragan Sr., the affable octogenarian who made his fortune as an auto dealer in Birmingham before moving to Jacksonville and buying the Suns in 1984. Aside from Mr. Bragan, the next biggest fan at any Suns game is sure to be Southpaw, the floppy-eared hound who serves as the team mascot. The ushers also do their part to make the ballpark experience warm and inviting, wearing distinctive Panama hats.

The Suns treat their fans to fireworks shows every Friday night, while kids get to run the bases after every Sunday game. On "Throwdown Thursday," fans enjoy $1.00 Budweiser specials. "Report Card Day" is a popular annual promotion each June, when kids can bring their grade sheets to the ballpark to receive discounted ticket and concessions. Students with perfect attendance and/or a B average or higher are honored on the field in a pregame ceremony. A couple of times each year, a Christian concert follows the game. These nights draw especially large crowds. During the 2005 season, a local record 11,000 people turned out to hear "Avalon" play.

On the Town

Before games Suns fans congregate at the **Amsterdam Sky Cafe** (234 A. Philip Randolph Boulevard), right across the street from the ballpark. Owing to the park's location in an isolated sports complex, there really isn't much else to do around the park, aside from checking out the old church and the other historic buildings in the neighborhood.

Although Wolfson Stadium has been destroyed, baseball fans still have the chance to check out an historic ballpark during their stay in Jacksonville. **Durkee Field** (1701 Myrtle Avenue) served Jacksonville's minor league team and its Negro League Red Caps during the early 1900s. It also served as the spring training site of big league teams like the New

York Yankees, Philadelphia A's, and Brooklyn Dodgers. It was known at various times as Barrs Field, James P. Small Memorial Stadium, and Red Caps Field. Today, the park is preserved as an historic monument. Its arched brick façade and covered concrete seating bowl date back to the early 1920s. Visitors will be interested to note that the seating bowl is misaligned . . . or maybe the field is. Rather than sitting between the first and third base stands, home plate is in front of the first base grandstand.

ROGER DEAN STADIUM

Jupiter Hammerheads and Palm Beach Cardinals

Class A, Florida State League

(FLORIDA MARLINS AND
ST. LOUIS CARDINALS)

Roger Dean Stadium
4751 Main Street
Jupiter, Florida
561–630–1828

Roger Dean Stadium's claim to fame is that it hosts more than 170 professional baseball games per year. During spring training both the Florida Marlins and St. Louis Cardinals call the ballpark "home," meaning that every single day of the spring schedule offers a Grapefruit League game in Jupiter. Not a bad deal for local baseball fans, eh? After the big league teams head south and northwest respectively, the Florida State League season begins and Roger Dean Stadium does double duty again, serving as the home of both the Jupiter Hammerheads and the Palm Beach Cardinals. As if that weren't enough baseball to satisfy one small community's hankering for hardball, the stadium and its twelve adjoining practice fields host a number of national high school tournaments each year, like the USA Baseball Junior Olympic Championship in June and the Perfect Game/*Baseball America* World Wood Bat Championship in August. No, Roger Dean was not some visionary baseball enthusiast who helped create this hardball hotbed. He is a local auto dealer who shells out $100,000 a year for the stadium naming rights.

Roger Dean Stadium is nothing remarkable to look at from an aesthetic standpoint. It matches the cream stucco of most Abacoa Town Center edifices and has the same green aluminum roof that seems to cap all of the other buildings in this planned community. Roger Dean Stadium's most distinguishing exterior features are its arched entranceways and palm-encircled courtyard. The bricks that make up the courtyard are etched with the names of fans who paid $100 to support the ballpark's construction. Some of the bricks include short words of wisdom or praise for the teams that play at Roger Dean Stadium. Others memorialized lost loved ones. Others quote scripture. Others offer indiscernible gibberish.

Inside, the ballpark is very clean and well kept. A large press box level wraps around the diamond from dugout to dugout, also housing six luxury suites on the first base side. There is no sunroof over the seats although the press box provides a shadow for some fans during day games. The outfield view is dominated by two large clubhouse buildings, one beyond the fence in left that belongs to the Marlins and Hammerheads and one beyond the fence in right that belongs to the major league and minor league Cardinals. According to legend Mark McGwire hit a 450-foot home run during the very first game at Roger Dean Stadium in 1998, knocking loose a chunk of stucco from the upper levels of the building in left. Once spring training ended, Big Mac hit 70 home runs in the regular season.

When the ballpark originally opened, it served as the spring training site of the Cardinals and Montreal Expos. In 2002 the Expos and Marlins swapped spring sites, so that the Marlins could play closer to their regular season home in Miami. The Fish took up residence with the Cards at Roger Dean, while the soon-to-be-extinct Expos headed north to Space Coast Stadium in Viera. The Jupiter Hammerheads, who had previously been an Expos affiliate, became the Marlins Florida State League franchise at that time. The Palm Beach Cardinals debuted in the league a year later.

Game Day

Getting to the Park

Jupiter is 10 miles north of West Palm Beach on Florida's Atlantic coast. From I–95, take exit 83 and follow Donald Ross Road east. Turn left onto Central Boulevard, go through the rotary, and then turn right onto Main Street. On entering the Town Center complex, follow the signs to the park. The parking garages within the complex charge $3.00 per car.

Inside the Park

Roger Dean Stadium can hold 6,806 fans, but during the Florida State League season, crowds rarely approach capacity. The main

seating bowl extends deeper into left field than it does in right. There are fourteen rows of Field Box Seats below a midlevel walkway and twelve rows of Loge Box Seats above the walkway. Section 102 is in medium-depth right field, Section 113 is behind the plate, and Section 124 is in deep left.

The bleachers in deep left field foul territory can accommodate about 1,000 fans. The bleachers are angled nicely back toward the infield, but unless you have some compelling reason to sit near the Marlins bull pen, which is located parallel to the left field line, you're probably better off sitting closer to the infield. On the other side of the diamond, there is a small grass berm in left field foul territory that

Roger Dean Stadium

provides a comfortable viewing location for 300 lucky fans per game and a raised party deck for group functions.

The concession stands are on the concourse beneath the grandstand. The menu includes the trademark all-beef Roger Dean Dog, which weighs in at one-third of a pound. That's right, this wiener packs almost six ounces of meat. It's pretty tasty too, but the bratwurst steamed in beer is even better. Other treats include a couple of different barbecue items and smoked turkey legs. As for the beer, there is a decidedly Budweiser flavor at each stand. Here's guessing that has something to do with the long-standing relationship of the Cardinals with Anheuser Busch.

The Roger Dean Experience

The hardworking folks at Roger Dean Stadium do a nice job of keeping the mood light and festive, while also providing plenty of activities to keep the kids occupied.

Hamilton R. Head and Robbie the Redbird are constantly causing trouble and getting laughs, while a Fan Fest area on the right field concourse features a batting cage, a bouncy-house, and a speed-pitch booth. My fastball sat consistently at 56 miles per hour, but after I polished off my second Dean Dog, I touched the low-60s a couple of times. I'd be interested to hear from readers who notice that the Dean Dog has the same effect on their velocity.

An interesting ballpark tradition occurs in the middle of the third inning when the Roger Dean front office staff tosses free bags of peanuts out the press box window to the fans seated in the home plate Loge.

If you happen to find yourself accosted by slobbering canines on arriving at Roger Dean Stadium, that means you've shown up on one of the "Dog Days of Summer." On these nights fans are encouraged to bring their best friends to the ballpark. The pups receive free admission and treats. My best advice is to hold your Roger Dean Dog extra high on these nights and to watch for puddles on the concourse.

On the Town

Roger Dean Stadium is located within the confines of a planned community known as Abacoa Town Center. The ballpark sits a few miles south of downtown Jupiter on land that previously belonged to the MacArthur Foundation. All of the earth-toned stucco buildings that surround Roger Dean Stadium were built after the ballpark opened in 1998. The ubiquitous semi urban streets around Roger Dean offer a sixteen-screen Cineplex, office buildings, parking garages, an outdoor amphitheater, restaurants, boutiques, a cigar store, town houses, apartment buildings, and plenty of baseball fields. Florida Atlantic University's John D. MacArthur Campus is also located in Town Center.

J. J. Muggs Stadium Grill is a popular pre-game and post-game watering hole for baseball fans, directly across the street from the stadium. This sports bar specializes in grilled pizzas, Black Angus burgers, buffalo wings, and cold drafts.

Visitors looking to experience the wonders of Florida's Treasure Coast can head to **Bowling Rocks Beach**, **Jupiter Beach Park**, **Juno Beach Park**, or **Carlin Park Beach**, all of which are located just a few miles northeast of Roger Dean Stadium. Those looking for a bit more of an adventure can head south to West Palm Beach.

JOKER MARCHANT STADIUM

Lakeland Tigers

Class A, Florida State League
(DETROIT TIGERS)

Joker Marchant Stadium
2125 North Lake Avenue
Lakeland, Florida
863–686–8075

Far removed from the hustle and bustle of the coastal resort towns that host many of the franchises in the Florida State League, Joker Marchant Stadium offers an unpretentious minor league setting in the heart of orange country. Lakeland has been hosting Florida State League baseball since 1919, with just a few lapses through the years. It has also been the spring training home of the Detroit Tigers since 1934, except during the war years of 1943 through 1945 when travel restrictions forced the Tigers to train in Evansville, Indiana.

Prior to the construction of Joker Marchant Stadium in 1967, Lakeland's minor league and spring training yard was Henley Field, which debuted in 1923. Originally, Lakeland had an affiliation with the Cleveland Indians, but after the minor league Indians moved away in 1927, the Tigers came to town. Henley Field still stands just a mile away from Joker Marchant, and still sees regular use as an amateur venue. While Joker Marchant Stadium was being renovated in 2002, the Lakeland Tigers retuned to Henley Field to play their home games.

The City of Lakeland shelled out $500,000 in 1967 to build Joker Marchant Stadium, in an effort to better accommodate the throngs of Detroit snowbirds flocking to town each spring

during the Tigers successful 1960s era that culminated in a world championship in 1968. The ballpark was named after Marcus Thigpen Marchant, the Lakeland recreation director who led the effort to build the stadium and was famous for his inventive practical jokes. The new ballpark was built on the former site of the Lodwick School of Aeronautics, an abandoned World War II flight school.

In addition to the main stadium, the Tiger Town complex houses five practice fields, administrative and clubhouse buildings, batting cages, and a three-level dormitory that can sleep up to 190 minor leaguers during spring training.

Joker Marchant seated just 4,200 fans at the time of its opening, but renovations through the years have raised its capacity to 8,500, while also making it more a modern and fan-friendly park. A 1972 project made night games possible, adding a $160,000 lighting system, while a 1987 project built a towering bank of bleachers down the left field line, increasing capacity to 7,027. More recently, an $11 million project completed in 2003 built a hillside seating berm in left field home run territory, added 1,000 new field-level seats, and added six luxury boxes behind home plate. The luxury boxes are named after famous Tigers Ty Cobb, Charlie Gehringer, Hank Greenberg, Willie Horton, Al Kaline, and Hal Newhouser.

The stadium exterior is as distinctive as it is delightful. The tan stucco façade embraces a Mediterranean flare and features two tall towers, one that houses an elevator shaft and one that houses a stairway, both providing access inside the stadium to the press box and luxury suites. The tower nearest to the main entrance is adorned with a colorful mural of a real-life tiger peeking through a cluster of palm fronds, getting ready to pounce on its prey. As fans move past this noble creature and toward the turnstiles, they find a large patio made of bricks and concrete inlayed with the Tigers old-English *D*.

Inside the stadium the sight lines showcase a row of palm trees at the back of the berm in left, a scoreboard that displays the old-English *D* and the old-English *L* of the Lakeland Tigers in right-center, and eight covered batting tunnels beyond the fence in right. Most of the outfield fence is plastered with advertising signs, except for a stretch in right-center where see-through chain-link allows fans to peer into the home and visiting bull pens. A small roof provides cover for the fans in the last rows of grandstand seats, while openings in the back of the stadium allow for a cool breeze to waft into the stadium on hot summer nights. Fans who sit in the top rows of the bleachers along the left field line can peer over the cloverleaf of practice fields beyond the right field fence and see motor boats tracing ripples in the surface of Lake Parker, ½ mile away.

The Lakeland field is large by Class A standards, measuring 340 feet down the lines and 420 feet to center, but the stands are cozy and intimate, and the first row of seats is right down at field level, bringing every row that much closer to the action.

The Lakeland Tigers enjoyed an historic 2005 season, posting an 85–48 record, the best mark in franchise history. The team's .639 winning percentage was tops among all professional baseball teams in North America that season. When it came time for the best-of-five-game Florida State League championship series though, the Tigers lost a five-game tilt against the Palm Beach Cardinals, dropping the finale in ten innings.

Game Day

Getting to the Park

Lakeland is in the middle of the Sunshine State, between Viera on the east coast and Tampa on the west coast. Tiger Town is 2½ miles south of I–4, not far from the groves of orange trees that fill the air with a sweet scent during the spring. From I–4, take exit 19 and follow Route 33 to the stadium. Parking is free.

Inside the Park

The main seating bowl starts at Section 100, just past the infield dirt on the first base side, continues to Sections 105 though 108 behind home plate, and ends at Section 112, even with the third base bag. The Field Box Seats are in first three rows between the dugouts in Sections 105 through 108. The Box Seats appear behind the Field Boxes and in the rest of the section below the midlevel walkway. Behind the walkway, Reserved Seats provides comfortable plastic seats, many of which are beneath the roof. The Bleachers in left field foul territory provides thirty-four steep rows of metal benches. The lower ten rows offer back supports. The upper twenty-four rows have no backs. The Berm in left is raised and nicely sloped, allowing for excellent views of the game and of the ospreys that circle their nests in the outfield light banks. The shaded concourse beneath the stands offers Little Caesar's Pizza, provided as a nod to Detroit Tigers owner Mike Ilitch, who made his fortune in the pizza business before buying the team. If you're not in the mood for bland stadium pizza, visit the Joe Lewis barbecue stand instead, where there are full slabs of ribs and mouthwatering pulled pork sandwiches. Other stands sell boiled peanuts, baked potatoes, roasted corn, turkey legs, and fresh fruit. The strawberry shortcake at the Dairy Queen stand is quite popular.

A display case on the right field concourse houses all six of the different baseball caps and jerseys currently being worn by players in the Detroit system, including gear from the big league Tigers, Triple-A Toledo Mud Hens,

Joker Marchant Stadium

Double-A Erie SeaWolves, high-A Lakeland Tigers, low-A West Michigan Whitecaps, short-season Oneonta Tigers, and Gulf Coast League Tigers.

The Joker Marchant Stadium Experience

Rather than bombarding fans with blaring sound bites and flashy promotions, the Lakeland Tigers cultivate a simple old-time ballpark atmosphere that keeps the focus on the game.

Southpaw is the local mascot. This happy go lucky cat dances on the dugout roof during the traditional playing of "Cotton Eye Joe" each night. And when a member of the home team hits a long ball, the public-address system plays the team's theme song, "Who Are the Baddest Cats in Town?" as the player circles the bases.

Summer-long promotions include "Way Back Wednesdays," when hot dogs, peanuts, and popcorn sell for $1.00, and "Thirsty Thursdays," when twelve-ounce beers sell for just $1.00.

On the Town

Lakeland is a quaint but growing city of nearly 80,000 people. It offers streets named after different types of citrus fruit, access to eleven lakes, a bird sanctuary, an art museum, and a symphony hall. **Henley Field** (Florida Avenue) is home to the Florida Southern University Moccasins and the Lakeland High School Dreadnoughts. Its exterior is similar in appearance to Joker Marchant, but much smaller, featuring tan stucco, tiny ticket windows, and small palm trees flanking its narrow entrance. A metal roof covers the cozy bleachers behind home plate.

To visit another historic ballpark while you're in citrus country, head 10 miles east to Winter Haven and see where the Cleveland Indians play their spring training games. **Chain O' Lakes Park** (500 Cletus Allen Drive) sits on the banks of Lake Lulu, where it has hosted Grapefruit League play since 1966. The Indians arrived in 1993, supplanting the Boston Red Sox as Winter Haven's spring resident. Chain O' Lakes Park offers a unique seating bowl built right into the side of a large hill, making it unnecessary for the stadium to offer much in the way of exterior walls. The effect is similar to the design of Dodger Stadium in Los Angeles, only on a much smaller scale.

TRADITION FIELD

St. Lucie Mets

Class A, Florida State League
(NEW YORK METS)

Tradition Field
525 Northwest Peacock Boulevard
Port St. Lucie, Florida
772–871–2100

Fittingly, Tradition Field is a scaled-down version of Shea Stadium. That may sound like a slight, since many baseball fans consider Shea Stadium to be one of the worst major league stadiums, but I don't mean it to be. The truth is that watching a Florida State League or Grapefruit League game at this little park in St. Lucie is much more enjoyable than enduring one at the behemoth in Queens. Still, there are several aesthetic similarities between the two stadiums.

Shea's main problems are that its upper levels are too high above field level and that the streets surrounding it are filthy. Neither is the case at Tradition Field. The seating bowl rises more steeply from field level than at most Florida State League venues, but there's only one level, not four like at Shea, and the last row of seats in St. Lucie is still closer to the field than any second-level seat in New York. And instead of the postindustrial wasteland of auto repair shops surrounding Shea, practice diamonds and a swampy pine forest surround Tradition Field.

So, now that I've defended Tradition Field, let me get back to explaining how it is similar in some ways to its big league cousin. To begin the field itself replicates the dimensions of the field in New York—338 feet down the lines, 371 feet to the power alleys, and 410 feet to straightaway center—and offers the same

royal blue outfield fences. These similarities may seem harmless enough, but the games would certainly be more interesting for fans if Tradition Field offered asymmetrical dimensions as many new parks do. Outside, both stadiums rise up from barren parking lots. Neither is part of a neighborhood. Both are the tallest structures on their blocks. Tradition Field's main entrance is more attractive than the one at Shea, at least at ground level. But the ballpark's redbrick base soon gives way to gray concrete, blue-and-white trim, and then an ugly gray cement sunroof. Like Shea Stadium, Tradition Field offers lots and lots of concrete inside and out and fails to evoke the elegance and charm that many ballparks do. The outside of the stadium is not particularly attractive. The inside is nondescript. If these seem like subjective criticisms, too ephemeral to quantify, take a trip to Holman Stadium in Vero Beach, or Joker Marchant Stadium in Lakeland, or Al Lang Field in St. Petersburg, and I think you'll get a better idea of what this ballpark lacks. It just doesn't feel very warm and inviting. There's nothing to distinguish it and make it special.

I was hoping that the renovation Tradition Field underwent prior to the 2004 season would provide for some paint to that ugly concrete roof. The $10 million project did give the main entrance a face-lift and add the already-mentioned redbrick base, but the roof stayed the same and the ballpark's aura didn't change all that much. The renovation also added three rows of premium Box Seats at field level, a new lawn seating area in right field, a new protective screen behind home plate, and three luxury boxes atop the seating bowl behind home plate. The New York Mets footed $7.25 million of the bill for the work, while the balance came from a new hotel tax in St. Lucie.

Prior to the renovation the ballpark had been known as Thomas J. White Stadium since opening in 1988. Mr. White donated the original one hundred acres on which the ballpark and its accompanying practice fields were built. Lest readers make the assumption that St. Lucie was trying to lend an air of royalty to the ballpark by renaming it in memory of all of the great traditions in Mets history, I should tell you that the stadium dropped Mr. White's name in order to fetch some easy naming-rights dollars from Core Communities, the developer of a nearby residential and commercial complex called "Tradition Place."

One final note regarding the atmosphere outside the stadium: Don't be alarmed by the row of granite monuments you'll encounter as you cross the parking lot and approach the main gates. They're not actual tombstones. I repeat, Casey Stengel is not buried in the Tradition Field parking lot. Nor is Rusty Staub (who to my memory is still alive). One of these quasi tombstones memorializes Andy Kaplan, the first general manager in St. Lucie Mets history; another remembers Joe McShane, who coordinated the initial effort to build the stadium; another pays tribute to the people of St. Lucie who voted to support the tourist tax that helped finance the original $11 million stadium project; and another remembers George McClelland, a public relations director with the team from 1988 through 2000.

Tradition Field

Game Day

Getting to the Park

Port St. Lucie is on Florida's so-called Treasure Coast, 25 miles south of Vero Beach, and 35 miles north of Jupiter. From I–95, take the exit for St. Lucie Boulevard. Drive east on St. Lucie Boulevard to the first traffic light and turn left onto Northwest Peacock Boulevard. Follow Peacock for 2 miles and the stadium will be on the right.

Inside the Park

The main seating bowl extends only as far as the corner bases on either side. A walkway bisects the seating bowl, offering Box Seats below and Reserved Seats above. In both locations comfortable blue stadium seats fill the rows, the rows are roomy, and the seating bowl rises steeply. Section 101 is behind home plate. The odd-numbered sections continue down the first baseline to Section 113. The even-numbered sections continue down the third baseline to Section 112.

A bank of metal bleachers—rarely filled, except during spring training—sits along the foul line in right field. Across the diamond a picnic terrace begins where the seats end after third base.

The most unique and interesting place to sit at Tradition Field is on the small grass berm in right field home run territory. Beginning behind the fence and a narrow gap, the lawn slopes back nicely to allow fans—whether sitting or standing—an excellent view of the action. Decorative palms provide shady areas on the back of the embankment, while picnic tables on the leveled top of the hill provide a place where fans can eat while keeping an eye on the game. The berm has its own concession stand and bathrooms.

The stands on the covered concourse behind the main seating bowl serve a trio of Big Apple favorites. Just like at Shea, Tradition Field sells knish, Carvel ice cream, and pretzels grilled over hot charcoal. The concourse also features banners that pay tribute to great moments in New York Mets history, in the same fashion that banners at Shea Stadium do. If you're a Red Sox fan and lived through the debacle of 1986, brace yourself. A trip from your seat to the men's room can be a pretty depressing experience. Try as you might, there's no avoiding images of Ray Knight, Gary Carter, Jesse Orosco, and other players whose names are still anathema in New England.

The Tradition Field Experience

A visit to Tradition Field offers fans the rare opportunity to check out an authentic bat house. You may be wondering what a bat house is or jogging your memory to recall what rarely turned to page of the baseball encyclopedia may have defined this term for you at one point. Rest assured, your baseball vocabulary isn't lacking. This isn't a baseball term, and it's not the cutesy name for some overhyped equipment shed where the St. Lucie clubhouse attendants stash the local lumber after the game either. The St. Lucie bat house is a place where living, breathing, flying bats live. That's right, those winged rodents that can often be spotted circling the light towers high above minor league ballparks. Back in the mid-1990s, a flock of free-tailed bats decided to roost at Tradition Field. The little buggers sneaked into the press box, the concourses, the belfries, and so on, until the ballpark became completely overrun. Realizing that it just wasn't fun for fans to go to the ballpark anymore, the St. Lucie County Commission took action, voting to bring a bat exclusion expert to town all the way from Wisconsin to purge the stadium of its several thousand nocturnal nuisances. But where would the bats live after being "excluded," local residents wondered? Would these angry creatures of the night besiege townsfolk with Hitchcockian splendor? Would they start nesting in joggers' hair, flying off with local lap dogs, bombarding phone booths? To guard against any of these unsettling possibilities, the county commission wisely voted to build a new home for the bats. In 1998 the county installed a 4-by-8-foot bat house adjacent to the stadium. The house is 14 feet off the ground, supported on four stilts. It can house 10,000 bats comfortably, or 15,000 if they all squeeze their wings in tight to their bodies. To see the bat house from ground level, head to the east entrance of the stadium and follow the signs. Bring a pocketful of moths and you'll make about 10,000 new friends faster than you can say, "Adam West wears blue tights."

On the Town

When the Mets originally arrived in St. Lucie in 1988, fewer than 40,000 people made their home in the city. Within ten years the population had more than doubled, and today it is approaching 100,000. It's easy to see why. This stretch of the Florida coast is known for its gorgeous white sand beaches and warm Atlantic waters. **Hutchinson Island,** accessible from Route 1 via Route 1A, a few miles north of St Lucie, offers beachgoers access to Fort Pierce Inlet State Park, South Jetty Park, South Beach Ocean Park, Surfside Park, and Frederick Douglass Memorial Park.

The Treasure Coast also offers access to the small fleet of eighteenth-century Spanish warships sunk just off the shore. The coast's unique nickname refers to the bounty of riches that went under aboard these ships in the 1700s. If you're hoping to find a treasure chest to finance the second leg of your road trip, you're a little late. This isn't *Pirates of the Caribbean*; it's Florida. The ships have already been picked over by the same retirees you'll see combing area beaches with metal detectors each day at dusk. But the water's warm, the fish are friendly, and the ships are just a few hundred yards from the beach. **Blue Planet Dive and Surf** (1317 St. Lucie West Boulevard) is just one of several local outfits that guides visitors to these unique underwater ruins.

If you prefer indoor recreation and like thin-crust pizza, forget about the seaside activities in St. Lucie and head to **Val's Tomato Pies** (7240 U.S. Route 1). Val's serves New York–style pizzas that will make your stomach think it's in Little Italy. The **St. Lucie Draft House** (6630 U.S. Route 1) is another popular pregame and postgame destination.

ED SMITH STADIUM

Sarasota Reds

Class A, Florida State League
(CINCINNATI REDS)

Ed Smith Stadium
12th Street and Tuttle Avenue
Sarasota, Florida
941–954–4464

Ed Smith Stadium reminds me of a lot of cars I've driven. It's not particularly pretty to look at, but it gets the job done. The ballpark is unspectacular in every way, but also comfortable, unpretentious, and highly functional in its capacity as home to the Florida State League's Sarasota Reds and Grapefruit League's Cincinnati Reds. From the sidewalk outside, the three-story structure behind home plate looks more like the balcony of a discount hotel than the backside of a professional ballpark. More than a dozen narrow doors appear here on two levels, allowing balcony walkers access to the press box and adjoining function rooms. Gray concrete—always fun and festive—composes the façade.

Inside, the environs are not quite so bland. The seats are light blue, while the railings between them are painted a garish blood red. The sunroof is blue to match the seats. Colorful advertising banners blanket the outfield fence, except for where tiny chain-link windows in right field and left field allow the bull pen pitchers to view the game. The foul poles bear the name and phone number of a local plumbing company, with the information appearing vertically on the slender billboards. What a great innovation, advertising on foul poles. You never know. You just might find yourself leaping up out of your seat late in the game to see if a long drive by one of the Reds players stays

fair, when it will suddenly occur to you: Gee, my toilet's been backed up lately, and I just ate three Big Red Smokey's and a plate full of pulled pork. I might need a reliable plumber and I might need one fast.

Clusters of palm trees, that thankfully do not feature any advertising on their trunks, grow beyond the outfield fence, combining with four practice fields and a practice infield to make for a decent view in center and left. In right field, though, three hideous gray buildings are visible. Plopped down on the landscape like concrete blocks, these provide administrative space and clubhouse facilities for the Reds.

Ed Smith Stadium was built in 1989 to replace Sarasota's Twin Lakes Park as the spring home of the Chicago White Sox. The stadium and complex surrounding it cost $9.5 million. When the Pale Hose decided to ditch the Grapefruit League in favor of a Cactus League home in Tucson in 1998, the Reds swooped in and filled the void, moving from Plant City, where they'd played for ten years, to Sarasota.

The history of professional baseball in Sarasota dates all the way back to 1923 when Mayor E. J. Bacon convinced local residents Calvin and Martha Payne to sell the city sixty acres of land at the discount price of $18,000. Upon this parcel the city built a wooden stadium called Payne Park. The ballpark was enough to lure John McGraw's New York Giants to town in 1924, beginning a long tradition of spring training baseball in Sarasota. The late Buck O'Neil, the grandfatherly Negro Leagues star made famous by Ken Burns's *Baseball* documentary, was a child in Sarasota during the 1920s. Buck fondly recalled that he and his friends once nailed two-by-fours to a big pine tree beyond the outfield fence at Payne Park so that they could scale the tree, peek over the fence, and watch McGraw's Giants play Babe Ruth's Yankees in an exhibition. The Giants spent four

Ed Smith Stadium

springs in Sarasota before opting not to return. In 1933 the Boston Red Sox began a spring affiliation with the city that would last until 1959. Then in 1960 the White Sox arrived.

Game Day

Getting to the Park

Sarasota is 60 miles south of Tampa on the Gulf Coast. From I–75 South, take the exit for University Parkway and follow University West to Tuttle Avenue. Turn left onto Tuttle and follow the signs to the stadium parking lot. From I–75 North, take the exit for Fruitville Road and follow Fruitville west until you come to Tuttle. Turn right and follow the signs to the ballpark's grassy parking lot.

Inside the Park

Rather than building a towering seating bowl that extends no farther than the corner bases on either side of the infield, the ballpark architects opted to build a low seating bowl that extends farther into the outfield. I think this was a good call. I'd always choose to sit five rows from the field in shallow left than twenty-five rows from the field behind the dugout. Ed Smith Stadium offers three different ticketing options: Box Seats, Reserved Seats, and General Admission. The Boxes are in the seven rows below the midlevel walkway. The Reserved Seats are raised above the walkway. And a General Admission ticket is good for a seat on the metal bleachers in medium-depth left and right field. Section 101 is in right field,

Section 113 is behind the plate, and Section 125 is in left field. The Reds average fewer than 500 fans per game, so there's no need to order tickets in advance.

The most popular concession item on the concourse behind the seating bowl at ground level is the Big Red Smoky. If you've been to Great American Ballpark in Cincinnati, chances are you're familiar with this mouthwatering kielbasa sandwich. I think the Sarasota version holds up pretty well against the original.

Plaques on the first base side of the concourse honor two influential members of the Sarasota baseball community. One remembers Howard "Red" Ermich, who worked for the city's Recreation Department and served as public-address announcer at every spring training game the White Sox ever played in Sarasota from 1960 through 1991. The other remembers Ed Smith, who was the president of the Sarasota Sports Committee that brought the White Sox to town in 1960, after the Red Sox bolted for Scottsdale, Arizona, in 1959.

The Ed Smith Stadium Experience

This ballpark offers a very sparsely populated minor league experience. During spring training the atmosphere is a bit livelier, as between-inning promotions entertain fans and pitch the services of local businesses.

Sarasota's laid-back equilibrium was thrown off kilter during the 1994 Grapefruit League season when the White Sox arrived for spring training with a national icon. That season the national media descended on Sarasota to witness the professional baseball debut of basketball superstar Michael Jordan. Previously, Jordan's most notable accomplishment as a hardballer had occurred in 1975 when the Dixie Youth Association named him North Carolina's Mr. Baseball in the twelve-year-old division.

Although Jordan was at the pinnacle of his basketball career in 1994, he mysteriously quit the sport he'd spent his whole life playing to give baseball a try. For one memorable, though not altogether pleasant spring, Sarasota and its ballpark faced the type of spotlight more commonly reserved for major league cities. Jordan-mania brought hundreds of reporters to Sarasota, tens of thousands more fans than usual, national cable networks that beamed live reports across the country, and a Nike van that set up on the plaza outside the stadium selling "Air Jordan" apparel. And that was before the Grapefruit League season even began. Once the games started, Jordan played sparingly as a right fielder wearing number 45 for the White Sox, but crowds exceeding 7,000 people packed Ed Smith Stadium every day. Even minor league workouts involving Jordan on the stadium's surrounding fields drew crowds that swelled into the thousands. After playing in a big league exhibition game against the Rangers early in the spring and being called out at first base by umpire Drew Coble on a close play, Jordan committed a memorable goof when he referred to Coble as "the ref" in a postgame interview. Fortunately, all was well that ended well for residents of Sarasota. Jordan was shipped out to the Double-A Birmingham Barons after spring training, and life returned to normal in Sarasota.

On the Town

Sarasota bills itself as Florida's "Cultural Coast," which means that if you want to go to an art exhibit, symphony, ballet, or opera while visiting, you'll have plenty of options to choose from. There are ten theaters in town and more than thirty art galleries. Wow. As Shoeless Joe wondered aloud in *Field of Dreams,* "Is this heaven?" Okay, maybe it's not so much for traveling baseball fans. But at least there are plenty of beaches nearby, spanning **Longboat Key** (accessible by Route 789 West) and **Siesta Key** (758 West). If you're looking for the quintessential Sarasota experience, you should probably head to **Siesta Key Beach,** which claims to have the whitest sand in the world, owing to its unique composition. Unlike most beaches that feature sand made of crushed coral, the sand at Siesta Key Beach is 99 percent quartz. As a result it never heats up, not even on the sunniest of summer scorchers. Be warned, however, this beach is always jammed with visitors, and the parking lot fills up early in the morning. For a more rustic beach experience, I suggest **North Lido Beach** (John Ringling Boulevard).

If you're interested in checking out some area ballparks that don't see much action in the summertime anymore but have played important roles in this region's hardball history, swing by **Twin Lakes Park** (6700 Clark Road), which served as Sarasota's minor league and Grapefruit League headquarters prior to the construction of Ed Smith Stadium. The complex currently sees use as the Baltimore Orioles minor league camp each spring, although the big league Orioles play across the state in Fort Lauderdale. Meanwhile, 15 miles north in Bradenton the spring training home of the Pittsburgh Pirates, **McKechnie Field** (1611 Ninth Street West), stands on a site where baseball has been played since 1923. The ballpark was rebuilt in 1992.

If you work up an appetite during the short walk from Ed Smith Stadium's grassy parking lot to the stadium gates, stop by **Gus' Twelfth Street Cafe**, right beside the stadium on Euclid, and recharge your batteries.

LEGENDS FIELD

Tampa Yankees

Class A, Florida State League
(NEW YORK YANKEES)

Legends Field
One Steinbrenner Drive
Tampa, Florida
813–875–7753

Legends Field provides relocated (read: retired) New Yorkers with a taste of the Big Apple on Florida's Gulf Coast. By Florida State League standards the 10,386-seat stadium is hulking, to say the least, but it is nine-tenths empty on most nights. It's not hard to imagine why. The Tampa Bay Devil Rays play big league ball, or something marginally approximating it, in the dome just across the bay in St. Petersburg. Tropicana Field is air-conditioned, and thankfully so. Legends Field, meanwhile, is open to the unbearable heat, humidity, and late-day thunderstorms that besiege this part of Florida all summer long.

Nonetheless, Yankee boss George Steinbrenner makes his year-round home in Tampa and frequents Legends Field, as do many big leaguers sent to the Yankees extended spring training base each year on rehabilitation assignments. In addition to housing the Class A Yankees, Legends Field is also home to the big league Yankees during the Grapefruit League season, when the temperatures are cooler and the crowds are much larger.

Built by the city of Tampa for $30 million and opened in 1996, Legends Field evokes many of the design quirks that distinguish the House That Ruth Built. For example, the white arches and filigree that decorate the top of the seating bowl at Legends Field mimic the arches that span the outfield façade at Yankee Stadium.

Similarly, Legends Field houses its own Monument Park, to pay tribute to the all-time great Yankees. While the hallowed ground in the South Bronx sits beyond the left field fence in an area of the ballpark that was once in play, the monuments in Tampa appear outside the stadium entrance, surrounded by an attractively landscaped duck pond, palm trees, and tropical flower gardens. The monuments in Tampa take the form of baseball-shaped, white-and-blue-pinstriped plaques that honor Joe DiMaggio, Lou Gehrig, Babe Ruth, Yogi Berra, Mickey Mantle, and the rest of the fifteen Yankees whose uniform numbers have been retired by the team. Yes, there's even a plaque for Phil Rizzuto, the worst hitting Hall of Famer ever.

The Bambino's plaque reads, "Single-handedly lifted baseball to new heights with his unlimited talent and unbridled love for the game," which is hard to dispute. Meanwhile, the Yankee Clipper's plaque reads, "I want to thank the good Lord for making me a Yankee." The idea of some omniscient superbeing playing fantasy baseball in heaven and overloading one team with as much talent as the Yankees have had over the years doesn't seem to ring true to me, but apparently it did to the Great DiMaggio. Who knows? Maybe he's right. Maybe God wears pinstriped pajamas and has a Derek Jeter bobblehead doll on his nightstand.

Legends Field is a ballpark befitting a team that has won more championships than any other two teams combined. Unfortunately, the major league Yankees only play thirteen or fourteen games a year here, while the Tampa Yanks spend the whole season at the joint. You have to wonder if the Tampa players ever find themselves embarrassed by their riches when a visiting team like the Sarasota Reds pulls into town after slumming its way through a homestand at Ed Smith Stadium. The three-story façade of Legends Field features an open-aired concession concourse behind the seating bowl on the second level, giant windscreens that spell out Y-A-N-K-E-E-S above the seating bowl between the second and third tiers, and a blue roof at the very top.

The playing field replicates the big league yard of the Yankees, measuring 314 feet down the right field line, 408 feet to straightaway center, 399 feet to Death Valley in left-center, and 318 feet down the left field line. The only difference between the two fields is that there isn't as much foul territory behind home plate in Tampa as there is in New York. The outfield fences, like the ballpark seats, take the hue of royal Yankee blue. A JumboTron, massive by Florida State League standards, sits behind the wall in left-center, partially obstructing the view of the passing traffic on Dale Mabry Highway.

Legends Field was part of a publicly financed construction project that also furnished the Tampa Bay Buccaneers with Raymond James Stadium, which is located right next to the ballpark. Prior to opening Legends Field with a spring training tilt between the Yankees and Indians on March 1, 1996, the spring Yankees and high-A Yankees played across the state in Fort Lauderdale.

Game Day

Getting to the Park

Legends Field is located near the Tampa Airport. Take I–275 to exit 41B and follow Dale Mabry Highway north for 3 miles. The ballpark is on the left, while the stadium parking lot is on the right, next to Roland James Stadium. Fans can check out the 103-foot fake pirate ship in the north end zone of the football grid, then use a pedestrian bridge to safely cross the highway.

Inside the Park

This is a large stadium that places all of its seats in a concrete seating bowl that rises steeply around the infield. The seats are comfortable stadium chairs that appear in sixteen rows of Field Box Seats on the low side of the midlevel walkway and sixteen rows of Grandstand Seats on the high side. The sunroof provides cover for those in the top rows of the Grandstands. Section 102 is in shallow right field, Sections 110 and 111 are behind the plate, and Section 120 is in shallow left. The Tampa Yankees average only 1,100 or so fans per game, so you should be able to sit wherever you like.

Unfortunately, there is no view of the game from the concourse midway up the seating bowl, but the ballpark food is pretty good. The Scooter Dog is named after the aforementioned weak-hitting Phil Rizzuto, while the Iron-Man Dog is named after Yankee icon Lou Gehrig, and the Foot-Long Dog is named, I assume, after Barry Foote, the catcher who played in fifty-seven games for the Yankees between 1981 and 1982. They all tasted the same to me.

The concourse is decorated with classic black-and-white photos of Yankee greats like Billy Martin, Whitey Ford, and the light-hitting Rizzuto, while there are also team shots of the many Yankee championship editions. Also worth checking out, before or after the game, is the large clubhouse shop outside the park near the main entrance.

The Legends Field Experience

Due to its size and the formality imposed by its ostentatious design, Legends Field does not lend itself to the type of intimacy or fan involvement found at many of the glorious bush league ball fields across our great land. The truth is that not many Florida State League ballparks do. Most are way too big for their local fan bases. During spring training the atmosphere is livelier, as the ground crew dances along to the Village People's "YMCA," while fans try to spell out the song lyrics with their arms and legs. Have you ever seen anything like it? Hmm. Think hard.

The best time for autograph seekers is also spring training when former Yankee and area celebrities make regular appearances at Legends Field. Wayne Gretzky, Reggie Jackson, Rudy Giuliani, Regis Philbin, Dick Vitale, and Jeb Bush have all been spotted in the stands and luxury boxes at one point or another. Like I always say, a road trip's just not a road trip, until you get Regis Philbin's autograph on the back of a ticket stub.

On the Town

If Tampa seems like a city absolutely teeming with strip clubs, that's because, well, it is a city absolutely teeming with strip clubs. In fact, at last check there were three such establishments within a mile radius of Legends Field. For a better family atmosphere, follow I–175 across the Bay into St. Petersburg.

In St. Pete baseball fans can catch a major league game at **Tropicana Field** (One Tropicana

Legends Field

Field Drive) and stroll along **Baseball Boulevard**, a mile-long footpath that begins at the spring training home of the Devil Rays, **Al Lang Field** (Bayshore Drive), and ends at the Trop. The walk is adorned with bronze home-plate-shaped plaques that celebrate more than eight decades of spring baseball in Florida.

Al Lang Field is located just a block south of **The Pier**, a St. Petersburg landmark that has been a tourist destination since 1899. On this long wharf travelers rent rods and reels to cast for snook, feed friendly pelicans, and lounge in the sun. The inverted pyramid at the end of the half-mile pier houses restaurants, gift shops, and an aquarium.

For a high-end meal back in Tampa, **Malio's Steak House** (301 South Dale Mabry Highway) offers the chance to check out one of Steinbrenner's and Lou Piniella's favorite hangouts. Piniella grew up with owner Malio Iavarone in West Tampa, while Steinbrenner has his own private room in back.

HOLMAN STADIUM

Vero Beach Rays

Class A, Florida State League
(TAMPA BAY DEVIL RAYS)

Holman Stadium/Dodgertown
4101 26th Street
Vero Beach, Florida
772–569–4900

Holman Stadium is one of the simplest and most delightful ballparks on the professional baseball landscape. The stadium is not so much a stadium as it is a field surrounded by rows of seats carved into a man-made embankment. The small hillside surrounds the entire diamond. There are no wooden, cement, or steel walls surrounding the field to pen in visitors, just the hill and a small chain-link fence. Players sit on benches in foul territory instead of in dugouts. The wooden press box is smaller than the one at your local Little League field. The home run fence is a low chain-link fence. There is no flashy scoreboard in the outfield. Live oak trees rise between the seats, casting the only shade fans will find during day games. Home runs sail into a grove of kumquat trees that grow on the outfield hill. The seats are right on top of the action. This is baseball the way it ought to be, baseball the way it was during a simpler time, baseball the way it was when Holman Stadium first opened as the spring training home of the Brooklyn Dodgers in 1953.

Despite moving cross-country to Los Angeles shortly after establishing a spring camp in Vero Beach in 1949, the Dodgers have returned to Florida's east coast every year since. The Florida State League's Vero Beach Dodgers played at Holman Stadium from 1971 through 2006, before Los Angeles moved its Class A prospects closer to home—relocating them to Inland Empire of the California League. The Devil Rays filled the void, signing on with Vero Beach in time for the start of the 2007 season.

Despite the local minor league team's new affiliation, the massive hardball haven that surrounds Holman Stadium is still called Dodgertown. The complex was the brainchild of baseball visionary Branch Rickey, and the pet project of longtime Dodgers owner Walter O'Malley. At a time when most big league clubs had player development agreements with more than twenty minor league teams, Rickey dreamt of establishing a "baseball college," where every member of the Brooklyn organization would learn to play the game the Dodger Way. Rickey was also interested in creating an island of sorts, where the racial segregation of the Jim Crow South, which made it impossible for Dodgers like Jackie Robinson, Don Newcombe, and Roy Campanella to train with the team, would not come into play.

To shelter Robinson from the racism he had faced during the spring of 1946 when he was barred from competing against whites at ball fields across Florida, the Dodgers spent the spring of 1947 in Havana, Cuba. In 1948 they traveled to Santo Domingo in the Dominican Republic. Then, in 1948 Vero Beach businessman Bud Holman approached Rickey and proposed converting a decommissioned World War II naval air base into a spring training camp. Holman and Rickey brokered a deal whereby Vero Beach leased the former military barracks and airport to the Dodgers for $1.00 per year, plus the proceeds from one spring exhibition game. During the winter of 1948, several baseball fields were chiseled into the hard ground of the airstrips, and the barracks were prepared for the arrival of professional baseball players.

In February of 1949, Rickey's Dodgers pulled into town—all of them. More than 600 players, representing twenty-six different teams trained in Vero Beach that first year, all wearing different colored uniforms depending on their anticipated level of play during the upcoming season. The players performed conditioning drills, participated in scrimmages, and sat through classroom sessions that instructed them on the finer points of baseball strategy. Rickey, a former army officer who had commanded a troop of baseball players in Europe during World War I, reportedly wandered throughout the Vero Beach barracks each morning at 6:00 A.M. waking up his players with a drill sergeant's whistle.

When Rickey left the Dodgers in 1951 to take a position with the Pittsburgh Pirates, O'Malley became the champion of the Dodgertown vision. The young owner wasn't quite the disciplinarian Rickey was, though. He poured money into the Dodgertown complex to turn it into a preseason resort for his players and their families. The benevolent owner added a swimming pool, tennis courts, a golf course, a movie theater, and a man-made lake in the shape of a heart, which he presented to his wife Kay as a Valentine gift one year.

In 1965 O'Malley purchased the 110-acre complex from Vero Beach, then over the next decade he expanded its borders by acquiring and developing more than 300 acres of the surrounding countryside. Today, Dodgertown is a 450-acre complex with two public golf courses, a sixty-acre citrus grove, globe streetlights painted like baseballs, walking paths with quaint names like Vin Sculley Way and Don Drysdale Drive, and plenty of baseball fields. In 2001 Indian River County purchased the complex from the Dodgers for $9.8 million. As part of the deal, the big league and minor league Dodgers agreed to stay in Vero Beach through 2021 and to pay the county $1.00 per year in rent.

Through the years Dodgertown has hosted a number of international teams. The list of recent tenants includes the Tokyo Giants and the Chunichi Dragons of the professional Japanese league, the Samsung Lions of the Korean league, and the Sinon Bulls of the Taiwanese league. Several NFL teams have also used the complex to train, including the Buffalo Bills, Cleveland Browns, Green Bay Packers, Kansas City Chiefs, New England Patriots, New Orleans Saints, and Philadelphia Eagles. In 1993 the University of Miami played a home football game at Holman Stadium after Hurricane Andrew rendered the Orange Bowl unfit for play.

Game Day

Getting to the Park

Vero Beach is 25 miles north of Port St. Lucie, and 40 miles south of Viera, where the nearest league rivals play. Dodgertown is 4 miles west of I–95, and 2 miles east of the Atlantic Ocean. From I–95, take exit 147, follow Route 60 East, turn left onto 43rd Avenue, and then follow Aviation Boulevard to the main entrance on 26th Street.

Inside the Park

The seating bowl extends nearly from foul pole to foul pole, while there is also an outfield lawn where fans can recline in left field home run territory. The main seating bowl offers seventeen rows, except behind home plate in Sections 13 through 15 where the protrusion of the press box allows room for only eleven rows. The home bench is located in front of Sections 18 and 19 on the third base side; the visiting bench is located in front of Sections 9 and 10 across the diamond. The Vero Beach Rays

Holman Stadium

attract only about 750 fans per game, so getting a good seat is never a problem.

There are concession stands behind third base at the bottom of the hill and behind home plate atop the hill. The menu isn't eclectic, but if it were, it wouldn't quite fit at Holman Stadium. Grilled foot-long dogs are the treat of choice.

Fans looking for a scenic place to eat before the game can have dinner at the picnic tables on the shores of old man O'Malley's heart-shaped pond.

The Dodgertown Experience

The Vero Beach Rays involve the local community in the life of the baseball team as much as possible. Following every Sunday home game, the team invites its fans to have a game of catch on the outfield lawn. The team also offers an annual event that raises money for charity by allowing fans to bid on a lunch date at a local restaurant with their favorite Vero Beach player. More than one aspiring baseball wife has been known to net a hubby this way . . . or at least an evening out.

The trademark event at Dodgertown is the annual "Dodgertown Dash," which dates back to 1979. Each July, the team hosts a 5K road race before a Sunday afternoon game. After pounding the pavement beneath the Florida sun, the runners shower on-site, then head to

Holman Stadium to eat hot dogs and watch the game. Sounds like a pretty good day to me . . . except for the running part.

On the Town

Vero Beach is one of the smallest towns in the country to have a professional baseball team. Fewer than 20,000 people live in this sleepy seaside community, and judging from the informal survey I conducted when I visited Holman Stadium, about 85 percent of residents are in their eighth or ninth decade. Visiting fans who are looking for hopping nightlife and wild times involving sauced-up coeds in string bikinis won't find those types of shenanigans in Vero Beach. The right field beer garden at Holman Stadium is about as "happening" as it gets for that sort of thing. And trust me, the beer garden isn't all that happening.

Those who enjoy a day at the beach or a day on the golf course will find their visit to town a bit more fulfilling. **Dodger Pines Golf Club** and **Dodgertown Country Club** are both open to visiting hackers, while **Orchid Island** (accessible via Route 60) offers swimmers and sunbathers the pleasures of **Jaycee Park** and **Wabasso Beach**.

SPACE COAST STADIUM
Brevard County Manatees

Class A, Florida State League
(MILWAUKEE BREWERS)

Space Coast Stadium
5800 Stadium Parkway
Viera, Florida
321–633–9200

Space Coast Stadium provides a delightfully rustic setting for a ball game. Flat green cow pastures and irrigation ponds that are crystal clear surround the field. Space Coast Stadium doesn't exactly blend in with these rural surroundings, offering an exterior of white, gray, and blue ceramic tile, similar to the type popular in American bathrooms during the 1970s, but it isn't unpleasant to look at either. Here's guessing Brevard County saw a good deal on tiles at the local Home Depot after those new press-and-seal one-piece bathroom sets started catching on and figured *why not*?

With a seating capacity that exceeds 8,000 people, Space Coast Stadium is another larger-than-necessary Florida State League stadium that rises higher above the field than most Class A facilities. Still, the site lines are unobstructed, the park is comfortable if not cozy, and the outfield view is quaint.

Space Coast Stadium is unique in that it enjoys affiliations with two different major league organizations. During the Grapefruit League season, the Washington Nationals use Space Coast and its five practice diamonds as their spring training base. Then, during the Florida State League season, the Brevard County Manatees, a Milwaukee Brewers affiliate, use the stadium. Although the ballpark opened fairly recently, in 1994, the Nationals are the third major league team to use Space Coast Stadium for spring games. Originally, the Florida Marlins played their Grapefruit League games at the park. Then, in 2003 the Marlins swapped spring sites with the Montreal Expos, who became the Nationals in 2005. As for the Manatees, they were a Marlins affiliate, then an Expos affiliate, before entering into a player development contract with the Brewers in 2005.

The stadium is just a short drive from Cape Canaveral, where NASA's space shuttles launch and land at the Kennedy Space Center. Thus, it was christened Space Coast Stadium at the time of its opening. In addition to honoring the U.S. space program with the ballpark's name, the facility embraces NASA in a number of other ways. Outside the ballpark there stands a 13-foot-tall, 350-pound model of a space shuttle in launch position. The orbiter is made of fiberglass, while the external tank and rocket boosters are made of aluminum. NASA donated the one-fifteenth-scale model to the stadium site, funding the ship's $15,000 construction cost.

A bit closer to the stadium, stands a bronze statue of Casey, from the Ernest L. Thayer poem, "Casey at the Bat." The 14½-foot-tall statue stands beside a bubbling fountain pond. It is a replica of the one that stands outside the big league stadium in Miami where the Florida Marlins play. You know, the stadium previously known as Joe Robbie Stadium, Pro Player Field, Dolphins Stadium, and sure to be named something else by the time this book is published.

Inside, Space Coast Stadium's foul poles remember the crews of the two fallen space shuttles. The right field foul pole reads "Challenger," from top to bottom, and displays an image of the *Challenger* with its nose held high on the launch pad, along with the date that it exploded, 1-28-86. The left field pole remembers the *Columbia* in the same way, while displaying the date of its tragic end, 2-1-03.

In left field a distinctive manually operated scoreboard resides on the grassy hillside behind the fence. An attendant sits high above the field and uses a runway in front of the board to update the score as the game progresses.

Game Day

Getting to the Park

The Space Coast Stadium complex lays half in Viera and half in Melbourne. It is ½ mile west of I–95. From the south, take I–95 North to the Wickham Road exit, turn left onto Wickham, then turn right at the traffic circle onto Lake Andrew Drive. Follow Lake Andrew through the Brevard County government office complex. At the four-way stop, turn right onto Stadium Parkway. From the north, take I–95 South to the Rockledge exit and then turn left onto Stadium Parkway. There is ample room for parking in the dusty fields around the stadium. One of the first things new Manatees owner Tom Winters did on buying the team in 2006 was eliminate the stadium parking fee. Good call, Tom. The gesture is appreciated.

Inside the Park

Fans enter the ballpark by walking up a long ramp leading to turnstiles that spill onto a main

Space Coast Stadium

concourse midway up the seating bowl. Runways lead from the concourse to the walkway that runs between the Box Seats and Reserved Seats. Teal blue stadium chairs left over from when the Florida Marlins played at Space Coast Stadium fill most of the seating bowl, but past the corner bases metal bleachers fill the second level. The seating bowl beings with Sections 101 and 201 in right field, continues to Sections 110 and 211 behind home plate, and ends at Sections 119 and 221 in right field. The only viewing area in home run territory is a small grass hill behind the left field fence that hosts group functions.

The concession stands on the concourse embrace the NASA theme, bearing names like the "Loading Dock" and the "Orbiter Grill." I loaded up on the ballpark pizza, which was a lot better than I expected. Then I tried the taco-in-a-helmet, which was out of this world. By the time I got around to trying the smoked turkey leg, my stomach already felt like a black hole. Once I polished off the drumstick, I was feeling the effects of gravity and had to sit down for a while.

The Space Coast Stadium Experience

Manatees general manager Buck Rogers is known for his affinity for quirky ballpark promotions. Here's a funny one: In 2005 the Manatees and their fans set a new world record for the most honorary first pitches thrown before a baseball game. I know what you're thinking. You've sat through some unduly long pregame ball-tossing ceremonies in your day, right? Sure, we've all been there. Your wristwatch says it's game time, you've got a cold frosty in one hand, a dog in the other, and your scorecard on your lap. And just then the local Little League trots forty-eight twelve-year-olds onto the field and proceeds to delay the game for ten minutes as some backup catcher tries to be

a good sport. Well get this, before a Saturday night game between the Manatees and Palm Beach Cardinals on August 27, 2005, Space Coast Stadium was the scene of an eight-hour, ten-minute, 4,218-pitch, pregame ball-tossing ceremony. The event began at 10:44 A.M. when Space Coast Stadium groundkeeper Doug Lopas threw pitch number 1, and it continued without stop until 6:55 P.M. when Manatees fan Karl Bohne threw pitch number 4,218. In between all of the Manatees and Cardinals players tossed a pitch from the mound, as did the Manatees front office personnel, the umpiring crew, and more than 4,000 fans who participated. The event was broadcast by ESPN Radio AM 1060 of Melbourne, which kept count as listeners throughout Brevard County sat on the edges of their seats and beach blankets. The wacky promotion shattered the old record of 2,052 first pitches, which had been set by the fans of the Madison Mallards, a college wood-bat-league team in Madison, Wisconsin.

Thankfully, there was no drawn out pregame ceremony on the day I visited Space Coast Stadium, although I did enjoy the brief chicken dance the ushers performed on top of the dugout roofs in the middle of the fifth inning. I still haven't figured out why this little dance number hasn't caught on and replaced "YMCA" as the ballpark dance-along of choice at ballparks nationwide.

On the Town

Why not embrace the namesakes of the local team and ballpark while you're in Brevard County? Plan a visit to the **Kennedy Space Center,** and while you're at it do some manatee watching. The Space Center is located on Route 405, just 10 miles north of Space Coast Stadium. The visitors complex is open daily from 9:00 A.M. until 6:00 P.M., offering the Astronaut Hall of

Fame, two launch pads, space-related theatrical productions, a full-sized fake space shuttle, the actual capsules from the Gemini program, astronauts who field questions from visitors, and a five-story IMAX screen that provides a window into the cosmos.

After marveling at the wonders of outer space, gawk in amazement at the 1,800-pound mammals that swim in the warm waters of Florida's rivers and estuaries. The hulking herbivores body surf, barrel roll, and float on either side of Merritt Island, which is flanked by the Indian River on its eastern side and the Banana River on its western side. A good place for an afternoon of manatee watching is the **Merritt Island National Wildlife Refuge**, which sits on 140,000 acres of land right beside the Kennedy Center. The refuge is open daily from 8:00 A.M. until 4:30 P.M.

HOOVER METROPOLITAN STADIUM

Birmingham Barons

Class AA, Southern League
(CHICAGO WHITE SOX)

Hoover Metropolitan Stadium
100 Ben Chapman Drive
Hoover, Alabama
205-988-3200

A trip to Birmingham affords traveling baseball fans the chance to visit one of the most charming and historic ballparks in the country. Unfortunately, that park hosts just one Southern League game each year. The Birmingham Barons moved to a new stadium in the suburbs in 1988, but they still return to ancient Rickwood Field once a year for a turn-back-the-clock game called the "Rickwood Classic."

The oldest professional ballpark in the country, and a National Historic Landmark, Rickwood Field has been expertly preserved through the years thanks to the efforts of a local fan club called the Friends of Rickwood. The park features a manually operated scoreboard, 1940s-era outfield signs, and a large roof supported by steel pillars over the grandstand.

The first minor league ballpark in the country built entirely of steel and concrete, Rickwood Field was the brainchild of Barons owner A. H. "Rick" Woodward. After the Birmingham millionaire consulted with Connie Mack on the design for his new stadium and personally oversaw its construction, the facility that would eventually bear his name (sort of) opened before a sell-out crowd of more than 10,000 people on August 18, 1910. That first game was played a year and a half before

Fenway Park—the oldest current major league stadium—would open in Boston.

The Birmingham fans went home happy that first night, as the Barons scored twice in the ninth inning to beat the Montgomery Rebels. But really, the fans were just happy to have a real stadium where they could sit on real bleacher benches. At their team's previous home, they had been forced to sit on piles of mining debris that served as improvised bleachers. The "Slag Pile," which hosted minor league ball beginning in the 1880s, was located in the city's West End Park, along the Great Southern Railroad line. Due to the large piles of mining waste in the ballpark's outfield and to Birmingham's reputation as a mining town, the Birmingham team that joined the original Southern Association in 1901 was known as the "Coal Barons."

During eight decades of steady play, Rickwood Field did more than just stand the test of time. During its first few decades, it set the standard by which all other minor league stadiums should be judged, and it became a point of immense civic pride for those living in Birmingham. The fans turned out at the park in droves during the 1920s when the Southern Association's Barons drew more than 160,000 fans in eight different seasons, including a whopping 299,000 in 1927. The postwar 1940s represented another high-water mark for Birmingham baseball, as the Barons shared Rickwood Field with the Black Barons of the Negro National League. In 1948 the Barons, who were a Boston Red Sox farm club at the time, set a franchise record when they drew 445,926 fans.

Through the years the list of baseball greats that called Rickwood Field their home grew to include names like Burleigh Grimes, Pie Traynor, Rube Marquard (who played for the Barons at the tail end of his professional career), Reggie Jackson, Rollie Fingers,

Catfish Hunter, Vida Blue, Sal Bando, and Tony LaRussa. By the 1980s, though, the old park was showing its age, and the Barons jumped at the opportunity to move to a new yard when the city of Hoover volunteered $14.5 million to build Hoover Metropolitan Stadium on a plot 12 miles outside of downtown Birmingham. The Barons made the move in 1988.

The "Hoover Met" is a decent facility for what it is—a large suburban stadium built to the specs of the pre-Camden era, when classic design flourishes and modern inventions like the open concourse and outfield seating berm had not yet become paramount in the minds of ballpark architects. Inside, the Met is massive. It has room to seat nearly 11,000 people in a seating bowl that consists predominantly of bleachers with backs. But it is not the seating bowl, per say, that makes the stadium feel as large as it does. Behind the last row of seats, there is a towering concrete wall that separates the seating bowl from the concourse behind it. After this wall rises about 15 feet, the stadium's twelve luxury suites interrupt its expanse, then above the suites, the wall rises another 20 feet before eventually being topped by a large roof that is set at an angle so as to extend upward as much as it does outward. Why they didn't simply put a small roof immediately over the luxury suites, I can't imagine. Maybe the folks building the Met had some extra concrete that they simply wanted to use up, or maybe the idea was to create a minor league park that resembled—at least a little bit—another famous "Met," the domed Metropolitan Stadium in Minneapolis.

In any case the red metal roof is the stadium's dominant feature. To those approaching the facility from Ben Chapman Drive, the stadium looks like one giant roof, and could almost be mistaken for a dome. The cap begins only about 15 feet above street level outside and covers the entire concourse before the very top

of it emerges above the luxury suites inside the stadium. From the outside the Hoover Met reminds me of a miniature version of Olympic Stadium in Montreal. It also looks a bit like an alien space ship descended on Birmingham to covertly entrap and snatch away the city's baseball fans. Forgive me if I watched too many episodes of the *X Files* in the 1990s, but I did a quick lap around the stadium to make sure it was actually cemented down before I decided it was safe to head inside.

The Hoover Met is a bore, of course, when compared with Rickwood Field, but what park built in the 1980s wouldn't be? While the towering concrete wall behind the field makes the Met feel more vacuous and sterile than it should and blocks the view of the field from the concourse, as far as the sight lines from the seats are concerned, the stadium grades out pretty high.

The current Barons franchise arrived in Birmingham via Montgomery in 1981, as the Magic City rejoined the Southern League after a five-year hiatus. The Barons, who were a Detroit Tigers affiliate from 1981 through 1986, have been a Chicago White Sox affiliate since 1987. While many future stars have played for the Barons during the White Sox era—including Frank Thomas, Magglio Ordóñez, Bo Jackson, Carlos Lee, Joe Crede, Jack McDowell, Mark Buehrle, and Jon Garland—the team's biggest drawing card to date was a lanky right fielder named Michael Jordan. His Airness played for the Barons in 1994 during his first retirement from basketball. While a contingent of more than 500 journalists followed the Barons around the country, the Barons traveled in style aboard the "Jordan Cruiser" luxury bus. Birmingham manager Terry Francona faithfully penciled Jordan into the staring lineup each night, and Jordan worked hard to improve his skills, but the results were largely disappointing. The best basketball player on the planet batted just .202 with 3 HR and 51 RBI for the Barons, while leading the Southern League in outfield errors with 11. As a lone personal bright spot, Jordan finished tied for fifth in the Southern League with 30 steals. As an organizational bright spot, Jordan's presence drew a team-record 467,867 fans to the Hoover Met that season, and the Barons saw their merchandising revenues increase exponentially. The team also appeared on national and regional television several times.

The current incarnation of the Barons has claimed five Southern League championships, taking league bragging rights in 1983, 1987, 1989, 1993, and 2002.

Game Day

Getting to the Park

Birmingham is in the middle of Alabama, 90 miles north of Montgomery and 150 miles west of Atlanta. Hoover Metropolitan Stadium is located south of Birmingham in Hoover. The ballpark is on Ben Chapman Drive, a street named after the longtime city resident who spent fifteen seasons in the big leagues, near the intersection of U.S. Highway 150 and I–459. From I–459, take exit 10 and follow US 150 toward Hoover. At the third light, turn right onto Stadium Trace. There is a large parking lot behind the stadium.

Inside the Park

The Hoover Met can accommodate 10,800 fans in a seating bowl that extends about three-quarters of the way down the outfield lines on either side. Tiered grass hillsides fill the spaces between the ends of the seating bowl and the outfield fence, but these areas are not used for seating. There are two seating levels. The 100 Level offers red stadium chairs—except down the lines where the two outfield-most sections

on either side contain the same blue bleachers with backs as found above the midlevel walkway throughout the 200 Level. As such, only about 30 percent of the seats in Birmingham are individual stadium chairs.

On the 100 Level, Sections A and AA are behind the plate, and then single-letter sections continue down the first baseline, following the alphabet to L just past first base, while double-letter sections continue down the left field line, finishing at LL just past third. The 200 Level is more conventionally marked, offering Sections 200 and 201 behind the plate, odd-numbered sections along the first baseline that end at Section 215, and even-numbered sections along the third baseline that end at Section 216.

On the concourse behind the big cement wall, the concession highlights include Papa John's Pizza, Philly cheesesteaks, and foot-long brats. On Saturdays and Sundays the Dreamland Barbecue—a Birmingham institution—sets up shop on the concourse, selling its trademark ribs. If you want to buy a Birmingham Barons hat like the one Britney Spears wore in her video for the song "Every Time," visit the clubhouse store behind home plate.

The Hoover Met Experience

The field in Birmingham plays big, measuring 340 feet down the lines and 405 feet to center. Several of the Barons fans I spoke with indicated that they wouldn't mind seeing more home runs and fewer pitchers duels.

The Barons mascot is Babe Ruff, a friendly hound dog, who gets very excited when fans scratch his belly or feed him nachos. And a troop of cheerleaders known as the "Diamond Girls" have also been known to make appearances at the Hoover Met, dancing on the dugout roofs and encouraging the crowd to root for the home team.

Rickwood Field

On the Town

As I mentioned earlier, those traveling to Birmingham should be sure to visit **Rickwood Field** (2100 Morris Avenue). The old ballpark is usually open during daytime hours and a self-guided walking tour teaches visitors about the stadium's rich history. The park's green-and-white-exterior has been favorably compared with Forbes Field, which once stood in Pittsburgh. Its manual scoreboard was built when Hollywood came to Birmingham to shoot scenes for the movie *Cobb* in the 1990s. Its light banks extend off the roof on metal scaffolding so that they're over the field. A gazebo atop the grandstand roof replicates the original press box.

The **Alabama Sports Hall of Fame** (2150 Civic Center Boulevard) is another point of interest for sports fans visiting Birmingham. The Hall offers exhibits related to Dixieland legends like Hank Aaron, Bo Jackson, Carl Lewis, Joe Louis, Willie Mays, Satchel Paige, Jesse Owens, and Don Sutton. It is open Monday through Saturday, from 9:00 A.M. until 5:00 P.M., and admission costs $5.00.

If you visit the Hoover Met on a weekday and miss out on the delicious **Dreamland Barbecue** ribs served at the ballpark on Saturdays and Sundays, head to the restaurant's original location at 1427 14th Avenue in downtown Birmingham.

JOE W. DAVIS
MUNICIPAL STADIUM
Huntsville Stars

Class AA, Southern League
(MILWAUKEE BREWERS)

Joe W. Davis Municipal Stadium
Don Mincher Drive
Huntsville, Alabama
256–882–2562

As any good sports fan will tell you, Alabama is football country. It's the state where men like Bear Bryant and Bo Jackson—and countless others in between—transformed themselves into legends. And while the National Pastime is a nice summer diversion for the folks who live in the Heart of Dixie, by the time the calendars flip to August each year, everyone is chomping at the bit for the college and high school football seasons to begin. It should come as little surprise then that the Huntsville Stars—one of four Southern League teams in Alabama—play at one of the best stadiums in all of the minor leagues for watching a football game. Unfortunately for local minor league baseball fans, the multipurpose stadium does not set up quite so nicely for hardball.

Joe W. Davis Municipal Stadium was built in 1985, which makes it the oldest stadium in the ten-team Southern League. It was designed to house a franchise looking to get out of Nashville at the time, and also to serve as Huntsville's pigskin hub during the high school football season. And so, in an era when multipurpose cookie-cutter stadiums were all the rage at the big league level, Huntsville started pouring concrete. Lots and lots of concrete.

The resulting stadium, which was promptly named after the mayor who had championed

its construction, turned out to be a 10,200-seat facility that might best be described as three-quarters of a football stadium. Imagine a full football stadium, complete with a high-rising, two-level concrete seating bowl around the entire gridiron, then strip away the seats along one of the sidelines, and what you're left with is a stadium like "The Joe." When configured for football, the stadium offers seats that trace one sideline and wrap around the pylons to line the backs of both end zones.

When set up for baseball, those same seats trace the left field line and extend just a short distance down the first baseline and a short distance toward left field home run territory. More than half of the seats are in left field foul territory. Making matters worse, the foul territory is much wider than at most minor league parks, pushing fans back far from the action. The steep upper level also places many of its seats high above field level. And the lower and upper levels both angle many of the seats toward center field rather than toward home plate. And the seats are not stadium chairs, but bleacher benches. Other than all that, the place is great!

While there is no new stadium on the horizon for the Stars, the good news is that the team's current ownership group has put pressure on the city to renovate The Joe. The group, which is headed by New York attorney Miles Prentice, refused to renew the stadium lease inherited from the previous ownership group in 2001. After the Stars played without a stadium lease in 2004 and 2005, the team and city finally agreed to a new five-year deal in 2006, contingent on Huntsville making at least $1 million in capital improvements to the stadium in the years ahead. At the top of the to-do list is updating the stadium lighting system, which still did not meet Double-A standards during the 2006 season. Other renovations will likely endeavor to make the stadium more baseball friendly and to add luxury boxes along the first baseline, where currently there are none.

While the old ballpark lights may be dim, they're not so dim as to allow a view of the stars overhead during night games. Fans do, however, find two large video boards shaped like stars flanking the scoreboard in left-center. The Huntsville team named itself the "Stars" as a nod to the Marshall Space Flight Center—a NASA facility a few miles west of the stadium. Also just west of the stadium is the U.S. Space and Rocket Center, which is open to visitors looking to learn more about the space program. Due to its association with NASA, Huntsville is sometimes referred to as the Rocket City.

The Stars were originally an Oakland A's affiliate. That relationship ended following the 1998 season, and ever since Huntsville has been a Milwaukee Brewers farm club. The long list of future major leaguers who have played in Huntsville includes such former Stars as Jose Canseco, Mark McGwire, Scott Brosius, Jason Giambi, Miguel Tejada, Tim Hudson, Ben Sheets, Rickie Weeks, and Prince Fielder.

Joe W. Davis Municipal Stadium also serves as the home field of the University of Alabama-Huntsville baseball team. The Chargers, who belong to the Gulf South Conference, play an exhibition game each spring against the Stars. In the fall the stadium hosts high school football and soccer.

Game Day

Getting to the Park

Huntsville is located in the northern part of Alabama, about 20 miles from the Tennessee border. The city is just a two-hour drive south of Nashville via I–65, and two-hour drive north of Birmingham on the same road. The stadium is just south of downtown. Follow I–65 to I–565 East, then take exit 19A and follow Memorial Parkway South to the Drake Avenue exit. Turn right onto Don Mincher Drive and follow it to the stadium. This access road is named after the former big leaguer and former Stars owner who now serves as president of the Southern League.

Inside the Park

More than half of the seats at this concrete jungle are aluminum benches, but don't despair, there are still plenty of stadium chairs to go around. The Stars average less than 3,000 fans per game and the stadium has more than 4,700 real seats. So if you don't want to sit in the bleachers, you don't have to.

There are two distinct seating bowls, a lower one, down at field level, and an upper one, raised 8 feet above a walkway between the two levels.

In the lower bowl, the ten rows of blue stadium chairs around the infield sell as Lower Box Seats. These end just past first base on the right field side, giving way to a lawn that serves as a group picnic area. On the left field side, the Lower Boxes end at third base, but the lower bowl continues all the way out to the left field corner, housing metal bleachers that sell as General Admission down the lines.

The steeply graded upper bowl offers red stadium chairs around the infield that sell as Upper Box Seats, and then lots and lots of bleachers along the left field line. Oddly, there is one lone section of bleachers at the end of the second level on the first base side, even with the base.

Deep in the left field corner, the upper and lower seats turn abruptly toward the foul line, tracing the back of what serves as the end zone during football season. They end in foul territory right behind the foul pole.

The stadium's fifteen air-conditioned suites appear behind the Upper Box Seats between home plate and third base. In the spot where skyboxes would normally also appear along the first baseline, there is nothing but a big concrete wall. This contributes to an unbalanced, unfinished effect. It reminded me of the new cars that my father used to buy when I was a kid. To save money he'd order them stripped down with none of the luxuries. Where the clock should have been on the dashboard, there was instead a blank plastic plate. Where the buttons for the A/C should have been, more plastic plates. Where the tape deck should have been, another plastic plate. And so on. Obviously, football stadiums don't usually provide luxury suites at the backs of the end zones, but baseball stadiums usually provide them along both baselines, not just one.

The concourse runs inside the stadium, beneath the Upper Level. The city has made an effort to warm up this concrete corridor with some color. In addition to the ballpark basics and Domino's Pizza, fans enjoy fresh cooked treats at Billy Ray's Grill on the third base side.

The Joe Experience

The local mascot is Homer the Pole Cat, who wears a white Stars jersey and bright red sneakers. The kids in Huntsville enjoy Homer at the ballpark during the summer months and at various community events all year long. Homer makes his services available to non-profit groups for no charge. His favorite night of the year is the "Stars Scouts Night" when local Boy Scout troops camp out on the field after a game and watch movies on the stadium video board.

The Stars offer several season-long promotions. On "Two for Tuesdays," fans enjoy two-for-one ticket, hot dog, pizza, and soda prices. If the Stars win on "We Wanna Win Wednesdays," fans can use their ticket stubs to get free admission to the next home game.

On "Thirsty Thursdays," the team offers $1.00 soda and beer specials until the fifth inning. On Fridays, fans enjoy a fireworks show after the game. On Sundays, fans bring their church bulletins to the game to get tickets for half price.

On the Town

Before and after games Stars fans congregate at **Applebee's** (3028 Memorial Parkway), right near the stadium. Just southeast of the stadium, **Wings Sports Grille** (4250 Balmoral Drive) also sees its business pick up on game days. **John Hunt Park,** which is named after the Freemason who first settled these parts and after whom the city would eventually be named, is south of the stadium on Memorial Drive. And a bit farther south the **Huntsville Municipal Golf Course** is the site of the annual Huntsville Stars Boosters Club's "Golfing with the Stars" event. The tournament pairs Stars players and coaches with local fans in a four-person scramble.

The **U.S. Space and Rocket Center** (1 Tranquility Base) is just west of the stadium, easily accessible via exit 15 off I–565. The center offers a museum, rocket park, and IMAX theater, and interactive attractions like a Mars rock-climbing wall, lunar lander, and launch simulator that propels people 140 feet in 2.5 seconds with 4 G's of force. The center is open seven days a week from 9:00 A.M. until 5:00 P.M. Admission costs $18.95 for adults and $12.95 for children.

Finally, barbecue junkies will be happy to hear that one of Huntsville's signature events is the **Whistle Stop Festival & Rocket City BBQ**, which takes place each May at the Huntsville Depot. The competition awards cash prizes in five categories—chicken, pork ribs, pulled pork, beef brisket, and dessert—while festival-goers enjoy entertainment and music.

HANK AARON STADIUM

Mobile BayBears

Class AA, Southern League
(ARIZONA DIAMONDBACKS)

Hank Aaron Stadium
755 Boiling Brothers Avenue
Mobile, Alabama
251–479–2327

After a thirty-six-year hiatus, Mobile welcomed the affiliated minor leagues back to its city limits on April 17, 1997. Native son Hank Aaron—wearing a dapper gray suit and a smile from ear to ear—delivered the first pitch at the brand new ballpark bearing his name. Then, once the opening ceremonies were taken care of, the Mobile BayBears beat the Birmingham Barons 4–2 before a sell-out crowd of 6,523 people.

While many of the choices related to Hank Aaron Stadium's unusual design can be called into question, one thing that can't be is the stadium's name. Rather than prostituting its new ballpark for a potentially lucrative naming-rights deal like so many other minor league teams and cities have done in recent years, Mobile chose to honor one of its own. Aaron was born in Mobile in 1934 and grew up in a house in the Toulminville section of town. He played shortstop and third base, first at Central High School and then, after transferring, at the Josephine Allen Institute. Aaron had an unorthodox approach at the plate and actually hit "cross-handed," with his right hand down near the knob of the bat and his left hand above it. But his natural talent was undeniable. By the time he was fifteen years old, he was playing for the Pritchett Athletics,

a local semipro team that paid him $3.00 per game. Two years later, he joined the semipro Mobile Black Bears, who paid him $10.00 per game. After an exhibition between the Black Bears and Indianapolis Clowns of the Negro American League in 1952, Clowns business manager Bunny Downs offered Aaron his first professional contract and Aaron accepted, but his stay with the Clowns was short-lived. Aaron's acumen on the diamond attracted the attention of the Boston Braves, who bought his contract for $10,000 and sent him to their minor league affiliate in Eau Claire, Wisconsin, where he finished the 1952 season. The next year, Aaron dominated the South Atlantic League for the Boston's farm team in Jacksonville, and by 1954 he was in the big leagues.

Today, Hank Aaron Stadium stands as an enduring monument to the life and times of the quiet, humble man who endured countless threats and taunts on the way to breaking the most hallowed record in American professional sports. Hmm . . . I wonder if there will one day be a minor league park in Riverside, California, named after Barry Lamar Bonds. For some reason, I'm thinking . . . no.

Hank Aaron Stadium certainly earns points for bucking convention and embracing a unique design approach. Although it was built in an era that has witnessed the construction of ballparks across the country featuring sunken playing fields, open concourses, and luxury boxes hung up above the concourse, Mobile's $8 million stadium offers none of the above. The luxury boxes are actually down at field level, located between and behind the dugouts, offering two rows of outdoor seats protected by netting, and glassed-in seats right behind. A flat green roof covers the suites. Then the first row of seats available to ordinary fans begins, about 20 feet above the field. From there the seating bowl rises sharply to the small gray press box behind home plate. While I normally appreciate any ballpark that makes an effort to offer its own variation of the gameday experience, I have to think the common fan—the one who can afford $8.00 or $10.00 for a ticket, but not $1,500 to rent a luxury box—is getting shafted in Mobile.

Even the territory just beyond the corner bases—where there are decent field-level seats at most parks—is off limits to most fans in Mobile. The private Stadium Club—reserved for season-ticket-holders—sits along the foul line just past first, while a video arcade—complete with skeet-ball and air-hockey—takes up valuable space past third.

Although Hank Aaron Stadium falls short of providing the type of sight lines that some parks do, it succeeds in offering lots of peripheral activities for families and casual fans. Nonetheless, the BayBears have witnessed a steady decline in attendance in recent years. The team drew 332,639 fans in their inaugural 1997 season, but only 207,597 in 2006, which ranked eighth in the ten-team Southern League.

Sagging support aside, the BayBears enjoyed a successful first decade on the field. A San Diego Padres affiliate from 1997 through 2006, the team captured its first Southern League championship in its second season, going 86–54 during the 1998 season and breezing through the playoffs. For their efforts the BayBears were named the "Minor League Team of the Year" by *Baseball America*, beating out 177 other teams. Mobile won its second league title in 2004, when it was crowned league cochampion along with the Tennessee Smokies after Hurricane Ivan wiped out the Southern League playoffs.

The Padres traveled to Mobile for exhibition games in 1998, 1999, and 2001. In 1998 Tony Gwynn was the star attraction. In 2001 former BayBears Matt Clement, David Newhan, and Wiki González were the homecoming heroes. Mobile's affiliation with the Padres ended after the 2006 season though, as the Padres opted to move their prospects to San Antonio of the Texas League. Mobile swiftly filled the void, inking the Arizona Diamondbacks to a PDC prior to the start of the 2007 season.

Prior to the arrival of the BayBears, the Mobile Bay Sharks of the independent Texas-Louisiana League called Mobile "home" in 1994 and 1995. The Sharks played at Eddie Stanky Field on the campus of the University of South Alabama. Predictably, the team folded when it was announced that the Southern League would be coming to town in 1997.

While Mobile's connection to the minor league game dates back all the way to the late-1800s, its relationship with the game has been sporadic. The Mobile Bears enjoyed success in the Southern Association in the early 1900s, but the team moved to Knoxville in 1931. Then baseball returned to Mobile in 1944 when the Knoxville Smokies moved back to Mobile and renamed themselves the Bears. The Bears won the Southern Association championship in 1947 but disbanded in 1961.

Game Day

Getting to the Park

Mobile belongs to the parcel of Alabama territory that extends south between Florida and Mississippi, ending at the Gulf of Mexico. It is only 20 miles from Mobile to Mississippi via I–10, and only 40 miles from Mobile to Florida via the same road. The ballpark is located a mile north of I–10, just east of I–65. Take exit 1 off I–65 and turn right onto Satchel Paige Drive. Then turn right onto Boiling Brothers Boulevard, which leads to the stadium parking lot.

Inside the Park

The first three rows high above field level contain the Stadium Club Seats. A narrow walkway runs behind these. Above the walkway the first eight rows sell as Super Box Seats, while the back nine rows sell as Box Seats. Fans sitting in the first few rows of the Super Boxes contend with view-blocking traffic on the walkway.

Section 101 is just to the outfield side of first base, Sections 106 and 107 are behind home plate, and Section 114 is at the end of the seating bowl in shallow left field.

A roof extends off the top of the press box and covers the last few rows of seats in Sections 103 through 105 and 108 through 110. All of the seats are green stadium chairs, but only those in the Stadium Club offer armrests.

If you're bent on scoring a field-level view of the game, but unwilling to buy a season ticket or rent a luxury box, the only remaining option is to buy a ticket to BayBear Mountain, a berm seating area in left field home run territory.

The concourse beneath the seats offers a view of the game on the closed-circuit televisions above the concession stands. Popular treats include hand-dipped corn dogs, spicy Cajun sausages, and baskets of chicken tenders and French fries. The concourse is decorated with the jerseys and photographs of players in the BayBears Hall of Fame.

The Hank Aaron Stadium Experience

Outside the park the Field of Greens is a golf facility with a full-sized driving range and practice putting green. The range runs along the third base side of the stadium. You'll also find Gas Light Park, a festive picnic area with a 50-foot-long inflatable slide, a moonwalk, speed-pitch booth, basketball court, volleyball court, and eight gazebos, outside the park. Inside the park fans find a Wiffle Ball field behind the left field berm, and Bay Beach, which features an inflatable waterslide, beach volleyball court, and tiki bar. And don't forget about that video arcade along the third baseline. Whew, with so much to do at the ballpark, it's a wonder anyone has time to watch the baseball game.

Here's a ballpark feature that you've probably never considered (unless you've flipped ahead and read about the Oklahoma RedHawks and their Bricktown Ballpark). During the dead of winter, when the temperatures in Mobile plummet all the way down into the low 40s at night, the BayBears transform Gas Light Park into BayBears Snow Park, producing as much as forty tons of snow per day. Thus, between December and February, Southern kids who might otherwise never get the chance to play in the snow get to frolic to their hearts content in the white stuff outside the ballpark.

On the Town

The ballpark neighborhood doesn't offer much in the way of eating and drinking establishments for fans other than a handful of fast-food joints about ½ mile north on Government Boulevard.

If you'd like to check out the home park of the University of South Alabama Jaguars, where the city's independent league team played in the early 1990s, head to **Eddie Stanky Field** (USA campus). Named after the former Jaguars coach who played eleven seasons in the major leagues and managed the St. Louis Cardinals from 1952 through 1955 and the Chicago White Sox from 1966 through 1968, the ballpark recently underwent a $2.5 million renovation that was funded in part by alums John Lieber and Luis González. The Jags play in the Sun Belt Conference.

Travelers interested in learning more about African-American culture and history—including about baseball pioneers like Aaron, Satchel Paige, Willie McCovey, and Billy Williams, who all grew up in Mobile—can visit the **National African-American Archives Museum** (564 Dr. Martin Luther King, Jr. Avenue). The museum is open Tuesday through Friday from 8:00 A.M. until 4:00 P.M., and admission is free. If the old white building that houses the museum reminds you of a library, that's because it used to be one. From 1932 until the mid-1960s, it served as the Davis Avenue branch of the Mobile Public Library, the only branch open to African Americans at the time.

MONTGOMERY RIVERWALK STADIUM

Montgomery Biscuits

Class AA, Southern League
(TAMPA BAY DEVIL RAYS)

Montgomery Riverwalk Stadium
200 Coosa Street
Montgomery, Alabama
334–323–2255

The Montgomery Biscuits are one of only four teams in the affiliated minor leagues named after a popular menu item from their region's local cuisine. I'm not counting teams named after animals like bisons, warthogs, manatees, and sidewinders, which may be considered delicious by some but aren't eaten by most rank-and-file baseball fans. The other current teams named after regional foods are the Lakewood BlueClaws, Modesto Nuts, and Cedar Rapids Kernels. As a traveler who likes to sample a hearty portion of whatever the local specialty happens to be, I like this trend and hope it catches on. And I think that as teams continue to get more creative and inventive in search of those merchandising bucks, it probably will. Peering into the future, I see teams with names like the North Carolina Barbecue, Virginia Baked Ham, Vermont Sharp Cheddar, and Buffalo Wings.

Montgomery Riverwalk Stadium is more than just a unique place to order a biscuit and a beer, though. It is also a great place to watch baseball, thanks largely to its innovative use of the preexisting landscape. The ballpark was constructed at a cost of $26 million and opened in 2004, with the hopes that it would anchor an entertainment district along the banks of the Alabama River, which meanders through

Montgomery's northwest quadrant. The park was designed by HOK—the same firm that made the B&O Warehouse such a major part of Baltimore's Camden Yards—and it incorporates an old rail yard storage facility that has stood since 1898 into its design. The "train shed" is a long, thin building that rises at the back of the concourse along the first baseline. Fans pass through it as they enter the park and find concession stands and restrooms built into its first level. Upstairs, the shed houses six luxury boxes. Just to the first base side of home plate, the newly constructed ballpark structure meets seamlessly with the old building to round the corner and head down the third baseline. The new structure covers the open concourse behind the last row of seats and provides room upstairs for the press box and another fourteen luxury boxes.

The seating bowl consists of green plastic stadium chairs that look a lot like the ones in Baltimore. These seats are sunken below street level, allowing the concourse to run around the entire stadium behind the last row. The buildings of downtown Montgomery rise behind the first base grandstand, including the handsome RSA tower, which glows a delightful pink at night. From the walkway that runs atop the 14-foot-high left field wall, fans can spy a glimpse of the state capital.

Outside, an old brick building at the corner of Coosa Street and Tallapoosa Street sits behind the home plate grandstand, serving as the team's front office. The understated façade offers little to suggest a baseball field exists inside, other than the light towers mounted high above the stadium. The railway runs just behind the left field fence, and the Alabama flows right behind the tracks. The ballpark plot was the site of a Confederate military prison during the Civil War. A historic marker outside the park tells the story of the 700 Union prisoners who were held at the prison from

April through December of 1862, "in a foul vermin-abounding cotton depot . . . without blankets, and only the hard earth or wood planks as a bed." According to the sign nearly 200 of the prisoners died due to the inhumane living conditions before those remaining were transferred to a different prison in Tuscaloosa. I give Montgomery credit for freely providing this information on the sign. If I were running a city, though, I think that would be one of those embarrassing things I'd tried not to publicize, especially outside a popular tourist attraction.

The Biscuits arrived in Montgomery in 2004, via Orlando, where they had played as the Orlando Rays. The Disney tourists had their chance but proved themselves incapable of supporting a Double-A team. The Baby Rays barely averaged 2,000 fans a game at Cracker Jack Stadium. Meanwhile, Montgomery was proving itself once again able to support a minor league team during the early 2000s. The city had flourished as a minor league town for several decades before a lack of fan support caused the Southern League's Montgomery Rebels to move to Birmingham following the 1980 season. Twenty years later, an independent league team reaffirmed Montgomery's love of the game. Playing at old Paterson Field, the same 1950s-era stadium that the Rebels had called home, the Montgomery Wings fielded a team in the All-American Association in 2001. The team drew more than 78,000 fans to thirty-four home dates, more than doubling the attendance total of the league's next best draw. When the All-American Association folded after the Wings first season, the

Wings switched to the Southeastern League the next year and continued to attract big crowds. Recognizing the important role that baseball could play in Montgomery once again, the Montgomery city council passed a new ballpark proposal in December of 2002. A month later, the Southern League announced the Rays would be moving to Montgomery after one final lame-duck season in Orlando. After a "name the team" contest drew nearly 3,000 entries, Montgomery named its team the Biscuits in May of 2003. Two months later, construction began on a new ballpark near the river.

On April 16, 2004, an SRO crowd of 7,378 fans turned out to watch the first game at Riverwalk Stadium. A Blackhawk helicopter from Maxwell Air Force Base delivered the ceremonial first pitch, then Montgomery pitcher Jarod Matthews pitched an 8–0 shutout against the Huntsville Stars. The Biscuits went on to draw 322,946 fans in 2004, good for second-best attendance mark in the Southern League. The next year, they topped the 300,000 plateau

Montgomery Riverwalk Stadium

again and finished second in the league—again. Those fans got the chance to watch a number of the Devil Rays prospects in action, as Elijah Dukes, Joey Gathright, Scott Kazmir, B. J. Upton, and Delmon Young all played for the Biscuits in those first two seasons.

Montgomery's previous tenure as a Southern League outpost spanned the years from 1965 through 1980, during which time the Rebels were a Detroit Tigers farm club. Future Mo-Town stars like Lou Whitaker and Alan Trammell honed their skills in Montgomery, while future big league skipper Jim Leyland spent time at the Rebels helm. Before that Montgomery fielded teams in the South Atlantic League, Southeastern League, Southern Association, and Alabama-Florida League, dating back to 1903. Those teams had names like the Black Sox, Bombers, Capitols, Grays, and Senators.

Game Day

Getting to the Park

Alabama's capital city is in the southeastern part of the state, where it is easily accessible via I–85 and I–65. From I–65, take exit 172 and follow Herron Street a few blocks east, then turn left onto Coosa Street. Parking is provided by several privately operated lots on North Perry Street and Columbus Street, while early arrivals find free curbside spots around the stadium.

Inside the Park

Riverwalk Stadium offers 6,000 seats, room for 1,000 people on its right field berm, and room for another 1,000 at the group picnic area in center field.

The seating bowl offers seventeen rows of stadium chairs that extend almost to the foul pole on the left side but just a little way past the infield on the right side. The first few rows around the infield sell as Executive Boxes. The remaining infield seats sell as Super Boxes. Beyond the corner bases, Box Seats prevail.

The seating bowl begins at Section 101 in deep left field, continues to Section 106, the first section of Super Boxes at third base, makes the turn at Section 111 behind home plate, extends to Section 117, the last section of Super Boxes at first base, and ends at Section 120 in shallow right. Fans who sit down the left field line have difficulty seeing the scoreboard in left-center because it is angled toward the first baseline, but they do enjoy a view of the nicely illuminated train shed behind the first base seats.

The right field berm wraps around the foul pole and bulges out into the field of play, making for a wavy right field home run fence. The effect is similar to the bend in the right field wall at Banner Island Ballpark in Stockton, which follows a similar path to make room for its right field party deck.

Of course the signature concession item in Montgomery is the ballpark biscuit. Fans find these fluffy buttermilk treats at a stand on the concourse behind home plate called "Biscuits (of Course)." Biscuits can be ordered plain, topped with syrup, or sandwiched around chicken or ham. Other favorite treats include the footlong bratwurst, catfish fingers, Philly cheesesteak, barbecue items, and Mexican items.

Kids find a playground area called "Big Mo's Dugout" in left field. The gift store, called the "Biscuit Basket," is behind home plate. The elevated concourse atop the left field wall allows for views of the railroad and river behind the fence, and of the city skyline behind the first base stands.

The Riverwalk Stadium Experience

The Montgomery mascot is Big Mo. As far as I can tell, this furry brown creature must be the interspecies love child of an aardvark and anteater. I think old school *Sesame Street* viewers will agree that he also bears a slight resemblance to Snuffleupagus.

The Biscuits offer the usual array of between inning contests and promotions, including many that utilize the million-dollar LED screen in left field.

A couple of times per game a train passes by on the tracks behind the left field fence. The train conductor toots his horn. The engine puffs some smoke into the air. The crowd cheers. And then the train disappears into the night.

On the Town

Folks visiting Montgomery over Memorial Day Weekend will find a lively block party called **Jubilee Cityfest** taking place in the streets of downtown. The city's signature event is a family-friendly music festival that offers all kinds of entertainment and foods.

Even when the festival is not taking place, downtown Montgomery offers plenty of places to eat and drink, including the **Montgomery Brewing Company** (12 West Jefferson Street), just a block south of the stadium. The "Brew Pub" offers an array of home brews, a full lunch and dinner menu, and live music after the game on Friday and Saturday nights.

Just southwest of the ballpark, **Overlook Park** (Bell Street and Tallapoosa Street) offers a scenic perch where visitors can peer down at the city.

Montgomery's old ballpark, **Paterson Field** (Madison Avenue and Hall Street), still stands. Its exterior consists of little more than steel pillars holding up the ugly cement underbelly of the seating bowl. The former home of the Montgomery Rebels and Montgomery Wings serves as the site of the annual NCAA Division II baseball championship.

TRUSTMARK PARK
Mississippi Braves

Class AA, Southern League
(ATLANTA BRAVES)

Trustmark Park
1 Braves Way
Pearl, Mississippi
601–932–8788

After a five-year hiatus, the affiliated minor leagues returned to Mississippi's largest metro region in 2005 with the debut of the Mississippi Braves in the Jackson suburb of Pearl. Jackson, a longtime Texas League outpost, had hosted a New York Mets affiliate from 1975 through 1990 and a Houston Astros affiliate from 1991 through 1999, before watching its team moved to Round Rock in 2000. The market quickly regrouped, putting together a privately financed ballpark plan to lure the Southern League's Greenville Braves to town.

The Braves, who are owned and operated by the big league Atlanta Braves, had played in Greenville for twenty-one seasons, but had grown disenchanted with their aging ballpark there. Ironically, after losing its team Greenville built a brand new park and wound up joining the South Atlantic League, just as the Jackson market built a new park and joined a new league only after losing the Jackson Generals to Round Rock. In any case it would seem like things worked out well for all three cities involved.Geographically, Jackson makes more sense as a member of the Southern League than the Texas League, Greenville's market size is more suited for Single-A than Double-A, and Round Rock has emerged as one of the hottest minor league towns in the country.

Jackson's old park, Smith-Wills Stadium, was a basic facility from the 1970s that was still functional but offered neither the old-time charm nor modern comforts that give minor league teams the best chances to succeed these days. It was time for a change, and Greater Jackson got the wakeup call as soon as its team moved away. Better late than never, right?

The Mississippi Braves averaged about 4,000 fans per game during their first two seasons at Trustmark Park, which must have been slightly disappointing to the team, but as the neighborhood around the ballpark continues to develop into the bustling retail and entertainment center that is anticipated, the team should see its attendance numbers increase. A Bass Pro Shop and seventeen-screen movie theater have already opened near Trustmark Park, and several other projects are underway.

Trustmark Park is inviting and modern. It offers an open concourse atop the last row of seats that encircles the entire field, a grass outfield seating area, an on-site restaurant, a playground, twenty-two luxury boxes, a tiered group area, and a video scoreboard that anchors the gameday entertainment package.

While Trustmark Park is not terribly unique compared with the many other stadiums that have opened in recent years, you can't really hold that against it. There comes a point where eccentricities for the sake of eccentricities can become overkill, so it's okay with me that the ballpark's designers, which included HOK, didn't go overboard and make any bizarre outfield dimensions or weird seating areas.

The ballpark is notable for a larger-than-usual plaza behind home plate, much of which is uncovered. The press box is not set back in line with the glassed-in portions of the luxury suites on either side of it, but rather juts out over the home plate grandstand giving the scribes an excellent bird's-eye view of the game. The upper level is a warm cream color while the steel support trusses for the roof are dark green. The ballpark has an open and airy feel, thanks to the fact that the concourse is open to the field on one side and to the plaza on the other.

Since the Mississippi Braves are actually owned by Time Warner, which owns the big league Braves, it should come as no surprise that Trustmark Park is one of the most "wired" ballparks in the minors. The facility offers more than 150 televisions throughout its concourse, plaza, and various seating areas, and wireless Internet access at the Cellular South Cafe in right field.

Game Day

Getting to the Park

Pearl is an eastern suburb of Jackson, which is Mississippi's largest city and state capital. The cities are located near the intersection of I–20 and I–55, which locals refer to as the "Crossroads of the South." Trustmark Park sits on the outskirts of Pearl in an area currently being developed into a retail and entertainment center. From I–55, take I–20 East and then take Highway 49 South. Turn right onto Highway 80, then turn right again onto Bass Pro Drive, and the ballpark will be on the left.

Inside the Park

Trustmark Park has 6,000 fixed seats and room for 2,000 fans on a large outfield berm. On the right side of the park, the comfortable stadium chairs extend all the way to the foul pole. Across the diamond the seats end halfway down the left field line, giving way to a tiered picnic area. The seats are all close to field level and provide excellent sight lines. The infield sections house the Dugout Level Seats, beginning with Section 104 at third base, continuing down the line to Section 110 behind home plate, and extending to Section 117 at first base. Meanwhile, the sec-

tions along the outfield foul lines contain the Field Level Seats. Sections 101 through 103 are in shallow left, while Sections 118 through 124 are in right. The tiered patio in left wraps around the foul pole and continues a short distance into home run territory before the berm seating area begins. The berm continues into right-center.

On the concourse fans find plenty of televisions showing the game and concession stands with clever names like the Mendoza Line, Hot Corner Slice, Basket Catch, and Sweet Spot. The most unique item is the fried catfish basket, which comes with French fries, coleslaw, and hush puppies.

Those looking for a sit-down dining experience can venture out to the Cellular South Cafe, which overlooks the field in right field home run territory. The menu includes items like fried pickles, seafood gumbo, grilled rib eye, and Mississippi mud pie. The cafe is open daily for lunch and for dinner on game days.

The Trustmark Park Experience

If your baseball adventures take you into central Mississippi when the Braves happen to be on a road trip, don't despair. You can still check out Trustmark Park. That's because the team offers guided tours of the park on non-game days between 11:00 A.M. and 2:00 P.M. The $6.00 cost includes lunch (hot dog, chips, soda) at the park and a complimentary gift. Fans get to walk on the warning track, visit the home clubhouse, and peer into the luxury boxes. The only catch is that all tours must be booked in advance. Call 601–664–7604 for more information or to book your tour.

On game days two monsters serve as mascots, one named "Jackson" and the other named "Pearl." Both have bright blue fur, even brighter yellow hair, buggy eyes, and horns atop their heads. Although these creatures are exceedingly friendly, I'm pretty sure they'd have turned up in my nightmares when I was eight years old. They look like they came right out of the pages of *Where the Wild Things Are*.

As for the regular weekly promotions, the Braves offer fireworks every Friday night and let the kids run the bases on Sunday afternoon.

On the Town

While anglers will certainly find the **Bass Pro Shop** adjacent to Trustmark Park worth visiting, seam-heads will find it worthwhile to make the trip across the Pearl River into Jackson to check out a pair of baseball-related sites in the northeast corner of the city.

Smith-Wills Stadium (Cool Papa Bell Drive), longtime home of Jackson's Texas League entrant, currently serves the Jackson Parks and Recreation Department as a multipurpose facility. The stadium, which opened in 1975, got a new field in 2004 when the city replaced the natural grass and dirt with artificial Spinturf. The only dirt is on the pitchers mound. As for the stadium itself, it features a high concrete grandstand behind home plate, topped by a midsized roof. After Nolan Ryan's baseball group bought the Jackson Generals in 1999 and moved them to Texas to become the Round Rock Express, an independent league team made a go of it at Smith-Wills Stadium, calling itself first the DiamondKats and then the Senators. The team was a member of the Texas-Louisiana League in 2000, then the Central League from 2002 through 2005. The Senators and Mississippi Braves overlapped in the Jackson market during the 2005 season, before the Senators disbanded.

The **Mississippi Sports Hall of Fame and Museum** (1152 Lakeland Drive) is right next door to Smith-Wills Stadium. It boasts the largest collection of Dizzy Dean memorabilia in America, thanks to donations made by Dean's widow after his death in 1974. These items include Dean's 1934 World Series ring, his Hall of Fame ring, and personal photos of the wacky hurler posing with friends like President Eisenhower and Satchel Paige. Aside from offering memorabilia related to Dean and other southern sports legends, the museum features a popular Participatory Room where visitors can partake in interactive baseball, golf, football, and soccer exhibits. The museum is open Monday through Saturday from 10:00 A.M. until 4:00 P.M. and admission is $5.00.

ZEPHYR FIELD
New Orleans Zephyrs

Class AAA, Pacific Coast League
(NEW YORK METS)

Zephyr Field
6000 Airline Drive
Metairie, Louisiana
504–734–5155

When Hurricane Katrina ripped through New Orleans in late August of 2005, the Pacific Coast League season was just winding down. Though Zephyr Field sustained damage to its roof, and though its scoreboard blew down into the seats, when the big winds finally stopped blowing, the Zephyrs returned home to discover that their stadium had held up reasonably well. Thanks to its location on a hillside in the western suburb of Metairie, the ballpark and its neighborhood did not suffer the type of flooding that besieged much of New Orleans. And in the days immediately following the storm, FEMA used Zephyr Field as a National Guard outpost.

As New Orleans slowly recovered in the months ahead, the local NFL, NBA, and Arena Football League teams found it impossible to resume play at their heavily damaged facilities. The Zephyrs, though they had much work to do, resolved to repair Zephyr Field in time for the start of the 2006 season. After team owner Don Beaver spent more than $2 million on an aggressive reconstruction, the largest gathering to fill the ballpark in three years—a standing room only crowd of 11,006 people—turned out on opening day to watch the Zephyrs play the Round Rock Express. The players donned warm-up jackets emblazoned with the words "Proud to Call New Orleans Home," while many fans held up signs that read simply "Thank

You." Members of the home team were visibly moved by the fan outpouring, and the visiting players were too. The Express, a Houston Astros farm club, featured a lineup laden with former Zephyrs, since New Orleans was affiliated with the Astros through 2004.

Although the Express rallied in the ninth inning to claim a 5–4 victory, the first outdoor professional sporting event in New Orleans since Katrina played an important role in returning some degree of normalcy to a city that had already suffered so much and still had a long way to go in rebuilding. Throughout the rest of the 2006 season, baseball continued to do its part in the healing, just as it had in other tragedy-stricken cities like New York in 2001, when the Yankees played deep into October, and Oklahoma City in 1995, when the 89ers gave local fans a few reasons to smile.

In addition to housing Pacific Coast League baseball, Zephyr Field also showcased Conference USA ball in 2006, as the Tulane University team played its entire thirty-eight-game home schedule at Zephyr Field. The Green Wave's Turchin Stadium had been in the midst of a major renovation when Katrina hit, and the storm suspended the project. Thus, the Green Wave opened play at Zephyr Field even before the Zephyrs did, and once the minor league season began there were seven dates when both teams played games on the same day. Construction at Turchin Stadium eventually resumed.

Zephyr Field opened in 1997, five years after the Zephyrs brought minor league baseball back to the Big Easy, fielding the city's first team since the American Association's New Orleans Pelicans departed the Superdome in 1977. The Zephyrs played their first four seasons at Privateer Park on the campus of the University of New Orleans, then moved to Metairie in Jefferson Parrish, after the state of Louisiana built a $23 million stadium for them. The Zephyrs averaged more than 500,000 fans per season in their first three years at the new park, but their annual attendance has since dwindled to about 330,000.

Zephyr Field is small and relatively simple by Triple-A standards, but it offers clear views of the field and an environment in which the game is emphasized first and foremost, with fewer of the peripheral distractions than usual. The stadium exterior features redbrick pillars that form arched entranceways at ground level and tan bricks on the second level. A level higher, visitors can see the exposed steel underbelly of the second deck inside. A small sunroof tops the facility, forming a small crown over the press box and sixteen luxury suites.

Inside, the lower seating bowl extends three-quarters of the way down the lines, and the upper bowl hangs down over the open concourse and last few rows of lower-level seats. The upper bowl continues only so far as the corner bases. The luxury suites appear on either side of the press box at the back of the second level. The scoreboard is above the fence in left-center field, a large hillside offers outfield seating in right-center, and a swimming pool resides in straightaway right.

The Zephyr franchise arrived in New Orleans after getting booted out of Denver to make way for the Colorado Rockies when they joined the National League in 1993. The team brought its affiliation with the Milwaukee Brewers with it to the Big Easy, then switched to a PDC with the Astros in 1997. Given the relative proximity of New Orleans to Houston, the match made sense, and over the next several years, bayou fans enjoyed glimpses of future Astros like Lance Berkman, Adam Everett, Wade Miller, and Roy Oswalt. But when Nolan Ryan's ownership group bought the Edmonton Trappers and moved them to Round Rock in 2005, New Orleans lost its connection with the local big league team and became an affiliate of the Washington Nationals. New Orleans switched

big league parents again following the 2006 season, signing on with the New York Mets.

The highlight for the Zephyrs franchise to date came in 1998, during the team's first season in the Pacific Coast League. Previously, the Zephyrs had played in the American Association. That year, the Zephyrs set a city attendance record for a professional baseball team, drawing 519,584 fans. They also won the Pacific Coast League championship and Triple-A World Series—beating the International League's Buffalo Bisons in a series played in Las Vegas. Berkman hit three home runs and drove in six runs in the World Series clincher to earn the MVP award.

Game Day

Getting to the Park

New Orleans is 350 miles east of Houston, the nearest big league city, and 150 miles west of Mobile, the nearest minor league town. Zephyr Field is in a semiindustrial area a few miles west of downtown. To reach the ballpark, take I–10 to Clearview Parkway South. Turn right onto Airline Drive (U.S. Highway 61 West), and after 3 miles the ballpark will be on the left. Parking costs $3.00 in the stadium lot.

Inside the Park

Zephyr Field offers 10,000 stadium chairs in its two small seating decks, with room for another 1,000 fans or so on its right field hill. The rows are nice and wide in both levels.

The lower level begins at Section 110 in left field, continues to Section 119 behind the plate, and ends at Section 128 in right field. Sections 114 through 124 contain Infield Box Seats, while the four sections in outfield foul territory on either side of the field contain Lower Reserved Seats.

The second deck hangs down over the back rows of the lower level. Section 213 is at third base, Section 219 is behind the plate, and Section 225 is at first base. Second-level Grandstand Seats cost less than the Field Reserved Seats and offer better views.

The sloped hillside beyond the fence in right-center is called the Levee. The hill is barely as high as the outfield fence in left-center where it begins, but gradually it grows higher as it extends across center field and into right. The view from the Levee is distant, making it not quite as attractive as the berms at some minor league venues.

The concession highlights on the open concourse atop the first level include jambalaya, barbecued beef and pork, pigskin nachos, tricolored supreme nachos, cheese enchiladas, and Hebrew National hot dogs. Fans find the best selection of brews on the concourse behind first base. Kids find a playground behind the group party shack in right.

The Zephyr Field Experience

A family of nutrias inhabits the ballpark in New Orleans. If you're not familiar with the wildlife of the Gulf Coast and find yourself wondering what in the world a nutria is, let me tell you. A nutria is an aquatic rodent with brown fur, webbed feet, and buckteeth, that looks something like a beaver. When the Zephyrs first arrived at Zephyr Field, the local nut was Boudreaux D. Nutria, who the fans quickly took to calling "Boo." Soon thereafter, Boo placed a personal ad in *Gambit Weekly,* and when the ad was answered by a lovely young thing

named Clotile Picou, Boo had found his soul mate. The two were married at home plate in the August of 1998 before a sell-out crowd, and they've been churning out babies ever since. The pack of ballpark varmints has grown to include Beauregard, Cherie, Claudette, Jean-Pierre, Noelle, and Thibodaux, and according to several fans who visited Zephyr Field late in the 2006 season, Clotile appeared plumper than usual around the midsection, fueling speculation that another litter might be on the way.

On the Town

Near the ballpark fans find a string of fast-food joints on Airline Drive, but no place to rival the eats, drinks, and good times found in New Orleans's famous **French Quarter.** This one of a kind entertainment district was among the first sections of the city to reopen after the floodwaters receded, and is a must-visit for any fun-loving traveler. The most famous spot for nightlife is **Bourbon Street,** but there are other excellent restaurants and clubs throughout the French Quarter, so do take some time to explore.

Fans interested in seeing where the Zephyrs originally played can stop by **Maestri Field at Privateer Park** (6801 Franklin Avenue) on the campus of the University of New Orleans. This 4,200-seat ballpark sits near scenic Lake Pontchartrain. The UNO Privateers play in the Sun Belt Conference.

DICKEY-STEPHENS PARK

Arkansas Travelers

Class AA, Texas League
(LOS ANGELES ANGELS OF ANAHEIM)

Dickey-Stephens Park
East Broadway Avenue
North Little Rock, Arkansas
501–664–1555

In the spring of 2007, minor league baseball officially bid adieu to one of its five oldest ballparks. The Arkansas Travelers began their 101st season of play at brand new Dickey-Stephens Park. The team moved across the Arkansas River from Little Rock to North Little Rock after Ray Winder Field became too old, cramped, and clunky to host the only professional team in Arkansas any longer.

The relocation of the Travelers represented a major coup for North Little Rock, which has always enjoyed a friendly rivalry with its neighbors to the south. The city pejoratively referred to as "Dogtown" got its hands on the Travelers after its residents voted in a special election to approve a 1 percent sales tax increase over a two-year period to fund the construction of a $28 million stadium and the expansion of a local senior citizens center. That vote, along with the news that local businessman Warren Stephens had offered to donate eleven acres of land on the North Little Rock waterfront, sealed the team's relocation plans in August of 2005.

On November 30, 2005, Stephens and other city and team officials joined North Little Rock mayor Patrick Hays at a groundbreaking ceremony for the new park. At the ceremony it was announced that the facility would be named in honor of the Stephens family and the Dickey family. Wilt and Jack Stephens, Warren Stephens's father and uncle respec-

tively, were longtime Little Rock baseball enthusiasts who were friends and business associates with former Travelers players Bill and George Dickey. Bill Dickey, of course, is the Hall of Fame catcher, who played for the New York Yankees. The eleven-time All-Star returned to Little Rock after his playing career and spent his latter years in the city until his passing in 1993. His brother George enjoyed a less illustrious six-year career with the Boston Red Sox and Chicago Cubs.

As the stadium was built during the summer of 2006, there were some unexpected twists and turns, most notably a $4 million cost overrun, attributed to higher energy costs and to the Hurricane Katrina effect. There were also some rumblings from discontented Travelers fans who were dismayed that many decisions related to design and construction of the publicly funded ballpark were made behind closed doors rather than in a public forum. Just the same, the ballpark stayed on schedule to open with a game between the Travelers and Springfield Cardinals on April 5, 2007.

Dickey-Stephens Park was designed to showcase a stunning view of the Arkansas River and of the Little Rock skyline beyond the right field fence. From the seats on the third base side, fans enjoy a view of the Broadway Bridge crossing the river behind the right field grandstand. Following the modern mold, the HKS-designed ballpark offers a sunken playing field, a concourse atop the last row of seats, an upper deck for luxury suites, and berm in the outfield.

Even though Dickey-Stephens Park is cozy, offering just 5,500 seats, many Travelers surely miss the intimacy of the team's old ballpark at War Memorial Park in Little Rock. With its low grandstand roof and 55-foot-high Screen Monster atop the right field fence, Ray Winder Field was one of a kind. However, fans won't miss the cramped concourse area, the long lines at the bathrooms, and the aluminum bleachers. As for the players, they won't miss the musty little clubhouses, the feral cats that haunted the bowels of the stadium, and the "bomb shelter" dugouts that required them to sit on the ground in order to see the game.

Ray Winder Field opened in 1932, replacing Kavanaugh Field as home of the local nine. Originally, the park was named Travelers Field, but in 1966 it was renamed in honor of Ray Winder, the man who led the effort to resurrect the Travelers, after the team disbanded briefly in the late 1950s. Indeed, the Travelers have been a Little Rock institution since their debut in 1895. The team was originally known as the "Little Rock" Travelers. The name paid tribute to a mythical traveling salesman whose exploits provided fodder for storytellers throughout the state in the late 1800s. In 1957 the team became the "Arkansas" Travelers. After representing several leagues and teams through the years, the Travelers have been members of the Texas League since 1966 and have been affiliated with the Los Angeles Angels of Anaheim, California of Orange County, of the USA, of the planet earth since 2001. Previously, the Travelers were a St. Louis Cardinals affiliate from 1966 through 2000.

The great moments in Ray Winder Field history range from a 1937 exhibition in which the home team beat Bill Dickey's defending world champion Yankees to a 1991 rehab start by Fernando Valenzuela that attracted an overflow crowd of more than 12,000 people. And you probably thought Fernandomania was exclusively a Southern California thing. Recent Travelers who reached the major leagues include such stars as J. D. Drew, Chone Figgins, Bobby Jenks, Brian Jordan, Howie Kendrick, John Lackey, Francisco Rodríguez, and Ervin Santana. Despite being fed a steady stream of highly rated Angels prospects, the Travelers ranked near the bottom of the Texas League attendance ledger in their

final several years at Ray Winder Field, averaging less than 3,000 fans per game.

Now this proud franchise has a fan- and player-friendly ballpark across the river to reinvigorate its fan base.

Game Day

Getting to the Park

Little Rock and North Little Rock are in the middle of Arkansas, accessible by both I–40 and I–30. The closest minor league city is Memphis, 150 miles east. Dickey-Stephens Park sits on the south side of North Little Rock, just east of the Broadway Bridge. From I–30, take Route 167 North, then take Route 65 North. You will see the ballpark on the right as you cross the river. Take the first exit on the other side of the bridge and follow East Riverfront Drive to the stadium parking lot.

Inside the Park

The seats extend just a short distance into outfield foul territory. Once the seating bowl ends, the grass seating areas begin, tracing the outfield foul lines and wrapping around the foul poles into home run territory. The first several rows sell as Box Seats, while the rest of the comfortable stadium chairs sell as Reserved Seats. A General Admission ticket is good for a spot somewhere on the lawn areas or in the right field bleachers. The upper level contains twenty-one luxury boxes that have indoor couches, tables for up to fifteen people, and outdoor seats for twelve people.

The Travelers Experience

While the team from Greater Little Rock may not have as large a fan base as some minor league teams, the diehards in central Arkansas are very serious about their baseball. In writing and researching this book, I frequently gleaned information about the country's many teams and ballparks from fan-run Web sites and from blogs where fans took advantage of the opportunity to sound off about what was good and not so good about their local team and ballpark. Travelerocity.com was by far the most comprehensive and highly trafficked (judging from the frequency of new posts on the message board) site I had the pleasure of visiting. Run by an anonymous Travelers fan, the site consistently raised interesting questions throughout the 2006 season, like: Why didn't Little Rock step up to the plate and make more of an effort to keep the Travelers from moving across the river? Why did North Little Rock maintain a shroud of secrecy while designing and building the new park? Did the new road jerseys the Travelers sported in April—emblazoned with the initials NLR—foreshadow an upcoming name change for the team? And so on. Scores of fans weighed in with their opinions on each of these important issues, indicating that they care deeply about their team and are vigilantly rooting for its success.

On the Town

Little Rock is still in the process of deciding what to do with **Ray Winder Field** (Jonesboro Drive). Among the many suggestions under consideration by the city are proposals to turn the ballpark into an office park, into an RV park, or into part of the abutting Little Rock Zoo. Keeping the park as it is, for use as an amateur baseball venue, does not seem like a popular idea, so you may find that Ray Winder Field has been demolished by the time you stop by Little Rock in 2008 or later. In the meantime this historic ballpark is definitely worth checking out. Opportunities to visit relics like this are rare. And Little Rock actually offers two such opportunities. The other ancient ballpark in Little Rock is **Lamar Porter Field** (7th Street and Johnson Street), which was built in 1936, as a Works Progress Administration project. An amateur field from the start, Porter Field is used by the local Boys Club. It features the same wooden bleachers that it did when future Hall of Famer Brooks Robinson graced the diamond as a kid.

Another site to visit is Bill Dickey's grave at **Roselawn Memorial Park** (2801 Asher Avenue).

As for the watering holes and restaurants near the new ballpark, the hope is that some fan-friendly saloons and restaurants to complement the several fast-food joints in the neighborhood will open soon.

SECTION 3

THE MIDWEST

Texas, Oklahoma, Kansas, Missouri, Illinois, Indiana,
Ohio, Michigan, Wisconsin, Nebraska, Iowa

WHATABURGER FIELD

Corpus Christi Hooks

Class AA, Texas League
(HOUSTON ASTROS)

Whataburger Field
734 East Port Avenue
Corpus Christi, Texas
361–561–4665

Since entering the minor league baseball business, Nolan Ryan has proven to be an even better team owner than he was a pitcher. And that's saying something. After all, we're talking about a 300-game winner, a Hall of Famer, and baseball's all-time strikeout king. Oh yeah, and don't forget about those seven no-hitters Ryan threw. But seriously, everything Ryan has touched has turned to gold since he entered the minor league ownership game. On retiring, the legend from Alvin signed a lifetime personal services contract with the Houston Astros, then watched as the Texas Rangers erected a statue bearing his likeness at their ballpark in Arlington. Then he got to work, further cementing his place atop the pantheon of Texas baseball legends. Sorry Roger, you may have more Cy Youngs, but Ryan is still the king of this state. Rack up another thousand strikeouts, throw at least one no-hitter, and establish a couple of the most successful minor league baseball teams in the country, and *then* we'll talk.

Ryan and prominent Houston businessman Don Sanders formed Ryan-Sanders Baseball in 2000. That year, their Round Rock Express joined the Texas League and proceeded to set a new Double-A attendance record. Then the Express broke its own record in each of the next three years. At that point Ryan and Sanders decided Round Rock could probably support

a Triple-A team. So they bought the Edmonton Trappers and moved them to town. Thus, Round Rock joined the Pacific Coast League in 2005, while the Texas League team that had been playing in the city moved 230 miles south to a brand new ballpark in Corpus Christi.

The fledgling Corpus Christi Hooks fell short of approaching the eye-popping 700,277 fans that Round Rock's Dell Diamond attracted in its first season as a Pacific Coast League facility in 2005, but the Hooks did draw 505,189 fans to Whataburger Field—good for third best in all of Double-A—as Texas League baseball returned to the Gulf Coast city for the first time in forty-six years.

Designed by HKS and built for the city of Corpus Christi for $27 million—including the land acquisition costs and accompanying infrastructure improvements—Whataburger Field stands where abandoned cotton warehouses stood previously. The lucrative cotton industry helped put Corpus Christi on the map back in the first two decades of the last century, and the new ballpark was designed to reflect this heritage. The exterior façade features brick pillars and corrugated gray steel that rises to meet a flat gray roof. The design gives the park the look of an old cotton mill. Inside, fans find cotton presses sitting on either side of the scoreboard in left field. The ballpark was built around these small gray metal houses that stand on stilts. They were once used to compress cotton on its way to sea, but now they're purely decorative.

While this cotton-centric sensibility is enough to make Whataburger Field unique, the park also offers an outfield view unlike any other. The massive Harbor Bridge dominates the skyline, connecting the mainland to Corpus Christi Beach. The bridge stretches from right to center field, its steel skeleton seeming to hover just above the field. From the ballpark seats fans can also see the USS

Lexington aircraft carrier docked at Corpus Christi Beach, the Texas State Aquarium, and the large vessels that pass through the shipping channel behind the left field fence.

The ballpark also comes with more than the usual amount of modern bells and whistles. For starters there's a Little League field behind the batter's eye in center. The tiny park sees action all summer long, welcoming area youth teams to play their own games and then file into the big park to watch the pros. Fans also find a swimming pool, basketball court, and rock-climbing wall behind the outfield fence.

Also worthy of mention is the 18-foot-tall, 3,000-pound statue of a baseball player that stands amidst a cluster of palm trees outside the home plate entrance. The statue is believed to be the largest bronze portrayal of a baseball player in the world. *For the Love of the Game* depicts a player looking wistfully into space as he holds a baseball bat across his shoulders with one hand on the barrel and one on the handle. The $150,000 piece was commissioned by the city and funded by a public arts rider attached to the original stadium proposal.

For those unfamiliar with the fast-food chains indigenous to the Lone Star State, I can tell you that Whataburger is indeed a rapidly spreading burger franchise, that it was founded in Corpus Christi in the 1950s, and that it signed a fifteen-year stadium naming rights agreement with the Hooks in 2005. In addition to serving the Hooks, Whataburger Field is the site of the four-day Whataburger College Classic each March. The participants include Texas colleges like Rice, TCU, and Texas A & M.

Game Day

Getting to the Park

Corpus Christi is 215 miles southwest of Houston and 145 miles southeast of San Antonio. Make no mistake, this is Astros country. The ballpark is located in the port district on the shores of Corpus Christi Inlet. It is just east of the Route 181 Bridge. To reach the park, follow I–37 until it ends in downtown Corpus Christi, turn left onto Chaparral Street, then left again onto Port Avenue. The parking lot behind the grandstand charges $3.00 per car.

Inside the Park

Fans pass through the ballpark gates and then walk up a set of stairs to access the main concourse, which runs atop the last row of seats. The seating bowl extends into the outfield on either side, ending at the midpoint between the corner bases and foul poles. All of the 5,050 seats are dark green stadium chairs with cup holders. There are also two outfield berms that provide room for another 2,000 people. The Hooks averaged more than 7,000 fans per game during their first two seasons,

Whataburger Field

so you'd be wise to order tickets in advance of your visit to Corpus Christi.

The Hooks make things easy on the fans and ticket tellers by offering just two different ticket options. The seats all sell as Reserved Seats, and they're all priced the same whether they're in the first row or last, in Section 110 in left field, Section 114 behind the home dugout at third base, Section 119 behind home plate, Section 124 behind the first base dugout, or Section 128 in right field. Meanwhile, a General Admission ticket is good for a spot on the lawn in straightaway left or in right-center.

Small group picnic areas flank the seating berm in right-center, while the Apex Pool and Spa area beside the visiting bull pen in right field home run territory offers a pool and hot tub. A larger group area in deep right field foul territory is called Kieschnick's Korner. The covered party deck was constructed from lumber stripped from the old cotton mills that once stood on the ballpark grounds. The deck is named after local hero Brooks Kieschnick, who was born in nearby Robstown, attended Corpus Christi's Carroll High School, and played his college ball at the University of Texas in Austin. In 1993 the Chicago Cubs made Kieschnick their first-round draft pick. He was an outfielder at the time but would eventually become a left-handed relief specialist. After spending the 2004 season with the Milwaukee Brewers, Kieschnick appeared in five games with the Hooks in 2005 before being promoted to Round Rock. He was never recalled by Houston though, and retired after the season.

There are nineteen luxury boxes in all, seven on the first base side of the press box and twelve on the third base side. These indoor/outdoor suites hang over the concourse.

The concession offerings include a Whataburger restaurant behind home plate, juicy Texas beef at the Nolan Ryan Grill, and tangy Texas barbecue.

The kids area behind the scoreboard in left features a basketball court, 27-foot-high rock-climbing wall, and an elaborate playground.

The Whataburger Field Experience

The mascots here are Rusty the Fishhook and Sammy the Seagull. The between-inning festivities include mascot races (put the smart money on the Seagull), dizzy bat races, and video board features like trivia questions and the "kiss cam."

Not that fans seem to need much incentive to turn out at the ballpark in Corpus Christi, but the crowds are especially robust when the Hooks and their corporate partners give away bobbleheads of past and current Astros like Roger Clemens, Jeff Bagwell, and Craig Biggio.

On the Town

The ballpark is located in the industrial part of Corpus Christi, just across Route 81 from the city's waterfront hub. **Corpus Christi Beach** on the other side of the harbor is accessible via Route 181, which turns into Surfside Avenue. In addition to the tourist-friendly beach and accompanying hotels, restaurants, and pizza shacks, the peninsula is home to the **Texas State Aquarium** (2710 North Shoreline Boulevard) and the **USS *Lexington* Aircraft Carrier Museum** (2914 North Shoreline Boulevard). The aquarium features all kinds of Gulf marine life and a giant waterfall that visitors walk beneath to enter the facility. It is open daily from 9:00 A.M. until 6:00 P.M. The USS *Lexington* was the last operational World War II Essex class aircraft carrier until it was retired to Corpus Christi Bay in 1992. Visitors are allowed free run of the vessel and can also step inside a flight simulator that was once used for pilot training drills. The ship is open seven days a week from 9:00 A.M. until 5:00 P.M.

DR PEPPER/SEVEN UP BALLPARK

Frisco RoughRiders

Class AA, Texas League
(TEXAS RANGERS)

Dr Pepper/Seven Up Ballpark
7300 RoughRiders Trail
Frisco, Texas
972–334–1923

In 2001 the Mandalay Sports Entertainment group bought the Shreveport Captains and announced plans to move the team to Frisco, Texas. At the time Shreveport was a bustling metropolis of more than 200,000 people, while Frisco was a bedroom community 35 miles north of Dallas with a population of barely 30,000. It is easy to imagine Texas League fans hearing of these relocation plans and collectively asking the same question that Ray Kinsella heard all movie long in *Field of Dreams*: "You want to build a ballpark, where?" As the last decent Kevin Costner movie that's been made and the story of how baseball came to Frisco both demonstrate, oftentimes we mock our great visionaries before eventually coming to understand their genius.

After getting the Texas Rangers to waive their territorial rights to Frisco in exchange for a promise to make the RoughRiders an affiliate of the Rangers, Mandalay and Frisco built a new stadium that has been filled to the gills with fans ever since it opened in 2003. Dr Pepper/Seven Up Ballpark is the centerpiece of a $300 million Frisco Entertainment and Sports Complex. The stadium has spurred local economic development and interest in the city, and Frisco's population has more than doubled since the ballpark opened.

While this ballpark has one of the most heinous names fans must endure, especially for those like me who once threw up in the back seat of their parents' Dodge Caravan after drinking a sun-warmed can of Dr Pepper, the ballpark itself is gorgeous and innovatively designed.

In the interests of saving page space, preventing another rant about how much I loathe Dr Pepper, and safeguarding my keyboard from any splotches of vomit I may emit, for the rest of this chapter, I will refrain from calling this ballpark by its proper name. Please bear with me and realize that this is more than just another one of my rants at the ridiculous corporate naming phenomenon that has accelerated nationwide in recent years. I assure you, this time it's personal.

The blueprints for Frisco's new stadium were drawn up by HKS, the same Dallas firm that designed Ameriquest Field in Arlington. Even to the untrained eye, the similarities between these two sibling stadiums are apparent. Both feature attractive exterior towers flanking their main entranceways, and both offer expansive outfield lawns. The unique four-story press box structure that rises above the home plate seats in Frisco is reminiscent of the four-level office building above the center field plaza in Arlington. The fifteen-story Embassy Suites Hotel that rises behind the batter's eye in center field in Frisco is also reminiscent of the center field structure in Arlington. Incidentally, John Q. Hammons developed the new Frisco hotel. Hammons is the same fellow who built Hammons Field in Springfield, Missouri, where the Texas League's Springfield Cardinals currently play. (You'll hear more about him in a later chapter.)

The park in Frisco offers a number of features that make it unique from the ballpark in Arlington too. The bull pens are located right up in the stands, down the right field and left field lines. Fans sit between the pens and the field in the lower boxes, while above the pens fans watch the game from the picnic areas. In 2006 a 1,500-square-foot swimming pool was added to the right field berm. The pool is available to members of private parties who rent a spot in the trilevel picnic area. The stadium offers three posh Founder's Club restaurants that are open only to members. The Founder's Club II memorabilia case displays the Texas League championship trophy that was won by the RoughRiders in 2004. A high-resolution video board rises above the left field berm, and plasma screen video boards, similar to the ones at Rogers Centre in Toronto, are built into the outfield fences.

Last, but certainly not least, the ballpark offers six freestanding condolike structures scattered along the concourse atop the seating bowl. These "pavilions" provide concession and restroom space at ground level and porches for luxury box viewers on the second level. Skywalks connect the luxury levels of these buildings to one another, while down at ground level, fans on the concourse can see the field between them. The gaps allow air to flow into and out of the stadium on those sticky Texas nights. Several decorative trees grow between the pavilions, and several more grow atop the berm that spans the outfield.

More than 10,000 fans turned out to watch the RoughRiders play their first game against the Tulsa Drillers on April 3, 2003, but Jorge Piedra of the Drillers stole the show, hitting for the cycle. Nonetheless, professional baseball has been much appreciated by local residents from the outset. The RoughRiders finished fourth out of 223 minor league teams in home attendance in 2003, attracting 666,977 fans to seventy home dates. Every year since, the team has finished in the top ten overall, while consistently leading all Double-A teams in attendance.

Dr Pepper/7UP Ballpark

Due to its proximity to Arlington, Frisco is a popular destination for Texas Ranger players on rehab assignments. It's a lot easier to drive forty minutes north to Frisco than to fly to Oklahoma City, where Texas's Triple-A affiliate resides. The Frisco ballpark also attracts its share of local celebrity guests, including members of the Dallas Cowboys, Dallas Mavericks, and Dallas Stars. Nolan Ryan has visited the ballpark, as have Deion Sanders, Troy Aikman, Tommy Maddox, Bill Guerin, and Shawn Bradley.

How this for a jinx? On July 14, 2003, Frisco's Edwin Moreno had a no-hitter through seven and one-third innings against Round Rock when a power failure abruptly stopped the game. When the lights came back on and play resumed after a twenty-one-minute delay, Moreno immediately surrendered back-to-back hits.

On June 10, 2004, the Rangers sent Kevin Mench to Frisco to get a few swings in while he was recovering from a strained oblique muscle, and the slugger thrilled the crowd with a walk-off home run.

On June 21, 2005, the Texas League All-Star Game was played in Frisco and in an innovative twist the final round of the home run hitting contest took place between the third and fourth innings of the game.

In addition to hosting the RoughRiders, the ballpark in Frisco is the site of an annual High School tournament, called the "Tournament of Champions," that welcomes twelve local teams to Frisco for a three-day event. The field is also used for state high school playoff games.

Game Day

Getting to the Park

From Dallas, take the Dallas North Tollway and exit onto the Dallas Parkway, using the Highway 121 exit. Travel north on the Dallas Parkway through the intersection of Highway 121, then turn right onto Texas Rangers Parkway. The lots nearest the ballpark gates are reserved for season ticket holders, while common wayfarers park in the garage beyond the left field fence and at the Stonebriar Centre Mall, half a mile away. The mall offers a designated stadium parking area, and free shuttle buses ferry fans to and from the ballpark. Taking a shuttle bus to a minor league game is definitely a hassle. It's too bad the planners of this development didn't leave more room for parking.

Inside the Park

Tickets are sold in person at the stadium during business hours, while all other sales are handled by Ticketmaster. Considering the ghastly stadium name, the parking situation, and the ticket situation, that's three strikes against the RoughRiders. The team can get away with these offenses though, because it plays at a truly special ballpark.

Traveling fans who wait until game day to get their tickets will likely wind up on the outfield lawn. The seating bowl spans from foul pole to foul pole, offering 8,600 chair backs. There is room for another 2,000 people in the picnic areas, on the berms, and in the luxury boxes.

Sections 102 and 103 are between the home bull pen and the left field line, Sections 112 through 114 are behind the home plate area, and Sections 124 and 125 are between the visiting bull pen and left field line.

The seats in home run territory near the left field foul pole are available only to groups. There are designated group areas above the bull pen seats at either wing of the stadium and in outfield home run territory on the berm. The pavilions offer twenty-seven luxury boxes.

The barbecued beef brisket is the top seller at the concession stands, while the pizza and chicken tenders are also popular. Instead of Coke or Pepsi, the stands offer RC Cola. Instead of Sprite or Sierra Mist, they offer 7UP. Yes, Dr Pepper is also on the menu.

The Ballpark Experience

Two RoughRider players sign autographs before every game. One player is stationed at the main entrance gate and one at the outfield gate. Other players sign and mingle with fans between the dugouts and foul poles.

On the concourse fans encounter a number of costumed individuals dressed like western outlaws and sheriffs. Their presence makes slightly more sense once the game begins and they take the field between innings to perform skits with western themes.

The RoughRiders made national headlines with a bizarre promotion during the 2004 season. In an effort to demonstrate how quick and painless undergoing laser eye surgery was at a local Laser Eye Center, a lucky fan won free corrective vision surgery.

Before the game the lucky fan demonstrated how poor his eyesight was by trying to read an eye chart posted on the left field video board. Then a helicopter swooped down and brought the fan to a local eye surgery center. In the middle of the sixth inning, the helicopter landed in the outfield, and the fan made his way back to his original seat. The eye chart was reposted on the video board, and this time the fan read the letters perfectly thanks to his newly corrected 20/15 eyesight. To punctuate the moment, Deuce—the 6-foot 8-inch prairie

dog who serves as the RoughRiders mascot—took the fan's glasses out of his hands and stomped them to pieces on the field. The Frisco fans applauded wildly.

On the Town

Efforts to develop the area around the ballpark into an entertainment center are still taking place, but the project already has made major strides. A practice facility for the NHL Dallas Stars sits across the street from the ballpark, bearing an even lengthier corporate name than the baseball field. Yes, they're naming practice facilities now. Meanwhile, 3 miles away, **Pizza Hut Park** serves as the home field of the MLS Dallas MetroStars.

Right in the ballpark neighborhood, fans find a convenient place to stay in the **Embassy Suites Hotel**, and a convenient place to eat in the **Stonebriar Centre Mall**. I know you're probably thinking you're not going to drive 2,800 miles to Frisco to eat at a mall food court, right? Well this food court is probably a little bit bigger than the one back home at your local mall. It offers eighty different restaurants, including the California Pizza Kitchen, the Cheesecake Factory, Dave and Busters, and Chili's. It also features a 316-foot-wide mural that depicts important events in Frisco history.

The **Irish Rover** (8250 Gaylord Parkway) is a popular hangout not far from the ballpark. Fans eat corned beef and cabbage or Guinness stew, while watching West Coast games on TV.

CITIBANK BALLPARK
Midland RockHounds

Class AA, Texas League
(OAKLAND ATHLETICS)

Citibank Ballpark
5514 Champions Drive
Midland, Texas
432–520–2255

Citibank Ballpark offers a larger concourse than you'll find anywhere else in minor league baseball. Although that may sound like a back-handed compliment, it's not meant to be. The concourse really is huge. The ballpark, which opened in 2002 as home to the local Texas League outfit, distinguishes itself in a few other ways too, but man, that concourse . . . Following the recent trend, Citibank Ballpark features a seating bowl below street level and an open concourse that runs atop the bowl. While most ballparks provide concourses beneath their luxury level and leave it at that, Citibank Ballpark offers a concourse that extends back even farther than the back of the luxury level, creating a nice wide area where folks waiting in line for concessions don't block the flow of pedestrians on the concrete path that encircles the field. Down the lines the concourse gets even wider. In left field it quadruples in width to provide a large picnic area where fans can plop down and eat their ballpark treats while enjoying a view of the game.

Such are the benefits of building a ballpark outside of downtown, without the worries of fitting the park between preexisting city streets. Citibank Ballpark is part of Midland's Scharbauer Sports Complex, where it can take up as much space as it needs to.

There are five different seating berms scattered around the park, most noticeably a big hill in left field that towers over the field. Although gently sloping outfield lawns are the norm, this one rises quite sharply, providing a unique perch from which fans can enjoy the game. Also of interest are the uniquely placed bull pens, which make for some crazy nooks and crannies in the outfield. The visitors bull pen appears as a caged-in box at field level in the left field corner, situated perpendicular to the foul line. The pen is actually half in foul territory and half in home run territory, with the pitchers throwing from mounds in homer land toward catcher in foul ground. The home bull pen sits entirely in home run territory in straightaway right. Also at field level, it juts out into right field, creating a 70-foot-long home run depository where the promised land is closer to home plate than it is across the rest of right field.

The stadium structure features white steel girders and multiple shades of earth-tone bricks on an upper level that hovers over the concourse from dugout to dugout. A large metal roof extends over the luxury boxes and brick press box and covers the back several rows of lower seats, bringing some much-appreciated shade to the infield seats. The outfield view features a large scoreboard in right and the expanse of the berm seating areas across the rest of the outfield.

Outside the park fans find an attractive brick earth-tone façade decorated with white ironwork. A black iron fence supported by brick pillars separates the concourse inside from the sidewalk outside. A large rock sits just outside the main entrance gate behind home plate. This amorphous stone really emphasizes the "rock" in RockHounds, especially if you're not watching where you're walking and acciden-tally slam your knee into it.

Before moving to Citibank Ballpark, the RockHounds played at Max H. Christensen Stadium, a facility that had served Midland's baseball community since the local nine first fielded a team in the old Longhorn League in the 1950s. Midland joined the Texas League in 1972, and has been a member of the league ever since. Midland began its Texas League tenure as a Chicago Cubs affiliate and was, in fact, called the Midland Cubs from 1972 through 1985. Then came an association with the California Angels from 1986 through 1998, during which time the team was called the Midland Angels. Then the team became the RockHounds in 1999, when it first inked a PDC with the Oakland A's. Through its association with these three major league organizations, the franchise has filled out an impressive Midland Hall of Fame roster that includes Bruce Sutter, Joe Carter, Bryan Harvey, Tim Salmon, and Jim Edmonds.

Game Day

Getting to the Park

Midland is in the southwest part of Texas, about 40 miles east of the right angle formed at the border of Texas and New Mexico. If you look at a map, you'll see what I mean. Citibank Ballpark is on the west side of downtown, adjacent to the city's 15,000-seat football/ soccer stadium. From I–20, turn north onto the Route 250 Loop that encircles the city, and the entrance to the sports complex will appear at the intersection of the Loop and U.S. Highway 191. There is a large free parking lot at the sports complex.

Inside the Park

Citibank Park provides slightly more than 5,000 fixed seats and room for another 1,000 fans or so on its outfield lawns. The typical crowds in Midland run about 3,500 people. Between the blue stadium chairs in the main seating bowl and the five distinct lawn areas, there are seating options around the entire field, except for

where the grass batter's eye rises in center. A 360-degree concourse allows fans to walk laps around the entire field, and as mentioned it is quite wide around the infield and in the outfield corners. The concourse becomes little more than a paved footpath though, as it wends its way across the outfield, running behind and at points in front of the lawn seating areas.

The seating bowl extends into medium-depth foul territory on either side, keeping all of the seats low to the field. Sections 10 through 12, behind home plate, sell as Club Seats. The five sections along each baseline—Sections 13 through 17 on the first base side and 5 through 9 on the third base side—sell as Box Seats. The four sections beyond third base—1 through 4— and the three sections beyond first base—18 through 20—sell as Reserved Seats.

Fans in the Club Seats and Box Seats watch the game through the haze of a larger-than-usual protective screen that runs from dugout to dugout. If this sounds like the type of obstruction that would annoy you, or if you are planning to take a lot of pictures at the game, you had better order a Reserved Seat.

A General Admission ticket is good for a place on any of the lawn areas, including the small lawns in deep right field and left field foul territory, the large lawn that spans from the right field foul pole to the batter's eye in center, the small lawn between the batter's eye and mound in left center, and the mound in left.

Sixteen indoor/outdoor luxury boxes overlook the infield. The high rollers have access to the exclusive Diamond Club, which offers a nightly smorgasbord of delicacies like smothered chimmichangas, country fried steak, fried catfish, herb-encrusted pork, and popcorn chicken. If that menu isn't enough incentive to get you and nineteen of your friends to plop down a few hundred dollars to rent your own suite, I don't know what is.

Ordinary fans find concession stands with less extravagant menus. Tex-Mex prevails, as popular sellers include the chicken and beef burritos, taco salad, frito pie, and jumbo chili-dog.

The Citibank Ballpark Experience

The local mascot is a hound named "Rocky," who wears a white Midland jersey with number 99 on it. Rocky reminded me of a cross between Scooby-Doo, Mickey's friend Pluto, and a Saint Bernard I once knew.

For season-long promotions, Midland offers half-priced sodas and beers on "Thirsty Thursdays," Saturday night fireworks, a pregame Christian concert series, and $1.00 Reserved Seats on Mondays for fans who present the ticket sellers at the box office with a coupon downloadable at www.midlandrockhounds.org.

On the Town

East of the ballpark, Midland Drive and Illinois Avenue offer plenty of restaurants from which to choose. I suggest trying one of the many Mexican joints, like **Jorge's Mexican Cafe** (3323 N Midland Drive) or **Oscar's Super Burrito** (4306 Neely Avenue), since Mexican food is the local specialty. You can eat Domino's or Arby's back home any old time.

The former home of the RockHounds still stands and is worth a visit if only to see how much better the new park is. **Christensen Stadium** (Lamesa Road at Loop 250) offers a gaudy Smurf-blue exterior. From the street outside fans can see the underbelly of the aluminum bleachers that rise above the infield.

Also worth visiting, but only once a year, is the **College Baseball Hall of Fame** induction ceremony that takes place on the campus of Texas Tech as part of Lubbock, Texas's annual Fourth of July celebration. Lubbock, which is 100 miles north of Midland, has been hosting the "Fourth on Broadway Festival" for years, but the College Baseball Hall of Fame is a new creation. The College Baseball Foundation inducted its first class of former collegiate coaches and players in 2006. Among the inaugural class of ten individuals were Dave Winfield (Minnesota), Bob Horner (Arizona State), Robin Ventura (Oklahoma State), and Will Clark (Mississippi State).

THE DELL DIAMOND
Round Rock Express

Class AAA, Pacific Coast League
(HOUSTON ASTROS)

The Dell Diamond
3400 East Palm Valley Boulevard
Round Rock, Texas
512–255–2255

Before making a big splash in Corpus Christi, the Ryan-Sanders ownership group got its start in Round Rock, transforming an eighty-five-acre cornfield into a baseball field and then proceeding to set one Double-A attendance record after another. After failing to garner enough voter support for a downtown stadium in Austin, Ryan-Sanders set its sights on Round Rock, a bit farther north, forging an agreement with the city to build a jointly funded $25 million stadium that opened in time for the 2000 season. Right from the very start, the Express have been a smashing success. Led by budding Houston Astros prospects like Roy Oswalt and Morgan Ensberg, the team won the Texas League championship in its debut season while also breaking the all-time single-season Double-A attendance record. The Express attracted 660,110 fans that first year and then broke their own record in each of the next four seasons, culminating with an attendance total of 689,286 in 2004.

The team made the jump to Triple-A in 2005, after Ryan-Sanders purchased the Pacific Coast League's Edmonton Trappers and moved them to Round Rock. Meanwhile, the erstwhile Texas League Express headed to the brand new ballpark in Corpus Christi. Predictably, Round Rock didn't miss a beat on moving up a level, increasing its attendance for a fifth straight year to 700,277. In all of the minor leagues, only the Sacramento River Cats, who attracted 755,750 fans to their Raley Field, outdrew the Express in 2005.

Suffice to say, a long layoff whetted the appetite of Austin area fans while they waited for the minor league game to return after it left in 1967, and that appetite has not been sated yet. Prior to the arrival of the Express, the last Texas League team to play in Greater Austin was a Milwaukee/Atlanta Braves farm club known as the Austin Senators—and then later as the Braves—that played in the state capital from 1956 through 1967. After the team relocated to Shreveport, professional baseball would not return to the area until the "Ryan Express" came roaring down U.S. Highway 79.

The Dell Diamond was built for $20 million, a third of which came from the City of Round Rock in the form of funds derived from a municipal hotel tax, and the rest of which came from Ryan-Sanders Baseball. The ballpark is named after the Dell Computer Corporation, which committed $2.5 million over fifteen years for the naming rights. The Express itself has taken Nolan Ryan's old nickname, of course, and accordingly the ballpark's main entrance resembles a train depot. A façade made of yellow limestone slabs flanks a wide tunnel that serves as the entrance, while up above, the Dell trademark displays its off-kilter *E*.

Inside, the low seating bowl offers 8,688 green stadium chairs, while thirty indoor/outdoor luxury boxes hang over the concourse atop the seats. A nicely sloped outfield berm runs from foul pole to foul pole, except where a green shed serves as the batter's eye in center. The Express have made several additions to the ballpark already, installing accoutrements like a restaurant in right field and a double-decked home run porch atop the berm in left. When most teams realize they have greater demand for tickets than they have seats to sell, they plop down a few banks of cheap aluminum bleachers and leave it at that. But the Express did much better for their fans, adding a two-level outfield structure reminiscent of the one in right field at the major league stadium in Arlington. The home run porch provides 700 shaded seats, as well as a row of shaded Adirondack chairs down at ground level that are available on a first-come, first-served basis. This unique left field seating area was added prior to the 2005 season, at a time when the Express also added six new luxury suites in left field foul territory. A walking bridge behind the left field foul pole connects the two new areas.

The Dell Diamond sits beside wooded Old Settlers Park, but because the playing field is sunken below street level, and because the seats don't rise very high, the outfield view doesn't showcase much of this quaint country terrain. A few treetops are visible, but mostly the view from the seats is of the outfield berm, the left field home run porch, and the miniature amusement park behind the berm in right. While purists will surely bristle, the ballpark's recreation center features a 20-by-50-foot swimming pool, a 10-by-10-foot hot tub, a full basketball court, a volleyball court, a speed-pitch booth, a 26-foot-high rock-climbing wall, a video arcade, a playground, and other games and attractions. So be sure to bring your high-tops and kneepads to the ballpark, just in case a pickup basketball game breaks out.

In addition to hosting the Express, The Dell Diamond is also the site of various high school and college baseball tournaments, concerts, trade shows, conventions, weddings, and corporate events.

While Nolan Ryan is a frequent visitor to The Dell Diamond, another big right-hander who is a Texas legend himself stopped by Round Rock's ballpark during the 2006 season. Before an overflow crowd of 13,475 fans—including Lance Armstrong and Matthew McConaughey, who sat behind the Round Rock dugout—Roger Clemens faced the New Orleans Zephyrs on a warm night in mid-June. In his final minor league tune-up before rejoining the Astros, the Rocket allowed 3 runs over five and two-thirds innings, while allowing 10 hits and striking out 5.

Game Day

Getting to the Park

Round Rock is 15 miles north of Austin and 160 miles west of the final rung on the Astros player development ladder—Houston. The organization's Double-A outpost in Corpus Christi is 230 miles south of Round Rock. To reach The Dell Diamond, follow I–35 to US 79 east and the ballpark will appear on the left. There is plenty of room for parking in the stadium lot.

Inside the Park

In case you skimmed through the first part of this chapter and somehow didn't get the impression that you should order tickets in advance of your visit to Round Rock, let me state plainly that if you don't order tickets ahead of time, the best you will do is a spot on the outfield berm, which is not a bad place to watch a game, but it isn't the same as having your own seat. Counting the new double-decker atop the left field berm, there are about 9,400 fixed seats at The Dell Diamond. And the local nine draws an average crowd of more than 10,000 people per game. So, you can do the math.

The seating bowl begins at Section 110 in left field, continues to Section 114 at third base, turns the corner at Section 119 behind home plate, extends to Section 124 at first base, and finishes at Section 128 in right field. The seats on the infield in Sections 113 through 125 sell as Box Seats, while the seats in the three outfield sections on either side sell as Reserved Seats. Because the seating bowl angles back toward the infield, the sight lines from the Reserved Seats are quite good.

As is the case at many ballparks, the glare of the setting sun was a nuisance for fans seated on the first base side near the home dugout, but the Express solved that problem in 2006, installing a sun shield high above the luxury suites on the third base side. This is a ballpark innovation other teams would be wise to copy.

A General Admission ticket is good for a spot anywhere on the berm, while a Home Run Porch Seat is far from the field but offers a nice overview of the game.

The Texadelphia restaurant on the right field berm serves Philly cheesesteaks that aren't quite as good as the ones they sell at Rick's Steaks at Citizens Bank Park in Philadelphia, but they are as close an approximation of the real thing as you'll find deep in the heart of Texas. Express fans also enjoy Texas Barbecue at a Pok-e-Jo's stand, aged Texas beef at the Nolan Ryan Grill, and Buffalo wings at a Hooter's stand. On hot nights—and there are plenty of them in Round Rock—the kids cool off with shaved ice, while the adults sip frozen margaritas.

The Dell Diamond Experience

In an age when many major league players make more money to play a single game than most minor leaguers make in an entire season, the Round Rock fans carry out a unique ballpark tradition, passing around a helmet whenever a member of the home team hits a home run. Fans contribute a dollar apiece and the wad of singles is collected and given to the conquering player.

Here's another one you won't see at too many other parks: While kids scale the rock-climbing wall in right field, a team employee

stands by with a stopwatch and times them. At the end of the night, the three fastest climbers get to see their names and times on the video board in left field.

The Express offers several Nolan Ryan–related giveaways each season, doling out items like Nolan Ryan piggy banks, Nolan Ryan bobbleheads, and Nolan Ryan jerseys. There are also several giveaways related to Dell Computer, as the local company dispenses mouse pads and other computer accessories to fans.

On the Town

The story of how Round Rock derived its unique name dates back to the late-1800s when cattle herders traveling in covered wagons would cross Bushy Creek on their way from South Texas to Kansas. The low-water point in the creek was marked by a large round rock that travelers used as a guide. Hence the town that would eventually grow around the creek became known as Round Rock. The namesake rock still sits along Chisholm Trail Street in Round Rock's Old Town district.

From those humble beginnings Round Rock has grown into a municipality of approximately 85,000 people. The city is best known in the high-tech world as the home of Dell, which was founded by University of Austin student Michael Dell in 1984, when he was still an undergrad. For baseball fans Round Rock doesn't offer much to do in the ballpark neighborhood, nor does it offer the type of nightlife found in nearby Austin. Downtown Austin offers lots of barbecue and Tex-Mex joints, as well as brewpubs and clubs. The **6th Street** entertainment district is a good place to start and end an evening, as the 7 city blocks between Congress Avenue and I–35 offer trendy places to eat, drink, and enjoy live music that ranges from jazz, to blues, to country, to rock, to hip-hop.

NELSON W. WOLFF MUNICIPAL STADIUM

San Antonio Missions

Class AA, Texas League
(SAN DIEGO PADRES)

Nelson W. Wolff Municipal Stadium
5757 West U.S. Highway 90
San Antonio, Texas
210–675–7275

The San Antonio Missions played the 2006 season with their future in limbo as rumors swirled that San Antonio was one of the three or four cities on the short list of possible relocation sites for the Florida Marlins. While San Antonio civic leader Nelson W. Wolff tried to sell Marlins officials on a plot of land northeast of downtown along the I–35 corridor as the future home of a $300 million stadium to be financed largely by a motel and rental car tax, the Marlins used the offer as bargaining leverage in Florida, where they continued to try to get state funding for a new ballpark. Whether or not San Antonio winds up getting the Marlins, it is a city that appears poised to join the big boys eventually. It has a population of 1.2 million people, making it the eighth-largest metropolis in the United States. It is home to a highly successful NBA team. And it ranks high on the NFL's list of possible expansion sites as the result of the New Orleans Saints playing three games at the Alamodome during the wake of the Hurricane Katrina disaster.

Of course the Portland Beavers and Las Vegas 51s also played the 2006 minor league seasons wondering if they might be affected by a Marlins move to their cities. Those teams struggled to hang onto fans and advertisers as their markets turned their attention to the possible arrival of the big league game. Yet, in San Antonio the Missions carried on business as usual. The x-factor for the Texas Leaguers, no doubt, was their modern ballpark, which is both fan-friendly and aesthetically pleasing.

Named after Wolff, a former San Antonio mayor, the ballpark is visually distinctive, both inside and out. Fans find two stately bell towers flanking the main entrance. These cream stucco towers look like they belong outside one of the many Spanish missions that stand in San Antonio. Immediately behind the towers, the dark green skeleton of the seating bowl and the maroon ballpark roof unify an earthy design flavor.

Inside, the roof is the most distinctive feature. It extends off the top of the cream stucco luxury box level that houses the press box and twelve luxury boxes, situated high above the last row of seats. Decorative lighting makes the roof's underbelly glow an eerie green, giving it the appearance of a hovering UFO stopping by the park to watch a few innings. For first-time visitors to the park, it is really a nice surprise when the roof lights up just after sunset. Not since my visit to Tropicana Field in St. Petersburg, where the roof glows fluorescent orange, had I seen anything like this roof in San Antonio.

The scoreboard in right field also deserves mention, as it is contoured to resemble the shape of the Alamo. Rather than appearing as a plain rectangle, the top of the board rises to a peak just like the sloped roof of the most famous Spanish mission in the country, which just happens to sit 8 miles east of the ballpark in the heart of downtown San Antonio.

While local baseball fans would certainly welcome the arrival of a big league team, the necessary departure of the Missions would represent a significant blow to the Texas League. Of the original six charter cities that formed the circuit in 1888—Austin, Dallas, Fort Worth, Galveston, Houston, and San Antonio—San Antonio is the only one still fielding a team. The city has remained a stalwart of the league for nearly twelve decades, which is pretty remarkable when you think about just how much the country and its National Pastime have changed during that time.

In the 1930s and 1940s, San Antonio was a St. Louis Cardinals outpost, and Dizzy Dean pitched at old Tech Field. During the 1950s the local team was affiliated with the Baltimore Orioles and the Chicago Cubs, as future stars like Brooks Robinson and Ron Santo graced Mission Stadium. During the 1960s San Antonio was affiliated with the Houston Astros and future Hall of Famer Joe Morgan collected his share of Texas leaguers at Mission Stadium. The Milwaukee Brewers, Cleveland Indians, and Texas Rangers were next, all enjoying brief affiliations with San Antonio in the 1970s when the team played at V. J. Keefe Memorial Stadium, a ballpark that still stands a couple miles north of Wolff Stadium. During the affiliation with the Indians, future Cooperstown inductee Dennis Eckersley pitched for San Antonio. In 1977 San Antonio began the longest relationship it has enjoyed with any big league organization, signing a player development contract with the Los Angeles Dodgers that would last through the 2000 season. During this extended relationship, San Antonio was a proving ground for future major leaguers like Fernando Valenzuela, Orel Hershiser, Steve Howe, Mike Piazza, Pedro Martínez, Eric Karros, and Paul Konerko.

San Antonio switched to a PDC with the Seattle Mariners in 2001 and then to one with the San Diego Padres in 2007. In recent years, the most electrifying player to pass through the Alamo City has been Felix Hernández, who went 5–1 with a 3.30 ERA in ten games for the Missions as an eighteen-year-old during the

second half of the 2004 season, then started the next season at AAA Tacoma, and finished it in Seattle.

Game Day

Getting to the Park

San Antonio is 200 miles west of Houston, 280 miles south of Dallas, and 140 miles from the closest Texas League rival, the Corpus Christi Hooks. Wolff Stadium sits amidst a residential neighborhood, 8 miles west of downtown, near the entrance to Lackland Air Force Base. The ballpark is on U.S. Highway 90. From the east or north, follow I–10 to US 90 West to the Callaghan Road exit and the stadium parking lot will appear on your left. From the west, follow US 90 East to the Callaghan Road exit and turn left onto Callaghan Road. From the south, follow Route 37 North to US 90 West and follow the directions above. Parking costs $3.00 at the stadium.

Inside the Park

Wolff Stadium has seating to accommodate 6,200 fans and room for about another 2,000 on its left field lawn. If there is one complaint to be made about this ballpark, it is that more than half of its seats are aluminum bleachers with backs instead of individual stadium chairs.

The seating bowl offers two levels. The 100 Level seats down at field level continue deep into the outfield corners on either side of the diamond, while the 200 Level seats appear behind the wide midlevel walkway and continue only to the corner bases.

In the 100 Level, the ten rows of green stadium chairs around the infield sell as Box Seats. Section 100 is directly behind home plate, while the odd-numbered sections continue down the third baseline, culminating with Section 113 beyond third base, and the even-numbered sections continue down the first baseline, culminating with Section 114 beyond first. The six field-level sections along the right field line and the five sections along the left field line sell as General Admission. These bleacher sections are angled back toward the infield.

The first four rows of the 200 Level offer green stadium chairs that sell as Upper Box Seats. These are raised above the walkway, so pedestrian interference with sight lines is not an issue. After the first four rows, the rest of these grandstand seats are bleachers that sell as Infield Reserved Seats. The roof covers most of these bleachers.

The berm seating area begins along the left field foul line and wraps around the foul pole into home run territory.

The main concourse runs behind the 200 Level. Here, fans find chicken and beef fajitas, roasted corn on the cob, roasted turkey legs, and the Catchers Mitt—a pita stuffed with chili and shredded cheddar cheese. Just be sure to stock up on napkins if you order a Catchers Mitt. A brick wall on the concourse serves as the team Wall of Fame, offering plaques that honor more than a century's worth of San Antonio baseball greats.

The Wolff Stadium Experience

The Missions embrace a Mexican motif with a trio of mascots reflective of local cuisine. There are two walking, talking jalapeños, known as Ball-apeño and Ball-apeño Jr., while the third mascot is a taco with a red tomato for a head and a pair of chili peppers for feet.

While a lot of teams offer drink specials on "Thirsty Thursdays," the Missions do their rooters one better, providing hot dogs, pizza, soda, and beer all for just $1.00 apiece on Thursdays. Saturday nights are also special in San Antonio, as the Missions put on a postgame fireworks show deep in the heart of Texas.

On the Town

No trip to San Antonio would be complete without paying the obligatory visit to the **Alamo** (100 Alamo Plaza). Head into downtown to see the Spanish mission upon which rocker Ozzy Osborne once famously urinated, that Paul Reubens visited during *Pee Wee's Big Adventure,* and that 189 Texans died trying to defend from the Mexican Army in 1836. A few blocks east of the Alamo, the city's **River Walk** traces the banks of the San Antonio River. A level below the streets of downtown, the River Walk dates back to the late 1930s when it was built as a Works Progress Administration project. It is lined with shops, bars, restaurants, and nightclubs. Perhaps the most famous spot along the river is **la Casa Rio**. Since opening in 1946 as the first riverside restaurant in San Antonio, this delightful river house has earned a reputation for serving the tastiest Mexican food in town.

San Antonio also offers the chance to visit family-friendly destinations like **SeaWorld San Antonio** (1604 Loop, west of the city), **Six Flags Fiesta Texas** (1604 and I–10), **Splashtown San Antonio** (3600 North/I–35), and the **San Antonio Zoo** (3903 North/St. Mary's Street).

Finally, baseball fans can visit the previous home of the Missions, **V. J. Keefe Memorial Stadium** (One Camino Santa Maria), which currently serves the NCAA Division II St. Mary's Rattlers baseball team. It offers a high-rising seating bowl of bright blue bleachers. In 1988 Keefe Memorial Stadium was the site of the longest scoreless game in Texas League history, as San Antonio and the Jackson Mets were still knotted at 0–0 after twenty-five innings and seven hours and ten minutes of play. That's right, the teams combined to hang fifty goose eggs on the scoreboard! Finally, the Texas League president declared the game a draw at 2:30 A.M. on July 16.

AT&T BRICKTOWN BALLPARK

Oklahoma RedHawks

Class AAA, Pacific Coast League
(TEXAS RANGERS)

AT&T Bricktown Ballpark
2 South Mickey Mantle Drive
Oklahoma City, Oklahoma
405–218–1000

After housing its Triple-A team at a ballpark on the remote State Fairgrounds for nearly four decades, Oklahoma City moved the local nine to town in 1998. The city's $34 million ballpark project was part of a larger effort to revitalize Bricktown, an aging warehouse neighborhood just east of downtown that has since evolved into a hopping entertainment district. In addition to building a classic redbrick ballpark and transforming the 1920s- and 1930s-era warehouses nearby into dining and retail space, the publicly funded Metropolitan Area Projects initiative filled Bricktown with colorful murals that pay homage to Oklahoma City's history and create an altogether pleasant place for a laid-back pregame stroll or a kicking postgame night on the town.

AT&T Bricktown Ballpark embraces the ethos of its neighborhood with an exterior to match its name and many indoor and outdoor nods to Oklahoma's proud baseball past. The streets around "The Brick" have been renamed Mickey Mantle Drive, Johnny Bench Drive, and Joe Carter Avenue, in tribute to three of the Sooner State's diamond kings. Mantle grew up in the small town of Commerce, up in Oklahoma's northeastern corner, while Bench and Carter were born right in Oklahoma City. Mantle and Bench are also honored with statues outside the park. Welcoming fans at the third base entrance is the Commerce Comet, captured in the follow-through of a mighty swing from the left-handed batter's box. The Mick's handprints are set in the cement down below. Meanwhile, in the shadows of the stadium's home plate façade, Bench strikes a pensive pose with his catcher's mitt resting on his hip. On the southwest side of the park, there are several colorful mosaics on the order of the ones found throughout Bricktown, and there is an overlook from which fans can peer down at the Bricktown Canal and entertainment district on either side of it.

Inside the park there are not nearly as many bricks as outside, but the ghosts of Oklahoma's baseball past are abundant. Banners and displays honor the three previously mentioned Oklahoma legends, as well as major leaguers like Dizzy Dean, Carl Hubbell, Bobby Murcer, Allie Reynolds, Warren Spahn, and Willie Stargell, who either grew up in Oklahoma or spent time in the state during their bush league days.

Atop the main seating bowl, the concourse runs around the entire field offering views of the game from beneath the overhang of the second deck. Fans find viewing locations around the entire diamond on the first level in the form of seats in foul territory, bleachers in left field, sloped outfield lawns above the fence in left-center and right, and standing room areas on the concourse. Other than just a few spots where the ballpark is a bit too cozy—like where the concourse narrows on the first base side due to the protrusion of the stairways that leads to the upper deck—the first level is fan-friendly and easy to navigate.

The second deck is larger than those at most minor league parks and is not symmetrical, owing to immovable entities on the preexisting landscape that forced the designers at the Oklahoma-based Architectural Design Group to put all of their creativity to good use. Around the infield the second deck offers Club Seats and two levels of luxury boxes. Where the Club Seats leave off, general second-level seats continue halfway down the left field line before giving way to a stadium restaurant with a view. Across the diamond, where there is no restaurant, the second level offers seats all the way down the right field line and even into home run territory, as the second deck wraps around the foul pole.

At field level in left, a set of bleachers just 325 feet from home plate makes for a unique home run porch, while tiered bull pens appear in straightaway left, running parallel to the outfield fence. The berm seating area runs across the rest of the outfield, above the dark green wall. A peaked brick building on the center field concourse serves as the batter's eye, along with the roped-off parcel of lawn below it. The main seating bowl does not allow for views of the outside world, as multiple-level advertising billboards rise at the back of the berm to seal in the park. Fans in the upper level in deep right field and on the right field berm do, however, enjoy views of the Oklahoma City skyline. The tall buildings west of Bricktown rise behind the stadium's third base stands.

Since opening, this ballpark has been known by five different names, which has to be some kind of a record for a facility that has yet to celebrate its tenth birthday. The park was originally named Bricktown Ballpark, before its name was changed to Southwestern Bell Park. Next, it was redubbed Southwestern Bell Bricktown Ballpark. Then it was called SBC Bricktown Ballpark. In 2006 its name was changed again, this time to AT&T Bricktown Ballpark. When—if ever—these corporate shenanigans might end, I have no idea. The locals have the right idea though, simply referring to the park as "The Brick."

Oklahoma City has been a Triple-A outpost of the Texas Rangers since 1983, first as a member of the American Association, and since 1998 as a member of the Pacific Coast League. Before that, the city enjoyed Triple-A affiliations with the Houston Colt .45s, the Cleveland Indians, and the Philadelphia Phillies.

Oklahoma City's team was known as the 89ers from 1962 until 1998, when it switched to the RedHawks. The 89ers nickname remembered the hearty settlers who rushed to Oklahoma territory in 1889 to claim a legal homestead. The folks who arrived too soon and claimed their land illegally became known as Sooners. The 89ers played at All Sports Stadium west of downtown, a facility that has since been demolished.

In addition to housing the RedHawks, the Brick hosts two of the three baseball games played between Oklahoma State University and the University of Oklahoma each year. The Big 12 Conference baseball tournament has also used the park on several occasions. And in September of 2006 the Pacific Coast League and International League used the field for the Triple-A World Series.

Game Day

Getting to the Park

Oklahoma City is southeast of the panhandle, smack in the center of Oklahoma. The nearest three minor league parks are all Texas League venues—in Tulsa to the east, Frisco to the south, and Wichita to the north, while the nearest Pacific Coast League rival is Albuquerque to the west. Oklahoma's two major highways run through the capital city, I–35 from north to south, and I–40 from east to west. Bricktown is east of the modern-day downtown. From I–40 East, take the Harvey Avenue exit and drive north on Harvey, then turn right onto Reno Avenue, which leads to the ballpark. From I–40 West, take the Robinson Avenue exit, stay in the far right lane, and follow Robinson north, before turning right onto Reno. The parking decks throughout Bricktown charge $5.00 on game days.

Inside the Park

Bricktown Ballpark can accommodate as many as 13,066 fans. More than half of the seating is provided in the form of the 7,500 green stadium chairs in the lower bowl. The RedHawks don't usually sell out, but they are a popular draw, averaging crowds of nearly 8,000 people per game.

The lower bowl begins at Section 100 in the left field corner, then continues down the left field line to Section 104 behind third base, makes the turn at Section 110 behind home plate, heads out to Section 116 behind first base, and ends at Section 120 in deep right field. Sections 103 through 117 contain Field Box Seats, while the three outfield-most sections on either side house General Admission Seats. The bleachers in left and outfield berms are also General Admission. If you want to make like a Sooner, arrive well before the game and claim a front-row seat in Section 118 just past first base.

The second deck offers ten sections of Club Seats, the press box, twenty-six luxury suites on two levels, four sections of Terrace Reserved Seats along the left field line, and nine sections of Terrace Reserved Seats along the right field line. The Terrace Reserved Seats are pretty good, especially if you can score tickets in Sections 202 or 203 on the third baseline, or 204 or 205 on the first baseline. Unless you're dying for that game-long view of the downtown skyline, Sections 208 through 212 in deep right should probably be avoided.

The ballpark treats include the trademark Fiesta Dog, which comes topped with chili, cheese, salsa, and sour cream, and other Mexican offerings like soft and hard tacos and burritos. The barbecued gyros and Hideaway Pizza are also fan favorites.

The Bricktown Ballpark Experience

The mascot in Oklahoma City is a big red hawk named "Rowdy," who is surely a lot more kid-friendly than a wagon-weary settler in 1889 garb, but not quite as colorful. Rowdy isn't the only fan wearing a baseball uniform in the stands on Wednesday nights, because that's when the RedHawks offer free admission to any youngster who wears his or her Little League jersey to the game. Kids who arrive early can even take a few pregame swings at the public batting cages in right field. The kids also get a kick out of Friday nights, when the RedHawks offer postgame fireworks, and Sunday afternoons, when the RedHawks let them run the bases and play catch on the field after the game.

From Thanksgiving through New Years, the Brick becomes more than just a dormant baseball park, but finds its winter groove, serving as a community "snowball park." The RedHawks install giant slides that run from the upper deck down to field level and inflate tubes and fill the field with snow. The kids ride down the slides on snow tubes, while their parents enjoy hot cocoa and coffee from the snowball park concession stands. Astute readers will remember, of course, that the Mobile BayBears offer their fans a winter wonderland too, only without any colossal slides.

On the Town

Fans find everything they could ask for in a ballpark neighborhood in Bricktown. There are places for pregame eats and drinks on either side of the canal, as well as pubs and clubs for afterward. Popular spots include the memorabilia-laden **Mickey Mantle's Steakhouse** (7 Mickey Mantle Drive); **Earl's Rib Place,** a saucy local chain (216 Johnny Bench Drive); the **Bricktown Brewery** (1 North Oklahoma Avenue); and **Abuelos Mexican Embassy** (17 East Sheridan Avenue).

The **State Capitol** (2300 Lincoln Boulevard) offers more than just a chance to see an impressive portrait of Mickey Mantle in the rotunda on the fourth floor, but a truly unique domeless structure that has a beautiful limestone and granite façade. Appropriately, active oil wells surround the building.

Somber though it may be, a visit to the **Oklahoma City National Memorial** (620 North Harvey Avenue) may be in order for those wishing to reflect on the 168 lives lost and countless lives changed forever on April 19, 1995, when terrorists bombed the Alfred P. Murrah Federal Building. The 3.3-acre park offers a quiet reflecting pool and part of the building's foundation still stands.

Fans who follow I–35 25 miles north to the town of Guthrie will find the **Oklahoma Sports Museum** (315 West Oklahoma Avenue, Guthrie). The museum pays tribute to all of the great athletes in state history and gives out an annual "Warren Spahn Award" to the top left-handed pitcher in Major League Baseball.

DRILLERS STADIUM
Tulsa Drillers

Class AA, Texas League
(COLORADO ROCKIES)

Drillers Stadium
4802 East 15th Street
Tulsa, Oklahoma
918–744–5998

Okay, I take it back. Earlier in this book, I seem to remember describing the seating bowl at Five County Stadium in Zebulon, North Carolina, as a one-of-a-kind phenomenon that fans won't find anywhere else in the minor league universe. Well, I wrote that chapter two months and fifty ballparks ago, before my sputtering Subaru rolled into Tulsa, Oklahoma. Here's the scoop: Like Five County Stadium, Drillers Stadium offers the majority of its seats in a second deck high above field level, rather than in its lower deck. The two parks are hardly identical twins, though. In Tulsa the second deck doesn't hang out over the first deck like in Zebulon, and the second deck in Tulsa doesn't rise nearly as steeply either. And Drillers Stadium, because it's built to Double-A specs, is much larger than its Single-A sister stadium. Drillers Stadium also offers a large roof over much of its second deck, a feature you won't find at the ballpark in North Carolina. Nonetheless, I will amend my previous analysis to conclude that the ball yards in Zebulon *and* Tulsa offer seating bowls unlike those found anywhere else. Interestingly, both unique facilities were built in series of fits and starts over several years. At the time of its opening in 1981, Drillers Stadium had a seating capacity of 4,800. Today, it is the largest stadium in the Texas League with room for 11,003.

Drillers Stadium sits smack dab in the middle of Tulsa, on a plot of county fairgrounds, alongside an amusement park and an old racetrack. The ballpark was built to replace Oiler Park—aka Texas League Park—that once stood just a few hundred feet west of its site.

Oiler Park was the scene of a near tragedy in 1977 when a large section of its wooden grandstands collapsed during an exhibition game between the Drillers and the Texas Rangers due to the weighty overflow crowd that turned out to see Tulsa's big league parent club. Fortunately, no one was seriously injured, and the Drillers and Rangers rushed into the stands to help extricate the fallen fans from the wreckage.

The incident underscored Tulsa's need for a new ballpark, and before long Tulsa County got to work building Drillers Stadium, which opened in 1981 as Sutton Stadium. The ballpark's name, like the artificial turf that originally covered its diamond, did not last long, as its chief benefactor and namesake, oilman Robert B. Sutton, was convicted of a white-collar crime in 1982, prompting Tulsa County to rename the park Tulsa County Stadium, and then a few years later, Drillers Stadium.

Aside from offering an unusual seating layout, Drillers Stadium is noteworthy for its old-time look. Many poles rise up between the upper-level seats to support the roof, recalling memories of Tiger Stadium in Detroit. Also unique is the enormous American flag that flies above the batter's eye in center field, waving a steady beat in the constant breeze that blows out toward the fences. There is a large net suspended over the left field fence to keep home run balls from flying onto 15th Street.

The Drillers rejoined the Texas League in 1977, again hooking up with the circuit they had belonged to from 1933 to 1942 and from 1946 to 1965. Tulsa's baseball history actually goes back much further than the 1930s though, as the first minor league team to take the field in Tulsa did so in 1905, two years before Oklahoma became an official U.S. state. The 1905 Tulsa Oilers were members of the Class C Missouri Valley League. Over the next three decades, the Oilers switched leagues often, playing in the South Central League, Oklahoma-Arkansas-Kansas League, Western Association, Oklahoma State League, and Western League. After the Oilers posted the Western League's best record, 98–48, in 1932, and bolstered by a new ballpark on the Tulsa fairgrounds, the team began its first long association with the Texas League in 1933. After leaving the Texas League following the 1965 season, the Oilers played in the Pacific Coast League (1966–68) and then in the American Association (1969–76) as a St. Louis Cardinals affiliate. When Tulsa rejoined the Texas League in 1977, the "Drillers" became a Texas Rangers farm club. The affiliation would last twenty-five years, until Texas decided to move its Double-A players closer to home in 2003, signing a PDC with Frisco. Fortunately for the baseball fans in Tulsa, the Colorado Rockies quickly filled the void.

During the affiliation with the Rangers, future stars like Dave Righetti, Sammy Sosa, Juan González, Kevin Brown, Ruben Sierra, Dean Palmer, Ivan Rodríguez, Kevin Mench, Travis Hafner, and Mark Teixeira played for Tulsa. Righetti still holds the Texas League record for the most strikeouts in a game. The lefty punched out 21 Midland batters on July 16, 1978, but wound up with a no-decision in a 4–2 loss. After the season "Rags" was part of a ten-player deal between the Rangers and the Yankees that landed him in pinstripes.

While Righetti passed through Tulsa on his way to a successful major league career, one of his former teammates stayed behind to establish permanent roots in the city. Like Righetti, Chuck Lamson was a hard-throwing lefty who thought he was on the fast track to the major leagues when he suited up for the Drillers in 1978. But Lamson's career was derailed by elbow problems, and by 1980 he was working in the Drillers ticket office and on their grounds crew. During the 1980s he was promoted to director of stadium operations, then to assistant general manager. Then, in the early 1990s, he became general manager of the team and acquired a minority ownership share. In 2006 Lamson completed his remarkable transformation when he purchased the Drillers from former owner Went Hubbard. If there's anyone who knows every single aspect of the minor league business, from the top to the bottom, it's got to be Chuck Lamson.

In addition to hosting seventy Texas League games a year, Drillers Stadium also sees use as an NCAA venue. Although the University of Tulsa no longer fields a varsity baseball team, Tulsans enjoy three high-level Division I games each spring. Drillers Stadium is the site of the annual "Bedlam Series" game played between the Oklahoma State Cowboys and the Oklahoma Sooners, and both Big 12 teams play an additional "home" game at Drillers Stadium. Drillers Stadium also hosts the "Drillers High School Showcase," an annual spring event involving eight teams.

Game Day

Getting to the Park

Tulsa is 100 miles northeast of Oklahoma City; 180 miles west of Springfield, Missouri; and 230 miles north of Frisco, Texas. Drillers Stadium is located on Expo Square at the corner of 15th Street and Yale Avenue. From the east or west, take I–44 to I–244, exit 9, then follow Harvard Avenue south to the ballpark. From the north or south, take U.S. Highway 75 to I–244 and then follow the directions above. Parking is free at the fairgrounds.

Inside the Park

The Drillers typically attract crowds of about 5,000 fans per night, so unless you're hell bent on sitting in the first level, there's no urgent need to order tickets in advance. The lower and upper seating bowls both extend nearly all the way out to the foul poles, offering metal stadium seats throughout. There is no home run territory seating or lawn seating, and there are just a few luxury suites on either side of the press box atop the second deck.

The first row of lower-level seats is raised about 6 feet above field level so that the dugouts, rather than jutting into the stands and taking up potential seat space, are recessed below the first few rows. In Sections 9 through 25 around the infield, there are eight rows of Dugout Box Seats. Meanwhile, the eight rows of Field Box Seats are along the outfield foul lines in Sections 0 through 8 in right, and Sections 26 through 34 in left.

The second level offers three times as many seats as the first. The Terrace Boxes are found behind home plate in Sections 35 through 37. The Reserved Seats are the first four rows, both on the infield and along the outfield foul lines. Section A is in deep right field, Section E is at first base, Sections I and J are behind home plate, Section N is at third base, and Section T is in deep left field. Other than these first four rows, the rest of the second-level seats sell as General Admission. On the rare rainy night, the upper seats are most desirable, since they are covered.

The one complaint I have related to Drillers Stadium is that fans sitting down the baselines on both the lower and upper levels have some difficulty seeing into the nearest outfield corner. This is due to the limited amount of foul territory and to the high wall that rises to separate the field from the stands.

The concourse is hidden behind and beneath the grandstand. Here, fans find tasty fajitas and burritos, dill pickles, smoked turkey legs, and Oscar Mayer wieners.

The Drillers Stadium Experience

The Drillers have resisted the obvious temptation to feature an oily roughneck as their mascot and instead offer fans a big blue moose named "Hornsby." Hornsby wears a pinstriped Tulsa uniform and has two proud horns that protrude from beneath his baseball cap. He is affable and entertaining and isn't at all scary like a dirty old oilman would be.

Over the course of the typical season, the Drillers treat their fans to about eight fireworks nights. Also popular is the annual Bark in the Park, when fans bring their pups to the game.

The Drillers also offer three or four bobblehead nights a year, usually honoring one of their former players. But in 2006 the Drillers staged one of the most unusual bobblehead nights ever, handing out Moses bobbleheads. No, I'm not talking about former big league outfielder John Moses. The other Moses. The one from the Old Testament. The figurine depicted the Big M holding the Ten Commandments.

On the Town

With a population of more than 400,000 people, Tulsa is the second-largest city in the Sooner State. Visiting fans find a wide selection of restaurants, taverns, and gentlemen's clubs in the downtown area. The pregame watering holes just north of the ballpark include the **Eleventh Street Pub** (6119 East 11th Street), the **Cockleburz Saloon & Grill** (6327 East 11th Street), and the **Hardwood Bar & Grill** (3148 East 11th Street).

As mentioned earlier the stadium shares the fairgrounds with an amusement park. **Bell's Family Fun Park** (3901 East 21st Street) has been a Tulsa institution since the 1950s. What began as a simple operation featuring Shetland pony rides now includes more than fifty rides, including the Zingo, a terrifying wooden roller coaster, and the Chili Pepper, a wet-and-wooly water plunge. The park is open Monday through Friday from 6:00 P.M. until 10:00 P.M. and Saturdays and Sundays from 1:00 P.M. until 10:00 P.M. Visitors have the option of purchasing all-day passes or paying a la carte by the ride.

Although he is best remembered for his prowess on the gridiron, legendary Oklahoman Jim Thorpe also played parts of six seasons in the National League between 1913 and 1919. Thorpe batted .252 with 7 homers and 82 RBI in 289 career games with the Giants, Reds, and Braves. The **Jim Thorpe Home** (706 East Boston Street, Yale) displays many awards and items from Thorpe's childhood. From Tulsa head west on U.S. Highway 51/Jim Thorpe Memorial Highway and follow the signs.

LAWRENCE-DUMONT STADIUM

Wichita Wranglers

Class AA, Texas League
(KANSAS CITY ROYALS)

Lawrence-Dumont Stadium
300 South Sycamore Street
Wichita, Kansas
316–267–3372

Ironically, the oldest ballpark in the Texas League—Lawrence-Dumont Stadium, which dates back to 1934—features bright green Astroturf on its infield. Think Busch Stadium in the 1980s, only with a little more neon in the spray paint, and you're approaching the type of plastic they've got on the infield in Wichita. The outfield lawn, however, is natural grass. So why would Wichita, whose park features old-fashioned pillars rising up from the grandstand seats to support the press box overhead and a concourse full of plaques that honor the old-time hardballers who played there, take the easy way out and install a rug? Well, you'll be happy to know that the team isn't merely trying to skimp on grounds keeping and watering bills. There's actually a pretty good reason for this anomaly. You see, the Wranglers aren't the only entity to call Lawrence-Dumont Stadium "home." The ballpark is also the site of the National Baseball Congress (NBC) World Series, an amateur tournament that amazingly plays more than eighty games at the park during a two-week period each summer. Such heavy use beneath the unforgiving Kansas sun subjects the field to the kind of wear and tear that natural grass just can't withstand.

The story of Lawrence-Dumont Stadium really is the story of the National Baseball Congress, or maybe it is the other way around. Maybe the story of the tournament is the story of the ballpark. The NBC was formed in 1935 by Raymond "Hap" Dumont, a Wichita sporting goods salesman who liked to dream big. In the midst of the Great Depression, Dumont envisioned a national tournament that would welcome all of the best semipro and barnstorming baseball teams from across the country to Wichita. Dumont had previously run a successful state tournament at an island ballpark on a bluff amidst the Arkansas River, but after that park burned down, he convinced Wichita to build him a bigger park by promising to make his tourney a national event. The city complied, building a new park on the western banks of the Arkansas as a WPA project, and naming it after Robert Lawrence, a prominent Wichita civic leader who had died the year before.

The first NBC World Series was a smashing success. Satchel Paige, lured to town by Dumont's promise of a $1,000 payday, put the tournament on the map. Paige struck out sixty batters while winning four games and leading his Corwin-Churchill team of Bismarck, North Dakota, to the title. In the seven decades since, more than 600 future and former major leaguers have played in the NBC tournament, but no one has approached Paige's strikeout record.

Today, the NBC serves as an interesting proving ground for up-and-coming players on collegiate summer league teams and aging players who still want to compete at a high level. Several dozen teams arrive in Wichita at the end of July, and then the games begin. And lots of them. For a three-day stretch in the middle of the tournament, Lawrence-Dumont Stadium sees action literally around the clock, hosting seventeen games in fifty-six hours. The marathon is called "Baseball Around the Clock," and those hearty fans who stay inside the park for all fifty-six hours receive a commemorative T-shirt and free pass to watch all of the remaining tournament games.

Fans of this unique tournament will tell you that Prairie Pine & Gravel of the Illinois Suburban League won three games in the pouring rain on the final day of the 2005 tournament to take home the title; that in the mid 1980s Barry Bonds and Rafael Palmeiro teamed up on the Hutchinson Broncos of the Kansas Jayhawk League; that in 1980 fan-favorite Joe Carter, of Wichita State University fame, blasted a pitch over the right field fence and into the Arkansas River while playing for a team from Boulder, Colorado; that in 1964 Tom Seaver went 2–0 on the mound and hit a game-winning grand slam for a team from Fairbanks, Alaska; that in 1954 Whitey Herzog won the NBC batting title with a .453 average for a team from Fort Leonard Wood, Missouri. And on and on goes the list of future major leaguers who have left their mark in Wichita.

The city's history as a minor league town is also impressive. Wichita hosted professional baseball as early as 1887 when the Wichita Braves were members of the Western League. Wichita enjoyed an on-again, off-again relationship with the Western League through the mid-1950s, before beginning one with the American Association. The Wichita Aeros were a stalwart in the now-defunct Triple-A circuit from 1970 through 1984, representing at various points the Cleveland Indians, Chicago Cubs, Texas Rangers, Montreal Expos, and Cincinnati Reds. After the American Association left town, Wichita joined the Texas League in 1987 when the Beaumont Golden Gators relocated to become the Wichita Pilots. A San Diego Padres affiliate, the Pilots changed their name to the Wranglers after just two seasons. Future big leaguers like Roberto and Sandy Alomar and Andy Benes made stops in Wichita while it was a Padres outpost, then the Wranglers switched to a PDC with the Kansas City Royals in 1995. Since then

Johnny Damon, Mike Sweeney, Carlos Beltrán, David DeJesus, and Alex Gordon have honed their skills at Lawrence-Dumont Stadium.

Although the stadium has undergone extensive renovations through the years, it maintains its old-time charm, until your eyes fall on that ghastly Astroturf infield. The view from the seats showcases the scenic Wichita skyline just across the river. The main entrance is adorned with a gigantic baseball bat that supports a round sign bearing the name of the stadium. The ballpark was renamed to honor Dumont as well as Lawrence in 1972, a year after Dumont's death.

Game Day

Getting to the Park

Wichita is 150 miles north of Oklahoma City and 180 miles southwest of Kansas City. From Oklahoma City, follow I–35 North to Wichita. From Kansas City, follow I–35 South to Wichita. Lawrence-Dumont Stadium is located across the Arkansas River from downtown, at the intersection of West Douglas Avenue and South Sycamore Street. From I–35, take the I–135 connector, which bisects Wichita from north to south, and exit onto Route 54/Kellogg Avenue. Follow Route 54 west for about 2 miles. After crossing the river, turn right onto Seneca Street, then right again onto Maple Street and the ballpark will be on the left. There is ample free parking at the stadium.

Inside the Park

Lawrence-Dumont Stadium can seat just over 6,000 fans, but the Wranglers are lucky if they draw 2,000 on most nights. This may be partly attributable to the fact that more than half of the seats at this historic stadium are bleacher benches.

The seating bowl is shaped like an L, with the seats on the right field side of the diamond extending only as far as the first base bag, and the seats on the left field side continuing all the way into medium-depth outfield territory.

The Marshall Seats and Sheriff Seats are below the narrow midlevel walkway upon which fans step as they exit the runways from the interior concourse to the seating bowl. The Marshall Seats are the six to eight rows of blue box seats along the first and third baselines, while the Sheriff Seats are the six rows of box seats behind home plate.

Why the Wranglers call their different ticket levels by quaint cowboy names, I have no idea, but I'm glad that other teams aren't following suit. It only serves to make things more confusing than need be. You could wake me up at 4:00 A.M. and ask me whether I'd prefer a Box Seat, a Reserved Seat, or a General Admission Seat for tomorrow's game, and I'd be able to tell you to put me in the Boxes without even opening my eyes. Ask me at four in the morning if I'd prefer a Marshall Seat, Sheriff Seat, or Deputy Seat, and I'll have to run a pot of coffee before I'll be able to sort out the hierarchy of Old West law enforcement officials and make my choice.

In any case the Deputy Seats are red stadium chairs that appear in the first four rows above the interior walkway behind home plate and in the entirety of the sections above the walkway along the first and third baselines. The remainder of the second-level seats behind home plate and the ones beyond the third base bag are General Admission bleachers known as Outlaw Seats. Ordinarily, I would caution fans to be wary of the stilt-like poles that rise amidst the Outlaw Seats behind home plate to support the press box, but because games are so sparsely attended in Wichita, the poles are not a problem. If you find that a pole is blocking your view, you can always scoot down a seat or two, or row or two, for a better view.

The four luxury boxes on either side of the press box all have indoor and outdoor seating. They can be rented for just $400 per night, so if you get nineteen of your friends to chip in $20 apiece you can enjoy a bird's-eye view of the game and a catered three-hour dinner for less money than it would cost to get that oil change your road-trip car has been begging for since you left Toledo in your rearview.

The main concourse is behind and beneath the Outlaw Seats. Here, fans find a diverse concession menu that includes several tasty barbecue options, Mexican specialties, red-hot sausages, brats, burgers, and more. The Souvenir Shop behind home plate is called the "General Store," but it was out of grain and spurs when I visited.

The concourse features an array of historic exhibits related to Wichita's minor league baseball history and the NBC. Here, fans find lore related to Messieurs Dumont and Lawrence, and NBC players like Paige, Carter, Seaver, Mark McGwire, John Olerud, and Roger Clemens. There are also plaques commemorating old minor league teams like the Wichita Jobbers and Wichita Witches who were members of the Western League in the 1910s and 1920s.

The Lawrence-Dumont Stadium Experience

The Wranglers offer fans the campy antics of two different mascots, a horse named "Wilbur" and an outlaw named "Angus." There is also a "trash monster" that makes appearances on particularly windy nights, encouraging fans to pick up after themselves.

Three or four times per season, the Wranglers treat local youngsters to "Scouts Night," when Boy Scouts and Girl Scouts get to watch the game and then camp out under the stars. I'm guessing they pitch their tents in the real grass outfield, not on the Astroturf infield.

Recurring "Faith Nights" offer the post-game incantations of Christian singers.

On the Town

Like a lot of cities in the Midwest and West, Wichita is laid out in a nice neat grid and isn't too cramped or crowded even in the heart of downtown. For a guy like me who grew up in and around Boston, a trip to Wichita is like a breath of fresh air after a big gulp of smog. Make no mistake, though, this is a good-sized city. In fact it's the largest in the Sunflower State, with a population of nearly 350,000.

Baseball fans find several restaurants just northwest of the ballpark, including **Ruben's Mexican Grill** (520 West Douglas Avenue) and the **Vagabond Cafe** (614 West Douglas Avenue),

while popular pregame and postgame watering holes include the **Stadium Sports Bar** (620 Maple Street), south of the stadium, and the **Southwinds Bar & Grill (**400 West Waterman Street), across the river.

The **Kansas Sports Hall of Fame** (238 North Mead Street) honors Wilt Chamberlain, Walter Johnson, Barry Sanders, and scores of other Kansas natives who made names for themselves in the wide world of sports. The museum is open Monday through Saturday from 9:00 A.M. until 5:00 P.M. and Sunday afternoons from 1:00 until 5:00. Admission costs $7.00 for adults and $6.00 for students and senior citizens.

HAMMONS FIELD

Springfield Cardinals

Class AA, Texas League
(ST. LOUIS CARDINALS)

Hammons Field
955 East Trafficway Street
Springfield, Missouri
417–863–2143

When developer John Q. Hammons announced in early 2002 that he planned to build an 8,000-seat ballpark in Springfield, Missouri, to lure a high-level minor league team to town, he faced some expected skepticism. People wondered aloud why a successful hotel baron with a company worth more than half a billion dollars would commit to building an expensive new park before he had even secured a team to play in it. You can't blame folks for wondering. After all, usually the sequence of events transpires in the reverse order. Disgruntled Team X states its preference to play in a new ballpark. Budget Strapped City X says it can't afford to build a new ballpark. Eager City Y steps up to the proverbial plate with the promise of a new ballpark. And Team X heads to City Y. John Q. Hammons took a different tack. First, he identified southwestern Missouri as a potentially lucrative minor league market. Second, he built a sparkling new ballpark in downtown Springfield. And then he got around to finding a team to play at his new yard.

In early 2004 Hammons broke ground on the $32 million stadium that would eventually bear his name. The park was built to Double-A specifications, with indoor batting cages, an indoor practice infield, posh player clubhouses, thirty luxury boxes, an open concourse above the seating bowl, and one of the snazziest video boards in all of the minor leagues.

While this construction was taking place, the Springfield-Ozark Ducks of the unaffiliated Frontier League were attracting decent crowds at Price Cutter Park, 10 miles away, and Hammons still hadn't found an affiliated team to play in Springfield. Just the same, Hammons maintained that not only would the new ballpark be finished in time for Opening Day 2005, but Springfield would have an affiliated team to play in it by then.

Still, the doubters bristled that Hammons was building a state-of-the-art stadium that would wind up hosting a lowly Frontier League team. Then, when he was good and ready, Hammons silenced his doubters on August 24, 2004, with the announcement that he had brokered a deal to bring a Texas League franchise to Springfield. And not just any franchise. The team would be affiliated with Missouri's major league darlings, the St. Louis Cardinals.

To pull off this coup, Hammons had to convince the St. Louis Cardinals to purchase the Texas League's El Paso Diablos for $9.8 million. The Diablos, an Arizona Diamondbacks affiliate, would relocate to Springfield and sign a player development contract with St. Louis. At the same time St. Louis would sever ties with its former Double-A Southern League affiliate in Sevierville, Tennessee, making way for its Double-A players to report to Springfield.

The Diamondbacks wound up moving their Double-A team to the spot vacated in Tennessee, and in the end, the loser in the shuffle appeared to be El Paso. Despite possessing a history in the Texas League that dated all the way back to 1962, the border town was suddenly left without a team. All was not lost, though. In 2005 a new incarnation of the Diablos began to play in El Paso as a member of the unaffiliated Central Baseball League and

Hammons Field

set a league attendance record drawing more than 190,000 fans.

Baseball's seminal season in Springfield was just as resoundingly successful as John Q. Hammons said it would be. The Cardinals received more than 8,000 season ticket requests before the season even began and went on to draw 526,630 fans. That total ranked Springfield fourteenth in minor league baseball and second among the thirty Double-A teams, behind only Frisco.

The first game at Hammons Field was an exhibition between the St. Louis Cardinals and the Springfield Cardinals in April of 2005. The next spring, the Springfield Cardinals returned the favor, traveling to the new Busch Stadium in St. Louis to open the new big league park with a preseason game against the Triple-A Memphis Redbirds. In between these two memorable moments in Springfield Cardinals history, the team treated its fans to many exciting highlights during its first year. The locals are still buzzing about a 485-foot home run that Juan Díaz hit to center field, about the three-homer game that Jeremy Brown of the visiting Midland RockHounds had at Hammons Field, and about Andre Eithier, who won the Texas League MVP award for Springfield and then got traded to the Los Angeles Dodgers for big leaguer Milton Bradley.

In the years ahead the Cardinals will doubtless make many more memories, beginning what should be a long run for minor league baseball in Springfield. In addition to hosting the Cardinals, Hammons Field is also the home of the Missouri State Bears.

Game Day

Getting to the Park

Springfield is 210 miles southwest of St. Louis and 250 miles southeast of Kansas City. From I–44, take U.S. Highway 65 South and then pick up the Chestnut Expressway West. Turn left onto National Street, then right onto Trafficway Street, and Hammons Field will appear on the right. There is no stadium parking lot. Most fans pay to park in the lot across the street from the stadium on Trafficway, or at the Jordan Valley Park parking garage just past the stadium. There are also several smaller lots in downtown Springfield where the prices range from $2.00 to $7.00 per car.

Inside the Park

Weekend games typically sell out in advance, while tickets to the left field lawn area are usually available at the box office during the week. All of the seats in Springfield are comfortable red stadium chairs, except for the last row around the top of the entire seating bowl, which takes the form of a bleacher bench. The Diamond Boxes are the first eight rows of seats between the dugouts in Sections D through L. Section D is at first base, Section H is behind the plate, and Section L is at third base. Behind the Diamond Boxes, Rows 9 through 24 sell as Infield Field Boxes. Past the corner bases Sections A through C in right field and Sections M and N in left field offer three rows of Dugout Boxes, then Outfield Field Boxes in Rows 4 through 24.

The Cardinals release 3,000 General Admission tickets for each game. The seating lawn begins in left field foul territory, curves around the left field foul pole, continues to the grove of pine trees that serves as the batter's eye in center field, and continues for a short stretch into right-center.

The wraparound concourse allows for a view of the game, serving hot dogs, brats, cheesesteaks, Domino's Pizza, and other treats. The huge souvenir store offers all kinds of Springfield and St. Louis Cardinals gear, and the kids area offers speed-pitch booths, batting cages, and other diversions.

The Hammons Field Experience

The Springfield mascot is Louie the Redbird, who claims to be the kid brother of Fredbird, the St. Louis Cardinals redbird. Another popular ballpark entertainer is superfan Marty Prather, a season ticket holder known as the "Sign Guy." Marty brings a different sign to the ballpark every game and holds his clever message up to get a chuckle out of his fellow fans and the players on the field. This may not seem like a big deal at first, but it is pretty impressive when you consider that the Cardinals play seventy home games each season, and Marty faces the constant pressure to be witty and original. Past favorites have included messages like, "Is this Heaven? No, it's Hammons," and "Who's Your Papo?" in homage to Springfield Cardinal bopper Papo Bolivar.

Before every game at Hammons Field, several members of the home team welcome fans as they pass through the turnstiles. Your chances of meeting the game's scheduled starting pitcher or cleanup hitter are slim, but you'll at least get to shake hands with a backup middle infielder, which is more than you can do at most parks.

Between innings, the video board in left-center educates fans with nuggets of inane trivia, some having to do with baseball, some having to do with science, some having to do with both, and some with neither. Here's a sampling:

➤ The silhouette on the MLB logo is of Harmon Killebrew.
➤ In the course of a lifetime, the average person sheds forty-four pounds of skin.
➤ Des Moines has the highest per capita Jell-O consumption rate in the U.S.
➤ Maine is the only state that borders on only one other state.
➤ The Amazon rainforest produces half of the world's oxygen supply.
➤ The most hits a team can collect in an inning without scoring is six.

The question I leave you with is: Do you feel smarter or dumber for knowing all of this useless information?

On the Town

Springfield is on the edge of the Ozarks, about 35 miles north of the Arkansas state line. On game days **Ebbet's Field** (1027 East Walnut Street) fills with fans, beginning in the late afternoon. After games many fans continue the party at **Trolley's Downtown Bar and Grille** (107 Park Central Square).

Fans who want to learn about Missouri sports history can visit the **Missouri Sports Hall of Fame** (3861 East Stan Musial Drive). The features include a "heavy-hitters" exhibit that pays tribute to sluggers like Babe Ruth, Willie Mays, Mike Schmidt, Mark McGwire, and Reggie Jackson, as well as other baseball exhibits, and displays related to motor sports, football, fishing, track and field, tennis, and other sports. The first person ever inducted into the Hall—way back in 1951—was former big league pitcher Carl Hubbell, who hailed from Carthage, Missouri. The Hall is open Monday through Saturday from 10:00 A.M. until 4:00 P.M. and Sunday from noon until 4:00 P.M. The cost is $5.00 for adults and $3.00 for children.

Half an hour south of Springfield along US 65, the town of **Branson** is a major tourist destination. The resort town is nestled between Table Rock Lake and Lake Taneycomo and is famous for its country music, theaters, showboats, theme parks, golf courses, and quaint Ozark landscape.

ELFSTROM STADIUM

Kane County Cougars

Class A, Midwest League
(OAKLAND ATHLETICS)

Philip B. Elfstrom Stadium
34W002 Cherry Lane
Geneva, Illinois
630–232–8811

Here's a case study that challenges the assumption that a minor league team needs its own exclusive market in order to thrive. Although we've been led to believe that if two teams are placed in cities too close together, they'll split the area's fan base, advertising dollars, and corporate partnership opportunities, and neither will be successful, the Kane County Cougars provide evidence to suggest that this is not necessarily true.

The Cougars play at Elfstrom Stadium in the western Chicago suburb of Geneva. The ballpark fits neither the retro mold, nor the modern fan-friendly mold. It is neither charming, nor intimate. It is a functional stadium that was built in 1991 near the site of a community landfill. The park sits on the outskirts of a town that had a population of less than 20,000 people at the time of the most recent census.

As for competition the Cougars must compete with the two major league teams 40 miles away, who draw a combined six million fans per season to their ballparks, as well as with five independent league teams in the area. Just 25 miles from Geneva, the Schaumburg Flyers of the Northern League draw more than 200,000 fans per season to their forty-eight home dates. Just 32 miles away, the Joliet Jackhammers of the Northern League draw 200,000 fans to Silver Cross Field. Just 40 miles away in Crestwood, the Windy City Thunder-

bolts of the Frontier League draw 80,000 fans to Hawkinson Ford Field. And just 60 miles away each—still within an hour's drive of Geneva—the Northern League's South Shore Railcats draw 150,000 fans to their park in Gary, Indiana, and the Frontier League's Rockford River Hawks draw more than 100,000 fans to their park in Rockford, Illinois.

Talk about some stiff competition for the Kane County Cougars. Well, as you might have already deduced, the Cougars do very well for themselves at the box office, despite a deck that would appear to be stacked against them. The team drew a surprisingly robust 240,000 fans in its inaugural 1991 season. The next year, the Cougars set a Midwest League attendance record, drawing 322,000 fans. And the year after that, attendance rose again. Today, despite the presence of the several minor league competitors nearby, and despite the presence of a decent major league park on Chicago's South Side, and of a revered ancient park on its North Side, the Cougars annual attendance totals continue to rise. In 2005 the Cougars attracted 519,000 fans to Elfstrom Stadium, drawing more fans than every other Class-A team, except for the Dayton Dragons. The Cougars placed sixteenth nationally in minor league attendance.

While the Cougars Midwest League rivals in Dayton enjoy the double benefit of playing at a dynamic new ballpark and of owning a player development contract with the nearby Cincinnati Reds, the Cougars play at a nondescript park and are affiliated with a major league team that's half a continent away. The obvious question, then, is, Why do the Cougars succeed to the degree that they do? It would take a comprehensive study—of the type beyond the scope of a book like this—to fully answer this question, but surely the answer would revolve around a collective love of baseball evidenced in Midwesterners and a long cultural tradition of enjoying minor league ball in this part of the country.

Elfstrom Stadium features an open design that does not leave much shade on sunny days or cover on rainy nights. The uncovered main concourse runs atop a seating bowl that extends all the way out to the foul poles on either side of the diamond, thanks to large grass berms that pick up where the seats leave off in shallow outfield territory and continue to the outfield wall. The berms actually wrap around the foul poles and into home run territory, providing group party areas in right field and left field. The bulk of the seating throughout the stadium comes in the form of metal bleachers. Several one-story structures stand at the back of the concourse, housing the concession stands and restrooms, while the press box is behind the home plate grandstand in front of the concourse. The outfield view showcases plenty of green trees, especially in left field.

At the time of its opening, Geneva's new ballpark was named in honor of Philip B. Elfstrom, the Kane County Forest Preserve president who worked tirelessly to bring a team to town, eventually landing a Midwest League club that had previously played in Wausau, Wisconsin. During their first two seasons, the Cougars were affiliated with the Baltimore Orioles. Future big leaguers like Joe Borowski, Curtis Goodwin, José Mercedes, Brad Pennington, and Alex Ochoa came to town in those early days of Kane County baseball. Then, in 1994 the team began a ten-year relationship with the Florida Marlins that would bring to town future stars like Josh Beckett, A. J. Burnett, Luis Castillo, Charles Johnson, Kevin Millar, Ryan Dempster, Scott Podsednik, Édgar Rentería, and Dontrelle Willis. Since the Cougars began their current affiliation with the A's in 2003, alumni Joe Blanton and Huston Street have found their way to Oakland.

In addition to hosting the Cougars, Elfstrom Stadium is the home of the Illinois State High School Association Division AA baseball tournament each June.

Game Day

Getting to the Park

Geneva is 40 miles directly west of Chicago. Elfstrom Stadium is located in the Kane County Events Center, just south of the intersection of Roosevelt Road/Route 38 and Kirk Road. From Chicago, follow I–290 West to I–88 West. Take the Farnsworth Road exit and follow Farnsworth until it becomes Kirk Road. After another 5 miles turn left onto Cherry Lane, which leads to the ballpark. Free parking is available in a large lot on the first base side of the stadium, or fans may pay $2.00 for a preferred parking spot closer to the entrance gates.

Inside the Park

The ballpark can accommodate 7,400 fans, and crowds typically exceed 7,000 people, meaning that if you show up on game day without a ticket, you'll probably wind up on one of the outfield lawns. The Field Boxes are in the first two rows of comfortable red stadium chairs in Sections 115, 116, and 117, on the outfield side of the visitors dugout on the third base side. These seats are practically right down on the field. The ten rows of stadium chairs throughout the rest of the seating bowl, whether behind home plate or in shallow outfield foul territory, sell as Box Seats. The thirteen rows of metal bleachers with backs behind the Boxes sell as Reserved Seats. Section 103 is in shallow right field, Sections 106 and 107 are behind the Cougars dugout, Section 110 is behind home plate, Sections 113 and 114 are behind the visitors dugout, and Section 118 is in left field.

When it comes to the matching berm areas on either side of the field, don't be fooled by their names. The "First Base Lawn" is actually in right field, and the "Third Base Lawn" is in left field. Many fans bring their own lawn chairs into the park.

The Cougars offer an excellent selection of concession treats, highlighted by Chicago Red Hots, pork chop sandwiches, dipped Italian beef, brats, and funnel cakes. The local beer on tap is from Two Brothers Brewing Company, based in Warrenville, Illinois, while Goose Island and Leinenkugel are also available.

After they've filled their bellies with hot dogs and soda, young fans visit the bouncy pens and other playground attractions behind the left field group area.

The Elfstrom Stadium Experience

The Cougars offer postgame fireworks after just about every evening home game. Less frequently, but still often, they offer fans the chance to witness Jake the Diamond Dog in action. Although he claims to be unrelated to Dinger the Home Run Dog, who wows fans at Coastal Federal Field in Myrtle Beach, Jake is every bit as talented. This well-trained golden retriever delivers balls and water bottles to the umpires between innings and keeps the barking to a minimum. Jake's good buddy is team mascot Ozzie the Cougar. No, this isn't a real cougar, just a heavyset guy in a furry suit. Ozzie is a mellow cat whose eyelids are usually at half-mast, giving him a half-baked look.

On the Town

Elfstrom Stadium is an excellent "eating" park, but for those who prefer to indulge before or after the game, there are several fast-food options half a mile north on State Street. From the ballpark lot, take a left onto Kirk Road and then a left onto State Street, and you'll soon encounter several familiar chains, as well as **Charlie Fox's Pizzeria** (1188 East State Street), **Bada Beef** (1188 East State Street), **Tia Maria's Mexican Restaurant** (730 East State Street), **Genoa Pizza** (705 East State Street), and **Gen Hoe Chop Suey** (537 East State Street).

A bit farther away, **Stockholm's** (306 West State Street) and **Three Stags Brew Pub** (319 West State Street) are popular spots among microbrew aficionados, while **The Little Owl** (101 West State Street) has been a Geneva landmark since 1920.

For the last six decades, Geneva has paid homage to its Swedish heritage by hosting a **Mid-sommar Festival**. The big blond block party takes place in the last week of June, offering food, drinks, entertainment, and family fun in the downtown business district.

O'BRIEN FIELD

Peoria Chiefs

Class A, Midwest League
(CHICAGO CUBS)

O'Brien Field
730 SW Jefferson Avenue
Peoria, Illinois
309–680–4000

There are so many things about the Midwest League that make it special: the knowledgeable local fans who fill the circuit's ballparks with enthusiasm, the warm summer nights that provide perfect settings for ballgames, the native corn on the cob at the concession stands, the palm trees that sway blithely in the breeze. Wait a minute, palm trees? In the Midwest League? You probably think your humble author is off his rocker, right? Well, rest assured, I haven't confused the Midwest League with the Florida State League. Strange as it may seem, O'Brien Field features a whole bunch of palm trees on its outfield berms, offering fans a tropical oasis in central Illinois.

When the Chiefs opened this ballpark in 2002, they wanted to distinguish it from all of the others nearby, so as strange as it may seem, they planted palm trees in the outfield, both inside and outside the park. They potted twenty palms prior to christening the new ballpark with a 3–0 win over Dontrelle Willis and the Kane County Cougars on May 24, 2002, then they went on to post the best record in franchise history. The Chiefs compiled a 47–24 record at home on their way to an 85-win season. After the Chiefs beat Lansing in the playoffs to claim the Midwest League championship, they announced their new park had helped them draw a franchise-best

254,407 fans. A great year in the two-decade-old history of the team ended on a down note, however, when the chilly winds of November and December assailed O'Brien Field's beloved palms, it severely sickened the majestic trees. Undeterred, the Chiefs planted a fresh batch of palms when the ground thawed the following spring, this time using a heartier tree known as the Queens Palm. Every spring since, the Chiefs have continued the tradition of refreshing their palm garden with new Queens Palms. Today, the trees continue to make an already pleasant ballpark environment unique.

O'Brien Field sits in the midst of downtown Peoria. It was built as part of a $24 million project. While the city helped fund the cost of acquiring the 2 city blocks on which the park was built, the Peoria Chiefs Community Baseball Club privately financed the $17 million stadium. The driving force behind the initiative was longtime city resident Pete Vonachen. "Mr. Baseball," as the locals call him, bought the Chiefs back in the mid-1980s, helping to stabilize the franchise shortly after it arrived via Danville in 1983. After establishing the Chiefs as one of the more successful minor league teams in the region, Vonachen sold them to a group of investors from Chicago in 1988. He kept turning out at the ballpark, though, and was honored in 1992 when the Chiefs remodeled Meinen Field and renamed it "Pete Vonachen Stadium." Previously, the ballpark had been named after John Meinen, a baseball coach at Bradley University.

Despite the update to the ballpark, the Peoria team fell on hard times in the early 1990s. Mirroring the overall decline of business and entertainment in downtown Peoria, the Chiefs struggled to attract crowds. Rumors swirled that the team was up for sale and might be bought by investors interested in moving it out of Peoria. The community turned to Vonachen once again, asking him to help reinvigorate the franchise. Vonachen delivered, forming a group of forty-one local investors to buy the team.

Over the next several years, Vonachen worked tirelessly to see to it that the Chiefs would have a new home, even though the city refused to offer the type of public support other cities have offered their teams in recent years. When O'Brien Field opened, the seventy-seven-year-old Vonachen told the *Peoria Journal Star*: "I'm going to die a happy man now because this is the climax of 18 years of professional baseball here. I'll go to my grave knowing that generations ahead in Peoria will be able to enjoy baseball. Good family entertainment is what we need."

Predictably, the new ballpark started a wave of economic development in downtown Peoria along the waterfront, helping to lift the profile of the city as a whole. If only every city had a Pete Vonachen to serve as the guardian of its local nine, there would be far fewer franchise relocations, far more top-notch ballparks, and our nation's urban communities would be a little bit healthier and a little bit happier across the board.

O'Brien Field was designed by HNTB and named after a local automobile dealership that bought the naming rights. It features a sunken playing field, an open concourse atop the seating bowl that allows fans to walk around the entire field, and a luxury box level above the concourse around the infield. Narrow grass berms appear in left and right field home run territory. To protect passing cars on Adams Street and Jefferson Avenue from foul balls, nets supported by poles rim the top of the stadium. Meanwhile, at ground level wrought-iron fences separate the stadium grounds from the streets outside, allowing visitors on the sidewalks to peer down into the seating bowl and to see parts of the field. From the seats fans enjoy a panoramic view of the downtown skyline, which features Peoria's twin towers.

The Born Paint Company building looms over the outfield, allowing its rooftop visitors a free view of the game. O'Brien Field is comfortable, scenic, and festive. It provides an excellent blueprint for success to any other community interested in integrating a new ballpark with a preexisting urban landscape.

Peoria has been a member of the Midwest League since 1983. Originally, the team was a farm club of the California Angels and was known as the Peoria Suns, but a year after moving to Peoria, the Suns renamed themselves the Chiefs, as a nod to a Peoria club that went by the same name while playing in the Three-I League from 1953 through 1957. After future major leaguers Mark McLemore, Wally Joyner, and Devon White starred for the Chiefs in their first Midwest League season, Vonachen purchased the team in 1984 and netted a new affiliation with the Cubs. Greg Maddux went 13–9 with a 3.19 ERA for the Chiefs in 1985, while Rafael Palmeiro batted .297 and drove in 55 runs. In 1995 the Chiefs began a ten-year PDC with the St. Louis Cardinals, heralding the arrival of future stars like Albert Pujols, Plácido Polanco, and Rick Ankiel in Peoria. In 2005 Peoria signed on to be a Cubs affiliate once again. The season was a memorable one. On April 20, Chiefs pitchers Sean Gallagher, Walt Nolen, and Jon Hunton combined to pitch the fifth no-hitter in Peoria history, leading the team to a 3–2 win at Cedar Rapids. On June 21, O'Brien Field hosted the Midwest League All-Star Game. On July 27, 2004, fans turned out at O'Brien Field to watch Nomar Garciaparra make a rehab appearance with the Chiefs. The next day, a franchise record 9,602 fans jammed into the park to cheer for Garciaparra. Just a week later, on August 2, Kerry Wood made a rehab appearance at O'Brien Field, striking out three of the four Kane County Cougars he faced. To finish the season on a high note, the Chiefs unveiled a new statue of Vonachen inside the front gates of O'Brien Field in early September, then announced they had set a new team attendance record by attracting 256,612 fans during the season.

Today, Pete Vonachen's son Rocky Vonachen serves as president of the Peoria Chiefs Community Baseball Club. Fans interested in learning more about Pete Vonachen and the history of the Peoria Chiefs should pick up a copy of *The Boys Who Would Be Cubs* by Joseph Bosco. The book chronicles the story of the 1988 Chiefs, a club managed by future big league skipper Jim Tracy.

Game Day

Getting to the Park

Peoria is located in central Illinois, 170 miles southwest of Chicago and 170 miles northeast of St. Louis. It makes for a great stopover on any major league trip to those two cities. From Chicago, take I–55 to I–74 and once in Peoria follow I–74 across the Murray Baker Bridge. Take the Glen Oak Avenue exit and follow Jefferson Avenue to the ballpark. From St. Louis, take I–55 to I–155 to I–74 and then follow the directions above. There are more than 3,000 parking spaces within a 5-block radius of the stadium, including 500 curbside spots. The parking lots directly north and east of the stadium charge $5.00 per car, while there are lots that charge less a couple of blocks east at the Peoria Civic Center.

Inside the Park

The seating bowl has an official capacity of 7,500 people, but the Chiefs are willing to sell as many lawn tickets as they have customers to buy them. The seating bowl extends into shallow outfield foul territory, providing comfortable stadium chairs throughout. Grass berms continue along the foul lines then wrap around the foul poles into home run territory. The nine sections around the infield sell as Club Box Seats. Section 104 is even with first base, while Section 108 is directly behind home plate, and Section 112 is at third base. The two sections in shallow left field, Sections 113 and 114, and the three sections in shallow right field, Sections 101 through 103, sell as Box Seats. Lawn tickets are good for a spot on the left field or right field berm. Fans can bring their own beach blankets into the stadium, but lawn chairs are not permitted. The twenty-two luxury boxes are above the concourse on the infield.

A large gift shop sits behind Section 110 on the first base side. The playground is behind the batter's eye in center. The concourse offers eight main concession stands, as well as vendor carts spread throughout the park. The menu includes brats, pork chop sandwiches, sweet corn, fresh roasted nuts, and snow cones.

The O'Brien Field Experience

The Peoria mascot is Homer, a human-sized Dalmatian who wears overalls and a fire chief's helmet. The between innings entertainment package is directed by a roaming MC who wanders the stands with a microphone in hand, while the video board in right field features prominently in the proceedings.

Peoria's popular annual promotional nights include Country Music Night, Hip-Hop Night, and Irish Night.

Former Cubs star and National Baseball Hall of Fame inductee Ferguson Jenkins makes occasional appearances at O'Brien Field to sign autographs and raise money for his Fergie Jenkins Foundation, which supports various American and Canadian charities.

On the Town

Visiting fans find a cluster of conveniently located watering holes just a few blocks east of O'Brien Field. The options include **Kelleher's**

Irish Pub (619 SW Water Street), the Waterhouse (619 SW Water Street), Cafe 401 (401 SW Water Street), Hooters (418 SW Water Street), and the Big Easy Cafe (100 State Street).

Those interested in visiting the Chiefs' old park will find Pete Vonachen Stadium (Nebraska Avenue) on the campus of Bradley University. The university is reportedly going to convert the ballpark into a soccer stadium soon, since its baseball team plays at O'Brien Field these days.

VICTORY FIELD

Indianapolis Indians

Class AAA, International League
(PITTSBURGH PIRATES)

Victory Field
501 West Maryland Street
Indianapolis, Indiana
317–269–3542

Indianapolis is one of the largest cities in the United States without a major league baseball team to call its own. Or, to put a more positive spin on the situation, it is one of the largest cities *with* a minor league team. As such, visiting fans get to enjoy minor league baseball at its highest level, while also taking in the peripheral attractions of a big league caliber city. Indianapolis is home to 800,000 people, an NFL team, an NBA team, the Indianapolis Motor Speedway, and the NCAA Hall of Fame. It is also home to one of the finer minor league ballparks. Since Victory Field opened midway through the 1996 season, numerous national media outlets—along the order of *Baseball America, Sports Illustrated,* and ESPN—have showered it with accolades. And deservedly so.

The park is basically a scaled-down version of a major league stadium. If you doubled both the lower deck and upper deck in size, you would have a facility suitable for the big league game. The $20 million stadium was funded jointly by the team and city. It was designed by HOK and offers a combination of modern amenities and old-time charm.

On the outside Victory Field offers a snazzy multicolored brick façade that features green steel trusses and large windows that shed light onto the concourse inside. The main entrance at the corner of West and Maryland Streets funnels fans between auburn brick columns topped by an arched green sign that displays the stadium name. After passing through the gates, fans step onto a large center field plaza that connects to a concourse that allows for easy wandering around the entire first level.

Seating surrounds the entire field in the lower bowl, except in straightaway center field where a patch of pines serves as the batter's eye. The concourse offers open views of the field and is covered in parts by a large second deck that extends three-quarters of the way down the foul lines on either side. The interior façade is a pale yellow, while the seats are all Camden-green.

The outfield view showcases the tall buildings of downtown. The familiar white parachuted top of the RCA Dome looms beyond the right field fence, while the three smokestacks of a power plant rise high above the ballpark's right field grandstand. There is a small tepee on the back of the left field berm that recalls memories of the outfield wigwams that once stood at Fulton County Stadium in Atlanta and Municipal Stadium in Cleveland.

Victory Field is named after its predecessor, which, though it wasn't called "Victory Field" in its latter years, did bear that name from 1942 through 1967. Originally introduced as "Perry Stadium" in 1932, the venue that would house minor league baseball in Indianapolis for more than six decades was renamed for the first time to celebrate the United States victory in World War II. It was renamed again in 1967 to honor former Indians player, manager, and team president Donie Bush, and it bore the name "Bush Stadium" until the new Victory Field opened on July 11, 1996. Oklahoma City's Rick Helling struck out 14 Indians that night— a mark that still stands as the record for the most K's by a visiting pitcher at the park.

Bush Stadium housed teams in the Negro American League and all three recent Triple-A leagues: the American Association, International League, and Pacific Coast League. Dating back long before that ballpark was built, Indianapolis actually got its feet wet in the professional game as a member of the National League. The Indianapolis Browns finished eighth in the eight-team Senior Circuit in 1887, with a record of 37–89. The team played two more seasons in the NL, finishing seventh both times, ahead of only Washington, before taking a few years off to revaluate the local landscape and then join the Western League in 1892. After sitting out the 1893 season, the Indians rejoined the Western League in 1894, and they have fielded a team every season since—including 1900 when they were members of the American League. The team spent most of the twentieth century in the American Association, but when that league dissolved in 1998, the Indians joined the International League.

Over the past two decades, the Indians have been affiliated with the Montreal Expos (1984–1992), Cincinnati Reds (1993–1999), and Milwaukee Brewers (2000–2004). In 2005 they signed a PDC with the Pittsburgh Pirates, rekindling a relationship that previously existed between 1949 and 1951. The list of Indians to eventually achieve enshrinement in the National Baseball Hall of Fame includes Grover Cleveland Alexander, Luke Appling, Charles Hartnett, Harmon Killebrew, Nap Lajoie, Al Lopez, Rube Marquard, Joseph McCarthy, Bill McKechnie, Ray Schalk, and Bob Uecker. Other Indianapolis stars have included Bernie Carbo, Sean Casey, Eric Davis, Zach Duke, Andrés Galarraga, Ken Griffey Sr., Randy Johnson, Paul Konerko, Hal McRae, Roger Maris, Herb Score, Ben Sheets, and Frank Viola.

Game Day

Getting to the Park

Indianapolis is smack dab in the middle of Indiana, and Victory Field is right in the middle of the city's downtown. In the Hoosier State, all roads lead to the capital. The I–465 beltway, which surrounds Indianapolis, is accessible via I–65, I–69, I–70, I–74, and a number of state highways and smaller roads. The stadium is part of the White River State Park, which features a number of other cultural, educational,

Victory Field

and recreational venues. To reach the stadium from I–65 South, take the Martin Luther King, Jr. Street/West Street exit. From I–65 North, take I–70 West to the West Street exit.

Most fans park in the garage at the corner of Maryland Street and West Street, right across the street from the main entrance. If you like keeping an eye on your carport during the game, then this is the place for you. The garage looms just beyond the field in left and center. It charges $5.00. You'll find options that are less expensive a bit farther away, including the lots at the Indiana State Museum or White River State Park, where the cost is $3.00 per car. There are also on-street spaces in the stadium neighborhood.

For fans staying at downtown hotels, the Indy-Go Blue Line circulator stops right at Victory Field. The free bus runs every ten minutes from 10:00 A.M. until 10:00 P.M., seven days a week.

Inside the Park

Victory Field offers 12,500 stadium chairs, 1,000 bleacher seats, and room for about 2,000 on its outfield lawns.

The lower bowl starts with Section 101 in the left field corner and continues down the left field line to Section 105 behind the Indians bull pen, 108 and 109 behind the Indians dugout, and 112 behind home plate. Then the bowl makes the turn and heads down the right field line to Sections 115 and 116 behind the visitors dugout and 119 behind the visitors bull pen. It ends at Section 124 in the right field corner. Sections 105 through 119 house Box Seats, while the outfield-most sections house Reserved Seats.

The upper deck is accessible via numerous staircases on the first-level concourse. The upper level offers both Box Seats and Reserved Seats, like the level below, but it doesn't continue all the way out to the foul poles. It ends

high above the bull pens in outfield territory. Sections 205 through 215, between the dugouts, house Box Seats, while Sections 201 through 204, in left field, and Sections 216 through 219, in right field, house Reserved Seats.

The Bleachers are above the concourse on the first level, appearing in three steep sections of aluminum benches in foul territory. These are the worst seats in the house, both in terms of comfort and sightlines. The Lawn Seating areas are above the home run fence in right and left. They are long, narrow, and appropriately sloped. Fans can bring their own coolers into the game, provided that they don't bring any glass bottles, alcoholic beverages, or offensively smelly cheeses.

Because the Reserved Seats, Bleacher Seats, and Lawn all cost the same, I suggest buying a Reserved Seat, either in the lower or upper bowl. That way you'll have a comfortable seat waiting for you, even if you decide to spend most of the game on the Lawn or in the Bleachers.

The twenty-eight luxury suites flank the press box atop the second deck. A green roof extends over the outdoor seats, also covering the back rows of general seats.

The main concourse runs atop the first-level seats, offering views of the field and seven main concession stands. The trademark ballpark treat is a creation known as Tribe Fries. Tribe Fries are spicy potato wedges. I suggest a healthy dose of ketchup to cool them off. Other Victory Field superlatives include the brats, breaded tenderloin, Coney Island dogs, and rib sandwich. To wash it all down, the ballpark offers Old Style to keep the Cubs fans happy, Pabst Blue Ribbon, Ram Blond, Razzwheat, and Victory Amber. There is also an ice-cream stand with picnic tables behind the batter's eye in center.

The center field plaza has a speed-pitch booth, a pop-shot game, and face painting for the kids. The Hot Corner Gift Shop is on the third base side of the concourse, while there is a smaller stand on the first base side.

The Victory Field Experience

You know your city is *that* close to being a big league town when the local minor league mascot is so inundated with autograph requests that the team has to designate one inning per game, and one inning only, during which he can sign for fans. Then again, Rowdie, the big red bear with a baseball for a nose, who has been the Indians mascot since 1993, has paws instead of fingers and can only sign his name about three times every fifteen minutes. So maybe his limited autograph availability doesn't mean that much after all. In any case the public-address announcer lets the young fans know when Rowdie is ready to lay some ink, and the kids line up to get in on the action.

Speaking of the kids, the Indians have a great program to engage fans fourteen and younger in the life of the team. Members of the Knot Hole Club pay just $12 per year for a season-long pass to the park, an Indians T-shirt, and a monthly newsletter. Hey, the Indians are no fools. If every kid brings along at least one paying adult to the game, and every adult shells out something like $30 per kid for Cracker Jack, ice cream, corn dogs, and memorabilia. . . .

Traditionally, the Indians show their appreciation for their fans before every Sunday game, offering a free souvenir to the first 4,000 to enter the park. The giveaway item varies from week to week.

On the Town

Indianapolis offers lots of attractions for those times when the games are not in progress. For ballpark junkies the list starts with **Bush Stadium,** which still stands at 1501 West 16th Street. During its six decades of use, Bush Stadium featured an ivy-covered brick wall across the outfield, a hand-operated scoreboard in left, concourse murals of great players that graced its field, and a large covered grandstand. You may recognize the park from its scenes in *Eight Men Out,* in which it was dressed up to resemble both Comiskey Park and Crosley Field. After the Indians moved to their new digs, Bush Stadium was converted into an auto-racing track, but the racing company pulled up stakes after just two seasons. Now the stadium sits idle, awaiting either the arrival of another sporting venture or the unforgiving pendulum of the wrecking ball.

Another location tied to Indianapolis baseball history is **Oscar Charleston Park** (2800 East 30th Street), a city-run facility named for the local Negro League standout who was inducted into the Hall of Fame in 1976. "The Hoosier Comet" served as a batboy for the Indianapolis ABCs in his youth, then starred for the team when he grew up. The park that bears his name is located near the spot where he grew up.

Racing enthusiasts will want to visit the **Indianapolis Motor Speedway Hall of Fame** (4790 West 16th Street), located within the Brickyard oval northwest of downtown. The museum features more than seventy cars, an extensive trophy collection, an exhibit related to the evolution of the scoring and timing at the 500, and low-speed bus tours of the 2.5-mile track. It is open from 9:00 A.M. until 5:00 P.M. every day of the year except Christmas, and admission is just $3.00 for adults and $1.00 for children under fifteen.

Finally, right in the ballpark neighborhood, visitors find the **National Art Museum of Sport at IUPUI** (850 West Michigan Avenue), the **NCAA Hall of Champions** (700 West Washington Street), and the **Indianapolis Zoo** (1200 West Washington Street).

MEMORIAL STADIUM

Fort Wayne Wizards

Class A, Midwest League
(SAN DIEGO PADRES)

Memorial Stadium
1616 East Coliseum Boulevard
Fort Wayne, Indiana
260–482–6400

When the Midwest League announced early in 2006 that the Fort Wayne Wizards had been sold to a group of out-of-town investors from Atlanta, the baseball fans in this large northeastern Indiana city shuttered. Just a few days later, though, the community breathed a collective sigh of relief when new owners Jason Freier and Chris Schoen announced that they planned to keep the Wizards in Fort Wayne, maintain the team's affiliation with the San Diego Padres, and retain all fourteen members of the front office staff. "We bought the team in Fort Wayne because of the way it's performing in Fort Wayne, because of the community support, and the people here," Freier said at a press conference shortly after purchasing the team. "We intend to be here as long as you guys will have us." Freier and Schoen went on to explain how committed they were to making the ballpark experience at Memorial Stadium even more festive and fun than it already was. They envisioned a new JumboTron and a display board in the outfield to track pitch speeds. They envisioned establishing a wider array of sponsors. They said their group liked the thirteen-year-old stadium but would remain open to the idea of building a new downtown ballpark in the future if there was widespread community support for one. Fort Wayne began a feasibility study in 2005 to investigate the possibility of building a new ballpark, and

speculation is that the new owners will accelerate the process.

From a business standpoint keeping the Wizards in Fort Wayne was actually an easy call for the new owners. This city of more than 200,000 residents was recently named the seventh-best minor league market in the country by *Street & Smith Sports Business Journal*, which rated 230 minor league baseball markets. The Wizards drew 318,506 fans to brand new Memorial Stadium on joining the Midwest League in 1993, and while they've failed to duplicate that lofty total in the years since, attendance increased six years in a row before the sale of the team. In 2005 the Wizards drew 278,631 fans, the second most in team history. In 2006, though, the team's attendance dipped to 253,564.

The Wizards were affiliated with the Minnesota Twins from 1993 until 2000, and they have had a player development contract with the Padres since 2001. Prior to playing in Fort Wayne, the franchise that became the Wizards spent ten seasons playing in Kenosha, Wisconsin. At the time of the team's arrival in 1993, Fort Wayne had been without a professional club since the Fort Wayne Daisies of the All-American Girls Professional Baseball League left town in the early 1950s. To accommodate the Wizards, Fort Wayne built Memorial Stadium at a cost of $5.6 million.

The stadium is part of a sports complex on the northern side of town that also includes the Allen County War Memorial Coliseum and Expo Center and parking lots that can hold 4,500 cars. Coliseum Boulevard runs behind the stadium in left field and center field, while a net suspended above the fence protects passing traffic from home run balls. Meanwhile, a historic U.S. Army tank sits behind the fence in right where it is visible to fans within the stadium. The stadium itself is big, gray, concrete and not particularly easy on the eyes.

Notable Wizards alumni include A. J. Pierzynski, Torii Hunter, Matt Lawton, Corey Koskie, Sean Burroughs, Jake Peavy, and Oliver Pérez. Large signs on the stadium concourses pay tribute to these past stars and other big leaguers who once called Fort Wayne "home." The stadium is also notable for being the site of Alex Rodríguez's first professional home run, as A-Rod went deep against the Wizards as a member of the visiting Appleton Foxes.

Past visitors to Memorial Stadium have included actor James Earl Jones, who came to Fort Wayne to promote a youth reading program; Hall of Famer Ernie Banks, who visited in 2004; and former major leaguers Ken Griffey Sr. and Andre Dawson, who visited in 2005 in an event coordinated by a local baseball card shop. The team's Christian Speaker Series has also brought former major leaguers like Dave Dravecky, Scott Sanderson, and Frank Tanana to Memorial Stadium.

In addition to the Wizards, local high schools use Memorial Stadium each spring, along with a Division 1 college baseball team—Indiana-Purdue-University, Fort Wayne.

Game Day

Getting to the Park

Fort Wayne is in northeastern Indiana, 10 miles west of the Ohio state line and 45 miles south of the Michigan line. From I–69, take the Coldwater Road exit and follow Coldwater Road south to Coliseum Boulevard/U.S. Route 30. Turn left on Coliseum Boulevard and after ½ mile, the stadium parking lot will be on the right. There is ample room for parking within this lot, located behind the stadium and adjacent to Johnny Appleseed Park. Parking costs $3.00.

Inside the Park

"The Castle," as Memorial Stadium is sometimes called, can accommodate 6,500 fans. The main grandstand rises between the dugouts, while a separate bank of bleachers resides down the left field line, and a picnic deck resides in right.

The main bowl offers Box Seats that begin about 10 feet above field level, then a midlevel walkway, and then Grandstand Seats—that are actually metal bleachers with backs. Section 101 is at first base, Section 106 is behind home plate, and Section 111 is at third base.

The Bleachers in left field are bleachers without backs. The first bleacher section, 301, is just past third base, while the last section, 304, is in deep left field.

The luxury boxes are located on the first level of the concrete structure behind home plate, and the press box is on the second level.

There is a large concession stand on the lower concourse just inside the main entrance gates that serves grilled hamburgers, barbecue chicken sandwiches, brats, Italian sausages, turkey legs, and hot dogs. There is no view of the game from here, but another stand, located down the left field line, serves the same items while allowing for a view of the action to those waiting in line. There are also three concession stands on the upper concourse above the main seating bowl—one on the first base side, one on the third base side, and one behind home plate.

Memorial Stadium offers a wide range of adult drinks, including LaBatt Blue, Heineken, Moosehead, Honey Brown, Rolling Rock, Corona, Smirnoff Ice, Bacardi Silver, Barcardi Razz, Bahama Mama Cooler, and Bahama Blast.

The Memorial Stadium Experience

The new owners sound intent on making the ballpark experience more lively and exciting than ever, and the team has done a good job in the past of embracing and engaging the local community. All fans are allowed to run the bases after every game. This is a refreshing policy in an age when the fourteen and under crowd seems to catch most of the breaks at the American ballpark. Haven't we adults all had our hearts broken at least once by a pimple-faced ballpark intern who tells us that we're too old to get a bobblehead doll or baseball card set out of the mound of cardboard boxes piled inside the turnstiles? Well, in Fort Wayne the kindly ballpark folks don't discriminate on the basis of age. So get out there and see if you can haul your bloated carcass from home plate to first base in less than four seconds. Don't worry about those kiddies in front of you . . . just push 'em out of the way.

Each year the Wizards host annual Boy Scout and Girl Scout overnight events, allowing the local troopers to camp out on the Memorial Stadium lawn. The team also holds ice-cream eating contests on summer Saturdays, courtesy of a local ice-cream distributor. On Saturdays and Sundays, the team offers clowns, face painters, and balloon benders to keep the kids occupied while their parents gnaw on turkey legs and drink beer.

On a nightly basis fans look forward to each game's potato chip race—a takeoff on the famous sausage race staged by the Milwaukee Brewers—that pits three contestants who run around the outfield in oversized potato chip bags.

Team mascot Dinger D. Dragon is a warty green fellow who dances in the crowd, signs autographs, hugs unsuspecting fans, and participates in on-field contests.

Keep your eyes open whenever a member of the Wizards hits a home run and you'll notice that the two poles on the right field scoreboard light up as the team plays a siren through the public-address system.

On the Town

Fort Wayne houses the **Children's Zoo** (3411 Sherman Boulevard), the **Lincoln Museum** (200 East Berry Street), the **Fort Wayne Museum of Art** (311 East Main Street), and a number of other cultural destinations. As game time approaches, fans congregate at the chain-type restaurants located near the ballpark.

One of Fort Wayne's claims to fame is that its **Archer Park** (adjacent to the Memorial Coliseum) is the final resting place of legendary American frontiersman Johnny Chapman, better known as "Johnny Appleseed." Back in the early 1800s, when the Midwest was still being explored, Chapman traveled the countryside on foot planting orchards. Chapman sowed the seeds for one of those orchards in Fort Wayne, and then decided to make the city his home. Today, Chapman's gravesite is designated a National Historic Landmark, and each year since 1976, Fort Wayne has held a festival at Archer Park to honor Johnny Appleseed's unique contribution to the American landscape. **The Johnny Appleseed Festival** offers vendors, musicians, and demonstrators who all wear nineteenth-century garb and pretend to be fascinated and perplexed by such alien modern novelties as festival-goers' wristwatches, cell phones, and ballpoint pens. Entering the festival grounds is like entering another century, a century in which it was admirable to roam the country spreading good cheer and apple seeds. Unfortunately for traveling baseball fans, the festival takes place in mid-September, after the minor league season has ended, but it's still worth visiting Archer Park during your visit to town to check out the gravesite of this unique American adventurer. After all, doesn't every traveling baseball fan have a bit of the same pioneering spirit in him that led Johnny Appleseed from field to field across the country? Only instead of leaving beautiful apple trees in our wake, we leave crumpled hot dog wrappers, crushed plastic beer cups, and clogged stadium toilets.

COVELESKI STADIUM
South Bend Silver Hawks

Class A, Midwest League
(ARIZONA DIAMONDBACKS)

Stanley Coveleski Regional Stadium
501 West South Street
South Bend, Indiana
574–235–9988

Throughout the 2005 season fans of the Midwest League's South Bend Silver Hawks faced persistent rumors that their team would be flying the coop after the season. The Palisades Baseball group had recently put the team up for sale and word was that a consortium of investors from southern Illinois was the most likely suitor. As the town of Marion, Illinois, began constructing a $16 million, 4,000-seat stadium in anticipation of the arrival of the Silver Hawks, the fans in South Bend could only hope and pray that the team they'd supported for nearly two decades would find a local buyer. Despite concerns that the local nine would soon desert them, more than 200,000 fans turned out at Coveleski Stadium to watch the Silver Hawks post the best record (84–56) in the Midwest League and then win the playoff tournament to claim their first Midwest League championship.

Nonetheless, shortly after the season, the league announced that the Hawks had indeed been sold to the Chautuaqua Heights baseball group, which was on record as saying it would move them to Marion. The Midwest League officially approved the sale in February of 2006, but issued no word at that time as to whether it would approve the relocation plan. This gave the fans in South Bend a glimmer of hope. Marion was 200 miles away from Peoria, which would be its closest Midwest League rival if

the league approved the move, and Marion was more than 500 miles away from some of the other cities in the Midwest League. A chance remained that the other teams in the league would balk at having to travel all the way to Marion for games.

Even so, as Coveleski Stadium was made ready for the 2006 campaign, many fans prepared themselves for one final lame duck season before the Hawks flew south. But then the saga took an unexpected turn for the better, at least as far as the fans in South Bend were concerned. In early March the Midwest League informed the Chautuaqua Heights group it would not be allowed to move the team to Marion on the grounds that several major league organizations with ties to the Midwest League didn't want their prospects suffering through ten-hour bus trips to and from Marion. Next, the Chautuaqua Heights group asked out of the deal it had just signed to purchase the Silver Hawks for an estimated $6 million. The league and the Palisades Baseball group consented to terminate the sale, then a group headed by former South Bend mayor and Indiana governor Joe Kernan swooped in and purchased the team. The group, which calls itself the South Bend Professional Baseball Club, quickly announced that it had no intention of moving the team out of South Bend.

The local fans breathed a collective sigh of relief, then more than 3,100 of them turned out at Coveleski Stadium on April 10, 2006, to watch the Silver Hawks drop their home opener to the West Michigan Whitecaps, 7–0. Oh well, it was a storybook ending, or new beginning, at least, until the first pitch was thrown.

"The Cove" is named in honor of former South Bend resident Stanley Coveleski, a member of the National Baseball Hall of Fame who won 215 games between 1912 and 1928. After his career Coveleski returned to South Bend, where he lived until the time of his death in 1984. The stadium opened when the Silver Hawks joined the Midwest League in 1988. At the time of its debut, it introduced a revolutionary design concept to minor league fans, placing its main concourse atop the seating bowl, allowing spectators to look down at the field while waiting in line for concessions. Previously, ballpark designers had been placing concourses within the bowels of stadiums, beneath the stands.

In the two decades since the Cove opened, the sunken field and raised concourse have become standard ballpark features. But this important link in ballpark evolution does not, in fact, allow spectators a view of the field from all locations on its concourse. That's because rather than locating its luxury boxes and press box upstairs on a second level, Coveleski Stadium houses them right behind the last row of seats. As such, fans find the view of the field blocked by the backs of the press box and luxury boxes for significant stretches on the concourse.

The Cove is located 2 miles south of the University of Notre Dame. With its redbrick exterior it meshes well with Union Station, which rises above the ballpark roof on the first base side, lending its signature to an industrial setting that includes several other large buildings, steeples, and smokestacks. Attractive grass berms appear on either end of the seating bowl in outfield foul territory, but these are only opened to fans when all of the other seats have sold. The dark green outfield fence continues across the field uninterrupted by advertising, while the usual colorful outfield advertising signs are mounted above and behind it, rather than on it.

The Silver Hawks derive their nickname from an extinct automobile. The Studebaker Silver Hawk was manufactured in South Bend

between 1957 and 1959. Today, the Studebaker National Museum sits near the ballpark at the corner of Thomas Street and Chapin Street.

The Silver Hawks, who were originally affiliated with the White Sox, have enjoyed their current PDC with the Arizona Diamondbacks since 1997. The team's alumni roster includes Mike Cameron, Joey Cora, David Dellucci, Lyle Overbay, Scott Radinsky, Brandon Webb, and Bob Wickman, while Hall of Famer Carlton Fisk once completed a rehab assignment in South Bend.

Game Day

Getting to the Park

South Bend sits along the Michigan border in north-central Indiana. The ballpark is just south of downtown at the intersection of South Street and Taylor Street. From the east or west, take I–80/90 to exit 77 (marked Notre Dame) and follow Route 31 south into downtown. Turn right onto Western Avenue, then left onto Taylor Street, and the stadium will be on your left. From the north or south, take Route 31 into South Bend, then head west on Western Avenue, then turn left onto Taylor Street. There are several parking lots near the stadium that charge a few dollars per car.

Inside the Park

The Cove has room for 5,000 fans in a seating bowl that extends into shallow outfield foul territory on either side of the diamond. Sections 105 though 114, between the dugouts, offer comfortable blue stadium chairs that sell as the Box Seats. Then, beginning at first and third base and continuing into the outfield, metal bleachers with backs sell as Reserved Seats. I recommend a front row Reserved Seat in either Section 104 at first base or Section 115 at third base. A picnic area sits in right field foul territory, while eight luxury suites are scattered behind the Box Seats on either side of home plate.

The general concession stands are at the back of the concourse, while a grill in right field sells brats, chicken, and other items hot off the flames.

The concourse displays plaques that celebrate South Bend's baseball history. One honors Stanley Coveleski, while others pay tribute to stars of the All-American Girls Professional Baseball League, which once fielded a team in South Bend.

The Coveleski Stadium Experience

Several different mascots entertain fans at the Cove. The leader of the flock is a Silver Hawk named "Swoop" who likes to sit on the dugout roof and play spin the bottle with any attractive young ladies who happen to be seated nearby.

The Silver Hawks offer several different season-long promotions tied to the different days of the week. On Sundays, fans who bring a bulletin from any house of worship to the ballpark receive $2.00 off their tickets. On Mondays, fans can purchase $1.00 Reserved Seats, $1.00 hot dogs, and $1.00 sodas. On Wednesdays, fans can clip a coupon in the *South Bend Tribune* and receive a Reserved ticket, hot dog, soda, candy bar, and scorecard, all for $5.00. On Fridays, in June, July, and August, there are postgame fireworks.

On the Town

Traveling baseball fans will find an assortment of eating and drinking establishments about a half mile northeast of the stadium on South Michigan Street. I recommend the **222 Italian Steakhouse** (222 South Michigan Street) or **Vesuvio Pizza** (230 South Michigan Street).

Auto buffs can visit the **Studebaker National Museum** (201 South Chapin Street), which showcases dozens of Studebakers built between the late 1890s and 1966 when the company closed up shop. The museum is open Monday through Saturday from 10:00 A.M. until 5:00 P.M. and Sunday from noon until 5:00 P.M. Admission is $8.00 for adults and $5.00 for kids.

Headstone hunters can visit the resting place of Hall of Famer Stanley Coveleski, who lies at **St. Joseph's Polish Roman Catholic Cemetery** (24980 State Road 2).

Finally, those visiting South Bend for the first time can swing by the famous university that put this city on the map. The 1,250-acre **Notre Dame** campus sits on unincorporated land just north of South Bend. It includes two lakes, the trademark Basilica of the Sacred Heart, and the 80,000-seat Notre Dame Stadium, which you've probably seen a half zillion times on NBC during college football season. The Fighting Irish baseball team plays before slightly smaller crowds at Frank Eck Stadium. The 2,500-seat ballpark opened in 1994.

CANAL PARK
Akron Aeros

Class AA, Eastern League
(CLEVELAND INDIANS)

Canal Park
300 South Main Street
Akron, Ohio
330–253–5153

Canal Park is named after a scenic stretch of the Ohio Canal that runs right behind its left field fence. The beautiful ballpark, which many consider to be the finest in the Eastern League, provides further proof—as if we needed any more—that a downtown ballpark can reinvigorate a franchise and fan base in the way that a suburban park simply cannot. Prior to moving to Akron in 1997, the team that would become the Aeros played at Thurman Munson Stadium, 20 miles south in Canton. During eight seasons in Canton, the Canton-Akron Indians attracted small crowds, due partly to the substandard conditions at Munson Stadium, and partly to the facility's location in an out-of-the-way residential neighborhood.

While it's easy to see why this franchise jumped at the opportunity to move to a new ballpark half an hour closer to Cleveland along I–77, no one could have predicted the Aeros and Canal Park would turn out to be as wildly successful as they have been. Or maybe they could have. After all, Akron followed the same blueprint to success that so many other major league and minor league cities have followed since Oriole Park at Camden Yards opened in Baltimore in 1992. Not only did Akron decide to plop its new ballpark smack in the heart of downtown—preexisting structures be damned—but it embraced a classic ball-park design, hiring the same architects who

designed Camden Yards. The city provided HOK with a healthy budget for the new park— $31 million, in fact—and the firm delivered.

Where the Anthony Wayne Hotel, First National Bank of Akron, and the Prinz Office Supply building once stood, there now stands a beautiful redbrick ballpark that offers an old-time look, a panoramic outfield view of downtown Akron, and modern amenities like extra wide rows, twenty-five luxury suites, a large restaurant overlooking the field, and one of the largest free-standing scoreboards in all of the minor leagues. The ballpark light stanchions are also delightfully old-timey, as the banks above the first and third base seats are both supported by four steel pillars that support fancy metal arches and latticework.

The seating bowl at Canal Park follows the same pattern as many of the new ballparks, offering a low bowl that extends all the way down the foul lines, rather than a high grandstand merely around the infield. This park is larger than many of the newbies, though, with a seating capacity of more than 9,000 people. The extra seats have been put to good use during the park's first decade. The Aeros set single-season Eastern League attendance records in each of their first three seasons, while also finishing first among all Double-A teams each year. The turnstiles clicked 473,272 times in 1997, 521,122 times in 1998, and 522,459 times in 1999. Attendance has since leveled off, but the Aeros still vie for the Eastern League attendance crown each year, as they and the Reading Phillies draw season's crowds in the 450,000 range.

The Aeros team name pays tribute to Ohio's proud history of innovation in aviation, and while the ball doesn't exactly "fly" out of Canal Park, which is a bit bigger than most Eastern League fields—measuring 331 feet down the left field line, 376 to left-center, 400 to center, 375 to right-center, and 337 down the right

Canal Park

field line—future Indians like Milton Bradley, Coco Crisp, Jhonny Peralta, Victor Martínez, and Grady Sizemore all launched their share of long balls while playing for the team in Akron. Future Tribe hurlers like Cliff Lee, C. C. Sabathia, and Jaret Wright have also toiled in Akron, as well as rehabbing big leaguers like Sandy Alomar Jr., Dwight Gooden, Manny Ramírez, and Jim Thome.

Game Day

Getting to the Park

Akron is 40 miles south of Cleveland and 20 miles north of Canton. From the north, take I–77 South to Route 59 East. Exit at Exchange/Cedar and turn right onto Cedar Street. Turn left onto Main Street and the ballpark will appear on the left. From the south, take I–77 North to the Main Street/Downtown exit and follow Broadway Street to Exchange Street. Turn left onto Exchange, then right onto Main, and the ballpark will appear on the left. There are more than a dozen privately operated parking decks and surface lots in the ballpark neighborhood that charge in the $5.00 range. The nearby city-run lots are free after 6:00 P.M.

Inside the Park

All of the seats in the main bowl are comfortable blue stadium chairs. In addition there are three sections of bleachers in right field home run territory. The Aeros keep things simple by selling all of the Reserved Seats for the same price—a reasonable $10 as of the 2006 season. There are twenty rows in most sections, and the sections continue all the way to the foul pole in right field and nearly all the way to the pole in left. Section 100 is directly behind home and the odd-numbered sections continue down the right field line, finishing with Section 125, while the even-numbered sections continue down the left field line, finishing with Section 124. Because the foul territory is kept to a minimum down the lines, fans seated in many of the sections along the baselines are unable to see into the nearest outfield corner. The Bleachers are plain metal benches set beside the right-center field bull pens, which run parallel to the outfield fence and beneath the scoreboard. The group picnic area is in left field home run territory between the outfield fence and canal.

The wide concourse atop the seating bowl is lined with attractive brick buildings that house the concession stands, restrooms, and souvenirs. The ballpark treats include pulled pork, grilled chicken, and Ballpark Franks served with authentic Stadium Mustard, the condiment of choice in Cleveland. The Menches Brothers restaurant in right field offers a large window overlooking the field and an outdoor seating area. It specializes in hamburgers, specialty sandwiches, salads, and pasta dishes, and also has a full bar. Menches is open to the general public from 11:00 A.M. until 2:00 P.M. whether there's a game or not, and then reopens for ticket holders only two hours before the first pitch on game days.

The Canal Park Experience

The local mascot is a bright red cat named "Orbit" who wears an Akron jersey and sometimes straps a jetpack onto his back.

The Aeros should be applauded for aggressively promoting a couple of unique events each year that improve the community. Each April, just before the season starts, the team hosts the "Canal Park Home Run Trot," a 5K run/walk that raises money for the Akron Aeros Charitable Foundation, which supports the Juvenile Diabetes Research Fund and other worthy causes. More than 600 people participate in the Trot in a typical year. Another important annual event is "Pet Day," when the team partners with the Akron Animal Humane Society to parade some 300 or 400 homeless animals around the field before the game in the hope that the fans in attendance will step to the plate and adopt them.

On the Town

The ballpark's namesake is well worth a visit before the game. The stone-lined banks of the canal are nicely landscaped and the locks that raise and lower the water level are something you don't get to see in too many cities.

While the ballpark neighborhood offers a more bustling environment during day games—when the downtown restaurants and bars cater to a business crowd—than night games, a number of establishments stay open at night. The top choices include **Panini's Bar and Grill** (271 South Main Street), the **Diamond Deli** (378 South Main Street), and **Brubaker's Brew Pub** (376 South Main Street).

There are two attractions in nearby Canton that fans may find worth visiting, Thurman Munson Stadium and the Pro Football Hall of Fame. After losing the Canton-Akron Indians to Akron, **Thurman Munson Stadium** (Allen Avenue SE, Canton) hosted a Frontier League team from 1997 through 2002, but it now sits dormant. The stadium offers a whole lot of aluminum and is fairly unattractive, inside and out. Number 15 hangs in center field to honor Munson, who attended Canton's Lehman High School, played eleven seasons for the New York Yankees, and died in a plane crash in 1979. The **Pro Football Hall of Fame** (2121 George Halas Drive NW, Canton) is open from 9:00 A.M. until 8:00 P.M. daily, and admission costs $15.00 for adults and $8.00 for children.

COOPER STADIUM

Columbus Clippers

Class AAA, International League
(WASHINGTON NATIONALS)

Cooper Stadium
1155 West Mound Street
Columbus, Ohio
614–462–5250

If Cooper Stadium rates high on your list of ballparks to see before you die—or before your wife tells you to stop gallivanting around the country and to come home and cut the lawn—then you'd better make your travel arrangements soon. The stadium that has served as the center of minor league activities in Columbus since 1932 and as home of the Clippers since 1977 will be replaced by a new ballpark in 2008. On the day Cooper Stadium closes its gates for the final time, the mantle of oldest ballpark in the International League will be passed to McCoy Stadium in Pawtucket.

In 2006 Franklin County, which owns the Clippers, secured eight acres of land at the corner of Nationwide Boulevard and Neil Avenue in the Columbus Arena District and embarked upon a $65 million stadium project. The new facility, which will stand 2½ miles northeast of the current home of the Clippers, will be called Huntington Park, thanks to a twenty-three-year, $12-million naming-rights deal the county signed with Huntington Bank. Huntington Park will feature two seating decks that are both close to field level and that both extend nearly all the way to the foul poles. It will also offer berm seating across the outfield and a festive plaza in center field.

In the meantime Cooper Stadium will continue to welcome Columbus baseball fans, just as it has since the Clippers returned baseball

to Ohio's capital city after a seven-year hiatus that began when the International League's Columbus Jets moved to Charleston, South Carolina, in 1970, and just as it had long before that. The facility originally opened as home of the Columbus Red Birds, an affiliate of Branch Rickey's St. Louis Cardinals that played in the American Association. The brick-and-California-redwood stadium was built, in fact, by the Cardinals, who shelled out $450,000 during the Great Depression to construct what would quickly come to be considered one of the finest ballparks in the country.

The stadium was originally called Red Birds Stadium, then later Franklin County Stadium, then in 1977 it was renamed Cooper Stadium after the county commissioner, Frank Cooper, who was instrumental in luring the International League back to Columbus. Thanks in large part to Cooper's influence the stadium that would soon bear his name received an extensive renovation prior to the Clippers arrival. The makeover included adding skyboxes to the roof over the grandstand and covering the field with Astroturf. While the skyboxes are still in place, the plastic grass was replaced with real turf in 1999.

Cooper Stadium's exterior façade features a pale brick first level and crisscrossed steel beams up above that support the underside of the seating bowl. Inside, the roof covers the back two-thirds of a fishhook-shaped seating bowl that extends just a little way beyond first base, but into medium-depth foul territory in left field—and all the way to the foul pole, in fact, if you include the large bank of uncovered bleachers that run parallel to the visitors bull pen along the left field line. The outfield fence is low and see-through in most locations, allowing fans to watch the game from the beer garden in left field home run territory.

Beyond the fence in right, fans find the Columbus version of Monument Park. The

Clippers were originally affiliated with the Pittsburgh Pirates, but that relationship lasted only two years. From 1979 through 2006 they were the top New York Yankee farm club, and just about every homegrown Yankee in the George Steinbrenner era passed through Cooper Stadium. The Monument Park in Columbus is not quite as impressive as the one in the Bronx, but for the minor leagues, it is pretty good. It consists of nine large stone monuments arranged at the positions where the nine fielders normally stand on a baseball diamond. The stones always play straightaway; they don't shift into right field when a left-handed pull hitter like David Ortiz comes to the plate. Each monument is etched with the names of the future Yankees who starred at that corresponding position on the field while in Columbus. Notable former Clippers honored at Monument Park include Jay Buhner, Robinson Canó, Derek Jeter, Mike Lowell, Andy Pettitte, Don Mattingly, Jorge Posada, Mariano Rivera, and Bernie Williams. Following the 2006 season the Clippers switched to a relationship with the Washington Nationals.

Before Cooper Stadium's construction, professional baseball was played in Columbus at a field near the old Union Depot on High Street. In the late 1800s Columbus belonged at various times to the International Association, the Western League, and the American Association, and fielded teams with names like the Buckeyes, Colts, and Senators. In 1905 the city built its first concrete-and-steel stadium, Neil Park, which hosted the minor league game for the next twenty-five years, until the Cardinals bought the Senators after the 1931 season and secured a plot of land between West Mound Street and Glenwood Avenue upon which to build the new stadium.

Now Columbus is at a hardball crossroads once again. Maybe some book written seventy

years from now will tell the story of how Huntington Park has stood the test of time through as many decades as its predecessor endured, or maybe Huntington Park will have long since faded into the annals of history by 2078. One thing for certain though is that Cooper Stadium will be long gone. While Franklin County has yet to officially announce its plans for the forty-seven-acre stadium site, the Coop will surely be demolished within the next few years. According to a report commissioned by the county in 2005, possible uses for the stadium grounds include turning them into an industrial park, racetrack, or auto/motorcycle sales lot.

Game Day

Getting to the Park

Columbus is in central Ohio and easy to reach via I–70 or I–71. From the east, take I–70 West to the Mound Street exit and go straight at the first light into the stadium driveway. From the west, take I–70 East to the Broad Street exit and turn left onto Broad, then right onto Glenwood Avenue, then left onto Mound. The stadium driveway will appear on your right. From the north or south, take I–71 to I–70 West to the Mound Street exit and follow the directions as above. Parking in the stadium lot costs $3.00.

Inside the Park

The Coop offers 15,000 seats, all of which are in foul territory. The good news is that most of the seats are individual chairs, not bleachers. The bad news is that these aren't the comfy new stadium chairs that we soft-bottomed fans have become accustomed to in recent years. They're narrow, hard, and squished close together, and there isn't much legroom between the rows. The Box Seats consist of the first ten rows at field level. These begin with Section 101 at first base, continue to Section 109 behind home plate, and finish with Section 119 in left field foul territory. A wide walkway runs behind the Box Seats. At the back of this concrete path the grandstands begin their steep incline beneath the covering of the roof. Between the dugouts the first several rows of the grandstand house Club Seats and Reserved Seats. But the vast majority of grandstand seats sell as General Admission. If you arrive early enough before the game, you can find a seat in the grandstand that isn't obstructed by one of the many steel pillars that support the roof. If you don't arrive early, you may get stuck behind a pole or out in the bleachers, which serve as an overflow seating area in deep left. The Clippers average about 7,500 fans per game, but that figure often swells to more than 10,000 per game during the summer months, so if you want to ensure that you get at least a Reserved Seat, you may want to order your tickets in advance.

There is a group picnic pavilion in deep right field foul territory, and the Quencher Corner group area is behind the fence in left. The souvenir store, which sells noisemaking Clippers cowbells, among other items, is located in deep right field near the pavilion. On the main concourse beneath the grandstands fans find the Clipper nacho ship, hot dogs, burgers, chicken wings, and Donato's Pizza.

The Cooper Stadium Experience

For many years the Columbus mascot was a salty seaman named "Captain Clipper," but he accepted a golden parachute from the Clippers in the mid-1990s and moved to a retirement home in nearby Grove City. Thus, a spot was created at Cooper Stadium for Lou Seal. This friendly fellow was discovered entertaining fishermen on the Scioto River at just the time when the Clippers were looking for a new kid-friendly mascot. Lou Seal loves to dance atop the dugout roofs and to act goofy in just about every other way imaginable. His good friend Krash, a krazy ballpark parrot, enhances his hijinks.

The Clippers offer a special promotion for every day of the week. On Sunday through Wednesday, there are ticket and food specials. On Thursday, the team offers fun and games all game long at Quencher Corner. On Friday, the Clippers offer a pregame party with food, drinks, and tunes at the right field pavilion. On Saturday, the team welcomes special entertainers to the park and shoots off fireworks.

On the Town

The relocation of the Clippers from their present location in the southwest corner of Columbus to the lively Arena District will certainly suit local fans just fine. The current ballpark neighborhood is about as lively as you would expect of a ballpark that stands between two cemeteries. The Coop sits between the Green Lawn Cemetery and the Mount Cavalry Cemetery. Fortunately, there are a few watering holes a bit east on West Mound Street, highlighted by Ron's Sports Pub (1690 West Mound Street), and a few fast-food joints too.

It remains to be seen how the opening of the new ballpark in Columbus will affect the fate of the unaffiliated Frontier League team that plays 35 miles south of Columbus in Chillicothe, but hopefully there will continue to be room for both the Clippers and Chillicothe Paints to coexist. The Paints have played at **V. A. Memorial Stadium** (north of Chillicothe on State Route 104) since joining the Frontier League as one of its charter members in 1993. Although Memorial Stadium opened in 1954, it has a thoroughly modern field, thanks to a $1 million renovation in 2006 that covered its lawn with field turf. Even the pitchers mound and home plate area are covered with field turf. The Paints, who are named after a breed of horse, will never have to paint lines on their field again. All of the areas that normally feature dirt on a regulation baseball field are covered with brown field turf, while the areas that are normally grass are covered with green turf. The foul lines and outline of the batters box are permanently painted onto the field in white.

FIFTH THIRD FIELD

Dayton Dragons

Class A, Midwest League
(CINCINNATI REDS)

Fifth Third Field
220 North Patterson Street
Dayton, Ohio
937–228–2287

Since opening in 2000, when the Dayton Dragons joined the Midwest League, Fifth Third Field has sold out every one of its 7,230 seats for every game of every season in its history. Not only have the seats all sold, they've sold well before each season has even started. Thanks to an expansive right field lawn and party decks that offer room for even more fans, the ballpark has averaged more than 8,300 fans per game over its seven seasons. At the time of this book's printing, the Dragons were closing in on their 500th straight sellout and setting their sights on the country's professional sports record of 814 consecutive sellouts, a mark set by the NBA's Portland Trailblazers from 1977 to 1995. The Dragons have ranked as the top Single-A franchise in attendance seven years running, perennially attracting upward of 570,000 fans, and have finished in the top ten in attendance in all of minor league baseball in each of those years.

It's no wonder the team draws well. The Dragons play just 50 miles from their big league parents, the Cincinnati Reds, which keeps fans interested in the on-field talent. Meanwhile, Fifth Third Field provides great sight lines and

Fifth Third Field

a highly entertaining experience on game day. Nestled in downtown, Fifth Third Field combines the look of an old-time ballpark while offering the amenities and comforts made possible by modern advances in stadium construction.

To pedestrians on the street outside, the stadium projects a regal brick-and-steel façade. Inside, it offers seating options aplenty surrounding the entire field, except in straight-away center where a black batter's eye rises behind the outfield fence. In left-center, a seven-story video board rises behind the outfield wall, flanked by two gigantic green dragons. When a member of the home team connects for a home run, the dragons' eyes turn red and smoke comes billowing out of their nostrils. The playing field is asymmetrical, offering a few nooks and crannies in left field—where the fence varies from 8 feet to 10½ feet in height—before following a more linear path around the outfield in center and right.

To accommodate a local business community that is shamelessly Dragon crazed, thirty luxury suites sit atop the seating bowl, featuring laptops with high-speed Internet connections, cable TV, swank furniture, private refrigerators, balcony seating, and a whole bunch of other perks that common fans like your humble author never get to enjoy and, frankly, never miss. The list of notable bigwigs who have visited these posh parts of the stadium includes the only two-time Heisman Trophy winner in history, Archie Griffin, who played his college ball at Ohio State University, then played eight seasons with the Cincinnati Bengals; basketball legend Magic Johnson; former major leaguer Mike Schmidt, a native Daytonian; and former Reds Johnny Bench and George Foster.

Several future Reds have played for the Dragons in the team's short history, including Wily Mo Peña, Adam Dunn, and Austin Kearns. José Rijo, the 1990 World Series MVP, also made an appearance in Dayton during a short-lived comeback attempt. Local fans still talk about a ridiculously hot stretch of hitting by Kearns in the stadium's inaugural season. During an eight game home stand against the Fort Wayne Wizards and Lansing Lugnuts in 2000, Kearns hit 10 home runs and reached base in fourteen straight plate appearances. The slugger went 18 for 25 (.720) in eight games, while driving in 20 runs and scoring 19 runs. The next season, Peña hit a 489-foot home run that cleared the batter's eye and touched down outside the confines of Fifth Third Field. The blast still ranks, anecdotally at least, as the longest dinger in stadium history.

In addition to serving as the home of the Dragons, Fifth Third Field has also hosted the Atlantic-10 college baseball championship, the Ohio High School State finals, and numerous other amateur tournaments.

Game Day

Getting to the Park

Dayton is in southwestern Ohio, 50 miles north of Cincinnati and 75 miles west of Columbus. The local ballpark does *not* stand at the intersection of Fifth Street and Third Street. Rather, it derives its name from Fifth Third Bank, which was formed when the Third National Bank of Ohio merged with the Fifth National Bank of Ohio. From I–75, take the First Street exit and follow First Street east until the stadium comes into view. From Route 35, take the Jefferson/Main Street exit. Take a right onto Jefferson and follow it to First Street. Take a right onto First and continue to the stadium.

The Dragons don't offer a stadium parking lot. Instead, a number of private businesses manage lots that charge from $3.00 to $5.00

per car. There are also metered spots on First Street, Second Street, Patterson Monument, and Jefferson Street that are free after 5:00 P.M. on weekdays and all day on weekends.

Inside the Park

Fifth Third Field offers five different seating options, four of which sell out before the season begins. Unless you have the foresight to plan your trip in February, or unless you have a "connection" in Dayton, you will wind up sitting or standing on the right field lawn, assuming you arrive at the ballpark early enough to score a ticket before the Lawn tickets also sell out.

The seating bowl begins at Section 104 just beyond first base, continues to Sections 109 and 110 behind the plate, and ends at Section 116 in medium-depth left field. It offers comfortable plastic stadium chairs with cup holders. The seats below the midlevel concourse are known as Premier Seats and Field Seats, except at the outfield most wings, where Sections 104, 115, and 116 contain Plaza Seats entirely. The first couple of rows above the midlevel walkway sell as Premier Seats, while the back rows sell as Box Seats.

There are small Lawn areas between the ends of the seating bowl and foul poles, then the big Lawn stretches from the right field pole to the batter's eye in center. A smaller lawn in left field, known as the Dragon's Lair, is reserved for groups. Each ticket to the Dragon's Lair comes with a complimentary Dragon's Lair baseball cap, which cannot be found in the team's clubhouse store or anywhere else on the premises. There are also private party decks above the concourse on the first and third base sides.

In 2005 the Dragons opened the Fifth Third Cafe, an on-site restaurant on the first base side of the concourse that is open to the public. The cafe specializes in daiquiris, roast beef sandwiches, and barbecue. Also in 2005, an interactive Fun Zone opened behind the batter's eye. Here, kids find a speed-pitch booth, a bouncy pen, face painting, a dragon slide, and other activities.

The open concourse offers a view of the field and ballpark treats like Donato's Pizza and Red Osier roast beef. The adult beverage choices include margaritas, frozen daiquiris, and Anheuser-Busch products. For those looking for a bit more of a kick to their drinks, there is a full bar at the Fifth Third Cafe.

The Fifth Third Field Experience

The Dragons loveable mascot is Heater, a friendly dragon who delights in challenging kids to races round the bases, games of tug of war, and other feats of strength. Heater usually gets off to a fast start in each of these events, but his stamina isn't all that great, and he inevitably finds a way to snatch defeat from the jaws of victory.

Another popular nightly spectacle is the fifth-inning Instant Replay on the video board that shows funny clips of fans who are unknowingly captured doing weird things during the first half of the game. So, be on your best behavior in Dayton or you might find yourself the laughingstock of about 8,000 people midway. Keep your shirt on and limit your beer consumption for the first four and one-half innings, then feel free to let it all hang out in the game's second half.

Among the many between-inning features are the always-hilarious Fifth Third Field hamster races. Fans put on furry hamster costumes, then allow themselves to be zipped inside giant inflatable hamster balls. Once inside, they race other hamster-ized fans around the field by walking inside their balls. Like I said, limit your beer consumption early in the game or you never know what these friendly Midwesterners will do to you for their amusement.

On the Town

Dayton is a midsized city famous for being the birthplace of aviation. Back in the early 1900s, Orville and Wilbur Wright built the first power-driven, heavier-than-air flying machine in their downtown bicycle shop. If you'd like to check out the 1905 Wright Flyer for yourself, visit **Carillon Historical Park** (1000 Carillon Boulevard), where it is displayed with other relics from Dayton's pioneering history.

A bit closer to the stadium, the banks of the Great Miami River provide a gorgeous location for a pregame stroll in **RiverScape Metro Park**. The path along the river is etched with historic information about Dayton that dates back to 1795. So, if you're interested in learning more about the Great Flood of 1913 or another memorable happening in the city's long life, here's your chance to enhance your knowledge of all-things-Dayton. During the summer months there are also nightly laser light shows along the riverbanks after Dragons games.

Across First Street from Fifth Third Field, fans congregate at **Brixx Ice House,** a tavern near the right field entrance that is less than 500 feet from home plate. The front of the establishment offers a giant window and many of the seats inside face outward, allowing fans a glimpse of the action at the ballpark. A festive outdoor patio is ideal for beer guzzling or chicken-wing eating on warm summer nights.

CLASSIC PARK

Lake County Captains

Class A, South Atlantic League
(CLEVELAND INDIANS)

Classic Park
35300 Vine Street
Eastlake, Ohio
440–975–8085

The Lake County Captains provide yet another example of a minor league team that thrives due at least in part to its geographic proximity to its big league parent club. Just as Red Sox fans pack McCoy Stadium in Pawtucket, and Reds fans pack Fifth Third Field in Dayton, the Indians fans in the Cleveland suburb of Eastlake get to watch the Tribe's prospects come of age at a ballpark less than 30 miles from downtown Cleveland. Since opening as the home of the Tribe's South Atlantic League affiliate in 2003, Classic Park has drawn average crowds of nearly 6,000 fans per game. In each of their first three seasons, the Lake County Captains ranked among the top thirty minor league teams nationally in attendance.

While geography has no doubt contributed to the Captains success, the overall quality of Classic Park should not be discounted, as it also plays an important part in the winning equation. The $20 million stadium lives up to its name, even if it is a name derived from a naming-rights deal between Eastlake and the Classic Automotive Group. Among the features that help make this ballpark an instant classic are its low-to-the-field seating bowl that contains comfortable stadium chairs throughout, its open concourse that runs atop the seats where it is sheltered nicely by the overhang of the luxury-suite level, and its festive outfield seating areas.

The stadium is uncluttered and comfortable, offering a wide concourse and roomy stairways and rows, yet at the same time, it is cozy and intimate, thanks to a seating bowl that contains only seventeen rows. Rather than rising steeply around the infield, the low seating bowl continues farther into the outfield than is usual at many Class A parks, thus keeping all of the seats close to the field. The outfield lawns are relatively narrow, appearing between the top of the home run fence and the advertising billboards that rise up to seal in the stadium from the suburban world outside. A large white building sits behind the foul pole in right field—housing both the home and visiting clubhouses—and long homers have been known to clank off its roof.

Prior to arriving in Eastlake, the team that would become the Captains played in Columbus, Georgia, where it was known as the Columbus Red Stixx. In anticipation of the team's arrival, Eastlake broke ground on a publicly financed stadium project in March of 2002. The new facility was completed in time for the Captains to post a 5–3 Opening Day win against the Charleston Alley Cats on April 10, 2003. More than 7,000 fans turned out for that first game, and as the season continued, the fans kept coming back. By the time the inaugural campaign in Lake County ended, the Captains had drawn 437,515 fans, and they have averaged more than 400,000 per season ever since.

Although the Captains have yet to send one of their alums on to major league fame, they have welcomed big league stars like Bob Wickman and Omar Vizquel to Classic Park on rehab assignments.

In addition to hosting minor league baseball, Classic Park has also hosted classic rock concerts. Bryan Adams and Def Leppard played the ballpark during the summer of 2005.

Game Day

Getting to the Park

Classic Park is just a half-hour drive northeast of Cleveland. From Cleveland, take I–90 East to Route 2 East and then follow Route 2 to the Eastlake exit. Turn left onto U.S. Highway 91 north and the stadium will appear on the right. The main parking lot is across the street, and fans use a pedestrian bridge to get from their cars to the ballpark.

Inside the Park

Classic Park has a listed capacity of 7,273 people, but the Captains keep selling Lawn tickets until every fan is accommodated. The park offers three different ticketing options: Box Seats, Bleacher Seats, and Lawn Seats. The Box Seats are the comfortable blue stadium chairs that fill the main seating bowl, beginning with Section 101 in medium-depth right field, continuing around the infield, and finishing with Section 120 in medium-depth left. Although it may seem odd that a first row seat behind home plate in Section 111 sells for the same price as a seventeenth row seat in right or left field, it is worth noting that the seating bowl does an exceptional job of angling its outfield sections back toward the infield. Sections 101 through 103 in right field and Sections 118 through 120 in left are practically perpendicular to the foul lines. This affords the fans in these sections a great view of the infield, but it also obstructs their views of the nearest outfield corner, which is situated practically behind them. The Bleachers are on the left field lawn just to the fair side of the foul pole. The Captains don't release Lawn tickets until all of the Box and Bleachers tickets have been sold. The Lawn areas are in left-center and right.

There are picnic areas in left field and in right field beneath large tents on the concourse.

The stadium's upper level hangs twenty luxury suites over the concourse on the infield.

Thanks to a $48,000 construction project that the Captains embarked on prior to the 2006 seasons, fans are now able to walk laps around Classic Park while remaining inside the stadium. The 360-degree concourse project connected the right field and left field lawn areas behind the batter's eye. The project allows youngsters seated in all parts of the park easier access to the outfield Kids Zone, which features a Bungee Run and inflatable games, while making it easier for adults to peruse the offerings at the different concession stands throughout the park. The concessions are managed by the Captains not by an outside vendor, and the team does an excellent job. This is a ballpark where you'll want to shop around before deciding what to eat for supper, since every stand has a different menu. The trademark items include the all-beef Captains Dog, and "The Barge," a foot-long bratwurst. The Captains Galley behind home plate serves barbecue pork sandwiches and Philly cheesesteaks, while the nearby Grill Works serves sausage subs loaded with peppers and onions. The Captains Deli on the third base side serves healthy salads and a variety of wraps, as well as macaroni and cheese. The All-American Grill on the first base side serves traditional ballpark fare as well as chili cheese fries. There is a pizza stand on the third base side and an ice-cream stand in left field. The Beers of the World counter behind Section 108 serves a wide selection of brews.

The Classic Park Experience

Popular annual promotions in Lake County include "80's Night," when fans wear big hair, big collars, and thin leather ties; "Italian Heritage Night" and "Croatian Heritage Night," when the ballpark concession menus are adjusted accordingly; and "Jimmy Buffett

Night." One night each summer is put aside for the local Boy Scout troops to camp overnight on the outfield grass.

During the summer a fireworks display follows every Friday night game. All season long Monday is "Buck Night," when fans buy hot dogs, ten-ounce beers, and twelve-ounce sodas for $1.00, and get $1.00 off the price of Box Seats.

The Captains mascot is Skipper, a pear-shaped goof ball who claims to share some common blood with Slider, the mascot who haunts the stands at Jacobs Field. Skipper has green fur all over his body, a shock of purple hair atop his head, and a big yellow nose. He wears a Captains jersey with the number 0 on it.

While the folks in Milwaukee enjoy their famous sausage races, the folks along the banks of Lake Erie enjoy fish races. The competitors each night include Willy the Walleye, Buster the Bluegill, and Pauly the Perch.

On the Town

In addition to housing a Wal-Mart and Kmart, the urban sprawl around the ballpark offers more than two dozen fast-food restaurants on either side of Vine Street. The greatest concentration of pizza shacks, sub shops, and burger joints is east of the ballpark between U.S. Highway 91 and Lake Shore Boulevard.

A visit to Classic Park affords baseball pilgrims the chance to get some sun and ride some waves at the largest beach in all of Ohio. Just a few miles north of the ballpark sits **Headlands Beach State Park** (Lakeshore Boulevard), which offers a mile of sandy shore along Lake Erie. During the summer the park opens half an hour before sunrise and closes half an hour after sunset.

A visit to Cleveland is also in order for baseball wanderers. In addition to housing **Jacobs Field** and the **Rock and Roll Hall of Fame**, the city offers the still-standing remnants of **League Park** (East 66th Street and Lexington Avenue), which served as the home of the Indians from 1910 through 1946. The old ballpark's ticket office is now part of a community recreation center. Don't bother looking for the ballpark that replaced League Park: Municipal Stadium. The "Mistake by the Lake" was demolished in 1996 to make room for a new stadium for the Cleveland Browns.

FIFTH THIRD FIELD
Toledo Mud Hens

Class AAA, International League
(DETROIT TIGERS)

Fifth Third Field
406 Washington Street
Toledo, Ohio
419–725–4367

Although professional baseball has been played in Toledo since the late-1800s, and although the local outfit had often referred to itself as the Mud Hens though the decades, the Mud Hen didn't officially enter America's pop culture lexicon until the 1970s. During the second season of the hit sitcom *M*A*S*H,* the cast welcomed an eccentric new character named Corporal Max Klinger. Over the next eleven years, Klinger—who was trying to convince the army that he was crazy in the hopes of receiving a Section 8 discharge—wore women's dresses. He also wore a Mud Hens cap and various other pieces of Mud Hens apparel. And why not? The Mud Hens were his favorite team from back home, a little slice of Americana to keep him sane during the madness of the Korean War. Viewers from across the country could relate, and Mud Hens gear started flying off the shelves in Toledo. Even today, the Mud Hens receive Internet orders from around the world wherever *M*A*S*H* reruns are airing.

While the story of how Jamie Farr—the actor who played Klinger—put his hometown team on the national baseball map is an interesting one, there is an even bigger story making headlines around Toledo these days. After playing their games at suburban Ned Skeldon Stadium for years, the Mud Hens opened a $39 million downtown ballpark in 2002, and the team has been one of the most popular draws in the

International League ever since. The Mud Hens broke their single-season attendance record in Fifth Third Field's inaugural season, welcoming 547,204 fans through the gates, then they surpassed that mark in 2005, drawing 556,995. The Mud Hens have become so popular that they recently capped their season ticket membership base at 3,500 seats. They sell more than 300,000 tickets before the season begins and average twenty-five sellouts per season.

The Mud Hens have also enjoyed success on the field of late. In 2005 they claimed Toledo's first Governor's Cup since 1967, beating Indianapolis three games to none in the International League championship series. Prior to the playoffs the Mud Hens won more regular season games than any other minor league team in 2005, going 89–55 under manager Larry Parrish. For their efforts they received the 2005 Triple-A Bob Freitas Award, which is given each year to the team that excels on and off the field.

Following the modern trend, Fifth Third Field was built in a rundown section of downtown with the hopes that it would blend in aesthetically with the preexisting landscape and begin the area's return to respectability. In both regards this jewel of a park has succeeded. Rather than knocking down three old warehouses in right field to make room for the stadium, Toledo incorporated the buildings into the design, wedging a section of elevated right field seats between them, snaking the 360-degree concourse around them, and renovating one building to house the team's clubhouse shop, offices, and banquet facilities. Toledo didn't skimp when it came time to order new bricks for the new structures that needed to be built either. The stadium offers an attractive brick façade along North Huron Street and Washington Street, while a smaller brick building stands at the corner of Clark

Street and Monroe Street in center field. It is here, behind the batter's eye, that most fans enter the park, spilling onto a large plaza that connects on either side to the concourse that runs around the entire field atop the last row of first-level seats. The concourse is at street level, while the field and first-level seats are sunken down below. Along the baselines the second level hangs down over the back several rows below, positioning the club seats and luxury suites close to the field.

The outfield view showcases several old warehouse buildings in right and more modern buildings beyond the fence in left and center. The presence of these looming buildings makes for a cozy urban backdrop for a game.

Another little eccentricity that makes Fifth Third Field unique is the design of the dugouts. Both dugout roofs are L shaped. The short leg of each L juts into the first-level seats to cover the runway that leads to the clubhouse beneath the stands. The field itself is a bit unusual too. The grounds crew maintains a dirt path between the pitcher's mound and home plate, just like the one they have at Comerica Park in Detroit, and just like the one they used to have at Ned Skeldon Stadium.

Ned Skeldon Stadium, a converted racetrack originally known as Lucas County Stadium, housed the Mud Hens from 1965 through 2001. The facility was actually not in Toledo but in nearby Maumee. Before moving to the suburbs, the Mud Hens had played at Swayne Field in Toledo, which stood at the corner of Monroe Street and Detroit Avenue from 1909 through 1956.

Through the decades big names like Jim Thorpe, Casey Stengel, Hack Wilson, and Kirby Puckett have called Toledo their baseball home. Another big name—professional golfer Phil Mickelson—got a tryout with the Mud Hens in 2003, working a bull pen session under the watchful eye of pitching coach Jeff Jones, but

the lefty's low-80s fastball and looping curve weren't enough for him to make the cut.

The Mud Hens current affiliation with the Detroit Tigers dates back to 1987 and should continue for a good long time, thanks to the geographic sense it makes for both teams, and to the beautiful ballpark that now stands in Toledo.

Game Day

Getting to the Park

Toledo is in the northwest part of Ohio, just 62 miles from Detroit. Fifth Third Field sits between Monroe Street, Morse Way, and Huron Street, 2 blocks west of the Maumee River. From the Ohio Turnpike (I–80/I–90), take exit 64 and follow I–75 North to exit 201B. Turn left onto Erie Street, then turn right onto Washington Street. From I–75 South, take exit 202A and turn right onto Washington Street. From I–75 North, take exit 201B and turn left onto Erie Street, then right onto Washington Street.

According to the Mud Hens, the many public and private parking lots within a quarter-mile radius of Fifth Third Field offer 6,623 parking spaces. I'm not sure which intern counted all of these spots, but I appreciate the precision of the count. Most of these lots charge $6.00. Public transportation is also an option for fans staying in town. The TARTA runs shuttles between the ballpark and twelve pickup locations in Toledo.

Inside the Park

Fifth Third Field offers 10,300 seats between its first and second levels, its luxury boxes, and its creatively designed outfield party areas. As mentioned earlier the team draws very well, so order your tickets in advance if possible.

The first-level seating bowl extends all the way to the foul poles. All of the seats sell at the same price, whether they're in Section 101 in deep left field, Section 106 behind the home dugout, Section 111 behind the plate, or Section 119 in deep right.

Upstairs, the Club Seats appear in a narrow band in front of the thirty-two luxury suites. The upper deck continues about two-thirds of the way down either foul line.

Fifth Third Field's trademark feature is its "Roost" seating area in deep right field. This elevated seating deck is wedged between, and attached to, two old warehouse buildings behind the right field foul. Meanwhile, nestled on the concourse below, fans find the "Coop A Cabana" party area. The "Swamp Shop," also located in the right field corner, sells all kinds of Hens gear, including the popular Muddonna bobblehead doll. There are tent-covered party terraces for groups in right and left field home run territory.

The concessions in Toledo rate well above average. The highlights include the trademark Fowl Balls—deep-fried chunks of chicken that taste better than they sound, as well as fresh-cut french fries and onion rings, pork tenderloin sandwiches, barbecued ribs, burritos, taco salads, meatball subs, Italian sausages, Philly cheesesteaks, gyros, Black Angus burgers, and Marco's Pizza.

The Fifth Third Field Experience

Like the old saying goes, if it looks like a chicken, walks like a chicken, dances like a chicken, poses for photos like a chicken, goofs on fans like a chicken . . . and so on . . . it must be a chicken. Well, not in this case. Muddy, the friendly fellow who serves as the Toledo mascot, is not in fact a chicken, even if he looks and acts like one. Supposedly, he is a mud hen, which is a dark marsh bird that has short wings, long bony legs, and big wide feet. When Toledo's baseball team adopted the Mud Hen as its moniker in 1896, these birds were found in great abundance in the city. But as Toledo

grew up and the surrounding swamplands diminished, so too did the flocks of mud hens. At least Toledons still have Muddy and his girl friend Muddonna to entertain them at the local ballpark. If you ask me, Muddy bears a definite resemblance to the San Diego Chicken—with his big yellow body, orange beak, and bright red legs—but everyone I spoke to assured me that he was a mud hen through and through. Go figure.

One of the great things about the bush leagues is that just when you think you've seen everything, a team surprises you with a new promotional night or marketing ploy that grabs your attention and makes you say, "Hey, that's a pretty good idea." Well, the Mud Hens do all of the usual promotions, like Friday night fireworks, scouts sleepovers, and various giveaway nights, but in 2006 they came up with a whole new way to get extra fans to turn out at the ballpark. On several nights during the season, the Mud Hens invited local high school teams to Fifth Third Field to participate in postgame home run derbies against rival high schools. Other minor league teams looking for an easy way to sell an extra few hundred tickets a night would be wise to take note. Not only do the schoolboys turn out at the park and feed the concession coffers, but their families and friends do too. And all it costs the team to stage the dinger derbies is the price of keeping the lights on for an extra half hour after the game.

Fans should keep their eyes peeled for Jamie Farr, who still visits the ballpark at least once a year, wearing the same Toledo hat he used to wear on *M*A*S*H*.

On the Town

As has been the case in so many U.S. cities in the past two decades, Toledo's new ballpark has helped transform a rundown section of town into a burgeoning entertainment district. There is still some work to be done in Toledo's Warehouse District, but by all accounts the difference between the neighborhood now and ten years ago is like night and day. A popular pregame hangout is the **Maumee Bay Brewing Company** (27 Broadway Street), while other options include **Bagpipers Pub & Eatery** (152 North Summit Street), **Jackson's Lounge & Grill** (233 North Huron Street), **Michael's Bar & Grill** (901 Monroe Street), and **Blueprint Sports Bar & Lounge** (1919 Monroe Street).

The Mud Hens old ballpark still stands, or at least part of it does. **Ned Skeldon Stadium** (Key Street in Maumee, Ohio) now serves as the Lucas County Recreation Center. The old baseball bleachers have been removed and the field is now used for youth games.

FIFTH THIRD BALLPARK
West Michigan Whitecaps

Class A, Midwest League
(DETROIT TIGERS)

Fifth Third Ballpark
4500 West River Drive
Comstock Park/Grand Rapids, Michigan
616–784–4131

Not to be confused with Fifth Third Field—home of the Midwest League's Dayton Dragons—or Fifth Third Field—home of the International League's Toledo Mud Hens—Fifth Third Ballpark serves as the home of the West Michigan Whitecaps. It disturbs me greatly that three ballparks have essentially the same name and leads me to wonder if one day not too far off, every ballpark in this great land of ours will be named after the three or four largest corporations in the country. Nonetheless, West Michigan's Fifth Third Ballpark is a thoroughly enjoyable place to visit. Since opening this park in 1994 and returning professional baseball to the Grand Rapids area for the first time in forty years, the Whitecaps have seemingly achieved one remarkable milestone after another, both on and off the field. Baseball came to West Michigan when a group of Grand Rapids businessmen led by Denny Baxter and Lew Chamberlin purchased the Madison Muskies and announced the team would relocate to Grand Rapids. In 1993 construction began on a 5,700-seat ballpark just north of the city near the Grand River. West Michigan Baseball Inc. built the $10 million ballpark entirely with private money, and the local fans wasted little time before showing the group that it had made a wise investment. In their debut season of 1994, the Whitecaps broke the

all-time Single-A attendance record, drawing 475,212 fans to the stadium then known as Old Kent Park. To understand the magnitude of this accomplishment, consider that the record had stood since 1949 when the Denver Bears drew 463,039 people to their park in the Mile High City. But the Whitecaps were just getting started. The next year, the team broke its own mark, ushering 507,989 fans through the turnstiles, and in 1996 West Michigan broke the record again, drawing 547,401. If you've done some quick math, you may be wondering how a 5,700-seat ballpark could accommodate an average of nearly 8,000 fans per game. Well, it couldn't. After each of their first three seasons, the Whitecaps expanded their ballpark to meet the demands of the insatiable local fan base. Then, they expanded the park again after the 1998 season. Today, Fifth Third Ballpark—as Old Kent Park was renamed in 2001, switching its name from one local bank to another—is the largest facility in all of Single-A, with room for 11,123 people in its seats, party areas, luxury suites, and on its lawns.

Why did baseball thrive so immediately and to the degree that it has in Grand Rapids? Well, the city had been hungry for a baseball team for a long time, since the Grand Rapids Chicks of the All-American Girls Professional Baseball League disbanded in 1954, in fact. Before that, Grand Rapids had always had a minor league team to call its own, dating back to the 1880s and continuing through the first half of the twentieth century when it was represented by clubs with names like the Furniture Makers, Rustlers, Gold Bugs, Black Sox, Bissell Sweepers, Dodger Colts, Orphans, Jets, and Joshers, which competed in a variety of leagues. Even though many of the folks who watched those teams play had passed on, they had also passed down to younger generations their love of the game and longing for a Grand Rapids team.

When the new ballpark opened in 1994, fans quickly determined that management hadn't skimped on any aspect of the park. The ballpark, the gameday experience, and the concessions were all top-notch, and so too was the team on the field. As an Oakland A's affiliate, the Whitecaps qualified for the Midwest League playoffs in their first season, then won the league championship in 1996. The next season, the Whitecaps celebrated a new affiliation with the Detroit Tigers by posting the best record in all of professional baseball. The Whitecaps were 92–39 in the regular season, then lost in the 1997 Midwest League playoffs. They were still named *Baseball America*'s "Minor League Team of the Year." In 1998 the Whitecaps won their second Midwest League crown. Then, in 1999 *Baseball America* named West Michigan the "Class A Organization of the Decade." With the team consistently winning, the national accolades pouring in, and the delicious Swimming Pig practically flying off the ballpark concession counters, it's easy to see how interest in the Whitecaps continued to gain momentum like white water cascading along the banks of the nearby Grand River.

Fifth Third Ballpark is set up on a small hill. It features a tan exterior covered by a green roof. Fans walk up a set of stairs to reach the entrance gates and then spill through the turnstiles onto a main concourse that overlooks the field. The seating bowl runs into shallow outfield foul territory, then gives way to grass lawns that continue down the foul lines. The spacious upper level houses twenty-four luxury suites, wrapping around the infield and covering the entire concourse. Four separate party areas span the outfield, set in front of a dense expanse of trees that seals in the ballpark.

While the Whitecaps have fielded some great teams, the local fans have yet to watch a truly great player pass through West Michigan on his way to major league stardom. The team's alumni roster contains B-level major leaguers such as Francisco Cordero, Jeff DaVanon, Robert Fick, Brandon Inge, Dave Newhan, Fernando Rodney, and Jeff Weaver. Here's betting that Tigers prospect Joel Zumaya becomes the first West Michigan alum to make a really big splash in the big leagues.

Game Day

Getting to the Park

Grand Rapids is 70 miles west of its league rival in Lansing and 30 miles east of Lake Michigan. Fifth Third Ballpark sits outside the Grand Rapids city limits in the town of Comstock Park. From the east or west, take I–96 to Route 131 North, then take exit 91 and follow West River Drive to the ballpark. From the north or south, follow Route 131 to the West River Drive exit. There is ample parking space on the forty-seven-acre ballpark grounds, but due to the large crowds, fans must often endure long lines to escape the lot after the last out.

Inside the Park

Fifth Third Ballpark offers comfortable red Box Seats in the first dozen rows down at field level, followed by an interior walkway, and then blue Reserved Seats, which are actually bleachers with backs. Section 109 is in shallow right field, Section 117 is behind home plate, and Section 125 is at the end of the seating bowl in shallow left.

Attendance has leveled off in recent years, as the Whitecaps average about 5,500 fans per game these days. There are only about 2,000 Box Seats, so most traveling fans will likely wind up in the Reserved bleachers. If those tickets are sold out, the only other option is a spot on the right field or left field lawn. The pavilion seats in right-center field are reserved for groups, as are the party decks in left field home run territory and in the right field corner.

This ballpark does as good a job as any I've seen at leaving the view of the field open to those on the concourse. It also excels in offering more concession treats than even the most gluttonous baseball wanderer could sample in just one visit. In addition to the stands on the concourse, there are grill areas in right field and left field that provide fresh meat and raised platforms where fans can sit and watch the game while chowing down. The signature concession item is the Swimming Pig, a center-cut boneless pork chop smothered in barbecue sauce that comes served on a sauce-soaked roll. Other tasty treats include the steak sandwich, grilled sausage, bratwurst, pulled chicken, pulled pork, pot roast sandwich, meatball sub, loaded mashed potatoes, chicken and beef tornados, chicken Caesar salads, Little Caesar's Pizza, deep-fried cheesecakes, cheese-filled breadsticks, chicken fries, roasted nuts, stuffed pretzels, and an array of frozen treats. The brews on tap include Bud, Miller, and Coors products, as well as Labatt, Leinenkugel, and Foster's.

While the adults eat and drink themselves silly, the kids can enjoy the playground behind the center field fence. The kids park features slides, crawl tubes, ladders, and other structures designed for creeping, crawling, and climbing.

The Fifth Third Ballpark Experience

The Whitecaps have always prided themselves on providing a carnival atmosphere for fans, complete with lots of promotions and between-inning contests, but in 2006 they took their mission a bit more literally than usual. At the start of the season, the team arranged to bring an actual carnival to the stadium parking lot. During the entire first week of the Midwest League season, West Michigan fans enjoyed carousel and bumper car rides before heading into the game to be amused, as usual, by the antics of the Whitecaps many mascots. The mascot who leads the cheers and revelry at Fifth Third Ballpark is a furry creature named "Crash." While it is unclear whether Crash is a beaver or a badger or some other kind of aquatic mammal, one thing for certain is that he must be a stronger swimmer than he is a runner. Crash entered the 2006 season having lost 820 consecutive races around the bases against the young fans who challenge him on a nightly basis. He's a good sport about it though, even if he faces teasing afterward from his nephew Crush, and his friends Hush Puppy and Franky (a swimming pig who wears a life preserver).

The Whitecaps are very innovative when it comes to on-field promotions, but one of their stunts went awry in April of 2006 when two young fans suffered minor injuries as they scrambled along with 300 other kids to pick up money being dropped from a helicopter. The "money drop" was part of the team's annual "Tax Relief Day." As the chopper dropped 900 $1.00 bills and a single $100 bill onto the field, some of the kids got overzealous and started throwing elbows, resulting in injuries to a pair of seven-year-olds. One of the children received treatment from paramedics at the ballpark for a bloody lip, while the other had to be taken to the Spectrum Health Butterworth Campus to be treated for various bumps and bruises.

On the Town

Because Fifth Third Ballpark is outside of town alongside the highway, the ballpark neighborhood doesn't offer much in the way of pregame eating or drinking options, other than a few fast-food restaurants on West River Drive. Fortunately, the food and drinks at the ballpark are as excellent as they are diverse, so fans don't need to tank up before the game.

As for after the game, visitors will find plenty of places to satisfy their tastes in downtown Grand Rapids. This midsized city offers an entertainment district just east of the Grand River that features lots of steakhouses, pubs, and seafood restaurants. Drive along Monroe Avenue, and you'll be sure to find a place that suits your fancy.

Those looking to fish or swim in Lake Michigan will find the state's western shore just a 45 minute drive from Grand Rapids. There are more than a dozen beaches between Muskegon and Douglas. From Grand Rapids, follow Route 45 West, then head north on Route 31, which leads to a concentration of state parks.

OLDSMOBILE PARK

Lansing Lugnuts

Class A, Midwest League
(TORONTO BLUE JAYS)

Oldsmobile Park
505 East Michigan Avenue
Lansing, Michigan
517–485–4500

When the city of Lansing decided to bring a Midwest League team to town in the mid-1990s and end a dearth of minor league ball in Michigan's capital that stretched over five and one-half decades, it didn't skimp. The city built a ballpark that is huge by Single-A standards but also unique and beautiful. After the city did its part, the local fans did theirs, filling the stands with nearly 8,000 people per game in the Lugnuts debut season of 1996. A decade later, the Lugnuts still average more than 5,000 fans per home date.

Oldsmobile Park can accommodate 11,000 spectators. The $12 million city-owned ballpark was designed by HNTB of Kansas City, financed by a consortium of local banks, and built by Clark Construction of Lansing. Naming the park after the Oldsmobile Corporation was a natural fit since the company has been a huge part of Lansing's identity for decades. More than just bearing the car manufacturer's name, the ballpark embraces the auto theme with creative displays and exhibits on its concourse.

While an 11,000-seat stadium can't be expected to match the intimacy of a 3,000-seat ballpark like the one at the Midwest League outpost in Burlington, Oldsmobile Park offers a festive gameday atmosphere and plenty of eccentricities that give it a character all its

own. Outside, fans find a distinctive main entrance that features a brick walkway, green lawns, park benches, and bronze statues of baseball players and young fans. The stadium exterior offers a brick front with green awnings and arched roofs over the entrances.

Inside, the seating bowl is sunken below street level, a 360-degree open concourse runs behind the last row of seats, an upstairs level houses twenty-six luxury suites, and the outfield features large grass seating berms. Among the downtown structures that fans can spot from inside the stadium are the capitol dome and a smokestack that has been outfitted with a giant faux lugnut. Perhaps the most unique aspects of the ballpark are the 23-foot-high green cement walls that begin just past the outfield-most ends of the seating bowl in foul territory and continue around the foul poles about 30 feet into fair territory before abruptly ending and giving way to more conventional outfield fences. The foul poles are just 305 feet from home plate, but in order for players to homer down either line, they must clank the ball off the cyclone fencing that extends above the tops of these cement minimonsters. Fans who stand behind the fencing on the outfield concourse enjoy a unique bird's-eye perspective of the game.

The most memorable game in Oldsmobile Park history to date will be hard for the Lugnuts to ever top. It offered visitors the chance to witness two extremely rare ballpark occurrences on the same day. On Easter Sunday of 2003, three Lugnuts pitchers—Justin Jones, Wes O'Brien, and Mark Carter—combined to throw a no-hitter against the Dayton Dragons. Meanwhile, Lugnuts third baseman Donny Hood hit for the cycle. The Lugnuts won the game 15–0 to account for the largest margin of victory in a no-hitter in Midwest League history. While that no-no was the first ever for the Lugnuts, Hood's cycle was the second in team history. Future major leaguer Corey Patterson turned the single-double-triple-homer trick for the Lugnuts against South Bend in 1999.

The Lugnuts served as an affiliate of the Kansas City Royals and Chicago Cubs before signing a player development contract with the Toronto Blue Jays in 2005. In addition to Patterson, the Lugnuts alums to reach the big leagues include Jeremy Giambi, Carlos Beltrán, Carlos Zambrano, Andy Sisco, Hee Seop Choi, and Jeremy Affeldt.

Lansing's early forays into the world of minor league baseball included teams that played intermittently in the Michigan State League, Southern Michigan League, and Central League between 1889 and 1941, usually as the "Senators." Native son Jack Morrissey, who played for the Cincinnati Reds in 1902 and 1903, managed and played for the Lansing nine between 1907 and 1914. The Senators went 35–78 in their final Michigan State League season in 1941. Then, the league folded, and thus began a long wait for Lansing fans until the game would eventually return fifty-five years later.

Game Day

Getting to the Park

Lansing sits smack dab in the middle of Michigan, about 90 miles west of Detroit. From the Motor City, take I–96 to U.S. Highway 127 North, then take the Grand River/Saginaw exit and turn left. Follow Grand Avenue west for 3 miles, then turn left onto Cedar Street and the stadium will appear on the left at the intersection of Cedar Street and Michigan Avenue. From the west, take I–96 East to the Saginaw Highway and follow Saginaw East for 5 miles before turning onto Cedar Street. Due to its location within downtown, Oldsmobile Park does not offer a parking lot for fans, but there are plenty of parking options in the ballpark neighborhood at city-run lots on Cedar, Grand, Larch, and Michigan.

Inside the Park

As mentioned earlier, this is a huge park by Single-A standards. The seating bowl extends nearly all the way to the foul poles on either side, and there is room for fans in home run territory, thanks to the berms in left and right and to the group picnic areas that overlook the berms. About half of the seats are individual stadium chairs that sell as Box Seats, while the other half are bleachers with backs that sell as Reserved Seats. The Box Seats are in the first dozen rows or so around the infield, while the Reserved Seats are in the rows behind them. Then, once the seating bowl passes the corner bases, it provides nothing but Reserved Seats from the first row to the last. All of the Box Seats are excellent, from the ones in Section B at first base, to the ones in Section H directly behind the plate, to the ones in Section P at third base. While many of the Reserved Seats provide good views of the field, especially those in Section A, just beyond first base, and in Section Q, just beyond third, this is a park where you might as well spring for Box Seats. As of 2006 Box Seats cost $8.00, while Reserved Seats cost $7.50. Heck, if you're going to drive all the way to Lansing for a baseball game, you might as well spend the extra fifty cents. As for the Lawn seating areas, the well-maintained grass embankments above the walls are nicely sloped and ideal for families traveling with children who will want to spend some time at Big Lug's Playground in left.

The concourse runs atop the seats, offering views of the field and colorful murals that trace the evolution of automobiles and minor league baseball from the early 1900s to the present day. The concession stands offer names and decor that also embrace the auto theme. The menu offers spicy burritos, jumbo brats, smoked turkey legs, and cheesesteak subs. Parents looking to enjoy a few frosties while their kids visit the playground can make a pit stop at the Bullpen Bar and Grill out by the left field foul pole. On Thursdays, twenty-ounce Molson drafts are just $2.00.

The Oldsmobile Park Experience

The Lugnuts have an avid fan base that does whatever is required and then some to support the local team. Falling into the "and then some" category, a few years ago the local fans launched a fund-raiser to create a stainless steel lugnut weighing in at two and a half tons. Then they mounted it atop the smokestack of a factory building across the street from the ballpark on Cedar Street. Today, the nuts and bolts of the endeavor serve as a proud beacon on the downtown skyline that lures folks to the ballpark.

Need further evidence that the folks in Lansing go nuts for their Lugnuts? When *USA Today* conducted an online readers poll in 2004 to see which minor league baseball team had the most imaginative nickname, the Lugnuts ran away with the competition, garnering 27 percent of the vote nationally. The Southern League's Montgomery Biscuits—who are owned by Tom Dickson and Sherrie Myers, the same duo that owns the Lugnuts—finished second with 17 percent of the tally. While I agree that both teams have nicknames that reflect the unique identities of their respective cities, I think the Savannah Sand Gnats, Albuquerque Isotopes, Augusta GreenJackets, and Auburn Doubledays at least deserve a seat at the table when it comes time to hash out who has the most creative nickname in minor league baseball.

But how many of those other teams have their own theme song? The Lugnuts do. "Go Nuts" is a real scream for the kids as well as for the loveable purple dinosaur named "Big Lug"

who keeps them entertained. Adult fans may find this song a bit cheery and simplistic when it plays through the stadium loudspeakers, but here's betting that many find themselves humming along to the melody during the car ride home after the game. The song starts:

> *You've got inhibitions,*
> *Lose 'em.*
> *You've got vocal chords,*
> *Use 'em.*
> *You've got the rhythm,*
> *You got the beat,*
> *You gotta clap your hands,*
> *You gotta stomp your feet.*
> *You gotta Go Nuts! Go Nuts, Go Nuts,*
>   *Go Nuts!*

On the Town

After learning a little bit about the history of the automobile on the ballpark concourse, head to the **R. E. Olds Transportation Museum** (240 Museum Drive) to learn more. The museum is just a block southwest of Oldsmobile Park, off Michigan Avenue. It offers the chance to see rare old models like the REO, the Star, the Durant, and the Viking, as well as many precursors to the modern automobile like modified buggies and bicycles. It is open Tuesday through Saturday from 10:00 A.M. until 5:00 P.M. and Sunday from noon until 5:00. Admission costs $5.00 per adult or $10.00 for the whole family.

Another popular spot in Lansing, especially on sunny spring days, is **Riverfront Park**. This walking trail traces the western banks of the Grand River for several miles. There is an access point just a block west of the ballpark between Cedar Street and Grand Avenue.

Those seeking a cold drink or bite to eat before the game can visit the **Nuthouse Sports Grill**, right across the street from the ballpark at the corner of Cedar and Michigan. This festive sports bar opened in 1996 at the same time as the ballpark, and it quickly became the pre-game and postgame hangout of choice for Lug-nuts nuts. The eclectic menu offers everything from calzones to Mexican, seafood, barbecue, jambalaya, and New England clam chowder.

Keeping in mind that sometimes you feel like a nut and sometimes you don't, the streets around the ballpark also offer the **Schnitz Delicatessen** (333 Cedar Street), **Lansing City Market Cafe** (333 Cedar Street), and **Capital City Grill** (111 Grand Avenue). There are also several fast-food chains north of the ballpark.

DOW DIAMOND

Great Lakes Loons

Class A, Midwest League

(LOS ANGELES DODGERS)

Dow Diamond
State Street and Buttles Street
Midland, Michigan
989–837–2255

For the first time ever, Midland was set to field a professional baseball team as the 2007 minor league season began and this book hit the shelves of bookstores. Midwest League baseball arrived in town after the Southwest Michigan Devil Rays bolted from Battle Creek, 150 miles south of Midland, where they enjoyed only marginal fan support. On opening day 2007, the new Midland team and its fans christened a brand new ballpark designed by the renowned ballpark architects at HOK of Kansas City. The franchise also celebrated a new big league affiliation, having signed on with the Los Angeles Dodgers over the winter.

The relocated team originally joined the Midwest League in 1995, first serving as a New York Yankees affiliate, then serving the Tampa Bay Devil Rays. But baseball in Battle Creek never caught on. The team tried a variety of nicknames and marketing strategies and even posted nine straight winning seasons between 1997 and 2005. But it consistently drew fewer than 1,400 fans per game to C. O. Brown Stadium. In a last-ditch effort to save professional baseball in Battle Creek, the team's former ownership group pledged to build a new stadium if the local fans bought 1,800 season tickets prior to the start of the 2006 season. When only 300 fans signed up, the team was sold to a group intent on moving it to Midland. News of the sale, which was announced in January, did

not come as much of a surprise to the people in Battle Creek or anywhere else in minor league baseball circles. The team had previously come close to moving to Dubuque, Iowa, in 2003, before residents in Dubuque balked at plans for a publicly financed stadium.

The team's move to Midland brought baseball to a city with a population of just 42,000 people, but the surrounding cities of Saginaw, Bay City, and Mount Pleasant help create a regional fan base of more than 400,000 people within 30 miles of the ballpark. Midland, Bay City, and Saginaw are so close to one another that they are often referred to as the "Tri Cities." While Midland is a brand new destination on the minor league baseball map, the Tri Cities have seen more than their share of teams pass through the region. Saginaw, located just a few miles southeast of Midland, has a long hardball history, as does Bay City, located a few miles to the east on the shores of Lake Huron. In 1883 Saginaw and Bay City were charter members of the Northwestern League, which is regarded by many as the first true minor league circuit that fielded franchises affiliated with major league organizations. In 1890 Saginaw and Bay City shared ownership of an International League team nicknamed "The Hyphens," which played half of its home games in each city. From 1883 to 1951 Saginaw fielded teams in ten different professional leagues. But no team called the region home in the five and a half decades since the Central League's Saginaw Bears left town after the 1951 season. Bay City waved good-bye to its most recent minor league team after the 1926 season.

The 2007 move from Battle Creek to Midland was made possible by Midland-based Dow Chemical Company, which bought the team through a newly formed nonprofit organization called the Michigan Baseball Foundation. The foundation also led the effort to build a new ballpark on downtown riverfront property previously owned by Dow. The city broke ground on the $18 million Dow Diamond in the spring of 2006. The stadium was designed to make baseball a top priority while also outfitting it for a range of multiuse capabilities. The stadium is equipped to host outdoor concerts and other warm-weather events, as well as conferences and inside activities during the cold Michigan winters.

The ballpark's name, while corporate in nature, is not so inappropriate. After all, Dow has been based in Midland since 1890. The company is as much a part of the community's identity and history as the Midland Center for the Arts.

Game Day

Getting to the Park

Midland is 120 miles northwest of Detroit. Its new ballpark is just off Business Route 10, on the east side of State Street and the south side of Buttles Street. From BR 10, follow State Street 1/10 mile to the intersection with Buttles.

Inside the Park

The stadium offers 3,500 comfortable plastic seats, several luxury suites, and a large lawn seating area that can accommodate more than 1,500 people. The main concourse runs above the last row of seats, allowing fans to walk down wide aisles to their rows. The main seating bowl extends from first base on the right side of the diamond, behind the plate, and then into medium-depth left field foul territory. Section 101 is in left field, Section 107 is behind home plate, and Section 113 is at first base. The first three to five rows, depending on the section, are Premier Box Seats and the rest are Box Seats. The lawn seating area begins where the seats leave off behind first base, wraps around

the right field foul pole, and extends across the outfield to where it ends in center field.

The Dow Diamond Experience

As the stadium did not open until after this book went to print, it is impossible for me to sum up the qualities that make a trip to Midland unique and special. The same goes for Lou E. Loon; I just can't tell you if this newbie mascot knows how to work a crowd or not. I would welcome correspondence from baseball travelers who get the chance to visit this new ballpark before I do. Feel free to e-mail me at minorleagueballparks@yahoo.com to tell me about the menu offerings, the game-day festivities, the fan traditions, the unusual configuration of the bathroom urinals, or anything else that distinguishes this park from the rest. You know, tell me about all of the stuff that I usually tell you about in this part of each chapter. Thanks.

On the Town

Midland is known as the "City of Science and Culture." Kurt Vonnegut readers will recall that beleaguered science fiction writer and *Breakfast of Champions* protagonist, Kilgore Trout, was on a mission to attend the Midland City Festival for the Arts throughout much of the book. Mr. Trout finally arrived at the **Midland Center for the Arts** in the book's waning pages. The real-life center is located at the corner of Eastman Street and St. Andrews Road. Nearly every month brings a new festival to town, so make like Kilgore Trout and Dwayne Hoover and check out the happenings while you're in town. There's more to life than just baseball, you know . . . like college basketball, football, golf, hockey, ping-pong, darts, road bowling, Vonnegut novels . . . and, oh yeah, the arts.

FOX CITIES STADIUM

Wisconsin Timber Rattlers

Class A, Midwest League
(SEATTLE MARINERS)

Fox Cities Stadium
2400 North Casaloma Drive
Appleton/Grand Chute, Wisconsin
920–733–4152

As the 1990s dawned, Wisconsin could boast that it fielded five teams in the Midwest League. Today, the only teams that remain in the state are the Beloit Snappers, who play along the Illinois border in southern Wisconsin, and the Wisconsin Timber Rattlers, who play in the northeastern part of the state, not far from Green Bay. Wisconsin's losses can be traced to an over reliance on old-time ballparks and to the refusal of many of its cities to update their old parks or build new ones. In the early 1990s, the National Association of Professional Baseball Leagues and Major League Baseball reached an agreement stipulating that all minor league parks had to meet certain standards in terms of their dugout and clubhouse accommodations and their field lighting. The agreement heralded the end of minor league baseball at old-time Wisconsin ballparks like the ones in Madison, Kenosha, Wausau, and Wisconsin Rapids. Those communities and the teams that called them home chose not to replace their aging ballparks, while Appleton's Goodland Field, which had sat on Spencer Street since 1940, was replaced with a new stadium. The Appleton Foxes, a Midwest League stalwart since 1962, opened Fox Cities Stadium in 1995. The team changed its name to the Wisconsin Timber Rattlers at that time.

The privately financed $5 million ballpark was built outside of downtown on the outskirts of Grand Chute. Local fans greeted the new ballpark's arrival with enthusiastic support. Attendance jumped from 76,000 in the team's final season at Goodland Field to 209,159 in the first season at the 5,500-seat stadium. The spike in attendance wasn't a one-year phenomenon, either. The next year, the Timber Rattlers drew 233,797 fans, and within five years the team had drawn more than a million visitors to its new yard.

Fox Cities Stadium makes an unspectacular first impression, as fans encounter its one-level tan façade and aluminum roof, but the ballpark inside the turnstiles is extremely fan-friendly and cozy. The field is sunken below street level, the seating bowl keeps fans close to the action, the open but shaded concourse runs atop the last row of seats, and the outfield berms are ideal for sunbathers and families. Strangely, the bull pens are located immediately after the dugouts where the infield dirt meets the outfield grass. But the pens aren't located in foul territory. Instead, they appear where the field-level seats normally appear. Other distinctive aspects of this ballpark include its asymmetrical playing field, which is much deeper in right-center field where the fence measures 405 feet from home plate, than in left-center where the fence measures 385 feet, and its series of three pitched roofs behind home plate that cover the press box and luxury boxes.

In addition to housing the Timber Rattlers, Fox Cities Stadium has also seen use in the annual Wisconsin Athletic Association High School baseball tournament, as the venue for Brett Favre's Celebrity Softball Challenge, and as an occasional home field of the NCAA Division III Lawrence University Vikings.

The Timber Rattlers have been a Seattle Mariners affiliate since 1993, during which time future major leaguers like Alex Rodríguez, Joel

Piñeiro, Gil Meche, Rafael Soriano, and Felix Hernández have played in Appleton. In 2002 some notable current major leaguers played in Appleton, too, including Ichiro Suzuki who along with his Mariners teammates played an exhibition game against the Timber Rattlers on April 29.

Before hitching on with the Mariners, the Appleton Foxes were affiliated with the Kansas City Royals (1987–1992), Chicago White Sox (1966–1986), and Baltimore Orioles (1962–1965). Their alumni roster from that era includes such luminous baseball names as Harold Baines, Bucky Dent, LaMarr Hoyt, Goose Gossage, Ron Kittle, Bobby Thigpen, and Tom Gordon.

Delving back a bit further into the annals of Appleton baseball history, household names like Boog Powell, Earl Weaver, Pat Gillick, and Cal Ripken Sr. all played for the Foxes in the 1950s and early 1960s when Appleton was a member of the Triple-I League. Before that, in the 1940s, Appleton was a member of the Wisconsin State League, and before that, the Appleton Papermakers played in the Illinois-Wisconsin League, between 1909 and 1914.

Today, the minor league game would seem to have a firm footing in the Fox Cities for years to come, thanks to the presence of Fox Cities Stadium and to the team's supportive fan base.

Game Day

Getting to the Park

The Timber Rattlers play their home games about 25 miles southwest of Green Bay and just a few miles north of Lake Winnebago. Fox Cities Stadium sits within the town limits of Grand Chute, but the Timber Rattlers consider Appleton their home, and Appleton seems happy to claim the team as well. The stadium is just a few miles northwest of downtown Appleton, near the Fox River Mall and Fox Valley Technical College. From U.S. Highway 41, take the Wisconsin Avenue exit and drive west. Then turn right onto Casaloma Drive and the stadium will appear on your right. There is ample on-site parking for $3.00 per car. The lots open two and one-half hours before game time, and many fans arrive early to cook brats and drink beer before heading into the stadium.

Inside the Park

Fox Cities Stadium offers three different seating options, and the view of the field is superb from all three locations. The main seating bowl extends only a little way into outfield territory and then large grass berms fill the areas between the ends of the stands and the foul poles. The first ten rows around the infield sell as Box Seats. These are comfortable stadium chairs. Immediately behind the Boxes, are the Reserved Seats, which are actually metal bleachers with backs. In shallow outfield foul territory on either side of the diamond, there are two additional sections that contain Reserved Seats entirely. These sections—114 and 116 on the first base side and 113 and 115 on the third base side—are behind the bull pens. If you're easily distracted, or just don't like the idea of having to look around a pitcher warming up, you should avoid the first few rows of these sections.

The lawn areas allow ample room for fans to spread out. Some choose to stand right down near the field, while others lounge on blankets higher on the hills. Unlike at some parks, fans are not permitted to bring lawn chairs into the stadium.

The concourse allows for a view of the game for those waiting in line for concessions. The menu offers traditional ballpark favorites like hot dogs, hamburgers, brats, pizza, and french fries, as well as healthy alternatives like vegetable trays and fruit. You've got to have at least one brat while you're in Wisconsin, but for an even more diverse menu, head to the last concession stand on the first base side where the Brew City Grill serves Polish and Italian sausages, grilled chicken, grilled steak, pork chop sandwiches, beer-battered onion rings, mozzarella sticks, and cheese curds with waffle fries. And you probably thought ballpark curds died a slow and painful death with the closing of Olympic Stadium in Montreal. Lest we fans forget that Wisconsin is known for more than just its tasty cased meat and fresh cheese, the concessions stands also offer a couple of varieties of ice cream and an array of brews on tap. The local favorite is Timber Rattler Brew.

Finally, for those hot summer days, Fox Cities Stadium offers an air-conditioned bar that overlooks the field on the first base side.

The Fox Cities Stadium Experience

Tailgating is a big part of the sporting culture in Wisconsin, so why not embrace it yourself? Shake the ashes out of that old hibachi in your garage and toss it into the trunk of your road-trip car, along with some charcoal, a cooler, and maybe some antacids. Pick up some beer and brats on game day, and you'd better grab some Uncle Phil's Dusseldorf Mustard too. Then join the party in the parking lot.

In 2006 the Timber Rattlers offered a unique ballpark experience every Friday, outfitting the local nine with throwback uniforms that resembled those worn by the Appleton Foxes in 1960. At the end of the season, each player autographed his special jersey, and then they were auctioned off to fans.

On the Town

While a trip to this neck of the woods offers the chance to visit Green Bay for an evening or Lake Winnebago for some fun in the sun, there is actually plenty to do in Appleton. In addition to finding the second-largest shopping mall in Wisconsin right near the ballpark, visiting fans who head downtown will be pleasantly surprised to find a hip, modern city. This community of 70,000 is home to Lawrence University, and as such, the center of Appleton's restaurant and bar scene is located near campus on College Avenue. In addition to the usual chain-type restaurants, local establishments cater to stereotypical Midwestern tastes and also offer unexpected delights like Mongolian, Greek, and Italian food. Football fans will want to visit the green-trimmed, memorabilia-packed **Vince Lombardi's Steakhouse** (333 West College Avenue), which serves delicious Wisconsin beef and offers an expansive wine list.

Those with inquiring minds may enjoy spending some time at the **Outagamie Museum** (330 East College Avenue). The museum provides a rare glimpse into the life and times of Appleton's most famous resident: Ehrich Weisz. I know what you're thinking: Never heard of him, right? Well actually, you have. Outside of Appleton, Mr. Weisz is more commonly remembered by his stage name: Harry Houdini. The museum offers hands-on exhibits that enable visitors to experience some of the great magician's trickery for themselves. The museum is open Monday through Saturday from 10:00 A.M. until 4:00 P.M. and Sunday from noon until 4:00. Admission costs $5.00 for adults and $2.50 for children.

POHLMAN FIELD

Beloit Snappers

Class A, Midwest League
(MINNESOTA TWINS)

Harry C. Pohlman Field at Telfer Park
2301 Skyline Drive
Beloit, Wisconsin
608–362–2272

Having a community-owned minor league team to root for must be something of a mixed blessing for local fans. On the one hand, you don't have to worry about the team ever being sold to a group of out of town investors and abruptly moved to some far off city. As long as the community group that runs the team is able to maintain its affiliation with a big league organization, there will always be a ballgame in town. On the other hand, the community-owned team's undying commitment to its home city costs it quite a bit of leverage when it comes time to update or replace its ballpark. In most communities the threat of losing the local team to another city serves as a powerful motivator for the city, county, and state officials who ordinarily allocate funding for ballpark projects. In cities with community-owned teams, though, the threat of the team moving to another city doesn't exist, so teams have less bargaining power when it comes time to lobby with local legislators for help in building new stadiums.

The community-owned Beloit Snappers play Midwest League baseball at a ballpark that clearly needs to be either significantly updated or completely rebuilt. While it would be inaccurate to portray this southern Wisconsin border town as one that has completely neglected its local park over the years—the city has made efforts to update Pohlman Field since its opening in 1982—there's no getting around the fact that this park comes up well short of meeting the comfort and aesthetic expectations of today's minor league baseball fans.

There is no real façade around the exterior of the ballpark, just the backsides of the long thin buildings that house concession stands and restrooms at ground level. Narrow pillars rise at the back of the stadium to support the metal roof over the home plate grandstand. A tiny press box, smaller than the ones at many high school fields, sits atop the bleachers behind the plate. Fans enter the seating bowl at ground level near the field and spill onto a pedestrian walkway that runs between the field and the seats. From this poorly placed interior concourse, fans walk up narrow stairways between sections to their rows. There are just a few hundred individual seats, while aluminum bleachers fill the rest of the park.

Pohlman Field apologists might suggest that the park offers visitors the chance to travel back in time to the early 1980s when the minor leagues truly were the "bush leagues," providing simple utilitarian venues for games. This may be true in a sense, but even so, there were certainly many ballparks of the era that offered fans more in the way of charm and intimacy than the ballpark in Beloit. There is a reason why the Snappers attract only 1,200 fans per game, while many of their Midwest League rivals draw crowds several times that size. Pohlman Field has outlived its era.

Realizing this, the Beloit Professional Baseball Association, which has run the team since its inception in 1982, has been trying to rally support for a new ballpark project since 2000. It has been a slow process. At the time of this book's publishing, the project still had not progressed beyond feasibility studies, site evaluations, and fund-raising efforts. The hope remains, though, that by 2008 or 2009 the team will be playing at a new stadium between Beloit and the larger city of Janesville, along I–90.

For the first twenty-three years of its existence, the Beloit team was affiliated with the Milwaukee Brewers. The Brewers decided to move their low-A prospects out of the Midwest League in 2005, though, to begin an affiliation with the South Atlantic League's West Virginia Power. Why would a team from Wisconsin prefer to send its prospects all the way to West Virginia, rather than keep them close to home in Beloit? Well, the Power opened a brand new ballpark in 2005 and that surely weighed heavily in the decision. Fortunately for the fans in Beloit, the Minnesota Twins signed on with Beloit shortly after the Brewers pulled up stakes. The Twins and Snappers have a PDC that runs through the 2008 season.

Pohlman Field was known as Telfer Park at the time of its opening in 1982. Harry C. Pohlman, a long-time baseball coach in the Beloit public school system and a charter member of the Beloit Brewers board of directors, threw out the ceremonial first pitch before Beloit fell to the Danville Suns, 7–2, in the team's first home game. Five years later, the ballpark would be rededicated Harry C. Pohlman Field. The home team was actually known as the Beloit Brewers through 1994, before switching to the "Snappers," as a nod to the many snapping turtles floating in the nearby Turtle River.

The list of future big league stars to play for Beloit includes Ronnie Belliard, Chris Bosio, Tom Candiotti, Jeff Cirillo, Cal Eldred, Bill Hall, Teddy Higuera, Geoff Jenkins, Troy O'Leary, Kevin Seitzer, B. J. Surhoff, Greg Vaughn, Rickie Weeks, and Prince Fielder. While on the fast track to the big leagues, Fielder spent the 2003 season with the Snappers, batting .313 with 27 homers and 112 RBI. The effort was reminis-

cent of Vaughn's dominant 1987 season, when he paced the Beloit club with a .305 average, 33 homers, and 105 RBI.

Game Day

Getting to the Park

Beloit is located along the Wisconsin-Illinois border, 75 miles southwest of Milwaukee and 55 miles south of Madison. The Rock River runs through the center of Beloit, while the swampy Turtle River meanders into town from the northeast. Visitors coming from Milwaukee should follow I–43 into Beloit. On crossing the Beloit town line, I–43 becomes Milwaukee Road. Shortly after entering town, turn right onto Cranston Road and follow Cranston for 1½ miles. Pohlman Field will appear on the right just past the intersection of Cranston and Shopiere Road. From the north or south, take I–90 to exit 185A. At the third stoplight, turn right onto Cranston Road and follow the directions above. There is a free parking lot between the stadium and the Edwards Ice Arena, while visitors also find curbside parking in the streets surrounding the ballpark.

Inside the Park

While Pohlman Field makes the top-five list of smallest full-season minor league parks, it isn't close to winning the competition. With a seating capacity of 3,500, Pohlman has 300 more seats than Community Field in Burlington, Indiana, and 1,800 more seats than Recreation Park in Visalia, California. Nonetheless, Beloit's ballpark belongs to the dying breed of small parks designed and built during a prolonged stretch of down years for the minor leagues. The main seating bowl offers just fifteen rows in six sections around the infield, while separate banks of bleachers provide additional room along the foul lines. In the main bowl the first seven rows contain Box Seats, which are molded blue plastic chairs with armrests. Behind the Boxes are eight rows of Reserved Seats, which are metal bleachers with backs. The Reserved Seats are the best bet on a rainy night, since they are beneath the grandstand roof. These seats are still very close to the field, and fortunately the metal pillars that support the roof are thin enough to not detract much from sight lines. The General Admission sections consist of two banks of bleachers down either baseline. These are plain bleacher benches without backs. The first bank of bleachers on either side sits behind a dugout, while the second bank sits just to the outfield side of the nearest base.

The main concession stand is located behind the home plate grandstand. Here, fans find hamburgers, hot dogs, and other ballpark basics. At the smoky stand down the first baseline, fans find grilled chicken strips and Italian chicken sandwiches. There is a full bar at the deck on the first base side, while Snappy's Pad offers Dippin' Dots and other sweets for the kids. On Thursday nights, Leinie's Lodge in left field serves an all-you-can-eat, all-you-can-drink buffet for $17. The menu includes hot dogs, Polish sausages, baked beans, potato chips, soda, and an assortment of Leinenkugel beers.

The Pohlman Field Experience

Snappy, a friendly snapping turtle, is the local mascot. He wears his Snappers hat backward, just like Ken Griffey Jr. wears his during home run hitting contests. Snappy also wears a white Snappers jersey and floppy blue and white sneakers. He has a green turtle beak and a big shell on his back.

The local fans forgive Snappy, of course, if he shrinks into his shell a bit when Beloit hosts "Outdoorsman Night," an annual promotion that encourages fans to wear orange and camouflage hunting garb to the park.

Also popular in Beloit are the bobblehead giveaway nights when the home team honors select alums who went on to achieve success in the major leagues. In 2006 there was a Bill Hall bobblehead night and a Greg Vaughn bobblehead night. Who would have thought that long after his major league playing career ended, Vaughn's old Single-A team would still be honoring him? Apparently, they still remember that magical 1987 season in Beloit.

On the Town

While Beloit is a small city, it offers ample lodging options on Milwaukee Road, along with a wide selection of taverns and restaurants. Those looking for a quick bite to eat before the game will find several fast-food chains half a mile north of the stadium on Prairie Avenue. For those with more refined taste, there are many bars and restaurants on the south side of town near Beloit College. The options include **The Turtle Tap** (1344 East Grand Avenue), **Suds O'Hanahan's Irish Pub** (435 East Grand Avenue), **The End Zone** (616 4th Street), **Grand Slam** (173 West Grand Avenue), and other establishments on either side of the Rock River.

JOHNNY ROSENBLATT STADIUM

Omaha Royals

Class AAA, Pacific Coast League
(KANSAS CITY ROYALS)

Johnny Rosenblatt Stadium
1202 Bert Murphy Avenue
Omaha, Nebraska
402–734–2550

Although it is better known as the site where the College World Series has taken place every year since 1947, Rosenblatt Stadium is also the longtime home of the Omaha Royals. Owing to its duel use, "The Blatt" has welcomed more fans through its gates, and showcased more rising stars, than any other minor league ballpark. The College World Series has drawn more than six million visitors to Omaha through the years, while the Royals are one of just twelve minor league clubs to have attracted more than ten million fans in their history. The other minor league giants, in case you're wondering, are the teams in Buffalo, Columbus, Des Moines, Indianapolis, Louisville, Oklahoma City, Pawtucket, Richmond, Rochester, Syracuse, and Tacoma.

Rosenblatt Stadium is the biggest facility in all of the minor leagues, with a seating capacity of 24,000, and it's a good thing, because the ballpark is sold out during ten days each June when the eight best college teams in the country square off in Omaha. The College World Series attracts more than 260,000 fans a year. The largest crowd ever to fill the Rosenblatt Stadium—a gathering of 28,216 strong—turned out on June 23, 2004, to watch a doubleheader featuring the University

of Texas versus Georgia, and the University of South Carolina versus Cal State-Fullerton.

The list of college stars that have graced Omaha's diamond includes the likes of Huston Street, who helped pitch the University of Texas to a championship in 2002; fellow Longhorns Roger Clemens and Calvin Schiraldi, who led Texas to the World Series title in 1983; Pat Burrell, whose Miami squad lost to LSU in the 1996 finale; Mark Kotsay, who won the tournament MVP award as a pitcher and outfielder for Cal State-Fullerton in 1995; Todd Walker, who led LSU to the title in 1993; Terry Francona, who starred for champion Arizona in 1980; Dave Winfield, who pitched and played outfield during a streak of five straight seasons that USC won in the early 1970s; and James O'Neill, who pitched little Holy Cross to the top of the college game against Missouri in 1952. The list even includes former president George H. W. Bush, who captained the 1947 Yale squad that fell to California in the very first College World Series championship game on a homer by future Red Sox star Jackie Jensen.

Although the Blatt has undergone several renovations through the years, it still offers a cohesive feel and plenty of charm. It is large for the minor league game, and the NCAA's drug-testing room beneath the stands and the RV parking stalls in the lot outside may seem a bit peculiar, but that's okay. It is a comfortable and friendly place to watch a game. The exterior offers handsome red brick at ground level, bright red-and-blue beams supporting the massive press box, and a bright blue press box roof above the home plate grandstand. There is a unique decorative peak in the middle of the roof. Inside, the large seating bowl offers levels of blue, gold, and red seats, layered something like the seats at Dodger Stadium, while bleachers span the outfield. The field measures 335 feet down the lines, 375 feet to the outfield power alleys, and 408 feet to center. The outfield fence measures 8 feet high, except for a stretch in center where it is 2 feet taller to offer a better backdrop for hitters.

Recent renovations to the ballpark have added an LED scoreboard in left field, a new sound system, and new bleachers in the outfield. The city built a large entry plaza prior to the 1999 season and added a statue outside that depicts four players celebrating after winning the College World Series. The press box, which was added in 1996, has ninety seats, fifteen broadcast booths, and a lounge that can accommodate 125 scribes and talking heads.

Rosenblatt Stadium is named after the former Omaha mayor who championed its construction in the mid-1940s. It originally opened as Municipal Stadium and had that tag until it was rededicated in 1964. During its first five seasons of use as a minor league facility, the park was home to a St. Louis Cardinals affiliate that played in the Class-A Western League. Then, from 1955 through 1959 it served as home to the Double-A farm club of the Cardinals. In 1961 and 1962 Omaha made the jump to Triple-A, fielding an American Association team that was affiliated with the Los Angeles Dodgers.

Omaha has been the Kansas City Royals top farm club since 1969. You just don't find too many relationships as enduring as this one in the minor league game, so this is a relationship to be celebrated, even if the big league parent is the hapless Kansas City team.

Omaha belonged to the American Association until the league was eliminated in the minor league consolidation after the 1997 season. Since then, Omaha has been a member of the Pacific Coast League. The team experimented with a new nickname from 1999 through 2001, calling itself the "Golden Spikes," but switched back to the "Royals" in 2002.

During the nearly four-decade-long partnership between Omaha and Kansas City, the fans at Rosenblatt Stadium have been treated to glimpses of virtually every future major leaguer to come through the Royals system, including stars like George Brett, Frank White, John Wathan, Carlos Beltrán, Johnny Damon, Mike Sweeney, and Jermaine Dye.

Today, one of the Omaha club's owners is a fellow with a little bit of cash named Warren Buffett. If only Mr. Buffett would buy the Kansas City Royals and give the front office some real money to spend, maybe the organization would hold onto more of the prospects who pass through Omaha, rather than losing them as free agents.

Game Day

Getting to the Park

Omaha is in eastern Nebraska, just across the state line from Iowa. The city is accessible from either I–29, which runs north to south, or I–80, which runs east to west. Rosenblatt Stadium sits near the Missouri River and Henry Doorly Zoo, just south of I–80. The stadium is visible from the highway and easy to reach off exit 454. From the exit, 13th Street South leads right to the large lots north and west of the stadium.

Inside the Park

Even if the Royals don't open the outfield bleachers, Rosenblatt Stadium is plenty big enough for the local minor league team's fan base. The Royals draw in the neighborhood of 300,000 fans per season during the course of their seventy-two-game home schedule, or about 40,000 fans more than the College World Series attracts in ten days.

The large seating bowl extends all the way into the outfield corners, beginning at Section AA, near the right field foul pole, and continuing to Section DD, midway to the infield. Sections A through D appear in the shadows

Johnny Rosenblatt Stadium

Omaha Steak burgers, juicy brat-wurst, honey popcorn, and frozen malts. The Stadium View Club, high above the field on the first base side, offers three levels of air-conditioned seating, a full bar, and a dinner menu. Stadium View Club members get first dibs on seats once the ballpark opens, but any ticket holder can call ahead (402–733–0333) and reserve a table before the game.

The Rosenblatt Stadium Experience

The Royals offer fewer bush league shenanigans than most teams, and that's probably a good thing. Early in the 2006 season, Omaha outfielder Kerry Robinson had to ask out of a game at the Blatt when he laughed so hard during the pregame antics of a local youth league team that he hurt himself. Robinson was at his position in center field when the National Anthem played. Meanwhile, a group of children who had lined up with the players when the starting lineups were announced stood at attention. When the anthem ended, rather than just running off the field, the kids all took a turn sliding into third base as team officials looked on helplessly. In their haste to all get a slide in, the kids wound up piled on top of each other and all tangled up. The sight triggered Robinson's center field laughing fit, during which he felt a twinge in his chest. Although the muscle spasm only kept the outfielder out of the lineup for a couple of days, it earned him mention in *Sports Illustrated* and spots on several national talk shows.

The Omaha mascot is a royal lion named "Casey." Casey is at the Blatt and comes through for fans, rain or shine, seventy-two games a year.

Royals fans enjoy two-for-one ticket prices on Tuesdays, drink specials and live music

of the Stadium View Club restaurant, which sits atop the grandstand along the right field line, then Sections E and F fill the space along the first baseline. Section I is directly behind home plate. Sections M and N are along the third baseline. And the seats end at Section X in deep left field. The first four sections in right field and last six sections in left field are not part of the original seating bowl but additions that angle nicely back toward the foul line, rather than simply running parallel to it. There's no reason to sit in these parts of the stadium though, since the typical crowd in Omaha consists of only about 4,500 fans, leaving plenty of room for everyone closer to the infield.

The first several rows are blue Box Seats. The gold Lower Reserved Seats come next, then a midlevel walkway, and then the red Upper Reserved Seats. Fans sitting in the Upper Reserved in Sections F through L must contend with the view-blocking support pillars of the press box, but otherwise the sight lines are sound throughout the park.

The concession stands are on the concourse behind the grandstand. They feature grilled before the game on Thursdays, and fireworks after the game on Fridays.

On the Town

Among the sights to see in Nebraska's largest city—population 400,000—is the landing on the banks of the Missouri River where Lewis and Clark first set foot in 1804. True, they weren't looking for baseball parks, but any traveling fan has to admire the pioneering spirit of these old-time road-trippers. A historical marker on Sixth Street marks the duo's arrival in Nebraska territory, while nearby a twenty-three-acre complex along the river's edge offers a boardwalk, restaurant, and walking and biking trails.

Just beyond the right field bleachers of Rosenblatt Stadium, visitors find the **Henry Doorly Zoo** (3701 South 10th Street). The zoo's trademark attractions are its indoor desert—which it claims is the largest in the world—a rainforest, a 70-foot underwater tunnel, and an IMAX Theater. The zoo is open daily from 9:30 A.M. until 5:00 P.M. Admission costs $10.50 for adults and $6.75 for children, ages five through eleven.

Sixty miles southwest of Omaha in the Nebraska's capital city, the Lincoln Saltdogs play independent league baseball as members of the new American Association. The club plays at 4,500-seat **Haymarket Park** (403 Line Drive, Lincoln), where it previously represented the Northern League before switching to the American Association in time for the league's 2006 debut. The new circuit fields ten teams, including the mother of all indies, the Saint Paul Saints, and clubs from as far south as El Paso and as far east as Pensacola.

COMMUNITY FIELD

Burlington Bees

Class A, Midwest League
(KANSAS CITY ROYALS)

Community Field
2712 Mount Pleasant Street
Burlington, Iowa
319–754–5705

The Burlington Bees are minor league baseball's equivalent of the Green Bay Packers. Just like the professional football team that plays in one of the NFL's smallest markets, the Bees are community owned and operated. And just as the Packers play at a historic field revered by locals, the Bees play at Community Field, which has nobly served this border town in southeastern Iowa for more than six decades. The Burlington Baseball Association is the nonprofit company that manages the Bees player development contract with the Kansas City Royals and oversees the operation of Community Field. The association consists of a volunteer-based board of directors and a staff of five full-time paid employees. The local American Legion post owns the land on which the stadium resides and leases the land to the city of Burlington, which owns the stadium and leases it to the Burlington Baseball Association. As you can see, everyone in this small community is doing their part to keep Burlington viable as a minor league baseball town.

The community has maintained a grassroots commitment to renovating the stadium through the years, with local residents pitching in to modernize Community Field and make improvements whenever necessary. A recent grant from Vision Iowa, a foundation that contributes to projects involving recreation and tourism in Iowa, funded a number of capital improvements to the park that were made in 2005 and 2006, with others scheduled for 2007. These include the construction of a new front office building, the expansion of the visiting clubhouse, the expansion of the press box, the enlargement of the stadium's main concourse, and the installation of a canopy roof over the concourse and part of the grandstand.

The small grandstand is unique looking from outside Community Field, offering a ground-level brick front, topped by the strange slant of the press box roof. Slender towers atop the press box anchor suspension cables that hold the canopy roof in place. These cables were designed to mirror the look of the cables on the Great River Bridge, which spans the Mississippi River, connecting Burlington to Illinois. Brick pillars at ground level support wrought-iron signs that spell out "Bees" in stylish cursive over the entrance gates. Inside, fans find a predictably quaint and small-time atmosphere. There is a public park beyond the ballpark's footprint, so the outfield view consists of pleasant green trees.

It should come as no surprise that the folks in Burlington are proud of their ballpark and work hard to maintain and improve it. Community Field dates all the way back to 1947 when it debuted as home to a Cleveland Indians affiliate. Previously, the Bees had played at a different field on the south end of Burlington where the airport currently sits.

The team has changed big league affiliations more than a dozen times since Community Field opened, but the local residents love of baseball has never wavered. The Bees joined the Midwest League in 1962 as a Pittsburgh Pirates affiliate and have remained a member of the league ever since. On June 9, 1971, Community Field burned to the ground after hosting a high school baseball game while the Bees were on a road trip. The community pulled together to gradually rebuild the stadium over the next two seasons, while play continued at the ball-park/construction site.

Through the years more than 160 future major leaguers have passed through Burlington on their way to the Show. The Bees most notable former players include Vida Blue, Billy Williams, Sal Bando, Paul Molitor, Mark Buehrle, Larry Walker, Javy López, Kenny Rogers, and Rubén Sierra. Blue, Williams, and Molitor are members of the Burlington Baseball Hall of Fame, and their old uniform numbers have been retired by the Bees. In 1968 Blue struck out 231 batters, a mark that still stands as the team's all-time single-season record. Molitor played his only minor league season in Burlington, winning Midwest League MVP and leading the Bees to the league championship in 1977, before making the Milwaukee Brewers out of spring training in 1978 and beginning his Hall of Fame career. Future big league managers Rene Lachemann, Terry Bevington, and Grady Little began their managerial careers in Burlington as well.

While no current high school or college team uses Community Field as its regular home, each year the Bees make sure that all of the local high school teams get to play at least one game at the stadium. Southeastern Community College in West Burlington also uses the field periodically. In 2003 Southeastern hosted the junior college state tournament at Community Field. In 1999 the sixteen-year-old Babe Ruth League World Series took place in Burlington and the tournament MVP was Sergio Santos, who is currently a top prospect in the Toronto Blue Jays system.

Game Day

Getting to the Park

From the east or west, take Route 34 to U.S. Highway 61 North. Proceed north on US 61 to the Mount Pleasant Street exit and then follow Mount Pleasant east to the ballpark. There is a grass field in front of the stadium where parking is always free. Check out the 150-foot-tall flagpole in the parking lot. It is the tallest one in the entire state of Iowa. If you arrive at the ballpark to find the stadium lot full, a small shopping center nearby serves as an overflow parking area.

Inside the Park

This is a tiny ballpark with a seating capacity of just 3,200. All of the seats are around the infield. The main seating bowl is located between the dugouts, while an extra bank of bleachers on the left side of the diamond is situated even with the third base bag. The majority of seating consists of General Admission bleachers, while 280 Box Seats occupy the four rows closest to the field.

A group area known as the Brat Garden is on the first base side past the seating bowl. The elevated wooden deck is open to the general public on nights when it isn't reserved for groups. The Brat Garden has its own concession stand and is surrounded by a patio, a playground, and a grass common area. On the other side of the diamond, a rooftop group seating area has room for up to forty people, mimicking the atmosphere of the rooftop viewing locations across the street from Wrigley Field on Waveland Avenue in Chicago.

The ballpark offers just one luxury box, a Hall of Fame suite in the press box that opened in 2005. The suite can accommodate up to twenty fans and is available for rent on a game-by-game basis. So if you're traveling with a large party and want to watch a game in style while you're in Burlington, have at it.

The concession stands are at ground level behind the seating bowl. The local favorite is the Macho Nacho plate, a heaping pile of toasted corn chips loaded with meat, cheese, salsa, and jalapeño peppers. If you think you can handle this monstrous plate of chips, give it a try. If not, opt for a less adventurous ballpark treat, like the Lippy Dog, which appears at Community Field courtesy of the Chicken Lip. I know this one sounds gross at first. You're probably thinking that it's a chicken hot dog that shamelessly markets the unique taste of chicken lips stuffed into natural casing. That's what I thought at first too, but it's actually not like that at all. The Chicken Lip is a local restaurant, and the Lippy Dog is a jumbo boneless buffalo wing, slathered in Lip's signature sauce and served on a hot dog bun. It's pretty good. The third base stand is the most popular one because it offers an up close view of the game and because it has a greater selection of adult beverages than the other stands. Here fans can order a wine cooler, hard lemonade, or any other fruity alcoholic beverage that may or may not serve as a good chaser for the Macho Nacho plate.

The Community Field Experience

Following the traditional singing of "Take Me Out to the Ball Game" midway through the seventh inning, the Community Field public-address system blares the Elvis Presley classic, "I Got Stung." The locals really get into this, singing along and dancing up a storm, so be prepared to buzz like a bee and shake your stinger. If you need inspiration, just make like Buzz, the Bees mascot. This big yellow bumble-bee may look harmless enough, dressed in his baseball uniform and flapping his wings, but think twice before you tell him to buzz off. This bee's got a stinger and knows how to use it.

Another popular figure at Community Field is Dancing Bobby, a superfan who attends almost every home game. Dancing Bobby stands at the top of the far ramp on the first base side behind the visitors dugout and dances to the music in between innings.

If you have a copy of the Bees current home schedule in front of you as you're reading this chapter, and you find yourself wondering why some weekday games begin at 11:30 A.M., rest assured there's a good reason for these matinees. The Bees designate several games each spring as "Honor Roll and Reading Club Days," welcoming local school kids to Community Field to celebrate their accomplishments in the classroom.

On the Town

Burlington is one of the smallest communities in the United States to have its own full-season affiliated minor league baseball team. If you're looking for a unique place to bunk down while in town, I suggest staying at **Fun City,** the recently remodeled former Best Western Plaza Hotel, 2 blocks south of the ballpark on Winegard Drive. This is one-stop shopping at its finest. You can sleep here, eat, drink, get some exercise, and even rub elbows with professional ballplayers and any groupies they should happen to leave in their wake. Fun City, which is the visiting team's hotel when Midwest League rivals come to Burlington, also features a full bar and restaurant, an arcade, a bowling alley, a go-cart track, a laser tag course, a 3-D theater, and an indoor/outdoor water park. If that's not enough to keep you occupied while you're in Burlington, head to the **Burlington Regional Rec Plex** to take a few swings in the batting cages. The Rec Plex is located inside a business park off Agency Street and Broadway, about 1½ miles southwest of Community Field.

VETERANS MEMORIAL STADIUM

Cedar Rapids Kernels

Class A, Midwest League
(LOS ANGELES ANGELS OF ANAHEIM)

Veterans Memorial Stadium
950 Rockford Road Southwest
Cedar Rapids, Iowa
319–363–3887

Veterans Memorial Stadium is a comfortable facility that provides a thoroughly enjoyable setting for a Midwest League baseball game. In this league that offers fans such widely varied ballpark experiences as those at the baseball-crazed environments in Dayton and Geneva, which seem more like Triple-A markets, and those at tiny ballparks in tiny towns like Beloit and Burlington, which seem like summer collegiate league markets—Cedar Rapids offers a happy middle ground. The city's ballpark can accommodate 5,300 fans, but the average crowd is only about half that size.

As visitors approach Veterans Memorial Stadium, they encounter an old army tank parked in front of a unique exterior façade composed of gray bricks down below and white metal up top. The main entrance is on the left field side, and from there fans spill onto a concourse that runs atop the small seating bowl. The metal roof over the infield grandstand is reminiscent of the one that once existed at the original Veterans Memorial Stadium, which was demolished after the current park was built adjacent to it in time for the 2002 season. Unlike the original Veterans Memorial Stadium, the current one features a mezzanine level with indoor/outdoor luxury boxes and an upstairs group-seating area on the first base side. The overhang of the second level shades

the home plate grandstand and part of the concession concourse on sunny summer days. Farther down the baselines, but still on the infield, the concourse is uncovered, airy, and spacious, offering fans room to mingle or just stretch their legs for an inning or two while enjoying an excellent view of the field.

There is a large video scoreboard in right-center, which the team makes steady use of all game long, even providing a video feed of the game in progress at times. The outfield view showcases green trees that rise immediately behind the home run fence, creating a nice backdrop for a game.

While some local fans still wax nostalgic about the old park, the reality is that it had only four rows of stadium seats, while the rest of the seating came in the form of bleachers; it didn't have any luxury boxes; and its press box, built into the roof, was accessible to scribes and team employees via a narrow and somewhat harrowing catwalk. Thankfully, when it came time to replace the circa-1949 stadium, the community-owned Kernels and the Cedar Rapids Veterans Memorial Commission did things right, building a small park with seats that are just as close to the field, if not closer, than they were at the old yard.

Over the past four decades, Cedar Rapids has served as a Midwest League affiliate of several teams, including the St. Louis Cardinals, Houston Astros, San Francisco Giants, and Cincinnati Reds. The Kernels have been affiliated with the Anaheim Angels since 1993. The franchise's alumni roster includes such notables as Eric Davis, Chili Davis, Rob Deer, Rob Dibble, Ken Hill, Casey Kotchman, Dallas McPherson, Bengie Molina, Paul O'Neill, and Reggie Sanders.

Prior to joining the Midwest League in 1962, Cedar Rapids fielded a number of different teams in a number of leagues, starting with the Cedar Rapids Rabbits, who played in the

Western League as early as 1897; the Bunnies, who played in the Mississippi Valley League in the 1920s; and the Raiders, who played in the Three-I League in the 1940s and 1950s.

Today, in addition to providing a home to the Kernels, Veterans Memorial Stadium sees use as an amateur facility, hosting high school games, Eastern Iowa Senior League games (a league for players age twenty-seven and older), American Legion games, and Perfect Game USA showcases. During the summer of 2005, Bob Dylan and Willie Nelson became the first musical acts to play the stadium, drawing a sell-out crowd.

Game Day

Getting to the Park

Cedar Rapids is centrally located between Iowa's other four minor league cities. Assuming you have a decent set of wheels—in other words, something other than a bicycle—you should be able to reach the "City of Five Seasons" in under an hour and a half from Burlington, Clinton, Davenport, or Des Moines. Veterans Memorial Stadium is part of a sports complex that also includes a football stadium and an ice arena within a nice residential neighborhood in the southwest quadrant of the city. The ballpark is located about 1 mile west of I–380, which bisects Cedar Rapids from north to south. From I–380 South, take the First Avenue exit and follow First Avenue West, then turn left onto 15th Street and the ballpark will appear on your left. From I–380 North, take the Wilson Avenue exit and turn left onto Wilson, then right onto Rockford Road and the stadium will appear on your left. Parking is free on the left field side of the ballpark.

Inside the Park

All of the seats in the main grandstand around the infield are comfortable red stadium chairs.

The seating continues past the corner bases, taking the form of a grass hillside along the left field line and of bleachers with backs along the right field line. In deep left field foul territory, and continuing for a short stretch into home run territory out near the foul pole, fans find a tiered Pavilion seating area similar to the tiki bar seats at Bright House Networks Field in Clearwater, Florida, and the Green Monster seats at Fenway Park. The Pavilion in Cedar Rapids is reserved for groups, whose lucky members enjoy not only four tiers of tableside seating and a unique view of the field, but a small hot tub. Section 104 is at first base, Sections 111 and 112 are behind home plate, and Section 118 is at third base. The first eight rows sell as Premier Seats and the remainder are the Club Seats. The Plaza Seats, actually bleachers, are in Sections 100 through 103 in right field. On a rainy night shoot for a Club Seat beneath the overhang that covers the back rows of Sections 108 through 114 between the dugouts. The second level, in addition to housing the press box and twelve luxury boxes, offers an upstairs group area on the first base side.

The concourse runs atop the last row of Club Seats, offering a view of the field from most locations. The concession menu serves local flavor in the form of corn dogs, pulled pork sandwiches, pork tenderloin sandwiches, bratwurst, and cheddar-wurst. The diverse beer list includes the usual macro-brews, as well as Goose Island and several types of Leinenkugel's.

The clubhouse shop on the third base side of the concourse houses the Kernels Hall of Fame, while a playground area on the third base side has attractions for the kids.

The Veterans Memorial Stadium Experience

When a foul ball makes its way into the stands at any ballpark across the country and a fan makes a nice catch while at the same time managing not to spill his beer or drop his nachos, someone inevitably yells the tired line, "Give that fan a contract." Sometimes it's another fan. Sometimes it's the ballpark public-address announcer. Sometimes it's one of the field managers if his team is having a difficult time of it in the field. I'm not sure who started this saying, or why anyone would actually assume that the ability to snag a pop fly in the grandstands would translate into the ability to hit a 90-mile-per-hour heater or fall-off-the-table curve, but the saying is as much a part of our National Pastime as the old axiom that says baseball's "cardinal sin" is making the first or third out of an inning at third base. Did you ever stop and ask yourself just what the heck a cardinal sin is? Or why this is a term that we only seem to use in our everyday vocabulary when a runner gets thrown out in a baseball game? Anyway, back to my original point. When a fan at Veterans Memorial Stadium catches a foul ball, he doesn't just get the obligatory contract talk tossed his way, he gets an actual contract from the team. All that ball-catching fans have to do is take their ball to the Guest Services Center on the concourse and they receive an honorary lifetime contract from the Kernels. Hey, if nothing else the contract bestows its holder with the ability to honestly say someday at a cocktail party, "Well, I was offered a professional baseball contract from a Midwest League team, an Angels affiliate, in fact, but I decided instead to concentrate on my career in (sales, marketing, window washing, or whatever)."

The Kernels mascot is a fellow known as "Mr. Shucks." Surprisingly, he doesn't really resemble an ear of corn. In fact he doesn't really resemble any identifiable life form or animate or inanimate object that I can think of. He has a gray, pear-shaped body and an over-sized baseball for a head. He wears bright red socks pulled all the way up to his knees like Jim Thome wears his, and a Kernels hat on his big round head. I was similarly disappointed to note that although the team offered many promotions between innings there was no corn-shucking contest. This may have been due to the fact that I visited in May. One local fan told me that as long as the corn stalks are "knee high by the fourth of July," the crop is on schedule.

On the Town

Cedar Rapids is widely considered to be one of only three cities in the entire world that houses its municipal headquarters on a river island. The Cedar Rapids city hall and county courthouse reside on Mays Island, in the midst of the Cedar River. Okay, trivia buffs: Can you name the other two cities whose municipal buildings sit on inland islands? For the answer, see the very end of this chapter.

In the center of downtown Cedar Rapids, visitors find the *Tree of Five Seasons* sculpture where First Avenue meets the river. Here along the riverbanks, visitors also find the city's trademark **Czech Village**, which includes ethnic restaurants, historic buildings, and the National Czech & Slovak Museum & Library.

Closer to the ballpark, thirsty, hungry baseball fans find the **Viking Lounge** (1971 16th Avenue Southwest), the **1810 On 6th Steakhouse Bar** (1810 6th Street Southwest), and **Sam's Pizza** (824 6th Street Southwest).

As for the trivia answer, the other two cities that offer island views to their municipal employees are Paris, France, which sits amidst the Seine River, and Osaka, Japan, which sits between the Dojimagawa and Tosaborigawa Rivers.

ALLIANT ENERGY FIELD
Clinton LumberKings

Class A, Midwest League
(TEXAS RANGERS)

Alliant Energy Field
Sixth Avenue North and First Street
Clinton, Iowa
563–242–0727

The Clinton LumberKings are the oldest continuously operated franchise in the Midwest League with a history that dates all the way back to when the league was known as the Ohio Valley League. Clinton was one of three expansion teams in 1954, along with Dubuque and Mississippi, to join the Ohio Valley League. In 1956 the circuit became officially known as the Midwest League when a number of teams relocated from Southern Illinois to larger cities in Iowa. Clinton is the only city to make this shift that still fields a team in the league today. The next-oldest franchise in the Midwest League is Quad City in Davenport, which joined in 1960.

Fittingly, the LumberKings play at a historic ballpark. Alliant Energy Field was built in 1937. It was known as Riverview Stadium until 2003 when Alliant Energy, a Wisconsin-based energy services provider, shelled out $450,000 in a ten-year naming-rights deal. The stadium is the centerpiece of Clinton's Riverview Park, a sixty-five-acre recreation center on the western banks of the Mississippi River. Here baseball fans find a simple old-time ballpark experience. The river meanders past the ballpark just a few hundred feet from the outfield fences, while a riverboat bobs beyond the left field wall. Although a levee built for flood control blocks the view of the river from the grandstands, the ballpark still offers a rustic

view. A grass lawn and a number of decorative trees fill the well-landscaped space between the stadium and the riverbanks. Beyond the left-center field fence a fountain shoots water high into the air. The field's most distinguishing characteristic is the S-shaped protrusion of an outfield seating berm in straightaway left that projects fans right out into the field on a small bluff. This is a great place to wait for home run balls.

Riverview Stadium was built as a Works Progress Administration project. When it opened in 1937, it harkened Clinton's second life as a minor league baseball town. Clinton's first foray into organized baseball occurred in 1906 when the Clinton Orphans played at Ringwood Park as a member of the Class D Iowa State League. Over the next twelve years, the Clinton nine were known as the Infants, Teddies, and Pilots while playing in several different leagues. The onset of World War I began a nineteen-year dearth of professional baseball in Clinton though, as able-bodied young men left the baseball fields of America for the battlefields of Europe.

Riverview Stadium welcomed the Clinton Owls, a Brooklyn Dodgers affiliate that played in the Three-I League, to Clinton in 1937. After the 1941 season Clinton's baseball light went dark again, this time due to World War II. A local industrial league team played at the ballpark throughout the war, and then in 1947 the Clinton Cubs brought pro ball back to town, playing in the Central Association. In the six decades since then, the franchise has had a number of different names and has had affiliations with nine different major league teams, including the Pittsburgh Pirates twice, but minor league baseball has continued to be played in Clinton without interruption. The team adopted the LumberKings nickname in 1994 when it was a San Francisco Giants affiliate. After severing ties with the Giants after that season, the LumberKings enjoyed a relationship with the San Diego Padres, Cincinnati Reds, and Montreal Expos, before inking a player development contract with the Texas Rangers in 2003.

Clinton alumni include famous bashers Gorman Thomas, Ron Kittle, and Matt Williams, who used to send long balls toward the river, and pitchers Dave Stewart, Orel Hershiser, and Denny McLain. Future big league managers Tom Kelly and Mike Scioscia both appeared in Clinton as players. In 1956 pitcher Arturo Miro won 19 straight games on his way to a Midwest League record 22 wins in the season for Clinton. On August 3, 2000, LumberKings pitcher Scott Dunn pitched a perfect game against Lansing at Riverview Stadium.

Game Day

Getting to the Park

Clinton is in the easternmost part of Iowa that bulges like a peninsula into Illinois territory. From Illinois, take U.S. Highway 30 West to South Third Street. Turn right onto South Third and follow it to Sixth Avenue North. Turn right onto Sixth and follow it across the railroad tracks to the ballpark. From the south and west, take US 30 East to U.S. Highway 67 North to Sixth Avenue North, then follow the directions above. A free parking lot sits behind the third base grandstand.

Inside the Park

The ballpark offers one small deck of covered seating around the infield. Berm seating extends from behind third base, around the foul pole, and into left-center. The Lumber Lounge party deck sits in right field home run territory.

In the main seating area around the infield, the first three rows are comfortable Box Seats that were installed in 2006. A walkway comes next, then fifteen rows of General Admission bleachers that account for the bulk of the stadium's 4,000 seats.

The concourse behind the grandstand offers a small souvenir stand, an arcade, a speed-pitch booth, a bouncy pen, and the usual ballpark concessions. The local favorite is fresh sweet corn, available at the ballpark in the late summer months. So put some dental floss in your pocket, butter up an ear, roll up those sleeves, and start chomping.

The Alliant Energy Field Experience

Kids run the bases after every Sunday home game. The ubiquitous dizzy bat race and unique minitractor race are popular nightly festivities.

The team mascot is Louie the LumberKing. Clinton was once considered the lumber capital of America, and this unique mascot pays tribute to that boarding legacy. Louie is a muscle-bound lumberjack who wears a gold crown on his head, a green flannel shirt, and a black handlebar mustache. Instead of a Louisville Slugger, he swings an armful of two-by-fours. It has been suggested by some fans that Louie is an odd, if not downright creepy, mascot and I agree. Something about Louie strikes me as a bit sinister. The locals adore him though, and that's what counts.

On the Town

Clinton is a small community of approximately 30,000 people, located half an hour from the Quad Cities and three hours from Chicago. The city's trademark event is a weeklong Fourth of July bash known as **Clinton Riverboat Days.** The event brings several musical groups to town for concerts that take place on multiple stages along the banks of the Mississippi River. An array of other outdoor exhibits and carnival attractions round out the event.

Field of Dreams

Those looking for a riverboat gambling experience can visit the **Mississippi Belle II**, a casino boat located right beyond the stadium's left field wall.

One of the most unique pop-culture/baseball landmarks you'll come across is located about 60 miles northwest of Clinton in tiny Dyersville, Iowa. Here you'll find the **Field of Dreams** movie site, a little piece of heaven on earth. Even though the movie, starring Kevin Costner and James Earl Jones, appeared on the silver screen way back in 1989, fans from across the country and around the world still flock to this quaint parcel of farmland to have a game of catch on the same field that the ghosts of Shoeless Joe Jackson and the other banned Chicago Black Sox haunted. Today, the field is surrounded by the same delightful cornstalks that ensconced it in the movie. Previously, tobacco was grown on Don Lansing's farm, but after Universal knocked on Lansing's door and made him an offer he couldn't refuse to build a baseball park on his land, he decided to keep the cornfields and baseball field as a tourist attraction. One thing you probably didn't notice in the movie that a visit to the field reveals is the stretch of telephone wires that bisects the baseball diamond. The wires were edited out of the movie. The Field of Dreams is open daily from 10:00 A.M. until 6:00 P.M. during the summer months. From Clinton, take Route 30 west to Route 61 north and follow Route 61 to Dubuque. Then take Route 20 west to Lansing Road in Dyersville. Take a right and follow the signs to the familiar white farmhouse.

JOHN O'DONNELL STADIUM
The Swing of the Quad Cities

Class A, Midwest League
(ST. LOUIS CARDINALS)

John O'Donnell Stadium
209 Gaines Street
Davenport, Iowa
563–328–2000

While the big league ballparks in cities like San Francisco, Cincinnati, and Pittsburgh offer traveling seam-heads striking water views beyond their outfield fences to enhance the game day experience, the ball fields of the game's minor leagues also do their part to embrace the scenic shorelines and rustic riverbanks that distinguish their respective cities from the zillions of other municipalities across this vast land of ours. No minor league ballpark does a better job of showcasing its local waterfront than John O'Donnell Stadium in Davenport. From the ballpark seats fans can see the mighty Mississippi River, the expansive Centennial Bridge, downtown Davenport, and the downtown skylines of Moline and Rock Island, Illinois.

Although minor league baseball has been played in Davenport on the banks of the Mississippi dating all the way back to 1931 when the ballpark opened as Municipal Stadium, the view wasn't always as breathtaking as it is today. During the ballpark's first seven decades, only a small stretch of the water was visible beyond the stadium in right field foul territory. But a $10 million renovation in 2004 fixed that slight, rotating the baseball field to the right by several degrees so that today the river is visible from the entire left side of the seating bowl. The river runs from behind the first base grandstand to out beyond the grass berm atop the fence in right-center.

After the renovation was approved by the Davenport City Council in 2003, the new ballpark design was drawn up by HOK, the same architectural firm that seamlessly meshed PNC Park with its riverside locale in downtown Pittsburgh. In addition to improving the sight lines, the renovation endowed O'Donnell Stadium with a concourse that enables fans to walk all the way around the field, a grass berm area that spans the outfield, a new luxury suite level, two team stores, a new video board, batting and pitching tunnels beneath the stadium, and expanded restroom and concession areas.

On three separate occasions O'Donnell Stadium has weathered major floods when the Mississippi breached its banks—in 1965, 1993, and 2001. To protect against this ever happening again, the 2004 renovation also equipped the stadium with a high-tech flood protection system. Let's hope that the stadium is as waterproof as currently advertised, but I suppose we won't find out for sure until another once-in-a-generation flood comes along to test the levies.

All that remains of the original ballpark structure is the unique stadium exterior on Gaines Street that welcomes fans through glorious redbrick archways. Municipal Stadium was renamed after *Davenport Times Democrat* sports editor John O'Donnell in 1971, after O'Donnell's death. It has hosted more than a dozen different minor league teams since beginning its professional life as home to the Davenport Blue Sox from 1931 through 1937.

Prior to entering into a player development contract with the St. Louis Cardinals and becoming The Swing of the Quad Cities, the team was known as the Quad City River Bandits from 1992 through 2003. The Bandits were affiliated with the Houston Astros from

John O'Donnell Stadium

1993 until 1998, then with the Minnesota Twins from 1999 through 2004.

Recent Quad City alums who have made a splash in the major leagues include Johan Santana, Joe Mauer, Billy Wagner, Garrett Anderson, and Jim Edmonds. Hall of Famer Jim Bunning also once pitched for Davenport. In 2005 a former major leaguer came to town for an extended visit, former Cardinals pitcher Rick Ankiel, who finished second in the National League's Rookie of the Year balloting in 2000 before throwing five wild pitches in the third inning of the first game of the National League Championship Series against the Braves and never regaining his control. Trying to resurrect his career as an outfielder, Ankiel crushed 11

home runs in fifty-one games for The Swing in 2005, while slugging .514.

As for the team's current identity, the "Quad Cities" are four geographically clustered cities on either side of the Iowa-Illinois state line, separated by the Mississippi River. Davenport and Bettendorf are in Iowa, Rock Island and Moline are in Illinois. The "Swing" moniker pays tribute to the region's rich jazz history. The legendary Bix Beiderbecke hailed from Davenport, as did several other famous names in jazz. The Centennial Bridge, which spans from Davenport to Rock Island, is one of four bridges that connect Davenport to the Illinois side of the Quad Cities. The Centennial opened in 1940 and was redecked in 1995.

Game Day

Getting to the Park

O'Donnell Stadium is on the southwest side of downtown Davenport. From I–74, which bisects the Quad Cities from south to north, take the Grant Street exit and follow Grant west to River Drive (Route 67). The ballpark is at the corner of River Drive and Gaines Street. The stadium parking lot is north of the stadium and charges $2.00. The lot hosts a farmers market on Sunday and Thursday mornings throughout the summer, so if you find yourself soiling your new Nikes as you step on abandoned eggplants and rotting rhubarb on your walk to the ballpark, that's why. If you are looking to take a ½-mile walk, or if you're just too stingy to shell out the whopping two bucks for parking, or if you really do have new Nikes, free on-street parking is plentiful on Second and Third Streets in downtown Davenport.

Inside the Park

The simple grandstand around the infield can accommodate 4,024 fans, and seats are always available on game day. The biggest crowds turn out when the Peoria Chiefs, a Chicago Cubs affiliate, come to town. Even at this low minor league level, the rivalry between the Cubbies and Redbirds runs strong. Section 1 is even with the first base bag, Section 6 is directly behind home plate, and Section 11 is even with third base. The first few rows of Sections 4 through 8 between the dugouts sell for a few dollars more than the rest as Club Seats, while all of the other seats are called Box Seats. I recommend sitting anywhere in Sections 8 through 11 on the third base side, where the outfield view is best.

A General Admission ticket bequeaths its holders with the choice of sitting anywhere in the metal bleachers in shallow left field foul territory or on the left field or right field berms. For folks hell-bent on going home with a game-used Midwest League baseball—river views be damned—your best bet is to sit on the right field berm where incoming home runs often touch off mad scrambles among the local ball hounds. The asymmetrical outfield is quite a bit deeper in left field than in right, so for that reason the right field berm sees more homer action.

Twenty luxury boxes flank the press box and wrap around the upper deck. Beyond Suite 20 in left field is a private party deck.

The concession stands are located above the seats on the concourse behind home plate, first base, and third base, and they offer a view of the game to those waiting in line. One stand has a Mexican theme and serves a pretty decent burrito, while another serves a delicious pork chop sandwich. A kids zone on the right field picnic plaza offers a speed-pitch booth, moonwalk pen, obstacle course, and other diversions.

The O'Donnell Stadium Experience

The Swing mascot is a seven-foot-tall orangutan named "Clyde," who loves to eat, play baseball, and act like, well, an orangutan. There's a serious side to Clyde too. The big ape also leads a local reading program that involves fifty area grammar schools and more than 11,000 Quad City students. Hey Clyde, here's an idea for you: Why not make this book I wrote about minor league baseball parks required reading in your syllabus?

As if Clyde weren't enough to keep fans amused and carefully guarding their ball-park treats, a trip to Davenport also offers the chance to see Banana Man in action. Banana Man is a fellow who dresses all in yellow and streaks across the outfield berm whenever a player on the home team hits a home run. And yes, the big orangutan sometimes tries to eat Banana Man.

On the Town

There are several riverboat casinos within a short walk or drive of O'Donnell Stadium, so if you're feeling lucky, head down to River Drive and pick an outfit that gives you good vibes.

My suggestion, throw a few chips on 33 black at the roulette table. I've just got a feeling it will work out for you. Don't ask me why.

Front Street Brewery (208 East River Drive) makes a special beer called Swing Ale during baseball season. I didn't get a chance to try it myself, but according to locals, the brewmaster really hit a home run when he came up with the recipe for this one. See what you think.

PRINCIPAL PARK

Iowa Cubs

Class AAA, Pacific Coast League
(CHICAGO CUBS)

Sec Taylor Field at Principal Park
350 South First Street
Des Moines, Iowa
515–243–6111

Ironically enough, the minor league city most closely associated with the Chicago Cubs, and the one that houses their top farm club, is also known as the place where night baseball originated. The Cubs waited longer than any other big league team before finally giving in to the interests of commercialism and modernity and adding lights at Wrigley Field in 1988. More than half a century earlier, the night baseball era dawned a few hundred miles west of Chicago in Des Moines, Iowa.

The first night game in professional baseball history was played at Western League Park on May 2, 1930. The Des Moines Demons defeated the Wichita Aviators 12–6 before 12,000 fans and a national radio audience, thanks to the collection of 10-feet-wide, 90-feet-tall light towers that Demons owner Lee Keyser had installed at a cost of more than $20,000 during the preceding off season. Keyser's ploy to make baseball more accessible to Des Moines community members—at a time when they were working long hours during the throes of the Great Depression—worked, and eventually it led to the arrival of the first night games in the major leagues. After the Cincinnati Reds erected light towers at Crosley Field in 1935, eight other teams followed suit and added lights to their ballparks before the end of the 1941 season.

Among the reporters present for the inaugural night game in Des Moines was Willis Garner "Sec" Taylor, who covered the contest for the *Des Moines Register*. Taylor would also be on hand in 1947, when the local nine opened a brand new park known as Pioneer Memorial Stadium, and in 1959, when that park was renamed Sec Taylor Stadium. Taylor, who was the sports editor of the *Register* from 1914 until his passing in 1965, died just four years before Des Moines became a Triple-A city in 1969 as the American Association affiliate of the Oakland A's.

Although much has changed on the Des Moines hardball front in the past four decades, much has remained the same. The city still fields a Triple-A club. Des Moines stuck with the American Association through its final season and then joined the Pacific Coast League in 1998. The local team still plays on the same plot that it did when Sec Taylor covered games. Although Sec Taylor Stadium no longer stands, a new ballpark was built on the same footprint in 1992.

Des Moines has been affiliated with the loveable losers of the National League since 1982. During that time prospects like Mark Grace, Greg Maddux, Rafael Palmeiro, Mark Prior, and Kerry Wood have helped the team consistently attract large crowds. The I-Cubs set a single-game franchise attendance record in 2005 when 13,669 fans jammed into newly renamed "Principal Park" to watch Wood make a rehab start. Then, when Wood returned the next year for another minor league tune-up, some 13,830 fans turned out.

Principal Park got its new name late in 2004, when Des Moines signed a naming-rights agreement with the Principal Financial Group. The playing field is still named after Taylor, for whatever that's worth. The ballpark sits at the confluence of the Des Moines and Raccoon

Rivers, but there really aren't any water views from the seats. The stadium was designed by HOK and built at a cost of $12 million. It isn't as flashy as some of the newer parks that have opened, but it certainly gets the job done, offering clear sight lines throughout a large one-deck seating bowl. The stadium underwent a few small renovations in its first decade, then a much larger one between the 2005 and 2006 seasons. The recent work included the installation of a new lighting system. Somewhere, no doubt, the ghost of old Lee Keyser was smiling.

Game Day

Getting to the Park

Des Moines is in south-central Iowa and accessible from the east or west via I–80 and from the north or south via I–35. Interstate 235 connects to both interstates and runs through the northern half of the city. Principal Park is on the south side of downtown. To reach the ballpark, take the Third Street exit off I–235 and follow Third Street south through downtown. Turn left onto Line Drive, which leads right to the park. The I-Cubs provide free parking to Cubs Club members, leaving other folks to find spots in the privately operated lots nearby.

Inside the Park

The recent renovation added 1,082 new seats down the right field line and replaced all of the other seats in the ballpark with comfortable green stadium chairs. The work brought the stadium's capacity to 10,800. The I-Cubs attract more than 500,000 fans per season, or about 7,500 per game, so if you plan on visiting Des Moines during the summer months, you should consider ordering tickets in advance.

The seating bowl offers lettered sections below the midlevel walkway and numbered sections above the walkway. The lower seats begin at Section AA in the left field corner. Section A comes next, and then the sections follow the alphabet down the left field line to Section F at third base and Section M directly behind home plate. Along the right field line, Section T is at first base, Section V is where the infield dirt meets the outfield grass, and Section ZZ is tucked into the right field corner. The seats in Sections C through W sell as Club Boxes, while the outfield sections sell as Field Boxes.

The seats above the walkway are nicely elevated so that the pedestrian traffic does not detract from sight lines. Sections 1 through 3 are in left field foul territory, Section 4 is where the outfield grass and infield dirt meet behind third base, Section 10 is behind home plate, Section 16 is behind first base, and Section 19 is in deep right. The seats in Sections 4 through 16 around the infield sell as Reserved Grandstands, while the seats in the three outfield sections on either side sell as General Admission. These are all good seats. For the best view of the gold-domed capitol beyond the center field fence, aim for seats behind home plate. For the best view of Des Moines skyscrapers, aim for seats along the first baseline.

A multi-tiered group picnic area sits in deep left field foul territory on the second level. The Cub Club is in left field home run territory. Most of the forty-five skyboxes appear on a small second level at the back of the infield grandstand, while the rest are built into the Cub Club.

The concourse runs behind and beneath the seating bowl. Here fans find several different types of hot dogs and brats, as well as fried bologna sandwiches, tenderloin sandwiches, beef brisket, barbecue nachos, chili cheese fries, fresh fruit bowls, and Papa John's Pizza. Road-trippers from Chicago can drink Old Style beer, while those with finer palates find several other brews available. The Cub Club restaurant is open to members only during games, but it is open to the public for breakfast and lunch on weekdays from 7:00 A.M. until 2:00 P.M.

The Principal Park Experience

With a big goofy smile on his face and a blue I-Cubs jersey on his back, Cubbie Bear is as jovial a minor league mascot as you'll find. But beware, he stands nearly 7 feet tall, weighs close to 300 pounds . . . and he likes to give hugs . . . big bear hugs. Cubbie Bear also enjoys tossing peanuts into the crowd after the second inning, leading fans in the traditional singing of "Take Me Out to the Ball Game" during the seventh-inning stretch, and shining bald heads with towels.

On the Town

Des Moines is the largest city in the Hawk-eye State, with a population of nearly 200,000 people. While fans won't find the type of night-life in Des Moines that they find around the Cubs' big league park, there are several local establishments worth a visit in the Court Avenue District just north of the stadium.

On the way out of town, fans headed west . . . perhaps to the ballpark in Omaha . . . can stop by the small town of Van Meter to visit the hometown of Bob Feller. The **Bob Feller Museum** (310 Mill Street) contains many items donated from the Hall of Famer's own collection, as well as autographs and collectibles for sale. The museum is just 10 miles from Des Moines along I-80. It is open daily from 10:00 A.M. until 5:00 P.M.

Fans in search of an independent league side trip can follow I-35 North 300 miles from Des Moines to the Twin Cities of Minnesota. While the local big league team plays inside a sterile dome, the most famous indy team of them all, the American Association's Saint Paul Saints, plays at charming **Midway Stadium** (1771 Energy Park Drive, St. Paul). The crazy Goldklang Group owns the Saints, and without the constraints of a big league affiliate to appease, the genius of Mike Veeck shines the brightest. Bill Murray coaches third base, a potbellied pig waddles onto the field to deliver fresh baseballs to the umpires, and an elderly nun gives massages in the stands. And that's on a normal night!

SECTION 4

THE WEST

Colorado, New Mexico, Arizona, Utah, Nevada,
California, Oregon, Washington

SECURITY SERVICE FIELD
Colorado Springs Sky Sox

Class AAA, Pacific Coast League
(COLORADO ROCKIES)

Security Service Field
4385 Tutt Boulevard
Colorado Springs, Colorado
719–597–1449

Sixty-five miles south of Denver, the Colorado Rockies top farm club plays at a ballpark more altitudinous than any other professional yard in North America. While Coors Field is the loftiest big league park at nearly a mile above sea level, Security Service Field is higher still, perched at an elevation of 6,531 feet. In this thin mountainous air, Rockies pitching prospects face a cruel baptism by fire while the organization attempts to sort out who among them will have a chance to survive the unique pitching conditions at the stadium up the interstate in Denver. Though its power alleys measure a distant 395 feet from home plate, make no mistake, Security Service Field is every bit the home run hitter's paradise that Coors Field is. A comparison between the two parks stops there. While Colorado's big league facility offers a backdrop of the stunning if distant Rocky Mountain peaks, the state's Pacific Coast League ballpark features an outfield view of peaked roofs, belonging to the many identical houses in the development just beyond the outfield walls.

Known as Sky Sox Stadium from the time of its opening in 1988 until 2004, Security Service Field underwent a $6.5 million renovation prior to the 2005 season that enlarged what was then and still is the smallest seating bowl in Triple-A. The project increased the number of seats from 6,000 to 8,500—all of which appear around the infield. The renovation also outfitted the park with underground batting cages and pitching tunnels, an enlarged luxury suite level, a remodeled main entrance, and a new entry plaza. The Sky Sox privately funded the renovation, just as they had previously picked up the tab for the stadium's original $3.7 million price tag.

Even after this recent work, Security Service Field is a basic structure that is serviceable but without many of the frills that the newer parks provide. The seating bowl is uncovered, and the concession concourse is open to a view of the field on either side of the small press box atop the home plate grandstand. The small suite level covers the concourse between the dugouts. There is a large grass berm down the left field line behind the visitors bullpen. Meanwhile, across the diamond in right field foul territory, fans find a tiered picnic terrace and an eight-person hot tub. There is no seating in home run territory, just two levels of advertising and a left field scoreboard that is topped by a faux silhouette of the Rocky Mountains.

The Sky Sox entered the Pacific Coast League in 1988 as a Cleveland Indians affiliate, at the time adopting the moniker of the old Class A Western League team that played in Colorado Springs from 1950 through 1958. Colorado Springs was a Chicago White Sox outpost then, hence the Sox nickname. Baseball's long-awaited return to Colorado Springs came about when the Hawaii Islanders decided to relocate to the mainland. The franchise that played in the Land of Magnum from 1961 through 1987, traces its origins all the way to the founding of the Pacific Coast League. Prior to playing in Colorado Springs and Hawaii, the club played in Sacramento from 1903 through 1960.

When the Colorado Rockies entered the National League in 1993, Colorado Springs switched allegiances, beginning a relationship with the local big league team. But despite this exciting development, the local market has struggled to demonstrate that it deserves a Triple-A team. The Sky Sox draw only about 3,000 fans per game, and once the International League team in Ottawa moves to the States in 2008, Colorado Springs will be the weakest Triple-A market.

We'll have to stay tuned to see if an eventual reshuffling of the minor league deck brings a lower level of ball to Security Service Field. In the meantime the ballpark that has witnessed the emergence of sluggers like Albert Belle and Todd Helton will continue to offer up close and personal looks at players just a phone call . . . and hour's drive . . . from the major leagues.

Game Day

Getting to the Park

While the drive from Colorado Springs to Albuquerque—the next closest Pacific Coast League city—is scenic, it's also a haul of about 385 miles. Colorado Springs is close to Denver though, and it makes for an ideal side trip to a Coors Field adventure. Security Service Field is located east of downtown, near the intersection of Powers Boulevard and Barnes Road. From I–25 South, take the Woodmen Road exit (149) and turn left onto Woodmen, then right onto Powers, then left onto Barnes. From I–25 North, take I–25 to U.S. Highway 24 East, which turns into Fountain Boulevard and then turn left onto Powers and right onto Barnes. Parking costs $5.00 in the large lot west of the ballpark. Tailgating is allowed, but alcoholic beverages are prohibited, which some would say defeats the purpose of tailgating altogether.

Inside the Park

The seating bowl offers a 100 Level below a narrow walkway and a 200 Level above the walkway. The 100 Level seats sell as Lower Boxes, while the 200 Level contains Upper Reserved Seats and General Admission seats. Sections 100 and 200 are located near first base; Sections 109, 110, 206, and 207 are behind home plate; and Sections 119 and 213 are at first base. For a view of Pike's Peak, which rises behind the first base grandstand, shoot for a seat on the third base side. If you're going to a day game, wear plenty of sunscreen, as the sun's rays are particularly strong in the thin mountain air. If you're going to a night game, bring an extra layer of clothing, as it often gets chilly after sunset at this lofty elevation.

For concessions fans find the Hot Corner Grill located not at third base as its name would suggest, but on the concourse behind home plate. Also nearby is the Hall of Fame Bar & Grill on the other side of the main entrance. A Mexican stand sells tasty burritos and jalapeño poppers. The ballpark's Bar-S hot dogs cost just 25 cents on Sundays, with patrons limited to buying eight at a time. According to the Sky Sox, they sell about 15,000 dogs on a busy Sunday.

The Fox Den souvenir stand is to the right of the home plate entrance, while a Family Fun Park is behind the left field berm.

The Security Service Field Experience

The Colorado Springs mascot is a fox named "Sox," who has puffy white cheeks and a long brown nose.

Fireworks are a big part of the ballpark experience in Colorado Springs, as the team shoots them off to celebrate homers, which the Sky Sox usually hit in abundance.

Aside from the cheap dog special on Sunday, "Two for Tuesday" makes for a popular promotional night, as the Sky Sox charge just $2.00 apiece for parking, tickets, and beer.

On the Town

While Security Service Field is outside of downtown, **Harry's Sports Bar** (4767 North Carefree Circle) and a few other nearby pubs make for a decent pregame scene. There are also a couple of pizza joints in the ballpark neighborhood.

Colorado Springs sits just east of **Pike National Forest** where gorgeous natural rock formations abound. **Garden of the Gods Park** (1805 North 30th Street) is easy to reach from I–25 and well worth a visit. The park offers 8 miles of trails through a paradise of red rock that almost seems extraterrestrial. The garden is free and open daily from 5:00 A.M. until 11:00 P.M.

Colorado Springs is also home to the **World Figure Skating Hall of Fame** (20 First Street) and the **Pro-Rodeo Hall of Fame** (101 Pro Rodeo Drive). If there are two more disparate halls of excellence in any other U.S. city, I've yet to discover them.

For diehard Rockies fans, a drive 350 miles north to Casper, Wyoming, may be in order. The Equality State's only professional ballpark, **Mike Lansing Field** (Crossroads Park, North Poplar Street) serves as home to this short-season Pioneer League affiliate of the Rockies. The grandstands are simple and offer little to distinguish the park from your typical high school facility, but at least the home team's mascot is unique. Hobart is a purple platypus who reportedly emanated from the nearby Platte River.

ISOTOPES PARK

Albuquerque Isotopes

Class AAA, Pacific Coast League
(FLORIDA MARLINS)

Isotopes Park
1601 Avenida Cesar Chavez SE
Albuquerque, New Mexico
505–924–2255

Does art imitate life, or does life imitate art? This question has been pondered by many a philosopher, ad executive, and *American Idol* contestant throughout the years. Now base-ball fans get their chance to weigh in on the subject while rooting for Homer Simpson's favorite team at beautiful Isotopes Park. This southwestern ballpark was rechristened in 2003 following a $25 million renovation that transformed it from the aging Albuquerque Sports Stadium into one of the more aestheti-cally appealing ballparks in the Pacific Coast League.

The stadium's reopening coincided with the return of minor league ball to Albuquer-que after a two-year hiatus and brought a new moniker to the local nine. The Isotopes name was derived from a minor league team often depicted on the popular FOX-TV show *The Simpsons*.

Isotopes Park

Previously, Albuquerque's team had been known as the Dukes, owing to Albuquerque's nickname as the Duke City. The Dukes played in the Pacific Coast League from 1972 through 2000, and in the Texas League before that. But in 2001 they left town, heading for Portland, Oregon. Clearly a new ballpark was needed if the Duke City wanted to reclaim its place in the Pacific Coast League, so the local politicians got to work on the matter and a fierce debate was soon to follow regarding the best location for the proposed park. Some civic leaders wanted to build a brand new ballpark in the city's downtown, while others wanted to keep Albuquerque's hardball hub right in its current location, in the city's southeast quadrant beside the University of New Mexico. Eventually, a public vote determined Sports Stadium would receive an extensive makeover.

With the stadium project underway, an Albuquerque group purchased the Pacific Coast League's Calgary Cannons and announced it would be moving them to New Mexico. All that was left to do was find a name for the new team, and that's where the cartoon connection came into play. As viewers of The Simpsons will surely recall, Homer Simpson was his hometown team's biggest fan, even serving as the mascot of the Springfield Isotopes in one episode. Later in the series, when the Isotopes announced their plans to move to Albuquerque, Homer chained himself to part of the stadium and began a hunger strike that eventually prevented the team from leaving.

Back in the real world, Albuquerque's search for a catchy name for its new team culminated in the good-humored Albuquerque Baseball Group dubbing its club the Isotopes. "In bringing baseball back to Albuquerque, we wanted to bring something that was fun, that was playful," the group's president, Ken Young, explained at the time of the announcement. While most fans took to the name immediately,

Albuquerque's top elected official was not amused. Mayor Marin Chavez told reporters, "This isn't a second-rate city that should be taking our name from a cartoon show."

The mayor's objections aside, there's no disputing that the unique name, along with the unique ballpark Albuquerque built, has put Albuquerque back on the proverbial baseball map. The "Topes" have attracted more than 575,000 fans per season since opening Isotopes Park, and their merchandise continues to sell like hotcakes . . . or like donuts . . . as Homer Simpson might put it. And for those who agree with the mayor that its absurd for a minor league club to name itself after a cartoon team, well, Albuquerque is known for its contributions to the U.S. nuclear program and the nearby Sandia National Laboratories has a notorious nuclear waste dump, so the name makes some sense, even to those who don't watch FOX-TV.

When fans arrive at Isotopes Park, the first thing they encounter is a large baseball sculpture in the middle of a wide cement walkway that runs from the parking lot to the main entrance. The ballpark exterior projects an artsy southwestern flair, highlighted by a four-story tower that features windows and colorful tiles that light up at night. The tiles take on a variety of earth tones, like olive green, orange, and pale yellow. At the top of the tower, funky orange-and-yellow letters display the stadium's name, while a cutout sign offers the team logo: an A with a baseball whizzing around it like an atom with an electron in orbit. To the left and right of the tower, the façade offers earthy red, brown, and cream adobe.

Fans enter the stadium and spill onto a rotunda on the first base side where mounted high above ground level huge cutouts of old-time baseballers are caught in the middle of their throwing and catching motions. The entryway leads to the open concourse that runs atop the last row of first level seats. This lower seating bowl extends out to the foul poles, while second-level seats appear in deep right field and left field. Uniquely, there are three levels of luxury seating locations around the infield, as rather than constructing one long suite level that extends well down the baselines as at virtually every other minor league park, Albuquerque decided to stack its posh seats on top of one another between home plate and the corner bases. So there are actually four levels of infield seats at Isotopes Park—the lower bowl, then a club level, and then two levels of indoor/outdoor luxury suites. The press box is located on the top level in the middle of the uppermost suites.

Isotopes Park sits at an altitude of 5,300 feet above sea level, and coupled with the hot, dry air in Albuquerque, the fly balls hit there really fly. Accordingly, the field is enormous, measuring 360 feet down the left field line, 340 feet down the right field line, 428 feet to the deepest points in right-center and left-center, and 410 feet to straightaway center. A 120-foot-long, 4-foot-high hill rises within the field of play in center, similar to the one in the outfield at Minute Maid Park in Houston. At the top of the hill, the outfield wall makes a big bubble, protruding toward home plate and accounting for the unusual field dimensions already cited. Behind the fence a darkly mulched garden serves as the batter's eye. Beyond the fences the outfield view showcases the Sandia Mountains east of the city. The Sandias get their name from the Spanish word for watermelon, as they glow a rich red color at sunset.

The Isotopes, who have been a Florida Marlins farm club since their inception, are one of the best draws in the Pacific Coast League, usually finishing behind only Sacramento, Round Rock, and Memphis in the sixteen-team circuit's attendance rankings. The Topes average more than 8,000 fans per game and

regularly top the 10,000 mark during the summer. In 2006 they established a new record for the largest crowd ever to watch a professional baseball game in Albuquerque when 15,020 fans turned out on July 3, to watch them play the Memphis Redbirds and to see a postgame fireworks show.

Albuquerque's minor league history has actually spanned the life of three ballparks. The local nine originally played at Rio Grand Park, located near the current site of the Rio Grand Zoo. Later renamed Tingley Field, the yard featured a telephone pole in the field of play in shallow left. It was home to the Class D Texas League's Albuquerque Cardinals from 1937 through 1941, to the Class D West Texas-New Mexico League's Dukes in 1942, to the Class A Western League's Dukes from 1956 through 1958, and to the Texas League's Dukes from 1963 through 1969. With the construction of Albuquerque Sports Stadium in 1969, the Dukes left the old yard, and in 1972 they joined the Pacific Coast League. Albuquerque's first Triple-A season was spent as a Dodgers affiliate, and it was a season to remember as a young skipper named Tommy Lasorda guided the team to a 92–56 record and the first of eight league championships Albuquerque has won.

In addition to hosting the Isotopes, Isotopes Park is also the home of the University of New Mexico baseball team.

Game Day

Getting to the Park

Albuquerque makes for a midway stop between visits to the big league stadiums in Denver and Phoenix. The city is located at the junction of I–25, which runs north to south, and I–40, which runs east to west. The ballpark is in the southeastern part of town, just east of I–25. From I–25, take the exit for Avenida Cesar Chavez East and the ballpark will appear at the intersection of University Boulevard. From I–40 take the exit for University Boulevard South. Parking is free on the campus of the adjoining University of New Mexico.

Inside the Park

Isotopes Park offers 11,075 seats, all of which are comfortable green stadium chairs. There is room for another 4,000 fans or so on the outfield berm. The lower bowl offers Box Seats around the infield, with Sections 101 and 102 behind home plate, the even-numbered sections continuing to Section 116 just past first base, and the odd-numbered sections continuing to Section 115 just past third. The first level also offers Reserved Seats along the outfield foul lines. The Club Seats are on the second level around the infield, while there are three sections of second-level seats in deep right field and three in shallow to medium left that sell as Reserved Seats. The Club Seats are not connected to the Reserved Seats on a continuous deck but sit in separate structures that hang out over the first-level concourse and the back rows of seats. Interestingly, the stairways from the concourse to the second level extend out over the seats in the lower bowl.

The concession highlights include the green chili cheeseburger, and other southwestern specialties like burritos, churros, tacos, barbecue nachos, and blooming onions with chipolte dipping sauce. The beer of choice among Topes fans is the locally brewed Isotopes Ale.

The Isotopes Park Experience

In a perfect world there would be Duff Beer at the concession stands and the mascot would be "Dancing Homer." But alas, lawsuits would be sure to follow, so the locals must settle for the Isotopes Ale and a furry mascot named "Orbit," who looks more like a big orange teddy bear than a subatomic particle. Then again, the microscope in my tenth-grade science lab at Shepherd Hill Regional High School in Dudley, Massachusetts, wasn't strong enough to let us look at a subatomic particles, so what do I know?

Here's a ballpark effect you've likely never seen before and likely never will. In a nod to Albuquerque baseball tradition, Isotopes Park was originally outfitted with a drive-in viewing deck high above the berm in right field where fans would be able to pull up in their cars and watch the game. A similar viewing location had existed for years on the ballpark grounds at Albuquerque Sports Stadium. Due to fears that the area would be difficult to police and that patrons would suddenly turn their headlights on or off and interfere with play, the drive-in deck never opened at the remodeled ballpark, however. The only other professional baseball park I can think of that had drive-in viewing spots was Sun City Stadium. The Cactus League facility of the Milwaukee Brewers from 1973 through 1985, Sun City Stadium was built in the middle of an Arizona retirement community designed by former Yankee owner Del Webb. It offered special parking spaces on its wide right field concourse where old timers could pull up in their golf carts and watch the ballgame.

On the Town

Historic Route 66 and the Rio Grand River both pass through Albuquerque, a hip city of nearly 450,000 people. If you like Mexican food, you'll feel like you've arrived in heaven when your road-trip car sputters into town. You really can't travel 3 blocks in Albuquerque without running into a fast-food or full-service Mexican eatery. After the game follow University Boulevard north from the ballpark and within a mile you'll run into Route 66/Central Avenue, where plenty of clubs and restaurants stay open late and offer outdoor seating on warm summer nights.

TUCSON ELECTRIC PARK

Tucson Sidewinders

Class AAA, Pacific Coast League
(ARIZONA DIAMONDBACKS)

Tucson Electric Park
2500 East Ajo Way
Tucson, Arizona
520–434–1021

When the Arizona Diamondbacks joined the National League as an expansion team in 1998, the Pacific Coast League's Phoenix Firebirds were forced to vacate their nest in the Phoenix suburb of Scottsdale and to relocate to Fresno, California. That gave the big league team exclusive access to the Phoenix market and left Tucson, where Pacific Coast League baseball has been played since 1969, as the only high-level minor league town in the state. Further sweetening the deal, the Tucson club entered into a new player development contract with the hometown Diamondbacks in 1998, changing its name from the Toros to the Sidewinders and opening a gorgeous new ballpark that offers striking views of the Santa Catalina Mountains. Toss in a tasty Mexican stand at the ballpark and some fresh-popped kettle corn, and you've got all the ingredients for a minor league success story. Right? Well, not exactly. Despite all of the check marks in its favor, Tucson Electric Park barely averages 4,000 fans per game, a paltry figure by Triple-A standards. Unfortunately, it seems the local fans prefer watching big league ball at the air-conditioned stadium in Phoenix or on TV in the air-conditioned comfort of their homes to sitting outside in the Arizona heat.

Another factor for the low attendance in Tucson may be the lingering discontent among Pima County taxpayers stemming from the stadium's construction details. Many local residents feel like the Diamondbacks and Chicago White Sox—who share Tucson Electric Park during spring training—took advantage of the local government. At the time the stadium deal came together in 1996, the Pima County Board of Supervisors agreed to finance construction of the $35 million stadium and adjoining training complex and to allow the two major league teams to use the facilities each spring virtually rent free.

In 1997 the county mortgaged the county jail to fund the early stages of the project, while three different tourist taxes—hotel, car rental, and RV parking—were imposed to help cover the additional construction costs. By the time the county has fully paid off the stadium—two years after the Cactus League leases with the Diamondbacks and White Sox expire in 2014—the county will have paid nearly $47 million for the ballpark with interest.

In the meantime the county allows the Diamondbacks and White Sox to split the $2 million that Tucson Electric Company agreed to pay over ten years for the naming rights to the stadium. And the county gives the major league teams 80 percent of the spring training ticket and parking revenues, as opposed to the county's 20 percent take, while the county bears the full cost of staffing the stadium and parking lot. The big league teams also receive 100 percent of the broadcast revenue and 100 percent of the profits from hard concession items like T-shirts and hats.

The small consolation for local taxpayers is that during the regular season the county receives all of the proceeds from food and beverage sales during Sidewinders games. The problem is that the ballpark is packed during spring training, then sits two-thirds empty during the minor league season. Hosting two Cactus League teams during the month of March, Tucson Electric Park attracts as many fans as it does during the five-month minor league season.

While its inception may have represented a rather obvious case of corporate welfare, Tucson Electric Park's construction was necessary for the survival of spring training baseball in the Tucson market. Without the new stadium and without the addition of two new Cactus League teams to Tucson, it seems unlikely the Colorado Rockies, who play their spring games across town at Hi Corbett Field, would have stuck around. In the years before Tucson Electric Park opened, many players had complained about the two-hour bus trips back and forth to Phoenix. Now, at least a couple of days a week, the three Tucson teams can square off against each other, limiting travel to just a few miles.

Tucson Electric Park is conceptually similar to Maryvale Baseball Park, the spring home of the Milwaukee Brewers that also opened in 1998, and Surprise Stadium, the spring home of the Texas Rangers and Kansas City Royals that opened in 2003. All three stadiums feature playing fields and seating bowls sunken below street level, expansive seating berms across the outfield, and open concourses that allow fans to walk laps around the entire stadium.

The ballpark is located within the 158-acre Kino Veterans Memorial Sports Complex beside the Kino Community Hospital and Davis-Monthan Air Force Base. In addition to the main stadium, the sports complex includes six practice fields for the White Sox on the stadium-side of Ajo Way and six fields for the Diamondbacks across the street. There is a clubhouse building for the White Sox, one for the Diamondbacks, and one for the Sidewinders. Both big league teams enjoy seven batting cages and ten practice pitching mounds. The White Sox have one practice infield, while the Diamondbacks have two. The complex also includes a community recreation center, youth fields, walking trails,

picnic areas, and a memorial to Tucson area war veterans. A pedestrian bridge decorated to look like a rattlesnake spans Ajo Way, connecting the two campuses of the complex.

Tucson's Pacific Coast League team enjoyed a long history at Hi Corbett Field before moving 5 miles to its new digs in 1998. Between 1968 and 1997, the Toros were affiliated at different times with the White Sox, A's, Rangers, Astros, and Brewers. During those years such future big league stars as Phil Garner, Johnny Ray, Danny Heep, and Glen Davis played in the Old Pueblo. The 1998 season was chaotic, as well as exciting, for the newly christened Sidewinders and the fans who turned out at their new ballpark. Owing largely to the fact that the Diamondbacks didn't have a Double-A affiliate established ahead of time to feed them players, the Sidewinders made a record 132 transactions during the 144-game minor league season. Predictably, the team struggled to a 57–85 record.

Tucson's minor league history dates back to even before the inception of the Toros. In 1928 Randolph Municipal Baseball Park—as Hi Corbett Field was then known—hosted the Tucson Cowboys of the fledgling Arizona State League. After three seasons the league merged with the Texas League to form the Border Conference, and Tucson placed entrants in the new league throughout the next three decades. From 1937 through 1950, the team was known as the Lizards, then from 1951 through 1958, it was known as the Cowboys again. From 1959 through 1968, the city didn't field a team, then the Toros debuted in 1969.

Game Day

Getting to the Park

From Phoenix, take I–10 East to Tucson. Take the Ajo Way exit and follow Ajo Way east to the sports complex. There are nearly 4,000 parking spots behind the stadium and even more across the street at Veterans Memorial Park.

Inside the Park

The stadium offers 8,000 fixed seats on two levels and room for 4,000 fans on the outfield lawn. Generally speaking, the best "view seats" are in the top rows along the first baseline and behind home plate. From these areas the peaks of the Santa Catalinas beyond the left field fence are most visible.

The lower bowl offers twenty-two rows. The Field Level Infield Seats are located on the infield. Sections 113 and 114 are behind home plate, while Section 107 is even with first base and Section 120 is even with third. The Field Level Grandstand Seats are the three sections in right field—104 through 106—and the one section in left—121.

The Lower Bleachers are bleachers with backs that appear in three sections in deep right field—Sections 101 through 103—and two in left—Sections 122 and 123.

The Covered Mezzanine Seats are upstairs on either side of the press box and luxury boxes, appearing in four rows. Sections 201 through 204 are above the first baseline and Sections 205 through 208 are above the third baseline.

A Lawn ticket offers access to the small berm in left field foul territory and to the main lawn that extends across the entire outfield, interrupted briefly by the brick batter's eye above the fence in center. Mind you, this 40-foot-high brick wall is in play, so sluggers best not break into their home run trots too soon or they might find themselves being thrown out at second base.

The open concourse behind the last row of seats is nicely decorated with colorful works of art produced by area elementary and high school students, as well as by banners that feature tidbits of Tucson baseball history. As for concessions, the specialty offerings include tacos and burros, pulled pork, and kettle corn.

The Tucson Electric Park Experience

For kids the Sidewinders offer diamondback "rattlers" at the clubhouse store on the first base side of the concourse. These noisemakers are really loud and really annoying, so pack some extra Advil if you're bringing the kids to the game.

Tucson Electric Park offers a special deal every day of the week. On "Margaritaville Monday," fans enjoy two-for-the-price-of-one margaritas at the ballpark. On "Two Dollar Tuesday," fans pay just $2.00 each for tickets, draft beers, and certain food items. On Wednesday, the team hands out cash door prizes to lucky fans. On "Thirsty Thursday," fans pay just $1.00 for beer, lemonade, and soda. On Friday, the game is followed by a fireworks show. On Saturday, the first 2,000 fans to pass through the turnstiles receive a free souvenir. On Sunday, hot dogs cost $1.00.

On the Town

For a quick bite to eat and a few frosties before the game, head to **Home Plate Sports Pub** (4880 East 22nd), **Famous Sam's** (3933 East Pima), or **The Bull Pen** (4749 South 12th). As for Mexican cuisine, you really can't go wrong in this town. Compared to the Mexican you're used to eating back home . . . well, there's really no comparison.

A road trip to the Old Pueblo wouldn't be complete without stopping by **Hi Corbett Field** (3400 East Camino Campestre), just 5 miles south of Tucson Electric Park. It offers an elegant southwestern stucco façade and a regal Colorado Rockies clock on its decorative tower outside the ticket windows. At the time of its opening in 1928, "Randolph Municipal Baseball Park" was the only diamond in the state of Arizona to offer a grass infield. The other

Hi Corbett Field

fields in the state were "scratch" diamonds that consisted of gravel and hard-packed sand. Tucson welcomed Larry Doby's spring training Cleveland Indians to town in 1947, as the team sought a haven from the racism of the Deep South where most teams still trained. In 1951 Randolph Park was renamed Hi Corbett Field in honor of popular state senator Hiram Steven Corbett, a ninth-generation Tucsonian.

The **Saguaro National Park** offers hikers and sightseers two locations, one east of Tucson and one west of the city. The eastern portion of the park is larger and more spectacular, offering trails into the Rincon and Santa Catalina Mountains.

The border towns of Nogales, Arizona, and Nogales, Mexico, are known collectively as **Ambos Nogales**. The towns are 60 mile south of Tucson via Route 19. Visitors can park in Arizona and walk across the border to shop for bargains in Mexico.

FRANKLIN COVEY FIELD

Salt Lake Bees

Class AAA, Pacific Coast League
(LOS ANGELES ANGELS OF ANAHEIM)

Franklin Covey Field
West Temple and 13th Street South
Salt Lake City, Utah
801–325–2337

As I've mentioned in a few previous chapters, I'm a sucker for mountain views, and for that reason I highly recommend a visit to Franklin Covey Field. Although Utah may be an out of the way destination on your tour of the minors, the spectacular outfield views of the Wasatch Mountains make a trip to the state's only full-season minor league park worth the extra time and effort. The mountains, which are still capped with snow in the early months of the season, loom seemingly just beyond the outfield walls. When the sun reflects off the peaks at twilight during the early innings of an evening game, there is no more gorgeous site in all of baseball.

When Franklin Covey Field opened in 1994, it returned Pacific Coast League baseball to Salt Lake City for the first time since the Salt Lake Gulls, a Mariners affiliate, moved to Calgary following the 1984 season. Prior to the new park's construction, the Salt Lake Trappers of the short-season Pioneer League had made Salt Lake City their home.

Franklin Covey Field was designed by the ballpark savants at HOK and built on the site of Derk's Field, Salt Lake City's previous minor league yard. The construction cost of $22 million was paid in full by the city. On reentering the PCL, Salt Lake City was affiliated with the Minnesota Twins and its team was known as

the "Buzz," a nickname that paid tribute to Utah's Beehive State nickname as well as to team owner Joe Buzas, who moved the franchise to Utah from Portland, Oregon. The Buzz changed its moniker to the "Stingers" in 2001, though, and then to the "Bees" in 2005. The latest nickname is a nod to Salt Lake City's original Pacific Coast League franchise, which was known as the Bees from 1915 through 1925, before moving to Los Angeles to become the Hollywood Stars. As for Buzas, he has since passed away, and Larry Miller, who also owns the Utah Jazz, now owns the Bees.

Like most recent HOK creations, Franklin Covey Field offers a brick exterior. Two blocky towers flank the main entrance behind home plate and similar towers stand outside the stadium down either baseline. The ballpark has an open concourse that circles the entire field and family-friendly berms in home run territory. The views from both the lower and upper seating bowls are unobstructed and excellent, while the luxury boxes are tucked beneath the larger-than-usual roof atop the upper-level seats. For left-handed pull hitters especially, this is a home run hitter's paradise. The field is as altitudinous as it is scenic at 4,229 feet above sea level, and the Bees don't store their balls in a humidor like the Colorado Rockies do, so fly balls carry quite well. The outfield fence measures 345 feet down the left field line, 385 to left-center, 420 to center, 375 to right-center, and just 315 down the right field line. The cutout of the infield dirt is unique in that it isn't rounded where it meets the outfield grass but rather extends straight toward second base from either foul line, running parallel to the middle baselines. This is a unique touch that makes the infield seem even more like a diamond than usual.

After future stars like Torii Hunter and David Ortiz played for Salt Lake during its time as a Twins affiliate, the franchise signed a player development contract with the Anaheim Angels in 2001. This renewed an old relationship between the two cities, as Salt Lake City was an Anaheim outpost from 1971 through 1981. The recent connection has suited both cities well, as evidenced by the 2005 American League Championship Series, which featured no less than fourteen former Salt Lake players. Among the Salt Lake alumni representing the Angels were Jeff DaVanon, Brendan Donnelly, Darin Erstad, Chone Figgins, Kevin Gregg, Adam Kennedy, John Lackey, Bengie and José Molina, Francisco Rodríguez, and Ervin Santana. White Sox closer Bobby Jenks, himself a Salt Lake City alumnus, didn't play in the series, but he got his chance to shine in the World Series, notching two saves, including the Game Four clincher against the Astros. Jenks signed with the White Sox as a minor league free agent after posting an 8.76 ERA for Salt Lake in 2004.

In addition to hosting the Bees, Franklin Covey Field is the home of the University of Utah baseball team.

Game Day

Getting to the Park

Salt Lake City is in north-central Utah, more than 400 miles from the Bees closest Pacific Coast League rivals, the Las Vegas 51s. Franklin Covey Field is south of Salt Lake City's downtown business district. From I–15 North, take exit 309 and turn right onto 1300 South. From I–15 South, take exit 309 and turn left at the end of the ramp. Follow 1300 South to the intersection of West Temple. The ballpark will be on the right, and the stadium parking lot, which charges $5.00 per car, will be on the left. Another option for those staying at a hotel in town is to take the TRAX to Franklin Covey Field. The station at 1300 South is a block east of the ballpark.

Inside the Park

Evidently they were thinking big when they built Franklin Covey Field, because the stadium can seat 13,000 people in its two large decks and another 2,500 on its outfield lawns. With a seating capacity of 15,500, Salt Lake City's ballpark is the third-largest facility in the sixteen-team Pacific Coast League, trailing only the behemoths in Omaha and Portland. Unfortunately, they don't really need so many seats in Salt Lake City, where the Bees attract average crowds of about 6,500 fans. Even in the franchise's best year—its debut season of 1994 when it drew more than 700,000 fans—Franklin Covey Field was only filled to about two-thirds capacity. So don't feel like you need to order tickets in advance and don't be surprised to find plenty of empty green seats when you arrive to watch the Bees play.

The lower deck continues all the way into the outfield corners, while the spacious upper deck ends a couple of sections sooner. All of the seats are comfortable green stadium chairs. The plum seats on the first level are quite pricey, as the Babe Ruth Diamond Seats in the first few rows of the five sections between the dugouts—Sections 11 through 15—cost $20. The remaining rows in these sections sell as Mickey Mantle Home Plate Seats. The next six sections along either baseline sell as Hank Aaron Super Seats. The four outfield-most sections on either side sell as Roberto Clemente Fun Seats. Upstairs, the five sections between the dugouts—Sections 107 through 111—sell as Hank Aaron Super Seats, while the rest are Roberto Clemente Fun Seats.

Though for the life of me I tried, I was unable to discover just what exactly is supposed to make the Roberto Clemente Seats more "fun" than the seats in the other sections of the park. Most of the Hank Aaron Seats offered "super" views of the field, so that nickname made a bit more sense to me. As a rule the infield sections, either downstairs or upstairs, are preferable to the ones on the outfield wings, and not just because they offer better views of the infield, but because they also allow for the breathtaking backdrop of the looming Wasatch Mountains to become a part of your ballpark experience. The mountains aren't as evident if you're sitting in the outfield with your back or side to them. For that reason I don't recommend buying a Ted Williams General Admission ticket and sitting on the outfield lawn.

The open concourse runs beneath the upper deck in foul territory, then continues across the outfield atop the berms. The concession stands offer grilled sausages, barbecued ribs, burritos, crepes, and Wienerschnitzel hot dogs that only cost $1.00 on Wednesdays. The crepes can be rolled with your choice of cinnamon, sugar, or other spices, as well as with various fruits and meats.

There are speed-pitch booths and batting cages deep in right field foul territory, while the play area behind the berm in left-center features a small motorized train.

The Franklin Covey Field Experience

Although Utah is the Beehive State, apparently it's not the queen bee anymore when it comes to buzz. The Salt Lake mascot used to be a humble bumblebee named "Buzz" until Georgia Tech brought a lawsuit against the Bees, claiming that the Yellow Jackets had the sole legal right to the "Buzz" mascot moniker. Give me a break. Why in the world would Georgia Tech possibly care that a minor league baseball team 3,000 miles away had a mascot with the same name as its own mascot? Were the Yellow Jackets noticing a decline in appearance fee revenues from Buzz in Atlanta because Georgians were confusing the Salt Lake City Buzz with the local one? It seems pretty unlikely. In any case the new bee in Salt Lake City, named "Bumble," is more fun than

the mascot in Atlanta will ever be. Bumble's four-wheeler buzzes around the field while he spreads goodwill and acts goofy.

But Bumble isn't the only ballpark entertainer in Salt Lake City. While you wouldn't necessarily expect a minor league team that plays in the prim and proper Land of Mormon to feature a cheerleading squad at the ballpark, Salt Lake's Honey Bees put their bodies into motion for the gawking fans at Franklin Covey Field. I guess we'll chalk this one up to Bees owner Larry Miller and the lessons he's learned while owning an NBA team. Way to go, Larry. According to the application form on the Bees Web site, the prerequisites for becoming a Honey Bee are that you must be at least eighteen years of age, have strong oral communication skills, have an understanding of baseball, be outgoing and energetic, and have an athletic physique. If you'd like to see these Honey Bees for yourself and can't wait until your visit to the ballpark in Utah, check out the many photos of the Honey Bees on the Salt Lake team's Web site. There you'll also find Q-and-A-style bios for each Honey Bee, including answers to such pertinent questions as which celebrity each Honey Bee would most like to spend the night with, what's their favorite season, what's their favorite hobby, what's their biggest fear, and what's their idea of a great weekend. The answers aren't terribly revealing, but they do bring to light the fact that a high percentage of Utah gals consider Matthew McConaughey a "hottie."

On the Town

Salt Lake City is Utah's capital and largest city with a population of about 180,000 people. Those looking for a bite to eat or for a brew in the ballpark neighborhood will find several local dives in the blocks north of Franklin Covey Field and several fast-food joints on West 13th

Street and South State Street. Keep in mind that there are more tourist-friendly parts of Salt Lake City than this neighborhood, and if your schedule allows, you should take some time to explore the scenic downtown of this city famous for its **Temple Square** and Mormon Tabernacle.

Franklin Covey Field sits just a few miles from the shores of the Great Salt Lake. The lake is the largest salt lake in the Western Hemisphere and is currently the thirty-third largest lake in the world. I say "currently" because the rankings fluctuate quite a bit as lakes lose and gain volume each year in response to global weather patterns. The Great Salt Lake was created during prehistoric times and used to be much larger. Today, it is fed by three major rivers but has no natural outlet. As a result it can only lose volume via evaporation, a process that removes moisture but leaves behind the salt. As such, the lake is too salty to sustain most types of marine life, save for tiny little brine shrimp or "sea monkeys" as we sometimes call them, and algae. The **Great Salt Lake**

State Park (I–80, exit 104) is 16 miles west of Salt Lake City. It is open year-round and offers swimming in the shallow salty water, boating, and picnicking. Just be sure to take a good long shower after going for that swim . . . unless you're part brine shrimp, of course. The **Antelope Island State Park** (I–15, exit 332), north of Salt Lake City, is also a popular tourist destination, especially for campers and wildlife buffs who visit to see the wild antelopes, bison, and other animals that live near the lake.

A trip through Utah also offers two short-season Pioneer League ballparks. The Ogden Raptors play 35 miles north of Salt Lake City at a tiny downtown ballpark named **Lindquist Field** (2330 Lincoln Avenue). Like Franklin Covey, Lindquist offers stunning views of the Wasatch Mountains. Meanwhile, 40 miles south of the capital in the Provo suburb of Orem, the Orem Owlz play on the campus of Utah Valley State College. The Owlz have been affiliated with the Angels since entering the Pioneer League in 2001. They opened the 4,000-seat **Home of the Owlz** (970 West University Parkway) in 2005.

CASHMAN FIELD

Las Vegas 51s

Class AAA, Pacific Coast League
(LOS ANGELES DODGERS)

Cashman Field
850 Las Vegas Boulevard North
Las Vegas, Nevada
702–386–7200

Over the last couple of years, Las Vegas has occasionally been mentioned as the next big league city, perhaps as soon as the Florida Marlins' lease runs out at Dolphins Stadium in 2010. Most prognosticators rate Sin City and San Antonio as the favorites for a relocated team, ahead of Portland, Oregon, and Monterrey, Mexico. This represents real progress for Las Vegas. Even if Marlins owner Jeffrey Loria eventually works out a deal to keep his team in south Florida, at least now Las Vegas is being considered a "potential," "future," "possible," "someday soon," big league city, whereas in the past its gambling interests made it a municipality non grata among major sports leagues.

The effort to bring a big league team to Las Vegas clearly hinges on whether the city and state government will finance the construction of a new ballpark. The city's current Triple-A stadium, Cashman Field, is not suitable for the big league product. In fact, as the ballpark enters its third decade, it's barely hanging on as a viable Pacific Coast League facility. Cashman Field is located on Las Vegas Boulevard, north of the famous Strip, in the middle of a run-down neighborhood that could use a shot of urban revitalization any day now . . . the kind of shot a major league ballpark would surely provide . . . or even a new minor league park.

Cashman Field is functional, but basic. Little effort has been made to dress up its concourses and walkways, and much of the seating comes in the form of bleachers. Instead of facing the glitzy neon lights of the downtown casinos, Cashman Field is oriented so that its sight lines showcase the serene mountain peaks outside the city.

The ballpark was built in 1982 on land donated by James "Big Jim" Cashman, who is considered one of Las Vegas's pioneers. The park was constructed as part of a fifty-acre, $26 million project that also included the adjacent convention center. The ballpark, which is owned by the Las Vegas Convention and Visitors Authority, succeeded immediately in luring the Spokane Indians to town in 1983. With the move the team was rechristened the Las Vegas Stars. Cashman Field opened its gates for the first time on April 1, 1983, for an exhibition game between the Seattle Mariners and San Diego Padres. After an overflow crowd of 13,878 fans turned out to watch the major league game, Triple-A baseball debuted nine days later before a crowd of 10,622.

Since its opening Cashman Field has been known as a hitter's paradise. Fly balls travel well in the thin desert air. To keep home run totals in check, the fence is 20-feet-high across the entire outfield. In center the big blue fence measures a distant 433 feet from home plate, but in the power alleys it measures just 364 feet, owing to the field's unique square contour. Home plate is at one corner of the square, the right field foul pole is at another corner, straightaway center is at another, and the left field foul pole is at another.

The Stars were a Padres affiliate from 1983 through 2000, during which time they won league titles in 1986 and 1988 and sent prospects like Roberto Alomar, Sandy Alomar Jr., Carlos Baerga, Kevin McReynolds, John Kruk, Wally Joyner, Benito Santiago, and Ozzie

Guillen to the big leagues. Padres star Tony Gwynn played a series at Cashman Field while on a rehabilitation assignment. In 2001 the team switched to its current affiliation with the Los Angeles Dodgers and changed its name to the Las Vegas 51s. The name pays tribute to the top-secret government base 120 miles northwest of Las Vegas known as "Area 51." This is the mysterious site you always see in those *Discovery Channel* UFO docudramas that detail the alien autopsies that allegedly took place back in the 1950s. As Fox Mulder would say, "The truth is out there." Or, maybe not. In any case the most successful member of the 51s to reach the major leagues so far is Dodgers closer Eric Gagne, who—with those funny goggles he wears—looks a little like an alien himself. The Dodgers have sent a number of big league stars to Cashman Field on rehab assignments, including Kevin Brown, Adrián Béltre, Paul Lo Duca, Hideo Nomo, Milton Bradley, Brad Penny, and Gagne, who returned to his old stomping grounds in 2005 before opting to have arm surgery.

As for the most memorable moments in Cashman Field history, the local fans still talk about the no-hitter that Tim Worrell pitched against the Phoenix Firebirds in 1992; about the 4-homer, 10-RBI game that Eddie Williams had against the Calgary Cannons in 1998; and about the no-hitter Lindsay Gulin threw against the Tacoma Rainiers in 2003.

In addition to housing the local minor league team, Cashman Field also hosts at least one spring training game per year. Often, these games involve the Dodgers, but not always. The Mariners and Cubs are regular returnees too. In 1993 a stadium-record 15,025 fans turned out to watch the Cubs and White Sox square off.

In 1996 the Oakland A's played their first six regular season home games at Cashman Field while the Coliseum in Oakland was being renovated to accommodate the return of the NFL's Raiders.

Cashman Field has also hosted several Triple-A all-star games and the Triple-A World Series. In 2000 it was the site of the "Big League Challenge," a charity home run hitting contest that was broadcast on ESPN. It was at this event, according to *Game of Shadows*, the tell-all book by Mark Fainaru-Wada and Lance Williams, that Barry Bonds gawked at Jose Canseco's physique and then decided to start injecting himself with Winstrol, Deca-Durabolin, and other hard-core steroids.

While an association—however tangential—with Bonds certainly won't help Las Vegas in its quest to secure a major league baseball team, here's betting that one of these days the Las Vegas Craps, Las Vegas Tricks, or maybe the Las Vegas Fredo's will be playing at a new ballpark near the Strip. In the meantime the 51s will continue to be the only show in town . . . well, the only baseball show.

Game Day

Getting to the Park

From I-15 South, take Route 95 East toward Las Vegas, then take the Las Vegas Boulevard exit and turn left. Follow Las Vegas Boulevard north for about ¼ mile and the ballpark will appear on the right. There are parking lots on three of the stadium's four sides, all of which charge $3.00 per car.

Inside the Park

Despite the fact that Las Vegas has a population of half a million, the 51s draw a relatively low—by Triple-A standards—total of about 4,800 fans per game. Maybe strippers and blackjack dealers don't like baseball? Certainly the tourists that flock to Las Vegas don't make their presence felt too strongly at the ballpark. I suppose most folks can watch a minor league game back home, so why spend three hours of potential casino time at the ballpark during their vacation? In any case tickets are always available at the box office on game day, except on July 3, when the traditional fireworks night packs the house. Because Ticketmaster handles the advance ticket sales, even those fans who like to plan ahead are better off waiting to get their tickets at the box office. Why pay a surcharge if you don't have to, right?

The low one-deck seating bowl stretches into medium-depth outfield foul territory on either side of the diamond, then small grass berms begin where the seats leave off and continue to the foul poles. The pedestrian concourse is located atop the seating bowl, and fans use narrow stairways between the sections to access their seats. There are five different ticket-pricing levels. The Dugout Seats are located in Sections 9 through 15 between the dugouts. The Field Seats are the first six rows in all of the other infield sections. The Plaza Seats are the grandstand seats between the dugouts and are the best bet for day games, owing to their presence in the shade of the overhanging press box roof. The Reserved Seats are on the grandstand level down the base lines, which are actually bleachers with backs. The General Admission Seats are the outfield-most bleacher sections along either foul line. The field level Party Zone in left can accommodate 150 people. There are no luxury boxes.

The concession stands offer a view of the game for those waiting in line, and access to ballpark basics and Budweiser products.

The Cashman Field Experience

Keep your eyes peeled for B-level celebrities at the ballpark in Las Vegas, along the lines of Robert Goulet, Wayne Newton, and Celine Dion, who sometimes turn out at the game. Additionally, the team sometimes offers pre-game concerts by way-past-their-prime acts like the Beach Boys, Three Dog Night, and the Doobie Brothers.

The team mascot is Cosmo, an alien from planet Koufaxia, who is pretty friendly as far as aliens go. He told me that his mission is to serve man.

On the Town

Obviously, Las Vegas offers more dining, gaming, and theater highlights than I could possibly do justice to in the limited page space available here, so I'll just offer a couple of baseball-related visiting and gaming suggestions, and then leave it up to you to explore the rest of the Strip on your own. **The Vegas Club** (18 East Fremont Street) offers a façade designed to look like Ebbets Field, a casino modeled after Wrigley Field, and a Dugout Restaurant. Most of its memorabilia is Dodgers-related. For those looking to bet on major league baseball during your trip to Las Vegas, I recommend the Vegas Club, first and foremost, since it offers dime lines up to $2.00. As for other casinos, the **Rio** breaks from a dime line to 15 cents at exactly minus 180—that is, minus 170/plus 160, but minus 180/plus 165— which is still decent. The Coast Resort–owned casinos (**Barbary Coast, Gold Coast, Orleans, Suncoast, Plaza**) offer extra credits for hanging lines at night for the next-day's games. Have fun, and remember, what happens in Vegas stays in Vegas, unless she's got a ring on her finger when you wake up beside her the next morning, in which case she's probably going home with you.

MAVERICKS STADIUM
High Desert Mavericks

Class A, California League
(SEATTLE MARINERS)

Mavericks Stadium
12000 Stadium Way
Adelanto, California
760–246–6287

Amidst a vast wasteland of sand, tumbleweed, desert sage, and Joshua trees, Mavericks Stadium rises out of the Mojave Desert like a mirage. Providing a ballpark experience unlike any other in minor league baseball, the home field of the High Desert Mavericks treats fans to majestic Mojave sunsets, mountain views, and a stark otherworldly environment that is as strange as it is beautiful.

Daytime highs in this part of California average more than ninety degrees Fahrenheit in June, July, and August, but at night the temperatures usually settle into the sixties. The ballpark was wisely designed to allow for the desert winds to pass right through it, which goes a long way toward cooling it off at night. The simple, open-air concept sinks the field below street level, places the concourse above the seating bowl, and offers no exterior façade to speak of, other than the small brick structures that house the restrooms, concession stands, and press box. The ballpark awning covers the entire concourse and is suspended by slender pillars that don't obstruct views or block airflow.

Thanks to the dry desert air and an altitude half a mile above sea level, Mavericks Stadium has earned a reputation as a hitter's park. The outfield foul poles measure 340 feet from home plate, and the green batter's eye in center field measures 401 feet from the plate. Balls soar out of the park at record numbers. A large scoreboard rises above the fence in left-center, while nearby mountain peaks rise a few miles away in right. The views beyond the left field and center field walls are dominated by the expanse of heavy-duty utility lines and their support stanchions.

The team that became the High Desert Mavericks in 1991 had previously played in Riverside, California, where it was known as the "Red Wave." The team migrated after the city of Adelanto spent $6.5 million to build it a new stadium and after baseball's Brett brothers—George, Bobby and John—who own the team, agreed to the move. The Mavericks set a California League attendance record in their inaugural season, averaging nearly 3,000 fans a game and drawing more than 200,000 fans in 1991. That record has since been broken by several California League teams, and attendance in Adelanto has since sagged to about 1,500 fans per game.

Although the Mavericks enjoyed some early successes on the field, winning California League championships in 1991, 1993, and 1997, the team burned through a host of major league affiliations in short order. The team began as a San Diego Padres farm club before signing on with the Florida Marlins in 1993, playing as an unaffiliated co-op team in 1994, signing with the Baltimore Orioles in 1995, the Arizona Diamondbacks in 1997, the Milwaukee Brewers in 2001, and the Kansas City Royals in 2005. In 2007, the team switched to a PDC with the Seattle Mariners. Perhaps due to this instability, the Mavericks and their fans have suffered through more than their share of miserable seasons. High Desert has played five 140-game campaigns in which it failed to muster as many as 50 wins, including 1994 (45–91), 1995 (46–94), 2000 (48–92), 2003 (42–98), and 2004 (49-91).

In 2005 the Mavericks won the California League's South Division in dramatic fashion, beating Lancaster 11–10 on the final day of the regular season to finish with a record of 75–65. The JetHawks finished with an identical record, but with their win on the last day of the season, the Mavericks clinched the tie-breaker, with a better head-to-head record. In the deciding game High Desert set a new California League single-season home run record when Bernard Stephens blasted a three-run shot in the fifth inning. It was the 201st dinger of the season for the Mavericks. The previous record of 200 homers had been set by Visalia in 1971. In any case Lancaster avenged its season-ending loss to High Desert by besting the Mavericks two games to one in the first round of the 2005 California League playoffs.

High Desert's alumni list includes Rod Barajas, Alex Cintrón, Carl Everett, J. J. Hardy, Travis Lee, Matt Mieske, Vicente Padilla, Brad Penny, Duaner Sanchez and Junior Spivey.

Game Day

Getting to the Park

The town of Adelanto is 75 miles northwest of Los Angeles and 30 miles north of San Bernardino, even though it seems like it should be about 500 miles from both towns owing to its stark desert atmosphere. Mavericks Stadium is conveniently located along U.S. Highway 395. From Los Angeles, take I–10, to I–15 North, to U.S. Highway 395 North. Follow US 395 for about 13 miles, then take the Adelanto Road exit and the stadium will appear immediately on your left. Parking is free at the stadium.

Inside the Park

This tiny ballpark offers just 3,808 fixed seats in a low seating bowl that extends only to the corner bases on either side of the diamond. There is also a tiered bar area down the left field line and a grass seating berm down the right field line that only opens on fireworks nights or when a larger than–usual-crowd is expected.

Section 100 is behind home plate, the even-numbered sections continue down the first baseline to Section 118, and the odd-numbered sections continue down the third baseline to Section 119. The first ten rows house the red Lower Box Seats, and the back eight rows house the blue Upper Box Seats. All of the seats offer unobstructed views of the field. There is no intermediary walkway between these two seating levels, only the main concourse, atop the Upper Boxes, and stairways between the different sections.

The stadium offers six luxury boxes—three behind the last row of Upper Boxes behind the Maverick third base dugout and three behind the seats behind the visitors dugout. These are about as unluxurious as luxury boxes can be. They are nothing more than open-air brick cubbies on the concourse.

As for concessions fans find chicken sandwiches, hot dogs, and corn dogs at the stands on the concourse, as well as cookies, ice-cream sandwiches, and frozen lemonade cups. Sierra Nevada is the specialty beer on tap.

The Mavericks Stadium Experience

The local mascot is Wooly Bully, an oversized bull who wears a blue cowboy hat and red Mavericks jersey. I pity the fool who has to wear this thick and furry suit all game long when the temperature is hovering around 100 degrees. They must have to hook the guy up to an IV at least a couple of times a game to keep his electrolytes up.

The Mavericks make a real effort to create a family-friendly environment. When the players are introduced at the start of each game, they bring young fans with them out to their position, which is a really nice touch that I have seen at just a few other ballparks around the country.

Regular theme nights include "Family Feast Fridays," when hot dogs and sodas are only $1.00, and "Thirsty Thursdays," when twelve-ounce drafts of Budweiser, Miller, and Coors products are only $1.00. The team also offers a number of fireworks nights throughout the season.

On the Town

Adelanto is a small city, even by minor league standards, that has a population of about 20,000 people. Visitors may choose to spend the night in Victorville, which is a larger city located about 7 miles to the southeast.

For those who find that the Mexican food at the ballpark has awoken their appetites for all things hot and spicy, there are several authentic Mexican joints in this neck of the woods. North of the ballpark along U.S. Highway 395, fans find **Taqueria Las Amigas** (11416 Crippen Avenue) and **La Botana** (11720 Bartlett Avenue); south of the park they find **Fiesta Mexican** (13354 Winter Park Street, Victorville).

Travelers looking to get better acquainted with the Mojave Desert can visit the **El Mirage Dry Lake**, 13 miles northwest of Adelanto. This massive dry lakebed is a popular spot for auto racers, land sailors, model aircraft fliers, amateur rocket launchers, lizard harvesters, sun worshippers, and artists. I recommend a visit at sunset.

Those in search of a day trip or overnight adventure in the desert can follow I–15 north-east to the **Mohave National Preserve**. This massive national park offers mountainous hiking trails and camping. For campers **Hole-in-the-Wall Campground** offers thirty-five sites surrounded by volcanic rock walls, and **Mid Hills Campground** offers twenty-six sites among pinyon pines and juniper trees.

Just be sure to bring lots of water with you when you set out on any desert expedition. You'll be surprised by how much you need to drink when the mercury is over the one-hundred-degree mark, and you never know when your car might break down or when some other unforeseen complication—like a rattlesnake bite, rock slide, or sandstorm—will extend your visit.

SAM LYNN BALLPARK
Bakersfield Blaze

Class A, California League
(TEXAS RANGERS)

Sam Lynn Ballpark
4009 Chester Avenue
Bakersfield, California
661–716–4487

Okay, baseball fans, here's a new one for you. You're surely well acquainted with the ubiquitous rain delays and lightning delays that interrupt the National Pastime from time to time. And chances are you've experienced a few early season snow delays, a few mid-summer fog delays, and a few delays caused by ballpark power outages. Heck, I can remember a game in Texas that was halted due to a swarm of moths that attacked the players and a game in Baltimore that was postponed due to a chemical spill on the railroad tracks near the ballpark. And I remember Mike Hargrove, who during his playing days used to take so long to get into the batter's box that he earned the nickname "the Human Rain Delay." But how about a sun delay? Ever sat through one? Ever heard of one? Well, the baseball fans in Bakersfield, California, have. That's because historic Sam Lynn Ballpark was build backward, with its home plate facing west instead of east. As a result the setting sun descends directly behind the pitcher. Through the years this all-too-common phenomenon has caused many a California League batter to step out of the batter's box and ask the home plate ump for a time, while the fans and players wait for the blinding sun to sink below the horizon. Today, depending on the time of year, the Bakersfield Blaze starts its home games at 7:30

or 8:00 P.M., or sometimes even a little later, to wait for the sun to set so that baseball can be played. The team has also installed a 120-foot-long sun shield behind the ballpark fence in center and left-center field to help reduce the glare. And local fans have learned to bring their sunglasses, eye black, and visors to the ballpark.

I know what you're probably thinking. Whoever the hell Sam Lynn was, I hope he lost his job over this monumental ballpark design failure. Right? Well, I'll fill you in on exactly who Sam Lynn was in a minute, but no, he can't really be blamed for the ballpark's unorthodox orientation. That's because Sam Lynn Ballpark was built in 1940, at a time when night baseball was not yet in vogue. Accustomed to start times in the middle of the afternoon, Sam Lynn and his friends had no reason to worry about the wicked glare that would besiege the batter's box at 7:00 or 8:00 at night. Of course "the light fad" caught on during the ensuing decade, so that all of the major league teams except for the Chicago Cubs had installed stadium lights by 1948. Minor league teams gradually followed suit, including the Bakersfield club, which quickly realized the havoc the sun would wreak on 7:00 P.M. starts. True, Bakersfield's ballpark pioneer Sam Lynn didn't look too far into the future when he envisioned a new ballpark in his city, but the ballpark he built didn't pose any sun problem at the time of its opening.

Lynn was the owner of a Coca-Cola bottling plant in Bakersfield during the 1930s, and during that time he sponsored the semipro Bakersfield Coca-Colas. In the late 1930s he teamed with former San Francisco Seals president Charlie Graham to envision and found the Class C California League. After overseeing the construction of a new ballpark in Bakersfield, and making sure the city would be a charter member of the new league in

1941, Lynn passed away just a few months before the Bakersfield Badgers took the field for the first time. The local fans who appreciated Lynn's efforts to bring minor league ball to town named the stadium in his honor.

The other charter members of the California League, incidentally, were the Anaheim Aces, Fresno Cardinals, Merced Bears, Riverside Reds, San Bernardino Stars, Santa Barbara Saints, and Stockton Fliers. Since those early days Bakersfield has consistently fielded a team with just a few interruptions (1943–45, 1976–77, and 1980–81). Through the decades the local team has been known by many names and has enjoyed affiliations with nine different big league organizations. The team became the Blaze in 1995 and has been a Texas Rangers affiliate since 2005. Before that Bakersfield was most recently affiliated with the Tampa Bay Devil Rays, San Francisco Giants, and Los Angeles Dodgers.

The ballpark's original wooden grandstand stood until 1993 when a renovation replaced it with a concrete seating bowl. Aside from the gigantic sunscreen in left-center and the sun-blocking trees strategically placed on either side of it, the ballpark's most distinguishing feature is its cozy outfield dimensions. The distance from home plate to dead center is just 354 feet, making this the smallest professional ballpark in the country. As a result of the cozy confines, many Bakersfield players have padded their stats with inflated home run totals on their way to the big leagues. A pitcher's paradise, this is not.

Among the 220 players to wear a Bakersfield uniform before making it to the show are a quintet of Dodgers who won the National League Rookie of the Year awards between 1992 and 1996: Eric Karros, Mike Piazza, Raul Mondesi, Hideo Nomo, and Todd Hollandsworth. Hall of Fame pitcher Don Drysdale cut his teeth in Bakersfield, as did three-time

National League All-Star Rick Sutcliffe, and three-time Cy Young Award winner Pedro Martínez. Today, Sam Lynn Ballpark honors these players and others with large paintings high above the concourse along the back of the grandstand.

As for memorable moments in the park's recent history, on July 3, 1995, the Blaze set a new California League single-game attendance record, attracting 8,175 fans who turned out to watch the ballgame and then enjoy a fireworks show. In 2002 Devil Rays top draft pick Josh Hamilton hit an opposite field home run that the local fans still talk about. The blast shattered an auxiliary scoreboard behind the left field fence, showering the outfield grass with sparks just like Robert Redford's climatic home run in *The Natural*.

Game Day

Getting to the Park

Bakersfield is 70 miles south of Visalia, the next closest California League city, and 110 miles north of Los Angeles. From Los Angeles, take I–5 North to Route 99 North, then after entering Bakersfield take Business Route 99. Turn right onto Golden State Avenue, then enter the rotary and exit onto Chester Avenue. The ballpark will appear on your left. From Visalia, take Route 99 South to Bakersfield and then follow the directions above. Parking is free in the lot behind the stadium.

Inside the Park

Sam Lynn Ballpark can seat 3,500 fans, but its crowds are typically in the 1,500 range. The main seating bowl offers both stadium seats and bleachers around the infield, while a separate bank of bleachers sits in right field foul territory and a picnic area lies down the right field line. The Dugout Box Seats are located in the first few rows behind the plate and along the baselines where fans find comfortable bright blue stadium chairs. The same comfortable chairs fill the home plate grandstand above the interior walkway, selling as Box Seats. The sections behind the walkway on the first baseline are comfortable Reserved Seats, while behind the walkway on the third baseline are General Admission bleachers. The Hardball Cafe is a group area that angles back toward the infield in deep right.

There is no roof over any of the seats, just a small press box atop the home plate grandstand. The concession stands on the open-air concourse behind home plate and third base sell tri-tip sandwiches and delicious riblets.

The Sam Lynn Ballpark Experience

Fans who arrive early have the chance to take a few pregame swings at the Bakersfield Batting Range, located right beside the front entrance of the ballpark. Once the game begins, the Bakersfield experience is old-timey. The team doesn't go out of its way to inundate fans with noise and promotional hoopla.

Heater the Dragon is the local mascot. This green-and-yellow fellow stands 6 feet tall and wears bright red shoes. His favorite song is "Love Is Like a Baseball Game" by the Intruders, and his favorite movie is *Pete's Dragon*. Heater likes to challenge adult fans to tricycle races around the bases.

On the Town

Bakersfield is a rapidly growing city with a population of more than 400,000 people. The lively downtown entertainment district includes **Tailgater's Sports Bar and Grill** (900 Truxtun Avenue), **Sports and Spirits** (6633 Ming Avenue), and **Kosmos Sports Bar** (1623 19th Street). For country music fans, **Buck Owens' Crystal Palace Steakhouse** (2800 Buck Owens Boulevard) has been named the Country Music Association's nightclub of the year several times and was the spot where Garth Brooks proposed to Trisha Yearwood.

For outdoor enthusiasts the **Kern River Parkway** offers a walking/biking path that follows the Kern River for nearly 20 miles. The path begins at the California Living Museum northeast of downtown and ends near Cal State-Bakersfield southwest of downtown.

CHUKCHANSI PARK

Fresno Grizzlies

Class AAA, Pacific Coast League
(SAN FRANCISCO GIANTS)

Chukchansi Park
1800 Tulare Street
Fresno, California
559–320–4487

After a ninety-two-year hiatus, the Pacific Coast League finally returned to Fresno in 1998. And a sparkling new downtown ballpark was soon to follow. Grizzlies Stadium opened in 2002 and has treated fans to a terrific ballpark experience ever since. The facility was renamed Chukchansi Park in 2007, after the Grizzlies struck a 15-year $16-million naming rights agreement with a local casino.

Fresno's Pacific Coast League odyssey began in the league's fourth season when the Sacramento Solons moved to Fresno in 1906 and became the Fresno Raisin Eaters. The Raisin Eaters finished in last place that year, then they promptly packed up their bats and balls and headed back to Sacramento. More than nine decades would pass before the PCL would give Fresno a second chance, but minor league baseball found a steady following in Fresno through the years, most notably during the city's long run in the California League, which spanned from 1941 through 1988 and included long-standing relationships with two of the National League's more prestigious franchises: the St. Louis Cardinals (1941–56) and San Francisco Giants (1958–87).

The opportunity for Fresno to rejoin the Pacific Coast League arose when Phoenix was awarded one of the two major league expansion teams that would begin play in 1998. The impending arrival of a National League club in Phoenix meant that the Pacific Coast League team already in that city—the Phoenix Firebirds—had to relocate. Thus began a chain reaction that sent the Firebirds to Tucson, where they became the Tucson Sidewinders and displaced the incumbent Tucson Toros, who set their sights on Fresno, where they would become the Fresno Grizzlies.

The Grizzlies have been affiliated with the San Francisco Giants since their debut. They played their first four seasons at Beiden Field on the campus of Cal State-Fresno, before opening their new park on May 1, 2002. The $46-million city-owned facility was designed by the ballpark experts at HOK. Along with the adjacent Fulton Street pedestrian mall, the stadium is part of a larger plan to revitalize Fresno's Central Business District Loop.

As we've come to expect from HOK designs, this park offers an exterior that blends the better elements of the local landscape with the classic elements of old-time baseball parks. The result is a distinctly Californian façade that features tan cement, decorative green metal, and more than two dozen second-story arches that create large windows between the second and third seating decks inside.

Yes, you read that last sentence correctly. Chukchansi Park is that minor league anomaly that offers not one, not two, but three decks of seating. The lower bowl traces the foul lines and then continues a short distance into home run territory on both sides of the field. The second deck hangs down nice and low over the open concourse atop the seats on the first level. And a third level of luxury suites tops it all off, offering indoor and outdoor seating on either side of the press box. Remarkably, the stadium feels much cozier than this description makes it sound.

The second and third levels are J shaped. They extend just a little way past third base on the left field side but all the way into deep right field. Such a design will no doubt make it easier for Fresno to host soccer or football at the stadium should the opportunity to attract a team in one of those sports arise.

The view from the first base seats showcases some of Fresno's tall buildings, which loom just behind the concourse along the left field line. The buildings are made more visible by the abbreviation of the second and third levels. Fulton Street runs behind the left field wall, and fans often congregate on rooftops there to steal a peek at the game inside. At street level down below, the Fulton Mall isn't exactly Eutaw Street, but it does offer shops and cafes where fans can hang out before and after games.

As the Grizzlies owe their origin, at least in part, to the arrival of the Arizona Diamondbacks, it seems fitting that their stadium borrows one of the modern amenities that debuted at the big league park in Phoenix. In Fresno, as in Phoenix, the ballpark features an outfield swimming pool. The oasis in Fresno is no mere hot tub, either, but a good-sized in-ground pool that sits beyond the fence in left-center. As if to pacify old-timers and purists who might bristle at the idea of putting a swimming pool inside a ballpark, Chukchansi Park offers a manually operated scoreboard above the fence in right-center. The board even has an old-fashioned sign on it that says, "Hit Sign, Win Fruit."

The outfield dimensions at Chukchansi Park are irregular, measuring just 324 feet down the left field line, 385 to left, 400 to left-center, 394 to center, 400 to right-center, 380 to right, and 335 down the right field line. If you're having trouble visualizing this layout, I can tell you that the result is a field that plays smaller than usual down the lines and bigger than usual in the outfield gaps. The home run fence is similarly quirky. It begins at a height of just 3 feet near the right field foul pole, then gradually increases to 8 feet in right-center, then suddenly grows to 13 feet in left-center, and continues at that height to the left field foul pole.

Among the players who have called the ballpark in Fresno home are Dave Doster, who compiled a thirty-two-game hitting streak during the 2004 season, and future Giants Matt Cain, Noah Lowry, Lance Niekro, and Tyler Walker. Before the Grizzlies moved into their new digs, their roster included future big league stars Joe Nathan and Russ Ortiz.

It seems safe to say that this time around the Pacific Coast League has "stuck" in Fresno in a way that it failed to back in 1906. The Raisin Eaters have not been forgotten though. In 2006 the Grizzlies and their fans celebrated the one-hundredth anniversary of Fresno's first foray into the PCL every Wednesday night when the players wore throwback Raisin Eaters uniforms, and the fans enjoyed $1.00 outfield tickets.

Game Day

Getting to the Park

Fresno is 180 miles southwest of San Francisco and an easy drive from the California League ballparks in Bakersfield, Modesto, and Visalia. Chukchansi Park is located at the corner of Tulare Street and Broadway, just a few blocks north of where U.S. Highway 99 and U.S. Highway 41 form a V on the map. From 99 North, take the Ventura Street exit and turn right onto Ventura, then left onto Van Ness Avenue. Turn left onto Tulare and follow it to the ballpark. From 99 South, take the Fresno Street exit and turn left onto Fresno and then right onto Broadway, which leads to the park. Parking costs $5.00 in the stadium lots.

Inside the Park

Chukchansi Park can seat 12,500 fans, and although the Grizzlies attract average crowds of 7,000 fans, during the summer months crowds often swell to near capacity. There is just enough foul territory to leave room for the bull pens down the outfield lines, while past the pens the lower seating bowl curves in nicely, angling fans back toward the infield. The seats begin deep in left field foul territory with Section 102, continue to Section 114 behind the plate, and finish with Section 130 in right field home run territory. Between and behind the dugouts, Sections 108 through 120 offer Diamond Box Seats in the first several rows and Field Box Seats in the remaining rows. The rest of the seats on the first level sell as Field Reserved, except for the five small sections of bleachers in left field home run territory that sell as Power Alley Seats. The Power Alley Seats don't go on sale until game day and are a steal if you can get them.

The second deck offers Super View Seats—beginning with Section 208 at third base, continuing to Section 214 behind the plate, and finishing with Section 218 between home plate and the Grizzlies first base dugout. Because the view really is as good as advertised from this second deck, I recommend the Super View Seats over the Field Reserved Seats. As the second level continues down the first base line, the next five sections to appear are the 600 Club Seats, which have rows that are extra wide and offer in-seat wait service. These seats are not available on a game-by-game basis. All fans are free to buy, however, the seats in the seven sections to the right of the 600 Club. The Terrace View Seats offer decent upper-level looks at the game above the right field line. The luxury suites are located above this second level, along with the press box.

Just like in San Francisco, the concession stands in Fresno offer garlic fries. These are the perfect ballpark munchies to stave off the chill of a nippy spring night or to give the chill to a significant other whose love nips are distracting you from the game. The chicken strips and *Wienerschnitzel* hot dogs are also popular sellers. As for the sports bar on the first base side upstairs, unfortunately only fans with 600 Club Seats can access it.

The Chukchansi Park Experience

After a new ownership group took over the Grizzlies in 2005, the team launched a rebranding campaign that resulted in a new team logo that features a shield with a bear claw set in the middle, and colors that reflect the team's identity. The pine and cedar in the logo represent Yosemite Valley. The gold represents the Golden State. The orange represents the team's ties to the Giants.

As part of their identity makeover, the Grizzlies also retired their mascot Wild Thing. After sowing his wild oats at and around the ballparks in Fresno for eight years, Wild Thing finally settled down and married his longtime gal pal Wilda in an on-field ceremony after a game in April of 2006. Wild Thing carried Wilda off into the sunset and hasn't been seen or heard from since. Some reports have him raising a family with Wilda in pure marital bliss in the Sequoia National Park, while others have him wandering alone, barefoot and penniless around the streets of San Francisco. In any case it seems unlikely he'll be turning out at Chukchansi Park anytime soon.

To replace Wild Thing, the Grizzlies introduced a new mascot named "Parker." This big yellow bear is one part fuzz and two parts fun. Parker enjoys sitting on people and eating their garlic fries and sometimes waxes philosophic in the later innings of extra-inning games, asking questions like, "Is a vegetarian allowed to eat animal crackers?" and dispensing tidbits of wisdom like, "Don't sweat the petty things, and don't pet the sweaty things."

Parker and the other Fresno fans enjoy special ballpark promotions every Monday through Thursday. "Monday Madness" offers the chance to buy two Field Reserved tickets, two hot dogs, and two soft drinks for $14. Once the game starts fans compete in on-field stunts to determine who is the "maddest" of them all, and the winner at the end of the night gets a trophy. No word yet on whether the descendents of the late Fresno author William Saroyan—who penned *Madness in the Family*, among other books—have participated in the ballpark hysterics.

Also popular is "Thirsty Thursday," which features not only the $1.00 draft specials that many ballparks offer on Thursday nights, but also a fan competition to crown "Mr. and Mrs. Thursday." At the end of the night, the king and queen exit the stadium wearing beer-stein-shaped trophies on their heads.

On the Town

A few years ago Fresno closed Fulton Street to traffic and turned it into a pedestrian mall behind Chukchansi Park's left field bleachers. While the presence of this shop-laden strip hasn't resulted in a massive revitalization of the general ballpark neighborhood yet, it is certainly a step in the right direction. For baseball fans the mall offers pregame eats and drinks at quickie joints like the **Cafe Fulton Coffee Company** (1145 Fulton Mall), **China Express** (931 Fulton Mall), and **Los Panchos Mexican Restaurant** (1000 Fulton Mall).

Fans interested in seeing where the Grizzlies used to play can head 7 miles north to **Beiden Field** (Cal State-Fresno campus), which continues to serve as the home of the Western Athletic Conference's Bulldogs. The stadium, which opened in 1966, is named after former Bulldogs coach Pete Beiden. Its 6,575 seats take the form of stadium chairs around the infield and aluminum bleachers in the outfield.

THE DIAMOND

Lake Elsinore Storm

Class A, California League
(SAN DIEGO PADRES)

The Diamond
500 Diamond Drive
Lake Elsinore, California
951–245–4487

I suppose I could begin this chapter with a witty reference to Shakespeare's Elsinore Castle. Okay, maybe I couldn't. That would require some actual research because I haven't opened my *Riverside Shakespeare* anthology since sophomore year of college. Maybe a pop culture reference will work instead. Remember the scene in *Strange Brew* when Rick Moranis's character, Bob McKenzie, realized that the only way for him to escape the Elsinore Brewery was to drink his way out of a gigantic tank of beer? Remember how happy and drunk he became? Well, that's how the folks in Lake Elsinore, California, must have felt when their beautiful new ballpark, The Diamond, opened in 1994. As its name suggests, The Diamond is a gem. The ballpark is quirky, historic, modern, and fan-friendly, all in one.

Although Southern California is about as far from Boston, Massachusetts, as you can get in terms of geography, weather, attitude, and a million other categories, The Diamond borrows heavily from the design of Fenway Park. The ballpark architects at HNTB copied Fenway's field layout, only in a "flipped negative" sort of way. The Diamond features an asymmetrical playing field that is much deeper in left field than in right, and a 36-foot-high Green Monster in right.

The looming right field edifice begins at the foul pole just 310 feet from home plate and continues into right-center before dropping to a more conventional height. Straightaway right is just 330 feet from home plate, while the distance to the fence in center is 400 feet, and the deepest part of left-center measures 425 feet. The wall then abruptly changes course and cuts to the left field foul pole, which is just 330 feet from the plate. If you're having trouble envisioning this odd lot, picture a football field. Put home plate in the back corner of one of the end zones. Make the back line of the end zone the right field line and make the left sideline the left field line. Make the right sideline and back line of the far end zone the outfield fences. Now, pretend it would actually be feasible to play baseball on such an asymmetrical parcel. Voilà! That's the field in Lake Elsinore.

Out of respect to ancient Fenway Park, Lake Elsinore constructed its Mini-Monster 1 foot shorter than the original Green Monster. Although The Diamond's Wall is painted Fenway Green, it also features a slew of advertising on its face, giving it an appearance more akin to the Green Monster of the 1940s than the one that stands in Boston today. Like the original Monster, the Mini-Monster bears a scoreboard that displays the line score and is home to a fuzzy creature that lives inside its bowels. No, I'm not talking about a scruffy scoreboard operator, a few days late for a shave. I'm talking about Jackpot, a pink bunny who claims to be a distant cousin of Wally the Green Monster who lives inside the Wall in Boston. Jackpot emerges from the Mini-Monster whenever the Storm scores a run and proceeds to do a special dance on the outfield lawn.

The Diamond's other distinguishing feature is its 90-foot-tall brick clock tower that rises above the green roof of the press box. The tower is a nod to the region's minor league baseball history, as it evokes memories of the massive timepiece that once rose above the home plate grandstand at Wrigley Field in

Los Angeles. Wrigley served as home of the Pacific Coast League's Los Angeles Angels from 1925 to 1957, and then housed the American League's Angels in 1961. It also served as the home of the classic TV show "Home Run Derby," which was filmed on the grounds in 1959 and 1960. The ballpark, tower and all, met the wrecking ball in 1966.

Lake Elsinore was affiliated with the Angels from the time it joined the California League in 1994 until 2000. Previously, the team that became the Storm had played 45 miles east in Palm Springs. In 2001 the Storm switched allegiances, signing a player development contract with the San Diego Padres. The Storm's alumni list includes such major leaguers as Jarrod Washburn, Darin Erstad, Francisco Rodríguez, Khalil Greene, Xavier Nady, Phil Nevin, and Jake Peavy. During the 2005 sea-

son, Fernando Valenzuela's son, Fernando Jr., played for the Storm and the proud papa was a regular visitor to The Diamond.

In addition to housing the Storm, the Diamond is also used for trade shows, concerts, high school and college graduations, and Moto-X events. Moto-X star Mike Metzger is a Storm fan and has wowed the Lake Elsinore fans on many occasions with daring motorcycle jumps on the field.

Game Day

Getting to the Park

Lake Elsinore is 140 miles southeast of Anaheim as the crow flies, and a bit farther away by car since travelers can't cut through the middle of the Cleveland National Forest but must drive north on U.S. Highway 91 before

The Diamond

hooking a right onto U.S. Highway 15 South. From US 15, take the exit for Diamond Drive/ Railroad Canyon Road and turn right onto Diamond Drive. The three stadium lots all charge $3.00 per car.

Inside the Park

The Diamond offers 6,069 comfortable maroon stadium seats and additional room in its twelve luxury suites and on its grass berm. The Diamond only sells out on Opening Day, the Fourth of July, and when the Padres come to town for exhibition games. Still, the Storm averages a very respectable 4,000 fans per game.

The seating bowl extends into medium-depth left field and right field, offering twenty-five to thirty rows of seats, depending upon the section. The concourse runs atop the seating bowl, beneath the press box and luxury boxes.

The first eight rows behind home plate and along the base lines house Preferred Box Seats. The remaining infield seats sell as Boxes. Section 101 is behind home plate; the even-numbered sections continue down the first baseline to Section 112 and the odd-numbered sections continue down the third baseline to Section 113.

Past the corner bases, the first eight rows sell as Preferred Reserved Seats, while the seats behind them sell as Reserved Seats. Sections 114 and 116 are in shallow right, while odd-numbered Sections 115 through 123 are in left.

A General Admission ticket entitles its bearer to a spot on the lawn in "deep" right field foul territory, which really isn't that deep at all due to the field's unique configuration.

There are three concession stands on the first base side and two on the third base side. The Diamond specializes in burritos and soft tacos and serves mixed and frozen drinks.

The Diamond Club Bar and Grill in left field foul territory can seat up to 288 people on three levels. This festive ballpark restaurant opens an hour before the game and is open to all fans. The menu features some of the same Randy Jones Barbecue items available at Petco Park in San Diego, Mexican plates, and grilled sandwiches.

For kids the concourse houses a Fun Zone with a rock-climbing wall, bouncy pen, speed-pitch booth, slide, and prize wheel.

The Diamond Experience

While the ballpark in Lake Elsinore caters to the twenty-something crowd with its on-site sports bar and frozen drinks, it also provides a fun environment for the entire family. Every Sunday is "kids day," as parents save money on buy-one-get-one-free kids tickets (if this isn't incentive enough to have a second child, I don't know what is), and kids get to run the bases and collect autographs from their favorite Storm players after the game. Wednesday is "Family Day," as games start an hour earlier than usual—at 6:05 P.M.—and the team sells family ticket packages. And every workweek ends with a bang as Friday nights feature post-game fireworks.

In addition to Jackpot, the pink bunny who lives in the Mini-Monster, The Diamond also offers kids the chance to interact with Thunder, a big green dog, who loves to shake his belly and shoot Silly String into the stands.

On the Town

The town of Lake Elsinore sits north of the San Mateo Canyons and south of the Estelle Mountain Reserve. The town is built around southern California's largest natural lake, Lake Elsinore, which began drawing tourists to this part of the state in the 1920s. This is a small minor league town by most measures, but one that has seen rapid development in recent years.

The **Lake Elsinore Recreation Area** (Riverside Street) on the east side of the lake offers camping, fishing, swimming, boating, and picnicking. If you're like me, you'll want to take a few casts into the deep water in the hopes of catching Whiskers, a farm-raised blue catfish and channel catfish hybrid that was released into Lake Elsinore as part of a fish-stocking program in March of 2000. At the time of his release, Whiskers tipped the scales at forty-seven pounds, but local anglers estimate that he's doubled in size since then. There's no arguing, Whiskers would make for one heck of a fish fry. Can you say, extra tartar sauce? For those who set their sights slightly lower, the lake also offers the chance to catch rainbow trout, bass, crappie, carp, and the ubiquitous blue gill.

Those looking for a tasty dinner after catching nothing but blue gill and crappie will find plenty of options on Riverside Drive and Lakeshore Drive. Mexican food is well represented in this part of California. I recommend **Elvira's Mexican** (32391 Riverside Drive) and **Juan Pollo** (16989 Lakeshore Drive).

CLEAR CHANNEL STADIUM

Lancaster JetHawks

Class A, California League
(BOSTON RED SOX)

Clear Channel Stadium
45116 Valley Central Way
Lancaster, California
661–726–5400

When the Lancaster JetHawks went corporate and changed the name of their ballpark from Lancaster Municipal Stadium to Clear Channel Stadium in 2005, local fans weren't too distraught. After all, neither the team nor its fans had referred to the ballpark by its given name in the past, and there was no reason why they'd have to stop using its popular nickname once the naming rights deal took effect. As far as local fans are concerned the JetHawks still play at "The Hangar." This apt nickname reflects the ballpark's identity in more ways than one. First, the name is fitting because the ballpark is located not far from Edwards Air Force Base, where NASA's space shuttles land. This is also the spot where Chuck Yeager became the first man to breach the speed of sound, piloting the Bell X-1 to a sonic boom in 1947. Second, the nickname is fitting because the ballpark is known throughout the California League as a home run hitter's paradise. The ball really takes off here, due to the frequent 30-mile-per-hour wind currents that blow straight out toward center field. Hence, the center field wall is deep by California League standards—410 feet from home plate.

The Hangar opened in 1996 when the JetHawks debuted as a Seattle Mariners affiliate. Mariners prospect Ken Cloud delivered the first pitch in Hangar history against the Visalia Oaks. The Opening Day game marked the return of minor league baseball to Los Angeles County for the first time since September of 1957, when the Pacific Coast League's Hollywood Stars played their final game at Wrigley Field in Los Angeles, then left town to make way for the migrating Brooklyn Dodgers.

The Hangar's most interesting characteristic resides just outside its main entranceway where an actual FA-18 fighter jet is mounted atop a cement pedestal with its nose pointed skyward. This is a great spot to stop and coerce a passerby to snap a photo of you and your road-trip buddies with the jet angled above your heads and the stadium in the background. NASA donated the blue-and-white ship to the city of Lancaster, just as it donated a mock space shuttle to the city of Viera, Florida, for display outside Space Coast Stadium, home of the Brevard County Manatees.

Behind the jet, The Hangar's tan cement exterior is simple and understated. Although the team hasn't been around long enough to accrue a ton of history, inside the ballpark gates fans encounter old team photos and jerseys decorating the concourse and artifacts from the first game in stadium history in the lobby near the front office entrance. Although The Hangar was designed by HOK, which has a history of creating architecturally unique facilities, the inside of the stadium doesn't offer much to distinguish it from other ballparks, nor does the outfield view of trucks passing on Freeway 14 enhance the gameday experience.

The seating bowl is roomy and low to the field—both plusses, in my book—and runs from foul pole to foul pole if you count the grass berms in outfield foul territory on either side. The press box level sits immediately behind the last row of seats, offering six luxury suites on either side of the media area.

When a new ownership group purchased the JetHawks in 2006, plans were set in motion to erect a new state-of-the-art video board at The Hangar that should be in place by the time this book is released. The new owners also introduced their idea for a novel public art project called the "Re-launch Your Inner JetHawk" campaign, imploring fans to submit artwork to the team that depicts those elements that make living in the Antelope Valley special. Some of the artwork on display at the stadium celebrates the aerospace industry, the local poppy reserve, Joshua trees, and the local mountains.

The JetHawks didn't remain a Mariners affiliate for long. In 2001 they signed a player development contract with the Arizona Diamondbacks. Then in 2007 they switched to an affiliation with the Boston Red Sox. The future major leaguers who have passed through The Hangar include José Cruz Jr., Brian Fuentes, Joe Mays, Joel Piñiero, and Brandon Webb.

In addition to providing a home to the JetHawks, The Hangar also hosts the annual "First Pitch" tournament at the start of the high school baseball season in March.

Game Day

Getting to the Park

Lancaster is the northernmost city in Los Angeles County. The ballpark sits between Freeway 14, Lancaster Boulevard, Valley Central Way, and Avenue I. From Freeway 14, take the Avenue I exit and follow Avenue I West toward Valley Central. Turn left onto Valley Central, and you will see the main parking lot beside the stadium on your left. Parking at the stadium costs $3.00. Another option is to park in the dirt lot across the street on Valley Central for free.

Inside the Park

The Hangar offers 4,500 green stadium chairs

and room for more on the grass berms between the ends of the seating bowl and the foul poles. The JetHawks typically attract fewer than 2,000 fans per game, so ordering tickets in advance is not necessary.

The Dugout Box Seats are in the field-level sections immediately behind and between the dugouts. Section 111 is behind home plate. The even-numbered sections continue to Section 116 behind first base and the odd-numbered sections continue to Section 127 behind third base. The Box Seats are behind the mid-level walkway on the infield. The Reserved Seats are down the baselines on the outfield sides of the Dugout Boxes. A General Admission ticket is good for a spot on either outfield lawn.

There is a covered picnic patio behind the Dugout Boxes on the third base side and an open picnic area behind the Dugout Boxes on the first base side. The concession concourse is located beneath the Box Seats. The Hangar offers tri-tip steak, Angus Beef burgers, and a value meal known as the "Jet-Pack," which consists of a hot dog, chips, and a soft drink.

The Clear Channel Stadium Experience

The local mascot is KaBoom, whom the local fans call "KB" for short. KB is a large hawk who wears a pilot helmet and flying goggles. He also wears a custom-made JetHawks uniform. During a memorable 2005 game, KB launched an unmanned, aluminum-foil-wrapped ballpark hot dog more than 50 feet above the earth's surface using a miniature rocket. To cap the promotion the team celebrated the successful takeoff and landing of Hot Dog One by doling out free M&M's to the fans in the stands. I understand the team's rationale for wanting to launch things for the amusement of fans, given Lancaster's ties to the aeronautics industry and all, but don't ask me to explain why they would waste a perfectly good hot dog. Like a lot of fans, I take the matter of ballpark frankfurters very seriously, and I expect the teams to handle them responsibly. When a team doesn't value its cased meat, I start to wonder why I should. Did you ever notice how the teams with really good hot dogs don't sling-shoot them into the stands as promotional items? Every time I've caught a free hot dog at a baseball park or NBA arena, it's been lukewarm, rubbery, and at least partially rancid.

In addition to occasionally launching hot dogs into the stratosphere, the JetHawks celebrate every home run by the home team with a fireworks display above the outfield fence. And midway through the eighth inning, KB leads any child who wants to run across the outfield lawn onto the field for a quick sprint while the JetHawk outfielders stretch their throwing arms.

On the Town

Lancaster is on the western edge of the Mojave Desert. The city is northeast of the fertile Angeles National Forest, which lies between Lancaster and the greater Los Angeles metro area.

Edwards Air Force Base (405 South Rosamond Boulevard) offers a free museum that is open Tuesday through Saturday from 9:00 A.M. until 5:00 P.M. The museum's trademark attraction is an outdoor airpark with sixteen different aircraft.

The **California State Poppy Reserve** is another object of Antelope Valley civic pride. Located 15 miles west of Lancaster on Avenue I in Antelope Buttes, this 1,700-acre wildlife area offers multicolored wildflowers that typically bloom from March through May. I am told the peak viewing time occurs in mid-April, right as the minor league baseball season begins. The reserve offers 8 miles of hiking trails.

JOHN THURMAN FIELD

Modesto Nuts

Class A, California League
(COLORADO ROCKIES)

John Thurman Field
601 Neece Drive
Modesto, California
209–572–4587

The home ballpark of the Modesto Nuts enjoys the distinction of sitting right next to Modesto Municipal Golf Course. Just how close is John Thurman Field to the local muni? The ballpark's concession concourse is protected by driving range netting to prevent fans from getting beaned by Maxfli's as they wait in line for hot dogs. How many other ballpark concourses can you say that about? The stadium is rather unremarkable otherwise. It underwent a $3 million renovation in 1997 that included upgrading the seating area, redoing the field, and bringing the player and fan amenities up to California League specs. Yet, Thurman Field doesn't offer much in the way of quirks or nuances to distinguish it from your typical small-time minor league stadium.

Modesto's history in the California League dates all the way back to 1946 when the local nine played at Municipal Park. The team moved to its current ballpark site in 1952 to play at "Del Webb Field." The stadium was renamed "John Thurman Field" in 1983 to honor a popular California assemblyman who died of a heart attack that year.

Several major league teams have enjoyed affiliations with Modesto over the past sixty years, including the Oakland A's, who were the parent club of the Modesto A's for thirty seasons. When the A's decided to sever their relationship with Modesto after the 2004 campaign, the Colorado Rockies signed a player development contract with Modesto and the team launched a two-month-long fan contest to come up with a new name. The local hardball enthusiasts settled on the "Nuts," as a tribute to the region's proud history as a leading producer of almonds and walnuts. Of the five finalists, Nuts received 52 percent of the vote, followed by Dusters (34 percent), Steel (8 percent), Derailers (4 percent), and Strike (2 percent).

The list of Modesto minor leaguers who have gone on to reach the major leagues is long and impressive. The city's alumni roster includes such names as Reggie Jackson, Joe Morgan, Joe Rudi, Mark McGwire, Rollie Fingers, Rickey Henderson, Jose Canseco, Jason Giambi, Miguel Tejada, Tim Hudson, and Bobby Crosby. And both Tony LaRussa and Sparky Anderson managed in Modesto.

A historic exhibit in the team store pays tribute to many of these former Modesto stars. Meanwhile, Rudi's number 26 has been retired by the team and is displayed atop the right field fence. A Modesto native, Rudi lived his childhood dream of playing for the Modesto A's before launching a sixteen-year big league career.

If we are to believe the claims Canseco made in his 2005 book *Juiced*, the young slugger played his last "clean" season in Modesto before becoming a chronic steroid abuser. While spending the 1984 season in Modesto, Canseco celebrated his twenty-first birthday, took a leave of absence from the team to fly home to visit his dying mother, promised his mother to become the best baseball player in the world, and batted .276 while reaching a new personal best with 15 homers in 410 at bats. Canseco weighed 180 pounds that season, but by the time he reported to the A's spring training camp the next spring, he had added twenty-five pounds of muscle. He

John Thurman Field

started the 1985 campaign in Double-A Huntsville, then moved to Triple-A Tacoma, then joined the big league A's in Oakland. Before the whirlwind season ended, he belted 41 home runs and racked up 140 RBIs. The next year, he won the American League Rookie of the Year Award. As he blossomed into a big league basher, the folks who had watched Canseco play in Modesto could only scratch their heads and wonder how he had improved his game so quickly. Now they know.

Lest we associate the upstanding Modesto baseball community with baseball's self-proclaimed steroid ambassador, here's a more favorable association by which fans might remember the team. In 2006 the Nuts played an important role in an episode of *Seventh Heaven,* the popular WB Network television show. In a January episode Martin Brewer had to choose between attending college or heading to Modesto to play minor league ball for the Nuts. The team logo and jersey made frequent appearances throughout the episode as Martin mulled the pros and cons of both potential life paths.

Game Day

Getting to the Park

Modesto is 75 miles east of San Francisco and 75 miles south of Sacramento. From the north or south, take Route 99 to the Tuolomne Boulevard exit and turn right at the end of the exit ramp. Take the first left onto Neece Drive and the ballpark will appear on the right. From San Francisco, take Route 580 East, to Route 205

East, to Route 120 East, to Route 99 South, and then follow the directions as above. The parking lots on Neece Drive and Sunset Street charge $5.00 per car.

Inside the Park

This small, uncovered seating bowl holds 4,000 fans when it's chock-full of Modesto baseball nuts. It extends just a little way into the outfield on either side of the diamond. The five rows of green stadium chairs closest to the field are below a midlevel walkway and sell as Super Box Seats. Behind these, the six sections above the walkway behind the home plate area—Sections 201 thorough 206—sell as Upper Box Seats. These are also comfortable green stadium chairs. The rest of the ballpark offers aluminum benches that sell as Preferred Grandstand Bleachers along the baselines, and General Admission Bleachers in the two outfield-most sections on either side. The stadium offers two luxury boxes, one on either side of the small press box atop the grandstand, and two picnic areas, one beside the home bullpen down the right field line, one in left field foul territory.

The concession stands are located behind the bleachers on either side of the stadium. Appropriately, Thurman Field offers four different varieties of flavored almonds courtesy of Stewart and Jasper Orchards. The flavors are All-Star Smokehouse, Twin Killing Chili Cheese, High Heat Barbecue, and Round the Horn Ranch.

A game area on the concourse provides a number of fun activities for kids, including the ever-popular wet slide for those hot summer nights.

The Thurman Field Experience

Thurman Field offers special promotional nights throughout the year like "Noche de Bèisbol" and "Jimmy Buffett Night," and these games sometimes sell out.

On a nightly basis a trio of mascots keeps fans entertained: Al the Almond, Wally the Walnut, and Peanut the Elephant. The mascots love to race each other around the bases, do the chicken dance, and pick out special ladies in the stands to whom they award bouquets of flowers.

In 2006 the Nuts created a buzz in the local community before the season, opening their vacant public-address announcer position to members of the general public. The Nuts teamed with ESPN Radio 970 AM to audition any and all fans who expressed an interest in sitting behind the microphone for the team's home games. After more than one hundred people tried out, five finalists were chosen, and on April 1, the finalists tried out at Thurman Field as a panel of celebrity judges and local fans chose the winner.

On the Town

Modesto is a city of nearly 200,000, located in Central Valley. Regrettably, the city has recently made its share of appearances on sensational cable TV shows dedicated to unveiling the ugly side of human nature. First, there was the highly publicized disappearance of Chandra Levy, the Washington, D.C., intern who had been romantically involved with congressman Gary Condit, who represented Modesto's district. Then, the Christmas Eve murder of Modesto resident Laci Peterson made headlines across the country. But try to put these isolated incidents aside as you enter the city limits. Modesto's really not a bad place to live or visit, and chances are you won't find O. J. searching for the real killers on the city's municipal golf course. The course isn't nearly posh enough for his tastes. For visiting hackers though, a trip to Modesto offers a great opportunity to sneak in a round before the baseball game. The **Modesto Municipal Golf**

Course is a nine-hole, par 35 course that measures barely 3,000 yards from the blue tees. The Muni also offers three practice greens and a driving range.

Fans looking for a pregame or postgame watering hole can head to **Sidelines Pub and Grill** (2801 Mchenry Avenue), which features memorabilia related to the local baseball team. Sidelines often hosts Nuts-sponsored luncheons that bring the team's players and coaches together with fans for friendly question-and-answer sessions.

THE EPICENTER

Rancho Cucamonga Quakes

Class A, California League
(LOS ANGELES ANGELS OF ANAHEIM)

The Epicenter
8408 Rochester Avenue
Rancho Cucamonga, California
909–481–5252

Fans will be hard pressed to find another baseball park that burst onto the minor league scene in quite the dynamic way Rancho Cucamonga's Epicenter did in 1993. It would be an understatement to merely say the minor league game was "well received" by the fans in this eastern suburb of Los Angeles. The California League franchise that relocated to Rancho Cucamonga in 1993 was *ridiculously* well received. The Quakes and their new ballpark were so popular, in fact, that Rancho Cucamonga established a new single-season California League attendance record in 1993. And they set that record by July 15, with a month and a half of the season still to play. The team finished its inaugural campaign at The Epicenter with an eye-popping attendance total of 331,005. The previous California League high-water mark of 218,444 had been set just the year before by the High Desert Mavericks.

The Quakes were just getting started. After hastily installing two new banks of temporary bleachers down the right field and left field lines in May of 1993, increasing The Epicenter's capacity to 5,042, the team went back to work during the off-season and added 1,600 new permanent seats to a stadium that had still not celebrated its first birthday. In 1994 the Quakes topped the 300,000 mark in atten-

dance again, and the team marched toward its first California League championship. The Quakes beat the Modesto A's three games to one in the championship series, clinching the title on their home field.

Following the championship season Quakes attendance boomed again. In 1995 the team played its home games before crowds that averaged 97 percent of capacity, the highest such figure in all of professional baseball. The Epicenter attracted 446,146 fans to seventy home games while less than 12,000 seats went unsold all season long. The Quakes topped the 400,000 mark again in each of the next two seasons.

Today, the Quakes are still a popular draw, but the crowds at The Epicenter have thinned a bit since the opening of new California League parks in nearby San Bernardino and Lake Elsinore. Rancho Cucamonga still leads the league in attendance each year, but with totals in the range of 270,000 to 300,000, instead of in the stratospheric 400,000s.

As these attendance figures may have led you to conclude, The Epicenter is a special ballpark that is well worth a visit during your baseball road trip. The stadium was built at a cost of $20 million by the city of Rancho Cucamonga to lure the California League team previously known as the San Bernardino Spirit to town. The stadium's three-story white stucco façade features elegant arched windows on the second floor and an arched main entranceway three stories tall. The edifice projects a distinctly California flare, while the courtyard of palm trees outside enhances this effect.

A life-sized bronze statue of comedian Jack Benny stands at the main entrance of The Epicenter. The statue depicts Benny gazing philosophically into space while he holds a violin in one hand. While I never watched the *Jack Benny Show* myself, according to my

Great Uncle Vit, who is as old as dirt, Benny used to do a regular skit in which he would pretend to be a train conductor and would call out the names of different stops. One of the stops was Cucamonga. I'm not sure where the humor came from in this routine, but Uncle Vit chuckled while he was trying to describe it to me, so I'll assume it passed for "funny" in the early days of TV.

In any case, on either side of the high rising main façade, fans find that the attractive white arches continue beneath the grandstands along the full length of the seating bowl. An iron fence separates the sidewalk outside the park from the ground-level concourse beneath the arches inside. Inside the seating bowl fans find the same white stucco, highlighted by decorative green tiles.

The real eye-catcher inside the park is the expanse of the San Gabriel Mountains that span the outfield. Because the view of the mountains is the most striking beyond the left field fence, the main scoreboard is located in right field, while a smaller, less-obtrusive board sits atop the fence in left. The seating bowl provides two tiers of seats, while leaving room for the concession stands and bathrooms underneath the stands.

The franchise that renamed itself the Quakes in 1993 certainly deserves such a sparkling ballpark to call its own. Its roots trace all the way back to 1966, when the Lodi Crushers entered the California League hundreds of miles north of Rancho Cucamonga. The team played at Lodi's Lawrence Park (now known as Tony Zupo Field) until 1985, then moved to Ventura County to play on the campus of Ventura College. In 1987 the team moved again, this time to San Bernardino, to play at Fiscilini Field. After nearly three decades as transients, in 1993 the franchise finally settled in Rancho Cucamonga.

The Quakes were a San Diego Padres affiliate when they arrived in Rancho Cucamonga, then they switched to their current player development contract with the Anaheim Angels in 2001. Because The Epicenter is located so close to the big league park in Anaheim, the Quakes attract many big leaguers on rehab assignments. Usually teams send their major leaguers to their Double-A or Triple-A teams to get some at-bats or pitch a few innings, but the Angels send theirs to Single-A Rancho Cucamonga. In recent years the Quakes have welcomed big league stars like Garret Anderson, Wally Joyner, Raul Mondesi, Tim Salmon, Brendan Donnelly, Troy Glaus, Adam Kennedy, and Jarrod Washburn to The Epicenter. Back when Rancho Cucamonga was a Padres affiliate, lefty Bruce Hurst made a rehab start at the park.

Rancho Cucamonga has also been an important proving ground for future big leaguers on their way to the majors like Sean Burroughs, Matt Clement, Brian Lawrence, Derek Lee, Gary Matthews Jr., Dallas McPherson, and Francisco Rodríguez. In 2005 Quakes fans got to witness breakout seasons by two of baseball's brightest young stars. Shortstop Brandon Wood batted .321 and hit 43 homers while driving in 115 runs for Rancho Cucamonga, then Wood shattered the Arizona Fall League record with 14 homers in twenty-nine games. Meanwhile, Wood's double-play partner at Rancho Cucamonga, Howie Kendrick, batted .384 before being promoted to the Angels Double-A team in Arkansas.

Game Day

Getting to the Park

Rancho Cucamonga is 40 miles east of Los Angeles, 20 miles northwest of San Bernardino, and 40 miles north of Lake Elsinore. The Epicenter is located on a fault line, but don't worry, unless the Big One comes you should be safe during your visit. The stadium, as you might expect, is built to withstand the usual tremors that folks in this part of the country barely seem to notice. The Epicenter is conveniently located near the intersection of Freeway 15 and Freeway 10. From Los Angeles, take the 10 East, to the 15 North, and then take the exit for Foothill Boulevard. Turn left off the exit and then turn left onto Rochester Avenue. There are seven stadium parking lots along Rochester Avenue that combine to offer 2,400 spaces. They charge $3.00 per car.

Inside the Park

The Epicenter's main seating bowl extends only so far as the corner bases, offering eight rows below an interior walkway and fifteen rows above. The second deck is elevated well above the walkway, allowing for unobstructed views over the pedestrians. The picnic areas appear at field level, jutting into foul territory in shallow right and left, then banks of bleachers rise in deep left field and deep right field foul territory.

The Quakes offer three different seating options within the main bowl. The Super Box Seats are the first few rows down at field level between the dugouts. The Box Seats make up the rest of the seats on the first level. The Reserved Seats fill the second level. The protective screen behind home plate rises straight up between the dugouts, allowing foul balls to drop down into the stands to become souvenirs, while lower screens continue along the tops of the dugout roofs to protect fans from low liners. These screens didn't bother me, but some fans told me they that don't like looking through the netting, so they always get Reserved Seats instead of Boxes. As for the Bleachers, they begin in medium-depth outfield foul territory and extend all the way to the foul poles. These are aluminum benches with back supports.

The concession stands beneath the grandstands feature Hebrew National hot dogs, kettle corn, chicken tenders, and other ballpark staples, while a stand in right field serves hot items fresh off the grill.

The Epicenter Experience

The team's primary mascot is a scary green dinosaur known as "Tremblor," who is sometimes joined by his little brother "Aftershock." I describe Tremblor as "scary" because he has beady, soulless, reptilian eyes and 5-inch-long incisors. His little brother is smaller and less menacing.

Quakes fans get a kick out of the ballpark dance troupe, known as the "Trash Family." These young women perform a nightly dance routine down on the field midway through the game, dressed in tuxedos. After the performance they scurry around the lawn picking up any hot dog wrappers or napkins that may have blown onto the field during the first few innings.

On the Town

Rancho Cucamonga is a rapidly growing city that offers travelers plenty of restaurants and watering holes to choose from along the urban sprawl of Foothill Boulevard. In addition to the usual chains and fast-food establishments, the strip near the ballpark offers Japanese, Mexican, Italian, Chinese, and Thai places. Popular spots include the **Beer Hunter** (12809 Foothill Boulevard), **Omaha Jack's Steakhouse and Brewery** (11837 Foothill Boulevard), the **Red Hill Barbecue** (8111 Foothill Boulevard), and **Woody's Bar-B-Que** (11897 Foothill Boulevard).

RALEY FIELD

Sacramento River Cats

Class AAA, Pacific Coast League
(OAKLAND ATHLETICS)

Raley Field
400 Ballpark Drive
West Sacramento, California
916–376–4700

The Sacramento River Cats have been on quite a winning streak—both on and off the field—since they joined the Pacific Coast League in 2000. Just how hot are these cool Cats in capital city? Well, the River Cats have led all of the minor leagues in attendance in each of their first six seasons (and counting), including a record-breaking inaugural campaign in which they shattered the single-season Pacific Coast League attendance mark, drawing 861,808 fans. The old record—to put Sacramento's accomplishment in perspective—was 713,224, set by Salt Lake in 1994. Meanwhile, an affiliation with the Oakland A's has brought a steady stream of Billy Beane's moneyballers to Sacramento, and aided by rising stars like Joe Blanton, Eric Chávez, Bobby Crosby, Mark Ellis, Rich Harden, Huston Street, Nick Swisher, and Barry Zito, the River Cats have qualified for the Pacific Coast League play-offs in each of their first six seasons, including 2003 and 2004 when they won league championships. For good measure add to the River Cats many accolades one of the most lucrative naming-rights deals in all of minor league baseball—one from a regional supermarket chain that pays $15 million over twenty years—and you have all the makings of a dynasty.

To what does the Sacramento team owe this charmed life, you ask? Well, it's no secret that fan-friendly ballparks that provide exceptional sight lines all around the diamond are in vogue these days. And that's exactly what Sacramento has in Raley Field. In their first year of existence, the River Cats not only returned the Pacific Coast League to one of its founding cities (well, almost . . . keep reading), but they opened a $29.5 million ballpark that will serve as the centerpiece of their success for years to come. Yes, tickets and parking are on the pricey side, but the gameday experience at Raley Field is top-notch. What the ballpark is not, however, is located inside the Sacramento city limits. In fact Raley Field is in West Sacramento, a separate city that belongs to a whole different county from Sacramento.

Raley Field was designed by HNTB and built right at the end of the Tower Bridge that spans the Sacramento River, connecting West Sacramento to Sacramento. At the home plate entrance, fans find a colorful façade with the stadium's name in bold red letters above arched entries. Owing to a playing field 17 feet below street level, the stadium exterior only reaches two stories high. The first level consists of beige sandstone, while the second level is a pleasing off-white tone. To the left of the entry gates, a clock tower is topped by decorative metalwork that displays the team logo.

For the viewing pleasure of those inside the park, the two matching support stanchions of the Tower Bridge rise majestically beyond the right field fence. These tall yellow structures each present a crisscrossed pattern. The bridge is especially spectacular when lighted at night. Meanwhile a bit farther away, the tall buildings of downtown Sacramento make their imprint on the horizon. West Sacramento's distinctive Ziggurat Building is also a prominent part of the outfield view, as the pyramid-shaped office building sits in the distance behind the center field fence. As for the stadium scoreboard—another important part of every ballpark's outfield view—it is mounted high above the batter's eye in center. The bull pens are located at field level in right field home run territory where they are visible behind the 5-foot-high see-through fence. Across the rest of the outfield the dark green fence measures a more conventional 8 feet high.

Almost all of the seats at Raley Field are in the lower bowl. Although the ballpark is large enough to accommodate the ravenous local fan base—with a seating capacity of 14,680—it is also surprisingly intimate—thanks to a seating bowl that keeps all fans close to field level. The ballpark is also family-friendly, thanks to a larger-than-usual lawn seating area in right. The upper level is just large enough to house thirty-six luxury boxes and six sections of club seats and isn't a dominant part of the stadium design like at some Triple-A stadiums. The upper deck doesn't hang out over the lower seats, but it occupies the air space over the open concourse behind the last row of seats.

The concourse is not a true walk-around concourse, as it doesn't connect behind the batter's eye in center like at some parks, but it does allow for easy access at its ends to the small berm in left field home run territory and the much larger berm that begins in right field foul territory, wraps around the foul pole, and continues into center field.

The River Cats arrived in Sacramento via Vancouver, where they had played as the "Vancouver Canadians." After current team owner Art Savage purchased the Canadians in 1998, the team played a final lame-duck season in British Columbia while waiting for a new privately financed ballpark to be constructed in West Sacramento.

Sacramento's previous ventures in the Pacific Coast League include the league's in-augural 1903 season, a three-year run from 1909 through 1911, a lengthy run from 1918 through 1960, and a brief run from 1974 through 1976. Most of those teams were called the "Solons," owing to their presence in the city where California's state lawmakers made their wise decisions. The Solons played at Edmonds Field on Broadway, and although a Target department store now resides where the ballpark once stood, the River Cats pay homage to it and to their Sacramento predecessors with several historic exhibits at the Raley Field souvenir store. When the Solons departed northern California following the 1960 season, they did what few California teams have ever done—they headed west. The team became the Hawaii Islanders.

Game Day

Getting to the Park

Sacramento is just 85 miles northeast of Oakland, making it an ideal destination for rehabbing A's players looking to get in a few swings or innings, or for road-tripping fans looking to catch a minor league game while visiting the two big league stadiums in the San Francisco Bay Area. Raley Field is just west of Old Sacramento across the Sacramento River. From I–5 North, take Business Route 80, then take the Jefferson Boulevard/South River Road exit. Stay to the right on exiting and follow South River Road to the ballpark.

The several parking lots between the ballpark and river are operated by River City Parking and charge $8.00 per car. Even if they allow tailgating in their dusty lots, this price seems outrageous for a minor league baseball game. There are also two lots on West Capitol Avenue behind the left field fence. Another option is to find a spot in Old Sacramento and walk across the Tower Bridge, which takes fifteen minutes, but will save you the aggravation of fighting the traffic after the game. Sacramento Regional Transit also offers shuttles to the game from several downtown locations.

Inside the Park

The seating bowl offers 11,092 seats, all of which are comfortable green stadium chairs, while the outfield lawns and luxury suites offer room for a few thousand people more. As is the case at many of the more popular minor league facilities these days, the best seats in the house—those in the first several rows between the dugouts—belong to season ticket holders and are not put on sale for the general public. Those fans who order tickets well in advance, however, should be able to secure seats in the upper rows behind the plate or along the baselines. Section 112 is directly behind the plate and it, along with the four sections on either side of it, is part of the Senate Box ticket level. At $19 this was one of the priciest minor league tickets in 2006, but at least the view is excellent, especially from Sections 113 through 116 on the third base side of the plate, from which the bridge is most visible. The next four sections along the first baseline (104–107) and third baseline (117–120) sell as Gold Rush Seats. Next come the Delta Box Seats, with Sections 102 and 103 in shallow right field and Sections 121 through 123 in left field, then the Hot Corner Seats, with Section 101 in medium-depth right field and Sections 124 and 125 in deep left. In general I recommend the seats on the third baseline since they offer better outfield views of the skyline and don't face the setting sun like the seats across the diamond do.

A General Admission ticket is good for a spot on the large berm in right field or on the tiny one in left. Fans are permitted to bring beach blankets, chairs, and umbrellas into the stadium. The portion of the right field berm in foul territory along the right field line is nicely sloped and angles toward the infield.

The concession highlights include apple-chicken sausages, grilled vegetarian sandwiches, toasted subs, Mexican, barbecue, pizza, Alpine's hot dogs, and freshly squeezed lemonade. The real treats are served upstairs though, in the Solons Club on the first base side of the second deck. Unfortunately, you need to be a Founder's Club ticket holder or luxury suite goer to access this exclusive stadium sports bar. According to a lucky fan who has seen the inside, I can tell you that the Solons Club menu includes such ballpark favorites as pasta with wild salmon, sautéed rainbow trout with lemon-chive sauce, and fettuccine with Dungeness crab and Pacific rockfish. If a menu like that doesn't say, "Let's play two," I don't know what does.

The Raley Field Experience

The Sacramento mascot is a loveable gray character named "Dinger the River Cat" who isn't anywhere near as menacing as the saber-toothed, sharp-clawed kitty climbing out of the Tower Bridge in the Sacramento team's official logo. Dinger likes to throw hot dogs into the stands and to eat "mice-cream cones" on hot days.

The River Cats offer special theme nights all season long like "Faith and Family Night," "Boy Scouts Night," "College Night," and "Teacher Appreciation Night." In 2006 the team also offered "Marriage Night," when several thousand fans were on hand to watch a couple from Benicia tie the knot at home plate before the first pitch of a game against the Tacoma Rainiers. Another innovative 2006 promotion was "Take Her Out to the Ballpark Night," when the team offered pregame Baseball 101 classes for any ladies unable to define such rudimentary terms as the *splitter* and *suicide squeeze*. River Cats players and coaches taught the classes. Another hopping night was "Singles Night," when the team staged a pregame mixer at the Cuervo Cantina on the concourse behind third base.

On the Town

Set aside some time to check out **Old Sacramento,** where you'll find more than fifty historic buildings, many of which date back to the Gold Rush of the mid-1800s, as well as shops, restaurants, cafes, and saloons. The development of Old Sacramento began in 1839 when John Sutter established a fort near where the Sacramento and American Rivers meet. As the Gold Rush hit, the city continued to grow, despite fires and floods that set its progress back but did not deter its pioneering settlers. By the 1960s Sacramento's commercial hub had gradually shifted to the east, however, leaving Old Sacramento to become a blighted urban neighborhood. Fortunately, the city stepped forward with a redevelopment plan and succeeded in turning Old Sacramento into a popular tourist attraction that celebrates the area's glorious past. Today, visitors and locals enjoy trademark annual events in Old Sacramento like the Jazz Jubilee, Pacific Rim Street Festival, and Gold Rush Days. Popular destinations within the twenty-eight-acre old city include **Sutter's Fort** (2710 L Street), the **California State Railroad Museum** (111 I Street), and the **California State Capitol Museum** (10th and L Street).

ARROWHEAD CREDIT UNION PARK

Inland Empire 66ers

Class A, California League
(LOS ANGELES DODGERS)

Arrowhead Credit Union Park
280 South E Street
San Bernardino, California
909–888–9922

Arrowhead Park, previously known as "The Ranch," opened in 1996 to cement the California League's presence in San Bernardino. The resounding success of the new parks that opened in Rancho Cucamonga and Lake Elsinore in 1993 and 1994, respectively, convinced San Bernardino's decision makers that a new facility was in order to give its baseball community a shot in the arm. And they were right. Prior to The Ranch's opening in downtown San Bernardino, the local team played before small crowds at tiny Fiscalini Field on the outskirts of town. Ever since Arrowhead Park opened, San Bernardino has been drawing more than 200,000 fans per season.

The stadium was designed by HOK and constructed at a cost of $13 million. Inside, fans find a comfortable atmosphere and a seating bowl that provides clear views of the field. The San Bernardino Mountains span the horizon beyond the outfield fence, composing a gorgeous backdrop for a game, particularly in the early evening hours when the setting sun lingers on the mountain peaks.

Arrowhead Park's most distinguishing feature is outside, though, where fans find an exterior built in the tradition of the Spanish missions that sprung up in this part of the country back in the 1800s. The stadium's main entrance consists of several arched passageways. The pillars and arches, like the majority of the façade, are a delightful pastel yellow color. Upstairs on the second level, rectangular windows break up the expanse of yellow stucco, while an auburn roof caps the structure. While the stadium is certainly unique, it did remind me of a downsized version of Cracker Jack Stadium in Kissimmee, Florida. The spring training home of the Atlanta Braves embraces the same type of architecture and features a very similar yellow stucco finish.

As for the team that plays in San Bernardino, since the California League arrived in town in 1987, the local nine has changed its name, its ownership, and its big league affiliation so frequently that even some of the local fans with whom I spoke were left scratching their heads as they tried to recollect the details of the team's history. In 1987 the Ventura County Gulls moved to San Bernardino and fielded an unaffiliated California League team that was known as the "San Bernardino Spirit." The team was owned by a group led by Hank Stickney. After borrowing minor leaguers from several different major league organizations in 1987, the Spirit began a PDC with the Seattle Mariners in 1988. In the winter after the 1992 season, Stickney announced that he would be moving his operation to a new ballpark 20 miles away in Rancho Cucamonga. He took his affiliation with the Mariners with him, but renamed his team the "Rancho Cucamonga Quakes." To fill the void in San Bernardino, that same off-season the Salinas Spurs relocated to San Bernardino. The only problem was that they arrived in town without a big league affiliation. In any case the new ownership group resurrected the still warm Spirit identity and began scouring the minor leagues for players to play in San Bernardino in 1993. Before the season could begin though, the team was sold to the Elmore Sports Group. Under new management for the second time in one off-season, the Spirit pasted together a piecemeal roster of minor leaguers from several different parent clubs. The team played without a parent in 1993 and then again in 1994. In 1995 San Bernardino hooked on as a Los Angeles Dodgers affiliate as a new ballpark was being constructed downtown. The team changed its name to the "San Bernardino Stampede" and celebrated its last full season at Fiscalini Field by claiming San Bernardino's first California League championship. The Ranch opened in August of 1996. The next year, the Stampede attracted more than 270,000 fans to the new park. The team won back-to-back league titles in 1999 and 2000. In 2001 San Bernardino severed ties with the Dodgers and signed a PDC with the Mariners. Then in 2007 the team dumped the Mariners and renewed its relationship with the Dodgers.

In 2002 the city sold the naming rights to The Ranch to Arrowhead Credit Union. After the ballpark's name changed, the team changed its identity, dropping the "San Bernardino" from its handle and becoming the Inland Empire 66ers. The "Inland Empire" is local slang for the cluster of cities located northeast of Los Angeles. As far as I know, nothing particularly interesting happened in San Bernardino in 1966. Rather, the team is named after famous Route 66, which passes through town.

In March of 2002 the Mariners visited San Bernardino for an exhibition game against the 66ers. The event drew a large crowd, but no

Arrowhead Credit Union Park

one took the game too seriously. In fact actor Kevin Costner started the game at shortstop for the 66ers and even pitched an inning in relief. Seattle manager Lou Piniella stepped into the right-handed batter's box and took a few hacks, making a brief comeback after retiring as a player eighteen years earlier.

In addition to Costner, San Bernardino's alumni roster includes Ken Griffey Jr., Mike Hampton, Paul Konerko, Adrián Béltre, Mac Suzuki, and Felix Hernández.

Game Day

Getting to the Park

San Bernardino is 60 miles east of Los Angeles. The town is situated among the foothills of the San Bernardino National Forest. From the west, follow Freeway 10 East to Freeway 215 North, then take the exit for Inland Center Drive. Turn right onto Inland Center Drive, then turn left onto G Street, and follow G Street north to the stadium parking lots. Parking costs $3.00.

Inside the Park

The seating bowl keeps the majority of fans close to field level. Although the park can hold only 5,000 people, the seats continue almost all the way to the foul poles, as a result of there being so few rows. The first level offers eight rows of maroon seats. There is a small second tier consisting of twelve rows of dark green seats behind home plate, but this grandstand level extends only a third of the way down either baseline before giving way to the group patio areas.

The field level seats between the dugouts sell as Executive Boxes, while those farther down the baselines but still on the infield sell as Field Boxes. Seats on the first level in the outfield are called Bullpen Boxes. The seats in the small second tier behind home plate sell as Upper Boxes. When big crowds are expected,

the 66ers sell General Admission tickets to the grassy hill in left field. The twelve luxury boxes appear on either side of the press box behind the last row of Upper Boxes.

The concession menu is varied and tasty, offering Hebrew National hot dogs, hot dogs wrapped in bacon, grilled hamburgers, tri-tip steak sandwiches, chicken tenders, Dominoes Pizza, Hooters buffalo wings, roasted corn on the cob, baked potatoes, fruit cups, caramel apples, fresh baked cookies, funnel cakes, and cinnamon buns. Cuca's Mexican stand serves burritos, tacos, quesadillas, and salads. The ballpark also opens its Pastimes Cafe on Thursdays through Sundays. Located on the third base patio, this casual spot serves tri-tip, burgers, and grilled chicken sandwiches, as well as twenty-four-ounce drafts and sixteen-ounce margaritas.

The Little Cruisers Playland behind the third base patio offers a bouncy house, speed-pitch booth, and slide. On Fridays, the kids enjoy clowns, face painters, and pony rides. That's right, pony rides. This place used to be called The Ranch, after all.

The Arrowhead Park Experience

San Bernardino's popular mascot is Bernie, an amorphous, androgynous creature, who likes to spray fans with a Super Soaker and race youngsters around the bases. Bernie stands about 7 feet tall (counting the rainbow-colored mane atop his head), is covered with red fur all over, and wears a 66ers jersey with black tennis shoes. Judging from his appreciable girth, I think it's fair to say Bernie enjoys the excellent concession items at Arrowhead Park.

Bernie gets assistance in the on-field entertainment department from the 66ers dance team. The troupe consists of attractive young women who wear slinky blue pants and revealing blue tops that leave their midriffs and upper chest areas exposed. The Toronto Blue

Jays cheerleaders and the many cheerleaders of the Caribbean Winter League have nothing on these girls.

On the Town

As mentioned earlier the 66ers are named after Route 66, the historic road that passes through town on the way from Los Angeles to Chicago. Along Route 66 in San Bernardino visitors find the site of the very first McDonald's restaurant. The **San Bernardino McDonald's and Route 66 Museum** (1398 North E Street) is open from 10:00 A.M. until 5:00 P.M. daily, and admission is free. The museum features antique McDonald's playground items, Happy Meal collectibles, past promotional items, and a panel-by-panel mural that describes how the restaurant grew from a small hamburger joint in San Bernardino into a multinational leader in the cholesterol delivery business. Unfortunately, the building that houses the museum is not the original circular structure where folks were introduced to the Big Mac in 1940. That building was destroyed in 1972. Some may also consider it unfortunate that the museum doesn't serve any McDonald's food. But I suppose Morgan Spurlock, the producer/director/guinea pig of the 2004 documentary *Super Size Me,* would say it's just as well.

Fans looking to pay homage to the original hub of San Bernardino baseball activities can visit **Fiscalini Field** (1103 East Highland Avenue). Although it hasn't hosted a professional game since the San Bernardino Stampede moved to the city's new ballpark in 1996, Fiscalini Field still sees regular use as an amateur venue. The ballpark's dominant feature is the small mountain, known as Perris Hill, immediately behind its right field fence. The original ballpark that existed on this site was known as Perris Hill Park. Built in 1937, the field attracted the Pittsburgh Pirates to San Bernardino for spring training that year, and the Pirates returned every March through 1942. After training in Muncie, Indiana, during the war years, the Pirates returned to San Bernardino in the spring of 1946 for one final stint in the Inland Empire. The St. Louis Browns also trained at Perris Hill Park in 1946, then returned from 1949 through 1952. The city replaced Perris Hill Park with Fiscalini Field in 1986, building an aluminum stadium around the footprint of the original field.

SAN JOSE MUNICIPAL STADIUM

San Jose Giants

Class A, California League
(SAN FRANCISCO GIANTS)

San Jose Municipal Stadium
588 East Alma Avenue
San Jose, California
408–297–1435

With outfield views that showcase the Coastal Mountains that separate Silicon Valley from Santa Cruz County, San Jose Municipal Stadium offers a gorgeous setting for a baseball game on any clear spring day or warm summer night. The ballpark is brightly colored, festive, inviting, quirky, and everything else a minor league ballpark should be. The small grandstand extends no farther than the corner bases on either side, while evergreen trees rise behind the back of the stadium, sealing it in from the outside world. It is easy to see why this scenic park was featured on the cover of the annual *Baseball America* calendar in 1996.

An eccentricity that makes the field unique is the placement of several advertising signs above the outfield fence. Like most minor league parks, the outfield walls are plastered with colorful signs advertising the services of local companies. Unlike other parks several of these signs rise above the left field fence, almost like a set of oversized teeth. Balls that hit the signs and bounce back onto the field are still in play, while balls that slip through the gaps between them count as home runs. This unique ballpark feature drives California League umpires nuts but makes every long line drive that much more interesting for fans.

The main concourse beneath the grandstand is decorated with a painted mural that traces the history of organized baseball in San Jose all the way back to the 1800s. The mural tells the tales of the different players who have played at Municipal Stadium, representing nine different major league organizations since the stadium opened in 1942 as home to the San Jose Owls. With just a few lapses through the years, San Jose has consistently fielded a team ever since, thanks to affiliations with the Boston Red Sox, Pittsburgh Pirates, California Angels, Kansas City Royals, Cleveland Indians, Seattle Mariners, Montreal Expos, Baltimore Orioles, and San Francisco Giants. The timeline on the concourse pays tribute to every future major leaguer to have worn the San Jose uniform on his way to the big leagues. These alumni include such notables as California native George Brett, Alfredo Griffin, Rod Beck, Keith Foulke, Bill Mueller, Russ Ortiz, and Joe Nathan. The concourse also offers a wall of logos depicting other team logos from around the minors, various idyllic baseball scenes, and paintings of famous major leaguers. The women's restroom is painted in honor of the All-American Girls Professional Baseball League.

One of the most memorable seasons in recent San Jose history was 1986 when the San Jose Bees became known locally as the "Bad News Bees" thanks to the collection of banished former major leaguers on their roster. Many of the Bad News Bees had drunk or drugged their way back to the low minors. The team included former major leaguers Steve Howe, Mike Norris, Ken Reitz, Daryl Sconiers, Steve McCatty, Vern Ruhle, Todd Cruz, and Derrel Thomas. The cast of outcasts piqued the interest of local fans, as attendance jumped from 53,423 in 1985 to 87,235 in 1986, marking an increase of 60 percent.

One of San Jose's most memorable games occurred in May of 1995, when the Giants

San Jose Municipal Stadium

On March 8, 1942, more than 2,000 fans turned out to watch the first game in Municipal Stadium history, as the San Francisco Seals defeated the Portland Beavers. Through the years the stadium has been renovated and modernized, but it still retains an old-time atmosphere. In fact the renovations have done little to alter the main seating bowl or field. In 1988 the team added a left field barbecue stand called Turkey Mike's that serves some of the most delicious food in the minors. The home clubhouse underwent a major renovation in 1995, while in 1999 the dugouts got a makeover. In 2005 a VIP deck was added to the barbecue stand in left. Finally, a new video board was installed in 2006.

In addition to serving as the home of the San Jose Giants, Municipal Stadium also serves the San Jose State University baseball team and hosts the Central California State High School semifinals and finals each spring. In 1995 the San Jose Spitfires of Ladies League Baseball played their home games at Municipal Stadium, but they lasted just one season.

locked horns with the San Bernardino Spirit in a contest that seemed like it might never end. The game began on May 12, before being suspended after twelve innings with the score tied 0–0. The next day, the game resumed and the teams combined for another eight scoreless innings before the Spirit pushed across a run in the top of the twenty-first inning to end the longest shutout in California League history.

Today, more than 150,00 fans pass through Municipal Stadium's gates each season. San Jose has been affiliated with the San Francisco Giants since 1988, marking the longest current affiliation in the California League. This is a great fit for local fans, as the big league Giants play just 44 miles away.

The movement to build a professional baseball stadium in San Jose and to attract a minor league team began in 1940 when the city council voted to build a 2,900-seat ballpark at the corner of Alma Avenue and Senter Road. Municipal Stadium was built on the site of a former grain field for $80,000. Like many ballparks of the era, the project was part of Franklin Delano Roosevelt's WPA, an initiative designed to help the country rebound from the Great Depression.

Game Day

Getting to the Park

Municipal Stadium is located south of downtown, near San Jose State University and Kelley Park. From downtown, follow U.S. Highway 101 South to the Story Road West exit. Follow Story Road until you come to Senter Road and take a left, then turn right onto Alma Street, and the stadium will appear on the left. From I–280, take the 10th/11th Street exit and turn right onto 10th Street. Turn left onto Alma Street and the stadium will be on the right. The main parking lot is beside the stadium, while there is also an overflow lot across the street.

Parking costs $6.00 per car, while fans arriving early will find free spots on Alma Street.

Inside the Park

Municipal Stadium lists an official seating capacity of 4,000. The park usually sells out between July 1 and 4, when the promise of nightly fireworks packs the house. The first seven rows are comfortable Box Seats, while the remainder of the grandstand provides bleachers with backs that sell as General Admission. Smaller banks of bleachers without backs sit just past the main seating bowl on either side of the diamond.

There is no lateral walkway within the seating bowl, just four tunnels that lead from the covered concourse behind the seats to the stairways that rise between sections. A tiny brick press box sits amidst the bleachers behind home plate.

Down the left field line, Turkey Mike's offers delicious barbecued ribs, chicken dinners, Philly cheesesteaks, tri-tip steak, apple-chicken sausages, garlic fries, and orzo salads. Turkey Mike's also provides picnic tables where fans can enjoy a field-level view of the game while they eat. The general concession stands beneath the stadium offer meatball subs, lobster wraps, and the ballpark basics. Municipal Stadium serves a plethora of different bottled beers and drafts, including Pabst Blue Ribbon, Gordon Biersch, Red Hook, Sierra Nevada, and Heineken.

A number of peripheral activities enhance the Municipal Stadium experience for kids, including a speed-pitch booth, bouncy house, slide, and miniature golf hole.

The Municipal Stadium Experience

Here's one gameday tradition that I don't think you'll find anywhere else in this vast and wondrous baseball land of ours. In the middle of the eighth inning, an old bread truck drives onto the field in foul territory and three lucky fans are chosen to hand two baseballs each to a San Jose Giant player of their choice. Each player then takes aim at the truck with his two baseballs, and if he succeeds at breaking one of the truck's headlights, he and the fan both win $25. This is a very popular promotion with the local fans and with the local players, although the auto mechanic who has to keep installing new headlights on the truck is probably getting sick of the routine.

In 2006 the Giants introduced a new mascot—a gorilla named "Gigante." This hairy fellow wears a San Jose Giants shirt with number 1 on his back, a pair of torn shorts, and a pair of oversized shoes. What does a gorilla have to do with San Jose, you may be wondering? Well, the best I can figure is that he's supposed to be "giant."

On the Town

San Jose is the tenth-largest city in the United States, having recently surpassed Detroit in population. No offense to Detroit, but I'd much prefer to spend a weekend in sunny San Jose than grimy Motown, even if there are a few more people in San Jose these days.

San Jose features a number of excellent restaurants and an active nightlife scene. Sports fans looking to catch all of the games from the comfort of a bar stool will find plenty of TVs and an inviting atmosphere at the **San Jose Bar and Grill** (85 South Second Street), while **Tres Gringos Baja Cantina** (83 South Second Street) is famous for its El Guapo fish taco and other tangy Mexican entrees.

BANNER ISLAND BALLPARK

Stockton Ports

Class A, California League
(OAKLAND ATHLETICS)

Banner Island Ballpark
404 West Fremont Street
Stockton, California
209–644–1900

Sixty miles east of the major league stadium in San Francisco, where Barry Bonds made himself infamous by depositing baseball after baseball into the waters of McCovey Cove, traveling fans find the inland port city of Stockton. Although the Stockton Ports are currently affiliated with that *other* Bay Area team, the Oakland A's, long home runs to right field at their Banner Island Ballpark also culminate in dramatic splash landings. The ballpark, which opened in 2005, sits on the banks of the Stockton Deep Water Ship Channel, a waterway created in the early 1930s to allow for shipping access to the San Joaquin River. To reach the drink at SBC Park in San Francisco, major league long balls must clear the outfield fence, two rows of bleacher seats, and a public pier, which means they must carry a minimum of 420 feet. The water is a bit more reachable in Stockton, where California Leaguers need clear only the right field fence and the relatively narrow seating berm that runs behind the right field fence. Stockton's Deep Water Channel is only 389 feet from home plate.

While this unique right field waterway makes Banner Island Ballpark a sort of little brother to the stadium in San Francisco, Stockton's ballpark also conjures images of a certain old-time park on the East Coast. Just 300 feet from home plate in left field, fans find a 13-foot-high miniature version of Fenway Park's Green Monster. The fans in Stockton call this the "Mini-Monster." Ports owner Tom Volpe, a Boston native, surely appreciates this ballpark feature.

As you might have already deduced, the outfield in Stockton is anything but symmetrical. Unlike Fenway Park's Green Monster, which extends straight toward center field, in Stockton the Mini-Monster cuts back from the foul pole away from home plate at a very sharp angle, so that a ball hit directly down the foul line must travel only 300 feet to reach the wall, but a ball hit, say 20 feet inside the line, will have to travel about 350 feet. After shooting nearly straight back for 50 feet, the wall turns sharply again and continues a more traditional expanse toward center field, leaving room for both bull pens behind the wall in left and left-center. The wall in right field is nearly as odd, as a curved porch extends off the berm seating area to create a bubble in the wall. So, pay attention whenever a long fly ball heads toward one of the fences at Banner Island Ballpark, because chances are it is going to carom off at a crazy angle.

The arrival of Banner Island Ballpark to replace old Billy Hebert Field has really rejuvenated the Ports, and the hope is that the ballpark, as well as the several other new developments along the waterfront, will stimulate a downtown revitalization in Stockton. Hey, it worked in Denver and Baltimore, so why not in Stockton too? In addition to building a new ballpark for one of the California League's oldest teams, Stockton also recently built a sixteen-screen movie theater, restored its 1930s era Art Deco theater, and built a 10,000-seat indoor arena that houses minor league hockey, arena football, and indoor soccer. The hope is that all of these entertainment venues will attract new restaurants and shops to an area that had been in decline.

Banner Island Ballpark was built by the city for $22 million. HKS did the architectural work, and Volpe, who made his money as a Silicon Valley venture capitalist, kicked in more than a million dollars of his own money toward the construction. Talk about naming rights galore, just about every corner of the ballpark has been sold to one local business or another, but I suppose this is a good sign—the local community getting behind the new park and the new downtown vision.

Banner Island Ballpark opened on April 28, 2005, as the Ports beat the San Jose Giants 7–4 before an overflow crowd of 5,300 fans. Prior to the game the Ports had played their first nineteen games on the road, to allow for the ballpark to be completed. Buoyed by the arrival of the new park, and by the fact that the late start to their home schedule made for more home games than normal during the summer months, the Ports attracted a franchise-record 205,719 fans in the park's inaugural season.

While their ballpark is the newest in the California League, the Ports are one of the circuit's oldest franchises. Stockton fielded a team in the league's debut season of 1941 and then sat out the abbreviated 1942 season as the nation prepared for war. After the league took a time-out, Stockton was one of six cities to rejoin the league in 1946. The city held its place in the league for the next twenty-six years before dropping out in 1973. But Stockton jumped back into the fray in 1978, as a Seattle Mariners affiliate. The city has fielded a team ever since. Stockton switched to a PDC with the Milwaukee Brewers in 1979 and maintained that relationship until 2000, before signing on for shorter stints with the Cincinnati Reds and Texas Rangers. The current relationship with the A's began when the new ballpark opened in 2005. Notable players to suit up for Stock-ton include Pumpsie Green, Don Baylor, Cal Eldred, Bobby Grich, Dave Henderson, Glenn Braggs, Ben Sheets, and Gary Sheffield.

In the early 2000s, the Stockton team was known as the "Mudville Nine," in tribute to the Ernest Thayer poem, "Casey at the Bat," which was originally published in the *San Francisco Daily Examiner* in 1888. Stockton was home to a minor league team in the old California League at the time, and the team played on Banner Island, which was known as Mudville due to its tendency to flood. Although Stockton likes to take credit for inspiring the mythic Casey, Thayer always insisted the team, its ball field, and its players came straight out of his imagination.

Game Day

Getting to the Park

Before you set out to cruise the California shoreline in search of the port city of Stockton, remind yourself that Stockton is an inland port that is more than 50 miles from the Pacific Ocean. The city is a port by virtue of interconnected rivers and canals that make it accessible to the ocean by boat. Stockton is about 40 miles west of Oakland, 40 miles south of Sacramento, and 20 miles north of Modesto. U. S. Highway 5 runs through the western side of town from north to south. From the north, take the US 5 South to the Oak Street/Freemont Street exit and turn left onto Fremont. The ballpark will appear on the right at the corner of Freemont and Lincoln Streets. From the south, take the US 5 North to the Pershing Avenue exit. Turn right onto Flora Street, then turn right onto Orange Street, and finally turn left onto Freemont. There are several parking lots operated by the city that charge $8.00 per car, as well as a parking garage between the ballpark and the indoor arena. Those staying in town may want to save on parking by taking the Downtown Trolley (Route 19) to the ballpark. Trolley fare is only 25 cents.

Inside the Park

Banner Island Ballpark seats 4,200 fans in a low seating bowl that keeps everyone close to the action. There is room for an additional thousand fans on the berm and on the patio area in right field. The large concourse at the back of the seating bowl circles the entire field, allowing for additional standing room, and allowing fans to peer down into the bull pens in left. The Ports attract good crowds, so seats along the outfield foul lines may be the best visiting fans are able to do on arriving at the box office on game day. Don't bother fantasizing about the Scouts Seats, which are in the back rows behind home plate, or the Club Seats, which are in the back rows behind the Ports dugout on the first base side. These sell out before the season even begins. Lucky visitors might, however, score MVP Box Seats, between home plate and the corner bases, in the rows between the Scout Seats and Club Seats. Section 105 is at third base, Section 110 is behind home plate, and Section 116 is at first base. Past the bases, the MVP Boxes yield to the Field Boxes, which continue out to the foul poles. Keep in mind that a seat in deep left field is preferable to a seat in deep right field, since the left field foul pole is 26 feet closer to home plate than the one in right. Another option is to buy a pass to the Sprint Home Run Hill in right field, where fans are allowed to set up their own lawn chairs. Just don't get your hopes up about snagging one of the comfortable rocking chairs on the elevated home run porch in right, because they are reserved for group outings.

There are three main concession stands at Banner Island Ballpark: one behind home plate, one down the right field line out near the batting cages, and one down the left field line. These serve basic ballpark fare, as well as nontraditional items like beer-battered, deep-fried asparagus, which is a local specialty. Stockton holds an annual Asparagus Festival each April that draws crowds in the neighborhood of 100,000 people. As for me, I say, what will they think up next, deep-fried lima beans? The park also offers Slush Puppies, freshly brewed coffee, and frozen ice-cream bars. And best of all is the grill behind the batter's eye in straightaway center that serves sausages, barbecued ribs, and grilled chicken. Fans can grab a sandwich fresh off the grill and then settle down at one of the waterfront picnic tables along the back of the berm.

Fans can use the batting cages down the right field line. During the first four innings of each game, the machine throws 50 miles per hour (very hittable), then in the fifth and sixth innings it throws 65 miles per hour (relatively hittable), then in the seventh inning it lights up the radar gun with speeds that exceed 80 miles per hour (not at all hittable, especially if you've dulled your reflexes with a few beers and a few sausages during the early innings). Five swings cost a dollar, and the line moves quickly. Try not to embarrass yourself . . . too much.

The Banner Island Ballpark Experience

Stockton's loveable mascot is a creature of indeterminate species named "Splash." This larger-than-life fellow wears spiky blue hair, a Ports jersey, blue-and-white tennis shoes, no pants, and a smile on his face from ear to ear. A word to the wise: Hold onto your beer-battered, deep-fried asparagus or Splash is apt to steal it.

The Ports offer plenty of promotions to make the ballpark a fun and lively place. After Friday, Saturday, and Sunday games, the youngsters get to run the bases. On Wednesdays, the gray-hairs play baseball bingo, marking their cards after each out. On Thursdays, the party crowd enjoys twelve-ounce drafts for only a $1.00. On Fridays, a fifteen-minute fireworks show follows the game.

On the Town

Stockton is a good-sized city that offers ample hotels, restaurants, and bars for traveling fans. Located in the fertile San Joaquin Valley, Stockton has made its name importing goods from all over the world. In addition to the waterways cutting through town, there are quite a few railroad tracks. The ballpark neighborhood is still evolving, but there's every reason to think it will eventually become a lively entertainment district as the Ports and Stockton's other minor league sports teams help draw folks downtown.

Fans may want to check out the Ports old ballpark, **Billy Hebert Field** (at Oak Park). Baseball was played on this site as early as the 1890s, when fans turned out at Oak Park Baseball Field to watch Stockton's semipro teams. The park's original wooden grandstand was built in 1927, but after two fires the city built a concrete stadium in 1953 and named it after Billy Hebert—a local player for the Karl Ross Post American Legion team—who was killed in World War II. The ballpark was renovated in the early 1980s and then again in the early 2000s. Today, it serves Stockton as an amateur field.

Fans seeking a bite to eat or a few drafts on game day enjoy **Valley Brewing Company** (157 West Adams Street), **Garlic Brothers** (6629 Embarcadero Drive), and **Chitiva's Salsa & Sports Bar** (445 West Weber Avenue).

RECREATION PARK
Visalia Oaks

Class A, California League
(ARIZONA DIAMONDBACKS)

Recreation Park
440 North Giddings Street
Visalia, California
559–625–0480

The Visalia Oaks play at a ballpark that brings a whole new meaning to such clichéd ballpark adjectives as "intimate" and "cozy." Tiny Recreation Park is the centerpiece of a complex that also features a skate park, basketball courts, and picnic areas. The park offers only eleven rows of seats in its uncovered grandstand and a few small banks of bleachers along the right field foul line. It seats only 1,647 fans, making it the smallest full-season minor league facility.

Remarkably, the first row behind the backstop is just 28 feet from home plate. There is so little foul territory along the first and third base lines that fans in the front rows, should they be so inclined, could spit sunflower seeds at the corner infielders and have a legitimate chance of scoring a direct hit or two before being identified by the friendly ballpark staff and ushered out of the stadium. I'm not advocating this type of behavior, mind you, I'm just letting you know that it's actually possible in Visalia, in order to underscore just how close the fans are to the players.

It is fitting that Visalia is home to such a perfectly old-timey ballpark. The city's history in organized ball dates all the way back to the 1880s, when neighboring cities like Bakersfield and Fresno sent their best player to Visalia to compete for Central Valley bragging rights. Back then, the games were played on plots of farmland that would be modified to resemble baseball diamonds when necessary.

Visalia became a bona fide minor league town in 1946, when the city built Recreation Park. Since then the city has consistently fielded a team in the California League, except during the 1963 through 1967 seasons. In an effort to lure a minor league team back to town in 1967, Visalia rebuilt the stadium. The renovation replaced the old wooden grandstand with the current concrete seating bowl. At that time the city used soil from the trench that it dug to lay U.S. Highway 198 through central Visalia to build a mound around the exterior of the seating bowl. After building the mound the city encased it with cement and shot creek rock. The result is a bulbous concrete and rock façade that is highly unique on the landscape of today's professional baseball parks.

Buoyed by the new ballpark, Visalia succeeded in regaining its place in the California League in 1968. In the years since the city has gradually made additions to Recreation Park to keep it just big enough and modern enough to function as a minor league facility. An additional building was added on the left field side of the stadium in the 1990s to offer concession and restroom space. In 2003 the stadium underwent the most extensive renovation yet. The work added a tent-covered, 300-person picnic deck down the left field line and a ring of exterior fences around an enlarged concourse behind the seating bowl. The project also offered a bit of addition by subtraction, ripping out the old metal bleachers that had filled the seating bowl since 1967 and replacing them with comfortable green stadium chairs. This reseating dropped the stadium's official seating capacity from 1,800 to its current level.

In 2005 Visalia added a new clubhouse for the home team and gave the ballpark entrance gates a facelift. Attractive green-and-white awnings currently cover the gates, welcoming fans to the concourse behind the unusual concrete-and-rock mound that encases the seating bowl.

The Oaks have been an Arizona Diamondbacks affiliate since 2007. Previously, they enjoyed relationships with more than a dozen major league organizations. The team has been known as the Oaks since 1977, except for a brief stint as the Central Valley Rockies in 1993 and 1994. Through the years more than 140 Visalia players have gone on to play in the major leagues, including Kirby Puckett, who started his professional career in Visalia, and Jeff Francis, who pitched a no-hitter for the Oaks at Recreation Park. Other notables on the team's alumni roster include Kent Hrbek, Scott Erickson, Rich Harden, Barry Zito, Eric Chávez, and Nick Swisher.

In addition to the Oaks, Visalia's Redwood High School baseball team uses Recreation Park.

Game Day

Getting to the Park

Visalia is about 35 miles south of Fresno and 50 miles north of Bakersfield. From I–5 or U.S. Highway 99, take U.S. Highway 198 East to Visalia. Take the Mooney Boulevard exit and turn left on Giddings Street. The ballpark will appear on the right, 4 blocks north of US 198. From the east, follow US 198 to the Central Visalia exit. Drive 1 mile on Mineral King Avenue, then turn right on Giddings Street. Parking is free at the lots on Giddings Street and Murray Avenue.

Inside the Park

This stadium is so tiny that it's just plain silly. The seating bowl starts at first base and wraps around to third base, while three banks of separate bleachers provide additional seating down the right field line. The stadium offers fourteen luxury boxes, though there is nothing too luxurious about them. Located atop the seats on either side of a press box that provides room for about four people, these open-air boxes offer bar stools under beach umbrellas. All of the seats in the main bowl are stadium chairs with cup holders. The first three rows are below an interior walkway and sell as 100 Level Seats, while the eight rows behind the walkway are 200 Level Seats. Fans in Sections 100 through 107 around the plate enjoy a view of the batter's box that's about as up close and personal as that more commonly found at local Little League fields. The bleachers sell as General Admission. The picnic deck along the left field foul line is covered by an awning, but it's only available for group functions.

The concourse behind the stadium offers ballpark staples and tri-tip. The Corona Hut resembles the type of tin shanty featured in those Corona commercials on TV.

The Recreation Park Experience

The local mascot is Chatter the Squirrel, a furry creature who likes to beg for peanuts. At first I found myself wondering why the Angry Acorn emblem was so popular on hats and T-shirts among fans at Recreation Park. After all, who would want to walk around wearing a ticked-off nut on their person? Then I realized that it's because local fans share the Angry Acorn's contempt for Chatter and his insatiable appetite. You'll see what I mean during your visit. The real fun begins, for Chatter, I am told, when the Modesto Nuts come to town.

Recreation Park offers a nightly bus and trolley race that simultaneously entertains fans and promotes the Visalia Municipal Transportation Association. I say, put your money on the bus if you've been having a tough night at Mound Ball and are looking to recoup your losses. Put your money on the trolley if you want to do right by the environment.

The Oaks allow fans to run the bases after Friday, Saturday, and Sunday games.

On the Town

Visalia is a city of about 90,000 people, 35 miles west of **Sequoia National Park.** Those wishing to hike upon one of the many trails within the national forest's northern unit should follow Route 245 north toward Pinehurst, then follow the signs to where the tall trees grow. From Pinehurst fans can also access **King's Canyon National Park.** Baseball pilgrims who aren't really outdoor types can visit the **Visalia Adventure Park** (US 198 and Akers Street) to take a few swings in the batting cages and enjoy minigolf, laser tag, and bumper boats.

PGE PARK

Portland Beavers

Class AAA, Pacific Coast League
(SAN DIEGO PADRES)

PGE Park
1844 SW Morrison Street
Portland, Oregon
503–553–5400

With a history that dates back to 1926, PGE Park is the oldest facility still in use in the high minors, and one of the oldest yards in all of professional baseball, even if it didn't begin hosting the local nine on a regular basis until 1956. Want history? This plot at the corner of 18th Avenue and Morrison Street has it in spades. In 1893 the Multnomah Athletic Club began staging athletic events here at a humble venue known as Multnomah Field. Two years later, a group of barnstorming big leaguers passed through Oregon and stopped by the field just long enough to pummel the best local squad Portland could offer by a score of 22–4. By the time President William H. Taft visited Portland in 1909, a wooden grandstand that could hold 10,000 people had been erected at Multnomah Field. By the time President Warren G. Harding spoke at the field in 1923, plans to build a new 28,000-seat stadium were slowly gaining momentum. The new facility cost $502,000 to build and was funded largely by Portland citizens who shelled out $100 apiece to purchase their own plaque at the new stadium.

Multnomah Stadium opened on October 9, 1926, hosting a football game between the University of Oregon and the University of Washington. But for much of the next three decades, it was without a regular tenant. With U.S. presidents stopping by Portland only every three election cycles or so, and the Pacific Coast League's Portland Beavers content to stay at Vaughn Street Ballpark, the stadium sat empty for most of the year. From the early 1930s through the mid-1950s, it served primarily as home to the Multnomah Kennel Club. Finally, in 1956 the Beavers abandoned their old wooden park and moved to the biggest yard in town.

In 1966 Portland bought the stadium from the Multnomah Athletic Club for $2.1 million and renamed it Civic Stadium. In 1969 the stadium became the first outdoor baseball park in the United States to install artificial turf, beginning a trend that would soon spell an end to the natural grass fields at several big league stadiums.

Through the years the list of notable Americans to perform in their various areas of expertise at Portland's stadium grew to include such icons as Jack Dempsey, Joe DiMaggio, Elvis Presley, Pele, Bob Dylan, Bob Hope, Pete Rose, and Billy Graham. In addition to hosting Pacific Coast League baseball, Civic Stadium hosted major league and NFL exhibitions, World Cup soccer, and of course, the Rose Festival. In 1979 a group of major leaguers traveled to Portland for a home run derby and Willie Stargell hit a prodigious blast off the face of the Multnomah Athletic Club balcony, high above the right field fence. The Portland Breakers of the short-lived United States Football League played at Civic Stadium in 1985.

In 1991 Vancouver Canadians outfielder Rodney McCray crashed through the outfield fence in a game against the Beavers while trying to run down a fly ball. The play, which made national news programs, is still featured whenever ESPN or any other sports station compiles the best baseball bloopers of all-time. While the play was hilarious to watch—at least for those viewers not named Rodney McCray—it underscored the disrepair into which Portland's stadium was slowly slipping. After all, at the Triple-A level, teams can't have fielders running through outfield walls on a regular basis.

As is often the case in the minor leagues, it took losing the local team for a few years to get Portland to update its ballpark. In 1994 the Beavers moved to Salt Lake City, where a new ballpark awaited. A short-season Northwest League franchise moved into Civic Stadium to fill the void in 1995, and the Portland Rockies promptly broke the circuit's single-season attendance record, averaging more than 6,000 fans per game. Soon the wheels of local bureaucracy began slowly turning, moving toward a massive renovation that would bring Civic Stadium up to twenty-first century standards while preserving its old-time charm and atmosphere. The $38.5 million project began during the summer of 2000 and ended in time to welcome Pacific Coast League baseball back to the Rose City, a month into the 2001 season. Resurrected as a San Diego Padres affiliate, the Beavers played their first eight home dates at Dust Devils Stadium in Pasco, Washington, then moved to their refurbished home in Portland at the end of April.

The remodeled stadium was renamed PGE Park, thanks to a naming-rights deal with Portland General Electric. It resembles its old self, but features modern dugouts and bull pens, a new Nexturf playing surface, renovated concourses and concession areas, three levels of luxury boxes stacked on top of each other behind home plate, and a reseated lower half of the seating bowl full of green stadium chairs. The wooden benches from 1926 still remain in the upper half of the seating bowl, and the

PGE Park

3-D "Jantzen Diving Girl," who was a fixture atop the right field fence for years, has been relocated to the concourse behind home plate. The seven-story-high, 60-foot-wide manually operated scoreboard in left-center requires a staff of four to keep it up to date. The playing surface is well below street level, enabling passersby to peek down at the game through the wrought-iron gates that separate the stadium from 18th Avenue in left field. The Multnomah Athletic Club still stands on Salmon Street and towers over right field.

A large roof covers the steep upper half of the seating bowl that continues farther down the right field line than it does in left. The twenty-four luxury suites interrupt the expanse of upper-level seats behind home plate. Meanwhile, there are six field-level luxury suites behind the backstop on the third base side of home plate. The only home run territory seating comes in the form of a small party deck high above left-center field, out near the scoreboard.

Outside the park at the corner of 20th and Morrison, the home plate entrance is adorned by a massive piece of public art that is essentially a giant smiling face. A similar piece stands outside the left field gate at 18th and Morrison. The two sculptures, collectively titled *Facing the Crowd,* were created by local artist Michael Stutz. Behind them, the off-white stadium façade offers several narrow arches through which fans pass into the stadium.

All in all, Ellerbe Becket, who served as the chief architect for the renovation, and Turner Construction, who implemented the designs, did a nice job of blending the old with the new. But since reopening PGE Park, the Beavers have struggled to sustain the type of fan interest that exists in some Triple-A cities, making Portland's aspirations to one day become a big league city seem all the more unrealistic. The

Beavers currently average about 5,000 fans per game, or about half as many as turn out at the ballparks in the better Triple-A markets.

In addition to serving the Beavers, PGE Park hosts the Portland Timbers professional soccer team.

Game Day

Getting to the Park

Portland is in northwest Oregon, just across the Columbia River from Vancouver, Washington. PGE Park is a few blocks west of the downtown business district. From I–5 North, take I–405 to the West Burnside exit and then follow Southwest 20th Avenue to the stadium. Parking is limited, with fans at the mercy of private lots on 20th, 12th, and 10th Avenues and Taylor Street that charge between $5.00 and $10.00 per car. Another option is to take the MAX bus to the game. The MAX stops at the left field entrance to the ballpark.

Inside the Park

PGE Park can accommodate 19,566 fans when configured for baseball. There are forty-nine rows of seats, divided in the middle by an interior walkway. Below the walkway are 8,136 stadium chairs. Above the walkway are 10,681 bleachers seats.

The lower bowl begins in shallow left field with Section 101 and continues down the line to Section 107 at third base. The bowl makes the turn at Section 110 behind the plate and heads down the first baseline to Section 117 at the bag, before finishing at Section 123 in deep right. The first few rows in Sections 105 through 117, around the infield, sell as Club Seats—which belong to season ticket holders—while the seats behind them sell as Infield Reserved. The rest of the seats on the first level sell as Outfield Reserved. All of the wooden benches with backs in the upper bowl sell as General Admission. Owing to the stadium's status as a multiuse facility, there is more foul territory along the third baseline than on the first base side, so if you like to be as close to the action as possible, shoot for a seat near the visitors first base dugout.

The concession stands are located on the spacious concourse beneath the upper-level seats. The general stands offer the ballpark basics, along with decent Polish sausages. The Taco Del Mar stand has burritos, tacos, chili cheese dogs, and frozen margaritas. The Italian stand has pizza, sausages with peppers and onions, meatball sandwiches, and salads. The PGE Park Grill has bratwurst, hamburgers, garden burgers, and garlic fries. The Widmer Grill, at field level on the first base side, has seating for up to 400 people and a menu that includes half-pound burgers, double-smoked sausages, and cheesesteaks.

The PGE Park Experience

I was surprised to learn that beavers and feral cats can live together in apparent harmony. Get this: The Portland team employs more than twenty-five feral cats that live in the bowels of the stadium for the purpose of keeping a lid on the local rodent population. The cats are watered and fed (just not too much, they want to keep them hungry) at the Feral Cat Station behind the Beavers bullpen in left field. I asked team mascot Boomer the Beaver if the cats ever give him any trouble, and he told me, only when the grounds crew forgets to feed them, but otherwise they're good company.

On the Town

While the immediate ballpark neighborhood doesn't offer a wealth of things to do besides hunting for parking spots and watching baseball, there are plenty of joints just north and east of PGE Park where fans can grab a quick bite to eat as well as a drink before the game. The **Bullpen Tavern** (1730 SW Taylor Street) is a popular pregame and postgame hangout, while the **Kingston Bar & Grill** (2021 SW Morrison Street) is also right nearby.

Portland is a fun city that is well worth exploring. For entertainment and dining visit the **Hawthorne District** on the other side of the Willamette River, where there are lots of shops, restaurants, pubs, and cafes, or **Old Town**, which sits atop the supposedly haunted "Shanghai Tunnels" and offers a home to art galleries, Chinese restaurants, and the Portland Saturday Market.

To see the industrial park that now stands where **Vaughn Street Ballpark** (aka Lucky Beavers Stadium) stood from 1901 through 1956, visit 2409 NW Vaughn Street, where a historic marker memorializes the old yard.

For a Northwest League adventure, head 45 miles south on I–5 and watch the Salem-Keizer Volcanoes play at **Volcanoes Stadium** (6700 Field of Dreams Way, Keizer). Then head another 65 miles south and watch the Eugene Emeralds play at **Civic Stadium** (2077 Willamette Street, Eugene), a WPA facility built in 1938. The Volcanoes have been a San Francisco Giants affiliate since 1997, while the Emeralds have been a San Diego Padres farm club since 2001.

CHENEY STADIUM

Tacoma Rainiers

Class AAA, Pacific Coast League
(SEATTLE MARINERS)

Cheney Stadium
2502 South Tyler Street
Tacoma, Washington
253–752–7707

All it took for Tacoma to establish itself as a viable member of the Pacific Coast League was a second look from the historic circuit that visited its city limits back in the early 1900s and then did not return for more than half a century. While the fans in the rival city of Fresno waited ninety-two years for their town to get a second chance, the Tacoma faithful waited *only* fifty-five years to see their city rejoin the PCL. Tacoma originally belonged to the PCL in 1904 when the Tacoma Tigers took the league by storm, claiming a pennant in their very first campaign. But a midseason swoon in 1905, both on the field and at the turnstiles, prompted the team to move to Sacramento before that second season's end.

Flash forward one hundred years, and today the Tacoma Rainiers own the longest consecutive seasons played streak in the Pacific Coast League, a tenure that dates back to 1960. Much of the credit for Tacoma's success belongs to Cheney Stadium, a ballpark built prior to the start of the 1960 season using bits and pieces of San Francisco's recently demolished Seal's Stadium. Cheney Stadium still supports the game quite well, thanks to steady updates through the years by the city and Pierce County.

The effort to lure the PCL to Tacoma began in 1957, when local businessmen Ben Cheney and Clay Huntington began courting possible big league suitors to serve as Tacoma's parent club. The persuasive duo eventually convinced the San Francisco Giants to relocate their Triple-A team from Phoenix to Tacoma, contingent on the Tacoma City Council approving a plan to build a new stadium near Snake Lake. The city council came through, voting 8–1 in favor of the measure, and Cheney guaranteed the project's success by agreeing to pay for any cost overruns.

The inventor of the two-by-four stud wound up chipping in $100,000 toward the $940,000 project, and the stadium was completed in time for the opening of the 1960 season. The construction took just three months and fourteen days and utilized the wooden grandstand seats and outfield light stanchions from Seal's Stadium, which had served the PCL from 1931 until 1957 but was made obsolete by the arrival of the big league Giants and by the construction of Candlestick Park. Conveniently, Seal's Stadium was just about to meet the wrecking ball when the plans to build Cheney Stadium came together.

After the first scheduled game at Cheney Stadium was rained out—would you expect anything less in the soggy Pacific Northwest?—Tacoma christened its new yard with a doubleheader against the Portland Beavers on April 16, 1960. After losing the first home game in franchise history, the Tacoma Giants won the nightcap 11–0 behind the stellar hurling of an up-and-coming pitcher named Juan Marichal. The future Hall of Famer would begin his major league career in San Francisco later that season.

Ben Cheney was on hand that first day to witness the debut of the team he'd brought to town. And he's still on hand at Cheney Stadium today. A life-sized bronze sculpture of the affable lumber king sits in the stands between home plate and the Rainiers' first base dugout. Old Mr. Cheney has a bag of fresh roasted peanuts in his right hand, a scorecard and peanut shells at his feet, and a Cheney Studs emblem proudly displayed on his lapel.

Cheney Stadium possesses a 1960s-era charm that you won't find at too many other ballparks, owing to its construction at the end of the classic ballpark era when more utilitarian stadiums started going up. Most of those stadiums have since been destroyed, rather than preserved. Cheney Stadium's design features not the brick and steel popular in earlier and later stadium construction eras, but concrete, and lots of it. On pulling into the stadium parking lot, fans find an alarmingly stark façade that offers large concrete columns that rise not vertically but at an angle to support the underside of the concrete seating bowl. A separate one-story building serves as the ticket office, while a tiny press box sits high above the concrete stadium roof.

Surprisingly, Cheney Stadium is warm and cozy on the inside, despite all of the cement beneath and behind it, thanks to a small main seating bowl that is covered by a grandstand roof that is larger than normal. There are no luxury boxes atop the seats, so the stadium does not rise too high. The atmosphere is made warmer by the Rainiers' efforts to minimize the grayness of the concrete. For example, a colorful mural on the third base side of the concourse portrays eight players in a dugout, each wearing one of the different uniforms that Tacoma's teams have donned through the years. Along with the oldest and newest of the outfits—those worn by the Tacoma Tigers and Tacoma Rainiers—the mural also depicts the uniforms worn by the Tacoma Giants (1960–65), Tacoma Cubs (1966–71), Tacoma Twins (1972–77), Tacoma Yankees (1978), Tacoma Tugs (1979), and Tacoma Tigers (1980–94). The Tugs were affiliated with the Cleveland Indians, while the second incarnation of the Tigers was an Oakland A's farm club.

Recent renovations to Cheney Stadium have included the removal of most of the original wooden seats and bleacher benches that once occupied the top rows of the grandstand. In a nod to the stadium's history and to Mr. Cheney, who was not about to vacate his seat in Section K, Row 1, Seat 1, two small sections of the old wooden seats were left undisturbed. The recent work also lowered the outfield fences and added a new scoreboard in left-center that is topped with a faux Mount Rainier. As for the real Mount Rainier, its peak is visible on clear days beyond the first base seats. The outfield view is otherwise unremarkable, providing glimpses of a nearby school and of tall pines farther off. The outfield is the most spacious in the league, measuring 385 feet to the wall in the power alleys and 425 feet to the batter's eye in center.

Tacoma won two Pacific Coast League championships during its first decade—in 1961 and 1969—but has not won another outright championship since. Tacoma was declared a league cochampion, however, in 1978 along with Albuquerque, when the play-offs were rained out, and in 2001 along with New Orleans, when the terrorist attacks of 9/11 canceled the league's championship series.

Cheney Stadium draws about 330,000 visitors per season, which is low by Triple-A standards, but the team's place in the Pacific Coast League appears secure, given its long history in the league and their cozy relationship with the nearby Mariners. It remains to be seen, however, how much longer the Rainiers will continue to survive at Cheney Stadium without luxury boxes and without the revenue stream they provide. George Foster, the California poultry baron who owns the Rainiers, has been trying to sell the team since 2000. One of the hang-ups in finding a local ownership group has been the continued uncertainty as to whether Tacoma, Pierce County, and Washington State will chip in about $10 million to replace the concrete roof at Cheney Stadium with a more seismically safe steel one and to add some luxury boxes. We'll have to stay tuned to see if this neat old stadium gets another upgrade to ensure its continued success in the twenty-first century.

Game Day

Getting to the Park

Tacoma is 30 miles south of Seattle, positioned at the southern tip of Puget Sound. The nearest Pacific Coast League rivals are the Portland Beavers, who play 140 miles south. Cheney Stadium sits off U.S. Highway 16 at the intersection of Tyler Street and 19th Street. From I–5, take US 16 West and then take the 19th Street exit, heading east. Turn right onto Cheyenne Street and then either find a parking spot on the street outside for free or at the stadium lot for $5.00.

Inside the Park

Cheney Stadium offers 9,600 seats, all of which are in foul territory. The original seating bowl extends only to where the infield dirt meets the outfield grass on either side, then banks of bleachers with backs continue to the foul poles. Around the infield there are eight rows of lower seats, then a midlevel walkway, then seventeen rows above the walkway. The concourse runs behind the stadium at ground level, where it is sheltered by the underside of the grandstand. Section A is a little way past third base, while Sections G, H, and J are behind home plate, and Section P is just past first base. Sections A and K are the only ones to feature the old wooden seats from Seal's Stadium.

The Field Box Seats are the first two rows at field level. The Row Box Seats are the next six rows. After the walkway Rows 7 through 17—or the Reserved Seats—are beneath the roof.

The bleachers along the outfield lines are sold as General Admission. The bleachers on the left field side are preferable to those across the diamond, since the ones in right face the setting sun.

Cheney Stadium offers a group terrace above the bleachers in left and "bull pen barbecue" pits in front of the bleachers at field level in right and left. There is a food court on the concourse behind home plate and a small "pub" behind Section E. The ballpark barbecue is excellent, while the one-pound Mountain Burger topped with Canadian bacon is also a fan favorite. Don't worry lightweights, there's a half-pound burger on the menu too. The Rainier Dog is a meaty Cloverdale frank. The menu also includes pizza, Mexican, and several types of coffee. When it comes to suds, Tacoma fans enjoy Rainier Ale and Red Hook on tap, as well as microbrews like Fat Tire and Widmere Hefeweisen.

Be sure to check out the historic Tacoma mural on the third base side of the concourse, as well as the Tacoma Hall of Fame on the first base side, and stop by Section K to give Mr. Cheney a tip of your cap.

The Cheney Stadium Experience

The local mascot is a reindeer named "Rhubarb" who leads the youngsters onto the field midway through the game for a dash down the right field line. He also enjoys signing autographs. Rhubarb wears a full Rainiers uniform with a Tacoma cap nestled between his antlers. Rhubarb's antics aside, the atmosphere in Tacoma is agreeably low key, with fewer promotions and advertisements than at most parks these days.

The Tacoma fans got a treat during the 2006 season when Mariner great Edgar Martinez stopped by Cheney Stadium to watch a game. "Felix Hernández Bobble-Head Night" also drew a large crowd, as did "Seahawks Day," when members of the local gridiron squad stopped by the ballpark with some of their cheerleaders.

Thursday night is always "Dollar Night" in Tacoma when hot dogs, beer, soda and ice cream cost a buck each. Friday's game is followed by fireworks.

On the Town

Owing to Cheney Stadium's location in a residential neighborhood, there isn't much to do for road-tripping fans around the ballpark. Those intent on finding a pregame bite to eat can visit the cluster of fast-food joints a mile south of the stadium on Center Street.

While Tacoma has the general reputation of being Seattle's less-attractive and somewhat unpleasantly aromatic younger stepsister, there is at least one spot worth visiting in town before you head north to watch the big leaguers play at Safeco Field. **Point Defiance Park** (5400 North Pearl Street) juts out into the water between The Narrows and Commencement Bay, offering more than 700 acres of recreation space. The park includes hiking and biking trails through an old-growth forest, a replica lumber camp, batting cages and a go-cart racing track, a theme park for kids, a zoo and aquarium, a beach, and fishing piers. The park dates back to 1880 when it was established with help from President Grover Cleveland.

SECTION 5

SHORT-SEASON, ROOKIE, AND INDEPENDENT LEAGUES

NEW YORK–PENN LEAGUE

Class A, Short-Season

The fourteen-team New York-Penn League plays a seventy-six-game schedule that begins in the third week of June and ends in early September. The league is a frequent destination for just-drafted players, since league rules stipulate that no more than four players per team may exceed twenty-two years of age.

RIPKEN STADIUM, Aberdeen Ironbirds
(BALTIMORE ORIOLES)

> 873 Long Drive
> Aberdeen, Maryland
> 410–297–9292

Directions: Take I–95 to Route 22 West, then turn right onto Long Drive.

FALCON PARK, Auburn Doubledays
(TORONTO BLUE JAYS)

> 130 North Division Street
> Auburn, New York
> 315–255–2489

Directions: Take I–90 to exit 40 and turn right onto Route 34. Follow Route 34 for 8 miles to York Street and turn right, then turn left onto Division Street.

DWYER STADIUM, Batavia Muckdogs
(ST. LOUIS CARDINALS)

> 299 Bank Street
> Batavia, New York
> 585–343–5454

Directions: Take I–90 to exit 48 and turn left onto Route 98 South, then turn left onto Richmond Avenue, then left onto Bank Street.

KEYSPAN PARK, Brooklyn Cyclones
(NEW YORK METS)

> 1904 Surf Avenue
> Brooklyn, New York
> 718–449–8497

Directions: Take the Belt Parkway to Cropsey Avenue South and follow Cropsey until it turns into West 17th Street, which leads to Surf Avenue.

DUTCHESS STADIUM, Hudson Valley Renegades (TAMPA BAY DEVIL RAYS)

> Route 9D
> Wappingers Falls, New York
> 845–838–0094

Directions: Take I–84 to Route 9D North. Follow 9D for 1 mile to the stadium.

RUSSELL E. DIETHRICK, JR. PARK, Jamestown Jammers (FLORIDA MARLINS)

> 485 Falconer Street
> Jamestown, New York
> 716–664–0915

Directions: Take I–90 to Route 60 South, then turn left onto Buffalo Street and left onto Falconer Street.

EDWARD LELACHEUR PARK,
Lowell Spinners (BOSTON RED SOX)

450 Aiken Street
Lowell, Massachusetts
978–459–2255

Directions: Take Route 495 to the Lowell Connector and follow the connector to exit 5B, then follow Dutton Street to Father Morrissette Boulevard. Turn left onto Father Morrissette, then right onto Aiken Street.

EASTWOOD FIELD,
Mahoning Valley Scrappers
(CLEVELAND INDIANS)

111 Eastwood Mall Boulevard
Niles, Ohio
330–505–0000

Directions: Take I–80 to Route 82 West to Route 46 South. The stadium is located behind the Eastwood Mall.

DAMASCHKE FIELD, Oneonta Tigers
(DETROIT TIGERS)

95 River Street
Oneonta, New York
607–432–6326

Directions: Take I–88 to exit 15.

MEDLER FIELD AT LUBRANO PARK,
State College Spikes
(PITTSBURGH PIRATES)

Curtin Road and Porter Road
University Park, Pennsylvania
814–272–1711

Directions: Take I–80 to Route 150 South to Route 26 South. The stadium is located directly across from the South/East entrance to Beaver Stadium.

RICHMOND COUNTY BANK BALLPARK,
Staten Island Yankees
(NEW YORK YANKEES)

75 Richmond Terrace
Staten Island, New York
718–720–9265

Directions: Take I–95 to I–278 East and then take the Father Cappodanno Boulevard exit, which turns into Bay Street. The ballpark is beside the ferry terminal.

JOSEPH L. BRUNO STADIUM,
Tri-City Valleycats (HOUSTON ASTROS)

Hudson Valley Community College
80 Vandenburgh Avenue
Troy, New York
518–629–2287

Directions: From the north, take I–87, to Route 7, to I–787 South, then to Route 378 East, to Route 4 South, which leads to the Hudson Valley Community College campus.

CENTENNIAL FIELD, Vermont Lake
Monsters (WASHINGTON NATIONALS)

Colchester Avenue
Winooski, Vermont
802–655–4200

Directions: Take I-89 to exit 14W and turn right onto East Avenue. Follow East for 1 mile and then turn right onto Colchester Avenue.

BOWMAN FIELD, Williamsport
Crosscutters (PHILADELPHIA PHILLIES)

1700 West Fourth Street
Williamsport, Pennsylvania
570–326–3389

Directions: From the south, take Route 15 to Maynard Street and turn right, then turn left onto Fourth Street. From the north, take Route 15 to Fourth Street and turn left.

NORTHWEST LEAGUE
Class A, Short-Season

The eight-team Northwest League begins play in mid-June and finishes in early September. Recently drafted players are often assigned to the Northwest League to begin their professional careers. Each team in the league may have no more than four players over the age of twenty-two on its thirty-man roster.

MEMORIAL STADIUM, Boise Hawks (CHICAGO CUBS)

Western Idaho Fairgrounds
5600 North Glenwood Street
Boise, Idaho
208–322–5000

Directions: Take I–84 to Cole Road and continue north to the Western Idaho Fairgrounds.

CIVIC STADIUM, Eugene Emeralds (SAN DIEGO PADRES)

20th Avenue
Eugene, Oregon
541–342–5367

Directions: Follow I–5 to I–105 and take exit 2. Stay left and drive into downtown Eugene, picking up Eighth Avenue. Turn left onto Pearl Street and then follow 20th Avenue to the ballpark.

EVERETT MEMORIAL STADIUM, Everett Aquasox (SEATTLE MARINERS)

3802 Broadway
Everett, Washington
425–258–3673

Directions: Take I–5 to exit 192.

VOLCANOES STADIUM, Salem-Keizer Volcanoes (SAN FRANCISCO GIANTS)

6700 Field of Dreams Way
Keizer, Oregon
503–390–2225

Directions: Take I–5 to exit 260. Follow Chemawa Road west and then turn right onto Radiant Drive, which leads to Field of Dreams Way.

AVISTA STADIUM AT SPOKANE COUNTY FAIR AND EXPO CENTER, Spokane Indians (TEXAS RANGERS)

602 North Havana Street
Spokane, Washington
509–535–2922

Directions: From the east, take I–90 to the Broadway exit. Turn right onto Broadway and then left onto Havana. From the west, take I–90 to the Thor/Freya exit and follow Third Avenue east, then turn left onto Havana.

DUST DEVILS STADIUM, Tri-City Dust Devils (COLORADO ROCKIES)

6200 Burden Road
Pasco, Washington
509–544–8789

Directions: Take I–182 to Road 68 North. Turn right onto Burden Road.

NAT BAILEY STADIUM, Vancouver Canadians (OAKLAND ATHLETICS)

> Clancy Loranger Way
> Vancouver, British Columbia
> 604–872–5232

Directions: Take U.S. Highway 99 to Oak Street, then turn right onto 41st Avenue, left onto Main Street, and right onto Clancy Loranger Way.

YAKIMA COUNTY STADIUM, Yakima Bears (ARIZONA DIAMONDBACKS)

> Pacific Avenue
> Yakima, Washington
> 509–457–5151

Directions: Take I–82 to Nob Hill Boulevard West. Turn right onto Fair Avenue and then right onto Pacific Avenue.

APPALACHIAN LEAGUE
Rookie League, Advanced

The ten-team Appalachian League begins play in mid-June and finishes its sixty-eight-game schedule by the end of August. Players must have no more than two years of prior professional experience to be eligible.

BOWEN FIELD, Bluefield Orioles (BALTIMORE ORIOLES)

> Stadium Drive/Bluefield City Park
> Bluefield, West Virginia
> 276–326–1326

Directions: Take I–77 to Route 290 to Route 460 West. Turn right onto Leatherwood Lane, then left at the first light and then a right onto Stadium Drive.

BURLINGTON ATHLETIC STADIUM, Burlington Indians (KANSAS CITY ROYALS)

> 1450 Graham Street
> Burlington, North Carolina
> 336–222–0223

Directions: Take I–40 to Route 100 North/Maple Street. Turn right onto Mebane Street, then right onto Beaumont Street, then left onto Graham Street.

DEVAULT MEMORIAL STADIUM, Bristol White Sox (CHICAGO WHITE SOX)

> 1501 Euclid Avenue
> Bristol, Virginia
> 540–645–7275

Directions: Take I–81 to exit 3, Commonwealth Avenue. Turn right onto Euclid Avenue.

DAN DANIEL MEMORIAL PARK, Danville Braves (ATLANTA BRAVES)

> 302 River Park Drive
> Danville, Virginia
> 434–797–3792

Directions: Take the U.S. Highway 29 Bypass to the River Park Drive exit and follow the signs to the ballpark.

JOE O'BRIEN FIELD, Elizabethtown Twins
(MINNESOTA TWINS)

> 208 North Holly Lane
> Elizabethton, Tennessee
> 423–547–6441

Directions: Take I–81 to U.S. Highway 26 to the U.S. Highway 321 exit and then turn left onto Holly Lane.

PIONEER PARK, Greeneville Astros
(HOUSTON ASTROS)

> Tusculum College Campus
> Greeneville, Tennessee
> 423–638–0411

Directions: Take I–81 to exit 23 and merge onto West Andrew Johnson Highway. After 16 miles, turn right onto Tusculum Boulevard, then turn into the entrance for Tusculum College.

HOWARD JOHNSON FIELD, Johnson City Cardinals (ST. LOUIS CARDINALS)

> 111 Legion Street
> Johnson City, Tennessee
> 423–461–4866

Directions: Take I–81 to exit 32 and turn left onto East Main Street, then follow Legion Street to the ballpark.

HUNTER WRIGHT STADIUM, Kingsport Mets (NEW YORK METS)

> 800 Granby Road
> Kingsport, Tennessee
> 423–378–3744

Directions: Take I–81, to I–181 North, to the Stone Drive exit. Turn left onto West Stone Drive, then right onto Granby Road.

HUNNICUTT FIELD, Princeton Devil Rays
(TAMPA BAY DEVIL RAYS)

> Old Bluefield Road
> Princeton, West Virginia
> 304–487–2000

Directions: Take I–77 to exit 9 and follow Route 460 West. Turn left onto Stafford Drive, then onto Old Bluefield Road. The ballpark is behind the Mercer County Technical Education Center.

CALFEE PARK, Pulaski Blue Jays
(CURRENTLY UNAFFILIATED)

> Pierce Avenue
> Pulaski, Virginia
> 540–980–1017

Directions: Take I–81 to Route 11 North. Turn right onto Pierce Avenue.

PIONEER LEAGUE
Rookie League, Advanced

The Pioneer League is an eight-team league that plays a seventy-six-game schedule from mid-June until early September. Each team has a thirty-five-man roster that may include only seventeen players age twenty-one or older.

COBB FIELD, Billings Mustangs
(CINCINNATI REDS)

> Ninth Avenue
> Billings, Montana
> 406–252–1241

Directions: Take I–90 to 27th Street North, then follow Ninth Avenue North to the ballpark.

MIKE LANSING FIELD, Casper Rockies
(COLORADO ROCKIES)

> Crossroads Park
> Casper, Wyoming
> 307–232–1111

Directions: Take I–25 to the Poplar Street exit and follow Poplar Street North. Turn right into Crossroads Park.

LEGION PARK, Great Falls White Sox
(CHICAGO WHITE SOX)

> 25th Street North
> Great Falls, Montana
> 406–452–5311

Directions: Take I–15 to 10th Avenue South. Follow 10th Avenue for 4 miles, then turn left onto 8th Avenue North. Turn left onto 25th Street North.

KINDRICK FIELD, Helena Brewers
(MILWAUKEE BREWERS)

> Memorial Park
> Main Street
> Helena, Montana
> 406–495–0500

Directions: Take I–15 to the Cedar Street exit and follow Main Street West.

MCDERMOTT FIELD, Idaho Falls Chukars
(KANSAS CITY ROYALS)

> Mound Avenue
> Idaho Falls, Idaho
> 208–522–8363

Directions: Take I–15 to the West Broadway exit and turn left onto Memorial Drive, then right onto Mound Avenue.

MISSOULA CIVIC STADIUM, Missoula Osprey (ARIZONA DIAMONDBACKS)

> McCormick Park
> Missoula, Montana
> 406–543–3300

Directions: Take I–90 to Orange Street/Business Route 93 South. Turn right onto Craig Lane. The stadium is on the west side of McCormick Park.

LINDQUIST FIELD, Ogden Raptors
(LOS ANGELES DODGERS)

2330 Lincoln Avenue
Ogden, Utah
801–393–2400

Directions: Take I–15 to the 21st Street exit and follow 21st Street East. Turn right onto Lincoln Avenue.

HOME OF THE OWLZ, Orem Owlz
(LOS ANGELES ANGELS OF ANAHEIM)

Utah Valley State College
970 West University Parkway
Orem, Utah
801–377–2255

Directions: Take I–15 to exit 272 and follow University Parkway to the Utah Valley State College campus.

ARIZONA FALL LEAGUE
Developmental League

The Arizona Fall League offers the chance to see six teams in action during a thirty-two-game schedule that takes place in October and early November. The teams are composed of players who have less than two years of major league service time. Each team is stocked with prospects representing five different major league organizations. The teams utilize four ballparks that are also used as Cactus League venues during spring training.

SCOTTSDALE STADIUM, Grand Canyon Rafters and Scottsdale Scorpions

7408 East Osborn Road
Scottsdale, Arizona

Directions: Take Route 101 to the Indian School Road exit. Follow Indian School Road West, then turn left onto Drinkwater Road, then onto East Osborn. The ballpark will be on the left near the Civic Center.

HOHOKAM PARK, Mesa Solar Sox

1235 North Center Street
Mesa, Arizona

Directions: Take I–10 to Route 60, and then take Route 87 North. Turn right onto Brown Road and then left onto Center Street.

PEORIA STADIUM, Peoria Javelinas and Peoria Saguaros

1601 North 83rd Avenue
Peoria, Arizona

Directions: Take I–17 to the Bell Road exit and follow Bell Road to 83rd Avenue. Turn left onto 83rd Avenue.

PHOENIX MUNICIPAL STADIUM, Phoenix Desert Dogs

5999 East Van Buren Street
Phoenix, Arizona

Directions: Take I–10 to U.S. Highway 202 to the Priest Avenue exit. Follow Priest Avenue North for 1 mile to East Van Buren.

AMERICAN ASSOCIATION
Independent

Borrowing its name from the longtime Triple-A league that included teams from across the Midwest until disbanding in 1998, the new American Association debuted in 2006. The league features an assortment of teams that had previously played under the banners of the Central and Northern Leagues. The biggest coup for the American Association was convincing the mother of all indies, the St. Paul Saints, to leave the Northern League and join its members in time for the inaugural season. The Saints, who are owned by the wacky Goldklang Group, draw nearly 300,000 fans per season to Midway Stadium, making them far and away the hottest ticket in the AA.

The league is divided into Northern and Southern Divisions and plays a ninety-six-game split schedule that begins in mid-May and ends late in August. After the season, the first-half and second-half winners of each division meet in best-of-five-game play-off series, then the two play-off winners meet in a best-of-five-game league championship.

Each team has a twenty-two-man roster that must include at least five first-year pros and can include no more than four players with as many as four years of professional experience.

FAIRGROUNDS FIELD, Coastal Bend Aviators

U.S. Highway 44 and U.S. Highway 77
Robstown, Texas
361–387–8585

Directions: The ballpark is 12 miles west of downtown Corpus Christi at the junction of US 44 and US 77.

COHEN STADIUM, El Paso Diablos

9700 Gateway North Boulevard
El Paso, Texas
915–755–2000

Directions: Take I–10 to Route 54 East (Patriot Freeway) into Diana, then follow Gateway North Boulevard to the ballpark.

LAGRAVE FIELD, Fort Worth Cats

301 NE Sixth Street
Fort Worth, Texas
817–226–2287

Directions: Follow I–30 to I–35 North to North Side Drive to Main Street West. Take Main Street West to NE Sixth Street.

HAYMARKET PARK, Lincoln Saltdogs

403 Line Drive
Lincoln, Nebraska
402–474–2255

Directions: Follow I–80 to Cornhusker Highway West. Turn left onto First Street, then right onto Sun Valley Boulevard and left onto Line Drive.

PELICAN PARK, Pensacola Pelicans

University of West Florida Sports Complex
Campus Drive
Pensacola, Florida
850–934–8444

Directions: Take I–10 to Route 291 North (Davis Highway), to University Parkway, to Campus Drive.

PHIL WELCH STADIUM,
St. Joseph Blacksnakes

2600 SW Parkway
St. Joseph, Missouri
816–279–6777

Directions: From I–29, take U.S. Highway 36 West. Turn left onto 28th Street and follow to the stadium.

MIDWAY STADIUM, St. Paul Saints

1771 Energy Park Drive
St. Paul, Minnesota
651–644–3517

Directions: Take I–94 to Snelling Avenue North, then turn left onto Energy Park Drive.

FAIR GROUNDS FIELD, Shreveport Sports

Louisiana State Fairgrounds
Shreveport, Louisiana
318–636–5555

Directions: Take I–20 to Route 171 (Hearne Avenue) and follow to the State Fairgrounds.

LEWIS AND CLARK PARK,
Sioux City Explorers

3400 Line Drive
Sioux City, Iowa
712–277–9467

Directions: Take I–29 to Singing Hills Boulevard North, then turn right onto Line Drive.

SIOUX FALLS STADIUM,
Sioux Falls Canaries

1001 North West Avenue
Sioux Falls, South Dakota
605–333–0179

Directions: Take I–29 to Russell Street South, then turn right onto West Avenue.

ATLANTIC LEAGUE
Independent

The Atlantic League was founded in 1998. It is split into Northern and Southern Divisions and plays a 126-game split schedule that begins late in April and ends in mid-September. After the regular season, the first-half and second-half division winners play one another in best-of-three-game play-off series, then the two division champs meet in a five-game finale to decide the league title. The league's best draw each year is the Long Island franchise, which typically sells out all of its games and ushers more than 400,000 fans through the turnstiles each season.

THE SANDCASTLE, Atlantic City Surf

545 North Albany Avenue
Atlantic City, New Jersey
609–344–8873

Directions: Take the Atlantic City Expressway to exit 2, then follow Routes 40/322 East to the ballpark.

THE BALLPARK AT HARBOR YARD,
Bridgeport Bluefish

500 Main Street
Bridgeport, Connecticut
203–345–4800

Directions: Follow I–95 to exit 27, then take Routes 8/25 North to exit 1/Main Street.

CAMPBELL'S FIELD, Camden Riversharks

401 North Delaware Avenue
Camden, New Jersey
856–963–2600

Directions: Take I–676 to exit 5B and follow the signs off the exit ramp to the ballpark.

CLIPPER MAGAZINE STADIUM,
Lancaster Barnstormers

650 North Prince Street
Lancaster, Pennsylvania
717–509–4487

Directions: Take Route 30 to either the Fruitville Pike or Harrisburg Pike toward downtown Lancaster. The stadium sits at the intersection of Prince Street and the Harrisburg Pike.

CITIBANK PARK, Long Island Ducks

3 Court House Drive
Central Islip, New York
631–940–3825

Directions: Follow the Southern State Parkway East to Carleton Avenue North, then turn right onto Court House Drive.

RIVERFRONT STADIUM,
Newark Bears

450 Broad Street
Newark, New Jersey
973–848–1000

Directions: Follow the Garden State Parkway to I–280 East, to exit 15, or follow the New Jersey Turnpike to I–280 West, to exit 15A.

COMMERCE BANK BALLPARK,
Somerset Patriots

One Patriots Park
Bridgewater, New Jersey
908–252–0700

Directions: Take Route 287 North to exit 13B, or take Route 287 South to exit 13.

THE ROAD WARRIORS

The Road Warriors played all of their games on the road in 2006 and were still looking for a city to call home when this book went to print.

CAN-AM LEAGUE
Independent

The Can-Am League was formed in 2005. Its teams play a ninety-two-game split season that begins late in May and ends in early September. After the regular season, the league's first-half and second-half winners meet the two non-division-winning teams with the best overall records in best-of-five-game play-off series. Then the two first-round winners square off in a five-game series for the league title. League rules specify that each team's twenty-two-man roster must include no more than four players who have four years or more of professional experience and at least five first-year pros.

CAMPANELLI STADIUM, Brockton Rox

1 Lexington Avenue
Brockton, Massachusetts
508–559–7000

Directions: Follow I–24 to Route 123 East (Belmont Street). Follow Belmont for about a mile, then right onto West, and right onto Lexington Avenue. The stadium will appear on the right.

LE STADE MUNICIPAL DE QUÉBEC, Les Capitales de Québec

Parc Victoria
Quebec City, Quebec
481–521–2255

Directions: Take Highway 40 to Highway 173, exit 2, to Parc Victoria.

HOLMAN STADIUM, Nashua Pride

67 Amherst Street
Nashua, New Hampshire
603–883–2255

Directions: Take Route 3 to exit 7E and follow Amherst Street to the stadium.

YALE FIELD, New Haven Country Cutters

252 Derby Avenue
West Haven, Connecticut
203–777–5636

Directions: Take I–95 to Route 10 and follow the signs for the Yale Bowl.

YOGI BERRA STADIUM, New Jersey Jackals

Montclair State University Campus
Upper Montclair, New Jersey
973–746–7434

Directions: Take the Garden State Parkway to Route 46, then take the Valley Road exit to Montclair State University.

FRASER FIELD, North Shore Spirit

365 Western Avenue
Lynn, Massachusetts
781–592–0007

Directions: From Route 128, take Route 129 into Lynn, then turn left onto Chestnut Street and right onto Western Avenue.

SKYLANDS PARK, Sussex Skyhawks

94 Championship Place
Augusta, New Jersey
973–300–1000

Directions: Take I–80 to Route 15 North and follow to Ross Corner, then turn right onto County Road 565, which leads to Championship Place.

HANOVER INSURANCE PARK AT FITTON FIELD, Worcester Tornadoes

College of the Holy Cross Campus
Worcester, Massachusetts
508–792–2288

Directions: Take I–290 to exit 11. Turn right onto College Street, then left onto Fitton Avenue.

FRONTIER LEAGUE
Independent

With a history that dates back to 1993, the Frontier League is one of the two oldest currently operating independent leagues, sharing the distinction with the Northern League, which debuted the same year. The Frontier League plays a ninety-six-game season that begins late in May and ends in early September. The league includes East and West Divisions and after the season stages a playoff tournament involving the top two finishers in each division. Both the opening and championship rounds are best-of-five-game affairs. Teams have twenty-four-man rosters that must include at least ten first-year players. Players who are older than twenty-seven years of age are ineligible.

V.A. MEMORIAL STADIUM, Chillicothe Paints

State Route 104
Chillicothe, Ohio
740–773–8326

Directions: The stadium is 4 miles north of Chillicothe. Take Route 23 to Bridge Street, then take Route 35 West to Route 104 North.

CHAMPION WINDOW FIELD, Florence Freedom

7950 Freedom Way
Florence, Kentucky
859–594–4487

Directions: Take I–71/I–75 South to exit 180 and turn left onto U.S. Highway 42, then right onto Freedom Way.

BOSSE FIELD, Evansville Otters

1701 North Main Street
Evansville, Indiana
812–435–8686

Directions: Take Route 41 to Diamond Avenue West. Turn left onto Heidelbach Avenue and follow it to the ballpark at the intersection of Main Street.

GMC STADIUM, Gateway Grizzlies

2301 Grizzlie Bear Boulevard
Sauget, Illinois
618–337–3000

Directions: Take I–255 to Mousette Lane, then take Sauget Industrial Park Drive West to Goose Lake Road.

HOMER STRYKER FIELD,
Kalamazoo Kings

> 251 Mills Street
> Kalamazoo, Michigan
> 269–388–8326

Directions: Take I–94 to Sprinkle Road North, then turn left onto Business Loop I–94, left onto Kings Highway, and right onto Mills Street.

T. R. HUGHES BALLPARK,
River City Rascals

> 900 Ozzie Smith Drive
> O'Fallon, Missouri
> 636–240–2287

Directions: Take I–70 to exit 219 and follow T. R. Hughes Road North to the ballpark.

RIVERHAWKS STADIUM,
Rockford RiverHawks

> 4503 Interstate Boulevard
> Loves Park, Illinois
> 815–885–2255

Directions: Take I–90 to Riverside Boulevard East to Interstate Boulevard.

MARION STADIUM,
Southern Illinois Baseball Group

> The Hill District
> Marion, Illinois
> 618–998–8499

Directions: The stadium is located northwest of the intersection of Illinois Route 13 and I–57.

WUERFEL PARK,
Traverse City Beach Bums

> 333 Stadium Drive
> Traverse City, Michigan
> 231–943–0100

Directions: The ballpark is located just north of the Route 31 and Route 37 intersection. From the intersection, follow Chum's Village Drive to the ballpark.

FALCONI FIELD, Washington Wild Things

> One Washington Federal Way
> Washington, Pennsylvania
> 724–250–9555

Directions: From I–70, take exit 15 and turn right on Chestnut Street. Follow to the Washington Crown Center Mall and turn right onto Mall Drive, which leads to the stadium.

HAWKINSON FORD FIELD,
Windy City Thunderbolts

> 14011 South Kenton Avenue
> Crestwood, Illinois
> 708–489–2255

Directions: Take I294 to Cicero Avenue/Route 50 South, then turn left onto the Midlothian Turnpike and right onto Kenton Avenue.

GOLDEN LEAGUE
Independent

The Golden League, which includes Rickey Henderson and Jose Canseco among its alumni, debuted in 2005. Unlike traditional professional leagues, which are composed of independently owned franchises, the Golden League owns all of its franchises. The eighty-game split season begins in early June and ends in late August. The first-half and second-half winners meet in a best-of-five series to determine the league champion.

NETTLETON STADIUM, Chico Outlaws

400 West First Street
Chico, California
530–345–3210

Directions: Take Route 99 North to Route 32 West, then turn right onto Main Street and left onto West First Street.

GOODWIN FIELD, Fullerton Flyers

800 North State College Boulevard
Fullerton, California
714–526–8326

Directions: From the Orange Freeway/U. S. Highway 57, take the Yorba Linda Boulevard exit and follow Yorba Linda West. Turn left onto Associated Road.

BLAIR FIELD, Long Beach Armada

10th Street and Park Avenue
Long Beach, California
562–597–9787

Directions: From 405 North, take Seventh Street/22 West and then turn right onto Park Avenue.

PECCOLE PARK, Reno Silver Sox

University of Reno Campus
Reno, Nevada
775–348–7769

Directions: From I–80, take the Virginia Street exit and follow Virginia North. Turn right onto Ninth Street, which turns into Evans Avenue and leads to the park.

TONY GWYNN STADIUM, San Diego Surf Dogs

San Diego State University Campus
San Diego, California
619–282–4487

Directions: From I–8, take College Avenue South, then turn right onto Montezuma Road, and right onto 55th Street, which leads to campus.

DESERT SUN STADIUM, Yuma Scorpions

1280 West Desert Sun Drive
Yuma, Arizona
928–257–4700

Directions: From I–8, take Fourth Avenue and follow to Avenue A, which takes you directly to the stadium.

NORTHERN LEAGUE
Independent

Perhaps the most well known of the independent leagues, owing to the multitude of players it has graduated to affiliated ball and the major leagues since forming in 1993, the Northern League continues to thrive in the United States and Canada. One of the league's franchises drew some negative attention to the circuit in 2006 though, as the owner of the Schaumburg Flyers allowed his team's fans to run the club through Internet voting. The team floundered, while fans routinely set starting lineups that placed players out of their normal positions, and TV cameras from the TV production company LivePlanet followed every move the players made for a reality show.

FOOTHILLS STADIUM, Calgary Vipers

2255 Crowchild Trail NW
Calgary, Alberta
403–277–2255

Directions: The stadium is located at the intersection of Crowchild Trail and 24th Avenue.

TELUS FIELD, Edmonton Cracker-Cats

10233 96th Avenue
Edmonton, Alberta
780–423–2255

Directions: Follow Calgary Trail North to Queen Elizabeth Hill, turn right onto the Walterdale Bridge and then right onto 96th Avenue.

NEWMAN OUTDOOR FIELD, Fargo-Moorehead Redhawks

Albrecht Boulevard
Fargo, North Dakota
701–235–6161

Directions: Follow I–29 North to 19th Avenue North to FargoDome. Then turn right on Albrecht Avenue.

U.S. STEEL YARD, Gary Southshore Railcats

One Stadium Plaza
Gary, Indiana
219–882–2255

Directions: From I–90, take the exit for Broadway South and turn left onto Fifth Street.

SILVER CROSS FIELD, Joliet Jackhammers

Jefferson Street
Joliet, Illinois
815–726–2255

Directions: Follow I–80 to the exit for Route 53 North (Chicago Street) and turn right onto Washington Street, then right onto Jefferson Street.

COMMUNITY AMERICA BALLPARK, Kansas City T-Bones

State Avenue and 110th Street
Kansas City, Kansas
913–328–2255

Directions: Follow I–70 to I–435 North, then take the State Avenue exit. Follow State Avenue west for 1 mile.

ALEXIAN FIELD, Schaumburg Flyers

1999 South Springinsguth Road
Schaumburg, Illinois
847–891–2255

Directions: From I–290, take the Elgin-O'Hare Expressway West to the Irving Park Road exit. Turn left onto Springinsguth Road.

CANWEST GLOBAL PARK,
Winnipeg Goldeyes

> Water Avenue
> Winnipeg, Manitoba
> 204–982–2273

Directions: Take Route 75/Pembina Highway, to River Avenue East, to Main Street North, then to Water Avenue East.

UNITED LEAGUE
Independent

The United League debuted in 2006, offering fans six teams hailing from Texas and Louisiana. Like the Golden League, which owns all of its franchises, the United League is made up of teams that all operate under the central ownership of the league. The ninety-game season begins in mid-May and ends late in August. The top four teams participate in a two-round play-off tourney.

BRINGHURST FIELD, Alexandria Aces

> 1 Babe Ruth Drive
> Alexandria, Louisiana
> 318–473–2237

Directions: Follow I–49 North to exit 80 and follow Route 71 toward MacArthur Drive. Merge onto US 165 Business North/Masonic Drive, then turn left onto Babe Ruth Drive.

DILLA VILLA, Amarillo Dillas

> 3300 3rd Street
> Amarillo, Texas
> 806–342–0400

Directions: From I–40, take exit 72B onto E I–40 toward Grand Street. The ballpark is located a block west of Grand Street.

EDINBURG BASEBALL STADIUM,
Edinburg Coyotes

> 920 North Sugar Road
> Edinburg, Texas
> 956–386–0080

Directions: From I–281, take West Schurior Street to North Sugar Road. Turn right onto North Sugar.

VETERANS FIELD, Laredo Broncos

> 2211 Santa Maria
> Laredo, Texas
> 956–723–2273

Directions: From I–35 South, take exit 1B and follow Santa Ursula Avenue to Park Street. Turn right, then right again onto Santa Maria.

HARLINGEN FIELD,
Rio Grande Valley White Wings

> 1216 FairPark Boulevard
> Harlingen, Texas
> 956–412–9464

Directions: Follow Route 77 to the intersection of FairPark Boulevard and turn left.

FOSTER FIELD, San Angelo Colts

> 1600 University Avenue
> San Angelo, Texas
> 325–942–6587

Directions: From Route 87, take West Avenue Q, which turns into Knickerbocker Road, then turn right onto University Avenue.

BEST OF THE MINOR LEAGUES

The Best Old-Time Minor League Stadiums

➤ McCoy Stadium (Pawtucket Red Sox)
➤ Municipal Stadium (Hagerstown Suns)
➤ McCormick Field (Asheville Tourists)
➤ Grainger Stadium (Kinston Indians)
➤ Grayson Stadium (Savannah Sand Gnats)
➤ Rickwood Field (Birmingham Barons)
➤ PGE Park (Portland Beavers)
➤ Damaschke Field (Oneonta Tigers)
➤ Yale Field (New Haven County Cutters)
➤ FirstEnergy Stadium (Reading Phillies)

The Coziest Minor League Stadiums

➤ Holman Stadium (Vero Beach Rays)
➤ Knology Park (Dunedin Blue Jays)
➤ Centennial Field (Vermont Lake Monsters)
➤ Recreation Park (Visalia Oaks)
➤ Community Field (Burlington Bees)
➤ Sam Lynn Ballpark (Bakersfield Blaze)
➤ Bowen Field (Bluefield Orioles)
➤ McCormick Field (Asheville Tourists)
➤ Ernie Shore Field (Winston-Salem Warthogs)
➤ Lake Olmstead Stadium (Augusta GreenJackets)

The Best Outfield Views in Minor League Baseball

➤ The Roller Coaster at Blair County Ballpark (Altoona Curve)
➤ The Blue Ridge Mountains at Salem Memorial Baseball Stadium (Salem Avalanche)
➤ The Memphis Skyline at Autozone Park (Memphis Redbirds)
➤ The Harbor Bridge at Whataburger Field (Corpus Christi Hooks)
➤ The Ben Franklin Bridge at Campbell's Field (Camden Riversharks)
➤ The Mojave Desert around Mavericks Stadium (High Desert Mavericks)
➤ The Mississippi River at John O'Donnell Stadium (The Swing of the Quad Cities)

- The Wasatch Mountains at Franklin Covey Field (Salt Lake Bees)
- The San Gabriel Mountains at the Epicenter (Rancho Cucamonga Quakes)
- The San Bernardino Mountains at Arrowhead Credit Union Park (Inland Empire 66ers)

The Best Ballpark Playgrounds in Minor League Baseball

- FirstEnergy Park (Lakewood BlueClaws)
- Ernie Shore Field (Winston-Salem Warthogs)
- The Baseball Grounds (Jacksonville Suns)
- Hank Aaron Stadium (Mobile BayBears)
- Montgomery Riverwalk Stadium (Montgomery Biscuits)
- Whataburger Field (Corpus Christi Hooks)
- AutoZone Park (Memphis Redbirds)
- Oldsmobile Park (Lansing Lugnuts)
- Arrowhead Credit Union Park (Inland Empire 66ers)

The Best Ballpark Attractions in Minor League Baseball

- The Big Blue Bull, Durham Bulls Athletic Park (Durham Bulls)
- Monument Park, Legends Field (Tampa Yankees)
- Mickey Mantle's Handprints, Bricktown Ballpark (Oklahoma RedHawks)
- Judy Johnson Statue, Frawley Stadium (Wilmington Blue Rocks)
- The Giant Baseball Bat, Applebee's Park (Lexington Legends)
- The Jackie Robinson Statue, Jackie Robinson Ballpark (Daytona Cubs)
- The Model Space Shuttle, Space Coast Stadium (Brevard County Manatees)
- National Baseball Congress Hall of Fame, Lawrence-Dumont Stadium (Wichita Wranglers)
- The Murals, San Jose Municipal Stadium (San Jose Giants)
- The Ben Cheney Statue, Cheney Stadium (Tacoma Rainiers)

The Most Unique Seats in Minor League Baseball

➤ The Tiki Seats at Bright House Networks Field (Clearwater Threshers)

➤ The Hilton Garden Inn Hotel Courtyard, Merchantsauto.com Stadium (New Hampshire Fisher Cats)

➤ The Upper Deck at Five County Stadium (Carolina Mudcats)

➤ The KOA Campground, Smokies Park (Tennessee Smokies)

➤ The Train Shed Seats, Montgomery Riverwalk Stadium (Montgomery Biscuits)

➤ The Roost, Fifth Third Field (Toledo Mud Hens)

➤ The Right Field Rocking Chairs, Banner Island Ballpark (Stockton Ports)

➤ The Rail King Seats, Blair County Ballpark (Altoona Curve)

The Best Minor League Mascots

➤ Mr. Celery, Wilmington Blue Rocks

➤ Woolie the Caterpillar, Hagerstown Suns

➤ Buddy the Bat, Louisville Bats

➤ Conrad the Crawdad, Hickory Crawdads

➤ Guilford the Grasshopper, Greensboro Grasshoppers

➤ Clucky Jacobson, Tennessee Smokies

➤ Dinger, The Home Run Dog, Myrtle Beach Pelicans

➤ The Nutria Family, New Orleans Zephyrs

➤ Ball-apeno, San Antonio Missions

➤ Hobart the Purple Platypus, Casper Rockies

The Best Minor League Foods

➤ The Spiedie at NYSEG Stadium (Binghamton Mets)

➤ The White Hots at Frontier Field (Rochester Red Wings)

➤ The Beaver Tails at Lynx Stadium (Ottawa Lynx)

➤ The Flying Burrito at Durham Bulls Athletic Park (Durham Bulls)

➤ Dillard's Barbecue at Durham Bulls Athletic Park (Durham Bulls)

➤ Rendezvous Barbecue at Autozone Park (Memphis Redbirds)

➤ The Smokehouse Dog at Joseph P. Riley, Jr. Park (Charleston RiverDogs)

- Tribe Fries at Victory Field (Indianapolis Indians)
- The Swimming Pig at Fifth Third Ballpark (West Michigan Whitecaps)
- The Flavored Almonds at John Thurman Field (Modesto Nuts)

The Most Creative Team Names in Minor League Baseball

- Montgomery Biscuits
- Altoona Curve
- Savannah Sand Gnats
- Kansas City T-Bones
- Albuquerque Isotopes
- Cedar Rapids Kernels
- Kannapolis Intimidators
- Auburn Doubledays
- Chico Outlaws
- Frederick Keys

The Best Minor League Home Run Celebrations

- Hadlock Field (Portland Sea Dogs). A lighthouse rises in center field.
- First Energy Stadium (Reading Phillies). A train runs atop the right field fence.
- Bell South Park (Chattanooga Lookouts). A train runs behind the right field fence.
- The Baseball Grounds (Jacksonville Suns). The team owner rings a railroad bell.
- Joker Marchant Stadium (Lakeland Tigers). The P.A. system plays "Who Are the Baddest Cats in Town?"
- The Dell Diamond (Round Rock Express). Fans pass a hat and give the money to the player who homered.
- Fifth Third Field (Dayton Dragons). Two dragons atop the seven-story high scoreboard blow smoke out their nostrils.
- The Diamond (Lake Elsinore Storm). Jackpot, a pink bunny, emerges from the right field fence and dances on the field.

The Best Minor League Promotions and Traditions

➤ The Pony Race at Dodd Stadium (Connecticut Defenders)

➤ The Potato Chip Race at Memorial Stadium (Fort Wayne Wizards)

➤ The Fish Race at Classic Park (Lake County Captains)

➤ The Lobster Toss at Hadlock Field (Portland Sea Dogs)

➤ The Chicken Wing Toss at Pfitzner Stadium (Potomac Nationals)

➤ The Catfish Toss at Pringles Park (West Tennessee Diamond Jaxx)

➤ The Skits with Western Outlaws and Sheriffs at Dr Pepper/Seven Up Ballpark (Frisco RoughRiders)

➤ The Hamster Races at Fifth Third Field (Dayton Dragons)

➤ The Nightly Singing of "Go Nuts" at Oldsmobile Field (Lansing Lugnuts)

➤ The Nightly Key Shake at Harry Grove Stadium (Frederick Keys)

➤ The Nightly Singing of "I Got Stung" at Community Field (Burlington Bees)

The Best Minor League Super Fans

➤ The Toast-man (West Virginia Power)

➤ The Crazy Hot Dog Vendor (Reading Phillies)

➤ Homer Crafford (Winston-Salem Warthogs)

➤ Tony the Peanut Man (Charleston RiverDogs)

➤ Front Row Joe (Daytona Cubs)

➤ Dancing Bobby (Burlington Bees)

ACKNOWLEDGMENTS

AS ALWAYS, I owe a debt of gratitude to all of my friends and family members who share my love of baseball and support my writing, especially my wife Heather, parents Rich and Cathy, and brother Jamie. I also thank my editor at Lyons, Rob Kirkpatrick, and my agent at the Doe Coover Agency, Colleen Mohyde.

Writing this book was made infinitely more feasible thanks to the input I received from various individuals across the country who all do their part to support the minor league game. The following list of people who passed along insights related to their local teams and ballparks includes fans, sportswriters, ballpark employees, team employees, league executives, and even a couple of mascots. Major thanks go out to Sean Aaronson, Daniel Abashian, Ryan Alexander, Bill Ballew, Brian Barnes, Jim Byers, Jeff Calhoun, Chris Cameron, Ben Chiswick, Valerie Claus, Bill Cook, Mike Cummings, Jason Dambach, Meaghan Davis, Matt DeMargel, Eric Deutsch, Brian DeWine, Jeff Duggan, Pete Ehmke, Edmound Elzy, John Emmett, Tony Farlow, Bo Fulginiti, Jim Gemma, J. J. Gottsch, Todd Gretchen, David Haas, Tim Hagerty, Dick Harmon, Casey Hauan, Robin Hill, Chad Hodson, Shawn Holliday, Avery Holton, Kevin Huffine, Steve Hurlbert, C. J. Johnson, Andy Kauffman, Wendell Kim, Nate Kreinbrink, Chris Lampe, Jeff Lasky, Pete Laven, Steve Lenox, Michael Limmer, Mike Lindskog, Ryan Manuel, Colin McAndrew, Will Murphy, Brad Nicholson, Anthony Opperann, Timothy O'Reilly, Jared Parcell, Todd Parnell, Tony Patterson, Bill Potter, Ryan Roberts, Buck Rogers, Rachel Rogers, Owen Rosen, Norb Sadilek, Ryan Sakamoto, Jon Schaeffer, Doug Scopel, Greg Shelley, George Spelius, Jere Sisler, Andy Solomon, Brian Thomas, Jim Tocco, Laura Tolbirt, Bill Valentine, David Vincent, Jeff Vohs, Randy Wehofer, Tom Wess, Amanda Williams, Jarrod Wronski, John Zahr, and Meridith Zembal.

INDEX BY LEAGUE AND TEAM

CAROLINA LEAGUE

Frederick Keys, 75
Kinston Indians, 130
Lynchburg HillCats, 91
Myrtle Beach Pelicans, 172
Potomac Nationals, 88
Salem Avalanche, 102
Wilmington Blue Rocks, 69
Winston-Salem Warthogs, 141

FLORIDA STATE LEAGUE

Brevard County Manatees, 228
Clearwater Threshers, 188
Daytona Cubs, 191
Dunedin Blue Jays, 194
Fort Myers Miracle, 197
Jupiter Hammerheads, 205
Lakeland Tigers, 208
Palm Beach Cardinals, 205

St. Lucie Mets, 212
Sarasota Reds, 216
Tampa Yankees, 220
Vero Beach Rays, 224

Low-A

MIDWEST LEAGUE

Beloit Snappers, 339
Burlington Bees, 346
Cedar Rapids Kernels, 349
Clinton LumberKings, 352
Dayton Dragons, 315
Fort Wayne Wizards, 302
Great Lakes Loons, 334
Kane County Cougars, 291
Lansing Lugnuts, 330
Peoria Chiefs, 294
South Bend Silver Hawks, 305
Swing of the Quad Cities, 355

West Michigan Whitecaps, 326
Wisconsin Timber Rattlers, 336

SOUTH ATLANTIC LEAGUE

Asheville Tourists, 116
Augusta GreenJackets, 175
Charleston RiverDogs, 162
Columbus Catfish, 179
Delmarva Shorebirds, 81
Greensboro Grasshoppers, 133
Greenville Drive, 169
Hagerstown Suns, 78
Hickory Crawdads, 124
Kannapolis Intimidators, 127
Lake County Captains, 319
Lakewood BlueClaws, 42
Lexington Legends, 107
Rome Braves, 182
Savannah Sand Gnats, 185
West Virginia Power, 84

PHOTO CREDITS

Hadlock Field
  Photo by Josh Pahigian

Merchantsauto.com Stadium
  Photo by Josh Pahigian

McCoy Stadium
  Photo by Josh Pahigian

Dodd Stadium
  Courtesy of the Connecticut Defenders

NYSEG Stadium
  Photo by Daniel Abashian

Campbell's Field
  Courtesy of the Camden Riversharks

Blair County Ballpark
  Courtesy of the Altoona Curve

Lackawanna County Stadium
  Courtesy of the Scranton/Wilkes-Barre
  Red Barons

First Energy Stadium
  Courtesy of the Reading Phillies

Appalachian Power Park
  Courtesy of the West Virginia Power

Lynchburg City Stadium
  Courtesy of the Lynchburg Hill Cats

The Diamond
  Courtesy of the Richmond Braves

Louisville Slugger Museum
  Courtesy of the Louisville Slugger
  Museum

McCormick Field
  Photo by Tony Farlow

Durham Bulls Athletic Park
  Photo by Brian Fleming

First Horizon Park
  Courtesy of the Greensboro
  Grasshoppers

Five County Stadium
  Courtesy of the Carolina Mudcats

Ernie Shore Field
  Courtesy of the Winston-Salem
  Warthogs

Greer Stadium
  Courtesy of the Nashville Sounds
  Baseball Club

Joseph P. Riley, Jr. Park
  Courtesy of the Charleston RiverDogs

Golden Park
  Courtesy of the Columbus Catfish

Bright House Tiki Seats
  Photo by Josh Pahigian

Jackie Robinson Ballpark
  Courtesy of the Daytona Cubs

William Hammond Stadium
  Photo by Josh Pahigian

Roger Dean Stadium
  Photo by Josh Pahigian

Joker Marchant Stadium
  Photo by Josh Pahigian

Tradition Field
  Photo by Josh Pahigian

Ed Smith Stadium
  Photo by Josh Pahigian

Legends Field
  Photo by Josh Pahigian

Holman Stadium
  Photo by Josh Pahigian

Space Coast Stadium
  Photo by Josh Pahigian

Rickwood Field
  Courtesy of the Birmingham Barons

Montgomery Riverwalk Stadium
  Courtesy of the Montgomery Biscuits

Whataburger Field
  Courtesy of the Corpus Christi Hooks/
  Photo by Todd Yates

Dr Pepper/ Seven-Up Ballpark
  Courtesy of the Frisco RoughRiders

Hammons Field
  Courtesy of the Springfield Cardinals

Victory Field
  Courtesy of the Indianapolis Indians

Canal Park
  Courtesy of the Akron Aeros

Fifth Third Field
  Courtesy of the Dayton Dragons

Johnny Rosenblatt Stadium
  Courtesy of the Omaha Royals

Field of Dreams
  Photo by Kevin O'Connell

John O'Donnell Stadium
  Courtesy of the Swing of the Quad
  Cities

Isotopes Park
  Courtesy of the Albuquerque Isotopes

Hi Corbett Field
  Photo by Josh Pahigian

The Diamond
  Courtesy of the Lake Elsinore Storm

John Thurman Field
  Courtesy of the Modesto Nuts

Arrowhead Credit Union Park
  Courtesy of the Inland Empire 66ers

San Jose Municipal Stadium
  Courtesy of the San Jose Giants

PGE Park
  Courtesy of the Portland Beavers

About the Author
  Photo by Heather Pahigian

ABOUT THE AUTHOR

Josh Pahigian's other books with The Lyons Press include *The Ultimate Baseball Road-Trip* and *Why I Hate the Yankees*, which were both written with coauthor Kevin O'Connell. Josh is also the author of *Spring Training Handbook* and *The Red Sox in the Playoffs*. A Red Sox fan since birth, Josh holds a bachelor's degree in English from the College of the Holy Cross and a Master of Fine Arts in creative writing from Emerson College. Josh and his wife Heather live in Maine, where he teaches writing at the University of New England.